AWS Certified Solutions Architect - Associate (SAA-C03) Cert Guide

Companion Website and Pearson Test Prep Access Code

Access interactive study tools on this book's companion website, including practice test software, review exercises, Key Term flash card application, a study planner, and more!

To access the companion website, simply follow these steps:

1. Go to **www.pearsonitcertification.com/register.**

2. Enter the **print book ISBN: 9780137941582**

3. Answer the security question to validate your purchase.

4. Go to your account page.

5. Click on the **Registered Products** tab.

6. Under the book listing, click on the **Access Bonus Content** link.

When you register your book, your Pearson Test Prep practice test access code will automatically be populated with the book listing under the Registered Products tab. You will need this code to access the practice test that comes with this book. You can redeem the code at **PearsonTestPrep.com**. Simply choose Pearson IT Certification as your product group and log in to the site with the same credentials you used to register your book. Click the **Activate New Product** button and enter the access code. More detailed instructions on how to redeem your access code for both the online and desktop versions can be found on the companion website.

If you have any issues accessing the companion website or obtaining your Pearson Test Prep practice test access code, you can contact our support team by going to **pearsonitp.echelp.org**.

AWS Certified Solutions Architect – Associate (SAA-C03) Cert Guide

Mark Wilkins

Pearson

AWS Certified Solutions Architect – Associate (SAA-C03) Cert Guide

ISBN-13: 978-0-13-794158-2

ISBN-10: 0-13-794158-7

Library of Congress Control Number: 2023930964

5 2024

Trademarks

Warning and Disclaimer

Special Sales

For information about buying this title in bulk quantities, or for special sales opportunities (which may include electronic versions; custom cover designs; and content particular to your business, training goals, marketing focus, or branding interests), please contact our corporate sales department at corpsales@pearsoned.com or (800) 382-3419.

For government sales inquiries, please contact governmentsales@pearsoned.com.

For questions about sales outside the U.S., please contact intlcs@pearson.com.

Vice President, IT Professional
Mark Taub

Director, ITP Product Management
Brett Bartow

Executive Editor
Nancy Davis

Development Editor
Christopher Cleveland

Managing Editor
Sandra Schroeder

Senior Project Editor
Tonya Simpson

Copy Editor
Bill McManus

Indexer
Jen Hinchliffe

Proofreader
Jen Hinchliffe

Technical Editor
Ralph Parisi

Publishing Coordinator
Cindy Teeters

Cover Designer
Chuti Prasertsith

Compositor
codeMantra

Pearson's Commitment to Diversity, Equity, and Inclusion

Pearson is dedicated to creating bias-free content that reflects the diversity of all learners. We embrace the many dimensions of diversity, including but not limited to race, ethnicity, gender, socioeconomic status, ability, age, sexual orientation, and religious or political beliefs.

Education is a powerful force for equity and change in our world. It has the potential to deliver opportunities that improve lives and enable economic mobility. As we work with authors to create content for every product and service, we acknowledge our responsibility to demonstrate inclusivity and incorporate diverse scholarship so that everyone can achieve their potential through learning. As the world's leading learning company, we have a duty to help drive change and live up to our purpose to help more people create a better life for themselves and to create a better world.

Our ambition is to purposefully contribute to a world where

- Everyone has an equitable and lifelong opportunity to succeed through learning

- Our educational products and services are inclusive and represent the rich diversity of learners

- Our educational content accurately reflects the histories and experiences of the learners we serve

- Our educational content prompts deeper discussions with learners and motivates them to expand their own learning (and worldview)

While we work hard to present unbiased content, we want to hear from you about any concerns or needs with this Pearson product so that we can investigate and address them.

Please contact us with concerns about any potential bias at https://www.pearson.com/report-bias.html.

Contents at a Glance

Table of Contents

About the Author

Mark Wilkins is an electronics engineering technologist with a wealth of experience in designing, deploying, and supporting software and hardware technology in the corporate and small business world. Since 2013, Mark has focused on supporting and designing cloud service solutions with Amazon Web Services, Microsoft Azure, and the IBM Cloud. He is certified as an AWS Certified Solutions Architect – Associate. Mark is also a Microsoft Certified Trainer (MCT) and holds certifications in MCTS, MCSA, Server Virtualization with Windows Server Hyper-V, and Azure Cloud Services.

Mark worked as a technical evangelist for IBM SoftLayer from 2013 through 2016 and taught both SoftLayer fundamentals and SoftLayer design classes to many Fortune 500 companies in Canada, the United States, Europe, and Australia. As former course director for Global Knowledge, Mark developed and taught many technical seminars, including Configuring Active Directory Services, Configuring Group Policy, and Cloud and Virtualization Essentials. Mark currently develops AWS curriculum on AWS cloud services and certification for O'Reilly Media and LinkedIn Learning. To learn more about what Mark finds interesting about the cloud, visit The Cloud Thingy, at https://thecloudthingy.substack.com/. To learn more about the AWS cloud and AWS certification, check out Mark's YouTube channel at http://www.youtube.com/@SAA-C03.

Mark's published books include *Windows 2003 Registry for Dummies*, *Administering SMS 3.0*, *Administering Active Directory*, and *Learning Amazon Web Services (AWS): A Hands-On Guide to the Fundamentals of AWS Cloud*.

Dedication

I would like to dedicate this book to my grandson, Silas, a future nerd. And to Bruce, one of our cats, for making me take breaks when he wanted.

Acknowledgments

This manuscript was made truly great by the incredible project management of Tonya Simpson, who went above and beyond! Thanks so much.

I would also like to express my gratitude to Chris Cleveland, the development editor of this book. I was lucky to work with him on this text. Chris helped make this book several cuts above the rest.

Finally, thanks so much to Nancy Davis, my tireless acquisitions editor. Nancy very patiently made this book a reality.

About the Technical Reviewer

Ralph Parisi is a certified Champion Authorized Amazon instructor and has been teaching AWS courses for 6 years. Ralph has been an instructor for more than 20 years and has taught technical classes for Microsoft Exchange Server, Microsoft Windows Server, Active Directory, Group Policy, Citrix XenDeskop, and XenApp. Ralph has worked as a consultant to large corporations architecting Exchange Server and Active Directory solutions and migrations. Ralph has also worked with various companies as a technical writer. Ralph lives in North Carolina with his wife and Saluki, Dillon.

We Want to Hear from You!

As the reader of this book, *you* are our most important critic and commentator. We value your opinion and want to know what we're doing right, what we could do better, what areas you'd like to see us publish in, and any other words of wisdom you're willing to pass our way.

We welcome your comments. You can email or write to let us know what you did or didn't like about this book—as well as what we can do to make our books better.

Please note that we cannot help you with technical problems related to the topic of this book.

When you write, please be sure to include this book's title and author as well as your name and email address. We will carefully review your comments and share them with the author and editors who worked on the book.

Email: community@informit.com

Reader Services

Register your copy of *AWS Certified Solutions Architect – Associate (SAA-C03) Cert Guide* at www.pearsonitcertification.com for convenient access to downloads, updates, and corrections as they become available. To start the registration process, go to www.pearsonitcertification.com/register and log in or create an account*. Enter the product ISBN 9780137941582 and click Submit. When the process is complete, you will find any available bonus content under Registered Products.

*Be sure to check the box that you would like to hear from us to receive exclusive discounts on future editions of this product.

Introduction

There are many reasons to get certified in AWS technology. First of all, AWS certifications validate your AWS cloud knowledge. To fully understand the AWS cloud, preparing for the AWS Certified Solutions Architect – Associate (SAA-C03) exam is a great place to start. There are other AWS certifications that may be a better fit, depending on your technical level, your current knowledge of cloud concepts, and your current and future jobs with AWS technologies and services. Certifications are broken down into Foundational, Associate, Professional, and Specialty certifications. Full details can be found at https://aws.amazon.com/certification/. AWS frequently adds new certification tracks, but the following are the certifications that are currently available:

- **Foundational:** There is one Foundational certification: AWS Certified Cloud Practitioner. The recommendation is to have at least 6 months of fundamental AWS cloud knowledge before attempting this certification exam. You might be closer to this certification than you think, depending on your current level of technical skills. One advantage of taking the AWS Certified Cloud Practitioner exam first is that it helps you to get used to answering multiple-choice test questions and to learn about the foundational AWS cloud services.

- **Associate:** There are several Associate certifications:

    - **AWS Certified Solutions Architect – Associate:** For individuals working as solutions architects, designing AWS solutions using AWS services

    - **AWS Certified SysOps Administrator – Associate:** For individuals working as systems administrators, managing and operating AWS services

    - **AWS Certified Developer – Associate:** For individuals working as developers, deploying and debugging cloud-based applications hosted at AWS

    Each certification exam expects that you know how the AWS service that you are being tested on works. Each Associate certification has a specific focus:

    - **Architect:** The best design possible, based on the question and scenario

    - **SysOps:** The administration steps required to carry out a particular task

    - **Developer:** How to best use the service for the hosted application you are writing

For example, the three Associate exams would test different aspects of CloudWatch logs:

- **Architect:** The main focus of this exam is on how CloudWatch logs work and the main design features to consider based on specific needs—that is, design knowledge related to using CloudWatch logs for a variety of solutions.

- **SysOps:** The main focus of this exam is on how to configure Cloud-Watch logs based on specific needs—that is, configuration and deployment of CloudWatch logs using operational knowledge.

- **Developer:** The main focus of this exam is on what CloudWatch logs are useful for when developing applications for tracking performance of an application hosted on an EC2 instance—that is, knowledge of how a particular AWS service can help in the development and testing process with applications.

  Before you attempt one of the Associate certifications, AWS recommends that you have at least 1 year of experience solving problems and implementing solutions using AWS services. AWS really wants to ensure that you have hands-on experience solving problems.

- **Professional:** These certifications include the AWS Certified Solutions Architect Professional and the AWS Certified DevOps Engineer Professional. Professional certifications are not where you normally start your certification journey. AWS recommends that you have at least 2 years of hands-on experience before taking a Professional exam.

- **Specialty:** The Specialty certifications for Advanced Networking, Security, Machine Learning, Data Analytics, SAP on AWS, and Database require advanced knowledge of the subject matter. AWS recommends that you have an Associate certification before you attempt one of these certifications.

NOTE   The AWS Certified Solutions Architect – Associate (SAA-C03) certification is globally recognized and does an excellent job of demonstrating that the holder has knowledge and skills across a broad range of AWS topics.

The Goals of the AWS Certified Solutions Architect – Associate Certification

The AWS Certified Solutions Architect – Associate certification is intended for individuals who perform in a solutions architect role. This exam validates a candidate's ability to effectively demonstrate knowledge of how to architect and deploy secure and robust applications on AWS technologies. It validates a candidate's ability to

- Have knowledge and skills in the following AWS services: compute, networking, storage, and database and deployment and management services

- Have knowledge and skills in deploying, managing, and operating AWS workloads and implementing security controls and compliance requirements

- Identify which AWS service meets technical requirements

- Define technical requirements for AWS-based applications

- Identify which AWS services meet a given technical requirement

Recommended Prerequisite Skills

While this book provides you with the information required to pass the Certified Solutions Architect – Associate (SAA-C03) exam, Amazon considers ideal candidates to be those who possess the following:

- Experience in AWS technology

- Strong on-premises IT experience

- Understanding of mapping on-premises technology to the cloud

- Experience with other cloud services

The Exam Domains

The AWS Certified Solutions Architect – Associate (SAA-C03) exam is broken down into four major domains. This book covers each of the domains and the task statements.

- **Domain 1: Design Secure Architectures 30%**

  - Task Statement 1: Design secure access to AWS resources

  - Task Statement 2: Design secure workloads and applications

  - Task Statement 3: Determine appropriate data security controls

- **Domain 2: Design Resilient Architectures 26%**

  - Task Statement 1: Design scalable and loosely coupled architectures

  - Task Statement 2: Design highly available and/or fault-tolerant architectures

- **Domain 3: Design High-Performing Architectures 24%**

  - Task Statement 1: Determine high-performing and/or scalable storage solutions

  - Task Statement 2: Design high-performing and elastic compute solutions

  - Task Statement 3: Determine high-performing database solutions

- Task Statement 4: Determine high-performing and/or scalable network architectures

- Task Statement 5: Determine high-performing data ingestion and transformation solutions

- **Domain 4: Design Cost-Optimized Architectures 20%**

    - Task Statement 1: Design cost-optimized storage solutions

    - Task Statement 2: Design cost-optimized compute solutions

    - Task Statement 3: Design cost-optimized database solutions

    - Task Statement 4: Design cost-optimized network architectures

Steps to Becoming an AWS Certified Solutions Architect – Associate

To become an AWS Certified Solutions Architect – Associate, an exam candidate must meet certain prerequisites and follow specific procedures. Exam candidates must ensure that they have the necessary background and technical experience for the exam and then sign up for the exam.

Signing Up for the Exam

The steps required to sign up for the AWS Certified Solutions Architect – Associate exam are as follows:

Step 1.   Create an AWS Certification account at https://www.aws.training/ Certification and schedule your exam from the home page by clicking Schedule New Exam.

Step 2.   Select a testing provider, either Pearson VUE or PSI, and select whether you want to take the exam at a local testing center or online from your home or office. If you choose to take an online exam, you will have to agree to the online testing policies.

Step 3.   Complete the examination signup by selecting the preferred language and the date of your exam.

Step 4.   Submit the examination fee.

TIP   Refer to the AWS Certification site at https://aws.amazon.com/certification/ for more information regarding this and other AWS certifications.

How to Use This Book

This book maps directly to the domains of the AWS Certified Solutions Architect – Associate (SAA-C03) exam and includes a number of features that help you understand the topics and prepare for the exam.

Objectives and Methods

This book uses several key methodologies to help you discover the exam topics on which you need more review, to help you fully understand and remember those details, and to help you ensure that you have retained your knowledge of those topics. This book does not try to help you pass the exam only by memorization; it seeks to help you truly learn and understand the topics. This book is designed to help you pass the AWS Certified Solutions Architect – Associate (SAA-C03) exam by using the following methods:

- Helping you discover which exam topics you have not mastered

- Providing explanations and information to fill in your knowledge gaps

- Supplying exercises that enhance your ability to recall and deduce the answers to test questions

- Providing practice exercises on the topics and the testing process via test questions on the companion website

Book Features

To help you customize your study time using this book, the core chapters have several features that help you make the best use of your time:

- **Foundation Topics:** The sections under "Foundation Topics" describe the core topics of each chapter.

- **Exam Preparation Tasks:** The "Exam Preparation Tasks" section lists a series of study activities that you should do at the end of each chapter:

  - **Review All Key Topics:** The Key Topic icon appears next to the most important items in the "Foundation Topics" section of the chapter. The "Review All Key Topics" activity lists the key topics from the chapter, along with the number of the page where you can find more information about each one. Although the contents of the entire chapter could be tested on the exam, you should definitely know the information listed in each key topic, so you should review these.

  - **Define Key Terms:** Although the AWS Certified Solutions Architect – Associate (SAA-C03) exam may be unlikely to word a question "Define this term," the exam does require that you learn and know a lot of terminology. This section lists the most important terms from the chapter and asks you to write a short definition and compare your answer to the glossary at the end of the book.

- **Q&A:** Confirm that you understand the content that you just covered by answering these questions and reading the answer explanations.

- **Web-based practice exam:** The companion website includes the Pearson Test Prep practice test engine, which enables you to take practice exam questions. Use it to prepare with a sample exam and to pinpoint topics where you need more study.

How This Book Is Organized

This book contains 14 core chapters—Chapters 2 through 15. Chapter 1 introduces the foundations of AWS, and Chapter 16 provides preparation tips and suggestions for how to approach the exam. Each core chapter covers a specific task statement or multiple task statements of the domains for the AWS Certified Solutions Architect – Associate (SAA-C03) exam.

Companion Website

Register this book to get access to the Pearson Test Prep practice test software and other study materials plus additional bonus content. Check this site regularly for new and updated postings written by the author that provide further insight into the more troublesome topics on the exam. Be sure to check the box indicating that you would like to hear from us to receive updates and exclusive discounts on future editions of this product or related products.

To access this companion website, follow these steps:

Step 1.   Go to https://www.pearsonitcertification.com/register and log in or create a new account.

Step 2.   Enter the ISBN 9780137941582.

Step 3.   Answer the challenge question as proof of purchase.

Step 4.   Click the Access Bonus Content link in the Registered Products section of your account page to be taken to the page where your downloadable content is available.

Please note that many of our companion content files can be very large, especially image and video files.

If you are unable to locate the files for this title by following these steps, please visit https://www.pearsonITcertification.com/contact and select the Site Problems/Comments option from the Select a Topic drop-down list. Our customer service representatives will assist you.

Pearson Test Prep Practice Test Software

As noted earlier, the Pearson Test Prep practice test software comes with two full practice exams. These practice exams are available to you either online or as an offline Windows application. To access the practice exams that were developed with this book, please see the instructions below. For more information about the practice exams and more tools for exam preparation, see Chapter 16.

How to Access the Pearson Test Prep (PTP) App

You have two options for installing and using the Pearson Test Prep application: a web app and a desktop app. To use the Pearson Test Prep application, start by finding the registration code that comes with the book. You can find the code in these ways:

- You can get your access code by registering the print ISBN (9780137941582) on pearsonitcertification.com/register. Make sure to use the print book ISBN, regardless of whether you purchased an eBook or the print book. After you register the book, your access code will be populated on your account page under the Registered Products tab. Instructions for how to redeem the code are available on the book's companion website by clicking the Access Bonus Content link.

- Premium Edition: If you purchase the Premium Edition eBook and Practice Test directly from the Pearson IT Certification website, the code will be populated on your account page after purchase. Just log in at pearsonitcertification.com, click Account to see details of your account, and click the digital purchases tab.

NOTE   After you register your book, your code can always be found in your account under the Registered Products tab.

Once you have the access code, to find instructions about both the PTP web app and the desktop app, follow these steps:

Step 1. Open this book's companion website as shown earlier in this Introduction under the heading, "Companion Website."

Step 2. Click the **Practice Exams** button.

Step 3. Follow the instructions listed there for both installing the desktop app and using the web app.

Note that if you want to use the web app only at this point, just navigate to pearsontestprep.com, log in using the same credentials used to register your book or purchase the Premium Edition, and register this book's practice tests using the registration code you just found. The process should take only a couple of minutes.

Figure Credits

Cover: Yurchanka Siarhei/Shutterstock

Chapter opener: Charlie Edwards/Getty Images

Figures 1.1, 1.3 through 1.6, 1.10, 1.12 through 1.4, 2.1 through 2.4, 2.6 through 2.8, 2.13, 2.14, 3.1 through 3.4, 3.7 through 3.9, 3.11 through 3.24, 3.27 through 3.37, 3.39 through 3.48, 4.3, 4.4, 4.6 through 4.8, 4.11 through 4.14, 4.22 through 4.34, 5.2, 5.6 through 5.11, 5.14 through 5.16, 5.18, 6.7, 6.11 through 6.15, 6.17 through 6.20, 6.22, 6.23, 6.26 through 6.30, 7.5, 7.11 through 7.14, 7.33, 7.34, 8.1 through 8.13, 8.15, 8.17 through 8.23, 9.2 through 9.5, 9.7, 9.9, 9.10, 9.12, 9.13 through 9.29, 10.1, 10.4, 10.10 through 10.12, 10.17, 10.18, 11.3 through 11.7, 11.10 through 11.21, 11.23, 11.24, 11.27 through 11.31, 11.33, 11.34, 12.1 through 12.10, 12.12 through 12.17, 13.3 through 13.12, 14.1, 14.3 through 14.6, 14.13, 15.4, 16.1, 16.2: Amazon Web Services, Inc

Figure 2.11: Adam Wiggins

Figures 2.9a, 7.1: Andrei Minsk/Shutterstock

Figures 3.10, 3.38, 11.25: Microsoft Corporation

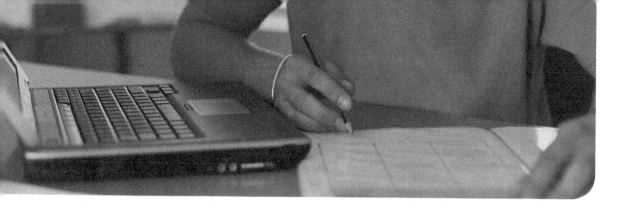

This chapter covers the following topics:

- Essential Characteristics of AWS Cloud Computing
- AWS Cloud Computing and NIST
- Moving to AWS
- Operational Benefits of AWS
- Cloud Provider Responsibilities
- Security at AWS
- Migrating Applications
- The AWS Well-Architected Framework
- AWS Services Cheat Sheet

CHAPTER 1

Understanding the Foundations of AWS Architecture

The AWS Certified Solutions Architect – Associate (SAA-C03) exam that we are discussing in this book measures your technical competence in architecting workloads to run successfully in the Amazon Web Services (AWS) cloud. For any of their associate certification exams, AWS does not expect you to be an expert in every single cloud service, as that is an impossible task. However, AWS does expect you to be able to display a high level of competence about how to architect (design, deploy, monitor, and manage) workloads running on AWS cloud architecture based on the exam domains of knowledge. You can find the SAA-C03 exam guide here: https://d1.awsstatic.com/training-and-certification/docs-sa-assoc/AWS-Certified-Solutions-Architect-Associate_Exam-Guide_C03.pdf. The SAA-C03 exam guide lists the AWS services that could be tested on the exam, and what AWS services are not covered.

The goal of writing this book is to include enough technical details for all readers to absorb and pass the AWS Certified Solutions Architect – Associate (SAA-C03) exam. The following list should help you to gauge whether you should read this entire chapter or skim through the topics:

- If you are coming from a technical background but don't know anything about the AWS cloud, start with this first chapter and read it carefully.

- If you have a background working in the AWS cloud but this is your first certification attempt, you might not need to read the entire chapter, but you should review the first chapter's content, and study the final section, "AWS Services Cheat Sheet."

- If you already are certified as an AWS Certified Solutions Architect – Associate and it's time to re-certify, you might not need to read this chapter, but you should study the final section, "AWS Services Cheat Sheet," to ensure that you're up to speed on the latest AWS services covered on the exam.

And let's be clear, the goal of this book is to help you pass the AWS Certified Solutions Architect – Associate exam. If you ace the exam, great! However, passing the exam should be your overall goal. You need to get roughly 72% of the exam questions right to pass the exam; Amazon is not clear as to the exact percentage for passing the exam but it's in this range. The AWS SAA-C03 exam is 65 multiple choice questions. However, it's very important to understand that 15 of the 65 exam questions are beta questions that don't count! Therefore, there are 50 questions you must answer successfully. Answering approximately 37 questions correctly out of the 50 questions that count will achieve your goal of becoming an AWS Certified Solutions Architect – Associate.

The SAA-C03 exam is marked using what is defined as *scaled scoring*. The questions that you are presented on your exam most likely will not be the same as those presented to other exam candidates; the difficulty of each exam question is weighted to ensure the total knowledge level of each exam as a whole is maintained. Additional details on how to prepare to take the exam are fully covered in the last chapter of this book, Chapter 16, "Final Preparation."

The following list of tasks will also help you greatly in the goal of becoming certified:

- **Read the FAQs:** Each AWS cloud service has a frequently asked questions (FAQs) summary that summarizes the service and its highlights. When learning about an AWS service, always start with the FAQ—you won't be disappointed. And be sure to take notes as you learn.

- **Read the AWS Well-Architected Framework PDFs:** The exam is based on the AWS Well-Architected Framework. Reading the PDF of each pillar is a great study aid for understanding the mindset of the exam questions, and will also prepare you to be a great AWS consultant/cloud architect. Make sure to review the Security Pillar, Reliability Pillar, Performance Efficiency Pillar, and the Cost Optimization Pillar. See https://aws.amazon.com/architecture/well-architected/.

- **Sign up for a free AWS cloud account:** This is the best method to practice hands-on tasks for the exam. Create multiple AWS accounts; you are not limited to one free AWS account, but a different e-mail address must be used as the root login for each AWS account that is created.

- **Complete AWS Well-Architected Labs:** Complete as many of the labs as possible that relate to the AWS Certified Solutions Architect – Associate exam topics. The labs are foundational (100), intermediate (200), and advanced (300), as partially shown in Figure 1-1 for the Security category. See https://wellarchitectedlabs.com/.

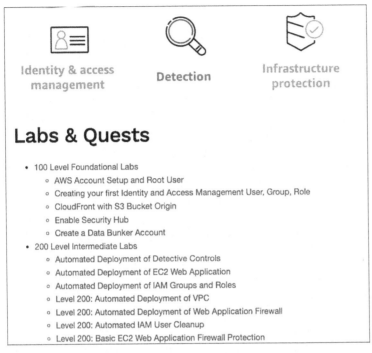

Figure 1-1   AWS Well-Architected Framework Hands-on Labs

■ **Use the AWS Well-Architected Tool:** The AWS Well-Architected Tool is a self-paced utility that consists of Well-Architected Framework questions from each pillar to make you consider which best practices and procedures should be considered when hosting your workloads at AWS. This is a great study aid for the exam, available at https://www.wellarchitectedlabs.com/well-architectedtool/.

■ **Complete the AWS security workshops:** AWS offers a variety of security workshops that will help you understand AWS security best practices; see https://awssecworkshops.com/.

■ **Answer as many sample exam questions as you can:** Included in this book is a test engine with hundreds of test questions. The hardest part of preparing to take the exam is getting used to answering multiple-choice test questions. The more practice you have, the better you will be prepared. AWS also has some sample questions for the SAA-C03 exam here:

https://d1.awsstatic.com/training-and-certification/docs-sa-assoc/AWS-Certified-Solutions-Architect-Associate_Sample-Questions.pdf and here:

https://explore.skillbuilder.aws/learn/course/external/view/elearning/13266/
aws-certified-solutions-architect-associate-official-practice-question-set-saa-
c03-english?saa=sec&sec=prep

■ **Browse the AWS Architecture Center:** The AWS Architecture Center
(https://aws.amazon.com/architecture/) has many examples of how to deploy
reference architecture for analytics, compute and HPC deployments, and databases, to name just a few. Walking through the step-by-step notes provides a
great overview of the associated AWS services and can be helpful in visualizing
how AWS architecture is designed and deployed.

Essential Characteristics of AWS Cloud Computing

In 2021, CEO Andy Jassy estimated that the cloud was currently less than 5% of
global IT spending, which suggests that moving workloads to the cloud for many
companies is really just beginning. The public cloud providers AWS and Microsoft
Azure have been established for well over a decade and have strong infrastructure as
a service (IaaS) and platform as a service (PaaS) offerings available around the world.
Google Cloud Platform (GCP), Oracle Cloud, and IBM Cloud are also viable alter-
natives. Figure 1-2 shows the Gartner Magic Quadrant for Cloud Infrastructure and
Platform Services (see https://www.gartner.com/en/research/methodologies/magic-
quadrants-research), which indicates the current favorite cloud technology providers
companies can choose to align with. In the Leaders quadrant, Amazon Web Services
leads, followed closely by Microsoft and then Google. Alibaba Cloud aligns with the
Visionaries quadrant, and Oracle, Tencent Cloud, and IBM currently occupy the
Niche Players quadrant.

When I started my career as a computer technician in the 1990s, most corporations
that I supported used several computer-based services running on mainframes that
were not located on premises. Accounting services were accessed through a fast (at
the time) 1200-baud modem that was connected using one of those green-screened
digital terminals. The serial cable, threaded through the drop ceiling to connect the
terminal, was strong enough to pull a car.

Today we rely more and more on one or more public cloud providers for hosting
many types of workloads on an ever-increasing collection of very specialized data
centers and cloud services. There is no hardware ownership, the cloud provider
owns the services, and customers rent cloud services as required.

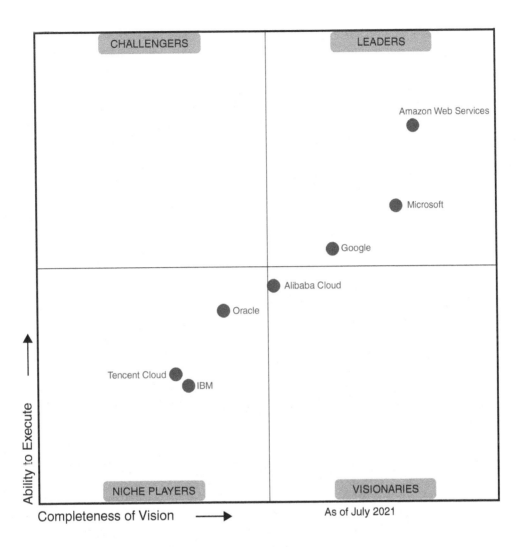

Source: Gartner (July 2021)

Figure 1-2 Gartner's Magic Quadrant of Top Public Cloud Providers (https://www.gartner.com/en/research/methodologies/magic-quadrants-research)[1]

You might think that the public cloud only offers virtual resources, but the AWS cloud and others *can* provide bare-metal servers if requested. AWS will happily host

---

1 Gartner does not endorse any vendor, product, or service depicted in its research publications and does not advise technology users to select only those vendors with the highest ratings or other designation. Gartner research publications consist of the opinions of Gartner's research organization and should not be construed as statements of fact. Gartner disclaims all warranties, expressed or implied, with respect to this research, including any warranties of merchantability or fitness for a particular purpose.

your applications and databases on bare-metal servers hosted at AWS, or in your own data centers. Of course, more commonly, AWS offers you a wide variety of virtual servers in many different sizes and designs. AWS is also quite happy if you continue to operate your on-premises data centers and coexist with cloud resources and services operating at AWS. AWS also offers AWS Outposts, which enables customers to run an ever-increasing number of AWS cloud services on premises. Microsoft Azure will offer to sell you a copy of its complete Azure cloud operating system, called Azure Stack, installed on servers in your data centers. It's getting harder to define the public cloud these days.

Applications that are hosted in the public cloud leverage virtual server, network, and storage resources combined with cloud services that provide monitoring, backup services, and more. Hardware devices, such as routers, switches, and storage arrays, have been replaced by AWS-managed cloud services built from the same virtual computers, storage, and networking components used by AWS themselves that are offered to each customer. This doesn't mean that companies aren't still using hardware devices on premises. However, it is possible to run hundreds or thousands of virtual machines in parallel, outperforming the functionality of a single hardware switch or router device. Most AWS cloud services are hosted on virtual machines called Amazon Elastic Cloud Compute (EC2) instances running in massive server farms powering the storage arrays, networking services, load-balancing, and auto-scaling services provided by AWS are part of Amazon Web Services (AWS). For example, AWS Config helps you manage compliance, and the AWS Backup service backs up AWS storage services.

AWS Cloud Computing and NIST

If you haven't heard of the National Institute of Standards and Technology (NIST), a branch of the U.S. government, you're not alone. Around 2010, NIST began documenting the emerging public cloud. After consulting the major cloud vendors, it released an initial report in June 2011, Special Publication 800-145, "The NIST Definition of Cloud Computing," defining the cloud services that were common across all public cloud vendors. The report's genius is that it defined in 2011 what the emerging public cloud actually became. NIST's cloud definitions have moved from mere definitions, to accepted standards that are followed by all of the public clouds we use today.

The five key NIST definitions of the public cloud have morphed into a definitive standard methodology of how cloud providers and thousands of customers operate in the public cloud. The report can be found here: https://nvlpubs.nist.gov/nistpubs/legacy/sp/nistspecialpublication800-145.pdf. The five essential characteristics of the cloud model defined by NIST are

- On-demand Self-Service

- Broad Network Access

- Resource Pooling

- Rapid Elasticity

- Measured Service

The sections that follow describe these essential NIST characteristics.

On-Demand Self-Service

These days companies don't just *expect* cloud service to be delivered quickly; they *demand* it.

Every cloud provider, including AWS, offers a self-service management portal (see Figure 1-3). Request any cloud service, and in seconds, or minutes, it's available in your AWS account, ready to be configured or used. Gone are the days of requesting a virtual server via email and waiting several days until it's available. At AWS, a virtual server can be ordered and operational in under 5 minutes. Creating and using an Amazon Simple Storage Service (Amazon S3) bucket is possible within seconds. It is also possible to procure a software-defined network (called an Amazon Virtual Private Cloud) and have it operational in seconds. Using the AWS management console enables customers to order and configure many cloud services across many AWS regions. Any cloud service ordered is quickly delivered using automated procedures running in the background.

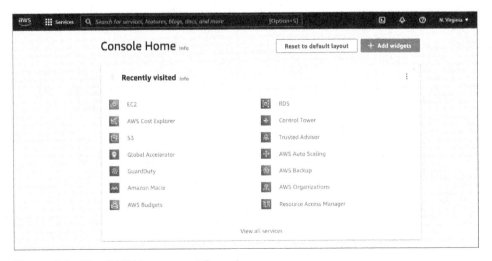

Figure 1-3 The AWS Management Console

Broad Network Access

Cloud services running at AWS can be accessed from anywhere there is an Internet connection, using just a web browser. AWS provides secure HTTPS endpoints to access every cloud service hosted at AWS. However, your company might not want or require what NIST defined as broad network access, which is public Internet network access to your workloads. Many companies that are moving to the AWS cloud have no interest in a publicly accessible software solution. They want their hosted cloud services to remain private, accessible only by their employees using private network connections. Each cloud customer ultimately defines their definition of broad network access: public Internet connections, private VPN or fiber connections, or both.

At AWS, applications and services can be made publicly available, or they can remain completely private. Virtual private network (VPN) connections from your place of work to AWS are commonplace. Customers can also order an AWS Direct Connect connection, a private fiber connection to AWS resources running at speeds up to 100 Gbps. Depending on the type of application you're hosting in the AWS cloud, high-speed network access may be essential.

It's also possible to administer AWS services from a smartphone by using an AWS app (see Figure 1-4). Certainly, accessing AWS from any device is possible.

Resource Pooling

Infrastructure resources for AWS cloud services are located across different geographical regions of the world in many data centers. A company running an on-premises private cloud will typically pool its virtual machines, memory, processing, and networking capabilities into one or two data centers offering a limited pool of compute and network resources.

AWS has clusters of data centers, stored in multiple availability zones (AZs) across each region, and each AZ has thousands of bare-metal servers and storage resources available and online, allowing customers to host their workloads with a high level of resiliency and availability. Without a massive pool of compute resources, AWS would not be able to allow customers to dynamically allocate compute resources to match their performance requirements and workload needs. Amazon S3 object storage is offered as unlimited; there is no defined maximum storage limit.

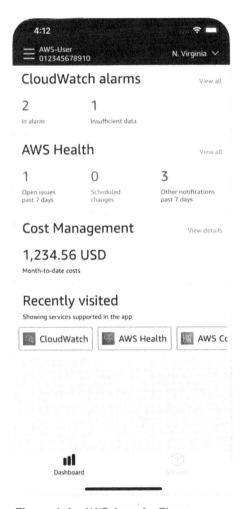

Figure 1-4   AWS Apps for Phone

Rapid Elasticity

Rapid elasticity in the public cloud is *the* key feature for hosted cloud applications. At AWS, compute and storage resources are defined as elastic. Workloads running in the AWS cloud for Amazon EC2 instances or Amazon Elastic Container Service (Amazon ECS) deployments have the capability to automatically scale using a scaling policy to dynamically resize an Auto Scaling group of web or application servers using several scaling policies, including target tracking (see Figure 1-5). In this example, EC2 Auto Scale will maintain CPU utilization of 65%; additional compute resources will be automatically added or removed to maintain the desired target value.

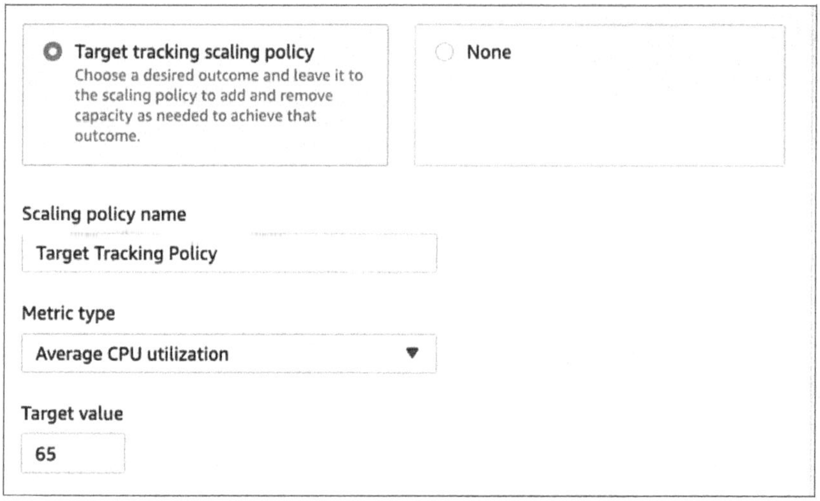

Figure 1-5   Workload Scaling Based on Demand

Elasticity—that is, dynamic scaling—is an automated solution scaling compute resources up or down in size based on workload needs. Administrators these days don't need to turn off virtual servers, add additional RAM, and turn the servers back on again; instead, they can deploy *horizontal scaling*—that is, automatically add or remove additional servers as required. AWS EC2 Auto Scaling is integrated with the Amazon CloudWatch monitoring service using metrics and event-driven alarms to dynamically increase or decrease compute resources as required.

Measured Service

In the AWS cloud, you are billed for only the services that you use or consume; this concept is referred to as a *measured service*. AWS charges can be broken down into compute, storage, and data transfer charges. Packet flowing inbound (i.e., ingress to the AWS cloud) is usually free. By contrast, outbound packet flow (i.e., egress traffic across the Internet, a private network connection, or network replication traffic between a primary and alternate database server hosted on subnets in different availability zones) is charged an outbound data transfer fee. In the case of computer services such as AWS EC2 compute instances, charges are per hour for EC2 usage calculated by the second based on the size of the EC2 instance, operating system, and the AWS Region where the instance is launched. For storage services such as Amazon S3 storage or virtual hard drives (Amazon EBS), storage charges are per gigabyte used per month.

If a cloud service in your AWS account is on, charges will apply. Running hosted workloads in the AWS cloud requires a detailed understanding of how costs are charged; the management of costs at AWS is one of the most important tasks to understand and control. AWS has many useful tools to help you control your cloud costs, including the AWS Simple Monthly Calculator, AWS Cost Explorer, and AWS Budgets (see Figure 1-6).

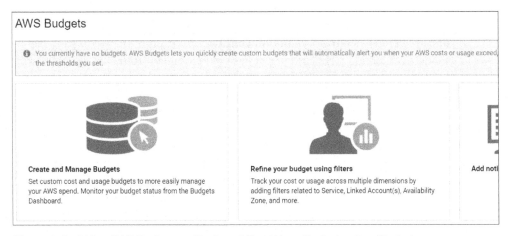

Figure 1-6   Using AWS Budgets to Track and Alert When Costs Are Over Budget

Being billed for consuming cloud services is a reality that we are all personally used to; for example, Netflix, Disney, and Dropbox are common services. However, billing at AWS is different from the flat per-month fees for personal software as a service (SaaS) services. Customers must understand and carefully monitor their compute, storage, and data transfer costs or else their monthly charges can become extremely expensive. For example, a load balancer can be ordered at AWS for approximately $18 per month. However, the data traffic transferred through the load balancer is also charged, so the overall monthly price could be substantial.

Moving to AWS

Once an organization has decided to move to the AWS cloud, countless moving parts begin to churn. People need to be trained, infrastructure changes must take place, developers need to develop applications with a different mindset, and administrators must get up to speed. Generally, people at companies beginning to utilize cloud services typically have several mindsets:

- **The corporate mentality:** You currently have data centers, infrastructure, and virtualized applications. Ever-increasing infrastructure and maintenance costs are driving you to look at what options are available in the AWS cloud. Your starting point could be to utilize the available IaaS offerings for servers, storage, monitoring, and networking services.

- **The born-in-the-cloud mentality:** You're a developer (or a nimble organization) with a great idea but not much startup funding. You also don't have a local data center, and want to get going as soon as possible. Your starting point could be to utilize the available IaaS offerings for servers, storage, monitoring, and networking, and the PaaS offerings, to speed up the development process.

- **The startup mentality:** You've just lost your job due to a merger or buyout and are determined to strike out on your own. Your brand-new company has no data center and lacks cash, but it has plenty of ideas. Your starting point will be the same as the born-in-the-cloud mentality example.

Each of these starting mindsets or outlooks will have differing points of view about how to migrate or design their cloud infrastructure and hosted applications. If you come from a corporate environment, you will probably expect the cloud provider to have a detailed service-level agreement (SLA) that you can change to match your needs. You will also probably have expectations about how much detail should be provided about the cloud provider's infrastructure and cloud services. AWS has service-level agreements for its cloud services and very detailed documentation for each hosted cloud service.

NOTE AWS has options for developers who want to craft and deploy applications hosted at AWS. Visit https://aws.amazon.com/startups/ for further information about how you might be able to qualify for AWS Promotional Credit. There's a possibility of getting up to $15,000 in credits over 2 years, including AWS support and training.

Infrastructure as a Service (IaaS)

Many cloud services offered by AWS are defined as IaaS services, and are defined in this book as foundational services that are used by every customer (see Figure 1-7). Virtualized servers (Amazon EC2), container services (Amazon ECS), and database services (Amazon RDS) are hosted on a fast private software-defined network (SDN). Each customer's IaaS services are isolated from all other AWS customers by default. A robust security service named AWS Identity and Access Management (IAM) enables each customer to secure and control every ordered IaaS service as desired. A wide variety of supporting services, defined as Management and Governance services, also shown in Figure 1-7, provide monitoring (Amazon CloudWatch), audit services (AWS CloudTrail), scaling of compute resources (AWS Auto Scaling), governance (AWS Config), and event-driven automation (AWS Lambda).

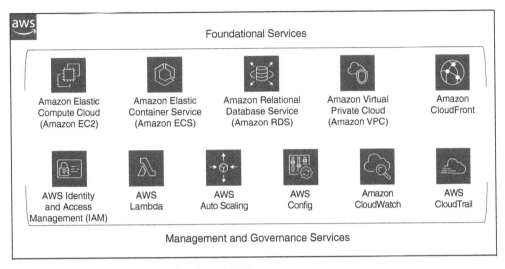

Figure 1-7 Infrastructure as a Service at AWS

Hosting compute workloads at AWS requires the creation of a network environment called Amazon Virtual Private Cloud (VPC) hosting web, application, and database services on subnets. Customers have the flexibility to create whatever architectural stack is required at AWS, using the vast number of IaaS services and management services available. Many companies moving to AWS typically start with IaaS services, because the IaaS services at AWS closely mirror their current on-premises virtual environment.

Here are some examples of the essential cloud services at AWS:

- **Compute services:** The previously introduced Amazon EC2 is a cloud service that provides virtual servers (dedicated, multi-tenant, or bare-metal) in an ever-increasing variety of options. Amazon Elastic Container Service (Amazon ECS) supports Docker containers running at AWS, or on-premises using AWS Outpost deployments. Amazon Elastic Kubernetes Service (EKS) supports Kubernetes deployments at AWS or on-premises using AWS Outposts.

- **Storage services:** Amazon S3 is a cloud service that provides unlimited object storage in Amazon S3 buckets or archived storage in vaults. There are shared storage arrays: Amazon Elastic File System (Amazon EFS) for Linux, and Amazon FSx for Windows File Server for Microsoft Windows deployments, and virtual block storage volumes using the Amazon Elastic Block Store (Amazon EBS) service.

- **Database services:** AWS offers a fully managed database service called Amazon Relational Database Service (Amazon RDS). Choose from Amazon Aurora (with MySQL or PostgreSQL compatibility), MySQL, PostgreSQL, Oracle, and Microsoft SQL Server engines. Using Amazon RDS, AWS builds, hosts, maintains, backs up, and synchronizes HA pairs or clusters of primary/ standby database servers, leaving customers the single task of managing their data records. Many other managed database services are also available at AWS, including Amazon DynamoDB, a NoSQL database; and Amazon ElastiCache, a managed in-memory caching service that supports Memcached and Redis deployments.

- **Automating AWS infrastructure:** AWS CloudFormation enables customers to automate the process of modeling and provisioning infrastructure stacks, complete with the required compute, storage, networks, load balancers, and third-party resources required for each workload. Template files are created using either JSON or YAML declarative code.

- **Auditing:** AWS CloudTrail is enabled in every AWS account, tracking and recording all application programming interface (API) calls and authentication calls. Customers can also configure AWS CloudTrail to store audit information in Amazon S3 Glacier archive forever.

- **Monitoring:** AWS CloudWatch is a powerful monitoring service with metrics for more than 70 AWS services that can be used to monitor resources and application operations using alarms to carry out automated actions when predetermined thresholds are breached.

- **VMware Cloud on AWS:** Many companies use VMware ESXi infrastructure for their on-premises application servers. Capital expenses and licensing costs are some of the biggest expenses incurred when running an ever-expanding on-premises private cloud. Virtualization was supposed to be the answer to controlling a company's infrastructure costs; however, the cost of hosting, running, and maintaining virtualization services became extremely high as deployments expand in size and complexity. Replacing on-premises VMware deployments with AWS-hosted virtualized servers running on AWS's hypervisor services removes a company's need for hypervisor administration expertise. Many applications used by corporations are also now widely available in the public cloud as hosted applications defined as a software as a service (SaaS) application. VMware ESXi is also available as VMware Cloud on AWS, using VMware's software-defined data center architecture running on AWS infrastructure.

NOTE At AWS, infrastructure and platform services and resources are spread across the world in 31 different regions (2022), and additional regions are scheduled to be added. If you are in a large population center, the odds are that access to AWS cloud resources is close by. If AWS is not yet close by, you still might be able to connect using an edge location or a local point of presence connection. To review the current AWS infrastructure, visit https://aws.amazon.com/about-aws/global-infrastructure/ regions_az/.

Platform as a Service (PaaS)

PaaS cloud providers enable your company's developers to create custom applications on a variety of popular development platforms, such as Java, PHP, and Python and Go. Your choice of language and development framework will determine the PaaS vendor you select. Using a PaaS provider means that developers don't have to manually build and manage the infrastructure components required for each workload; instead, the required infrastructure resources for each workload running in the development, testing, and production environments are created, hosted, and managed by the PaaS cloud provider. After an application has been developed and tested and is ready for production, end users can access the application using the application's public URL. In the background, the PaaS cloud provider hosts and scales the hosted SaaS workload based on demand. As the number of users using the workload changes, the infrastructure resources scale out or in as required. PaaS environments are installed on the IaaS resources of the PaaS cloud provider, as shown in Figure 1-8. In fact, IaaS is always behind all "as a service" monikers. Examples of PaaS providers include Google Cloud, Cloud Foundry, and Heroku.

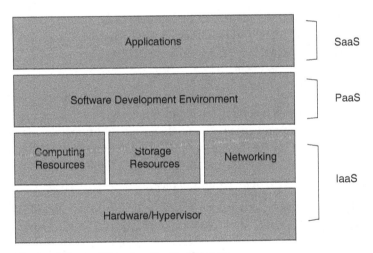

Figure 1-8   IaaS Hosting the PaaS Layer

The Cloud Foundry PaaS solution is offered for application development at IBM Cloud, running a customized version of the Cloud Foundry platform components. Developers can sign up and focus on writing applications. All application requests are handled by the PaaS layer interfacing with the IaaS layer, where the application's compute, storage, load-balancing, and scaling services operate.

Another popular solution for developing applications in the public cloud, Heroku, a container-based PaaS environment, enables developers to create and run applications using a variety of development platforms. Just as with IBM Cloud, once the workload is deployed into production, Heroku hosts, load-balances, and auto-scales each workload as required and sends each customer a bill for the infrastructure hosting costs used each month.

When developing applications at a PaaS provider, remember that programming languages change from time to time; therefore, the associated APIs offered by each cloud provider can change as well—and sometimes without much warning. Developers and companies must keep up to date with any ongoing changes or there can be issues when using a cloud-hosted PaaS development platform.

An additional reality is that one cloud provider's PaaS offering is not necessarily compatible with another cloud provider's PaaS offering. For example, Heroku and Microsoft Azure offer similar PaaS cloud services for developing applications, but internally, each cloud provider operates in a completely different fashion, with a completely different set of supporting APIs. There is no single standard for defining what PaaS must be. Compatibility issues can begin to reveal themselves at the lower levels of each vendor's proposed solution. RESTful interfaces, manifest file formats, framework configurations, external APIs, and component integration are not necessarily compatible across all cloud vendors.

AWS Elastic Beanstalk is Amazon's cloud service for deploying web applications. The service supports Java, .NET, PHP, Node.js, Python, Ruby, and Go. Code applications can be hosted on Apache, Nginx, Passenger, or IIS web servers, and containerized applications hosted on Docker.

Elastic Beanstalk acts as a managed service that frees customers from having to build out infrastructure configurations. It automatically handles scaling, load balancing, monitoring, capacity provisioning, and application updates. For additional details on AWS Elastic Beanstalk, see Chapter 6, "Designing Resilient Architecture." AWS has also recently purchased Cloud9, an AWS-hosted integrated development environment (IDE) that supports more than 40 programming languages.

AWS has several cloud services to assist in developing applications, shown in Figure 1-9, including AWS CodeBuild, AWS CodeCommit, AWS Cloud9, and AWS CodeDeploy, that can be key components in your application deployment workflow at AWS.

AWS Cloud9

AWS CodeBuild

AWS CodeCommit

AWS CodeDeploy

Figure 1-9 Platform Options at AWS

Operational Benefits of AWS

Operating in the public AWS cloud has certain benefits provided by the previously discussed NIST five essential characteristics. Unlimited access to the many cloud services available at AWS may make it easier than expected to operate and manage workloads in the AWS cloud. Consider the following:

- **Servers:** Underutilized servers in your data center are expensive to run and maintain. Moving applications to the public cloud can reduce the size of your on-premises data center. When you no longer host as many physical servers, your total hosting costs (racking, powering, heating, and cooling) could be lower as well. You also don't have to pay for software licenses at the processer level because you're not responsible for running hypervisor services; that's now Amazon's job. You might think that moving to the AWS cloud means virtualized resources and only virtualization. However, with AWS, you can get an ever-increasing variety of EC2 instances, including dedicated virtual servers or bare-metal servers. Sizes range from a single-core CPU with 512 MB of RAM to hundreds of CPU cores and terabytes of RAM.

- **Storage:** Using cloud storage has huge benefits, including having unlimited amounts of storage. Amazon has shareable file solutions for both Linux and Windows Server workloads. Virtual hard disks are available using Amazon EBS to create the required volumes. Unlimited storage and long-term archive storage are provided by Amazon S3 buckets and S3 Glacier archive storage.

- **Managed cloud services:** The AWS-managed cloud services, outlined in Table 1-1, may be able to replace or complement existing services and utilities currently used on premises after moving to the AWS cloud.

Table 1-1 Managed Services at AWS

IT Operation	On Premises	AWS Cloud
Monitoring	Nagios, SolarWinds	CloudWatch monitoring provides metrics for every AWS service with monitoring and logging data stored in unlimited Amazon S3 storage. Third-party monitoring solutions perform analysis of stored log data stored in S3 buckets.
Data backup	Backup tools such as Commvault and Veritas NetBackup	Many third-party vendors such as Veritas and Commvault (and many others) support the AWS cloud with compatible software appliances. AWS Storage Gateway can also be installed to move on-premises data records and virtual hard drive volumes to S3 storage while locally caching popular content. AWS Backup enables you to centrally manage the backup of most data storage services at AWS to S3 storage.

IT Operation	On Premises	AWS Cloud
Scale	Automation for increasing/decreasing the size of each virtual machine's RAM and CPU cores as required	Use EC2 Auto Scaling to automatically scale virtual machines (EC2 instances) or containers, dynamically increasing/decreasing the compute power required by applications.
Testing/development	Expensive provisioning of hardware for testing and development	Provisioning resources for short-term testing at AWS is incredibly inexpensive. Signing up for the AWS Free Tier enables customers to test a variety of AWS services for one year completely free of charge.
Identity management	Active Directory Domain Services for accessing corporate resources	It is possible to migrate or integrate on-premises Active Directory Domain Services to the AWS cloud using AWS Directory Services. Deploy AWS single sign-on (SSO) services using IAM Identity Center to manage access to popular cloud business applications hosted by AWS or a third-party cloud provider.

Cloud Provider Responsibilities

AWS has published service-level agreements (SLAs) for most AWS cloud services. Each separate SLA lists the desired operational level that AWS will endeavor to meet or exceed. Current details on the SLAs offered by AWS can be viewed at https://aws.amazon.com/legal/service-level-agreements. AWS defines its commitments in each SLA about security, compliance, and overall operations. The challenge is to live up to these agreements when all services fail from time to time. Each cloud service SLA contains details about the acceptable outage times and the responsibility of the cloud provider when outages occur. Each SLA also contains statements about their level of responsibility for events outside the cloud provider's control. SLAs commonly use terms such as "best effort" and "commercially reasonable effort."

AWS is responsible for overall service operation and deployment, service orchestration and overall management of their cloud services, the security of the cloud components, and maintenance of each customer's privacy. A managed services SLA also spells out how a cloud consumer is to carry out business with the cloud provider. Each cloud consumer must fully understand what each cloud service offered provides—that is, exactly what the cloud service will, and will not, do.

Is it acceptable to expect AWS failures from time to time? It is a reality; everything does fail from time to time.

What happens when a key service or component of your workload hosted in the AWS cloud fails? Does a disaster occur, or is the failure manageable? When operating at AWS, customers must design each hosted workload to be able to continue operating as required when cloud services, or compute and storage failures occur. Designing high availability and failover for hosted workloads running at AWS is one of the key concepts of many of the questions on the AWS Certified Solutions Architect – Associate (SAA-C03) exam. Many questions will be based on the concepts of designing with a high availability, failover, and durability mindset. Customers must design workloads to meet the application requirements, considering that cloud services *do* fail from time to time.

All public cloud providers really have the same SLA summarized in nine short words when failures happen: "We are sorry; we will give you a credit." Here's another reality check: If your application is down, you might have to *prove* that it was actually down by providing network traces and appropriate documentation that leaves no doubt that it was down because of an AWS cloud issue.

Here's another further detail to be aware of: If you don't build redundancy into your workload design, don't bother asking for a credit. Application designs that have a single EC2 instance hosting a workload with no failover or high-availability design parameters have no cloud provider SLA protection. AWS expects customers to be serious about their application design. Each customer needs to carefully design, deploy, and maintain each hosted workload based on the business needs and requirements, ensuring that any high availability and failover requirements have been met.

Security at AWS

As you move to the AWS cloud, you need to consider a number of security factors, including the following:

- **Data security:** The reality is that your data is typically more secure and durable when stored in the public cloud than in on-premises physical servers due to the multiple physical copies of any data records stored in public cloud storage. All storage mediums at AWS can also be easily encrypted with the Advanced Encryption Standard (AES). Amazon EBS volumes—both boot and data volumes—can be encrypted at rest and in transit, using customer master keys provided by AWS or keys provided by the customer. Shared storage services such as Amazon EFS and FSx for Windows File Server can also be encrypted at rest, as can all offered database engines. Amazon S3 buckets are encrypted with keys provided by the S3 service or the Key Management Service (KMS) shown in Figure 1-10. Data durability provides additional security as all data stored in the AWS cloud is stored in multiple physical locations.

For example, each EBS volume has multiple copies replicated within the data center where they are created.

Amazon S3 objects are replicated across at least three separate availability zones within the selected AWS region, producing a very high level of durability.

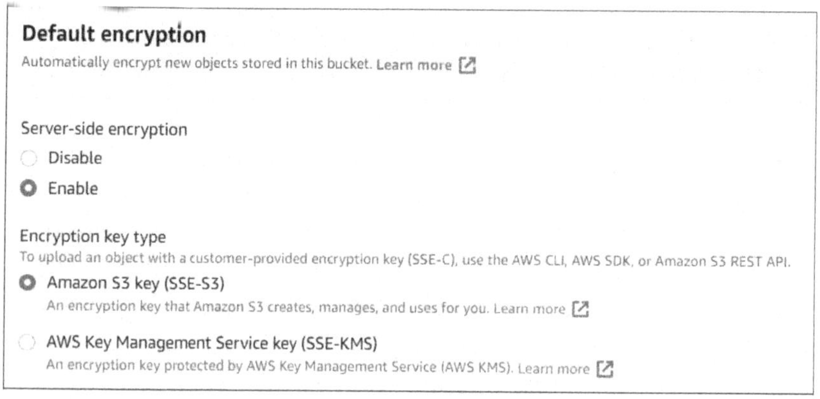

Default encryption

Automatically encrypt new objects stored in this bucket. **Learn more** ☑

Server-side encryption

○ Disable

● Enable

Encryption key type

To upload an object with a customer-provided encryption key (SSE-C), use the AWS CLI, AWS SDK, or Amazon S3 REST API.

● Amazon S3 key (SSE-S3)

   An encryption key that Amazon S3 creates, manages, and uses for you. Learn more ☑

○ AWS Key Management Service key (SSE-KMS)

   An encryption key protected by AWS Key Management Service (AWS KMS). Learn more ☑

Figure 1-10 Encrypting S3 Buckets Using S3 Keys or AWS-KMS Managed Keys

- **Data privacy:** Amazon ensures that each AWS account's stored data records remain isolated from other AWS customers. In addition, data records are always created as a private resource. Each S3 bucket can be shared publicly; however, each customer assumes the responsibility when changing a private S3 bucket to be publicly accessible across the Internet.

- **Data control:** Customers are fully responsible for storing and retrieving their data records stored at AWS. It's the customer's responsibility to define the security and accessibility of all data records stored at AWS.

- **Security controls:** AWS Identity and Access management permission policies can be defined at a very granular level to control access to *all* resources at AWS. Customers can also enable multifactor authentication (MFA) as an additional security control for all IAM users authenticating to AWS, and on S3 buckets when deletion of data records is attempted. Resource policies defining the precise level of security and access can be directly attached to resources such as S3 buckets.

Network Security at AWS

At AWS, networking is managed at the subnet level, and subnets are first created as private subnets with no direct access to the outside world. Subnets that reside on your private networks at AWS are hosted in a virtual private cloud (VPC). Only by adding gateway services to a VPC and route table entries are subnets able to be accessed from either the Internet, a private VPN connection, or from an external network location. The following are examples of networking services and utilities at AWS that help control network traffic:

- Each subnet's ingress and egress traffic can be controlled by subnet firewalls called *network ACLs* that define separate stateless rules for inbound and outbound packet flow.

- Each EC2 instance hosted on a subnet is protected by a firewall called a *security group*, which defines what inbound traffic is allowed into the instance and where outbound traffic is allowed to flow to.

- VPCs can be further protected by deploying the AWS Network Firewall, providing control over all network traffic, such as blocking outbound Server Message Block (SMB) requests, bad URLs, and specific domain names.

- VPC flow logs can be enabled to capture network traffic for the entire VPC, for a single subnet, or for a network interface.

Application Security at AWS

Both web and application servers hosted at AWS are usually located on private subnets, which are not directly accessible from the Internet. Customers requesting access to the application will be directed by DNS services (Route 53) to the DNS name of the load balancer, which in turn directs incoming traffic from the public subnet to the targeted web servers hosted in private subnets.

For example, the end-to-end traffic pattern for a three-tier web application can be designed using many encryption/decryption points on its path from source to destination, as described in the list that follows and as shown in Figure 1-11:

- **AWS Web Application Firewall (WAF):** AWS WAF is a custom traffic filter that can be associated with an Application Load Balancer to protect against malicious traffic requests.

- **Application Load Balancer:** An application load balancer can accept encrypted HTTPS traffic on port 443 and provide Secure Sockets Layer/ Transport Layer Security (SSL/TLS) decryption and, optionally, user authentication support.

- **EC2 instance hosting a web application:** EBS boot and data volumes can be encrypted using the AWS KMS service.

- **EC2 instance hosting an application server:** EBS boot and data volumes can be encrypted using the AWS KMS service.

- **RDS database server:** All boot and data volumes can be encrypted using the AWS KMS service.

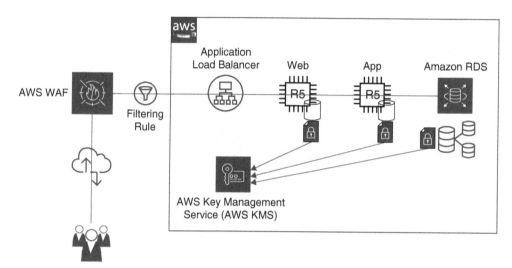

Figure 1-11   Encrypted Traffic Flow at AWS

Migrating Applications

For applications that have been chosen as starting candidates to move to the AWS cloud, several decisions need to be made about each application's journey or path. There are several options available for moving an application, depending on factors such as the age of the application and its operating system, and any local dependencies. The following sections walk through these options. Typical large organizations run many applications on thousands of virtual servers. When you move to AWS, you need to determine which applications can be moved to AWS and what applications should first be prioritized. Consider the following caveats before making these choices:

- **Define a value proposition:** Thousands of companies have successfully moved to AWS; you, too, can be successful. Start off with a defined value proposition that can be validated quickly—that is, in a matter of months rather than years. For developing applications, you could consider developing with AWS Cloud9 (see Figure 1-12), a cloud-hosted integrated development environment

(IDE) that supports more than 40 programming languages. Using Cloud9 and a browser, you can try your hand at developing a new application at AWS or at another PaaS provider such as Heroku. When you develop a completely new application at AWS, you are not constrained by factors such as the type of database that must be used, the type of programming language that must be used, or the type of compute that must be used. Starting new at AWS enables you to try out new methods to host applications, such as serverless computing, creating a mobile application using stateless components, or using DynamoDB as a NoSQL deployment instead of a SQL database. Developing and deploying a new workload at AWS without any legacy dependencies is where the real learning about what the AWS cloud can do for you begins.

Figure 1-12   Cloud9 IDE at AWS for Application Development

- **Start with low value/low risk:** When choosing what application to move to the AWS cloud, many consultants begin by suggesting a starting point of selecting an already virtualized application stack with high value and low risk. However, it's probably going to take you many months or longer to successfully move a production application to the cloud. Think about choosing an application with low value first. This will enable you to do some additional planning and analysis without any added pressure. Many companies make the pronouncement that applications will be moving to the cloud quickly. It rarely happens as quickly as expected because there are so many things to learn and consider. Take your time and select a working application that has been virtualized and running successfully. Consider using the AWS Application Migration Service to migrate your first application to AWS. After you are successful, document every step, including lessons learned and what to do differently for the next application chosen to be migrated. Moving additional applications to the cloud will generally be easier and faster thanks to the lessons learned and experience gained.

- **Solve a single problem:** Do you require additional storage? Perhaps that's a great starting point for moving resources to the AWS cloud. Archiving files in S3 Glacier could be as simple as ordering an external AWS Snowball device, connecting it up to your network, filling it with files that you would like to archive, and shipping it back to AWS. Archiving records in the AWS cloud would be an excellent first project in working with AWS.

- **Allowing access to on-premises data records:** The number-one problem for larger companies starting to work with cloud providers is working through the internal politics to allow access to on-premises data from the cloud. Be sure to consider data record access and the steps required for successful access before you begin moving to the cloud:

    - How can you access your on-premises data from the cloud?

    - What data records must stay on premises?

    - Are you bound by any compliance rules and regulations?

    - Is your current data in the right format for what you need?

Applications That Can Be Moved to AWS and Hosted on an EC2 Instance with No Changes

An application that fits into this category is referred to as *lift and shift* or *re-hosting*. Server migration tools and database migration tools can carry out these migrations quite effectively. AWS Application Discovery Service helps organizations plan migration projects by gathering information about their on-premises data centers and potentially thousands of workloads. Server utilization data and the mapping of any dependencies are useful first steps in the initial migration process. The collected data can be exported as a CSV file and used to estimate the total cost of ownership (TCO) of running workloads when planning migration to AWS.

AWS Application Migration Service (formally CloudEndure Migration) is the recommended migration service for performing lift-and-shift migrations to AWS because it automatically converts source servers from physical, virtual, or from existing third-party cloud providers to run at AWS. Supported physical servers include VMware vSphere and Microsoft Hyper-V. EC2 instances can also be migrated between AWS regions or between AWS accounts.

However, applications that are lifted and shifted to the cloud are likely to have dependencies and issues that need to be considered before beginning the migration, including the following:

- If the application stores its data in a database, will the database remain on the premises or will it be moved to the cloud? The Database Migration Service can help in migrating many types of on-premises databases to the cloud.

- If the database for the application remains on premises, are there latency issues that need to be considered when communicating with the database? Each AWS site-to-site VPN connection supports a maximum throughput of up to 1.25 Gbps.

- Will a high-speed connection need to be established between the AWS cloud and the database remaining on premises? A high-speed private fiber AWS Direct Connect dedicated connection ranges from 1 to 100 Gbps.

- Are there compliance issues regarding the application data? Does the data have to be encrypted at rest? Does communication with the database need to be encrypted? AWS Artifact, available in the AWS Management console, provides compliance reports and agreements to review current compliance standards.

- Do users need to authenticate to the application across the corporate network? If so, are federation services required to be deployed at AWS for single sign-on (SSO)? IAM Identity Center provides SSO for multiple AWS accounts and SaaS cloud applications.

- Are there local dependencies installed on the application server that will interfere with the application server's operation in the AWS cloud? AWS Migration Hub Strategy Recommendations can be useful for alerting customers about potential migration conflicts for application migrations.

- Are there licensing considerations for both the operating system and the application when operating in the cloud? AWS License Manager can help track license usage across your environments.

Applications with Many Local Dependencies That Cause Problems When Being Moved to the Cloud

For applications that fit in this category, consider the following:

- Application developers might have to refactor or restructure the source code of the application to take advantage of managed cloud services such as work queues (Amazon Simple Queue Service [SQS]), auto scaling (EC2 Auto Scaling), or hosted logging services (CloudWatch logs).

- Application developers might be able to take advantage of AWS cloud services by replacing the existing on-premises database with a database hosted in the cloud utilizing Amazon Relational Database Service (Amazon RDS).

Replacing an Existing Application with a SaaS Application Hosted by a Public Cloud Provider

With so many hosted cloud applications available in the public cloud, the odds are close to 100% that there will be an existing application that can replace a current on-premises application.

Applications That Should Remain On Premises and Eventually Be Deprecated

The following applications should not be moved to the cloud but should remain on premises or should be deprecated:

- The application is hosted on legacy hardware that is near end-of-life.

- The application cannot be virtualized.

- The application does not have technical support.

- The application is used by a small number of users.

The AWS Well-Architected Framework

Several years ago, AWS introduced the Well-Architected Framework to provide guidance to help cloud architects build secure, resilient, and well-performing infrastructure to host their applications. The framework describes recognized best practices developed over time, based on the experience of many AWS customers and AWS technical experts.

The documentation for the Well-Architected Framework (see https://docs.aws.amazon.com/wellarchitected/latest/framework) also presents many key questions customers should review. It is useful to discuss these questions with the other technical team members in your company to make key decisions about your infrastructure and workloads to be hosted at AWS. Each workload to be deployed at AWS should be viewed through the lens of the Well-Architected Framework following these six pillars:

- **Operational excellence:** Relates to how best to design, deploy, execute, and monitor applications running at AWS using automated deployment monitoring procedures, continuous improvement, and automated solutions for recovering from failures. Operational excellence questions to consider include:

- How are disruptions to applications handled—manually or automatically?
- How can you analyze the ongoing health of your applications and infrastructure components hosted at AWS?

- **Security:** Relates to how to best design systems that will operate reliably and securely while protecting customer information and data records. Security questions to consider include:

  - How are security credentials and authentication managed at AWS?
  - How are automated procedures secured?

- **Reliability:** Relates to how applications hosted at AWS recover from disruption with minimal downtime and how applications meet escalating demands. Reliability questions to consider include:

  - How do you monitor resources hosted at AWS?
  - How do applications hosted at AWS adapt to changes in demand by end users?

- **Performance efficiency:** Relates to how to use compute resources to meet and maintain your application requirements on an ongoing basis. Should your compute solution change from EC2 instances to containers or serverless? Performance efficiency questions to consider include:

  - Why did you select your database architecture?
  - Why did you select your current compute infrastructure?

- **Cost optimization:** Relates to how to design workloads that meet your needs at the lowest price point. Cost optimization questions to consider include:

  - How do you oversee usage and cost?
  - How do you meet cost targets?
  - Are you aware of current data transfer charges based on your AWS designs?

■ **Sustainability:** Relates to designing workload deployments that minimize waste. Sustainability questions to consider include:

■ How do you select the most efficient storage and compute?

■ What managed service offerings could reduce current infrastructure deployments?

The Well-Architected Tool

In the AWS Management Console, you can search and find the AWS Well-Architected Framework tool. This tool, shown in Figure 1-13, provides a framework for documenting your workloads against AWS best practices, as defined in the Well-Architected Framework documentation. For each of the six pillars, there are many questions to consider before beginning to deploy an application. As questions for each pillar are considered and debated, milestones can be created marking important points about the workload architecture as teams discuss the questions and make changes to their workload design.

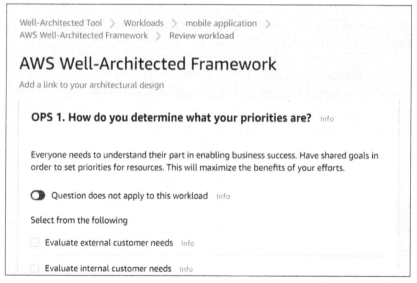

Figure 1-13   Evaluating Workloads Using the Well-Architected Framework Tool

The Well-Architected Framework tool provides tips and guidance on how to follow the best practices recommended by AWS while carrying out a full architectural review of an actual workload that you are planning to deploy at AWS. Your team will find that working with the Well-Architected Framework tool is well worth the time invested.

Before your architectural review begins, open the Well Architected Tool and select the AWS region where your application will be hosted, then define the workload and industry type, and whether the workload is in production or a pre-production environment. After all the pertinent questions have been answered, during the review process, the Well-Architected Framework tool helps you identify potential areas of medium and high risk, based on your answers to the questions. The six pillars of design success are also included in the plan for recommended improvements to your initial design decisions (see Figure 1-14).

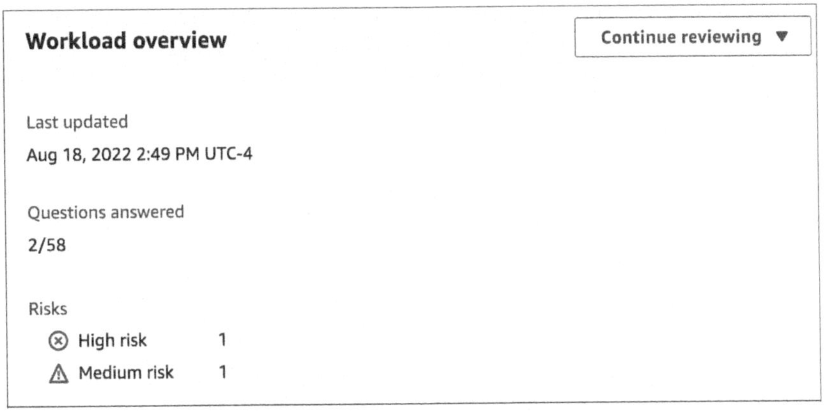

Workload overview   Continue reviewing ▼

Last updated
Aug 18, 2022 2:49 PM UTC-4

Questions answered
2/58

Risks
⊗ High risk   1
⚠ Medium risk   1

Figure 1-14   Recommended Improvements Using the Well-Architected Framework Tool Review

AWS Services Cheat Sheet

Each section of the exam domains for the AWS Certified Solutions Architect – Associated (SAA-C03) exam is covered in a separate chapter in this book. You can quickly understand a variety of AWS services that are covered by the exam domains via a short explanation provided by the following list. You can review additional details on each of these services by reading the related FAQs for each service. There might be exam questions about some of these services, and then again, there might not be. For the purposes of preparing for the exam, the following details for these particular AWS services should be sufficient in answering the test questions that may mention them.

- **AWS AppSync:** A service designed for mobile applications that require user and data synchronization across multiple devices. AWS AppSync supports iOS, Android, and JavaScript (React and Angular). Select data records can be synchronized automatically across multiple devices using the GraphQL query language.

- **Amazon AppFlow:** A hosted integration service for securely exchanging data records, such as events from external SaaS applications such as Salesforce and ServiceNow.

- **Amazon Athena:** A serverless query service that analyzes Amazon S3 data. Queries can be performed in a variety of standards, including CSV, JSON, ORC, Avro, and Parquet. Queries can also be executed in parallel, resulting in extremely high performance.

- **AWS Audit Manager:** Audit Manager's prebuilt frameworks map your AWS resources to industry standards such as CIS AWS Foundations Benchmark, the General Data Protection Regulation (GDPR), and the Payment Card Industry Data Security Standard (PCI DSS).

- **Amazon Comprehend:** A natural language processing (NLP) service that uses machine learning to find meaning and insights in text.

- **Amazon Cognito:** Add mobile user sign-up, sign-in, and access controls to your web and mobile apps using a hosted identity store that supports both social media and enterprise identity federation.

- **Amazon Detective:** Analyze, investigate, and quickly identify the root cause of potential security issues or suspicious activities collecting log data from your AWS resources using machine learning, statistical analysis, and graph theory, ingesting data from AWS CloudTrail logs, Amazon VPC Flow Logs, and Amazon GuardDuty findings.

- **AWS Device Farm:** An application testing service that lets you improve the quality of your web and mobile apps during development by running tests concurrently on multiple desktop browsers and real physical mobile devices hosted at AWS. Device support includes Apple, Google, and Android devices.

- **AWS Data Exchange:** Supports the secure exchange of third-party data files and data tables into AWS. Customers can use the AWS Data Exchange API to copy selected third-party data from AWS Data Exchange into Amazon S3 storage. Data Exchange third-party products include weather, healthcare, data sciences, geospatial and mapping services.

- **AWS Data Pipeline:** Process and move data between different AWS compute and storage services, and from on-premises siloed data sources, and transfer the results into Amazon S3 buckets, Amazon RDS, Amazon DynamoDB, and Amazon EMR.

- **Amazon EMR:** EMR is a big data platform for data processing, interactive analysis, and machine learning using Apache Spark, Apache Hive, and Presto. Run petabyte-scale analysis much cheaper than traditional on-premises solutions.

- **Amazon Forecast:** Provides accurate time-sensitive forecasts for retail, manufacturing, travel demand, logistics, and web traffic markets.

- **Amazon Fraud Detector:** A managed fraud detector that helps identify potentially fraudulent online activities such as online payment fraud and fake account creation.

- **AWS Glue:** A fully managed extract, transform, and load (ETL) service that helps discover details and properties of data stored in Amazon S3 and Amazon Redshift for analytics, machine learning, and application development. AWS Glue has the following key components:

  - **AWS Glue Data Catalog:** Stores structural and operational metadata, including its table definition, physical location, and the data's historical and business relevance.

  - **Glue Crawlers:** Crawlers are used to scan various data stores populating the AWS Glue Data Catalog with relevant data statistics.

  - **AWS Glue Studio:** Create jobs that extract structured or semi-structured data from a data source.

  - **AWS Glue Schema Registry:** Validate and control streaming data using registered schemas for Apache Avro and JSON.

  - **AWS Glue DataBrew:** A visual data preparation tool that can be used by data analysts to clean and normalize data for analysis and machine learning.

- **Amazon Kendra:** Highly accurate machine learning enterprise search service for all unstructured data stored in Amazon S3 and Amazon RDS databases.

- **Amazon Kinesis:** Allows customers to connect, process, and analyze real-time streaming data to quickly gather insights to the incoming data flow of information. The use case for Amazon Kinesis is for ingesting, buffering, and processing streaming video, audio applications, logs, website clickstreams, and IoT telemetry data for machine learning, analysis, and storage at any scale.

  - **Amazon Kinesis Video Streams:** Developers can use the Kinesis Video Streams SDK to develop applications with connected camera devices, such as phones, drones, and dash cams, to securely stream video to custom real-time or batch-oriented applications running on AWS EC2 instances. The video streams can also be stored and encrypted for further monitoring and analytics.

  - **Amazon Kinesis Data Firehose:** Streaming data is collected and delivered in real time to Amazon S3, Amazon Redshift, Amazon Open Search Service, custom HTTP/HTTPS endpoints, and to third-party service providers including Splunk, Datadog, and LogicMonitor. Kinesis Data Firehouse can also be configured to transform data records before the data is stored.

- **Amazon Kinesis Data Streams:** Collect and process gigabytes of streaming data that is generated continuously from thousands of locations such as log files, e-commerce purchases, game player activity, web click-stream data, and social media information. Multiple data streams ingested into Kinesis are sent into custom applications running on EC2 instances, or data stored in a DynamoDB table, Amazon S3 storage, Amazon EMR, or Amazon Redshift.

- **Amazon Lex:** Build conversational interfaces using voice and text powered by Alexa. Speech recognition and language understanding capabilities enable chatbots for applications published to Facebook Messenger, Slack, or Twilio SMS.

- **Amazon Managed Streaming for Apache Kafka (Amazon MSK):** Streaming data can be consumed using a full-managed Apache Kafka and Kafka Connect Clusters hosted at AWS, allowing Kafka applications and Kafka connectors to run at AWS without requiring expert knowledge in operating Apache Kafka.

- **Amazon Managed Service for Prometheus:** A monitoring and alerting service that collects and accesses performance and operational data from container workloads on AWS and on premises.

- **Amazon Managed Grafana:** Existing Grafana customers can analyze, monitor, and generate alarms on metrics, logs, and traces across AWS accounts, AWS regions, AWS CloudWatch, AWS X-Ray, Amazon Elasticsearch Service, Amazon Timestream, AWS IoT SiteWise, and Amazon Managed Service for Prometheus.

- **Amazon OpenSearch Service:** Perform log analysis and real-time application monitoring, providing visibility into your workload performance. Find relevant data within applications, websites, and data lakes using SQL query syntax. Data can be read using CSV tables or JSON documents.

- **Amazon Pinpoint:** An outbound and inbound marketing communications service allowing companies to connect with customers using email, SMS, push, voice messages, or in-app messaging to deliver promotional or transactional messages such as one-time passwords, reminders, or confirmation of orders.

- **Amazon Polly:** Turn text into lifelike speech for speech-enabled mobile apps and devices using lifelike voices in multiple languages; text sent to the Amazon Polly API returns an audio stream for use in your applications or devices.

- **AWS Personal Health Dashboard:** Receive notifications when AWS is experiencing issues on AWS services you are using, and alerts triggered by changes in the health of AWS services.

- **AWS Proton:** Allow platform teams to create rules for developers provisioning automated infrastructure as code. There are two supported methods:

  - AWS-managed provisioning uses CloudFormation templates to deploy infrastructure.

  - Self-managed provisioning uses Terraform templates to deploy infrastructure.

- **Amazon QuickSight:** A hosted business intelligence service powered by machine learning that provides data visualizations and insights from an organization's data records for reports or viewable dashboards. Accessed data records can be stored at AWS or stored in external locations including on-premises SQL Server, MySQL, and PostgreSQL databases, or in Amazon Redshift, RDS, Aurora, Athena, and S3 storage.

- **Amazon Rekognition:** Allows developers to add visual capabilities to applications using the following methods:

  - **Rekognition Image:** Searches, verifies, and organizes millions of images, detecting objects, scenes, and faces; identifies and extracts inappropriate content in images.

  - **Rekognition Video:** Extracts motion-based context from stored or live-stream videos for analysis, recognizing objects, celebrities, and inappropriate content in videos stored in Amazon S3 storage.

- **AWS Security Hub:** Provides a detailed view of your current security environment of a single or multiple AWS accounts by consuming and prioritizing the findings gathered from various AWS security services such as Amazon GuardDuty, AWS Config, Amazon Detective, AWS Firewall Manager, AWS IAM Access Analyzer, Amazon Inspector, Amazon Macie, and Amazon Trusted Advisor. Once enabled, AWS Security Hub executes continuous account-level configuration and security checks based on AWS best practices and industry standards.

- **Amazon SageMaker:** Build, train, and deploy machine learning (ML) models.

- **Amazon SageMaker Autopilot:** Automatically inspect raw data and apply feature processors picking the best algorithm training and tuning multiple models and ranking each model based on performance.

- **Amazon SageMaker Pipelines:** Create fully automated ML workflows.

- **Amazon Textract:** A document analysis service that detects and extracts printed text and handwriting from images and scans of uploaded documents.

- **Amazon Transcribe:** Converts speech to text.

- **Amazon Translate:** A neural machine translation service that delivers high-quality language translation.

- **AWS X-Ray:** Allows developers to analyze and debug applications in development and production to quickly identify and troubleshoot performance issues and errors, providing an end-to-end view of workload communication.

  - **Service map:** X-Ray creates a map of services and connections being used by your application and tracks all application requests.

  - **Identify:** Errors and bugs are highlighted by analyzing the response code for each request made to your application.

  - **Custom analysis:** X-Ray query APIs can be used to build your own analysis and visualization interfaces.

In Conclusion

In this initial chapter, we have looked at what the public cloud is and how AWS fits into the public cloud arena in terms of IaaS and PaaS services. This chapter also introduced the NIST definitions of the public cloud and how the AWS cloud fits into NIST's definition.

This chapter also introduced the AWS Well-Architected Framework, which is an essential guideline on accepted best practices for deploying and managing workloads in the AWS cloud using suggested best practices and procedures. If you are planning to take the AWS Certified Solutions Architect – Associate (SAA-C03) exam, you need to be familiar with the Well-Architected Framework. We finished with a summary of a variety of AWS services that you might encounter on the exam, with enough details to understand the purpose of each service for answering exam questions.

This chapter covers the following topics:

- The Well-Architected Framework
- Designing a Workload SLA
- Deployment Methodologies

This chapter covers content that's important to the following exam domain and task statements:

Domain 2: Design Resilient Architectures

Task Statement 1: Design scalable and loosely coupled architectures

Task Statement 2: Design highly available and/or fault-tolerant architectures

CHAPTER 2

The AWS Well-Architected Framework

Your organization may be developing applications to be hosted in the cloud, or they may want to move some or all of current IT operations to the cloud. Regardless of the reason or scenario, your organization's applications/workloads that are moved to the cloud will be hosted on a variety of cloud services maintained and provided by the cloud provider. The most popular public cloud provider competitors to AWS, Microsoft Azure and Google Cloud, have been in operation for well over a decade. During this time, there have been many lessons learned by all cloud providers and customers; what works and what needs to be refined. This learned experience has resulted in many best practices that have been tested and refined for a variety of development and deployment scenarios. Each customer, before moving to the public cloud should take advantage of this documented experience, called the Well-Architected Framework. Microsoft Azure has released the Microsoft Azure Well-Architected Framework (https://learn.microsoft.com/en-us/azure/architecture/framework/), and Google has a Google Cloud Architecture Framework (https://cloud.google.com/architecture/framework).

The focus of this chapter, and indeed the book, is the pillars of the AWS Well-Architected Framework. The AWS Certified Solutions Architect – Associate website states that "The focus of this certification is on the design of cost and performance optimized solutions, demonstrating a strong understanding of the AWS Well-Architected Framework."

Selecting the best architectural design for a workload by considering the relevant best practices that have been tested in production by thousands of customers allows organizations to successfully plan for success with a very high degree of confidence. Instead of reacting to a never-ending series of short-term issues and fixes, customers can plan for engineering and operating workloads in the AWS cloud with a proven long-term approach. Whether you have existing systems that you are trying to migrate to the cloud or are building a new project from the ground up, using the AWS Well-Architected Framework will ultimately save your organization a great deal of time by considering many scenarios and ideas for design and deployment that you might not have fully considered.

Keep in mind that you are engineering your workloads for people—your customers. Employees and contractors are building and operating your cloud-based or hybrid deployments, choosing when, where, and how to use the technologies that make sense for each workload deployment. The goal is architecting your operations and workloads to operate successfully in the cloud, meeting and exceeding your business needs and requirements.

"Do I Know This Already?"

The "Do I Know This Already?" quiz allows you to assess whether you should read this entire chapter thoroughly or jump to the "Exam Preparation Tasks" section. If you are in doubt about your answers to these questions or your own assessment of your knowledge of the topics, read the entire chapter. Table 2-1 lists the major headings in this chapter and their corresponding "Do I Know This Already?" quiz questions. You can find the answers in Appendix A, "Answers to the 'Do I Know This Already?' Quizzes and Q&A Sections."

Table 2-1 "Do I Know This Already?" Section-to-Question Mapping

Foundation Topics Section	Questions
The Well-Architected Framework	1, 2
Designing a Workload SLA	3, 4
Deployment Methodologies	5, 6

CAUTION   The goal of self-assessment is to gauge your mastery of the topics in this chapter. If you do not know the answer to a question or are only partially sure of the answer, you should mark that question as wrong for purposes of the self-assessment. Giving yourself credit for an answer you correctly guess skews your self-assessment results and might provide you with a false sense of security.

1. The AWS Well-Architected Framework Sustainability pillar provides guidance on what types of impacts?

    a. Reliability

    b. Sizing compute and storage to avoid waste

    c. Compute performance

    d. Storage sizing

2. Which other AWS Well-Architected Framework pillars does workload reliability also affect?

   a. Cost Optimization and Sustainability

   b. Operation Excellence and Sustainability

   c. Scale and Performance

   d. Security and Cost Optimization

3. A workload SLA is designed to meet what criteria?

   a. Cloud service SLA

   b. Service-level objective

   c. Mean time between failures

   d. Restore point objective

4. What are the metrics used in determining a workload SLA called?

   a. Service-level indicators

   b. CloudWatch metrics

   c. Rules and alerts

   d. AWS defined SLAs

5. Agile development means focusing on what processes at the same time?

   a. Design, coding, and testing

   b. Planning and testing

   c. Planning and coding

   d. Planning, design, coding, and testing

6. What companion process can also be used with the AWS Well-Architected Framework?

   a. Big Bang development

   b. Waterfall development

   c. Agile development

   d. Twelve-Factor App Methodology

Foundation Topics

The Well-Architected Framework

As previously mentioned, AWS, Microsoft Azure, and Google Cloud all have their own well-architected frameworks (WAFs) as guidance, broken up into essential categories. I strongly recommend AWS's guidance for workload deployment (and for preparing for the AWS Certified Solutions Architect – Associate exam; exam questions are based on the Reliability, Security, Performance Efficiency, and Cost Optimization pillars). AWS is in constant contact with its customers to evaluate what they are currently doing in the cloud, and how they are doing it. Customers are always asking for features and changes to be added, and AWS and other public cloud providers are happy to oblige; after all, they want to retain their customers and keep them happy.

New products and services may offer improvements, but only if they are the right fit for your workload and your business needs and requirements. Decisions should be based on the six pillars of the AWS Well-Architected Framework: Security, Reliability, Performance Efficiency, Cost Optimization, Operational Excellence, and Sustainability. Evaluating these pillars is necessary for both pre-deployment architecture design *and* during your workload solution's lifecycle. Each of the WAF pillars is a subdiscipline of systems engineering in itself. Security engineering, reliability engineering, operational engineering, performance engineering, and cost and sustainability engineering are all areas of concern that customers need to keep on top of.

The AWS Well-Architected Framework has a number of relevant questions for each pillar that each customer should consider (see Figure 2-1). The end goal is to help you understand both the pros and cons of any decisions that you make when architecting workload successfully in the AWS cloud. The Well-Architected Framework contains best practices for designing reliable, secure, efficient, and cost-effective systems; however, you must carefully consider each best practice offered to see whether it applies. Listed best practices are suggestions, not decrees; final decisions are always left to each organization.

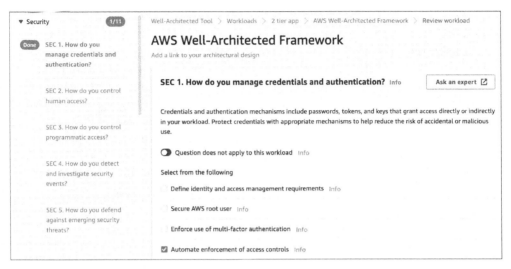

Figure 2-1   AWS Well-Architected Framework Security Pillar Questions

Before AWS launches a new cloud service, a focus on the desired operational excellence of the proposed service is discussed based on the overall requirements and priorities for the new service and the required business outcomes. There are certain aspects of operational excellence that are considered at the very start of the prepare phase, and there are continual tasks performed during the operation and management of the workload during its lifetime. However, one common thread is woven throughout the operational excellence pillar: performing detailed monitoring of all aspects of each workload during the prepare, operate, and evolve phases. There are four best practice areas for achieving and maintaining operational excellence:

- **Organization:** Completely understand the entire workload, team responsibilities, and defined business goals for business success for the new workload.

- **Prepare:** Understand the workload to be built, and closely monitor expected behaviors of the workload's internal state and external components.

- **Operate:** Each workload's success is measured by achieving both business and customer outcomes.

- **Evolve:** Continuously improve operations over time through learning and sharing the knowledge learned across all technical teams.

After operation excellence has been addressed, the next goal is to make each workload as secure as possible. Once security at all layers has been considered and planned for, workload reliability is next addressed. Next up is the performance efficiency of the workload; performance should be as fast as required, based on the business requirements. How do you know when there is a security, reliability, performance, or operational issue? To paraphrase: "There are known knowns; there are things we know we know. We also know there are known unknowns; that is to say we know there are some things we do not know. But there are also unknown unknowns—the ones we don't know we don't know." Ultimately, the answer to what we don't know always comes back to proactive monitoring. Without monitoring at every level of the workload, technical teams will not be able to monitor the operational health of each workload and won't have enough information to be able to solve existing and unexpected problems.

Let's look at the goals of each pillar of the AWS Well-Architected Framework in brief.

Operational Excellence Pillar

Operational excellence isn't a one-time effort that you achieve and are done with. Operational excellence is the repeated attempts to achieve greater outcomes from the technologies you choose and to improve your workload's operational models, procedures, principles, patterns, and practices.

Once security, reliability, performance, and cost have been addressed, you will have hopefully achieved a measure of operational excellence for a period of time, perhaps six months, perhaps longer. Then AWS will introduce a new feature, or a new service that looks interesting; this will send you back into the testing and development phase once again. Perhaps you will find that one of the recently introduced new features will vastly improve how a current workload could be improved. This cycle of change and improvement will continue, forever. Take any new or improved features into account. Operational excellence guidance helps workloads successfully operate in the AWS cloud for the long term.

Operational excellence has been achieved when your workload is operating with just the right amount of security and reliability; the required performance is perfect for your current needs; there is no waste or underutilized components in your application stack; and the cost of running your application is exactly right. Achieving this rarefied level of operation might seem like a fantasy, but in fact it's the ultimate goal of governance processes that have been designed by a Cloud Center of Excellence (Cloud CoE) team within an organization that is tasked with overseeing cloud operations for the organization. The Cloud CoE, and the culture of operational excellence it implements, is the driver that propals improvements and value throughout your organization. But getting there takes work, planning, analysis, and a willingness to make changes to continuously improve and refine operations as a whole.

Changes and improvements to security, reliability, performance efficiency, and cost optimization within your cloud architectures are best communicated through a Cloud CoE. It's also important to realize that changes that affect one pillar might have side effects in other pillars. Changes in security will affect reliability. Changes in improving reliability will affect cost. Operational excellence is where you can review the entire workload and achieve the desired balance.

NOTE   Operational Excellence design principles include organize, prepare, operate, and evolve. These best practices are achieved through automated processes for operations and deployments, daily and weekly maintenance, and mitigating security incidents when they occur.

Security Pillar

After the initial operational excellence design discussions, implementing a strong security foundation is next. After a workload has been deployed, the management of workload security is paramount. Organizations must design security into their cloud solution architectures to protect the workload and ensure its survival from attacks and catastrophic events.

If your online store or customer portal is knocked offline by hackers or corrupted with false or damaging information, your organization's reputation and customers could be maligned. What if customers' financial, medical, or other personal information is leaked from your systems? Organizations must design, deploy, test, monitor, and continuously improve security controls from the beginning. Security requires planning, effort, and expense, as nothing is more valuable than your customers and your ability to securely deliver applications and services meeting their needs. Strategies need to be employed to help achieve the security, privacy, and compliance required by each application and its associated components. These strategies are discussed next.

Defense in Depth

Defense in depth can be divided into three areas: physical controls, technical controls, and administrative controls. AWS as the cloud provider is responsible for security of the cloud; therefore, AWS is responsible for securing the physical resources using a variety of methods and controls. AWS also is responsible for providing technical and administrative controls for the cloud services its customers are using, so that they may secure and protect their application stacks and resources that are hosted in the cloud.

Each component of your application stack should have relevant security controls enabled to limit access. For example, consider a two-tier application consisting of web servers and an associated relational database. Both the web and database servers should be hosted on private subnets with no direct access to the Internet. Access to the Internet for updates and licensing should be controlled by using network address translation (NAT) services that allow indirect access from private subnets to the Internet for server updates. For public-facing applications, the load balancer should be placed on a public subnet accepting and directing requests to the web servers hosted on private subnets. Firewalls should be in place at each tier: To protect incoming traffic from Internet attacks, web application firewalls filter out undesirable traffic (see Figure 2-2). Each web and database server should be also protected by firewalls that allow only the required traffic through. Each subnet should be secured with network access controls that allow the required traffic and deny all other requests. Encryption should be deployed for both data in transit and data at rest.

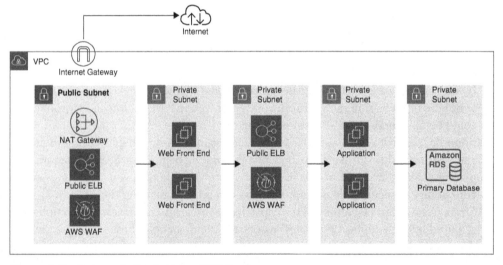

Figure 2-2   Defense in Depth Using AWS Services

Other security strategies include implementing the principle of least privilege using identity and authorization controls. AWS Identity and Access Management (IAM) allows customers to create permission policies for users, groups, and roles for cloud administrators, cloud services, and end users that access cloud resources from their mobile devices (see Figure 2-3).

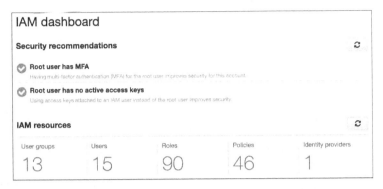

Figure 2-3   Identity and Access Management Security Controls

There are many security services you can enable in the cloud, allowing organizations to reap the benefits. For example, Amazon GuardDuty provides intelligent threat detection using machine learning to provide continuous monitoring of network traffic, DNS queries, and API calls, and protect access to RDS databases and Kubernetes deployments.

Reliability Pillar

Reliability is the most important requirement; without reliability, end users will eventually stop using the application. Each workload should be designed to minimize failure, keeping in mind there are many components in each application stack to consider. Over the past decade, many best practices have been published as to how to best deploy and manage workloads and associated AWS cloud services with a high degree of reliability.

Organizations must define the required level of reliability for each workload deployed in the AWS cloud. Cloud reliability is commonly defined as cloud service availability. Before the cloud, a *service-level agreement (SLA)* was an explicit contract with the provider that included consequences for missing the provider's service-level objectives. AWS SLAs indicate that they will do their best to keep their infrastructure and managed services up and available most of the time. Each AWS cloud service typically has a defined SLA that defines an operational uptime goal which AWS attempts to meet, and usually exceeds (see Figure 2-4). If failures occur, and they do occur from time to time, and you can prove that a workload was down because of AWS's failures, AWS will provide you with a credit on your bill. AWS SLAs can be found here: https://aws.amazon.com/legal/service-level-agreements/.

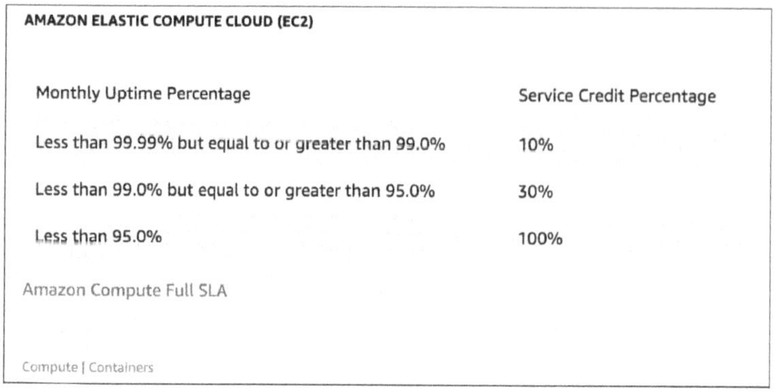

AMAZON ELASTIC COMPUTE CLOUD (EC2)	
Monthly Uptime Percentage	Service Credit Percentage
Less than 99.99% but equal to or greater than 99.0%	10%
Less than 99.0% but equal to or greater than 95.0%	30%
Less than 95.0%	100%
Amazon Compute Full SLA	
Compute | Containers	

Figure 2-4 AWS Service-Level Agreements

SLA numbers that define cloud service availability look better than they really are. For example, demanding a desired application availability of 99.99% is designing for the potential unavailability over a calendar year of roughly 52 minutes of downtime. Because potential downtime does not include scheduled maintenance, when is this 52 minutes of downtime going to occur? That is the big question to which there is no guaranteed answer. If your workload is streaming video delivery, 99.99% is the recommended availability target to shoot for. If your workload processes ATM transactions, a maximum unavailability of 5 minutes per year, or five nines (99.999%), is the recommended availability target to shoot for. For an online software as a service (SaaS) application involving point-of-sale transactions, the recommendation is 99.95%, or roughly 4 hours and 22 minutes of downtime per year. Other considerations when calculating workload availability include workload dependencies and availability with redundant components.

- **Workload dependencies:** On-premises workloads will have hard dependencies on other locally installed services; for example, an associated database. Operating in the AWS cloud, if a dependent database fails, a backup or standby database service can be available for automatic failover. In the AWS cloud, workloads can more easily be designed with a reliance on what are defined as *soft dependencies*. With each AWS region containing multiple availability zones, web and application servers deployed across multiple availability zones fronted by a load balancer provide a highly available design. Databases are also deployed across at least two availability zones, and the primary and secondary database servers are kept up to date with synchronous replication.

- **Availability using redundant components:** Designing with independent and redundant cloud services, availability can be calculated by subtracting the availability of the independent cloud services utilized by your workload from

100%. Operating a workload across two availability zones, each independent availability zone has a defined availability of 99.95%. Multiplied together and subtracted from 100%, availability is six nines, or 99.9999% (see Figure 2-5).

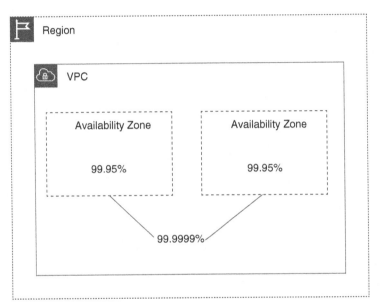

Figure 2-5 Multi-AZ Service-Level Agreements

NOTE Applications that are designed for higher levels of availability will also have increased costs. Workloads designed with high availability will have multiple web, application, and database instances across multiple availability zones.

Performance Efficiency Pillar

In information technology systems engineering, design specialists characterize workloads as compute oriented, storage focused, or memory driven, designing solutions tuned to efficiently meet the design requirements. To achieve your performance goals, customers must address how the design of workload components can affect the performance efficiency of the entire application stack.

How can you design around a compute bottleneck? How do you get around a limit of the read or write rate of your storage? Operating in the AWS cloud, customers can change compute and network performance as simply as turning off their EC2 instances and resizing the EC2 instance, changing the memory, processor, and network specs. Amazon Elastic Block Store (EBS) storage volumes can be changed in size, type, and speed at a moment's notice, increasing volume size and performance as needs change (see Figure 2-6).

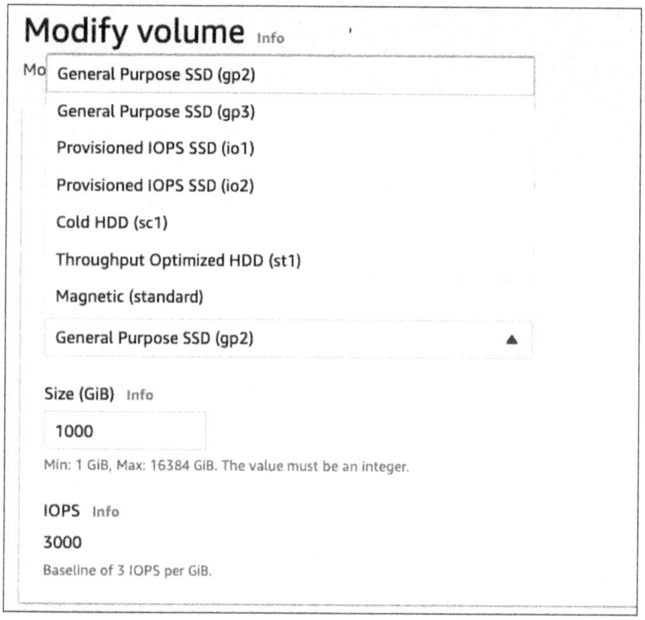

Modify volume   Info

Mo | General Purpose SSD (gp2)

General Purpose SSD (gp3)

Provisioned IOPS SSD (io1)

Provisioned IOPS SSD (io2)

Cold HDD (sc1)

Throughput Optimized HDD (st1)

Magnetic (standard)

General Purpose SSD (gp2) ▲

Size (GiB)   Info

1000

Min: 1 GiB, Max: 16384 GiB. The value must be an integer.

IOPS   Info

3000

Baseline of 3 IOPS per GiB.

Figure 2-6   Resize EBS Volumes

Maximizing performance efficiency depends on knowing your workload requirements over time. Measure workload limitations and overall operation by closely monitoring all aspects of the associated cloud services. After several days, weeks, and months of analyzing monitoring data for the computer, networking, and storage services utilized in your application stack, developers and operations teams will be able to make informed decisions about required changes and improvements to the current workload design. Learn where your bottlenecks are by carefully monitoring all aspects of your application stack. Performance efficiency can also be improved with parallelism, scalability, and improved network speeds:

- Parallelism can be designed into many systems so that you can have many instances running simultaneously. Workload transactions can be serialized using SQS caches or database read replicas.

- Scalability in the cloud is typically horizontal. But scale can also be vertical by increasing the size, compute power, or transaction capacity on web, app, or database processing instances or containers. Customers may find success by increasing the sizes of both the compute and networking speeds of database instances without having to rebuild from scratch, if this is a solution that can be carried out relatively quickly.

- Networking is critical to performance engineering in the cloud, because the host architecture that AWS offers its cloud services on, and the EC2 instances and storage arrays used for all workloads, are all networked. Networking speeds across private networks of AWS can reach 200 Gbps. Connecting to the AWS cloud from an on-premises location privately using VPN connections max out at 1.25 Gbps. Utilizing high-speed fiber AWS Direct Connections to the AWS cloud range from 1 to 100 Gbps.

Cost Optimization Pillar

Customers want to optimize their returns on investments in AWS cloud technologies. Successfully reducing cloud costs starts with assessing your true needs. Monitoring is essential to continually improving your performance efficiency, and it's also the key to unlocking cost benefits over time. AWS provides many cost tools for monitoring costs, including cost estimators, trackers, and machine learning–based advisors. Many of these services are free, such as AWS Cost Explorer or AWS Cost and Usage Report.

When analyzing the daily operation of services such as compute and storage, auto-scaling and true consumption spending are not the default configuration. Insights into spending trends and rates allow you to control what you spend in the cloud.

Sustainability Pillar

The Sustainability pillar addresses the impact of your workload deployments against long-term environmental issues such as indirect carbon emissions (see Figure 2-7) or environmental damage caused by cloud services. Because workload resources rely on cloud services that are virtual compute and storage services, areas where improvements in sustainability include energy consumption and workload efficiency in the following areas:

- Utilizing indirect electricity to power workload resources. Consider deploying resources in AWS regions where the grid has a published carbon intensity lower than other AWS regions.

- Optimizing workloads for economical operations. Consider scaling infrastructure matching user demand and ensuring only the minimum number of resources required are deployed.

- Minimizing the total number of storage resources used by each workload.

- Utilizing managed AWS services instead of existing infrastructure.

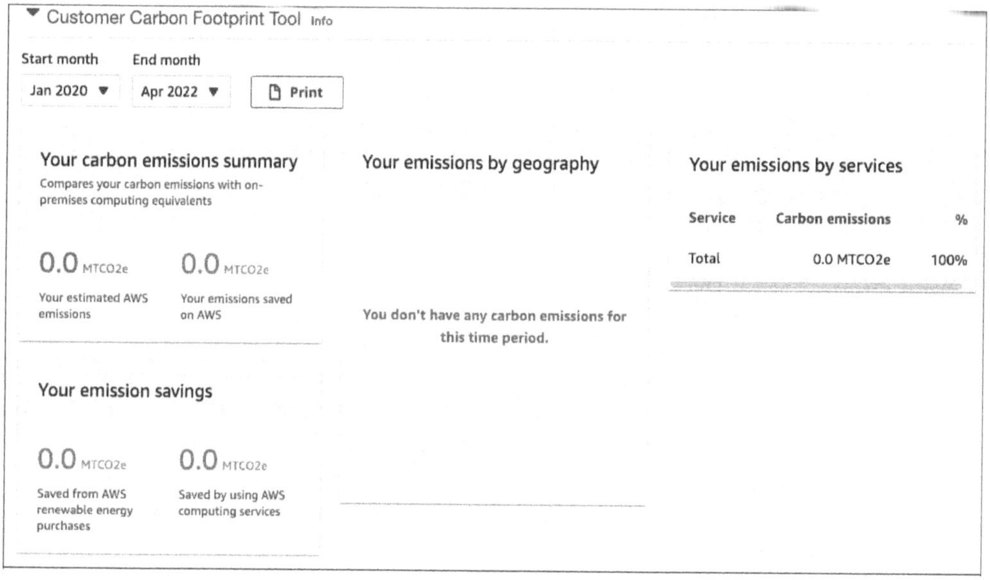

Figure 2-7 Customer Carbon Footprint Tool

Designing a Workload SLA

Organizations must design workload SLAs that define the level of workload reliability they require and are willing to pay for. It should be noted that AWS cloud services are online, very reliable, and up most of the time. The onus is on each AWS customer to design workloads to be able to minimize the effects of any failures of the AWS cloud services used to create application stacks. Note that each cloud service, such as storage and compute, that is part of your workload application stacks has its own separately defined SLA.

The AWS cloud services that are included in our workloads need to operate at our defined acceptable level of reliability; in the cloud industry this is defined as a *service-level objective (SLO)* and is measured by a metric called a *service-level indicator (SLI)*. For example, web servers must operate at a target of between 55%

and 65% utilization. By monitoring the CPU utilization of the web servers, you can be alerted using an Amazon CloudWatch metric linked to an event-driven alarm when the utilization exceeds 65%. You could manually add additional web servers, or EC2 Auto Scaling could be used to automatically add and remove additional web servers as required. There are numerous CloudWatch metrics that can be utilized for more than 70 AWS cloud services providing specific operational details and alert when issues occur.

Ongoing CloudWatch monitoring should be used to monitor each integrated cloud service for calculating the reliability of the workload as a whole using the cloud service metrics (see Figure 2-8). Each metric can be monitored over a defined time period, which can range from seconds to weeks; the default time period is typically 5 minutes. Every month the average amount of workload availability can be calculated by dividing the successful responses against all requests. By monitoring all integrated cloud services of a workload, valuable knowledge will be gathered regarding reliability issues, potential security threats, and workload performance.

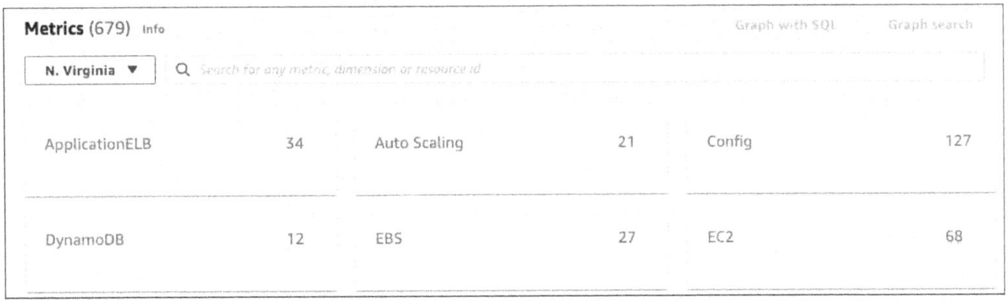

Metrics (679) Info				Graph with SQL	Graph search
N. Virginia ▼	Q Search for any metric, dimension or resource id				
ApplicationELB	34	Auto Scaling	21	Config	127
DynamoDB	12	EBS	27	EC2	68

Figure 2-8   CloudWatch Metrics

Service-level indicators are invaluable for all cloud services; here are a few examples to consider:

- **Availability:** The amount of time that the service is available and usable

- **Latency:** How quickly requests can be fulfilled

- **Throughput:** How much data is being processed; input/output operations per second (IOPS)

- **Durability:** The likelihood data written to storage can be retrieved in the future

Reliability and Performance Are Linked

Safety, testability, quality, maintainability, stability, durability, and availability are all aspects of a workload's overall reliability. Reliability is the critical design consideration. For example, if a workload crashes periodically but reboots and carries on, persistent end users who retry their requests might get their results eventually. But besides the obvious reliability issue, there is also a performance issue. Your workload's effective performance is lower because of the required retries.

An unresponsive website will eventually cause customer dissatisfaction, which negatively impacts trust and the reputation of the application. If it leads prospective or established customers to shop elsewhere, that could result in lost potential business. Maintaining redundant cloud services to improve workload reliability and performance will result in additional operational expense for some cloud services, such as multiple EC2 instances and multiple database instances providing redundant storage.

When designing for reliability, it's important to realize that not all workload dependencies will have the same impact when they fail. An outage for an application stack designed with some hard dependencies, such as a single primary database with no alternate database as a backup, will obviously cause problems that cannot be ignored when failure occurs. An outage with a soft dependency, such as an alternate database read-replica, will hopefully have no short-term impact on regular workload operation. Workload reliability can also positively affect overall performance. With the use of multiple availability zones utilizing separate physical data centers separated by miles, workloads can easily achieve a level of reliability and high availability as the web servers, and primary and alternate database servers, are hosted in separate physical locations. Database records can be kept up to date using synchronous replication between the primary and alternate database instances or storage locations.

Disaster Recovery

In addition to defining your availability objectives, you should consider disaster recovery (DR) objectives. How is each workload recovered when disaster occurs? How much data can you afford to lose, and how quickly must you recover? The application's acceptable *recovery time objective (RTO)* and *recovery point objective (RPO)* must be defined and then tested to ensure that the application meets and possibly exceeds the desired service-level objectives. Both the RTO and RPO for each workload need to be defined by your organization. RTO is the maximum acceptable delay between the interruption of an application and the restoration of service. RPO is the maximum acceptable amount of data loss.

Placing Cloud Services

It's critical that you choose where each workload component resides and operates. Some cloud services, such as DNS name resolution and traffic routing and content delivery networks (CDNs), are globally distributed across the world. But most AWS cloud services are regional in design. That is, they are *hosted* in one particular geographical location, even if they might be *accessible* globally. Techniques such as replication, redirection, and load balancing allow you to deploy workload cloud services as multi-region architecture.

Exam questions will ask you to consider several options when deciding where each workload and associated cloud services should be located to best meet the needs of the question's scenario: host location, data caching, data replication, load balancing, and failover architecture that is required.

Data Residency and Compute Locations

Running workloads in the cloud is essentially leasing time on storage and compute power in a cloud provider's data centers. Each cloud provider hosts services in regions throughout the world. For example, Amazon, Google, and Microsoft each host their cloud services somewhere in the state of Virginia, in a region near Tokyo, and in dozens of other regions around the globe.

How do you choose a region to host your services in? The first suggestion is to consider data residency. Do you have compliance guidelines, laws, or underwriters that suggest or dictate that you store your data within a certain country, state, or province? That might be your sole consideration. If data residency isn't strictly mandated or multiple AWS regions don't meet your criteria, you could instead place your data close to your customers or to your own facilities. Those regions might not be the same geography, depending on the nature of your business and markets you serve.

Let's use an example of a fictitious business called Terra Firma based in Winnipeg, Ontario, which is in the middle of Canada. Let's assume that Terra Firma has deployed its customer portal website in the AWS cloud somewhere in the central Canada region, near its offices and the majority of its users. If customers in the central Canada region have sufficiently fast, low-latency Internet connectivity to this AWS cloud region, their user experience could be adequate with the hosted website portal. Let's look next at whether caching could be a benefit to the Terra Firma website portal.

Caching Data with CDNs

CDNs serve up temporary copies of data to the client in order to improve effective network performance. Architecturally, the CDN servers are distributed around many global service areas. In the case of modern cloud CDNs, the service area is global; AWS hosts a global CDN world-wide *cache* called Amazon CloudWatch. How can a CDN cache benefit the web portal users?

Without a CDN cache, the web browsers of Terra Firma's central Canadian customers would send requests to the website address hosted at the cloud region hundreds of miles away. The speed of the website hosting and backend storage and databases for the site are a factor in the end-user experience. But the Internet latency from each user's Internet connection to the AWS cloud region chosen by Terra Firma can significantly contribute to the performance and overall experience.

Let's assume that Terra Firma's AWS cloud provider CloudFront has a CDN point of presence (POP) located in downtown Winnipeg. If Terra Firma's cloud architects and operations staff configured their website to use a CDN, their customers could benefit from a faster user experience. Customer Julian's web browser queries for Terra Firma's web address and receives a response from the CDN POP location in Winnipeg. Julian's browser next sends a request to load the website to that local POP in Winnipeg, which is a few miles away through the local Internet gateway instead of hundreds of miles and several network hops away to the location of the web server.

If Julian is the first user in the last 24 hours to load any of the requested files, the Winnipeg CDN POP won't find the files in its temporary cache. The POP would then relay a web request to the website origin address hosted in the cloud region hundreds of miles away.

When another customer in the Winnipeg region, Jan, visits the web portal site, her browser resolves the site name to the Winnipeg CDN POP just as Julian's had done recently. For each file that is still cached locally, the POP will send back an immediate local response; without consulting the web server hundreds of miles away, Jan gets a super-fast experience. And the hundreds, thousands, or millions of other customers who visit the Terra Firma web portal can get this performance benefit as well. AWS CloudFront, AWS's CDN, provides hundreds of POPs around the world (see Figure 2-9). Wherever users are located, there is likely a POP locally or within the same geographical area. Users close to the actual website AWS cloud region can also be serviced by a POP in that cloud region. People far away will get the same benefits once another end user in their area visits the Terra Firma website, which will automatically populate their local POP's cache.

Edge
Locations

Multiple
Edge Locations

Regional
Edge Caches

Figure 2-9 Amazon CloudWatch Edge Locations

NOTE CDN caching techniques must be explicitly programmed and configured in your application code and in the Amazon CloudWatch distribution. Deploying a CDN is designed to improve performance and alleviate the load on the origin services, as in our example of a web portal.

Data Replication

Although CloudFront focuses on performance, a CDN provides substantial security, reliability, cost, and operations benefits. But what if your workload design also stores persistent replica copies of your data, resulting in multiple copies of data? Let's look at the benefits of cloud storage and replicated data records.

The applications, cloud services, and data records that make up your workload solutions must be reliable. A single database or website is a single point of failure that could bring down the entire workload. Organizations don't want their business to fail, so they need to architect and engineer systems to avoid any single points of failure. To improve reliability in cloud solutions architectures, customers need to make choices about redundancy, replication, scaling, and failover.

AWS provides multiple replicas of data records that are stored in the cloud. Three copies is a common default, with options for greater or lesser redundancy depending on the storage service chosen. There are additional options for expanding or reducing additional data replication. Storage and replication are not free; customers must pay for the used storage infrastructure consumed per month. Network transfer costs are billed relative to the rate of change and duplicate copies are billed based on the stored capacity used. Always check with AWS for up-to-date and region-specific pricing of storage, databases, and replication for these services. Deploy the required configurations at AWS to enable the desired redundancy for every database, data lake, and storage requirement:

- Replicate within an availability zone if necessary

- Replicate between availability zones within your primary AWS region

- Replicate between your chosen primary AWS cloud region and one or more secondary regions

Operating in the AWS cloud requires security and replication at all levels. Customers should also consider deploying compute containers, virtual machine instances, or clusters of either to multiple availability zones and across regions to meet their needs.

Load Balancing Within and Between Regions

When we have more than one replica of an EC2 instance or containerized application, we can load balance requests to any one of those replicas, thereby balancing the load across the replicas (see Figure 2-10). Read operations, queries, database select statements, and many compute requests can be load balanced, as can writes to multi-master database systems.

- Network load balancers use Internet protocol addresses (IPv4 or IPv6), with a choice of TCP, UDP, or both on top of IP and with port numbers to identify the application or service running. Rules stating how to block or relay network traffic matching the source and target IP address, protocol, and port patterns dictate the load-balancing process.

- Application load balancers indicate that HTTP or HTTPS traffic is being load balanced, with balancing rules based on web URLs with rule choices of HTTP or HTTPS, domain name, folder and file name, web path, and query strings.

Application Load Balancer Info

Network Load Balancer Info

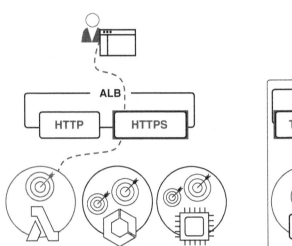
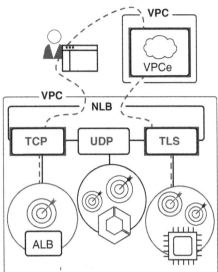

Figure 2-10 Load Balancer Options

Before load-balancing associations and connections can be established at load balancers, network communications using Internet technologies must perform name resolution. The Domain Name System (DNS) Amazon Route 53 service is used to *resolve* a domain name like www.pearson.com into other domain names (canonically), or into the IPv4 or IPv6 addresses needed to communicate. Rules and policies can be associated with a domain name so that round-robin, priority, failover, weighted, or geolocation will select the results for one end user versus another. Amazon Route 53 also provides *inter-region* load balancing across AWS regions.

One of the key advantages of the Network, Application, and Route 53 load balancers is that they can monitor the health of the targets they have been configured to distribute queries to. This feedback enables the load balancers to provide actual *balancing* of the load based on health checks, affinity, stickiness, and security filtering in order to better truly balance the load on your replicas, which allows you to better achieve cost optimization and performance efficiency. Load balancers are also key to application reliability as well.

Failover Architecture

Failover is a critical aspect of load-balancing resources. The ability to have your solutions *detect* failures and *automatically* divert to an alternate replica is essential. With *automatic failover*, you can quickly switchover and reassign requests to the surviving replicas. For database systems, primary–secondary relationships should be designed and deployed.

Failover allows for business continuity in the event of cloud service failure. If there were only two replicas of the application in question and one replica failed, in the failover state you are running without any redundancy. Customers must restore redundancy by either repairing the failed component and bringing it back online or by replacing it. If you deploy triple or greater degrees of redundancy in the first place, recovery from a failure state is not as immediate a concern.

Failover is a general topic that is not just limited to load-balancing technologies. Additional strategies of failover will be addressed in later chapters. It's important to note that replication, load balancing, and failover are related features that must be orchestrated so that they work in concert with one another. When configured properly, customers can achieve and maintain advantages in security, reliability, and workload performance.

Deployment Methodologies

Developers getting ready to create their first application in the cloud can look to a number of rules that are generally accepted for successfully creating applications that run exclusively in the public cloud.

Several years ago, Heroku cofounder Adam Wiggins released a suggested blueprint for creating native SaaS applications hosted in the public cloud, called the Twelve-Factor App Methodology. Heroku (https://www.heroku.com/) is a platform as a service provider (PaaS) owned by Salesforce and hosted at AWS. Heroku was attempting to provide guidance for SaaS applications created in the public cloud based on their real-world experience. Additional details on this methodology can be found at https://12factor.net/ (see Figure 2-11).

THE TWELVE-FACTOR APP

INTRODUCTION

In the modern era, software is commonly delivered as a service: called *web apps*, or *software-as-a-service*. The twelve-factor app is a methodology for building software-as-a-service apps that:

- Use **declarative** formats for setup automation, to minimize time and cost for new developers joining the project;
- Have a **clean contract** with the underlying operating system, offering **maximum portability** between execution environments;
- Are suitable for **deployment** on modern **cloud platforms**, obviating the need for servers and systems administration;
- **Minimize divergence** between development and production, enabling **continuous deployment** for maximum agility;
- And can **scale up** without significant changes to tooling, architecture, or development practices.

The twelve-factor methodology can be applied to apps written in any programming language, and which use any combination of backing services (database, queue, memory cache, etc).

Figure 2-11   The 12 Factor App Methodology

These guidelines can be viewed as a set of best practices to consider using when deploying applications at AWS that align with the AWS Well-Architected Framework. Depending on your deployment methods, you may quibble with some of the factors—and that's okay There arc many complementary management services hosted at AWS that greatly speed up the development and deployment process of workloads that are hosted at AWS. The development and operational model that you choose to embrace will follow one of these development and deployment paths:

- **Waterfall:** In this model, deployment is broken down into phases, including proper analysis, system design, implementation and testing, deployment, and ongoing maintenance. In the waterfall model, each of these phases must be completed before the next phase can begin. If your timeline is short, and all the technologies to be used in hosting and managing your workload are fully understood, then perhaps this model can still work in the cloud. However, cloud providers are introducing many cloud services that free you from having to know every technical detail as to how the service works; instead, you can just use the cloud service as part of your workload deployment. For example, an Amazon S3 bucket is used for unlimited cloud storage, without customers without customers needing to know the technical details of the S3 storage array. In the AWS cloud, all the infrastructure components for storage and compute are already online and functional; you don't have to build storage arrays or even databases from scratch; you can merely order or quickly config-ure the service, and you are off and running. When developing in the cloud, if your timeline for development is longer than six months, most hosted cloud services will have changed and improved in that time frame, forcing you to take another look at your design and deployment options.

■ **Agile:** In this model, the focus is on process adaptability, and teams can be working simultaneously on the planning, design, coding, and testing processes. The entire process cycle is divided into a relatively shorter time frame, such as a 1-month duration. At the end of the first month, the first build of the product is presented to the potential customers, feedback is provided, and is incorporated into the next process cycle and the second version of the product. This process continues until a final production version of the product is deliv-ered and accepted. This process might continue indefinitely if an application has continual changes and updates. Think of any cloud application installed on your personal devices and consider how many times that application gets updated. It's probably updated every few months at a minimum; for example, the Google Chrome browser updates itself at least every couple of weeks. AWS has a number of cloud services that can help with Agile deployments, including AWS Cloud9, AWS CloudFormation, AWS CodeCommit, AWS CodeBuild, and AWS CodePipeline.

■ **Big Bang:** In this model, there is no specific process flow; when money is available in the budget, development starts, and eventually software is devel-oped. This model can work in the cloud because there are no capital costs to worry about; work can proceed when there is a budget. But without proper planning and a full understanding of requirements of the application, long-term projects may have to be constantly revised over time due to changes in the cloud and changes from the customer.

Before deploying applications in the AWS cloud, you should carefully review your current development process and perhaps consider taking some of the steps pro-posed in the Twelve-Factor App Methodology described in the following sections. Applications that are hosted in the AWS cloud need the correct infrastructure; as a result, the rules for application deployment in the AWS cloud don't stand alone. Cloud infrastructure adhering to the principles of the AWS Well-Architected Framework is also a necessary part of the rules. The following sections look at the applicable factors of the Twelve-Factor App Methodology from the infrastructure point of view and also identify the AWS services that can help with adhering to each factor. This discussion can help you understand both the factors and the AWS ser-vices that are useful in application development and deployment and help you pre-pare for the exam with the right mindset.

Factor 1: Use One Codebase That Is Tracked with Version Control to Allow Many Deployments

In development circles, this factor is nonnegotiable; it must be followed. Creating an application usually involves three separate environments: development, testing, and production (see Figure 2-12). The same codebase should be used in each environment, whether it's the developer's laptop, a set of EC2 instances in the test environments, or the production EC2 instances. Each version of application code needs to be stored separately and securely in a safe location. Multiple AWS environments can take advantage of multiple availability zones and multiple VPCs to create dev, test, and production environments.

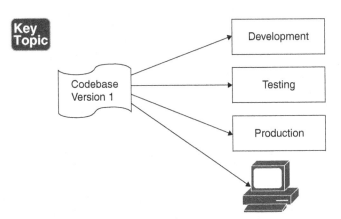

Figure 2-12   One Codebase, Regardless of Location

Developers typically use code repositories such as GitHub to store their code. Operating systems, off-the-shelf software, dynamic link libraries (DLLs), development environments, and application code are always defined by a specific version number. As your codebase undergoes revisions, each revision of each component needs to be tracked; after all, a single codebase might be responsible for thousands of deployments, and documenting and controlling the separate versions of the codebase just makes sense. Amazon has a code repository, called AWS CodeCommit, for applications developed and hosted at AWS.

At the infrastructure level at Amazon, it is important to consider all dependencies. The AWS infrastructure components to keep track of include the following:

- **AMIs:** Images for web, application, database, and appliance instances. Amazon Machine Images (AMI) should be version controlled and immutable.

- **Amazon EBS volumes:** Boot volumes and data volumes should be tagged by version number for proper identification and control.

- **Amazon EBS snapshots:** Snapshots used to create virtual server boot volumes are also part of each AMI.

- **Container images:** Each private container image can be stored in the Amazon Elastic Container Registry (ECR) and protected with Identity and Access Management (IAM) permission policies. Container images could be stored in the Amazon Elastic Container Registry.

- **Serverless applications.** The AWS Serverless Application Repository can be used to store, share, and assemble serverless architectures.

AWS CodeCommit

CodeCommit is a hosted AWS version control service with no storage size limits (see Figure 2-13). It allows AWS customers to privately store their source code and binary code, which are automatically encrypted at rest and at transit, at AWS. Code-Commit allows customers to store code versions at AWS rather than at Git without worrying about running out of storage space. CodeCommit is also HIPAA eligible and supports PCI DSS and ISO/IEC 27001 standards.

Figure 2-13   A CodeCommit Repository

CodeCommit supports common Git commands and, as mentioned earlier, there are no limits on file size, type, and repository size. CodeCommit is designed for collaborative software development environments. When developers make multiple file changes, CodeCommit manages the changes across multiple files. Amazon S3 buckets also support file versioning, but S3 versioning is meant for recovery of older versions of files; it is not designed for collaborative software development environments; as a result, S3 buckets are better suited for storing files that are not source code.

Factor 2: Explicitly Declare and Isolate Dependencies

A workload deployed in development, testing, and production VPC networks at AWS may require specific components, such as a MySQL database, a specific operating system version, and a particular utility, and monitoring agent. All dependencies for each workload must be documented so that developers are aware of the version of each component required by the application stack. Deployed applications should never rely on the assumed existence of required system components; ***dependencies*** need to be declared and managed by a dependency manager, ensuring that the required dependencies are installed with the codebase. Examples of dependency managers are Composer, which is used with PHP projects, and Maven, which can be used with Java projects. Dependency managers use a configuration database to keep track of the required version of each component, and what repository to retrieve it from. If there is a specific version of system tools that the codebase always requires, perhaps the system tools could be added to the operating system that the codebase will be installed on. However, over time, software versions for every component will change. The benefit of using a dependency manager is that the versions of your dependencies will be the same versions used in the development, testing, and production environments.

If multiple operating system versions are deployed, the operating system and its feature set can also be controlled by AMI versions. Several AWS services work with versions of AMIs, application code, and deployment of AWS infrastructure stacks:

- **AWS EC2 Image Builder:** Simplify the building, testing, and deployment of virtual machines and container images at AWS and on premises.

- **AWS CodeCommit:** Can be used to host different versions of the application code.

- **AWS CloudFormation:** Includes several helper scripts to automatically install and configure applications, packages, and operating system services that execute on EC2 Linux and Windows instances. The following are a few examples of these helper scripts:

  - **cfn-init:** This script can install packages, create files, and start operating system services.

  - **cfn-signal:** This script can be used with a wait condition to synchronize installation timings only when the required resources are installed and available.

  - **cdn-get-metadata:** This script can be used to retrieve metadata from the EC2 instance's memory.

Factor 3: Store Configuration in the Environment

Your *codebase* should be the same when it is running in the development, testing, and production network environments. However, your database instances will have different paths, or URLs, when connecting to testing or development environments. Other configuration components, such as API keys, plus database credentials for access and authentication, should never be hard-coded per environment. Use AWS Secrets Manager to store database credentials and secrets. Create IAM roles to access data resources at AWS, including S3 buckets, DynamoDB tables, and RDS databases. You can use Amazon API Gateway to host your APIs.

Development frameworks define environment variables through the use of configuration files. Separating your application components from the application code allows you to reuse your backing services in different environments, using environment variables to point to the desired resource from the development, testing, or production environment. Amazon has a few services that can help centrally store application configurations:

- **AWS Secrets Manager:** This service allows you to store application secrets such as database credentials, API keys, and OAuth tokens.

- **AWS Certificate Manager (ACM):** This service allows you to create and manage public Secure Sockets Layer/Transport Layer Security (SSL/TLS) certificates used for any hosted AWS websites or applications. ACM also enables you to create a private certificate authority and issue X.509 certificates for identification of IAM users, EC2 instances, and AWS services.

- **AWS Key Management Service (AWS KMS):** This service can be used to create and manage encryption keys.

- **AWS CloudHSM:** This service provides single-tenant hardware security modules allowing organizations to generate and manage their own encryption keys at AWS.

- **AWS Systems Manager Parameter Store:** This service stores configuration data and secrets for EC2 instances, including passwords, database strings, and license codes.

Factor 4: Treat Backing Services as Attached Resources

Many cloud infrastructure and platform services at AWS can be defined as backing services accessed by HTTPS private endpoints connected over the AWS private network. These include databases (for example, Amazon Relational Database Service [RDS], DynamoDB), shared storage (for example, Amazon S3 buckets, Amazon

Elastic File System [EFS]), Simple Mail Transfer Protocol (SMTP) services, queues (for example, Amazon Simple Queue Service [SQS]), caching systems (such as Amazon ElastiCache, which manages Memcached or Redis in-memory queues or in-memory databases), and monitoring services (for example, Amazon CloudWatch, AWS Config, AWS CloudTrail).

Backing services should be completely swappable; for example, a MySQL database hosted on premises should be able to be swapped with a hosted copy of the database at AWS without requiring any changes to application code; for this example, the only variable that would change is the resource handle in the configuration file pointing to the database location.

Factor 5: Separate Build and Run Stages

Applications that will be updated on a defined schedule or at unpredictable times require defined stages during which testing can be carried out on the application state before it is approved and moved into production. AWS Elastic Beanstalk allows you to upload and deploy your application code combined with a configuration file that builds the AWS environment required for the application.

The Elastic Beanstalk build stage could retrieve your application code from a defined repo storage location, such as an Amazon S3 bucket. Developers could also use the Elastic Beanstalk CLI to push application code commits to AWS CodeCommit. When you run the CLI command **EB create** or **EB deploy** to create or update an EBS environment, the selected application version is pulled from the defined AWS CodeCommit repository and the application and required environment are uploaded to Elastic Beanstalk. Other AWS services that work with deployment stages include the following:

- **AWS CodePipeline:** This service provides a continuous delivery service for automating deployment of applications using multiple staging environments.

- **AWS CodeDeploy:** This service helps automate application deployments to EC2 instances hosted at AWS or on premises.

- **AWS CodeBuild:** This service compiles source code, runs tests on prebuilt environments, and produces code ready to deploy without having to manually build the test server environment.

Factor 6: Execute an App as One or More Stateless Processes

Stateless processes provide fault tolerance for the EC2 instances or containers running applications by separating the application data records and storing them in a centralized storage location such as an Amazon SQS message queue. An example of a stateless design is using an SQS message queue (see Figure 2-14). EC2 instances that are subscribed to the watermark SQS queue poll the queue, for any updates; when an update message is received, the server carries out the work of adding a watermark to the video and storing the modified video in S3 storage.

Figure 2-14   Using SQS Queues to Provide Stateless Memory-Resident Storage for Applications

Other stateless options available at AWS include the following:

- **AWS Simple Notification Service (SNS):** This hosted messaging service allows applications to deliver push-based notifications to subscribers such as SQS queues or Lambda.

- **Amazon MQ:** This hosted managed message broker service, specifically designed for Apache Active MQ, is an open-source message broker service that provides functionality similar to that of AWS SQS queues.

- **Amazon Simple Email Service (SES):** This hosted email-sending service includes an SMTP interface that allows you to integrate the email service into your application for communicating with an end user.

- **AWS Lambda:** This service is used for executing custom functions written by each customer for a vast variety of event-driven tasks. Examples include AWS Config custom rules for resolving infrastructure resources that fall out of compliance, and automated responses for Amazon Simple Notification Services (SNS), and Amazon EventBridge and CloudWatch alarms.

- **Amazon AppFlow:** This service enables you to exchange data between SaaS applications and storage services such as Amazon S3 or Amazon Redshift.

- **AWS Step Functions:** This service enables you to build and run workflows that coordinate the execution of multiple AWS services.

Factor 7: Export Services via Port Binding

Instead of using a local web server installed on a local server host and accessible only from a local port, you should make services accessible by binding to external ports where the services are located and accessible, using an external URL. For example, all web requests can be carried out by binding to an external port, where the web service is hosted and from which it is accessed. The service port that the application needs to connect to is defined by the development environment's configuration file (see the section "Factor 3: Store Configuration in the Environment," earlier in this chapter. The associated web service can be used multiple times by different applications and the different development, testing, and production environments.

Factor 8: Scale Out via the Process Model

If your application can't scale horizontally, it's not designed for dynamic cloud operation. Many AWS services are designed to automatically scale horizontally:

- **EC2 instances:** Instances and containers can be scaled with EC2 Auto Scaling and CloudWatch metric alarms.

- **Load balancers:** The Elastic Load Balancing (ELB) load balancer infrastructure horizontally scales to handle demand.

  - **Amazon S3 storage:** The S3 storage array infrastructure horizontally scales in the background to handle reads.

  - **Amazon DynamoDB:** The DynamoDB service scales tables within an AWS region. Tables can also be designed as global tables that are asynchronously replicated across multiple AWS regions. Each region table copy is horizontally scaled within the region as required. Each copy of the regional table in each region has a copy of all table data.

  - **Amazon Aurora Serverless:** The Amazon Aurora v2 serverless deployment of PostgreSQL or MySQL can be deployed across three availability zones per AWS region, or as a global datastore across multiple AWS regions supporting highly variable workloads.

Factor 9: Maximize Robustness with Fast Startup and Graceful Shutdown

User session information can be stored in Amazon ElastiCache or in in-memory queues, and application state can be stored in SQS message queues. Application configuration and bindings, source code, and backing services can be hosted by many AWS-managed services, each with its own levels of redundancy and durability. Data is stored in a persistent storage location such as S3 buckets, RDS databases,

DynamoDB databases, or EFS or FSx for Windows File Server shared storage arrays. Workloads with no local dependencies and integrated cloud services can be managed and controlled by a number of AWS management services.

- **Elastic Load Balancer Service:** Load balancers targeting web application hosted on an EC2 instance stop sending requests when ELB health checks fail.

- **Amazon Route 53:** Regional workload failures can be redirected using Route 53 alias records to another region using defined traffic policies.

- **Amazon Relational Database Service (RDS):** When failure occurs, the RDS relational database instances automatically fail over to either the alternate or primary database instance. The failed database instance is automatically rebuilt and brought back online.

- **Amazon DynamoDB:** Tables are replicated across three availability zones throughout each AWS region.

- **EC2 Spot instances:** Spot instances can be configured to automatically hibernate when resources are taken back.

- **Amazon SQS:** SQS messages being processed by EC2 instances that fail are returned to the SQS work queue for reprocessing.

- **AWS Lambda:** Custom function can shut down tagged resources on demand.

Factor 10: Keep Development, Staging, and Production as Similar as Possible

With this factor, *similar* does not refer to the number of instances or the size of database instances and supporting infrastructure. Your development environment must be exact in the codebase being used but can be dissimilar in the number of instances or database servers being used. Aside from the infrastructure components, everything else in the codebase must remain the same.

- **AWS CloudFormation:** JSON or YAML template files can be used to automatically build AWS infrastructure with conditions that define what infrastructure resources to build for specific development, testing, and production environments.

Factor 11: Treat Logs as Event Streams

In development, testing, and production environments, each running process log stream must be stored externally. At AWS, logging is designed as event streams.

- **Amazon CloudWatch:** CloudWatch log groups or S3 buckets store EC2 instances' application logs. AWS CloudTrail event logs, which track all API calls to the AWS account, can also be streamed to CloudWatch logs for further analysis.

Factor 12: Run Admin/Management Tasks as One-Off Processes

Administrative processes should be executed using the same method, regardless of the environment in which the administrative task is executed. For example, an application might require a manual process to be carried out; the steps to carry out the manual process must remain the same, whether they are executed in the development, testing, or production environment.

Several AWS utilities can be used to execute administrative tasks:

- **AWS CLI:** Use the CLI to carry out administrative tasks with scripts.

- **AWS Systems Manager:** Apply OS patches and configure Linux and Windows systems.

Exam Preparation Tasks

As mentioned in the section "How to Use This Book" in the Introduction, you have a couple of choices for exam preparation: the exercises here, Chapter 16, "Final Preparation," and the exam simulation questions in the Pearson Test Prep Software Online.

Review All Key Topics

Review the most important topics in the chapter, noted with the Key Topic icon in the outer margin of the page. Table 2-2 lists these key topics and the page number on which each is found.

Table 2-2 Chapter 2 Key Topics

Key Topic Element	Description	Page Number
Section	Operational Excellence Pillar	44
Section	Security Pillar	45
Section	Defense in Depth	45
Section	Reliability Pillar	47
Section	Performance Efficiency Pillar	49
Section	Cost Optimization Pillar	51
Paragraph	Regular CloudWatch monitoring	53
Section	Caching Data with CDNs	56
Figure 2-12	One Codebase, Regardless of Location	63

Key Topic Element	Description	Page Number
Figure 2-14	Using SQS Queues to Provide Stateless Memory-Resident Storage for Applications	68
Section	Factor 8: Scale Out via the Process Model	69

Define Key Terms

Define the following key terms from this chapter and check your answers in the glossary:

defense in depth, service-level agreement (SLA), service-level objective (SLO), service-level indicator (SLI), recovery time objective (RTO), recovery point objective (RPO), dependencies, codebase

Q&A

The answers to these questions appear in Appendix A. For more practice with exam format questions, use the Pearson Test Prep Software Online.

1. Defense in depth can be divided into three areas: physical, technical, and _____.

2. Application availability of 99.99% means designing for the potential unavailability of roughly 52 minutes of _____.

3. Determine workload limits by _____ all aspects of the application stack.

4. Changes in security can affect _____.

5. Changes in reliability can affect _____.

6. Availability is defined as the _____ of time a cloud service is available and _____.

7. If your application can't scale _____, it's not designed for _____ cloud operation.

8. AWS CloudFormation can be used to automatically build infrastructure using a single _____.

This chapter covers the following topics:

- Identity and Access Management (IAM)

- AWS IAM Users and Groups

- Creating IAM Policies

- IAM Roles

- AWS Organizations

- AWS Resource Access Manager

- AWS Control Tower

This chapter covers content that's important to the following exam domain and task statement:

Domain 1: Design Secure Architectures

Task Statement 1: Design secure access to AWS resources

CHAPTER 3

Designing Secure Access to AWS Resources

It's only natural to think that the same security issues and concerns you face on premises could occur—and possibly be more widespread—when operating in the AWS cloud. Amazon is continuously patching and updating its entire cloud infrastructure, managed services, and all other integral system components. The latest security bulletins published by AWS (see https://aws.amazon.com/security/security-bulletins/) indicate Amazon has needed to consider various security advisories on behalf of all AWS customers.

AWS is responsible for maintaining the security of its cloud infrastructure, defined by AWS as security *of* the cloud. Our job is to maintain everything we host and store in the cloud. This concept is security *in* the cloud.

Indeed, the job of securing customer resources hosted in the AWS cloud never ends, just as security issues continue to be discovered. Way back in 2014, security vulnerabilities with the Bash shell were found. Bash shell security issues weren't new; they just hadn't been discovered until 2014.

To be successful when taking the AWS Certified Solutions Architect – Associate (SAA-C03) exam, a good understanding of the tools and methods available for maintaining the security of workloads, administrators, and cloud services is required.

"Do I Know This Already?"

The "Do I Know This Already?" quiz allows you to assess whether you should read this entire chapter thoroughly or jump to the "Exam Preparation Tasks" section. If you are in doubt about your answers to these questions or your own assessment of your knowledge of the topics, read the entire chapter. Table 3-1 lists the major headings in this chapter and their corresponding "Do I Know This Already?" quiz questions. You can find the answers in Appendix A, "Answers to the 'Do I Know This Already?' Quizzes and Q&A Sections."

Table 3-1   "Do I Know This Already?" Section-to-Question Mapping

Foundation Topics Section	Questions
Identity and Access Management (IAM)	1, 2
IAM Users and Groups	3, 4
Creating IAM Policies	5, 6
IAM Roles	7, 8
AWS Organizations	9, 10
AWS Resource Access Manager	11, 12
AWS Control Tower	13, 14

CAUTION   The goal of self-assessment is to gauge your mastery of the topics in this chapter. If you do not know the answer to a question or are only partially sure of the answer, you should mark that question as wrong for purposes of the self-assessment. Giving yourself credit for an answer you correctly guess skews your self-assessment results and might provide you with a false sense of security.

1. What process must happen before AWS IAM grants an IAM user access to requested AWS resources?

    a. Authorization

    b. Authentication

    c. Access granted

    d. Access denied

2. Which of the following entities is not controlled by AWS IAM?

    a. IAM groups

    b. IAM user

    c. Externally authenticated user

    d. Database authentication

3. What additional step can be added as a mandatory component when authenticating at AWS?

    a. Password policies

    b. Multi-factor authentication

    c. Resource policies

    d. Management policies

4. Which of the following AWS IAM entities cannot authenticate?

    a. Management policies

    b. IAM groups

    c. Job policies

    d. Secret keys

5. What type of permissions policy applies to resources?

    a. IAM managed policy

    b. Resource policy

    c. Job function policy

    d. Custom IAM policy

6. Which of the following options can be added to a policy as a conditional element?

    a. Explicit denies

    b. Tags

    c. Explicit allows

    d. Implicit allows

7. What essential component is not attached to an AWS IAM role?

    a. Security policy

    b. Credentials

    c. Multi-factor authentication

    d. Tags

8. What security service does an AWS IAM role interface with?

    a. AWS CloudTrail

    b. AWS Security Token Service

    c. AWS Config

    d. Amazon GuardDuty

9. How does an AWS organization help with managing costs?

    a. Organizational units

    b. Consolidated billing

    c. Service control policy

    d. Shared security services

10. Which of the following is the primary benefit of creating an AWS organization?

    a. Lower costs for linked accounts

    b. Centralized control of linked AWS accounts

    c. Distributed control

    d. Nesting OUs

11. What is a benefit of using AWS Resource Access Manager without AWS Organizations being deployed?

    a. Replacement of network peering

    b. Sharing of resources between AWS accounts

    c. Sharing of resources between regions

    d. Sharing of resources in different availability zones

12. Who is in charge of sharing resources using AWS Resource Access Manager?

    a. The resource user

    b. The principal ID

    c. The AWS account root user

    d. Any IAM administrator

13. How is governance carried out by AWS Control Tower?

    a. Account Factory

    b. Landing zone

    c. Guardrails

    d. Dashboard

14. What is the purpose of the AWS Control Tower Account Factory?

    a. Apply mandatory guardrails

    b. Provision new IAM accounts

    c. Standardize the provisioning of new AWS accounts

    d. Create OUs

Identity and Access Management (IAM)

The *Identity and Access Management (IAM)* service is used to deploy and maintain security using security policies and integrated security services. Security policies define what actions administrators (users and groups) and AWS cloud services can and can't carry out. IAM is a global AWS service that protects AWS resources located around the world across all AWS regions, with a global endpoint located at https://sts.amazonaws.com. There are different user types that require access to AWS resources, including an organization's AWS cloud administrators and end users who are not aware that they are even accessing the AWS cloud when they are using a SaaS application running on their phone. Many popular mobile SaaS applications have backend services hosted at AWS.

Identity and Access Management (IAM) (see Figure 3-1) was added as a feature to the AWS cloud on September 1, 2010, providing the capability for administrators to define the desired level of access to AWS workloads and the associated cloud services. Using the IAM dashboard, administrators must create IAM users, groups, and roles—no default users, groups, or roles are defined when an AWS account is created.

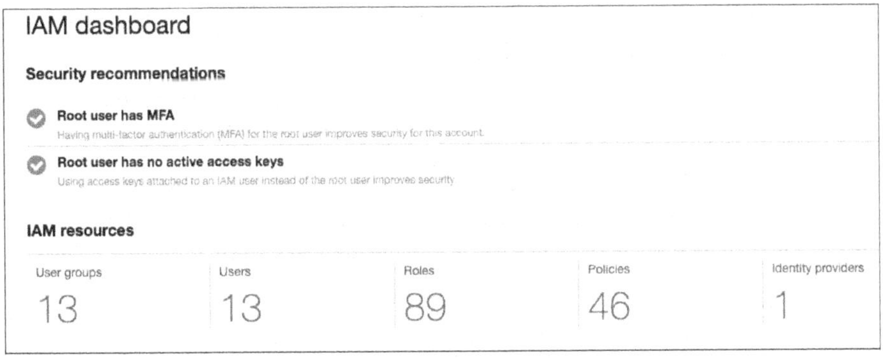

Figure 3-1   The IAM Dashboard

IAM is a paranoid security service, and we *want* it to be paranoid. IAM's default mindset is explicit denial with no default access to any AWS cloud service defined.

AWS is responsible for building, securing, and maintaining all the physical components that comprise the cloud services available through the AWS cloud portal. When operating in the public cloud, both the customers and the cloud provider have defined responsibilities, which is defined as a *shared responsibility model*.

The responsibilities of AWS are described as *security of the cloud*—protecting the infrastructure that hosts and runs the AWS cloud services. Each AWS customer's responsibility is defined as *security in the cloud*. Each cloud service ordered by a customer will have a default security configuration applied, and from this point forward each customer assumes the responsibility of managing and maintaining the cloud service's current and future security configuration. When an EC2 instance is deployed, Amazon is responsible for launching and hosting the EC2 instance on the subnet and availability zone chosen by the customer and ensuring it is initially accessible only to the customer that requested the instance. In the future, a customer may decide to share the EC2 instance with other AWS customers or across the Internet; the exact level of security is the customer's choice—and responsibility. Each AWS service follows the defined shared responsibility model; each party's responsibilities are clearly laid out in AWS documentation. AWS adheres to the ISO/IEC 27001 security standards, which define security management best practices in managing information security through defined security controls.

Amazon cloud services that access the resources in your AWS account on your behalf are also governed by special IAM policies called *service-linked roles* that define the maximum permitted level of access for each cloud service. Identity and Access Management's main features are as follows:

- **Full integration with all AWS services:** Access to every AWS service can be controlled using IAM security.

- **Cost benefits:** There is no additional charge for using IAM security to control access to AWS resources.

- **Controlled access to your AWS account resources in all regions:** Each IAM user can be assigned security policies controlling access to AWS resources in any AWS account in any AWS region.

- **Granular permission control:** IAM can control access to AWS resources to a granular level, for example, defining a policy that allows an IAM user the singular task of viewing a load balancer's attributes.

- **Define the level of access AWS services have to resources:** When you order an AWS cloud service such as AWS Config, the service is granted access to your AWS account through an IAM security policy controlled by a service-linked role (see Figure 3-2), ensuring that the AWS service can only carry out the approved list of tasks.

- **Multi-factor authentication (MFA):** An additional layer of authentication can be added to any IAM user, including the root user of each AWS account. *Multi-factor authentication (MFA)* provides a security code—from a software or hardware device that is linked to your AWS account—that must be entered and verified in order for authentication to AWS to succeed.

- **Identity federation/SSO access to AWS services:** IAM roles allow *externally authenticated users*—whose identities have been federated from a corporate directory or from a third-party identity provider such as Google or Facebook—to have temporary access to select AWS services.

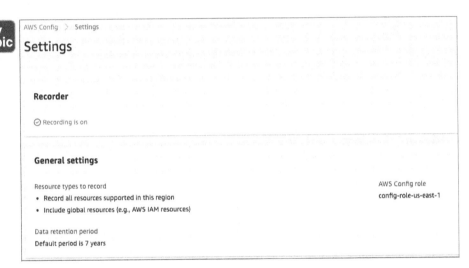

Figure 3-2 AWS Config Service-Linked Roles Defined by IAM

NOTE Because IAM is a global service, security changes and additions to the IAM service can take several minutes to completely replicate across the AWS cloud.

IAM Policy Definitions

Each IAM policy is a set of rules that define the actions that each AWS entity can perform on specific AWS resources; *who* is allowed to do *what*. To understand IAM, we need to understand the following terms:

- **User:** Only defined IAM users within each AWS account and externally authenticated users with assigned roles can authenticate to an AWS account. An example of an externally authenticated user could be a corporate user who first authenticates to the corporate Active Directory network that also requires access to AWS resources. After AWS verifies the externally authenticated user's attached IAM role, temporary credentials are assigned, allowing the external authenticated user access to the requested AWS resources. Google and

Facebook users are examples of externally authenticated users supported by IAM roles and AWS.

■ **Group:** A group of IAM users can access AWS resources based on the IAM policies assigned to the IAM group they belong to.

■ **Policy:** Each AWS service can be controlled by IAM policies created and managed by AWS or by custom policies created by customers.

■ **Statement:** Policy statements define what actions are allowed or denied to AWS resources.

■ **Principal:** The principal is an IAM user or application that can perform actions on an AWS resource.

■ **Resource:** A resource is an AWS resource (such as compute, storage, networking, or managed services) where actions are performed.

■ **Identity:** An identity is the IAM user, group, or role where an IAM policy is attached.

■ **Entities:** IAM entities that can authenticate are an IAM user, which is assigned permanent credentials, or an IAM role, which does not have attached credentials (that is, no password or permanent access keys). Temporary authentication credentials and session tokens are assigned to a role only after verification confirms that the identity is allowed to assume the policy assigned to the IAM role.

■ **Role:** An IAM role provides temporary access to AWS resources based on the attached IAM policy.

■ *Condition*: Specific conditions can be mandated. For example, a specific principal, IP address, date, or tag must be present before access is allowed. Conditions are optional.

IAM Authentication

Before tasks can be performed on AWS resources, you must first be authenticated as an IAM user signing in with a recognized IAM username and password or have been granted access using an IAM Role. If multi-factor authentication is enabled, you must also enter a numerical code during the authentication process before authentication is successful.

Authentication is also required when running commands or scripts using the AWS command-line interface (CLI) or software development kit (SDK). A valid *access key* and secret access key assigned to the IAM user account making the CLI or SDK request must be provided and validated before the command or script will execute.

When an IAM user account is created, two access keys are created; the first access key is the *ID key*, which is an uppercase alphabetic string of characters in the format AKIAXXXXXXXXXXXX, as shown in Figure 3-3. The second access key, the *secret access key*, is a Base64 string that is 40 characters in length.

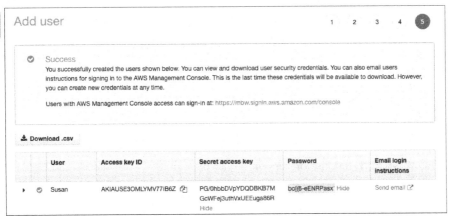

Figure 3-3 IAM User Account Access Keys

External authentication uses a set of temporary access keys issued by the AWS Security Token Service (AWS STS). Temporary access keys issued from STS are in the format ASIAXXXXXX. External authentication is covered in more detail later in this chapter.

Several forms of authentication are supported by AWS, including the following:

- IAM users and groups carry out administrative actions on AWS services and resources.

- Single sign-on (SSO) is supported using a federated identity with Active Directory Domain Services (AD DS) or a third-party provider that supports the Security Association Markup Language (SAML) 2.0 protocol.

- SAML external authentication is supported by IAM using IAM roles, which are attached to the externally authenticated user after identity verification of their external identity by the AWS Security Token Service. Active Directory credentials are stored in two locations: on the Active Directory domain controllers on premises, and on domain controllers hosted at AWS that have been synchronized with a current copy of the organization's Active Directory credentials and attributes.

- Amazon Cognito authenticates and controls access to AWS resources from mobile applications using IAM policies and IAM roles using an identity store and application data synchronization.

- AWS supports external authentication from mobile applications using public identity providers, Facebook, Google, Login with Amazon, and providers that support OpenID Connect, which generates the authentication token that is presented to AWS STS. Verification of the external authentication token by STS results in temporary security credentials being provided for access to the desired AWS resources.

- IAM RDS database authentication is supported by the following database engines:

  - MariaDB 10.6, all minor versions

  - MySQL 8.0, minor version 8.0.23 or higher

  - MySQL 5.7, minor version 5.7.33 or higher

  - PostgreSQL 14, 13, 12, and 11, all minor versions

  - PostgreSQL 10, minor version 10.6 or higher

  - PostgreSQL 9.6, minor version 9.6.11 or higher

  - PostgreSQL 9.5, minor version 9.5.15 or higher

Requesting Access to AWS Resources

Only after authentication is successful are IAM users allowed to request access to AWS resources. The following IAM components work together when requesting access to AWS resources:

- **Principal:** The principal defines which IAM user or external user with an assigned IAM role has requested access.

- **Operations:** Only after each request is authenticated and authorized are operations and actions to the requested AWS resource approved. Operations are always API calls executed from the AWS Management Console, through AWS Lambda function, a CLI command or script, or an AWS SDK using RESTful calls.

- **Actions:** Actions define the specific task, or tasks, the principal has requested to perform. Actions might be for information (**List** or **Get** requests) or to make changes (such as creating, deleting, or modifying).

- **Resource:** Every AWS resource is identified with a unique Amazon Resource Name (ARN), as shown in Figure 3-4.

- **Environmental data:** Environmental data indicates where the request originated (for example, from a specific IP address range) and can provide additional required security information such as the time of day.

- **Resource data:** Resource data provides additional details about the resource being accessed, such as a specific Amazon S3 bucket, Amazon DynamoDB table, or a specific tag attached to the AWS resource being accessed.

Figure 3-4 An Amazon Resource Name (ARN)

The Authorization Process

IAM reviews each request against the attached policies of the principal requesting authorization and determines whether the request will be allowed or denied, as shown in Figure 3-5. Note that the principal might also be a member of one or more *IAM groups*, which will increase the number of assigned policies that need to be evaluated before authorization is approved or denied. The evaluation logic of IAM policies follows these strict rules:

- By default, all requests are implicitly denied; there are no implicit permissions. Actions are not allowed without an explicit allow.

- Policies are evaluated for an explicit deny; if found the action is denied.

- An explicit allow overrides the implicit deny, allowing the action to be carried out.

- An explicit deny denies a requested action.

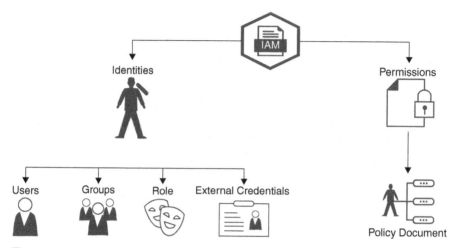

Figure 3-5 IAM Authorization

When a principal makes a request to access AWS resources, the IAM service confirms the principal is authenticated, signed in, authorized, and has the necessary permissions.

NOTE You probably experienced an IAM-like authorization process as a teenager. It might have sounded like this: "Hey, Dad, can I go to the movies?" "Nope. All requests are denied." So, you wait until Mom gets home. "Hey, Mom, can I go to the movies?" "I think so, but let me see whether you cleaned your room. Nope. You can't go to the movies because you didn't clean your room." Mom was sneaky and also used a condition; IAM policies can also use conditions for additional control.

The IAM security system reviews the policies assigned and approves or denies the request. As mentioned earlier, IAM implicitly denies everything by default. Requests are authorized only if the specific request is allowed. The following request logic maps to Figure 3-6:

1. The evaluation logic follows exact rules that can't be bent for anyone, not even Jeff Bezos; implicit deny by default. All requests are implicitly denied by default for IAM users.

2. Attached policies are evaluated.

3. An explicit deny denies any request. A default deny can only be overruled and allowed by an explicit allow permission.

4. Each explicit allow permission in the attached policies is allowed.

5. An explicit deny in any policy results in no access.

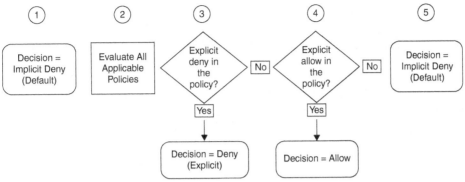

Figure 3-6 Policy Evaluation Logic

Actions

Actions are the tasks you can perform on an AWS resource, such as creating, editing, and deleting a resource. There can be many actions for each resource; for example, the EC2 service has more than 400 different actions that can be allowed or denied (see Figure 3-7). Once specific actions have been approved, only those actions, which are allowed in the policy, can be performed on the defined resource.

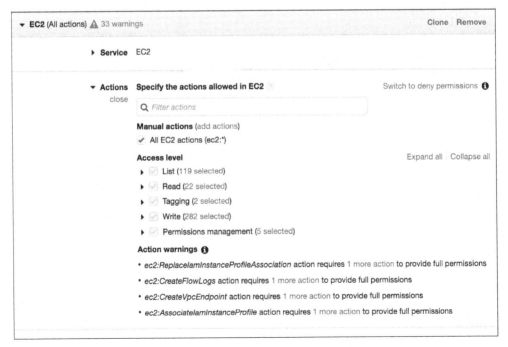

Figure 3-7 Actions Approved by IAM

Each AWS resource has several actions that can be carried out; the initial access level choices are typically **List**, **Read** (typically **Get** or **List**), and **Write** (typically **Create**, **Put**, **Delete**, **Update**). The type of AWS resource determines the action choices that are available.

IAM Users and Groups

When you think of the word *account*, you might think specifically of a user account or a group account in the context of an operating system. At AWS, the account that you initially signed up for was designed for organization-wide use, but each AWS account can be used by a single individual, or an organization. It can seem confusing at first.

It might help to think of your AWS account as a complete hosted cloud operating system with security features comparable to the Red Hat Enterprise Linux operating system or Microsoft Active Directory Domain Services.

Many organizations use many AWS accounts—perhaps one or more per developer. At AWS, all cloud services are available per AWS account—subject to the permissions and policies assigned to the authenticating IAM user accounts and roles.

Within each AWS account, IAM user identities or IAM roles are created for these requirements:

- An administrator who needs access to the AWS Management Console.

- An administrator or a developer who needs access to the AWS APIs using the AWS Management Console, and using the AWS CLI command-line interface typing single commands or running scripts, or development of applications using AWS SDKs, such as JavaScript or .NET.

> **NOTE**   All companies need to consider the number of administrator and developer user accounts that need to be created and the number of AWS accounts that need to be managed. The best practice is to create roles for external access (access to other AWS accounts or federated access) as much as possible. Roles are explained later in this chapter.

The Root User

Every AWS account has an initial root user per AWS account created when each AWS account is first provisioned. The root user is the owner of the AWS account, and root credentials are the email address and password provided during the initial creation of each AWS account.

The first time you logged in to a new AWS account, you used the root account credentials to authenticate; after all, there weren't any other administrator accounts available. Perhaps you're still using your root account credentials as your daily administrative account; however, doing so is not recommended, as the root user is not an IAM user controlled by IAM security. The root user has unrestricted access to all resources in the AWS account. Each root account has specific tasks that only the root account can perform. Think of the root account as a special administrator account that should only be used to perform specific tasks, such as billing, changing the AWS support plan, or reviewing tax invoices. The root user is not meant for daily administrative duties. If the root account is the only admin account available in your AWS account, you need to create several IAM users as administrators to properly safeguard your AWS account resources.

Here's a quick way to check if you're using an AWS account root account: What are the security credentials you use to log in to the AWS account? If you use an email address (see Figure 3-8), you are accessing this AWS account as the root user. Now think about how many other administrators could potentially be using the same root account login; each of these administrators could potentially delete everything in the associated AWS account when using the root user account logon. There's no way to disable root account actions because there are no IAM controls on the root account. And no controls can be added.

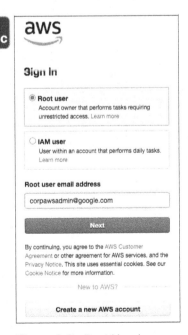

Figure 3-8 Root User Logon

Why would AWS create an initial user account that has unlimited power? The first account in any operating system must have the most power; think of an Active Directory Domain Services enterprise administrator or the root user for the Linux operating system. As in any other operating system, the root credentials need to be protected. AWS will alert you to create additional IAM users to protect your AWS account.

The following tasks can only be carried out in each AWS account when authenticated as the AWS root user:

- Modifying the root user account details, including changing the password of the root account

- Closing an AWS account

- Changing your AWS support plan from free to Developer, Small Business, or Enterprise

- Enabling billing for the account or changing your payment options or billing information

- Creating a CloudFront key pair

- Enabling MFA on an S3 bucket in your AWS account

- Requesting permission to perform a penetration test

- Restoring IAM user permissions that have been revoked

NOTE After you sign in for the first time using the root user for your AWS account, the best practice is to create an IAM user for administration duties, add the required administrative policies and privileges to your new IAM user account, and stop using the root account unless it is necessary to carry out a root administrative task.

The IAM User

An IAM user is an IAM security principal that can be used to access the following interfaces:

- Every IAM user with assigned username and password credentials can access AWS resources using the AWS Management Console.

- An IAM user with assigned username and password credentials and an active access key (access key ID and secret access key) is allowed both AWS

Management Console access *and* programmatic access from the AWS CLI. Script or CLI commands will not execute until the IAM user account's access ID and secret access keys are validated.

There are two ways to identify an IAM user:

- The most common way is the name of the user account listed in the IAM dashboard. This username also shows up in each IAM group's list of associated IAM users.

- An Amazon Resource Name (ARN) uniquely identifies each IAM user across all AWS user accounts. Every resource that is created at AWS also has a unique ARN. For example, if you create a resource policy to control access to an S3 bucket, you will need to specify the user's account ARN that can access the bucket in the following format: *arn:aws:iam::account ID:user/mark*.

Creating an IAM User

The easiest way to start creating IAM users is to use the IAM dashboard and click Add Users, which opens the dialog box shown in Figure 3-9.

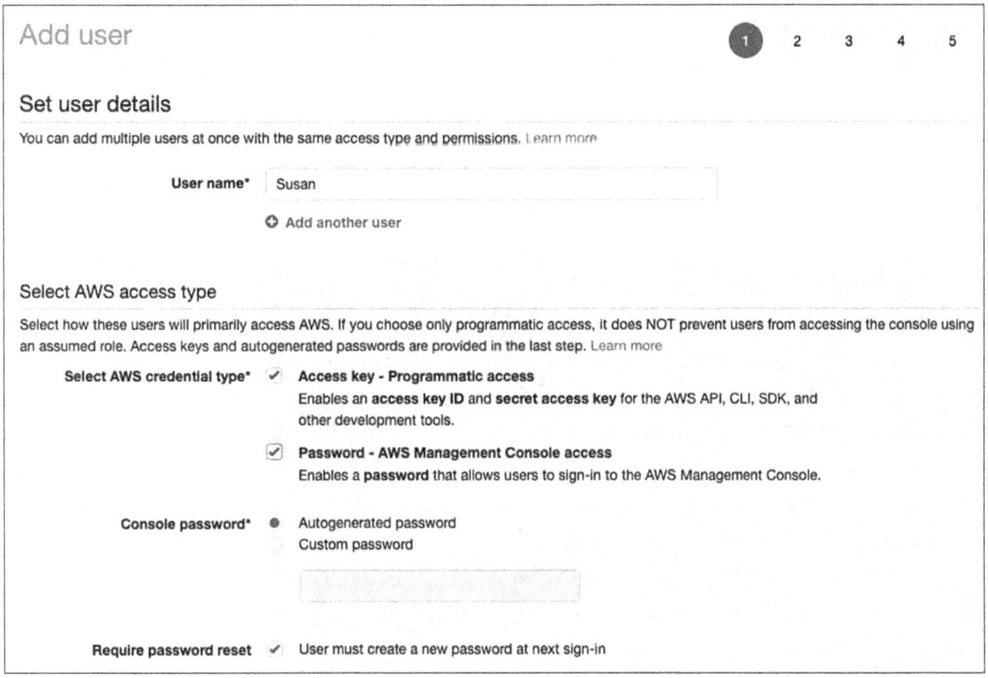

Figure 3-9 Creating an IAM User

The first decision you must make is the type of access you want to allow your new IAM user to have:

- **Password – AWS Management Console access:** With this type of access, users enter a username and password to authenticate. If console access is all that is required, access keys (an access key ID and secret access key) are not required.

- **Access key – Programmatic access:** This type of access also allows working from the command prompt using the AWS CLI or AWS SDK. Checking both boxes allows both types of access.

NOTE   If you're taking over an existing AWS environment, you might find that IAM users have access keys assigned to their accounts, but they don't actually carry out programmatic tasks. If this is the case, the current access keys can be deleted. In the future, if you decide that access keys are required, they can be added. It is a best practice to remove the root account access keys to make it impossible to run scripts and automation when logged in as a root user.

IAM User Access Keys

Each user account can have two access keys: the access key ID and a secret access key. As discussed earlier in this chapter, access keys are also required when using the AWS CLI (see Figure 3-10), when running scripts, when running PowerShell scripts, or when calling AWS APIs directly or through an application.

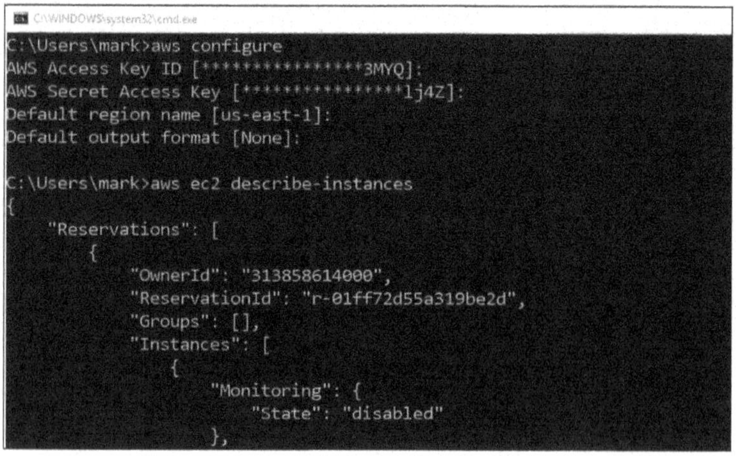

Figure 3-10   Access Keys Required for CLI Operation

Once an IAM user account has been created successfully, you can download a copy of the access keys (access key ID and secret access key). This option is a one-shot deal: If you don't download a copy of the secret access key at the completion of the user account creation process, you cannot view the assigned secret access key again. However, a new set of access keys for an already created IAM user (access ID and secret access key) can be requested.

There are three options available when creating a new IAM user using the IAM dashboard, as shown in Figure 3-11:

- Add the user to an existing IAM group
- Copy permissions from existing IAM users to the user being created
- Attach existing policies directly to the new IAM user

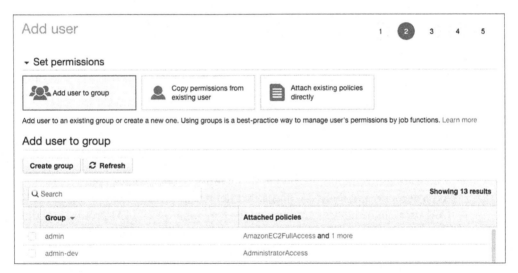

Figure 3-11 IAM User Account Creation Options

Creating a new IAM user without adding additional permissions or groups creates an extremely limited IAM user as there are no security policies assigned by default. One best practice to consider is to add the new IAM user to an existing IAM group that has the permissions needed for the IAM user account's required duties. Even if you are creating an IAM user for a specific AWS task that just this IAM user will carry out, you might want to think about adding this person to an IAM group if there's a possibility of multiple IAM users carrying out the same task in the future.

NOTE   What each IAM user can and can't do at AWS is defined either by an explicit allow permission to carry out a task against AWS resources, or by explicit deny permissions that prohibit the user from being able to carry out a task. Note that an explicit deny for a specific task in any policy assigned to an IAM user account overrides any allow permissions defined in any other attached IAM policies.

IAM Groups

An IAM group is a collection of IAM users. IAM groups are useful for delegating security policies to a specific group of IAM users. Attaching IAM groups to IAM user accounts makes assigning permissions much easier than having to modify each individual IAM user account. Each IAM user listed in an IAM group has their own authentication credentials and possible memberships in additional IAM groups. Each IAM group that IAM users are members of are assigned their IAM group permissions only after they have successfully authenticated to AWS. The characteristics of IAM groups are as follows:

- Each IAM group can contain multiple IAM users from the same AWS account.

- IAM users can belong to multiple IAM groups in the same AWS account.

- IAM groups can't be nested.

- IAM groups can only contain IAM users and not any additional IAM groups.

- There are initial quotas on the number of IAM groups you can have in each AWS account, and there is a quota that defines how many IAM groups an IAM user can be in. An IAM user can be a member of 10 IAM groups, and the maximum number of IAM users that can be created in a single AWS account is 5000.

Signing In as an IAM User

After IAM users have been created, to make it easier for your IAM users to sign in to the IAM console, you can create a custom URL that contains your AWS account ID, as shown in Figure 3-12.

NOTE   When creating and maintaining users, groups, and roles, you can manage IAM by using a third-party identity management product such as ForgeRock (https://www.forgerock.com), Okta (https://www.okta.com), or OneLogin (https://www.onelogin.com).

Figure 3-12 Using Custom URL for IAM Users

IAM Account Details

Each IAM user account displayed in the IAM console shows some useful information, including the IAM groups that the IAM user belongs to, the age of the access
keys assigned to the IAM user account, the age of the current password, the last
activity of the IAM account, and whether MFA has been enabled. Selecting an
IAM user account in the console, you can see several additional account options,
including the ARN of the account and information on the following tabs (see
Figure 3-13):

- **Permissions:** This tab lists the applied permissions policies and the policy
  types.

- **Groups:** This tab lists the policies attached due to group membership.

- **Tags:** This tab lists key/value pairs (up to 50) that can be added for additional
  information.

- **Security Credentials:** This tab enables you to manage credential-related
  parameters such as the following:

  - The console password of the IAM user

  - The assigned MFA device (which can be a virtual or hardware device)

  - Signing certificates

  - Access keys

- **Access Advisor:** This tab lists the service permissions that have been granted
  to the IAM user and when the AWS services were last accessed within the calendar year.

Figure 3-13 User Account Summary Information

Creating a Password Policy

Password policies can be defined by selecting Account Settings in the IAM console. After password policies are defined, they control all IAM user accounts created in the AWS account. Password options include password complexity, password expiration, password reuse, and whether IAM users can change their own passwords (see Figure 3-14).

Best practice is to review your corporate policy for passwords and consider whether more stringent rules need to be followed for working in the AWS cloud. If rules around password policy need to be tightened, the rules for the current on-premises password policy and the password policy defined in the AWS cloud should be analyzed and unified.

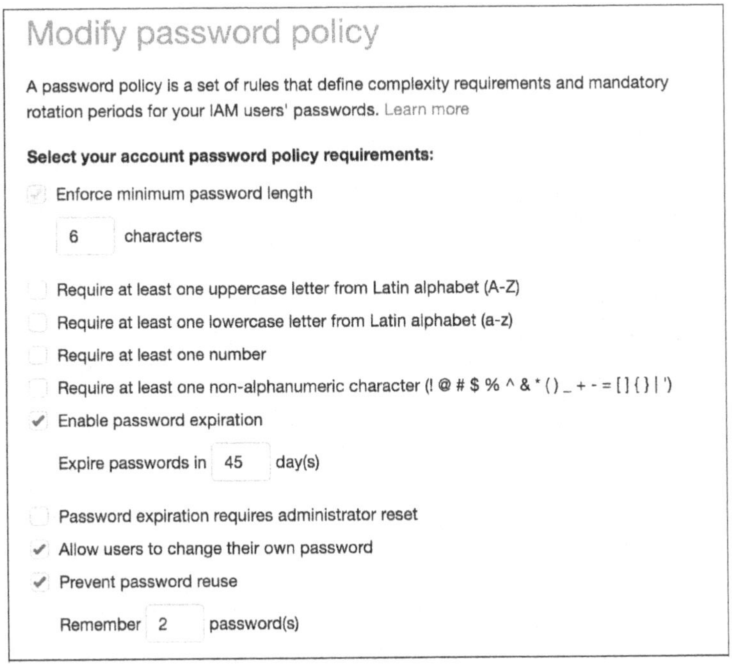

Figure 3-14   Password Policy Options

Rotating Access Keys

After an IAM user account has been created with access keys, the access keys are not changed unless they are manually rotated, or an automated process to perform the key rotation process is used such as a script or a custom Lambda function. Best practice is to rotate a user's access keys, preferably at the same time the IAM user password is changed, to maintain a higher level of security and avoid issues that can arise from compromised access keys. The access keys currently assigned to the IAM user can be viewed in the properties of the IAM user account on the Security Credentials tab. When a request is received to create a new access key, an associated secret access key is created along with the new access key ID, as shown in Figure 3-15.

The important task of rotating access keys, shown in Figure 3-16, should be assigned to a trusted IAM administrator account that will be carrying out the task of key rotation. Note that multiple **Get**, **Create**, **List**, **Update**, and **Delete** actions must be assigned to the selected IAM user in order to rotate access keys successfully.

Key Topic

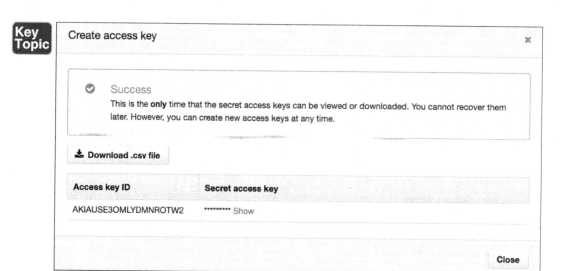

Figure 3-15 Creating an Additional Access Key Manually

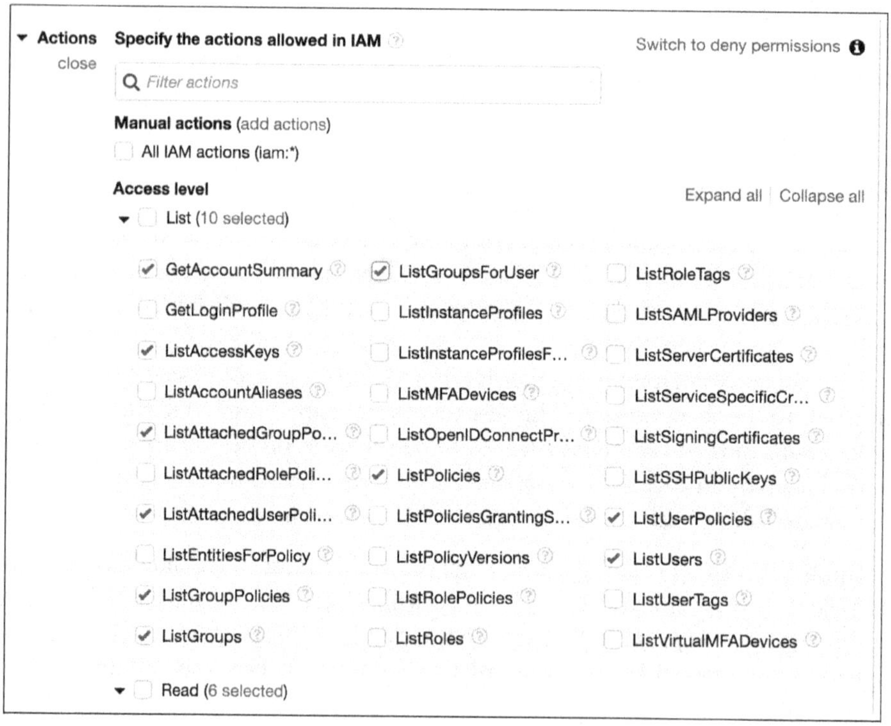

Figure 3-16 Policy Actions for Rotating Access Keys

Using Multi-Factor Authentication

Every AWS user account—including the root account and the IAM user account—supports MFA. With MFA enabled, during the process of authenticating to AWS, a user must provide a security code in addition to the username and password credentials provided to access AWS resources, as shown in Figure 3-17.

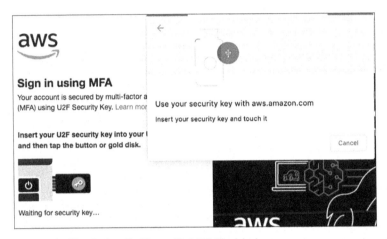

Figure 3-17   Authenticating with MFA Enabled

There are several options available at AWS for deploying MFA:

- **Virtual MFA device:** A software app such as Google Authenticator or Authy, that typically is installed on the user's phone, can generate the six-digit code to be entered during authentication.

- **U2F security key:** A U2F security key is generated by a USB device that generates a security code when tapped. These types of devices are approved by the Fast Identity Online (FIDO) Alliance. These keys are supported by many industry leaders, including Microsoft, Google, AWS, VMware, and Intel.

- **Hardware MFA device:** A hardware device such as a Thales SafeNet security appliance can also generate an MFA security code. Thales devices can provide end-to-end management of the entire encryption process.

Creating IAM Policies

Identity and Access Management enables you to use or create a large number of security policies. Identity-based policies use the Identity and Access Service to apply security policies to an identified IAM user, group, or role.

NOTE   The other type of security policy is called a resource-based policy. It is assigned to protect storage resources such as S3 buckets. Resource policies were available before the Identity and Access Management security service was introduced.

IAM Policy Types

The actions for controlling AWS services with IAM policies are forever increasing as new features are added frequently to existing and new AWS cloud services. Make sure to check the documentation for each AWS service for the up-to-date choices. This section looks at the policy types that can be attached to IAM identities (users, groups, or roles).

Identity-Based Policies

Identity-based policies are categorized as permission policies. Each identity-based policy contains permissions for specific actions an IAM user, group, or role can carry out. Polices can allow or deny access, and, optionally, indicate one or more mandatory conditions, must be met before access is allowed to the listed AWS cloud service or services defined in each policy.

There are three identity-based policy types:

- **Managed policies:** Managed policies, which are created and maintained by AWS, are read-only stand-alone identity-based policies that you can select and attach to IAM users, IAM groups, or roles created within each AWS account (see Figure 3-18). Listed are some concepts you need to understand when working with managed policies:

  - Managed policies can be attached to and detached from any identity (that is, user, group, or role).

  - A managed policy can be copied and saved as a custom policy.

  - Managed policies cannot be deleted. When you detach a managed policy, it is removed from the selected identity, user, group, or role; however, the managed policy is still available in the library of managed AWS policies for reuse.

  - Custom policies can be attached, detached, and deleted.

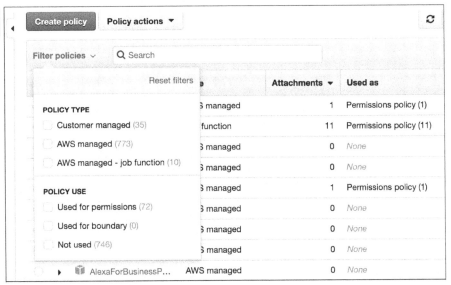

Figure 3-18 Managed Policies

- **Managed Policies for Job function:** Job function policies, which are also created and managed by AWS, are specialized managed policies based on generic job descriptions (see Figure 3-19). Job function policies might at first seem like an excellent idea. However, you need to be careful when assigning job function policies because a job function policy may assign more permissions than you need or wish to assign. For example, the SystemAdministrator job function policy allows the creation and maintenance of resources across many AWS services, including AWS CloudTrail, AWS CloudWatch, AWS CodeCommit, AWS CodeDeploy, AWS Config, AWS Directory Service, Amazon EC2, AWS IAM, AWS Lambda, Amazon Relational Database Service (RDS), Amazon Route 53, AWS Trusted Advisor, and Amazon Virtual Private Cloud (VPC). However, a job function policy can be useful as a starting policy template that once imported as a custom policy enables you to make further modifications to suit your organization's needs. The job function policies that can be selected are Administrator, Billing, Database Administrator, Data Scientist, Developer Power User, Network Administrator, Security Auditor, Support User, System Administrator, and View-Only User.

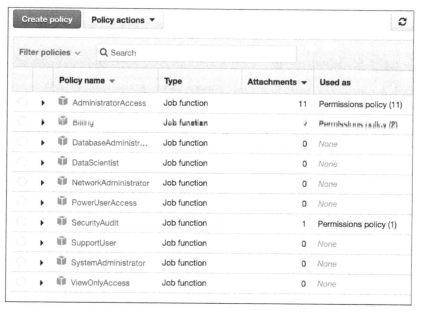

Figure 3-19   Job Function Policies

- **Custom policies:** You can select any managed policy as a starting template, modify it for your requirements, saving it as a custom policy in your AWS account. You can also elect to start with a blank page when creating a custom policy document and create the entire policy from scratch using the IAM dashboard. Each custom policy created is managed and maintained by each organization.

Resource-Based Policies

As previously discussed, identity-based policies are attached to an IAM user, group, or role defining what actions each attached identity is allowed, or not allowed to do. Resource-based policies are a little different in functionality because they are attached directly to AWS resources and are not created using the AWS Identity Access Management service. Resource-based policies are supported by several AWS storage services; the most common example is an Amazon S3 bucket, but there are other older AWS cloud services that support resource-based policies, including Amazon S3 Glacier vaults, Amazon Simple Notification Service (SNS), Amazon Simple Queue Service (SQS), and AWS Lambda functions. Because resource policies are attached directly to the AWS resource, each policy needs to define the access rules for the AWS resource and the IAM user, group, or AWS account that will access the resource. Resource-based policies are similar in functionality to

IAM *inline policies* due to the direct attaching of the resource policy to the AWS resource; if a resource is deleted, the resource policy is unattached and discarded. Resource-based policies are always a custom creation; AWS does not create any managed resource-based policies. Inline policies are discussed later in this chapter.

An IAM user can be assigned both a managed IAM identity policy and a resource-based policy for accessing the same AWS resource (see Figure 3-20):

- IAM User Mark has an identity-based policy that allows him to list and read from S3 Bucket A.

- The resource—in this case, the S3 bucket—has an attached resource-based policy that identifies that Mark can list and write on S3 Bucket A.

- S3 Bucket C has an attached resource-based policy that denies access to Mark. IAM User Julian also has a combination of identity- and resource-based policies.

- IAM User Jan has no managed policies assigned.

- Jan has access to S3 Bucket C because she is specifically listed in the resource policy using her IAM User ARN.

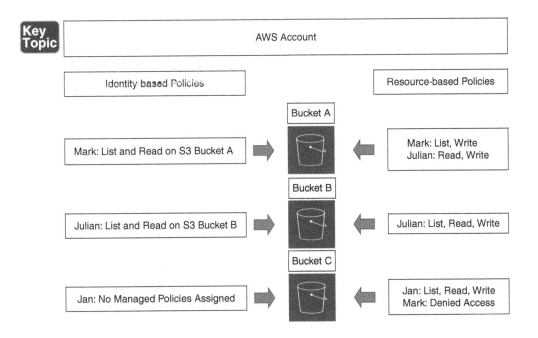

Figure 3-20 Identity and Resource Policies Working Together

> **NOTE**   Amazon S3 bucket policies are resource policies.

Inline Policies

Another method of attaching IAM policies is through the process of what is called an inline or directly attached policy, as shown in Figure 3-21. An IAM policy that is attached inline helps you maintain a strict one-to-one relationship between the attached policy and the entity the policy is attached to. When the entity is deleted, the attached policies are discarded. In comparison, using a managed policy allows you to apply the policy to multiple IAM users and groups.

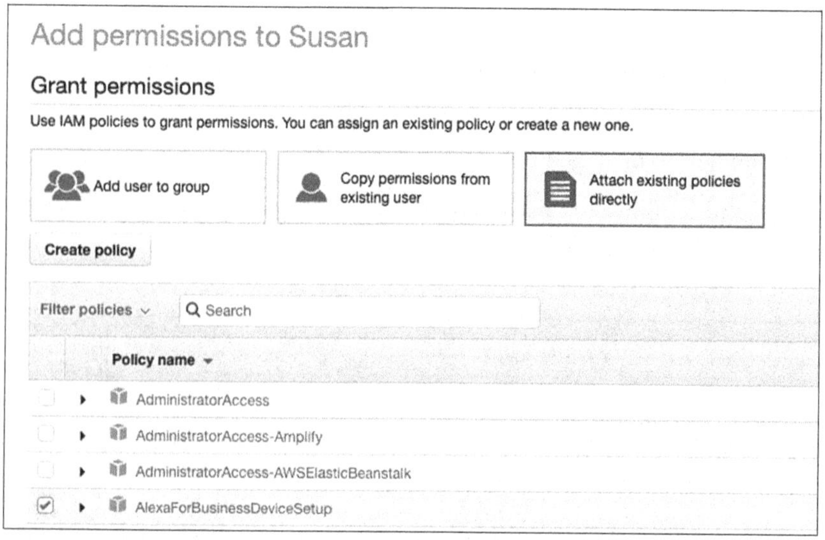

Add permissions to Susan

Grant permissions

Use IAM policies to grant permissions. You can assign an existing policy or create a new one.

Add user to group | Copy permissions from existing user | Attach existing policies directly

Create policy

Filter policies ∨   Q Search

Policy name ▾

- ▸ AdministratorAccess
- ▸ AdministratorAccess-Amplify
- ▸ AdministratorAccess-AWSElasticBeanstalk
- ☑ ▸ AlexaForBusinessDeviceSetup

Figure 3-21   Attaching Existing Policies Directly

For example, a specific user with high security clearance within your organization has been assigned the task of managing AWS CloudHSM, a security service that uses single-tenant hardware security modules (HSMs) for storing your organization's symmetric and asymmetric keys. You've decided to manage the security for this service by using inline policies that are attached to just one trusted administrator to ensure that only this person can carry out the specific tasks. Perhaps you have two security administrators, and you use inline policies to ensure that the policies are only assigned to these two individuals. You could use an IAM group but you don't want to make a mistake and accidentally add an additional IAM user to the existing group and weaken your security. If the administrator's IAM user accounts are deleted, the inline policies are discarded as well.

NOTE   IAM roles (which are discussed later in this chapter in the section "IAM Roles") are also attached directly to the IAM user or federated user.

IAM Policy Creation

Each IAM policy is crafted in what is called a lightweight data interchange format, JavaScript Object Notation (JSON) format. You can create and view any existing IAM policies by using the IAM dashboard or by using the AWS CLI and using the commands **create-policy** or **list-policies**. If you are just starting with AWS, it's probably best to start with the IAM dashboard, where you can easily view the IAM users and groups, policies, and roles. For crafting IAM policies using the AWS CLI, the AWS CLI command reference for Identity and Access management can be found here: https://awscli.amazonaws.com/v2/documentation/api/latest/reference/iam/index.html.

Each IAM policy can define a single permission statement or multiple permission statements. When you create custom policies, it is important to keep them as simple as possible to start with; don't mix AWS resource types in a single policy just because you can. It's a good idea to separate custom policies by AWS resource type for easier deployment and troubleshooting. You can create IAM policies by using several methods:

- Create IAM policies by using the visual editor in the IAM console.

- Create IAM policies by using the JSON editor in the IAM console (see Figure 3-22).

- Create and add IAM policies by using standard copy and paste techniques to import policy settings in JSON format into your JSON editor.

- Create IAM policies by using a third-party IAM tool that has been installed and properly configured. After authenticating to AWS using a recognized IAM user with valid access keys and appropriate administrative permissions, you can create IAM users, groups, and roles with third-party tools, such as OneLogin or Ping Identity, instead of using the IAM console.

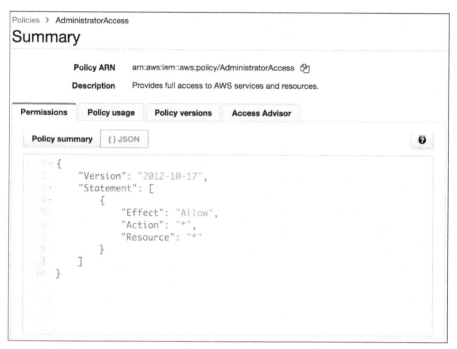

Figure 3-22   The JSON Editor

Policy Elements

Each IAM policy contains mandatory and optional elements that you need to understand and be familiar with:

- **Version:** (Mandatory) This element is the version of the policy language that the policy is using (see Figure 3-23). The latest policy language version is 2012-10-17; the date/time version number is added automatically to each policy document when you are manually creating a policy document using the IAM console. Add the latest version to all custom policies if they are created outside the IAM console to ensure that any new AWS features you are referencing in the custom policy are supported. If no version number is listed, the oldest IAM version number is used, which can potentially cause problems. For example, if you were using tags to determine access, or permission boundaries in a custom policy with no listed version number, these newer features would not work without the latest version number present at the top of the policy document.

Figure 3-23 Version Information

■ **Statement:** (Mandatory) Each IAM policy has at least a single statement; multiple statements are allowed in a policy. When beginning to craft custom policies, it might be cleanest or simplest to limit each policy document to a single policy statement.

■ **Sid:** (Optional) This element is a unique ID statement for additional identification purposes.

■ **Effect:** (Mandatory) The effect of any listed action is Allow or Deny.

■ **Action:** (Mandatory) Each action lists the API call(s) that is allowed or denied.

■ **Principal:** (Optional) The account, user, role, or federated user of the policy allows or denies access to a resource.

■ **Resource:** (Mandatory) This element identifies the AWS resource that the actions in the statement apply to.

■ **Condition:** (Optional) This element defines the absolute circumstances that must be met for the policy to be applied.

Reading a Simple JSON Policy

You need to follow a number of syntax and grammatical rules when creating custom IAM policies. One missing brace ({) or missed comma or colon can cause lots of pain when you're troubleshooting an IAM policy. These are the rules:

■ Text values—that is, string values—are always encased in double quotes.

■ A string value is followed by a colon.

- The data parts in a policy are defined as name/value pairs.

- The name and the value are separated with a colon (for example, **"Effect"**: **"Allow"**).

- When data in a policy has multiple name/value pairs, the name/value pairs are separated using commas.

- Braces { } contain objects.

- Each object can hold multiple name/value pairs.

- If square brackets are used, there are multiple name/value pairs, separated by commas.

Let's look at a simple IAM policy example in Example 3-1 and explore its construction. Note that the numbers shown are just for identification purposes.

Example 3-1   IAM Policy

```
1.{
2. "Version": "2012-10-17",
3. "Statement": {
4. "Effect": "Allow",
5. "Action": "s3:ListBucket",
6. "Resource": "arn:aws:s3:::graphic_bucket"
7. }
8. }
```

Each policy starts with a left brace that defines the start of the policy statement block. A curly right brace denotes the end of the policy statement block. In Example 3-1, line 1 and line 8 start and end the policy statement block.

Line 2 shows the current version of IAM policies; both **Version** and the version number are in quotation marks because the values within the quotes are string values. You can treat the version line in an IAM policy as a mandatory policy element. The version number is a name/value pair, and the name and the value are separated by a colon. Because there are multiple name/value pairs in this policy, there is a comma at the end of each line that contains a name/value pair (that is, lines 2, 4, and 5).

The first statement in the policy, line 3, is defined by **"Statement"** (note the quotation marks) followed by a colon (:) and another inner left brace ({) that denotes the start of the statement block, which includes **Effect**, **Action**, and **Resource**:

- Line 4, **"Effect"** (note the quotation marks), followed by a colon (:), is set to the value **"Allow"** (also in quotation marks). **"Effect"** can be set to either **Allow** or **Deny**.

- Line 5, **"Action"** in this policy, is set to allow the listing of an S3 bucket.

- Line 6, **"Resource"**, specifies that the resource being controlled by this policy is the S3 bucket **graphic_bucket**. The resource references the ARN—the unique Amazon name that is assigned to each resource at creation. Resource lines in policies don't have commas because a resource is a name/resource listing, not a name/value pair.

Line 7, the right curly brace (}), indicates that the statement block is complete. The final right curly bracket that starts line 8 indicates that the policy statement block is complete.

Policy Actions

When creating custom policies, you will typically have to provide several actions for the user to be able to carry out the required tasks. Take, for example, creating a policy for an administrator to be able to create, change, or remove their IAM user account password. The actions that need to be listed in the policy must include the following:

- **CreateLoginProfile:** The user needs to be able to create a login profile.

- **DeleteLoginProfile:** The user must be able to delete their login profile if they want to make changes.

- **GetLoginProfile:** The user has to be able to access the login profile.

- **UpdateLoginProfile:** After making changes, the user has to be able to update their login information.

For an IAM user to be able to perform administration tasks for a group of IAM users, the additional actions required include creating users, deleting users, listing users and groups, removing policies, and renaming or changing information. To be able to make changes to an AWS resource, you must be able to modify and delete. The statement in Example 3-2 provides the details for this policy.

Example 3-2   IAM Policy for Performing Administrative Tasks

```
"Statement": [
{
"Sid": "AllowUsersToPerformUserActions",
"Effect": "Allow",
"Action": [
"iam:ListPolicies",
"iam:GetPolicy",
"iam:UpdateUser",
"iam:AttachUserPolicy",
"iam:ListEntitiesForPolicy",
"iam:DeleteUserPolicy",
"iam:DeleteUser",
"iam:ListUserPolicies",
"iam:CreateUser",
"iam:RemoveUserFromGroup",
"iam:AddUserToGroup",
"iam:GetUserPolicy",
"iam:ListGroupsForUser",

"iam:PutUserPolicy",
"iam:ListAttachedUserPolicies",
"iam:ListUsers",
"iam:GetUser",
"iam:DetachUserPolicy"
}
],
```

Additional Policy Control Options

Several policy options give you great power in how you manage security options for IAM users and groups, including permission boundaries, service control policies, access control lists, and session policies.

Permission Boundaries

Permission boundaries are used to mandate the security policies that can be applied to an IAM user or role.

You can apply a permission boundary policy for both the IAM user and IAM role within a single AWS account. Without a permission boundary being defined, the applied managed or custom policy defines the maximum permissions that are granted to each particular IAM user or role. Adding a permission boundary provides a level of control by filtering the permissions that can be applied. The IAM user or role can only carry out the actions that are allowed by *both* the assigned identity-based policy and the permission boundary policy. Therefore, the permission settings defined are controlled by a permission boundary policy that establishes the specific listing of permissions that can be applied.

For example, suppose you want administrator Mark to be able to manage Amazon S3 buckets and EC2 instances—and that's all. In this case, you need to create the custom policy shown in Example 3-3, which defines the permissions boundary for Mark— namely, that he can fully administrate Amazon S3 buckets and EC2 instances.

Example 3-3   Mark's Permission Boundary

```
{
"Version": "2012-10-17",
"Statement": [
{
"Effect": "Allow",
"Action": [
"s3:*",
"ec2:*"
],
"Resource": "*"
}
]
}
```

Once a permission boundary has been added to Mark's IAM account, as shown in Figure 3-24, the only two AWS services that Mark will have full administrative control over are Amazon S3 Buckets and EC2 instances. In the future, an IAM policy is added to Mark's account to enable him to work with AWS CloudTrail and create alerts and alarms. However, when Mark goes to carry out actions using AWS CloudTrail, if the current permission boundary has not been updated, listing that Mark can also use the CloudTrail service, then this action will be denied. The permission boundary policy settings must match up with the IAM policy settings that are applied to Mark's IAM user account.

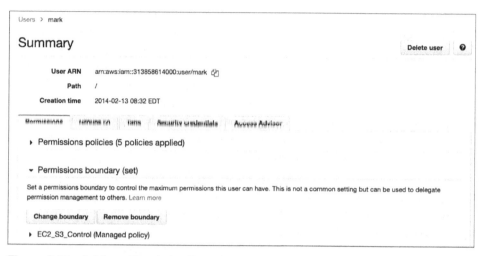

Figure 3-24 Adding a Permission Boundary to a User Account

The permission boundary shown in Figure 3-24 could be much more stringent; instead of listing full control, a permission boundary could mandate a specific listing of tasks that Mark could carry out for both Amazon S3 buckets and EC2 instances.

AWS Organizations Service Control Policies

AWS Organizations enables organizations to manage security settings and services across AWS accounts that are grouped together in a tree formation. (More details on AWS Organizations are discussed later in this chapter.) One of the security features of AWS Organizations is a service control policy (SCP), which provides a permission boundary located at the root of the tree controlling all AWS account members, or to specific OUs containing AWS accounts in the AWS Organization tree. The SCP and the entity being controlled must have matching permissions for the desired permissions to be allowed (see Figure 3-25). Once an SCP has been enabled, permissions are allowed only if the IAM policy and the SCP list the identical permissions in both policies. The types of permission policies that can be controlled by an SCP are identity-based policies for IAM users, roles, the root user in any AWS account, and resource-based policies.

NOTE   Service control policies do not affect service-linked roles that delegate the permissions assigned to each AWS service to carry out their assigned tasks.

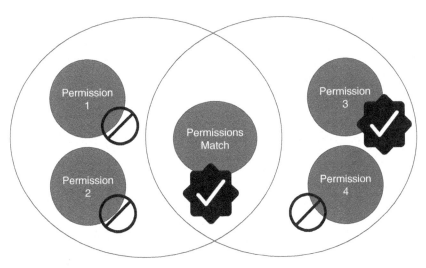

Figure 3-25 Effective Permissions Using a Service Control Policy

Access Control Lists

Access control lists (ACLs) are present for defining simple permission controls on objects in Amazon S3 buckets for cross-account permission access only between separate AWS accounts. ACLs cannot be used to grant permissions to entities in the same AWS account. ACLs are only present because of backward compatibility; it's a much better idea to use IAM roles to control cross-account access. Amazon recommends that ACLs not be used for applying security to S3 bucket contents. Instead use the Amazon S3 Object Ownership setting **Bucket owner enforced** to disable all of the ACLs associated with a bucket. When this bucket-level setting is applied, all of the objects in the bucket become owned by the AWS account that created the bucket and ACLs can no longer be used to grant access.

Session Policies

Session policies are another version of a permission boundary to help limit what permissions can be assigned to federated users or IAM users assigned roles (see Figure 3-26). Developers can create session policies when IAM roles are used to access an application. When session policies are deployed, the effective permissions for the session are either the ones that are granted by the resource-based policy settings or the identity-based policy settings that match the session policy permission settings.

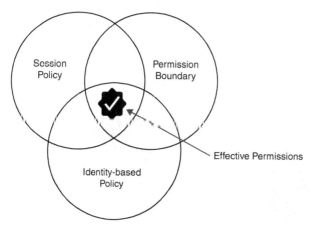

Figure 3-26 Session Policies

Reviewing Policy Permissions

For troubleshooting purposes, it may be necessary to review the assigned access levels, the required AWS resources, and any additional conditions that have been allowed or denied within each IAM policy. Thankfully, AWS provides these details in graphic *policy summary tables*, as shown in Figure 3-27, which make it easier to troubleshoot or analyze what an IAM user, group, or role combined with a select IAM policy can do. There are policy summaries on both IAM users and roles for all attached policies. View a policy summary by selecting the individual policy; on its summary page click Policy Summary. Information is displayed for the different types of policies: custom and AWS-managed policies and AWS-managed job function policies.

Permissions	Policy usage	Policy versions	Access Advisor

Policy summary   **{ } JSON**

Q Filter

Service ⌄	Access level	Resource
Allow (6 of 264 services) Show remaining 258		
CloudWatch	Full access	All resources
EC2	Full access	All resources
EC2 Auto Scaling	Full access	All resources
ELB	Full access	All resources
ELB v2	Full access	All resources
IAM	**Limited**: Write	All resources

Figure 3-27 Policy Summary Tables

Policy permissions information is contained in three tables:

- **Policy Summary (Services):** Information is grouped into explicit deny, allow, and uncategorized services when IAM can't figure out the service name due to a typo or when a custom third-party service is in use that has not been defined properly. Recognized services are listed based on whether the policy allows or explicitly denies the use of the service.

- **Service Summary (Actions):** Information displayed includes a list of the actions and permissions (for example, list, read, write) that have been defined in the policy for a particular service.

- **Action Summary (Resources):** Information includes a list of resources and the conditions that control each action. Details include the resources, the region where the resources have been defined, and what IAM accounts the actions are associated with.

IAM Policy Versions

After you've created an IAM policy, in the future you may want to make additions or deletions. Regardless of whether a policy is a custom policy that you have created or an AWS-managed policy, every time an IAM policy is updated, a new version of the policy is created.

AWS stores up to five versions of each IAM policy. To define the default version of an IAM policy to be used, after selecting the policy, select the Policy versions tab, and from the displayed versions, select the version of the policy that you want to define as the current version to be used. From this point forward, the selected version of the policy becomes version enforced, as shown in Figure 3-28. If you want to make changes later, you can change the current version of the policy to another version of the policy.

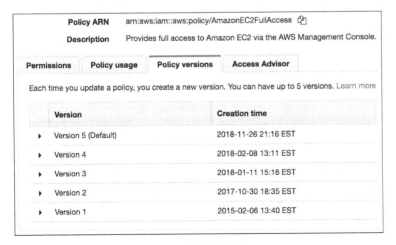

| Policy ARN | arn:aws:iam::aws:policy/AmazonEC2FullAccess |
| Description | Provides full access to Amazon EC2 via the AWS Management Console. |

Permissions   Policy usage   Policy versions   Access Advisor

Each time you update a policy, you create a new version. You can have up to 5 versions. Learn more

Version	Creation time
▸ Version 5 (Default)	2018-11-26 21:16 EST
▸ Version 4	2018-02-08 13:11 EST
▸ Version 3	2018-01-11 15:16 EST
▸ Version 2	2017-10-30 18:35 EST
▸ Version 1	2015-02-06 13:40 EST

Figure 3-28 Viewing Versions of IAM Policies

Using Conditional Elements

Conditional elements of a JSON policy allow you to dictate optional parameters that must be met before the policy action is approved. Conditional elements are global or service-specific, as shown in the examples in Table 3-2. An organization could use the **aws:SourceIP** element, for example, to control the range of IP addresses from which administrators can log on to AWS.

Table 3-2   Conditional Elements

Element	Description
Global Elements	
aws:CurrentTime	This element checks for date/time conditions.
aws:SecureTransport	The request must use Secure Sockets Layer (SSL/TLS).
aws:UserAgent	This element allows certain client applications to make requests.
aws:MultiFactorAuthPresent	With this element, you can use the **BoolIfExists** operator to deny requests that do not include MFA.
Bool	The value of this element must be true.
StringEquals	The request must contain a specific value.
Service-Specific Elements	
aws:PrincipalOrgID	With this element, the user must be a member of a specific AWS organization.
aws:PrincipalTag/*tag-key*	This element checks for specific tags.
aws:RequestTag/*tag-key*	This element checks for a tag and a specific value.
aws:PrincipalType	This element checks for a specific user or role.
aws:SourceVpce	This element restricts access to a specific endpoint.
aws:RequestedRegion	This element allows you to control the regions to which API calls can be made.
aws:SourceIp	This element specifies an IPv4 or IPv6 address or range of addresses.
aws:userid	This element checks the user's ID.

Using Tags with IAM Identities

Most AWS resources allow you to define a number of tags for the resource you are creating or using. You can add custom attributes using tags to both the IAM user and roles; for example, you can define a tag for an EC2 instance with the key **location** and the tag value **Toronto**.

Once you have tagged your resources, tags can be used to control IAM users and roles and their access to AWS resources. Tags can be added as a conditional element of each policy, mandating what tags need to be attached to the resource before the request is allowed. The following logic can be controlled using conditional tags:

- **Resources:** Tags can be used for IAM users and roles to determine whether access is allowed or denied to the requested resource based on the attached tags.

- **Principals:** Tags with Boolean logic can be used to control what the IAM user is allowed to do.

In Example 3-4, administrators can only delete users who have the **ResourceTag** set to **temp_user=can_terminate** tag and **PrincipalTag** attached to **useradmin=*true***. The tags in the example have been bolded for ease of reading.

Example 3-4   Using Tags to Control Deletions

```
{
 "Version": "2012-10-17",
 "Statement": [{
 "Effect": "Allow",
 "Action": "iam:DeleteUser",
 "Resource": "*",
 "Condition": {"StringLike": {"iam:ResourceTag/temp user":
    "can_terminate"}}
 }]
}
{
 "Version": "2012-10-17",
 "Statement": [
 {
 "Effect": "Allow",
 "Action": "iam:* ",
 "Resource": "*",
 "Condition": {"StringEquals": {"aws:PrincipalTag/useradmin": "true"}}
 }
 ]
}
```

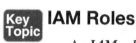

IAM Roles

An *IAM role* is an IAM identity with specific permissions that define what the identity can and can't do at AWS. IAM roles provide temporary access to AWS resources once a role is associated with the following identities:

- An IAM user in the same AWS account as the role

- An IAM user in a different AWS account than the role

- An AWS web service such as Amazon EC2

- An external user authenticated by an external identity provider (IdP) service compatible with SAML 2.0 or OpenID Connect

When IAM roles are assumed by an identity, there is an additional linked policy called a *trust policy*. The use of an IAM role establishes a trust relationship between your *trusting* account and other AWS *trusted* accounts. The trusting account owns the AWS resource to be accessed. The trusted account contains the IAM identity that needs access to the resource. The trust policy and the security policy are assigned to the identity who will assume the role, as shown in Example 3-5. Roles do not have attached credentials. Temporary authentication credentials and a session token are assigned to an IAM user or federated user only after verification that the identity can assume the role. Trust policies are created for roles as follows:

- When a role is set up using the IAM console, the trust policy document is created and applied automatically.

- When a role is assigned to a user in the same AWS account, no trust policy is required, as the IAM user is already known to the AWS account.

- When a role is assigned to an IAM user residing in another AWS account, a trust policy must be assigned to the IAM user to be able to gain access.

- When the AWS CLI is used to create a role, both the trust policy and the permissions policy must be created.

Example 3-5   IAM Role Trust Policy

```
{
 "Version":"2012-10-17",
 "Statement": {
 "Effect":"Allow",
 "Principal": {"AWS: "arn:iam::123456789:root" },
 "Action":"sts:AssumeRole",
 }
}
```

When to Use IAM Roles

IAM roles are used for these authentication scenarios:

- Access to AWS resources using service-linked roles

- EC2 instances hosting applications needing access to AWS resources

- Third-party access required to AWS Accounts resources

- Web identity federation authentication by an external identity provider requiring access to AWS resources

- SAML 2.0 federation authentication requiring access to AWS resources

- Cross-account access—AWS account identities requiring access to resources in another AWS account

The following sections describe these scenarios.

AWS Services Perform Actions on Your Behalf

Service-linked roles assign the required permissions that allow each AWS service to carry out its job. AWS Config, Amazon Inspector, Amazon CloudWatch logs, and Amazon Elastic File System (EFS) are examples of AWS services using service-linked roles with the required permissions attached and temporary credentials granting access to carry out the requested tasks as required.

EC2 Instances Hosting Applications Need Access to AWS Resources

AWS roles are useful for EC2 instances hosting applications that need access to AWS resources. For a workload to function properly, it needs valid AWS credentials to make its API requests to AWS resources. You could (but this a bad idea!) store a set of IAM users' credentials on the local hard disk of the application server or web server and allow the application to use those credentials.

Instead, implement the recommended best practice and create an IAM role that provides the required permission for the application hosted on the EC2 instance. The addition of a role to an EC2 instance creates an *instance profile* that is attached to the instance either during creation, as shown in Figure 3-29, or after creation.

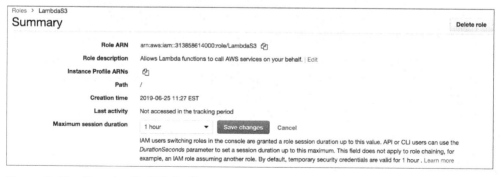

Figure 3-29   Attaching an IAM Role to an EC2 Instance

When the IAM role is used, temporary credentials are supplied, and the application can access the required AWS resources. Each EC2 instance can have a single role assigned; however, the single role can be assigned to multiple instances. Any future changes made to the role are propagated to all instances that are currently using that role.

Using IAM roles means that you don't have to manage credentials. Instead, the AWS Security Token Service (STS) handles the authentication and authorization management. Each role assigned to an EC2 instance contains a permissions policy that lists the permissions to be used, plus a trust policy that allows the EC2 instance to be able to assume the assigned role and access the required AWS service. Each approved role is allowed access for a defined period of time; 1 hour is the default, as shown in Figure 3-30. The temporary credentials are stored in the memory of the running instance and are part of the instance's metadata store under iam/security-credentials/role-name.

Figure 3-30   Changing the Validity Time Frame for Temporary Credentials

Using temporary security credentials for an EC2 instance provides an additional advantage: The security credentials are automatically rotated just before their temporary session expires, ensuring that a valid set of credentials is always available for the application. IAM roles that control web/application server access to AWS cloud services is a concept that the AWS Certified Solutions Architect – Associate (SAA-C03) exam will expect you to know and understand.

Access to AWS Accounts by Third Parties

Roles can be used to delegate access to third parties that require access to an organization's AWS resources. Perhaps the third party is managing some of your AWS resources. Granting access with a role and temporary security credentials allows you to grant access without sharing existing IAM security credentials. The role for the third party requires the following information:

- The third party's AWS account ID. The permissions policy specifies that identities from this AWS account number can assume the role.

- A secret identifier specified in the trust policy. The secret identifier is known to both the secure token service (AWS STS) and the third party.

- The permissions required by the third party to carry out their tasks.

Web Identity Federation

Mobile applications can be designed to request temporary AWS security credentials using a process called *web identity federation*. Temporary credentials can map to a role with the required permissions to allow the mobile application to carry out its required tasks. Amazon Cognito is designed for scalable and secure mobile web-based federation to provide authentication for hundreds of thousands of users using social media providers such as Google, Facebook, Amazon, or any third-party identity provider that supports the OpenID Connect protocol. Amazon Cognito also provides support for enterprise federation using Microsoft Active Directory and any external IdP that supports SAML 2.0. Amazon Cognito uses user pools and federated identities to manage sign-up and authentication to mobile applications:

- **Amazon Cognito user pools:** Cognito enables you to create user pools of email addresses or phone numbers that can be linked to the desired application along with the type of authentication needed: through the user pool or by federating through a third-party IdP.

- **Amazon Cognito federated identities:** Cognito manages multiple IdPs— both identity federation and web-based federation options that mobile applications use for authentication and controlling access to your backend AWS resources and APIs, ensuring users get only the requested access to AWS services such as Amazon S3, Amazon DynamoDB, Amazon API Gateway, and AWS Lambda (see Figure 3-31).

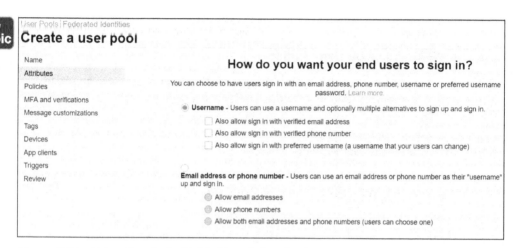

Figure 3-31   Using Cognito for Mobile User Authentication

SAML 2.0 Federation

The changes in authentication over the past 20 years have led to a number of options for single sign-on, including Cognito, AWS STS, Web Identity Federation, SAML 2.0, and Open ID Connect. Many companies use Active Directory Domain Services, which has supported SAML for many years. SAML is supported by all public cloud providers in order to support most major corporations' ability to authenticate to the cloud using SSO.

Before the rise of mobile phones, corporate computer/user accounts were linked to applications hosted in the cloud. Mobile applications on devices are now commonplace requiring a unique type of authentication linking phones and devices running an application hosted by the cloud provider.

If an organization's end users already authenticate to a corporate network using a security service such as AD DS, you don't have to create separate IAM users for access to AWS services and resources. Instead, your users' corporate Active Directory user identities can be *federated* and synchronized to AWS with access to AWS resources using IAM roles. If your corporate network is compatible with SAML 2.0, it can be configured to provide an SSO process for gaining access to the AWS Management Console or other AWS services as required.

AWS provides several services to handle the different levels of federation used today. Amazon Cognito allows you to manage the variety of authentication providers in the industry, including Facebook, Google, Twitter, OpenID, and SAML, and even custom authentication providers that can be created from scratch. The odds are that you will use several of these prebuilt third-party authentication providers for controlling authentication and access to applications hosted at AWS. AD DS deployments with Active Directory Federated Services installed can take advantage of AWS Directory Service to build a trust relationship between your corporate Active Directory network, your corporate users, and resources hosted in an AWS account.

Here are big-picture steps for linking your on-premises Active Directory environment with AWS. Registration of the organization identity provider with AWS is necessary before you can create IAM roles that define the tasks that your corporate users can carry out at AWS.

Step 1.   Register your organization's identity provider, such as Active Directory, with AWS. To do so, you must create and provide a metadata XML file, as shown in Figure 3-32, that lists your IdP and authentication keys used by AWS to validate the authentication requests from your organization.

Figure 3-32   Adding a Metadata XML

Step 2.   Create IAM roles that provide access to the AWS resources. For the trust policy of the role, list your IdP as the principal. This ensures that users from your organization will be allowed to access AWS resources.

Step 3.   Define which users or groups to map to the IAM roles, as shown in Figure 3-33, to provide access to the required AWS resources.

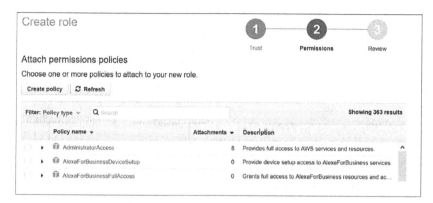

Figure 3-33 Selecting Policies for an IAM Role

Cross-Account Access

To allow access to resources in your AWS account from users in other AWS accounts rather than create an IAM user account within multiple AWS accounts for access, you can instead provide temporary *cross-account access* by using an IAM role. For example, a developer's IAM account located in the dev AWS account needs access to the S3 bucket **corpdocs** in the production AWS account. User identities in the dev AWS account use IAM roles to assume access to AWS resources in the production AWS account, using defined IAM roles and policies that authenticate using AWS STS. The following steps allow access to specific AWS services hosted in the production account from the dev AWS account:

Step 1.   Create an IAM policy called **access-s3** in the production account that controls access to the S3 resource. The policy created is a custom policy that allows access to a specific S3 resource, as shown here:

```
Statement": [
{
"Effect": "Allow",
"Action": "s3:ListAllMyBuckets",
"Resource": "*"
},
{
"Effect": "Allow",
"Action": [
"s3:ListBucket",
"s3:GetBucketLocation"
```

```
],
"Resource": "arn:aws:s3:::corpdocs"
},
{
"Effect": " Allow",
"Action": [
"s3:GetObject",
"s3:PutObject",
"s3:DeleteObject"
],
" Resource": "arn:aws:s3:::corpdocs/*"
}
]
}
```

Step 2. Create an IAM role called **get-access**, which is assigned to the developer's IAM account that is linked to the IAM role policy **access-s3**.

Step 3. Get the ARN of the **get-access** role. The ARN is required to populate the custom IAM policy that allows the developer's IAM group to successfully switch accounts and access the **get-access** role.

Step 4. Grant access to the role in the developer's IAM user account by creating a custom policy that allows the developer to access the **get-access** role, as shown here:

```
{
"Version": "2012-10-17",
"Statement": {
"Effect": "Allow",
"Action": "sts:AssumeRole",
"Resource": "arn:aws:iam:::PRODUCTION-AWS-ACCT-ID:role/
get-access"
}
}
```

Step 5. The developer can now switch roles by using the AWS Management Console and clicking Switch Role below the username, as shown in Figure 3-34, to gain access to the desired AWS resource.

NOTE All Amazon services except for AWS RoboMaker, Amazon QuickSight, AWS Amplify, and Amazon Rekognition allow the use of roles. The action in the policy **AssumeRole** triggers communication with STS for verification.

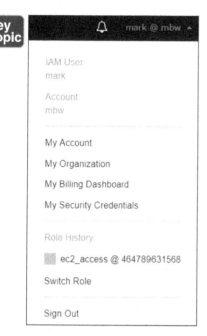

Figure 3-34   Using the Switch Role Option for Cross-Account Access

AWS Security Token Service

External authentication using identity federation is possible at AWS, including SSO federation with SAML 2.0, web-based federation (via Amazon, Google, or Facebook), and federation using OpenID Connect. To support the various types of identity federation, running in the background at AWS is a global security service that provides temporary credentials upon request for external and internal access to AWS services using an attached IAM role. AWS STS uses a default global endpoint located in the US-East Northern Virginia region at https://sts.amazonaws.com; you can also choose to make STS API calls to other AWS regions using a regional endpoint if faster responses are needed. Temporary security credentials are, indeed, temporary, whereas access credentials linked to an IAM user are permanent. Temporary credentials are provided only when access to AWS resources is requested using a role.

The action in the policy can be defined as **AssumeRole**, **AssumeRoleWithSAML**, or **AssumeRoleWithWebIdentity**, as shown in Figure 3-35.

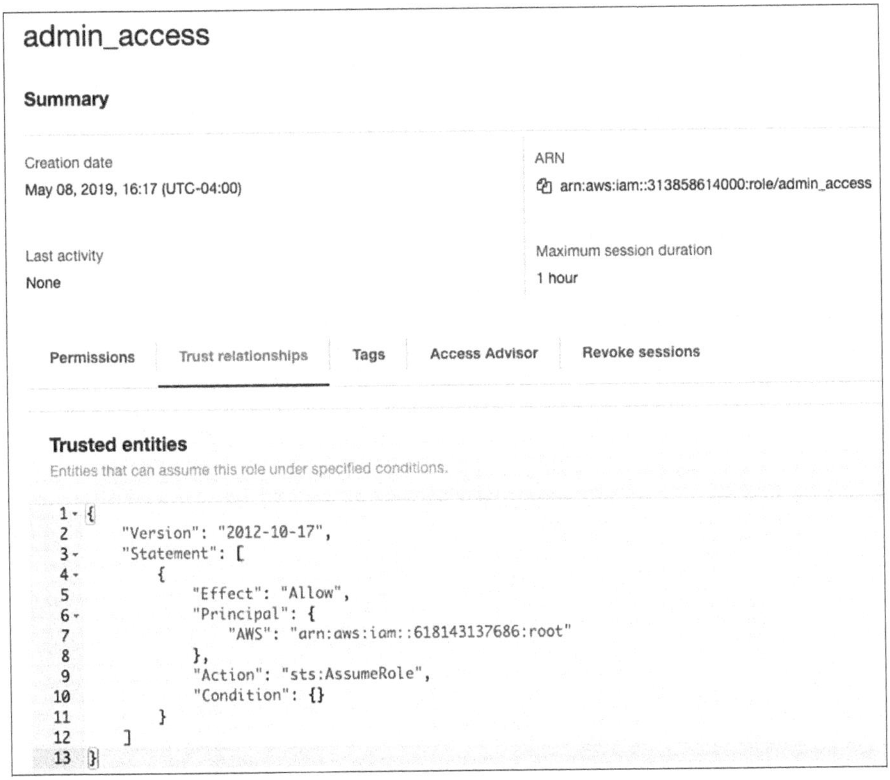

admin_access

Summary

Creation date
May 08, 2019, 16:17 (UTC-04:00)

ARN
⧉ arn:aws:iam::313858614000:role/admin_access

Last activity
None

Maximum session duration
1 hour

| Permissions | Trust relationships | Tags | Access Advisor | Revoke sessions |

Trusted entities
Entities that can assume this role under specified conditions.

```
 1 ▾ {
 2        "Version": "2012-10-17",
 3 ▾      "Statement": [
 4 ▾          {
 5                "Effect": "Allow",
 6 ▾              "Principal": {
 7                    "AWS": "arn:aws:iam::618143137686:root"
 8                },
 9                "Action": "sts:AssumeRole",
10                "Condition": {}
11            }
12        ]
13  }
```

Figure 3-35   Trusted Entities in Trust Policy

For either of these actions, STS is called. After verification, STS returns temporary credentials (access key, secret access key, and security token), which are valid for 1 hour by default. You can edit the maximum role session duration to control the exact length of time the assigned security credentials are valid (1 to 36 hours), or a custom length of time can be defined. The advantages of using STS to provide temporary credentials for accessing AWS services are as follows:

- There's no need to rotate security credentials; STS performs credential rotation when temporary credentials are renewed.

- Applications use temporary credentials when they're hosted on EC2 instances with assigned roles, so there is no need for IAM user account credentials and passwords to be embedded in the application.

- STS manages and secures temporary credentials.

- Access to AWS resources can be defined without requiring a full IAM user account.

■ Active sessions can be revoked at any time using the IAM dashboard, as shown in Figure 3-36.

Permissions   Trust relationships   Tags   Access Advisor   Revoke sessions

Immediately revoke all active sessions

If you choose Revoke active sessions, IAM attaches an inline policy named **AWSRevokeOlderSessions** to this role. This new sessions based on this role. If you need to undo this action later, you can remove the inline policy. Learn more

Revoke active sessions

Here is an example of the AWSRevokeOlderSessions policy that is created after you choose **Revoke active sessions**:

```
 1 ▾ {
 2       "Version": "2012-10-17",
 3 ▾     "Statement": [
 4 ▾         {
 5               "Effect": "Deny",
 6 ▾             "Action": [
 7                   "*"
 8               ],
 9 ▾             "Resource": [
10                   "*"
11               ],
12 ▾             "Condition": {
13 ▾                 "DateLessThan": {
14                       "aws:TokenIssueTime": "[policy creation time]"
15                   }
16               }
17           }
18       ]
19 }
```

Figure 3-36   Revoke Active Sessions

IAM Best Practices

There are several best practices you should consider following when managing user security with IAM:

■ **Root account:** Be careful with the AWS root account password. Don't create such a complicated password that you can't remember it and have to write it down. When you need access to the root account, reset the password. In addition, always enable MFA on a root account. Make sure your access keys for the root account have been deleted. You can check whether you have active access keys for your root account by logging on as the root user, opening the IAM console, and making sure the root account access keys have been removed (see Figure 3-37).

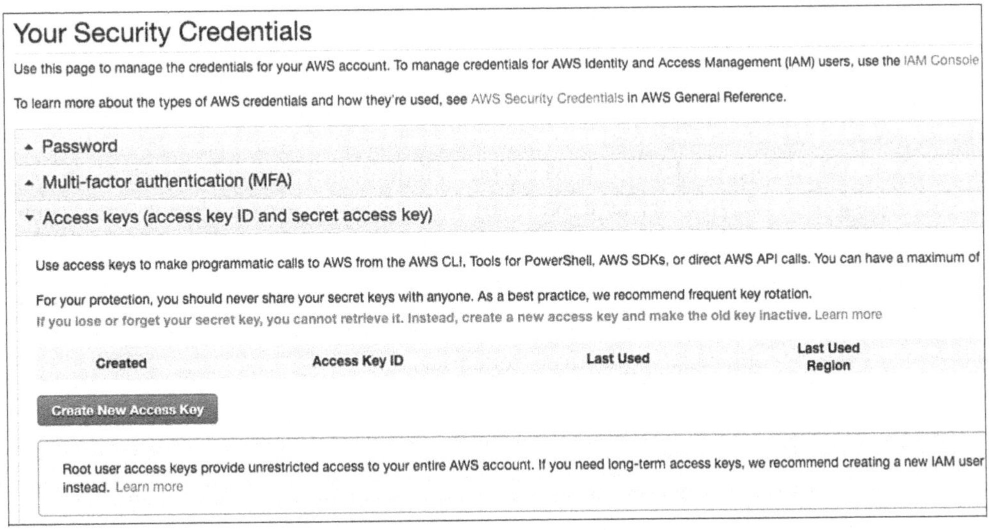

Your Security Credentials

Use this page to manage the credentials for your AWS account. To manage credentials for AWS Identity and Access Management (IAM) users, use the IAM Console

To learn more about the types of AWS credentials and how they're used, see AWS Security Credentials in AWS General Reference.

▲ Password

▲ Multi-factor authentication (MFA)

▼ Access keys (access key ID and secret access key)

Use access keys to make programmatic calls to AWS from the AWS CLI, Tools for PowerShell, AWS SDKs, or direct AWS API calls. You can have a maximum of

For your protection, you should never share your secret keys with anyone. As a best practice, we recommend frequent key rotation.
If you lose or forget your secret key, you cannot retrieve it. Instead, create a new access key and make the old key inactive. Learn more

Created	Access Key ID	Last Used	Last Used Region

Create New Access Key

Root user access keys provide unrestricted access to your entire AWS account. If you need long-term access keys, we recommend creating a new IAM user instead. Learn more

Figure 3-37 Properly Set Up Root Account

- **Individual IAM users and groups for administration:** Even when creating single IAM users, consider placing them in an IAM group. At some point, each single user's duties may need to be assumed by someone else due to holidays or illness. It's much easier to add a new IAM user to an existing IAM group than to manage separate individual IAM users.

- **Permissions:** Grant least privileges when assigning IAM permissions. Take the time to get proficient at deploying IAM management policies. If necessary, create custom IAM policies for specific administrative access. Remember that most IAM accounts are administrator accounts. The goal should be to use IAM roles wherever possible because roles use controlled access with temporary credentials that are assigned and completely managed by STS.

- **Groups:** If possible, don't manage by individual IAM users; instead, manage by delegating access using IAM groups.

- **Conditions:** Consider restricting access with additional policy conditions. Consider adding a mandatory IP address range for administrators who need to perform administrative tasks and force authentication and access from a specific range of IP addresses.

- **CloudTrail logs:** Create a custom CloudTrail trail that saves all API calls and authentications from all AWS regions to a defined S3 bucket forever.

- **Passwords:** Make sure to create a strong password policy that matches corporate requirements.

- **Security credential rotation:** Consider rotating the security credentials on a timeline that matches the password change for each account. Even better, redesign your IAM security to use IAM roles for administrative tasks to ensure temporary credentials are used and managed by STS/AWS.

- **MFA:** Enable MFA for IAM users, including the root user of each AWS account. At the very least, use a software-based security code generator such as Google Authenticator or Authy.

- **Use IAM roles for application servers:** Use IAM roles to share temporary access to AWS resources for applications hosted on EC2 instances. Let AWS and STS manage application credentials.

IAM Security Tools

Various security utilities and tools are available to make your job of managing IAM security easier. The following are tools to know for the SAA-C03 exam:

- **Credential Report:** From the IAM dashboard or using the AWS CLI, request and download a comma-separated values (CSV) report that lists the current status of IAM users in an AWS account (see Figure 3-38). Details include the status of the access keys (for example, usage, last used service, key rotation, passwords enabled/disabled, last time used, last changed, and MFA status. The information provided by the report is within the most recent 4-hour time status).

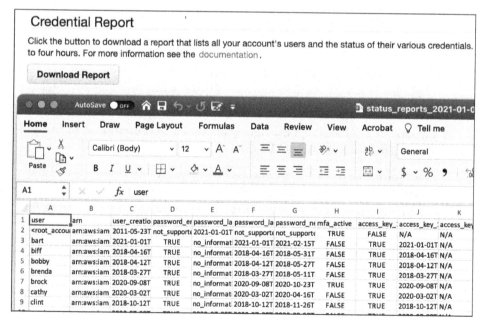

Figure 3-38   Credential Report

■ **Access Advisor:** Reports can be generated to display the last time an IAM user or role accessed an AWS service. View reports for each IAM entity by first selecting the IAM user, group, or role, selecting the Access Advisor tab, and then viewing the contents of the Access Advisor tab, as shown in Figure 3-39.

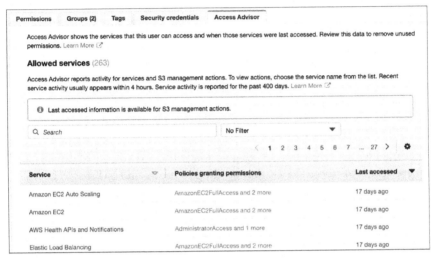

Figure 3-39   Access Advisor Details

■ **Policy Simulator:** After you've created your first policy, you might get lucky and have it work right away. If you are using the pre-created managed policies provided by AWS, they will usually work. However, a custom policy might not work as expected. Fortunately, Amazon has a simulator called the IAM Policy Simulator that you can use to test your policies (see Figure 3-40). The simulator evaluates your policy using the same policy evaluation engine that would be used if real IAM policy requests were being carried out.

Figure 3-40   IAM Policy Simulator

With the Policy Simulator, you can test IAM policies that are attached to IAM users, groups, or roles within an AWS account. You can select one or all security policies that are attached, and you can test all actions for what is being allowed or denied by the selected IAM policies. You can even include conditions such as the IP address that the request must come from. Both identity-based and resource-based policies can be tested with the Policy Simulator.

IAM Cheat Sheet

For the AWS Certified Solutions Architect – Associate (SAA-C03) exam, you need to understand the following critical aspects of IAM:

- New IAM users are created with no access to any AWS services.

- IAM users can be assigned access keys, passwords, and multi-factor authentication.

- By using identity federation in conjunction with IAM roles, you can enable secure access to resources without needing to create an IAM user account.

- IAM is a global service that is not restricted to a single AWS region.

- IAM roles use security credentials provided by AWS STS that provide temporary access to AWS services and resources.

- Temporary security credentials include an AWS access key, a secret access key, and a security token.

- Each AWS account root account has full administrative permissions that cannot be restricted.

- IAM roles define a set of permissions for allowing or denying actions to AWS services.

- IAM roles are assumed by trusted identities.

- IAM roles allow you to delegate access permissions to AWS resources without requiring permanent credentials.

- There are no credentials assigned to an IAM role.

- IAM roles have two policies:

  - The permissions policy defines the permissions required for the role.

  - The trust policy defines the trusted accounts that are allowed to assume the role.

AWS Identity Center

AWS Identity Center, the successor to AWS Single Sign-On, is a cloud-based SSO service that manages access and permissions to third-party cloud applications and applications that support SAML 2.0 for AWS accounts contained in AWS Organizations. AWS Identity Center integrates with AWS Organizations and enumerated AWS accounts supporting the following features:

- Provides SSO access to cloud applications for AWS accounts

- Provides SSO access to AWS applications such as SageMaker

- Provides SSO access to EC2 Windows desktops

- Provides SSO access to IAM users and groups, AWS-Managed Microsoft AD directory users, and external identity providers

- Provides SSO access to many popular cloud-hosted applications (Salesforce, Box, Office 365)

To get started with AWS Identity Center, complete the following steps:

Step 1.   AWS Organizations must first be deployed.

Step 2.   Sign in using the AWS Organizations Management account credentials, which are required to enable AWS Identity Center.

Step 3.   Choose the identity store that will have access to the AWS Identity Center user portal.

Step 4.   After opening the AWS Identity Center console for the first time, enable the AWS Identity Center service.

Step 5.   Add and configure applications that are to be integrated with AWS Identity Center, as shown in Figure 3-41.

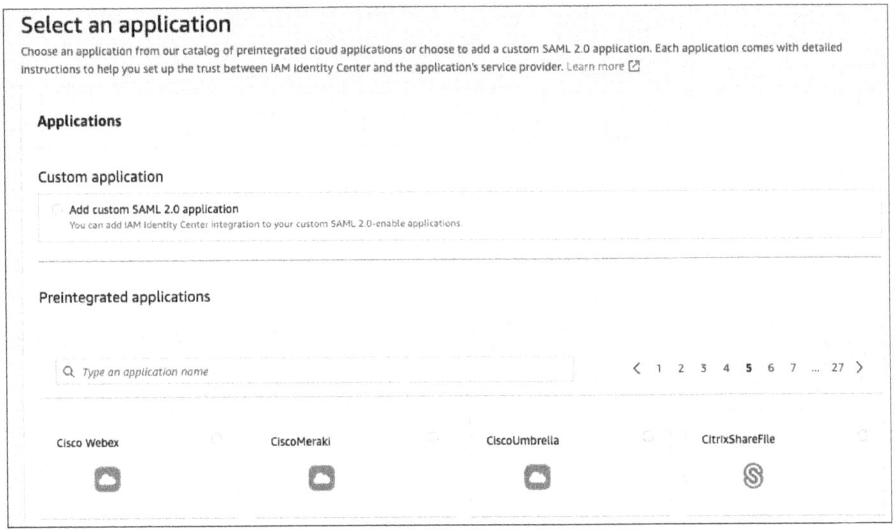

Figure 3-41   AWS Identity Center Cloud Applications

AWS Organizations

AWS Organizations enables centralized policy-based management for multiple AWS accounts that are grouped together in a tree structure. If you're lucky enough to not yet have multiple AWS accounts, you can look at AWS Organizations as a great starting point, especially if you know you're eventually going to have multiple AWS accounts to manage.

The first step to carry out with AWS Organizations is to create your initial organization with a specific AWS account; this account will henceforth be known as the *management account* (see Figure 3-42). The management account sits at the root of your AWS organization's tree.

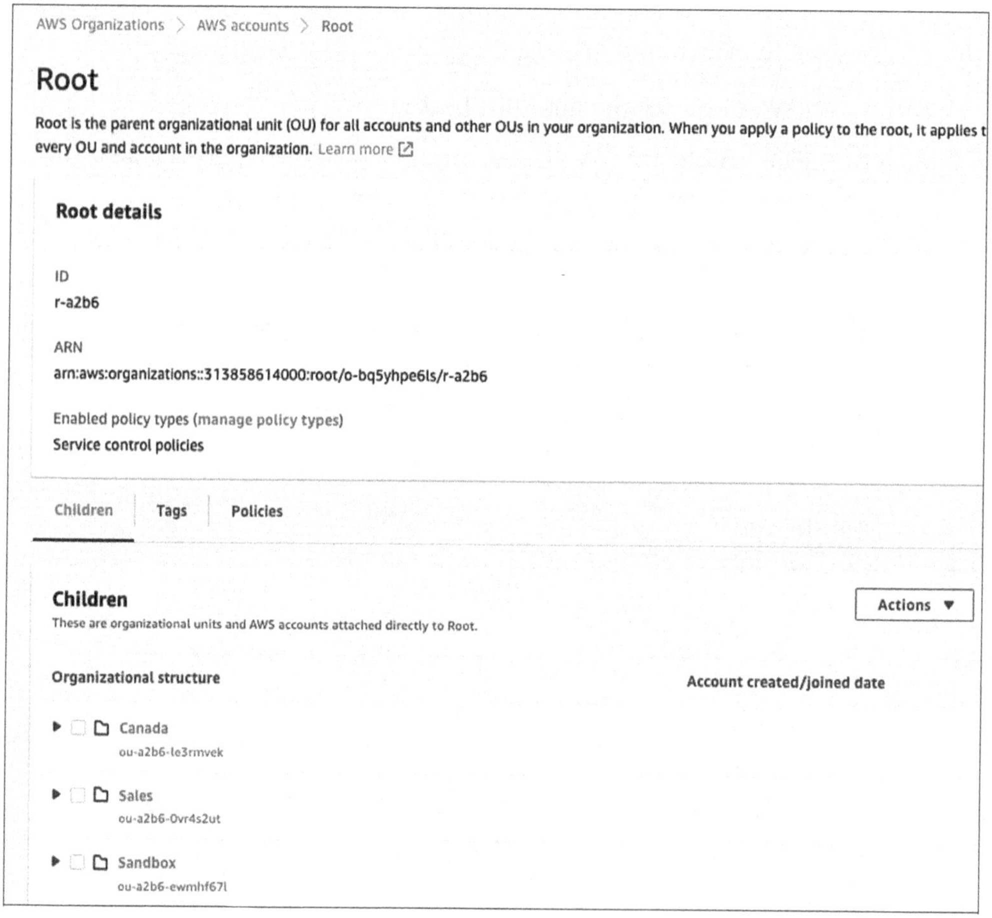

AWS Organizations > AWS accounts > Root

Root

Root is the parent organizational unit (OU) for all accounts and other OUs in your organization. When you apply a policy to the root, it applies to every OU and account in the organization. Learn more ☑

Root details

ID
r-a2b6

ARN
arn:aws:organizations::313858614000:root/o-bq5yhpe6ls/r-a2b6

Enabled policy types (manage policy types)
Service control policies

Children	Tags	Policies

Children
These are organizational units and AWS accounts attached directly to Root.

Actions ▼

Organizational structure   Account created/joined date

▶ ☐ 🗀 Canada
        ou-a2b6-le3rmvek

▶ ☐ 🗀 Sales
        ou-a2b6-0vr4s2ut

▶ ☐ 🗀 Sandbox
        ou-a2b6-ewmhf67l

Figure 3-42 AWS Organizations

NOTE The management account is also called the *payer account* because it is responsible for all the charges carried out by all the AWS accounts that are nested within AWS Organizations. AWS Organizations includes, by default, consolidated billing.

Using AWS Organizations, at the root, you can create new AWS accounts or add existing AWS accounts. All additional AWS accounts added to AWS Organizations are defined as member accounts. After grouping your AWS accounts, you can then apply security control policies to them. As introduced earlier in this chapter, the policies that can be applied to AWS Organizations are called service control policies (SCPs); these are permission boundaries that help define the effective permissions of applied IAM policies. If an SCP and an IAM policy assigned to a specific AWS account IAM user allow the same AWS service actions in both policy documents— that is, if the settings match—then the actions are allowed.

Within AWS Organizations, the AWS accounts can be organized into groupings called *organizational units (OUs)*, as shown in Figure 3-43. OUs can be nested to create a tree-like hierarchy that meets your organization's needs and requirements. Nested OUs inherit SCPs from the parent OU and specific policy controls that can be applied directly to any OU. SCPs can be defined for an entire AWS organization, for specific OUs, or for specific AWS accounts located within an OU.

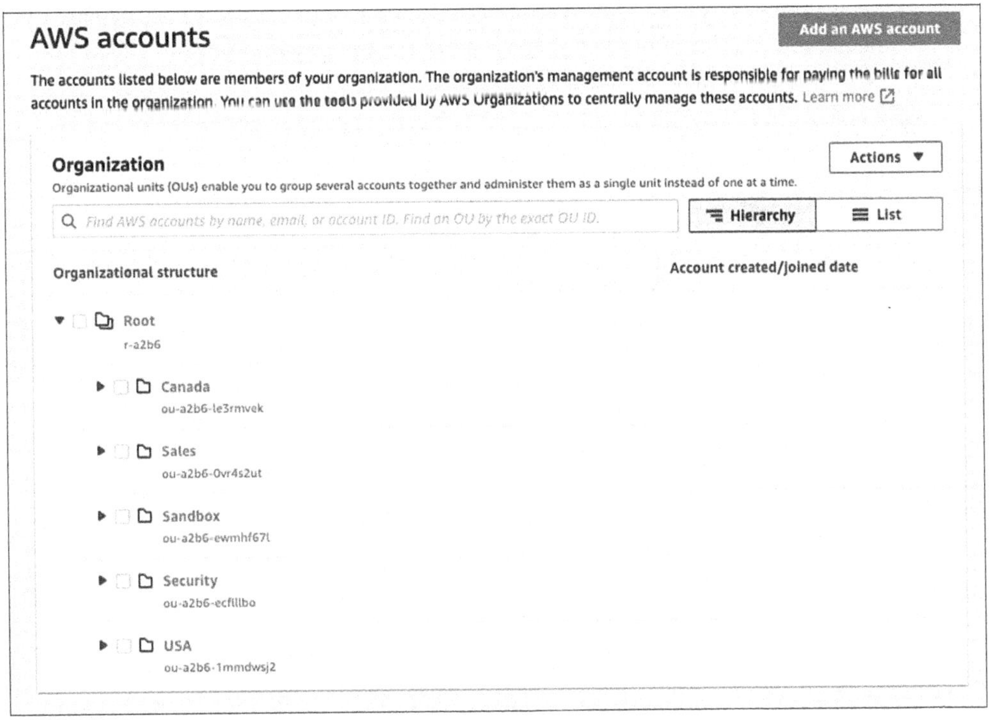

AWS accounts

Add an AWS account

The accounts listed below are members of your organization. The organization's management account is responsible for paying the bills for all accounts in the organization. You can use the tools provided by AWS Organizations to centrally manage these accounts. Learn more ☑

Organization

Actions ▼

Organizational units (OUs) enable you to group several accounts together and administer them as a single unit instead of one at a time.

🔍 *Find AWS accounts by name, email, or account ID. Find an OU by the exact OU ID.*

☰ Hierarchy   ☰ List

Organizational structure   Account created/joined date

▼ ☐ 🗂 Root
        r-a2b6

   ▶ ☐ 🗂 Canada
           ou-a2b6-le3rmvek

   ▶ ☐ 🗂 Sales
           ou-a2b6-0vr4s2ut

   ▶ ☐ 🗂 Sandbox
           ou-a2b6-ewmhf67l

   ▶ ☐ 🗂 Security
           ou-a2b6-ecfillbo

   ▶ ☐ 🗂 USA
           ou-a2b6-1mmdwsj2

Figure 3-43 OUs in AWS Organizations

AWS Organizations Cheat Sheet

For the AWS Certified Solutions Architect – Associate (SAA-C03) exam, you need to understand the following critical aspects of AWS Organizations:

- An AWS organization is a collection of AWS accounts organized into a hierarchy that can be managed centrally.

- Each AWS account in an organization is designated as a member account located in a container. There is no technical difference between the master account and a member account other than its location.

- AWS Organizations supports consolidated billing.

- AWS Resource Access Manager can be used to share resources within the organization tree.

- Service control policies (SCPs) can be applied to AWS accounts or OUs contained within the AWS organization controlling access to AWS resources and services.

- AWS CloudTrail can be activated across all AWS accounts in the organization and cannot be turned off by member accounts.

- An organizational unit contains one or more AWS accounts within the AWS organizational tree.

- Security tools (AWS IAM, AWS Config, AWS Control Tower) can manage the needs and requirements of the AWS accounts that are members of the same AWS organization.

- AWS Cost Explorer can be used to track costs across accounts.

AWS Resource Access Manager

AWS Resource Access Manager (RAM) allows you to centrally manage resources across AWS accounts and AWS Organizations.

AWS RAM allows you to share selected AWS resources hosted within a single AWS account with other AWS accounts. If you are using AWS Organizations, AWS RAM can also be used to share AWS resources between AWS accounts that are members of the same AWS Organization.

AWS RAM can share application or database servers between different AWS accounts instead of having to create duplicate resources.

To share resources using AWS RAM, first create a resource share (see Figure 3-44), configure the permissions to use for the resource, and select the principals that will have access to the resource.

With AWS RAM, the first task is to decide which resources that you own that you want to share. Next, you need to decide which principals to share the resource with;

resource principals can be AWS accounts, OUs, IAM users, or the entire AWS organization.

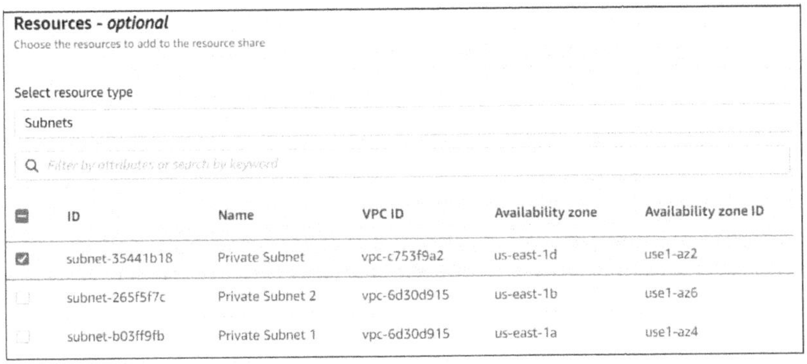

Resources - *optional*
Choose the resources to add to the resource share

Select resource type

Subnets

Q *Filter by attributes or search by keyword*

	ID	Name	VPC ID	Availability zone	Availability zone ID
☑	subnet-35441b18	Private Subnet	vpc-c753f9a2	us-east-1d	use1-az2
☐	subnet-265f5f7c	Private Subnet 2	vpc-6d30d915	us-east-1b	use1-az6
☐	subnet-b03ff9fb	Private Subnet 1	vpc-6d30d915	us-east-1a	use1-az4

Figure 3-44   Sharing Subnets with AWS RAM

If your AWS account is a member of an AWS organization, once sharing is enabled, any selected resource principal will be granted access to any resources shared by a resource share, as shown in Figure 3-45. If AWS Organizations is not deployed, the separate AWS account will receive an invitation from the AWS owner account that has created the resource share to join the resource share—after accepting the invitation, the AWS account will have access to the shared resource.

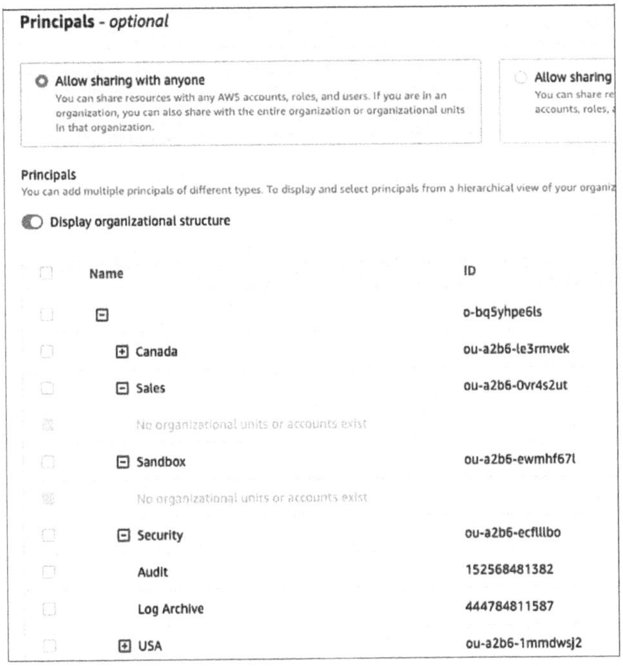

Principals - *optional*

○ **Allow sharing with anyone**
You can share resources with any AWS accounts, roles, and users. If you are in an organization, you can also share with the entire organization or organizational units in that organization.

Allow sharing
You can share re accounts, roles, a

Principals
You can add multiple principals of different types. To display and select principals from a hierarchical view of your organiz

🔘 Display organizational structure

	Name		ID
☐			
☐	⊟		o-bq5yhpe6ls
☐		⊞ Canada	ou-a2b6-le3rmvek
☐		⊟ Sales	ou-a2b6-0vr4s2ut
		No organizational units or accounts exist	
☐		⊟ Sandbox	ou-a2b6-ewmhf67l
		No organizational units or accounts exist	
☐		⊟ Security	ou-a2b6-ecflllbo
☐		Audit	152568481382
☐		Log Archive	444784811587
☐		⊞ USA	ou-a2b6-1mmdwsj2

Figure 3-45   Selecting Principals to Grant Access

The tasks that can be performed with the shared resource depends on the type of resource shared and the IAM security policies and service control policies that may have been applied. AWS resources that can be shared with the AWS Resource Access Manager include Aurora DB clusters, Capacity reservations, Dedicated hosts, Glue catalogs, Image Builder images, AWS Outposts, and Transit Gateways.

Key Topic

AWS Control Tower

AWS Control Tower automates the creation and governance of a secure, multi-account AWS environment using AWS Organizations, as shown in Figure 3-46. AWS Control Tower also automates the creation of a landing zone for onboarding AWS accounts using prebuilt blueprints that follow suggested best practices for configuring a default identity, federated access, and account structure. Deploying AWS Control Tower deploys and configures and integrates the following AWS services:

- AWS Organizations is deployed creating a multi-AWS account structure.

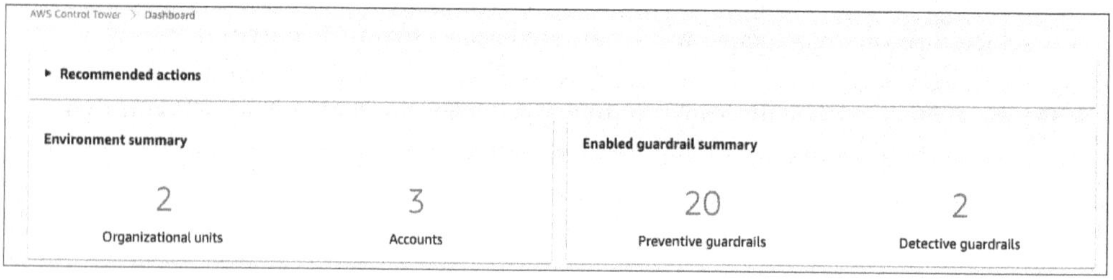

AWS Control Tower > Dashboard			
▶ **Recommended actions**			
Environment summary		**Enabled guardrail summary**	
2	3	20	2
Organizational units	Accounts	Preventive guardrails	Detective guardrails

Figure 3-46 AWS Control Tower Landing Zone

- AWS Organization's SCPs are deployed to prevent unwanted configuration changes.

- Federated access is enabled using AWS Identity Center.

- Central log archiving using AWS CloudTrail and AWS Config is stored in Amazon S3.

- Security audits are enabled across all AWS accounts using AWS Identity Center and Identity and Access Management.

- **Account Factory:** The account factory automates the provisioning of new AWS accounts in the deployed AWS Organization tree. Preapproved network configurations and AWS region selections can also be defined as the mandatory network baseline for all new AWS accounts, as shown in Figure 3-47.

Figure 3-47 Account Factory Preapproved Network Configurations

■ **Guardrails:** Guardrails are used to provide ongoing governance of the AWS environment by preventing deployment of resources that don't follow prescribed policies. Guardrails prevent deployment of resources that don't match your rules. Guardrails can also be detective in nature by continually monitoring the resources that are deployed for nonconformance. Guardrails are deployed using an AWS CloudFormation script that establishes the configuration baseline. SCPs create preventive guardrails that prevent unwanted infrastructure changes. Detective guardrails are created and enforced using AWS Config rules. There are also mandatory and optional guardrails that can be leveraged, as shown in Figure 3-48. For example, organizations can mandate that any changes to logging configuration for Amazon S3 bucket policies can be set to disallowed. An example of an optional guardrail that can be enabled is detecting whether MFA is enabled for the root user.

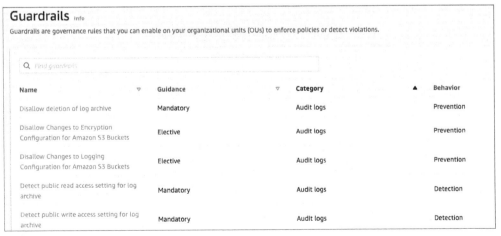

Figure 3-48 AWS Control Tower Guardrails

Exam Preparation Tasks

As mentioned in the section "How to Use This Book" in the Introduction, you have a couple of choices for exam preparation: the exercises here, Chapter 16, "Final Preparation," and the exam simulation questions in the Pearson Test Prep Software Online.

Review All Key Topics

Review the most important topics in the chapter, noted with the Key Topic icon in the margin of the page. Table 3-3 lists these key topics and the page number on which each is found.

Table 3-3   Chapter 3 Key Topics

Key Topic Element	Description	Page Number
Figure 3-2	AWS Config Service-Linked Roles Defined by IAM	81
Section	IAM Policy Definitions	81
Paragraph	IAM authentication	82
Figure 3-3	IAM User Account Access Keys	83
Figure 3-4	An Amazon AWS Resource Name (ARN)	85
Figure 3-6	Policy Evaluation Logic	87
Figure 3-8	Root User Logon	89
Figure 3-10	Access Keys Required for CLI Operation	92
Figure 3-12	Using Custom URL for IAM Users	95
Figure 3-15	Creating an Additional Access Key Manually	98
Section	Using Multi-Factor Authentication	99
Figure 3-18	Managed Policies	101
Section	Resource-Based Policies	102
Figure 3-20	Identity and Resource Policies Working Together	103
Section	Policy Elements	106
Example 3-2	IAM Policy for Performing Administrative Tasks	110
Section	Additional Policy Control Options	110
Section	AWS Organizations Service Control Policies	112

Key Topic Element	Description	Page Number
Section	IAM Policy Versions	115
Table 3-2	Conditional Elements	116
Section	IAM Roles	118
Section	When to Use IAM Roles	119
Figure 3-29	Attaching an IAM Role to an EC2 Instance	120
Section	Web Identity Federation	121
Figure 3-31	Using Cognito for Mobile User Authentication	122
Figure 3-34	Using the Switch Role Option for Cross-Account Access	126
Section	AWS Security Token Service	126
Figure 3-36	Revoke Active Sessions	128
Section	IAM Best Practices	128
Section	IAM Security Tools	130
Section	IAM Cheat Sheet	132
Section	AWS Identity Center	132
Section	AWS Organizations Cheat Sheet	136
Section	AWS Resource Access Manager	136
Section	AWS Control Tower	138
Figure 3-48	AWS Control Tower Guardrails	139

Define Key Terms

Define the following key terms from this chapter and check your answers in the glossary:

Identity and Access Management (IAM), multi-factor authentication (MFA), externally authenticated user, condition, access key, IAM group, password policies, IAM role

Q&A

The answers to these questions appear in Appendix A. For more practice with exam format questions, use the Pearson Test Prep Software Online.

1. How can you tell when you're using the root account?

2. What is the best way to give an application secure access to AWS services?

3. What is the advantage of using a resource-based policy instead of an identity-based policy to protect an S3 bucket?

4. What is the best method for controlling access to AWS resources?

5. Why should inline policies be discouraged in most cases?

6. Which tool can you use to check your policies for proper functionality?

7. How can AWS Organizations help you manage multiple AWS accounts?

8. What security components are required to run a script from the command-line interface?

This chapter covers the following topics:

- Securing Network Infrastructure
- Amazon Cognito
- External Connections
- Amazon GuardDuty
- Amazon Macie
- Security Services for Securing Workloads

This chapter covers content that's important to the following exam domain and task statement:

Domain 1: Design Secure Architectures

Task Statement 2: Design secure workloads and applications

CHAPTER 4

Designing Secure Workloads and Applications

Workload and application security at AWS refers to the measures and controls that are implemented to protect the data and associated cloud services used to process, store, and transmit data. This includes implementing security controls and practices to protect against potential threats and vulnerabilities that could compromise the security of workloads.

To properly secure workload network infrastructure in the cloud, organizations must design and deploy subnets and route tables, security groups (SG), and network access control lists (ACLs) to protect workload infrastructure hosted on subnets in each virtual private cloud (VPC). There are also security services to consider deploying at each edge location, including the AWS Web Application Firewall (WAF), AWS Shield Standard, and AWS Shield Advanced, to help protect workloads that are exposed to the Internet.

Workload security can also utilize a combination of security controls provided by the AWS, such as utilizing Amazon Cognito, which provides authentication, authorization, and user management for your web and mobile applications. There are also several AWS security services that can assist in securing the associated workload, including Amazon Macie, Amazon GuardDuty, AWS CloudTrail, AWS Secrets Manager, Amazon Inspector, and AWS Trusted Advisor.

"Do I Know This Already?"

The "Do I Know This Already?" quiz allows you to assess whether you should read this entire chapter thoroughly or jump to the "Exam Preparation Tasks" section. If you are in doubt about your answers to these questions or your assessment of your knowledge of the topics, read the entire chapter. Table 4-1 lists the major headings in this chapter and their corresponding "Do I Know This Already?" quiz questions. You can find the answers in Appendix A, "Answers to the 'Do I Know This Already?' Quizzes and Q&A Sections."

Table 4-1   "Do I Know This Already?" Section-to-Question Mapping

Foundation Topics Section	Questions
Securing Network Infrastructure	1, 2
Amazon Cognito	3, 4
External Connections	5, 6
Amazon GuardDuty	7, 8
Amazon Macie	9, 10
Security Services for Securing Workloads	11, 12

CAUTION   The goal of self-assessment is to gauge your mastery of the topics in this chapter. If you do not know the answer to a question or are only partially sure of the answer, you should mark that question as wrong for purposes of the self-assessment. Giving yourself credit for an answer you correctly guess skews your self-assessment results and might provide you with a false sense of security.

1. Which route table is associated with each new subnet at creation?

    a. Custom route table

    b. None, because route tables are not automatically associated

    c. The main route table

    d. The network access control list

2. What is a security group's job?

    a. To deny incoming and outgoing traffic

    b. To control incoming and outgoing traffic

    c. To block incoming and outgoing traffic

    d. To explicitly deny incoming and outgoing traffic

3. What services are analyzed by Amazon GuardDuty?

    a. Amazon EFS and FSx for Windows File Server logs

    b. AWS Route 53 logs and Amazon VPC flow logs

    c. Amazon Inspector logs and AWS Config rules

    d. Amazon RDS logs and Amazon EC2 system logs

4. What AWS service is used to automate remediation of Amazon GuardDuty issues?

   a. Amazon CloudTrail

   b. Amazon CloudWatch

   c. AWS Lambda

   d. Amazon Route 53

5. What VPN service needs to be installed before connecting to a VPC?

   a. AWS Direct Connect

   b. AWS Customer Gateway

   c. Virtual Private Gateway

   d. AWS VPN Cloud Hub

6. What type of network connection is an AWS Direct Connect connection?

   a. Public

   b. Single-mode fiber

   c. VPN

   d. IPsec

7. What type of data records are analyzed by Amazon Macie?

   a. Amazon S3 buckets

   b. Amazon EFS

   c. Amazon S3 Glacier

   d. Amazon FSx for Windows File Server

8. What process is used by Amazon Macie to begin a data analysis?

   a. Administrator

   b. Schedule

   c. Job

   d. Task

9. What does AWS Cognito use to authenticate end users to a user pool?

   a. Username/password

   b. Username/SNS

   c. Username/email/phone number

   d. MFA and password

10. What does Amazon Cognito require to authenticate mobile application users?

   a. User pool

   b. Identity pool

   c. Certificates

   d. MFA

11. Which of the following can you use to retain AWS CloudTrail events permanently?

   a. AWS Lambda function

   b. A custom trail

   c. AWS Step Function

   d. None of these; events can be retained for only 90 days

12. Which of the following does Amazon Inspector evaluate?

   a. Amazon S3 buckets

   b. Amazon Elastic Container Service

   c. Amazon EC2 instances

   d. Amazon Relational Database Service

Foundation Topics

Securing Network Infrastructure

Workloads can be protected with a variety of AWS security services. Connections to workloads running at AWS can utilize both public and private connections using one or more of the following AWS networking services (see Figure 4-1):

- **Internet connections (HTTPS/HTTP) to public-facing workloads:** An Internet gateway must be attached to the VPC hosting the workload, and the VPC's security groups and network ACLs must be configured to allow the appropriate traffic to flow through the subnets, load balancer, and web servers.

- *AWS Direct Connect*: Establish a dedicated network connection from your on-premises data center to your VPC (Virtual Private Cloud) at AWS.

- **An AWS VPN (Virtual Private Network) connection:** Provide a secure encrypted connection between an on-premises network and VPC at AWS. VPN connections allow access to your AWS resources and workloads as if they were on your on-premises network.

- **Edge locations for accessing cached data records using Amazon CloudFront, Amazon's content delivery network (CDN):** Edge locations are located at the edge of the AWS cloud and serve content to users more quickly and efficiently.

- **AWS Global Accelerator network:** Use Amazon's global network of edge locations to improve the performance of Internet applications routing traffic from users to the optimal AWS endpoint.

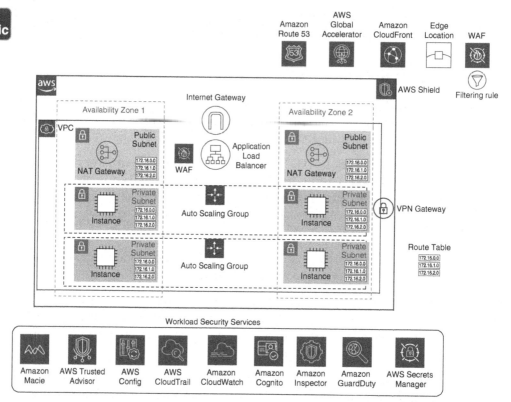

Figure 4-1   Connections and Security Services

Networking Services Located at Edge Locations

Edge locations are located at the edge of the AWS regions and are used to serve content to users more quickly and efficiently. These essential AWS services are located at each edge location:

- **Amazon Route 53:** Amazon-provided DNS services for resolving queries to Amazon CloudFront and AWS Global Accelerator deployments. Additional details on Route 53 operation can be found in Chapter 7, "Designing Highly Available and Fault-Tolerant Architecture."

- **AWS Shield:** Provides protection against distributed denial of service attacks (DDoS).

- **AWS Web Application Firewall (WAF):** Protect web applications from common web exploits that could affect application availability, compromise security, or consume excessive resources. AWS WAF enables you to create rules that block, allow, or monitor web requests based on conditions.

- **Amazon CloudFront:** CloudFront serves cached static and dynamic content from edge locations rather than from the origin data location (S3 bucket or application server), which can reduce the amount of time it takes to access static, dynamic, or streaming content. Additional details on CloudFront operation can be found in Chapter 11, "High-Performing and Scalable Networking Architecture."

 AWS Shield (Standard and Advanced)

What if a malicious request, DDoS attack, or a malicious bot attempts to enter an AWS edge location and attack a public-facing application? AWS Shield Standard protection protects AWS infrastructure and ingress paths at each edge location for all AWS customers. AWS Shield runs at each edge location, providing basic DDoS protection for known Layer 3 and Layer 4 attacks using AWS Web Application Firewall rules deployed and managed by AWS.

If organizations don't have the required expertise needed to solve ongoing security exploits that are attacking workloads hosted at AWS, they can contract with AWS experts to assist with real-time custom protection, known as AWS Shield Advanced, a paid version of AWS Shield that utilizes an expert AWS DDoS response team with a 15-minute SLA response protecting your workload components (Amazon EC2 instances, AWS Elastic Load Balancers, Amazon CloudFront distributions, AWS Global Accelerator deployments, and Amazon Route 53 resources). After analyzing the situation, the response team creates and applies custom WAF filters to mitigate DDoS attacks and other security issues. All AWS Shield Advanced customers get access to a global threat dashboard (see Figure 4-2) that displays a sampling of current attacks.

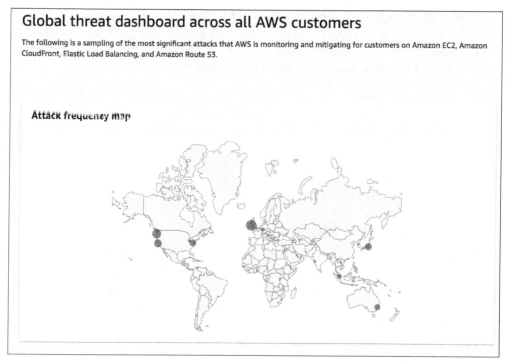

Figure 4-2   Global Threat Dashboard

AWS Shield Advanced also provides *cost protection*, which saves customers money when workload compute resources are required to scale due to illegitimate demand placed on the workload cloud services by a DDoS attack. AWS refunds the additional load balancer, compute, data transfer, and Route 53 query costs that accumulate during the DDoS attack for AWS Shield Advanced customers.

AWS Shield Advanced costs $3,000 a month with a one-year commitment. AWS WAF and AWS Firewall Manager are included with AWS Shield Advanced at no additional charge.

NOTE   Multiple WAF rules can be managed across multiple AWS accounts and workloads using AWS Firewall Manager.

AWS Web Application Firewall (WAF)

For custom workload protection at each edge location, the AWS Web Application Firewall (WAF) provides custom filtering of incoming (ingress) public traffic requests for IPv4 and IPv6 HTTP and HTTPS requests at each edge location, limiting any malicious request from gaining access to AWS cloud infrastructure. AWS WAF rules are created using the AWS Management Console or the AWS CLI. WAF rules are created using conditions combined into a web ACL. WAF rules allow or block, depending on the conditions, as shown in Figure 4-3. WAF rules can be applied to public-facing application load balancers, Amazon CloudFront distributions, Amazon API gateway hosted APIs, and AWS AppSync. To create a WAF rule, specify the conditions that will trigger the rule, such as the source IP address or the content of a web request. Next, specify the action that the rule should take when the conditions are met, such as blocking or allowing the request. Behaviors and conditions can be used to create custom rules that meet the specific security requirements for your web applications. WAF supports the following behaviors:

- **IP addresses:** Create rules that allow or block requests based on the source or destination IP address.

- **HTTP methods:** Create rules that allow or block requests based on the HTTP method used in the request, such as blocking all PUT requests.

- **Cookies:** Create rules that allow or block requests based on the presence or absence of cookies in the request, such as a specific cookie that is required for authentication.

- **Headers:** Create rules that allow or block requests based on the contents of the request header.

- **Query strings:** Create rules that allow or block requests based on the contents of the query string.

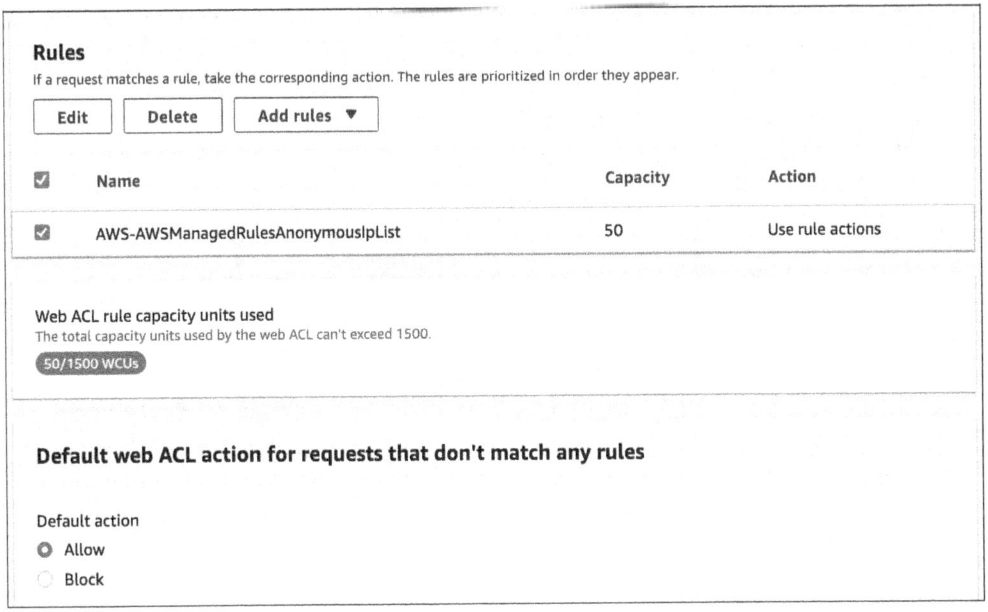

Rules

If a request matches a rule, take the corresponding action. The rules are prioritized in order they appear.

| Edit | Delete | Add rules ▼ |

	Name	Capacity	Action
☑	AWS-AWSManagedRulesAnonymousIpList	50	Use rule actions

Web ACL rule capacity units used
The total capacity units used by the web ACL can't exceed 1500.

50/1500 WCUs

Default web ACL action for requests that don't match any rules

Default action
- ◉ Allow
- ○ Block

Figure 4-3 Web Application Firewall Rules

AWS WAF provides three types of rules:

- **Regular rules:** Used to specify conditions that must be met in order for the rule to be triggered. For example, you might create a regular rule that blocks requests from a specific IP address or that allows requests that contain a specific string in the query string.

- **Rate based rules:** Used to limit the rate at which requests are allowed to be made to a web application. For example, you might create a rate-based rule that allows no more than 600 requests per second from a single IP address.

- **Group rules:** Used to group together multiple regular and rate-based rules, applying them as a single entity. For example, you might create a group rule that combines a regular rule that blocks requests from a specific IP address with a rate-based rule that limits the rate at which requests are allowed. This enables you to apply multiple rules to a web application with a single group rule.

VPC Networking Services for Securing Workloads

Each VPC provides a number of security features designed to protect workloads running in the AWS cloud. Features covered in this section include route tables, security groups, and network ACLs. It's important to realize that these security features are assigned to a specific VPC when they are created.

Route Tables

Each route table is used to control subnet traffic using a set of rules, called routes, that determine where network traffic is directed within each VPC. Workloads running on virtual servers or containers are hosted on EC2 instances located on subnets contained within a specific VPC. Subnets are associated with a specific availability zone within each AWS region.

Each subnet must be associated with a route table. If no specific route table association has been configured, the subnet will use the default route table that was created when the VPC was first created, called the main route table (discussed next), containing a default route that allows instances within the VPC to communicate with each other. Multiple subnets can be associated and controlled with a single route table that is assigned to multiple subnets. You might have multiple private subnets that need routes to the same service, such as a route to the NAT gateway service enabling resources on private subnets to get updates from a public location on the Internet, or a route to the virtual private gateway (VGW) for VPN connections from external locations.

The Main Route Table

Each VPC has a default route table called the main route table that provides local routing services throughout each VPC and across all defined availability zones (AZs), as shown in Figure 4-4. The main route table is associated with a VPC after it is first created. The main route table also defines the routing for all subnets that are not explicitly associated with any other custom route table. The main route table cannot be deleted; however a custom route table can be associated with a subnet, replacing main route table association.

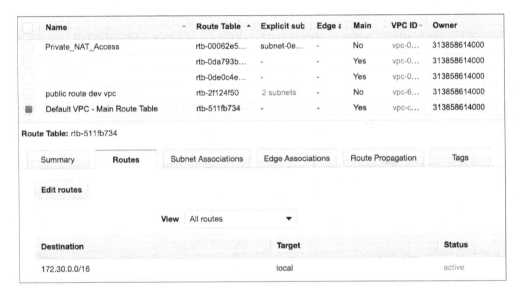

Figure 4-4 Main Route Table

Each custom or default route table has an entry containing the VPC's initial CIDR designations, and a local route used to provide access to the VPC's resources.

As mentioned earlier, you cannot delete the local route entry in a subnet route table, but you can change the local entry to point to another verified target such as a NAT gateway, network interface, or Gateway Load Balancer endpoint.

Custom Route Tables

A custom route table is a user-defined routing table that enables custom routes to direct traffic to specific destinations or implement more complex network architectures.

For example, suppose an organization named Terra Firma is considering starting with a two-tier design for the human resources customer relationship management (CRM) application hosted at AWS. For the production workload network, Terra Firma has decided to use two AZs within the VPC hosting the CRM servers to provide high availability and failover for the application and database servers. The following tasks must be carried out to create the required infrastructure for the CRM workload.

- Create public subnets in each AZ.

- Add Elastic Load Balancing (ELB) and NAT services to the public subnets.

- Create separate private subnets for the EC2 instances hosting the CRM application servers and the Amazon RDS MySQL database servers (see Figure 4-5).

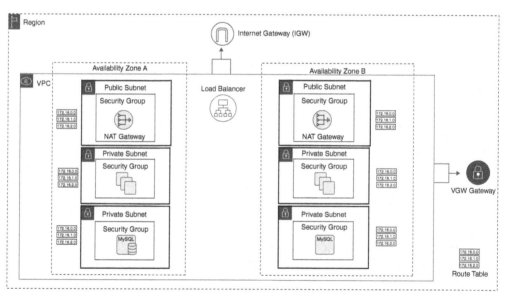

Figure 4-5   Proposed Two-Tier VPC Subnet Design

The RDS database servers use synchronous replication to ensure database records remain up to date. When synchronous replication is enabled for an RDS instance, the primary and standby instances are continuously connected, and all data changes made to the primary instance are immediately replicated to the standby instance. This ensures that the standby instance is always up to date and can be quickly switched over to if the primary instance fails.

For the initial infrastructure design, after the subnets have been created, Terra Firma's network administrators must create custom route tables for the following subnet groupings (see Figure 4-6):

- **Public subnets and custom route tables:** Public subnets host the AWS ELB load balancer and the AWS NAT gateway service. A custom route table will be created and associated with the public subnets, adding a route table entry for the AWS Internet Gateway service. Internet gateway routes are usually set with a destination route of 0.0.0.0/0 as client queries will typically come from multiple source locations across the public Internet.

- **Private subnets and custom route tables:** The application servers are hosted on private subnets within each AZ. The primary and standby database instances will be deployed and managed using the Amazon Relational Database Service (RDS). Separate AWS NAT gateway services with associated Elastic IP addresses will be ordered and attached to the public subnets in each AZ, enabling the application servers hosted on private subnets to connect to the NAT gateway service and receive any required updates from the Internet. Custom route tables and route table entries pointing to the NAT gateway service must be defined in each private subnet's route table.

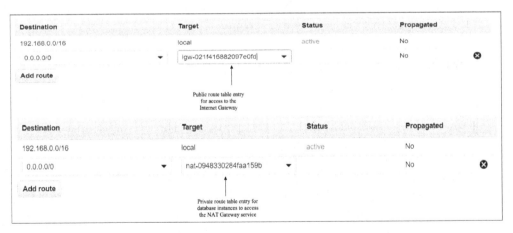

Figure 4-6 Using Custom Route Tables

NOTE A single route table can be assigned to multiple subnets within the same VPC.

Route Table Cheat Sheet

For the AWS Certified Solutions Architect – Associate (SAA-C03) exam, you need to understand the following critical aspects of route tables:

- Each VPC has a main route table that provides local routing throughout each VPC.

- Each subnet, when created using the VPC dashboard, is implicitly associated with the main route table.

- Don't add additional routes to a main route table. Leaving the main route table in its default state ensures that if the main route table remains associated to a subnet by mistake, the worst that can happen is that local routing is enabled. If additional routes are added to the main route table, the additional routes will be available from each new subnet due to the default association with the main route table.

- The main route table cannot be deleted; however, it can be ignored and will remain unassigned if you do not associate it with any subnets within the VPC.

- Create and assign a custom route table for custom routes required by a subnet.

- Subnet destinations are matched with the most definitive route within the route table that matches the traffic request.

Security Groups

A *security group (SG)* is a virtual software firewall that controls the incoming and outgoing network traffic for one or more EC2 instances hosted in a VPC. Security groups enable you to specify the protocols, ports, and source IP ranges that are allowed to reach your instances. Every attached elastic network interface (ENI) is protected by a security group. Each security group is associated with a specific VPC and has a set of inbound and outbound rules that designate the port(s) and protocol(s) allowed into and out of each network interface, as shown in Figure 4-7.

> **NOTE** It might not be obvious when you start creating VPC networking components but all components created using the VPC console are associated. Each subnet, route table, security group, network interface, and network ACL is assigned to a specific VPC during creation.

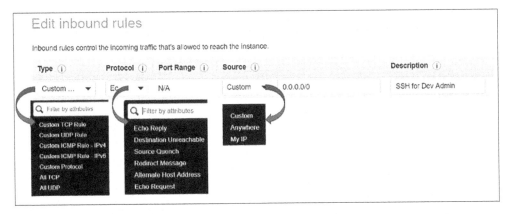

Figure 4-7   Security Group Details

After security groups have been assigned to an EC2 instance, changes made to security groups attached to an EC2 instance while the instance is online usually take effect within seconds.

The initial service quota limit for the number of security groups applied to an EC2 instance is five; you can request an increase using the Service Quotas utility. In addition, every custom security group can have up to 50 inbound and 50 outbound IPv4 or IPv6 rules. You can also increase the number of rules per security group.

Think of each security group as a reusable security template assigned to a particular VPC. Once a security group has been created, it can be assigned multiple times within the VPC where it was created to protect one or many EC2 instances.

One important concept to grasp about security groups is that they don't *deny* traffic flow. Instead, their job is to *allow* traffic flow. Another equally important concept is the direction of traffic flow both inbound and outbound each security group allows.

Security groups are defined as stateful, which means that if traffic is allowed in one direction, the security group automatically allows the traffic in the opposite direction. For example, if you allow incoming traffic on port 80 (HTTP), the security group will automatically allow outgoing traffic on port 80.

A defined inbound port request does not usually use the same port number for the outbound response. For example, if there's a rule defined allowing inbound HTTP traffic across port 80, the outbound traffic response is allowed out; however, the outbound traffic will not use port 80 for outbound communication. Outbound traffic uses a dynamically assigned port called an *ephemeral port*, determined by the operating system of the server making the response (you will learn more about ephemeral ports later in this chapter, in the upcoming section, "Network ACLs").

When a VPC is first created, a default security group is also created. Note that the default security group allows outbound traffic, but any inbound traffic is implicitly denied as inbound rules have not been defined (see Figure 4-8).

Figure 4-8   Default Security Group Rules

The default security group allows all outbound traffic but denies all inbound traffic. EC2 instances in a VPC associated with just the default security group can initiate outbound communications, but all inbound communication is blocked. The default security groups can't be deleted; however, the default security groups can be removed and custom security groups can be created and used instead.

Here are some additional details about security groups to know:

- A security group is always associated with a single VPC.

- Each elastic network interface assigned to an EC2 instance hosted within a VPC can be associated with up to five security groups by default.

- Security groups allow traffic; however, a security group cannot explicitly deny traffic. If either inbound or outbound access is not specifically allowed, it is implicitly denied.

- When a new security group is created, all outbound traffic is allowed if you don't review and change the default outbound rules before saving.

- Specify which protocols, ports, IP ranges, and security groups are allowed to access your instances.

- Outbound rules can be changed to direct outbound traffic to a specific outbound destination. For example, you could decree that all outbound traffic from a public-facing load balancer can only flow to a security group protecting the web tier.

Security group rules are defined as *stateful*. This means that inbound traffic flowing through a security group is tracked, logging the traffic allowed in, and any allowed inbound traffic is always allowed outbound. This process is called *connection tracking*; connections to a security group are automatically tracked to ensure valid replies. Some AWS services that can be associated with a security group include

- **Amazon Elastic Compute Cloud (EC2):** Security groups can be used to control network traffic to and from EC2 instances.

- **Amazon Elastic Kubernetes Service (EKS):** Security groups can be used to control network traffic to and from EKS clusters.

- **Amazon Elastic Container Service (ECS):** Security groups can be used to control network traffic to and from ECS tasks and services.

- **Amazon Relational Database Service (RDS):** Security groups can be used to control network traffic to and from RDS instances.

- **Amazon Elastic Load Balancer (ELB):** Security groups can be used to control network traffic to and from ELB load balancers.

Security Groups Cheat Sheet

For the AWS Certified Solutions Architect – Associate (SAA-C03) exam, you need to understand the following critical aspects of security groups:

- A security group acts like a firewall at the EC2 instance, protecting all attached network interfaces.

- Security groups support both IPv4 and IPv6 traffic.

- A security group controls both outgoing (egress) and incoming (ingress) traffic.

- For each security group, rules control the inbound traffic that is allowed to reach the associated EC2 instances.

- Separate sets of rules control both the inbound and the outbound traffic.

- Each security group includes an outbound rule that allows all outbound traffic by default. Outbound rules can be modified and, if necessary, deleted.

- Security groups allow traffic based on protocols and port numbers.

- Security groups define allow rules. (It is not possible to create rules that explicitly deny access.)

- Security group rules allow you to direct traffic outbound from one security group inbound to another security group within the same VPC.

- Changes made to a security group take effect immediately.

- Security groups don't deny traffic explicitly; instead, they deny traffic implicitly by defining only *allowed* traffic.

- Security groups are stateful; for requests that are allowed in, their response traffic is allowed out, and vice versa.

- For each rule, you define the protocol, the port or port range, and the source inbound and output destination for the traffic.

- The protocols allowed with security groups are TCP, UDP, or ICMP.

NOTE   It is impossible to block specific IP addresses by using a security group; instead, use a network access control list to block a range of IP addresses. Further details are provided in the section "Network ACLs" later in this chapter.

Custom Security Groups

When a custom security group is created, it is associated with a specific VPC. By default, a custom security group allows no inbound traffic but allows all outbound traffic. To create inbound rules and outbound rules, select the security group properties and use the following tabs to make changes (see Figure 4-9):

- **Inbound rules:** Define the source of the traffic—that is, where it is coming from—and what the destination port or port range is. The traffic source could be a single IP address (IPv4 or IPv6), a range of addresses, or from another security group.

- **Outbound rules:** Define the destination of the outbound traffic. The destination of the traffic could be a single IP address (IPv4 or IPv6), a range of addresses, or from another security group; EC2 instances that are associated with one security group can access EC2 instances associated with another security group.

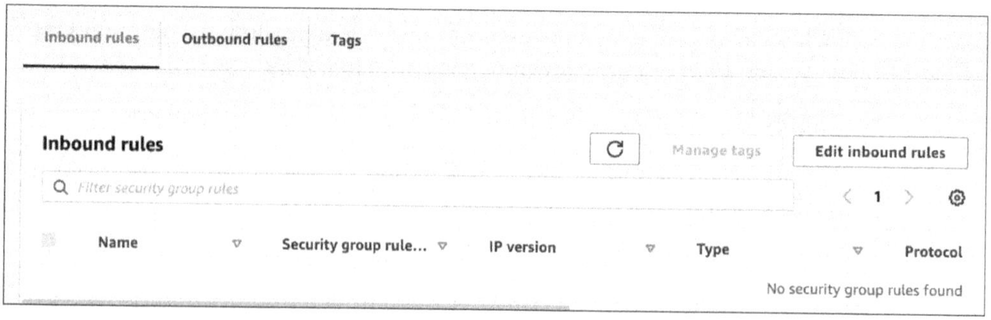

Figure 4-9   Default Security Group Inbound and Outbound Tabs

When designing security groups, the best practice is to minimize the ports allowed. Open only the specific ports that are needed for the services and applications running on your load balancer. The following sections provide some examples to consider for your security group configurations and setup.

NOTE Security groups "allow" access; however, security groups can also be said to "deny by default." If an incoming port is not allowed, access is denied.

Web Server Inbound Ports

Web server security group rules need to allow inbound HTTP or HTTPS traffic access from the Internet (see Table 4-2). Other rules and inbound ports can also be allowed, depending on workload requirements.

Table 4-2 Web Server Security Group Options

Web Server Inbound Ports

Port	Details
80 (HTTP)	Inbound IPv4 (0.0.0.0)
	Inbound IPv6 (::0)
443	HTTPS
25	SMTP
53	DNS
22	SSH

Database Server Inbound Ports

Several database server engines are available when deploying Amazon Relational Database Server database instances. The default port address assigned during deployment is based on the database engine's default port, which can be changed to a custom port number for additional security. Table 4-3 lists the default RDS security group database port options that are assigned per database engine during installation.

Table 4-3 RDS Database Inbound Ports

Port	Database Engine
3306	Microsoft SQL Server
3306	Amazon Aurora/MySQL
5432	Amazon Aurora PostgreSQL
1521	Oracle
27017	MongoDB

Administration Access

Connecting to an EC2 instance to perform direct administration requires associating a security group with an elastic network interface with inbound rules allowing either Secure Shell (SSH) or Remote Desktop Protocol (RDP) access, depending on the host's operating system (see Table 4-4). Deploying an EC2 instance as a bastion host on a public subnet would allow administrators to first authenticate to the bastion host and then "jump" to the associated EC2 instance in the private subnet.

A bastion host is a special purpose EC2 instance or third-party software appliance hosted on a public subnet exposed to the Internet, serving as a secure gateway or "jump box" for remote access to instances hosted on private subnets in the VPC without exposing a web or database server directly to the Internet (see Figure 4-10). Common security group settings for a bastion host could include the following:

- Allow incoming traffic on port 22 for SSH access.

- Allow incoming traffic on port 443 for HTTPS access.

- Allow outgoing traffic to allow the bastion host to access other machines on the network.

- Allow outgoing traffic linking specific security groups to allow the bastion host to access specific machines on the network.

- Set the source IP range for incoming traffic to a restricted range, such as the IP addresses of your office or trusted administrators.

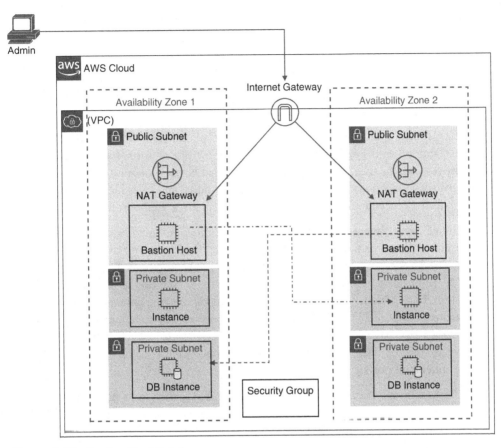

Figure 4-10 Bastion Host Solution

Table 4-4 Security Groups Inbound Ports for Administrative Access

Port	Operating System
22	Linux
3389	Windows

Understanding Ephemeral Ports

When configuring network security settings, such as a security group or network access control list, you need to allow for ephemeral port ranges for outbound communication from your instances or network services, such as load balancers.

Network design needs to consider where the traffic originated for both inbound and outbound traffic requests. Return traffic from an EC2 instance hosted in a VPC to a destination across the Internet communicates using a dynamic outbound or inbound *ephemeral port*.

Ephemeral ports are temporary, short-lived ports that are typically used by client applications for outbound communications from a predefined range of port numbers and are used for the duration of a communication session. When the session is complete, the port is released and can be used by another application.

TCP/IP communications don't utilize the same inbound and outbound ports; instead, the client or server's operating system defines the range of ports that will be dynamically selected for the return communication—that is, the outbound communication. Network connections require two endpoints: a source and a destination. Each source and destination endpoint has an IP address and an associated port number.

When a client system connects to a server, several components are employed: the server IP address, the server port, the client IP address, and the client port. The ephemeral port is a temporary port assigned by the computer's TCP/IP stack. The TCP/IP implementation chooses the port number based on the host operating system. In the case of Windows Server 2016 and above, the ephemeral port range is from 49152 to 65535. If Linux is the operating system, the ephemeral port range is from 32768 to 61000, as shown in Table 4-5. Different operating system versions may use slightly different ephemeral ranges; check what your operating system uses for ephemeral ports.

When communication is carried out from a source service to its destination, the traffic typically uses the named port for the destination traffic, such as port 22 on a Linux box accepting SSH connections. However, for the return traffic from the server to the client, an ephemeral port is typically used for the return traffic. An ephemeral port can be defined as a dynamically assigned port from a range of assumed available port addresses. Outbound packets travel through an outbound port allowed by the existing security group using an allowed ephemeral port.

Outbound communication from an EC2 instance hosted on a VPC must have an allowed outbound range of ephemeral ports. These ports remain available only during the communication session; each dynamically assigned port is released after the TCP connection terminates. If custom security groups or NACLs are deployed, ephemeral rules need to appear in both the inbound and outbound rules to cover the dynamic requirements of communication using ephemeral ports. Table 4-5 lists some common inbound port numbers that are typically used. The outbound port 443 is the exception as it answers outbound, using port 443.

Table 4-5 Inbound Port Numbers

Port #	Service	Protocol	Description	Port Type
20	FTP	TCP/UDP	File transfer data	Dynamic
21	FTP	TCP/UDP	File transfer control	Dynamic
22	SSH	TCP/UDP/SCTP	Secure Shell	Dynamic
25	SMTP	TCP/UDP	Simple mail transfer	Dynamic
67	BOOTPS	UDP	Bootstrap (BOOTP/ DHCP) server	Dynamic
68	BOOTPC	UDP	Bootstrap (BOOTP/ DHCP) client	Dynamic
69	TFTP	UDP	Trivial file transfer	Dynamic
80	HTTP	TCP	Hypertext Transfer Protocol	Dynamic
88	Kerberos	TCP	Kerberos	Dynamic
123	NTP	UDP	Network time	Dynamic
443	HTTPS	TCP	HTTP over TLS/SSL	443
143	Microsoft-ds	IMAP	Internet Message Access Protocol	Dynamic

Security Group Planning

For the AWS Certified Solutions Architect – Associate (SAA-C03) exam, you need to understand the following critical aspects of security group design:

- Create a security group for your public-facing application load balancer that accepts inbound traffic from the Internet (port 80 or port 443) and sends outbound traffic to your web tier security group, as shown in Figure 4-11.

- Create separate security groups for administrative tasks.

- Create a security group for your application tier that only accepts inbound traffic from the web tier and sends outbound traffic to your database tier security group.

- Create a security group for your database tier that only accepts inbound traffic from the application tier.

- Deploy a test application and test communication on a test VPC before deploying to production.

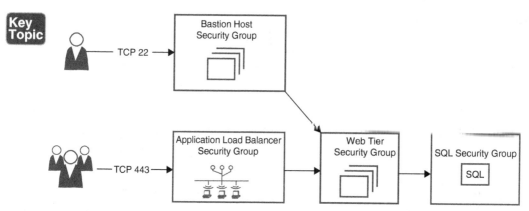

Figure 4-11 Security Group Design

Network ACLs

A *network access control list (NACL)* is an optional software firewall that controls inbound and outbound traffic for each subnet within a VPC. A NACL is a set of rules that allows or denies traffic based on the source and destination IP addresses, ports, and protocols. Both the Transmission Control Protocol (TCP) and User Datagram Protocol (UDP) are supported by network ACLs.

NACLs are used to supplement the security provided by security groups, which are associated with individual Amazon EC2 instances. Whereas security groups control traffic to and from specific instances, network ACLs control traffic at the subnet level, allowing you to set rules for the subnet.

Each VPC is associated with a default NACL that is merely a placeholder as the default network ACL allows all inbound and outbound traffic at the subnet level. Custom NACLs can and should be created, just like security groups. NACLs, once created, can also be associated with one or multiple subnets within the associated VPC.

Each NACL contains a set of inbound and outbound subnet traffic rules, from a starting lowest-numbered rule to the highest-numbered rule, as shown in Figure 4-12. Rules are processed in order to determine whether traffic is allowed or denied inbound or outbound on each subnet.

Inbound NACL

Rule#	Source IP	Protocol	Port	Allow / Deny	Comments
100	Private IP address range	TCP	22	ALLOW	Inbound SSH to subnet
110	Private IP address range	TCP	3389	ALLOW	Inbound SSH to subnet
120	Private IP address range	TCP	32768-65535	ALLOW	Inbound return traffic to subnet
*	0.0.0.0/0	All	All	DENY	Denies inbound traffic not handled by existing rule

Inbound return traffic from private subnet requests

Outbound NACL

Rule#	Source IP	Protocol	Port	Allow / Deny	Comments
100	Private IP address range	ALL	ALL	ALLOW	Outbound traffic to private network
120	Private IP address range	TCP	32768-65535	ALLOW	Outbound traffic to private network
*	0.0.0.0/0	All	All	DENY	Denies outbound traffic not handled by existing rule

Outbound responses to clients on private network

Figure 4-12   NACL Design

NACLs are located at the perimeter of each subnet and provide an additional layer of defense. A single NACL can protect multiple application servers at the subnet level. Rules can target an entire subnet or a block of IP addresses.

NOTE   Security protection provided by a NACL is at the subnet level. Blocked network traffic denied at the subnet level cannot get anywhere near your EC2 instances.

Network ACL Implementation Details

Both inbound and outbound rules should be numbered in an organized fashion with some separation between the numbers so that you can make changes if necessary in the future. It is best practice to number your inbound and outbound rules by 10s—10 for the first rule, 20 for the second rule, and so on.

NACL rules are *stateless*; this means that inbound and outbound NACL rules are independent from each other.

- Outbound rules are processed separately without any regard to the defined inbound rules.

- Inbound rules are processed without any regard to the outbound rules that have been defined.

Network ACL Cheat Sheet

For the AWS Certified Solutions Architect – Associate (SAA-C03) exam, you need to understand the following critical aspects of NACLs:

- A NACL is an optional security control for subnets.

- Each VPC is assigned a default NACL that allows all inbound and outbound traffic across all subnets.

- NACLs are stateless in design; inbound and outbound rules are enforced independently.

- Each NACL is a collection of deny or allow rules for both inbound and outbound traffic.

- The default NACL can be modified.

- A NACL has both allow and deny rules.

- A NACL applies to both ingress and egress subnet traffic; it does not apply to traffic within the subnet.

- You can create custom NACLs and associate them to any subnet in a VPC.

- A custom NACL can be associated with more than one subnet.

- A subnet can be associated with only one NACL.

- A NACL is a first line of defense at the subnet level; a security group is a second line of defense at the instance.

Network ACL Rule Processing

Both inbound and outbound rules are evaluated, starting with the lowest-numbered defined rule. Once a rule matches the traffic request, it is applied; there is no additional comparison with higher-numbered rules that may also match. A misconfigured lower-numbered rule that also matches the same traffic request could cause problems. If you designated a higher-numbered rule to deal with specific traffic, but instead a lower-numbered rule matched the traffic request, the higher-numbered rule would never be used, as shown in Table 4-6.

Table 4-6 NACL Rules with Incorrect Order

Rule Number	Source	Protocol	Port Number	Allow/Deny	Comment
100	0.0.0.0/0	TCP	22	Allow	Inbound SSH is allowed
110	0.0.0.0/0	TCP	3389	Allow	Inbound RDP is allowed
120	0.0.0.0/0	TCP	3389	Deny	Inbound RDP deny rule will not be evaluated
*	0.0.0.0/0	All	All	Deny	Denies all traffic not defined by any other rule

* All undefined traffic is blocked.

When inbound packets appear at the subnet level, they are evaluated against the incoming (ingress) rules of the network ACL. For example, the request is for port 443. Starting with the first rule, numbered 100, there is not a match because the first rule has been defined for port 80 HTML traffic (see Table 4-7). The second rule, numbered 110, has been defined for allowing HTTPS traffic. Therefore, HTTP traffic is allowed onto the subnet. All other traffic is denied access if it doesn't match any of the inbound allow rules. If the inbound communication is from the Internet, the source is defined as 0.0.0.0/0 because the traffic could come from any location.

Outbound or egress traffic also must be matched with an outbound rule for the traffic to be allowed to exit the subnet. The outbound rule for HTTPS traffic also uses port 443; the destination is 0.0.0.0/0 because the destination could be anywhere across the Internet. In this case, both the inbound and the outbound rules for HTTPS traffic is set to allow. A rule for the required range of dynamic ports allows outbound responses.

Table 4-7   Custom NACL Setup

Inbound Network ACL

Rule	Source Address	Protocol	Port Number	Allow/ Deny	Details
100	0.0.0.0/0	TCP	80	Allow	Allows inbound HTTP traffic from any IPv4 address on the Internet
110	0.0.0.0/0	TCP	443	Allow	Allows inbound HTTPS traffic from any IPv4 address on the Internet
120	IPv4 address range for administration	TCP	22	Allow	Allows inbound SSH traffic for administrators
130	IPv4 address range for administration	TCP	3389	Allow	Allows inbound RDP traffic for administrators
*	0.0.0.0/0	All	All	Deny	Denies all traffic not defined by any other rule

Outbound Network ACL

Rule	Destination IP Address	Protocol	Port	Allow/ Deny	Details
100	0.0.0.0/0	TCP	80	Allow	Allows outbound HTTP traffic from the public subnet to the Internet
110	0.0.0.0/0	TCP	443	Allow	Allows outbound HTTPS traffic from the subnet to the Internet

Outbound Network ACL

Rule	Destination IP Address	Protocol	Port	Allow/Deny	Details
120	0.0.0.0/0	TCP	32768–65535	Allow	Allows outbound responses to clients across the Internet
*	0.0.0.0/0	All	All	Deny	Denies all traffic not defined by any other rule

* All undefined traffic is blocked.

VPC Flow Logs

VPC flow logs enable you to capture information about the IP traffic going to and from a VPC. Flow logs can be used to monitor, troubleshoot, and analyze the network traffic in your VPC.

VPC flow logs can be enabled at the VPC, subnet, or elastic network interface level, capturing traffic flowing in and out of the specified resource. Flow logs record the IP traffic flowing in and out of your VPC, including information about the source and destination IP addresses, ports, protocols, and packet and byte counts.

Network traffic can be captured for analysis or to diagnose communication problems at the level of the elastic network interface, subnet, or entire VPC. When each flow log is created, define the type of traffic that will be captured—accepted traffic, rejected traffic, or all traffic. AWS does not charge for creating a flow log but will impose charges for log data storage.

Flow logs can be stored either as CloudWatch logs or directly in an S3 bucket, as shown in Figure 4-13. If VPC flow logs are stored as CloudWatch logs, AWS IAM roles must be created that define the permissions allowing the CloudWatch monitoring service to publish the flow log data to the CloudWatch log group. Once a log group has been created, you can publish multiple flow logs to the same log group.

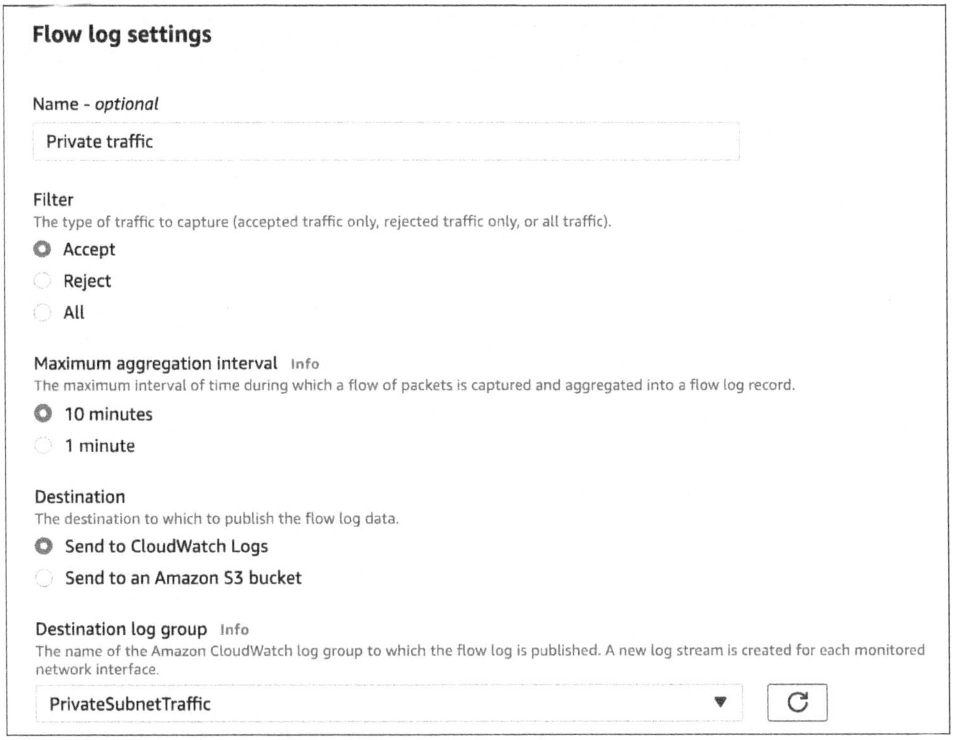

Flow log settings

Name - *optional*

Private traffic

Filter
The type of traffic to capture (accepted traffic only, rejected traffic only, or all traffic).

○ Accept

○ Reject

○ All

Maximum aggregation interval   Info
The maximum interval of time during which a flow of packets is captured and aggregated into a flow log record.

○ 10 minutes

○ 1 minute

Destination
The destination to which to publish the flow log data.

○ Send to CloudWatch Logs

○ Send to an Amazon S3 bucket

Destination log group   Info
The name of the Amazon CloudWatch log group to which the flow log is published. A new log stream is created for each monitored network interface.

PrivateSubnetTraffic	▼	⟳

Figure 4-13   Flow Log Storage Location Choices

If you create a flow log for a subnet, or VPC, each network interface in the subnet or VPC is monitored. Launching additional EC2 instances into a subnet with an attached flow log results in new log streams for each new network interface and network traffic flows.

Not all traffic is logged in a flow log. Examples of traffic that is not logged in flow logs include AWS Route 53 server traffic, Windows license activation traffic, EC2 instance metadata requests, Amazon Time Sync Service traffic, reserved IP address traffic, and DHCP traffic.

Any EC2 instance elastic network interface can be tracked with flow logs. Here are several examples of where VPC flow could be useful:

- **Amazon Elastic Compute Cloud (EC2):** VPC flow logs can be enabled for EC2 instances to capture traffic flowing to and from the instances.

- **Amazon Elastic Load Balancer (ELB):** VPC flow logs can be enabled for ELB load balancers to capture traffic flowing to and from the load balancer.

- **Amazon Elastic Kubernetes Service (EKS):** VPC flow logs can be enabled for EKS clusters to capture traffic flowing to and from the cluster.

- **Amazon Elastic Container Service (ECS):** VPC flow logs can be enabled for ECS tasks and services to capture traffic flowing to and from the tasks and services.

- **Amazon Route 53:** VPC flow logs can be enabled for Route 53 to capture traffic flowing to and from Route 53.

 NAT Services

At AWS, the purpose of network address translation (NAT) services is to provide an indirect path for EC2 instances hosted on private subnets that need Internet access to obtain updates, licensing, or other external resources. NAT is a networking technique that enables private network resources to access the Internet while hiding their true IP addresses. Several AWS services provide NAT capabilities:

- **Amazon Virtual Private Cloud (VPC) NAT Gateway:** Enables instances in a private subnet to access the Internet without exposing their private IP addresses.

- **AWS Transit Gateway NAT:** Enables instances in a VPC or on-premises network to access the Internet without exposing their private IP addresses.

- **AWS PrivateLink NAT Gateway:** Enables instances in a VPC to access resources in another VPC or on-premises network without exposing their private IP addresses.

NAT Gateway Service

Amazon VPC NAT Gateway is a service that provides NAT capabilities for Amazon VPC, allowing instances in private subnets to indirectly access the Internet. The NAT gateway translates the private IP addresses of the EC2 instance requesting access to its own public IP address, allowing EC2 instances hosted on private subnets to access the Internet without exposing their private IP addresses.

The *NAT gateway service* is hosted in a public subnet configure with an Elastic IP address (a static public IP address), as shown in Figure 4-14 for Internet communication. For multi-availability redundancy, Amazon recommends placing a NAT gateway in each availability zone. Route table entries need to be added to each private subnet's route table, allowing EC2 instances with a path to access the NAT gateway service.

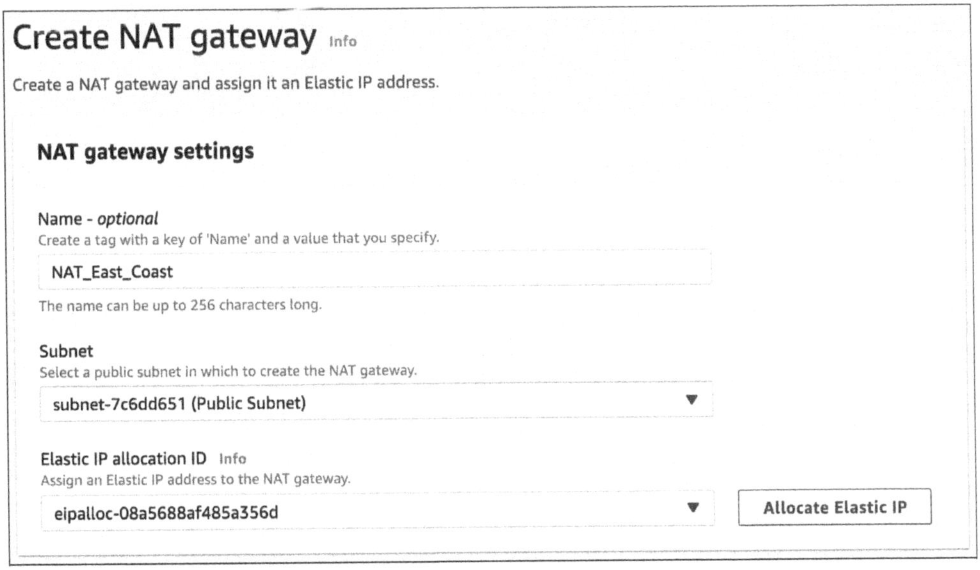

Create NAT gateway Info

Create a NAT gateway and assign it an Elastic IP address.

NAT gateway settings

Name - *optional*
Create a tag with a key of 'Name' and a value that you specify.

    NAT_East_Coast

The name can be up to 256 characters long.

Subnet
Select a public subnet in which to create the NAT gateway.

    subnet-7c6dd651 (Public Subnet)   ▼

Elastic IP allocation ID Info
Assign an Elastic IP address to the NAT gateway.

    eipalloc-08a5688af485a356d   ▼ | Allocate Elastic IP |

Figure 4-14   Creating a NAT Gateway

NOTE   The AWS NAT Gateway service initially supports up to 5 Gbps of bandwidth throughput and can scale up to 50 Gbps, as required.

NAT Instance

A NAT gateway third-party software appliance could also be deployed in a public subnet to allow EC2 instances in a private subnet to connect to the Internet and receive updates as necessary. However, you must configure and manage each NAT instance that is deployed. If you decide to use a third-party solution to provide NAT services, Amazon recommends that you create a high-availability pair of NAT instances for redundancy. Table 4-8 compares the NAT gateway service and the NAT instance.

Table 4-8   NAT Gateway and NAT EC2 Comparison

Parameter	NAT Gateway Service	NAT Instance
Management	By AWS	By the customer
Bandwidth	Up to 50 Gbps	Depends on the EC2 instance size
Maintenance	By AWS	By the customer

Parameter	NAT Gateway Service	NAT Instance
Public IP address	Elastic IP address	Elastic IP address
Security groups	Not supported	Required
Port forwarding	Not supported	Supported
Bastion host	Not supported	Supported

NOTE When deploying a NAT instance, source/destination checks must be disabled on the EC2 instance. By default, source/destination checks are enabled for all EC2 instances, which means that the instance can send and receive traffic only if the source and destination IP addresses match the private IP address of the instance.

AWS NAT Gateway Service Cheat Sheet

For the AWS Certified Solutions Architect – Associate (SAA-C03) exam, you need to understand the following critical aspects of the NAT Gateway service:

- An AWS NAT gateway must be hosted in a public subnet.

- An AWS NAT gateway uses an Elastic IP address as its static public IP address.

- The AWS NAT gateway service does not support security groups.

- The AWS NAT gateway service does not support port forwarding.

Amazon Cognito

Amazon Cognito provides authentication, authorization, and user management for web and mobile applications. Amazon Cognito enables users to sign into applications hosted at AWS using popular identity providers, such as Amazon, Facebook, and Google, without having to create new credentials. End users sign in using either a user pool or federated identity provider (see Figure 4-15).

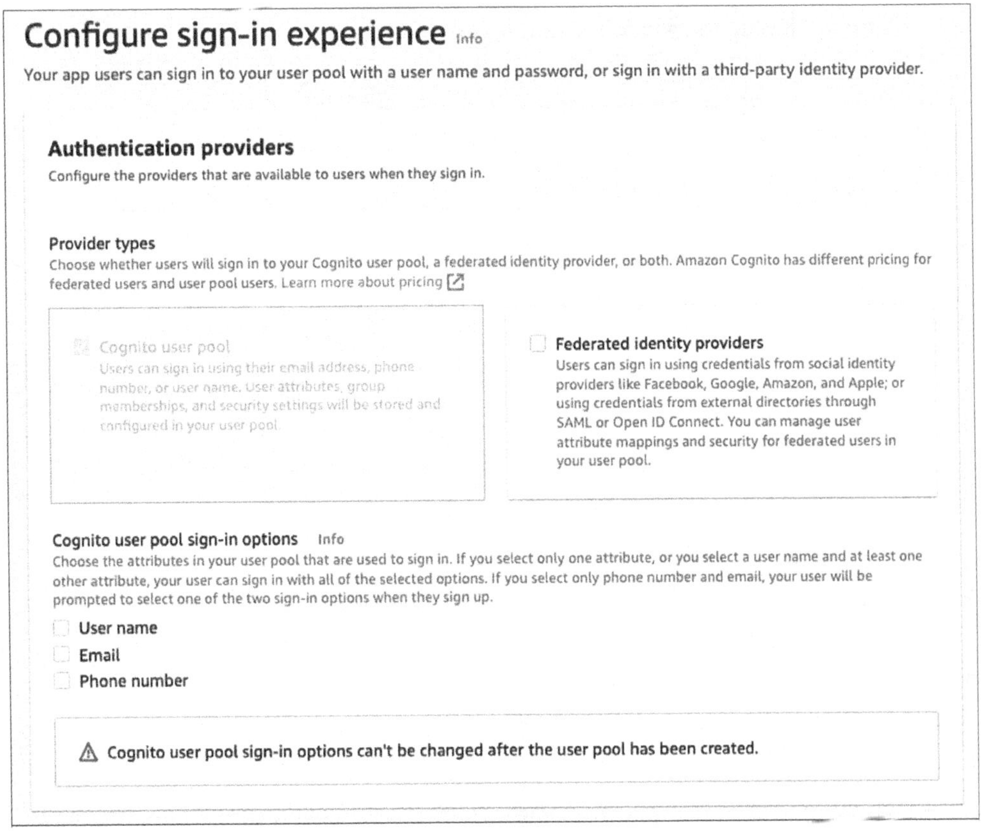

Configure sign-in experience Info

Your app users can sign in to your user pool with a user name and password, or sign in with a third-party identity provider.

Authentication providers

Configure the providers that are available to users when they sign in.

Provider types

Choose whether users will sign in to your Cognito user pool, a federated identity provider, or both. Amazon Cognito has different pricing for federated users and user pool users. Learn more about pricing [↗]

Cognito user pool

Users can sign in using their email address, phone number, or user name. User attributes, group memberships, and security settings will be stored and configured in your user pool.

☐ **Federated identity providers**

Users can sign in using credentials from social identity providers like Facebook, Google, Amazon, and Apple; or using credentials from external directories through SAML or Open ID Connect. You can manage user attribute mappings and security for federated users in your user pool.

Cognito user pool sign-in options   Info

Choose the attributes in your user pool that are used to sign in. If you select only one attribute, or you select a user name and at least one other attribute, your user can sign in with all of the selected options. If you select only phone number and email, your user will be prompted to select one of the two sign-in options when they sign up.

☐ User name
☐ Email
☐ Phone number

⚠ Cognito user pool sign-in options can't be changed after the user pool has been created.

Figure 4-15 AWS Cognito Authentication Options

User Pool

Amazon Cognito user pools are a fully managed user directory that enables you to create and manage user accounts for your application. User pools provide sign-up and sign-in options for your users, as well as user profile management and security features such as multi-factor authentication and password policies.

A member of a user pool can sign into a web application with a username, phone number, or email address. Multi-factor authentication (see Figure 4-16) is supported during the sign-in process using an authenticator app such as Authy or Google Authenticator or an SMS message for the time-based one-time password (TOTP).

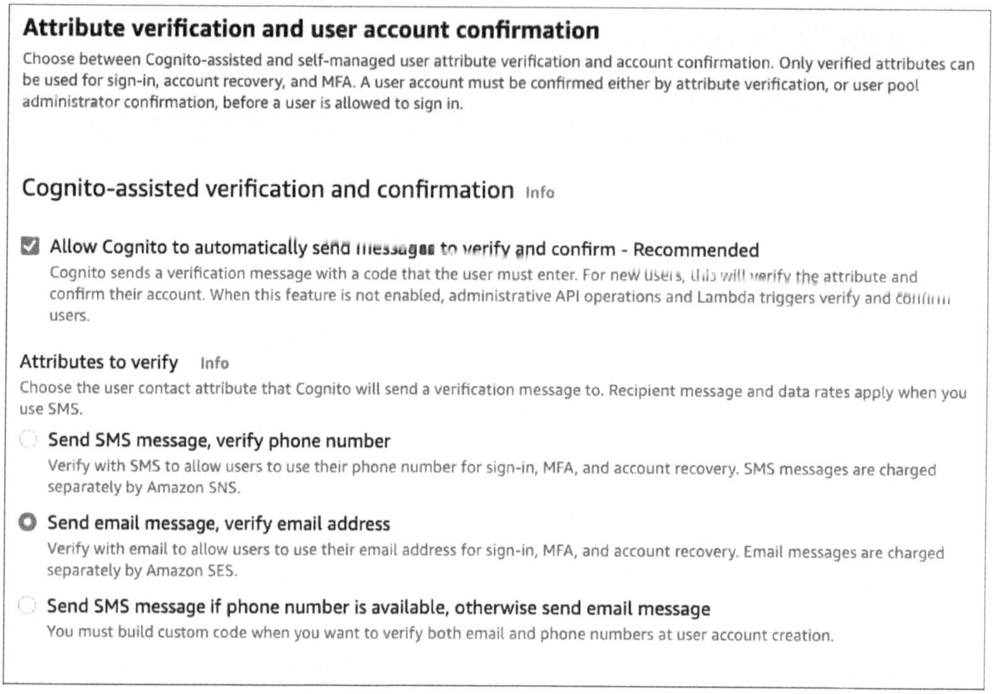

Attribute verification and user account confirmation

Choose between Cognito-assisted and self-managed user attribute verification and account confirmation. Only verified attributes can be used for sign-in, account recovery, and MFA. A user account must be confirmed either by attribute verification, or user pool administrator confirmation, before a user is allowed to sign in.

Cognito-assisted verification and confirmation Info

☑ Allow Cognito to automatically send messages to verify and confirm - Recommended

Cognito sends a verification message with a code that the user must enter. For new users, this will verify the attribute and confirm their account. When this feature is not enabled, administrative API operations and Lambda triggers verify and confirm users.

Attributes to verify   Info

Choose the user contact attribute that Cognito will send a verification message to. Recipient message and data rates apply when you use SMS.

○ Send SMS message, verify phone number

Verify with SMS to allow users to use their phone number for sign-in, MFA, and account recovery. SMS messages are charged separately by Amazon SNS.

◉ Send email message, verify email address

Verify with email to allow users to use their email address for sign-in, MFA, and account recovery. Email messages are charged separately by Amazon SES.

○ Send SMS message if phone number is available, otherwise send email message

You must build custom code when you want to verify both email and phone numbers at user account creation.

Figure 4-16   Multi-Factor Authentication Options

After an end user has been successfully authenticated using Amazon Cognito, a JSON Web Token (JWT) is issued to secure API communications or to be exchanged for temporary credentials allowing access to on-premises resources or AWS resources such as the S3 storage services used by the web or mobile application (see Figure 4-17).

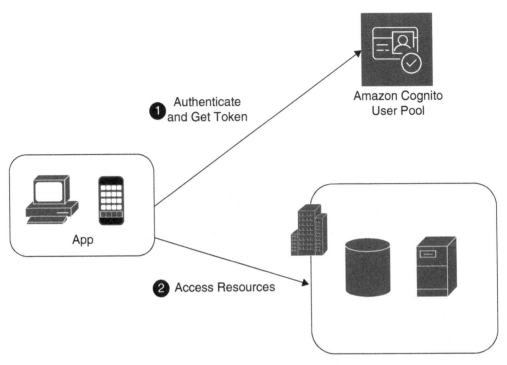

Figure 4-17 User Pool Sign-in

Federated Identity Provider

Users can authenticate to a web or mobile app using a social identity provider such as Google, Facebook, or Apple, or using a Security Association Markup Language (SAML) provider such as Active Directory Federation Services or OpenID Connect (OIDC). After a successful user pool authentication, the user pool tokens are forwarded to the AWS Cognito identity pool, which provides temporary access to AWS services (see Figure 4-18). Amazon Cognito identity pools enable you to grant your users access to AWS services, such as Amazon S3 and Amazon DynamoDB. Identity pools enable your users to sign in to your application and use AWS resources without having to create AWS credentials.

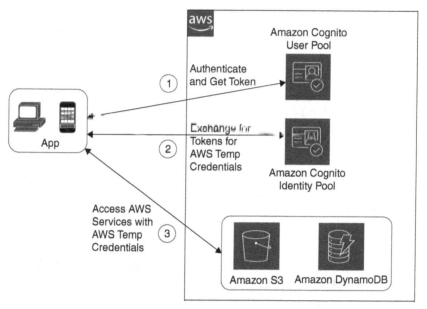

Figure 4-18   User Pool and Federated Identity Pool

> **NOTE**   The AWS Amplify framework can be used to create an end-user application that integrates with Amazon Cognito.

External Connections

Many companies design solutions using a private hybrid design, where the corporate data center is securely connected to AWS using an AWS VPN connection. Using an IPsec VPN connection to connect to your VPC provides a high level of security.

Before a VPN connection can be set up and connected from your corporate data center to a VPC from your remote network, you need a *virtual private gateway (VPG)* directly attached to the VPC where access is required.

> **NOTE**   Both an Internet gateway (IGW) and a VPG are directly attached to the VPC and not subnets. Gateway devices require route table entries on each subnet where access is required.

Routing types supported are either static or dynamic routes using Border Gateway Protocol (BGP). A VPN connection with a single static route is shown in Figure 4-19.

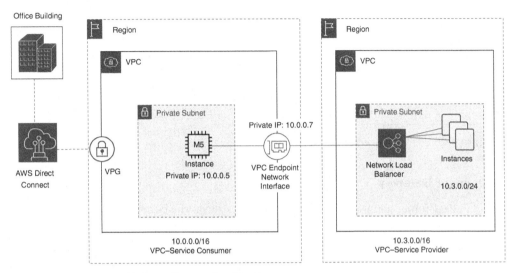

Figure 4-19 External Private Connection Choices

Each VPN connection at AWS is created with two endpoints; each endpoint is connected to a separate availability zone and assigned a unique public IP address.

Virtual Private Gateway

A virtual private gateway is the VPN concentrator on the AWS VPC. The virtual private gateway uses Internet Protocol Security (IPsec) to encrypt the data transmitted between the on-premises network and the VPC. When creating a site-to-site VPN connection, create a virtual private gateway on the AWS side of the connection and a customer gateway on the customer side of the connection.

Several AWS components are required to be set up and configured for an AWS VPN connection. Figure 4-20 shows the common components: the VPG, the customer gateway (CGW), and the VPN connection.

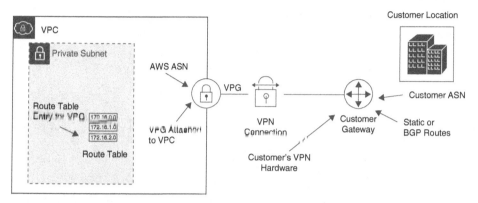

Figure 4-20   VPG Connection Components Choices

Customer Gateway

The customer gateway is the VPN concentrator on the customer side of a site-to-site VPN connection.

The customer gateway provides the VPN endpoint for your on-premises network and uses IPsec to encrypt the data transmitted between the on-premises network and the VPC. The customer gateway device provided must be compatible with AWS VPN connections. Customers use hardware or virtual devices for their customer gateway devices. AWS provides configuration steps for most of the popular customer hardware options. Examples of devices that AWS supports include Cisco, Check Point, Fortinet, Juniper, and Palo Alto.

During installation, you will be prompted to download the configuration file that matches your customer gateway device. Information contained in this document includes device details and tunnel configuration.

When creating a customer gateway, enter the public IP address or the private certificate of your customer gateway device and indicate the type of routing to be used: static or dynamic. If you choose dynamic routing, enter your private autonomous system number (ASN) for border gateway patrol (BGP) communications. When connections are completed on both the customer and AWS sides, traffic requests from the customer side of the AWS VPN connection initiate the VPN tunnel, as shown in Figure 4-21.

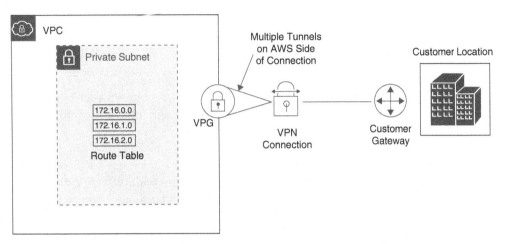

Figure 4-21   AWS VPN Tunnel Connections Choices

NOTE   During the configuration of an AWS VPN connection, you can accept the ASN provided by AWS or specify your custom ASN number.

Some of the most common routing options for AWS VPN connections include

- **Static routing:** Static routing enables you to specify routes for traffic over a VPN connection. With static routing, specify the IP address ranges and destinations for your traffic, and the VPN connection will use this information to route traffic.

- **Dynamic routing:** With dynamic routing, the AWS VPN connection will automatically add and remove routes as needed, based on the traffic paths available.

AWS Managed VPN Connection Options

Common solutions for AWS VPN connections include

- **AWS Site-to-Site VPN:** Enables you to create a secure connection between your on-premises network and your VPC. This type of VPN connection uses IPsec to encrypt the data transmitted between the on-premises network and the VPC.

- **AWS Client VPN:** Enables you to create a secure, encrypted connection between your VPC and your remote users. This type of VPN connection uses the OpenVPN protocol and is typically accessed using a client application installed on the user's device.

- **AWS Transit Gateway VPN:** Enables you to create a secure connection between your VPC and an on-premises network, as well as connections between multiple VPCs and on-premises networks. This type of VPN connection uses IPsec to encrypt the data transmitted between the networks.

- **AWS VPN CloudHub:** With CloudHub, multiple remote sites can communicate with the VPC and each other. CloudHub design follows the traditional hub-and-spoke model.

Deploying AWS VPN CloudHub, on the AWS side, there is a single VPG; however, there are multiple customer gateways required as there are multiple connection paths from multiple physical sites (see Figure 4-22). Each customer gateway requires a unique BGP ASN to distinguish its location. The maximum bandwidth of each AWS VPN connection at AWS is 1.25 Gbps.

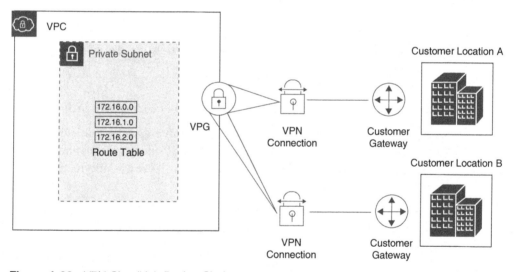

Figure 4-22   VPN CloudHub Design Choices

Understanding Route Propagation

After route table entries have been created to allow VPN connections from the customer gateway, you can enable the automatic provisioning of the available routes through *route propagation*. To enable automatic route propagation, choose the Route Propagation tab from the properties of the route table and then select the VPG to assign to the route table. Route propagation allows a virtual private gateway to automatically propagate routes to the route tables, ensuring efficient communications.

Each AWS VPN connection created in AWS has two tunnels for failover on the Amazon side of the connection. Each tunnel has a unique security association (SA) that identifies each tunnel's inbound and outbound traffic. If static routes are available, when an AWS VPN connection is activated, the static addresses for your customer data center and the CIDR ranges for the connected VPC are automatically added to the route table.

AWS Direct Connect

AWS Direct Connect is a service provided by AWS that enables you to establish a dedicated network connection from your on-premises data center to AWS. It offers two types of connections:

- **Dedicated connection:** This type of connection provides a dedicated, single-tenant network connection between your on-premises network and your VPC. The dedicated connection uses a physical network connection with a capacity of from 1 to 100 Gbps.

- **Hosted connection:** This type of connection enables you to establish a connection to AWS Direct Connect over the public Internet. The hosted connection uses a virtual interface with a capacity of 50 Mbps, 100 Mbps, or 200 Mbps.

Each AWS Direct Connect dedicated connection ordered is a single dedicated connection from your organization's routers to an AWS Direct Connect router. Virtual interface connections can be created to connect directly to AWS services or VPCs. A virtual public interface enables access to Amazon cloud services; a private virtual interface enables access to a VPC.

AWS Direct Connect dedicated connections support 1000BASE-LX or 10GBASE-LR connections over single-mode fiber using Ethernet transport and 1310 nm connectors.

A hosted connection is provided by an AWS Direct Connect partner from the customer data center to the facility where AWS Direct Connect connections can be made. The connection speeds available from the selected Amazon partner can range from 1 to 100 Gbps. To sign up for AWS Direct Connect, open the AWS Direct Connect Dashboard and complete the following steps:

Step 1. Request a connection, specifying the port speed and the Direct Connect location where the connection will be terminated. If your port speed required is less than 1 Gbps, you must contact a registered AWS Direct Connect vendor that is a member of the Amazon Partner Network (APN) in your geographic location and order a hosted connection at the bandwidth you desire. When this connection is complete, the setup of Direct Connect can continue in the console.

Step 2.   When AWS has approved your connection, download a Letter of Authorization-Connecting Facility Assignment (LOA-CFA) and present it to your provider as authorization to create a cross-connect network connection to AWS.

Step 3.   Create virtual interfaces for the required connections to either a VPC or a public AWS service.

Step 4.   After virtual interfaces have been created, download the router configuration file containing detailed router configuration information to successfully connect to the virtual interfaces.

There are many considerations for AWS Direct Connect, including your location, the AWS region you are operating in, the level of redundancy required, the number of VPCs, public AWS services, or AWS Direct Connect gateways that you connect (see Figure 4-23).

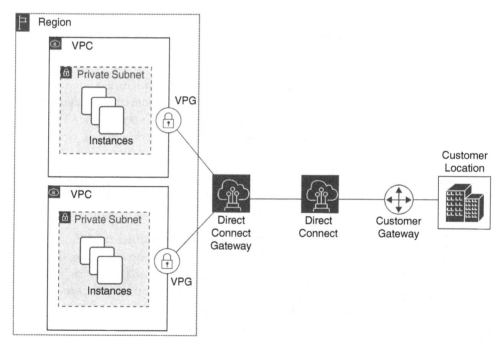

Figure 4-23   Direct Connect Choices

AWS Direct Connect Gateway

A Direct Connect Gateway is a component of AWS Direct Connect that enables you to connect multiple virtual private clouds to a single AWS Direct Connect connection. A Direct Connect gateway acts as a central hub for the VPCs that are connected to it, enabling the routing of traffic between the VPCs.

AWS Direct Connect Cheat Sheet

For the AWS Certified Solutions Architect – Associate (SAA-C03) exam, you need to understand the following critical aspects of Direct Connect:

- You can configure an AWS Direct Connect connection with one or more virtual interfaces (VIFs).

- Public VIFs allow access to services such as Amazon S3 buckets and Amazon DynamoDB tables.

- Private VIFs allow access only to VPCs.

- An AWS Direct Connect connection allows connections to all availability zones within the region where the connection has been established.

- You are charged for AWS Direct Connect connections based on data transfer and port hours used.

- AWS Direct Connect dedicated connections are available at 1 Gbps up to 100 Gbps speeds.

- You can order speeds of 50 Mbps up to 200 Mbps through a hosted connection through AWS Direct Connect partners.

- An AWS Direct Connect gateway allows you to connect to multiple VPCs.

- An AWS Direct Connect gateway can connect to virtual private gateways and private virtual interfaces owned by the same AWS account.

- An AWS Direct Connect gateway can be associated with AWS Transit Gateway, extending an organization's private network.

- An AWS Direct Connect connection can also be used with an IPsec VPN connection for additional security.

Amazon GuardDuty

Amazon GuardDuty is a threat detection service that continuously monitors and protects your AWS account, EC2 instances, container applications Amazon Aurora databases, and data stored in S3 buckets (see Figure 4-24). It uses machine learning and anomaly detection to identify potentially malicious activity in your AWS environment, such as unauthorized access or unusual behavior. GuardDuty provides alerts for any suspicious activity it detects, allowing organizations to take appropriate action to protect AWS resources. AWS GuardDuty also supports AWS Organizations.

Figure 4-24 GuardDuty Settings

Amazon GuardDuty relies on machine learning anomaly detection, network monitoring and malicious file detection using AWS, and third-party security knowledge to analyze AWS security services, including CloudTrail events, VPC flow logs, Amazon Elastic Kubernetes Service audit logs, and DNS query logs. Amazon GuardDuty performs near-real-time analysis and actions can be automated using AWS Lambda or Amazon EventBridge. Amazon GuardDuty is helpful when deployments are too extensive for organizations to adequately manage and protect AWS resources.

Once enabled, Amazon GuardDuty starts analyzing account, network, data activity, and AWS services enabled for analysis in near real time. Amazon GuardDuty monitors for many security issues, including the following:

- **Reconnaissance:** Amazon GuardDuty scans for unusual API activity, failed database login attempts using CloudTrail management event logs, and suspicious ingress and egress network traffic using VPC flow logs (see Figure 4-25).

- **Global events:** Amazon GuardDuty monitors CloudWatch global events for malicious IAM user behaviors, AWS Security Token Service, unauthorized Amazon S3 access, Amazon CloudFront, and Amazon Route 53 for malicious usage across AWS regions.

- **Amazon EC2 instance compromise:** Amazon GuardDuty monitors network protocols, inbound and outbound communication, and compromised EC2 credentials. Amazon GuardDuty Malware Protection, when enabled, scans EBS volumes attached to EC2 instances and container workloads.

- **Amazon EKS Protection:** Amazon GuardDuty monitors Amazon EKS cluster control plane activity by analyzing Amazon EKS audit logs for issues.

- **Amazon RDS Protection:** Amazon GuardDuty monitors access attempts to existing and new Aurora databases.

- **Amazon S3 Bucket compromise:** Amazon GuardDuty monitors for suspicious data patterns by analyzing AWS CloudTrail management events and

Amazon S3 data events, including **Get**, **Put**, **List**, and **Delete** object API operations from a remote host or unauthorized S3 access from known malicious IP addresses.

- **Amazon Route 53 DNS logs:** GuardDuty monitors Amazon Route 53 request and response logs for security issues.

Figure 4-25 GuardDuty Findings

Amazon GuardDuty Cheat Sheet

For the AWS Certified Solutions Architect – Associate (SAA-C03) exam, you need to understand the following critical aspects of GuardDuty:

- Amazon GuardDuty can also be deployed with AWS Organizations (AWS recommended deployment).

- When Amazon GuardDuty Malware Protection finds issues with EBS volumes, it creates replica snapshots of the affected EBS volumes.

- Amazon GuardDuty can also be integrated with AWS Security Hub and Amazon Detective Services to perform automated actions.

Amazon Macie

Amazon Macie is a security service provided by AWS that uses machine learning to automatically discover, classify, and protect sensitive data stored in S3 buckets. Amazon Macie helps you secure your data and prevent unauthorized access or accidental data leaks.

Amazon Macie uses machine learning and pattern matching to discover and protect sensitive data, such as personally identifiable information (PII) and intellectual property (IP). Discovered issues are presented as detailed findings for sensitive data, review, and remediation.

Amazon Macie runs data discovery jobs on a schedule or a one-time basis (see Figure 4-26), which starts the automated discovery, logging, and reporting of any security and privacy issues that are discovered. Each job selects the S3 bucket(s) and bucket criteria (name, account ID, effective permissions, shared access, and tags). Up to 1000 Amazon S3 buckets and AWS accounts can be selected per discovery job. The following sensitive data types are identified using data identifiers:

- Credential data such as private keys or AWS secret access keys

- Credit card and bank account numbers

- Personal information, health insurance details, passports, and medical IDs

- Custom identifiers consisting of regular expressions (regex) per organization, such as employee IDs, or internal data identifiers

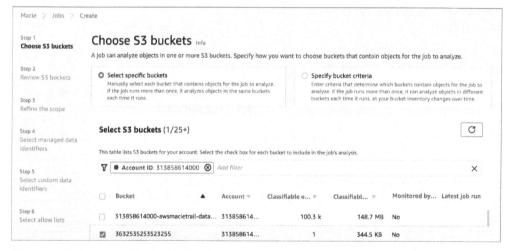

Figure 4-26   Amazon Macie Job Configuration

Amazon Macie data findings are published to the Amazon Macie console. Amazon EventBridge events can be configured that call a custom AWS Lambda function to perform automated remediation tasks.

Amazon Macie Cheat Sheet

For the AWS Certified Solutions Architect – Associate (SAA-C03) exam, you need to understand the following critical aspects of Amazon Macie:

- AWS Organizations uses multiple Amazon Macie accounts: an Administrator account that manages the Amazon Macie accounts for the organization and member accounts.

- Sensitive data can be identified using a custom data identifier or keyword.

- Amazon Macie can publish sensitive data policy findings automatically to Amazon EventBridge as events.

- A policy finding provides a detailed report of a potential policy violation (for example, unexpected access to S3 bucket), including a severity rating, detailed information, and when the issue was found.

- Amazon Macie publishes near-real-time logging data to CloudWatch logs.

- Amazon Macie can analyze encrypted objects with the exception of objects encrypted with customer-provided keys (SSE-C).

Security Services for Securing Workloads

For the AWS Certified Solutions Architect – Associate (SAA-C03) exam, you need to understand the use cases for the following AWS security tools for monitoring and managing hosted workloads:

- AWS CloudTrail

- AWS Secrets Manager

- Amazon Inspector

- AWS Trusted Advisor

- AWS Config

AWS CloudTrail

AWS CloudTrail records all AWS API calls carried out within each AWS account related to actions across your AWS infrastructure. AWS CloudTrail also logs all account authentications and event history for your AWS account, including actions taken through the AWS Management Console, AWS SDKs, the AWS CLI command prompt, and other AWS service activity. AWS CloudTrail is enabled by default for all AWS accounts, and events in the default CloudTrail trail are available for the last 90 days free of charge. Organizations can also create custom trails storing all activity indefinitely in an Amazon S3 bucket or Amazon CloudWatch log group. Amazon CloudWatch events are logged in AWS CloudTrail within 15 minutes of each API request. The following are common tasks that CloudTrail is useful for:

- Review event history and insights for resource management, compliance, and operational and risk auditing.

■ Review event history in AWS CloudTrail for information on successful and unsuccessful authentication requests.

■ Review API calls carried out in an AWS account.

Figure 4-27 shows the details of an AWS management console logon listing Amazon S3 Buckets by IAM user Mark, including the AWS account ID, username, time, source, and region.

Figure 4-27   Detailed CloudTrail Event

AWS CloudTrail is a regional service with a global reporting reach because the default trail automatically creates separate trails in each active AWS region. AWS CloudTrail events for each AWS region can be viewed using the AWS CloudTrail console and manually switching to the desired AWS region. IAM policies can be created using the AWS Identity and Access Management service to control which IAM users can create, configure, or delete AWS CloudTrail trails and events.

Creating an AWS CloudWatch Trail

To store AWS CloudTrail events longer than the default 90-day time frame, create a custom trail that stores the AWS CloudTrail event information in an Amazon S3 bucket or Amazon CloudWatch log group. Management read/write events, or just read-only or write-only events, can be added to your custom trail, as shown in Figure 4-28. Optionally, you can also create an AWS Simple Notification topic to receive notifications when specific events have been delivered to the Amazon CloudWatch log group.

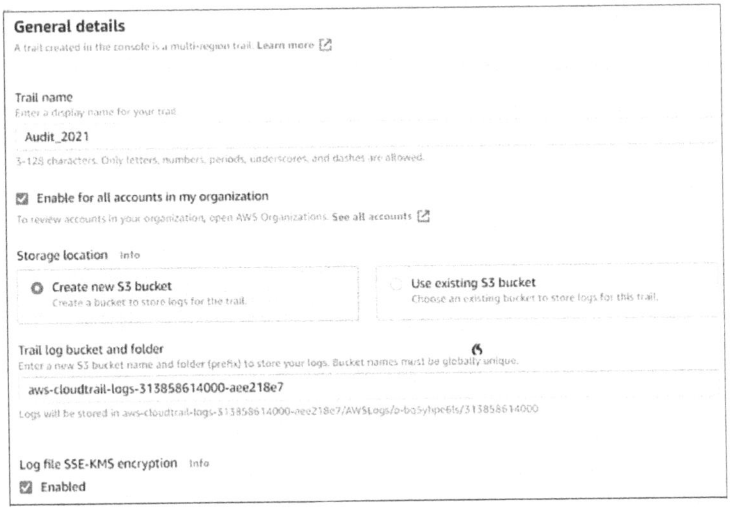

General details
A trail created in the console is a multi-region trail. Learn more

Trail name
Enter a display name for your trail

Audit_2021

3-128 characters. Only letters, numbers, periods, underscores, and dashes are allowed.

☑ Enable for all accounts in my organization
To review accounts in your organization, open AWS Organizations. See all accounts

Storage location Info

◉ **Create new S3 bucket**
   Create a bucket to store logs for the trail.

○ **Use existing S3 bucket**
   Choose an existing bucket to store logs for this trail.

Trail log bucket and folder
Enter a new S3 bucket name and folder (prefix) to store your logs. Bucket names must be globally unique.

aws-cloudtrail-logs-313858614000-aee218e7

Logs will be stored in aws-cloudtrail-logs-313858614000-aee218e7/AWSLogs/o-ba5yhpe6fs/313858614000

Log file SSE-KMS encryption Info
☑ Enabled

Figure 4-28 Creating a CloudTrail Trail

After data has been logged and stored in a custom trail, analysis and possible remediation can be performed using these methods:

- **Amazon S3 bucket:** API activity for the S3 bucket can trigger a notification to an AWS SNS topic or trigger an AWS Lambda custom function.

- **AWS Lambda function:** Custom AWS Lambda functions can respond to selected AWS CloudTrail data events.

- **AWS CloudTrail Insights:** CloudTrail Insights can be used to detect unusual activity for individual CloudTrail write management events within an AWS account.

- **AWS CloudTrail events:** A CloudTrail event can display a specific pattern, such as authentication as the root user, as shown in Figure 4-29.

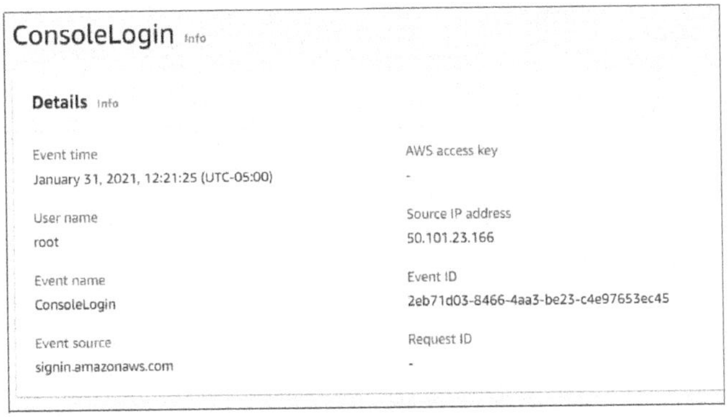

ConsoleLogin Info

Details Info

Event time	AWS access key
January 31, 2021, 12:21:25 (UTC-05:00)	-
User name	Source IP address
root	50.101.23.166
Event name	Event ID
ConsoleLogin	2eb71d03-8466-4aa3-be23-c4e97653ec45
Event source	Request ID
signin.amazonaws.com	-

Figure 4-29 CloudTrail Authentication Event

AWS CloudTrail Cheat Sheet

For the AWS Certified Solutions Architect – Associate (SAA-C03) exam, you need to understand the following critical aspects of AWS CloudTrail:

- AWS CloudTrail records all activity on an AWS account, including API calls and authentications.

- Custom AWS CloudWatch trails can deliver events to an S3 bucket or a CloudWatch log group.

- AWS CloudTrail events can be used for auditing AWS account activity.

- AWS CloudTrail reports activity for each AWS account.

- AWS CloudTrail can be integrated with an AWS Organization.

- AWS CloudTrail tracks both data and management events.

- AWS CloudTrail records can be encrypted using S3 server-side encryption.

AWS Secrets Manager

AWS Secrets Manager is a service that enables you to store, rotate, and manage organizational secrets used to access your applications, services, and IT resources. With Secrets Manager, you can securely store and manage secrets, such as database credentials and API keys, helping reduce the risk of secrets being compromised and meet compliance requirements. AWS Secrets Manager enables you to secure and manage secrets for SaaS applications, SSH keys, RDS databases, third-party services, and on-premises resources (see Figure 4-30). You can also store credentials for MySQL, PostgreSQL, and Amazon Aurora, and Oracle databases hosted on EC2 instances and OAuth refresh tokens used when accessing third-party services and on-premises resources.

Select secret type Info

- ◉ Credentials for RDS database
- ○ Credentials for DocumentDB database
- ○ Credentials for Redshift cluster
- ○ Credentials for other database
- ○ Other type of secrets (e.g. API key)

Specify the user name and password to be stored in this secret Info

User name

> mark

Password

> ••••••••••••••

☐ Show password

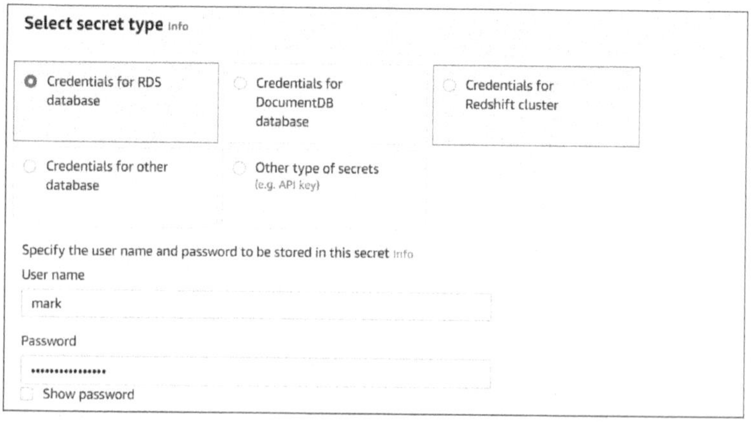

Figure 4-30   Storing RDS Credentials as a Secret

When database secrets are stored in AWS Secrets Manager, the rotation of database credentials can be automatically configured. Secrets are encrypted at rest using encryption keys stored in AWS Key Management Service. You can either specify customer master keys (CMKs) to encrypt secrets or use the default AWS KMS encryption keys provided for your AWS account.

NOTE   Use of the term *master* is ONLY in association with the official terminology used in industry specifications and/or standards, and in no way diminishes Pearson's commitment to promoting diversity, equity, and inclusion, and challenging, countering, and/or combating bias and stereotyping in the global population of the learners we serve.

Using the AWS Secrets Manager APIs, developers can replace any hard-coded secrets used in their applications with secrets retrieved from Secrets Manager. Access to secrets is controlled by the IAM policy, which defines the access permissions of users and applications when retrieving secrets.

Applications that are running on EC2 instances hosted within a VPC can use a private interface endpoint to connect directly to AWS Secrets Manager across the AWS private network.

Amazon Inspector

Amazon Inspector allows you to test the security levels of instances you have deployed. After you define an assessment target for Amazon Inspector, which is a group of tagged EC2 instances, Amazon Inspector evaluates the state of each instance by using several rule packages.

Amazon Inspector uses two types of rules: network accessibility tests that don't require the Inspector agent to be installed, and host assessment rules that require the Inspector agent to be installed (see Figure 4-31). Amazon Inspector performs security checks and assessments against the operating systems and applications hosted on Linux and Windows EC2 instances by using an optional Inspector agent installed on the operating system associated with the EC2 instance.

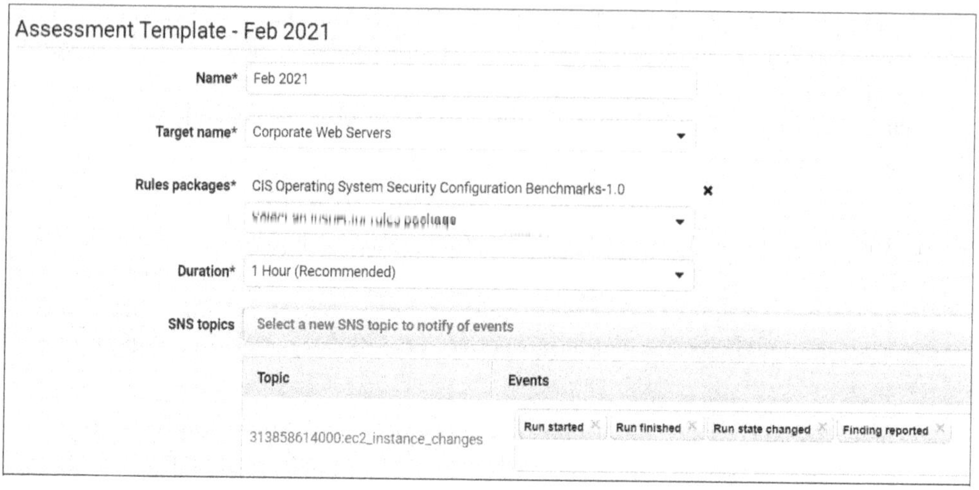

Figure 4-31   Amazon Inspector Options

Assessment templates check for any security issues on targeted EC2 instances. The choices for rule packages comply with industry standards. They include Common Vulnerabilities and Exposure (CVE) checks, Center for Internet Security (CIS) checks, operating system configuration benchmarks, and other security best practices. Current supported levels of CVE checks can be found at https://nvd.nist.gov/general. The Amazon Inspector Network Reachability rules package allows you to identify ports and services on your EC2 instances that are reachable from outside the VPC. Amazon Inspector gathers the current network configuration, including security groups, network access control lists, and route tables, and analyzes the accessibility of the instance.

Amazon Inspector rules are assigned severity levels of medium and high based on the defined assessment target's confidentiality, integrity, and availability. Amazon Inspector also integrates with Amazon Simple Notification Service (SNS), which sends notifications when failures occur. An AWS SNS notification can, in turn, call an AWS Lambda function, which can carry out any required task; AWS Lambda can call any AWS API. Amazon Inspector can alert you when security problems are discovered on web and application servers, including insecure network configurations, missing patches, and potential vulnerabilities in the application's runtime behavior.

AWS Trusted Advisor

AWS Trusted Advisor is a built-in management service that executes several essential checks against your AWS account resources (see Figure 4-32). Every AWS account has access to several core AWS Trusted Advisor checks, and access to the AWS

Personal Health Dashboard, which alerts you when specific resources you are using at AWS are having issues. The following are core AWS Trusted Advisor checks:

- Security checks include permission checks for EBS and RDS snapshots that are marked public, S3 buckets that have open access, checking for the creation of at least one IAM user, and root accounts that don't have MFA enabled.

- AWS Trusted Advisor checks various AWS services and alerts when usage is greater than 80% of the current service quota limits in force, including IAM users, Amazon S3 buckets created, VPCs created, and Auto Scaling groups.

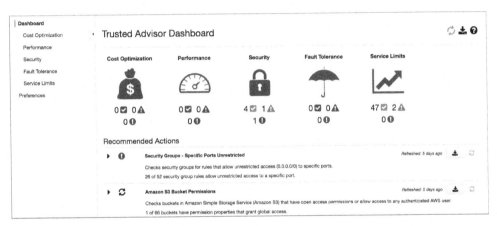

Figure 4-32   Trusted Advisor Security Checks

AWS Trusted Advisor can also provide additional checks if your organization has purchased Business or Enterprise support. Full AWS Trusted Advisor checks provide recommendations for improving performance, security, fault tolerance, and cost-effectiveness. AWS Trusted Advisor is useful to run against AWS account resources to review current security issues and any flagged service quotas (see Figure 4-33).

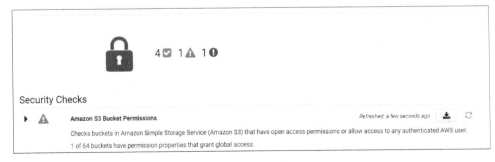

Figure 4-33   Trusted Advisor Security Checks Results

Once Business and Enterprise support has been purchased, AWS Trusted Advisor can alert you about issues to check, including the following:

- **Reserved Amazon EC2 instances:** AWS Trusted Advisor can calculate the optimized number of partial upfront reserved instances required based on an analysis of your usage history for the past month.

- **AWS ELB load balancer:** AWS Trusted Advisor checks current AWS ELB load balancing usage.

- **EBS volume check:** AWS Trusted Advisor warns if AWS EBS volumes in your AWS account are unattached or have low access rates.

- **Elastic IP addresses:** AWS Trusted Advisor warns if any Elastic IP addresses assigned to your account have not been associated. (Charges apply if Elastic IP addresses in your account are not used.)

- **Amazon RDS instances:** AWS Trusted Advisor checks for idle AWS RDS database instances.

- **Amazon Route 53 records:** AWS Trusted Advisor checks whether the creation of latency record sets has been properly designed to replicate end-user requests to the best AWS region.

- **Reserved reservation expiration check:** AWS Trusted Advisor warns you if your current reserved reservation is scheduled to expire within the next month. (Reserved reservations do not automatically renew.)

AWS Config

AWS Config enables customers to monitor, audit, and evaluate the deployed configurations of deployed IaaS resources, including EC2 instances, VPCs and components, IAM permissions, and S3 buckets deployed in a single AWS account or AWS accounts managed by an AWS organization. AWS Config provides detailed records of resource inventory, configuration history, and changes. Configuration data collected by AWS Config is stored in Amazon S3 buckets and Amazon DynamoDB.

The following are features of AWS Config:

- **Resource inventory:** Up-to-date inventory of selected AWS resources is recorded on an automated schedule.

- **Configuration History:** Configuration changes to AWS resources are tracked and stored, providing a historical view of changes over time.

- **Configuration Compliance:** Resources can be evaluated against predefined or custom rules, assessing the compliance of deployed AWS infrastructure components.

- **Management of Resources:** Centrally storing AWS resources helps an organization manage compliance and security standards.

- **Rules:** Managed rules created by AWS (see Figure 4-34) and custom rules can be used to evaluate resource configurations against predefined or custom criteria. Organizations can create their own custom AWS Config rules based on specific governance requirements such as security policies, compliance standards, or adhering to best practices. Custom rules are created using the AWS Lambda functions. Resource-specific rules could be created to evaluate the capacity of EC2 instances, the configuration of S3 buckets, or the configuration of a VPC.

- **Event Management:** SNS events can be generated when resource configurations change.

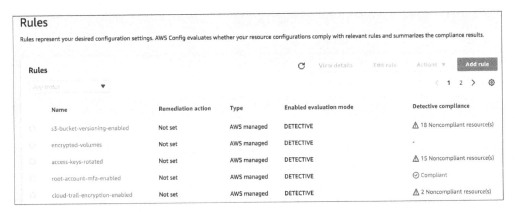

Figure 4-34   AWS Config Managed Rules

Exam Preparation Tasks

As mentioned in the section "How to Use This Book" in the Introduction, you have a couple of choices for exam preparation: the exercises here, Chapter 16, "Final Preparation," and the exam simulation questions in the Pearson Test Prep Software Online.

Review All Key Topics

Review the most important topics in the chapter, noted with the Key Topic icon in the margin of the page. Table 4-9 lists these key topics and the page number on which each is found.

Table 4-9   Chapter 4 Key Topics

Key Topic Element	Description	Page Number
Figure 4-1	Connections and Security Services	150
Section	AWS Shield (Standard and Advanced)	151
Section	AWS Web Application Firewall (WAF)	152
Section	The Main Route Table	155
Section	Custom Route Tables	155
Section	Route Table Cheat Sheet	158
Section	Security Groups	158
Section	Security Groups Cheat Sheet	161
Section	Understanding Ephemeral Ports	165
Figure 4-11	Security Group Design	168
Section	Network ACLs	168
Section	Network ACL Cheat Sheet	169
Section	VPC Flow Logs	172
Section	NAT Services	174
Section	AWS NAT Gateway Service Cheat Sheet	176
Section	Amazon Cognito	176
Section	External Connections	180
Section	AWS Direct Connect Cheat Sheet	187
Section	Amazon GuardDuty	187
Section	Amazon Macie	189
Section	Security Services for Securing Workloads	191
Section	AWS CloudTrail Cheat Sheet	194
Section	AWS Secrets Manager	194

Define Key Terms

Define the following key terms from this chapter and check your answers in the glossary:

AWS Direct Connect, security group (SG), network access control list (NACL), NAT gateway service

Q&A

The answers to these questions appear in Appendix A. Use the Pearson Test Prep Software Online for more practice with exam format questions.

1. What AWS networking services can replace existing hardware devices?

2. What can network ACLs do that a security group cannot do?

3. What is the benefit of using CloudTrail trails for all AWS regions?

4. What is the benefit of using AWS Secrets Manager?

5. What type of artificial intelligence is used to operate GuardDuty?

6. How can Direct Connect help with high-speed connections to multiple VPCs?

7. For what assessments are you not required to have the Amazon Inspector agent installed?

8. How do you enable all checks for Trusted Advisor?

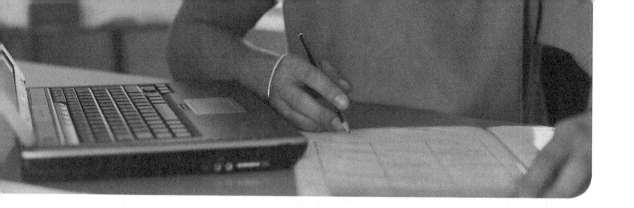

This chapter covers the following topics:

- Data Access and Governance
- Amazon EBS Encryption
- Amazon S3 Bucket Security
- AWS Key Management Service
- AWS Certificate Manager

This chapter covers content that's important to the following exam domain and task statement:

Domain 1: Design Secure Architectures

Task Statement 3: Determine appropriate data security controls

CHAPTER 5

Determining Appropriate Data Security Controls

Organizations have workloads and associated cloud services fail while operating at AWS. Amazon Elastic Compute Cloud (EC2) instances fail, Amazon Elastic Block Store (EBS) volumes crash, and cloud services can stop working. However, you shouldn't have go to your boss and announce, "We've lost some data." Fortunately, all data can be securely and redundantly stored at AWS.

All data stored at AWS using any storage service can be encrypted; organizations make the decision about whether encryption is required. However, Amazon S3 objects and S3 Glacier archive storage *is* automatically encrypted at rest. All other storage services at AWS store data records in an unencrypted state to start. For example, Amazon S3 buckets are encrypted using server-side encryption using Amazon S3, the AWS Key Management Service (KMS) with customer master keys (CMK) and data keys, or encryption keys supplied by each organization. Amazon EBS volumes—both boot and data volumes—can be encrypted at rest and in transit using CMKs provided by AWS KMS. Shared storage services such as Amazon EFS and Amazon FSx for Windows File Server can also be encrypted at rest, as can Amazon DynamoDB tables, Amazon Relational Database Service (RDS) deployments, and Amazon Simple Queue Service (SQS) queues.

NOTE Use of master/slave terms in the following chapter is ONLY in association with the official terminology used in industry specifications and/ or standards, and in no way diminishes Pearson's commitment to promoting diversity, equity, and inclusion, and challenging, countering, and/or combating bias and stereotyping in the global population of the learners we serve.

AWS does not have single-tenant persistent data storage for individual organizations; all storage services offered at AWS are multi-tenant by design. AWS has the responsibility to ensure that each organization's stored data records are isolated to the AWS account in which they are first created. Organizations can secure data at rest by choosing to encrypt all data records; protecting data in transit can be achieved using Transport Layer Security (TLS).

Each organization is in control of the storage and retrieval of its data records that are stored at AWS. It's the organization's responsibility to define the security and accessibility of all data records stored at AWS. All data storage at AWS starts as private storage only accessible across the AWS private network. Organizations can choose to make select Amazon S3 buckets public, but all other storage services offered by AWS remain private and are not publicly accessible across the Internet. AWS VPN and AWS Direct Connect connections from on-premises locations can directly access AWS storage services; however, EBS volumes can only be accessed through the attached EC2 instance. Figure 5-1 illustrates the options for data encryption at AWS that are discussed in this chapter.

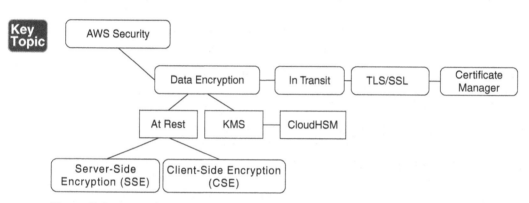

Figure 5-1   Encryption Choices at AWS

"Do I Know This Already?"

The "Do I Know This Already?" quiz allows you to assess whether you should read this entire chapter thoroughly or jump to the "Exam Preparation Tasks" section. If you are in doubt about your answers to these questions or your own assessment of your knowledge of the topics, read the entire chapter. Table 5-1 lists the major headings in this chapter and their corresponding "Do I Know This Already?" quiz questions. You can find the answers in Appendix A, "Answers to the 'Do I Know This Already?' Quizzes and Q&A Sections."

Table 5-1   "Do I Know This Already?" Section-to-Question Mapping

Foundation Topics Section	Questions
Data Access and Governance	1, 2
Amazon EBS Encryption	3, 4
Amazon S3 Bucket Security	5, 6
AWS Key Management Service	7, 8
AWS Certificate Manager	9, 10

CAUTION   The goal of self-assessment is to gauge your mastery of the topics in this chapter. If you do not know the answer to a question or are only partially sure of the answer, you should mark that question as wrong for purposes of the self-assessment. Giving yourself credit for an answer you correctly guess skews your self-assessment results and might provide you with a false sense of security.

1. What AWS service assists in protecting access to AWS?

    a. AWS Shield

    b. Amazon Macie

    c. Amazon EBS volumes

    d. Amazon DynamoDB databases

2. What is the purpose of using detective controls?

    a. To enable and enforce multifactor access

    b. To detect and alert when security controls change

    c. To manage AWS Organizations backups

    d. To analyze compliance levels

3. Which of the following determines whether an attached Amazon EBS volume can be encrypted?

    a. The type of Amazon EC2 instance

    b. The size of the Amazon EBS volume

    c. The type of the Amazon EBS volume

    d. The IOPS assigned to the Amazon EBS volume

4. Where are data keys stored when they are delivered to an Amazon EC2 instance for safekeeping?

    a. The associated Amazon EBS volume

    b. Unsecured RAM

    c. Secured RAM

    d. AWS Key Management Service

5. What security policy allows multiple AWS accounts to access the same Amazon S3 bucket?

    a. Amazon IAM policy

    b. AWS IAM server control policy

    c. Amazon S3 Bucket policy

    d. Amazon IAM policy

6. What type of encryption can be carried out before uploading objects to Amazon S3 to ensure absolute encryption outside AWS control?

    a. RSA encryption

    b. AES 128-bit encryption

    c. Client-side encryption

    d. Server-side encryption

7. What is the advantage of importing your organization's symmetric keys into AWS KMS?

    a. High level of compliance

    b. Faster encryption and decryption

    c. Absolute control of encryption keys

    d. None

8. What additional AWS service can work with AWS KMS as a custom key store?

    a. Encrypted EBS volume

    b. Encrypted Amazon S3 bucket

    c. AWS CloudHSM

    d. Encrypted AWS SQS queue

9. How does AWS charge for provisioning SSL/TLS certificates for AWS services using AWS Certificate Manager?

    a. It charges per certificate per year.

    b. It charges for private TLS certificates only.

    c. It does not charge for AWS services.

    d. It charges per certificate check.

10. Where are the security certificates for the AWS Application Load Balancer stored?

    a. Amazon S3 bucket

    b. Amazon EBS volume

    c. AWS Certificate Manager

    d. AWS KMS service

Data Access and Governance

Many on-premises and AWS-hosted workloads store their associated data records in the AWS cloud. Personal data stored in the public cloud is sometimes defined as personally identifiable information (PII). Sensitive data types, such as PII, must be protected to comply with privacy regulations such as the General Data Protection Regulation (GDPR), laws such as the Health Insurance Portability and Accountability Act (HIPAA), and industry standards such as the Payment Card Industry Data Security Standard (PCI DSS). More than 13 billion data records have been stolen since 2013, according to the *2022 Thales Data Threat Report* (https://cpl.thalesgroup.com/data-threat-report). AWS Artifact, located in the AWS Management console, provides on-demand access to all current AWS compliance and security reports, including Service Organization Control (SOC) and Payment Card Industry (PCI) reports and certifications from accreditation bodies validating the implementation and operating effectiveness of AWS security controls (see Figure 5-2).

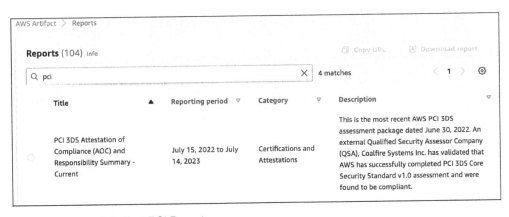

Figure 5-2   AWS Artifact PCI Report

Data Retention and Classification

When classifying data, it's important for each organization to implement data retention policies for each class of stored data. Organizations should design security policies using security zones for all data records, and data classification requirements based on how data is stored and who has access to it (see Figure 5-3). Defined security zones for data records range from highly protected to publicly accessible.

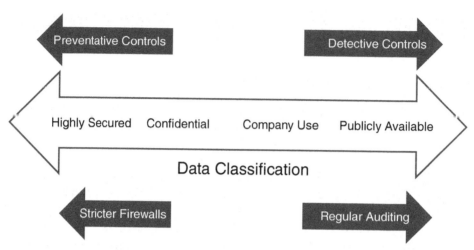

Figure 5-3   Classification of Data Records

Security zones are typically used to segregate different types of organizational data assets based on their sensitivity or importance, with the most sensitive or valuable data being placed in the highest security zone. This segregation enables organizations to implement different levels of security controls and access restrictions based on the sensitivity of the data, ensuring that only authorized users with the appropriate level of clearance can access and view sensitive data records.

Additionally, the creation of relevant security zones can help organizations prevent the spread of security breaches by limiting the potential impact to a specific area of the organization. Organizations also should create a network perimeter with defined network flow and access policies for data records defining where and how data can be accessed. Defense-in-depth security at AWS is applied using infrastructure security controls, AWS IAM security policies, and AWS detective controls (see Figure 5-4).

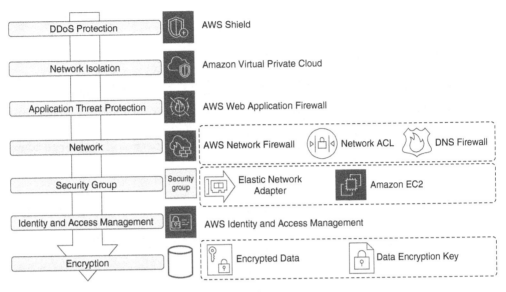

Figure 5-4 Preventative Controls

Infrastructure Security

Infrastructure security requires deploying the following protections:

- **DDoS Protection:** Amazon deploys AWS WAF and Shield to protect the AWS cloud from DDoS attacks.

- **Network isolation:** EC2 instances must be hosted in a virtual private cloud (VPC). Many AWS services can be accessed from a VPC with private VPC endpoints (Interface and Gateway endpoints), ensuring workload traffic remains on the private AWS network.

- **Application-layer threat protection:** The AWS Web Application Firewall (WAF) allows organizations to create rules and filters to accept or reject incoming requests to Amazon CloudFront distributions, Amazon API Gateway deployments, and Application Load Balancers, and HTTP/HTTPS traffic to web servers.

- **Security groups:** Security groups must be designed to allow ingress traffic from associated security groups.

- **Network ACL:** Design network ACLs to implement zone-based models for your workload (web/app servers/database), allowing only legitimate traffic to reach each subnet.

IAM Controls

AWS Identity and Access Management (IAM) policies are useful for controlling access to the data layer (database, queue, AWS EBS volumes, shared data [AWS EFS and AWS FSx for Windows File Server], and Amazon S3 storage) and managing IAM user and federated user activity and infrastructure security. Separate administrative tasks should be created for Amazon RDS with IAM policies (see Example 5-1) that control access to database data records. For authentication and authorization to any workload or organizational data records, enable multifactor authentication (MFA) for all administrators and end users.

Example 5-1   Administrative Access to Amazon RDS

```
"Version": "2012-10-17",
    "Statement": [
        {
            "Sid": " Controlled Admin Tasks",
            "Effect": "Allow",
            "Action": [
                "rds:CreateDBSnapshot",
                "rds:StopDBInstance",
                "rds:StartDBInstance"
            ],
            "Resource": [
                "arn:aws:rds:[AWS_region]:[_AWS_account_
id]:snapshot:*",
                "arn:aws:rds:[AWS_region]:[_AWS_account_
id]:db:demoDB"
            ]
        },
        {
            "Sid": "DescribeInstances",
            "Effect": "Allow",
            "Action": "rds:DescribeDBInstances",
            "Resource": "*"
        }
    ]
}
```

Detective Controls

Detective controls are a type of security control designed to detect and alert when potential security incidents or breaches occcur. Detective controls typically are used with preventive and corrective controls forming a comprehensive security strategy. Examples of detective controls at AWS include intrusion detection systems, and auditing or logging systems that monitor user activity and alert on suspicious behavior. The goal of detective controls is to identify potential security threats or vulnerabilities before they can cause harm, allowing organizations to take appropriate action to prevent or mitigate the impact of a security incident.

Detective controls are an important part of a defense-in-depth security strategy as they provide an additional layer of protection by detecting and responding to potential security threats. Detective controls at AWS include the following security services:

- **VPC Flow Logs:** A feature of Amazon VPC that monitors network traffic at the elastic network interface, subnet, or entire VPC. Captured network traffic can be used for troubleshooting connectivity issues and to check current network access rules.

- **AWS CloudTrail:** Continuously monitor and record API usage and user activity across AWS infrastructure.

- **AWS CloudWatch:** Monitors AWS cloud services such as Amazon RDS databases, EC2 instances, and DynamoDB tables and hosted applications by collecting and tracking metric data, application and operating system log files, and using automated responses to defined alarms.

- **Amazon GuardDuty:** Provides continuous threat detection and analysis of VPC Flow Logs, Amazon Route 53 DNS query logs, and AWS CloudTrail S3 data event logs, and protecting AWS accounts and data stored in Amazon S3 from malicious activity. AWS GuardDuty malware protection can help detect malicious files stored on EBS volumes, protecting attached EC2 instances and Amazon Elastic Kubernetes Service (EKS) clusters.

- **AWS Config:** Detects configuration changes in RDS AWS infrastructure including Amazon RDS, EC2 instances, VPC and database architecture, including security groups, database instances, snapshots, and subnet groups.

- **Amazon Macie:** Uses machine learning and pattern matching to protect Amazon S3 objects and sensitive data types.

- **Access Analyzer for S3:** Monitors Amazon S3 buckets and details public or cross-account access.

- **Amazon Detective:** Graphically analyzes AWS CloudTrail management events, VPC Flow Logs, AWS GuardDuty findings, and Amazon EKS audit logs to help identify the cause of potential security issues.

Amazon EBS Encryption

Amazon Elastic Block Storage (EBS) volumes provide persistent block-level storage volumes for EC2 instances. They can be used to store a wide variety of data, including operating system files, application data, and database records. EBS volumes are automatically replicated within their availability zone to protect against data loss due to failure, and support a range of performance levels and storage options to meet the needs of different workloads.

Amazon Elastic Block Store (EBS) provides the option to encrypt EBS volumes to protect the data records. Encrypting EBS volumes ensures that the data cannot be read or accessed by unauthorized parties, even if the underlying storage volume is compromised. Encryption is performed using a customer master key and data key managed by the AWS Key Management Service (KMS), which provides a secure and auditable encryption service for managing data encryption at AWS using encryption keys. EBS volumes can be encrypted when first created, or volumes can be encrypted after they have been created. EBS also provides the option to encrypt snapshots of EBS volumes, enabling you to create encrypted backups of your EBS volumes.

Both EBS boot and data volumes can be encrypted. Most EC2 instances support EBS volumes' encryption, including the C4, I2, I3, M3, M4, R3, and R4 families. AWS has made the encryption process incredibly easy to deploy; when creating an EBS volume, merely checking off the option to enable encryption starts the encryption process (see Figure 5-5), which is managed by AWS Key Management Service (KMS). More details on AWS KMS are provided throughout this chapter.

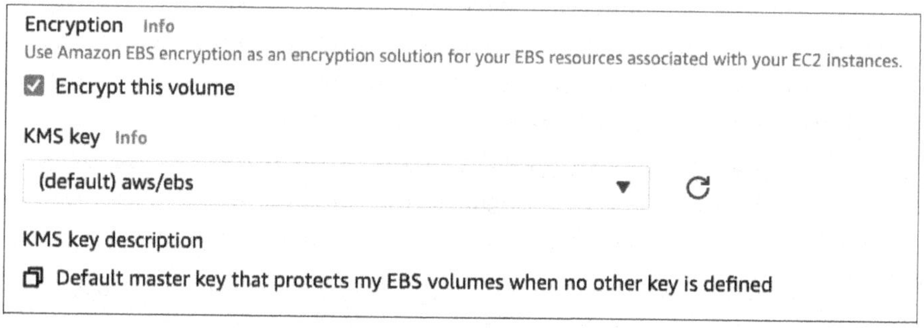

Encryption   Info
Use Amazon EBS encryption as an encryption solution for your EBS resources associated with your EC2 instances.
☑ **Encrypt this volume**

KMS key   Info

| (default) aws/ebs | ▼ | ⟳

KMS key description
⬚ Default master key that protects my EBS volumes when no other key is defined

---

Figure 5-5   Enabling EBS Encryption

NOTE   Data encrypted using the EBS encryption process is encrypted before it crosses the AWS private network. Data also remains encrypted in-flight and at rest and remains encrypted when a snapshot is created of an encrypted volume.

The CMK protects all the other keys issued for data encryption and decryption of your EBS volumes within your AWS account. All AWS KMS-issued CMKs are protected using envelope encryption, which means AWS is responsible for creating and wrapping the "envelope" that contains the CMKs of the respective AWS account. Envelope encryption encrypts the plaintext data with a data key, and then encrypts the data key using a key that is managed by the AWS Key Management Service (KMS). KMS keys are created inside AWS KMS and never leave AWS KMS unencrypted. AWS cryptographic tools and services support the Advanced Encryption Standard (AES) with 128-, 192-, or 256-bit keys. AES is combined with Galois/Counter Mode (GCM), which provides high-performance *symmetric key* operation using a block size of 128 bits and is used by AWS KMS. AES and GCM are documented as AES-GCM.

After enabling your customer key using KMS for your AWS account, for additional security, it's a good idea to add another key administrator and to allow key rotation of your Customer Master Keys. Administrators can use the KMS master key provided to create additional AWS KMS administrators, and to optionally enable key rotation of the CMK (see Figure 5-6).

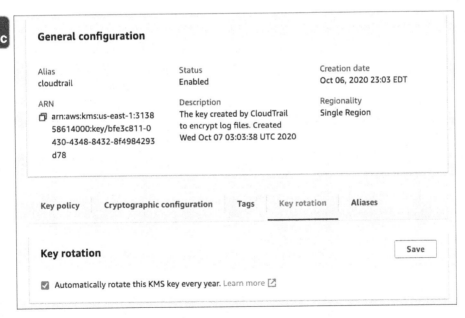

Figure 5-6 Enabling Key Rotation

To encrypt an EBS volume using the AWS Key Management Service, a CMK can be created by AWS and stored in AWS KMS. Optionally, organizations can choose to specify the key material for the CMK, which can be generated by KMS or imported from your own key management infrastructure. After a CMK has been created, you can create an encrypted EBS volume using the EC2 dashboard and specifying the ID of the CMK when creating the volume (see Figure 5-7). The EBS volume will be encrypted using the specified CMK, and the data on the EBS volume will be encrypted at rest on the underlying storage.

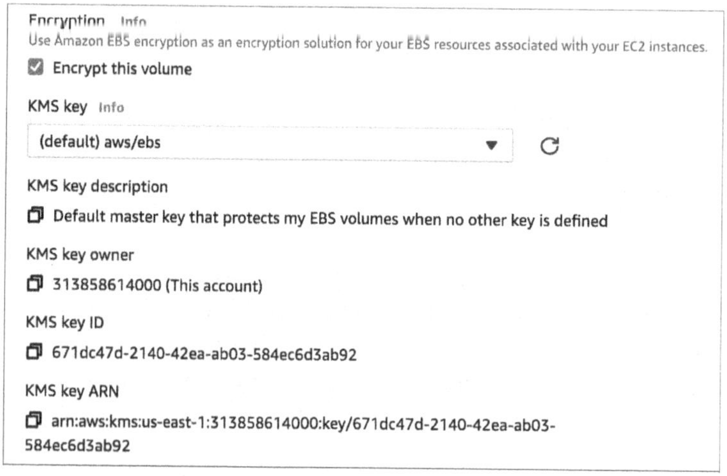

Encryption Info
Use Amazon EBS encryption as an encryption solution for your EBS resources associated with your EC2 instances.
☑ Encrypt this volume

KMS key Info

(default) aws/ebs ▼   ↻

KMS key description
⬚ Default master key that protects my EBS volumes when no other key is defined

KMS key owner
⬚ 313858614000 (This account)

KMS key ID
⬚ 671dc47d-2140-42ea-ab03-584ec6d3ab92

KMS key ARN
⬚ arn:aws:kms:us-east-1:313858614000:key/671dc47d-2140-42ea-ab03-584ec6d3ab92

Figure 5-7 Select KMS Key

When you attach the encrypted EBS volume to an EC2 instance, the instance will automatically download and install the necessary encryption and decryption components, including the appropriate version of the AWS Encryption SDK and the public key portion of the CMK. The instance will then use the CMK to encrypt and decrypt data as it is written to and read from the EBS volume. The private key portion of the CMK remains securely stored in AWS KMS, and is never made available to the EC2 instance.

When an EBS volume has been encrypted and attached to an EC2 instance, the following data types are encrypted:

- Data at rest inside the EBS volume
- All data that moves between the attached EBS volume and the EC2 instance
- All snapshots created from the EBS volume
- All volumes created from the encrypted snapshots

AWS KMS performs the following steps, as illustrated in Figure 5-8, to encrypt and decrypt the EBS volume:

Step 1.   AWS EBS sends a request to KMS, specifying the CMK to use for the AWS EBS volume encryption.

Step 2.   AWS KMS generates a new data key, encrypts it using the specified CMK, and sends the encrypted key to AWS EBS to be stored with the volume metadata.

Step 3.   The Amazon EC2 service sends a decrypt request to KMS.

Step 4.   EBS sends a request to KMS to decrypt the data key.

Step 5.   KMS uses the CMK to decrypt the encrypted data key and sends the decrypted key to the EC2 service.

Step 6.   EC2 stores the plaintext decrypted key in protected hypervisor memory on the bare-metal server where the EC2 instance is hosted and uses the key when required to perform decryption for the EBS volume.

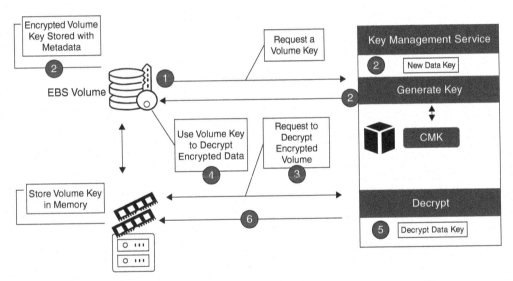

Figure 5-8   EBS Encryption Steps

NOTE   The default setting for each AWS region is that EBS encryption is not enabled. To enable EBS encryption in the AWS region, open the EC2 dashboard, and in the upper-right corner under Account Attributes click EBS Encryption. Click Manage and choose the desired AWS-managed CMK or another CMK. Next, click Enable and then click Update EBS encryption. Once encryption is enabled for the AWS region, all new EBS volumes and snapshots will be encrypted at creation.

Amazon S3 Bucket Security

By default, only the owner who created an S3 bucket has access to the objects stored in the bucket. There are several methods for controlling security for an S3 bucket (see Figure 5-9):

- **ACLs:** You can use *access control lists (ACLs)* to control primary access from other AWS accounts for list and write objects and read and write bucket permissions, public access, and access to S3 logging information. ACLs are available for purposes of backward compatibility and are the weakest type of S3 security (and therefore not recommended).

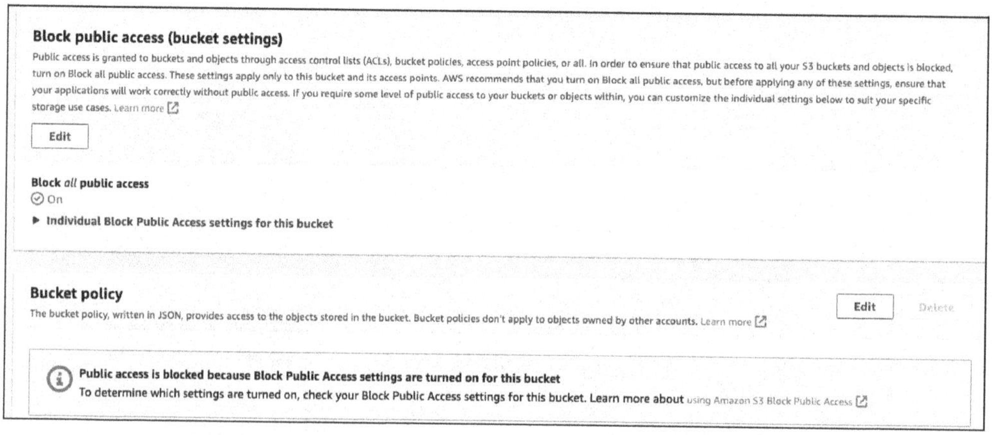

Block public access (bucket settings)

Public access is granted to buckets and objects through access control lists (ACLs), bucket policies, access point policies, or all. In order to ensure that public access to all your S3 buckets and objects is blocked, turn on Block all public access. These settings apply only to this bucket and its access points. AWS recommends that you turn on Block all public access, but before applying any of these settings, ensure that your applications will work correctly without public access. If you require some level of public access to your buckets or objects within, you can customize the individual settings below to suit your specific storage use cases. Learn more

    Edit

Block *all* public access
⊘ On
▶ Individual Block Public Access settings for this bucket

Bucket policy

The bucket policy, written in JSON, provides access to the objects stored in the bucket. Bucket policies don't apply to objects owned by other accounts. Learn more   Edit   Delete

ⓘ Public access is blocked because Block Public Access settings are turned on for this bucket
To determine which settings are turned on, check your Block Public Access settings for this bucket. Learn more about using Amazon S3 Block Public Access

Figure 5-9 S3 Permission Settings

- **IAM policy:** You can grant access to other AWS users and groups of IAM users by using IAM permission policies in partnership with resource policies.

- **S3 Bucket policy:** You can control direct access to an S3 bucket, as shown in Example 5-2, by creating a *bucket policy* assigned directly to the S3 bucket. An S3 bucket policy is a JSON-formatted document that defines which actions are allowed or denied on an S3 bucket and its contents. A bucket policy is attached directly to the bucket it is protecting, and the policy settings list who has access to the bucket and what they can do with the objects in the bucket. An S3 bucket policy might allow a specific IAM user to read and write objects in the bucket, while denying access to all other users. Or, the policy might allow any user to read objects in the bucket but allow only authenticated users to write objects.

S3 bucket policies are defined using the AWS Policy Language, which provides a set of keywords and operations that you can use to specify the conditions under which a policy takes effect. A bucket policy can also allow access from multiple AWS accounts to a single S3 bucket.

Example 5-2 S3 Bucket Policy

```
{
  "Version": "2012-10-17",
  "Id": "S3PolicyId1",
  "Statement": [
    {
      "Sid": "IPAllow",
      "Effect": "Deny",
      "Principal": "*",
      "Action": "s3:*",
      "Resource": [
                    "arn:aws:s3:::2021232reports",
         "arn:aws:s3:::2021232reports/*"
      ],
      "Condition": {
          "NotIpAddress": {"aws:SourceIp": "54.242.144.0/24"}
      }
    }
  ]
}
```

- **Query string authentication:** Query string authentication is a method to authenticate requests to an Amazon S3 bucket allowing organizations to generate a URL (see Figure 5-10) that can be shared with end users. When an end user clicks the URL, they are granted access to the specified S3 bucket and its contents.

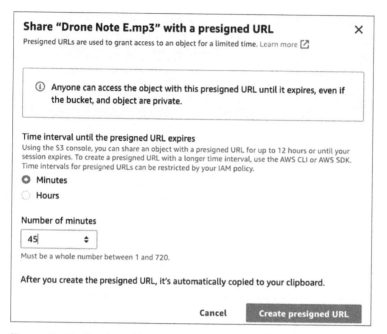

Share "Drone Note E.mp3" with a presigned URL   ✕

Presigned URLs are used to grant access to an object for a limited time. Learn more ⧉

ⓘ Anyone can access the object with this presigned URL until it expires, even if
   the bucket, and object are private.

Time interval until the presigned URL expires

Using the S3 console, you can share an object with a presigned URL for up to 12 hours or until your
session expires. To create a presigned URL with a longer time interval, use the AWS CLI or AWS SDK.
Time intervals for presigned URLs can be restricted by your IAM policy.

◉ Minutes

◯ Hours

Number of minutes

[45] ⬍

Must be a whole number between 1 and 720.

After you create the presigned URL, it's automatically copied to your clipboard.

                                              Cancel   **Create presigned URL**

Figure 5-10 Presigned URL for S3 Object Access

The URL includes a set of parameters that specify the credentials that grant access to the bucket. These parameters include the access key ID, an expiration time for the URL, and a signature that is calculated using the access key secret.

When someone attempts to access the URL, the Amazon S3 service checks the signature to verify that it matches the expected value. If the signature is valid, the user is granted access to the bucket; otherwise, the request is denied.

The use case for using query string authentication is useful for granting temporary access to an S3 bucket without having to create an IAM user or provide AWS access keys. However, query string authentication is not as secure as IAM policies or bucket policies because the URL and its parameters are included in each request; therefore, anyone who has access to the URL can potentially gain access to the bucket.

NOTE If you require public access to objects in an S3 bucket, it's recommended that you create a separate AWS account specifically for hosting the S3 buckets that will have public S3 object access.

■ **Blocking S3 public access:** S3 Buckets always start as private, with no default public access (see Figure 5-11). When the Block Public Access (Bucket Settings) setting is enabled, attempts at changing security settings to allow public access to objects in the S3 bucket are denied. You can block public access on an individual S3 bucket or on all S3 buckets in your AWS account by editing the public access settings for your account using the S3 console. Choices for blocking S3 public access include the following:

■ **Public:** Everyone has access to list objects, write objects, and read and write permissions.

■ **Objects Can Be Public:** The bucket is not public; however, public access can be granted to individual objects by users with permissions.

■ **Buckets and Objects Not Public:** No public access is allowed to the bucket or the objects within the bucket.

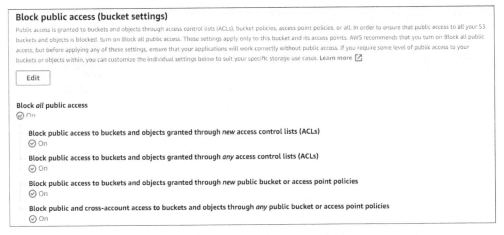

Figure 5-11   Blocking Public Access on an S3 Bucket by Default

NOTE   Amazon Macie is a powerful AWS security service that uses artificial intelligence (AI) and machine learning (ML) technology to analyze your S3 objects and access patterns. Amazon S3 data can be classified based on many file formats, such as Personally Identifiable Information (PII) and other file types. AWS SNS notifications can be generated by Amazon Macie when Amazon S3 objects are discovered to be compromised.

S3 Storage at Rest

For the AWS Certified Solutions Architect – Associate (SAA-C03) exam, the key topics to know about S3 storage at rest are as follows:

- **SSE-S3:** With SSE-S3, Amazon S3 manages the encryption and decryption of the data in the bucket. Organizations that select this option don't manage the encryption keys but can access the data in the bucket without having to manage the keys. SSE-S3 uses the Advanced Encryption Standard (AES) algorithm with a 256-bit key to encrypt the data in the bucket. The key is automatically generated by Amazon S3 and is regularly rotated to ensure the security of the encrypted data (see Figure 5-12). Note that SSE encrypts the object data but the optional tag object metadata remains unencrypted.

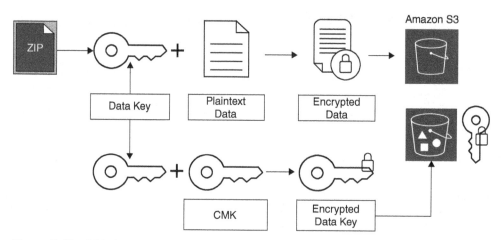

Figure 5-12 SSE-S3 Encryption Process

- **SSE-KMS:** Organizations can select AWS KMS to manage their encryption keys. Select the default CMK or choose a CMK that was already created in AWS KMS before starting an S3 encryption process. Accessing encrypted objects managed by KMS can be expensive: If you have an exceptionally large number of encrypted objects, a large volume of decryption requests will be made to KMS. You can configure SSE-KMS to significantly reduce the cost of the encryption and decryption process. When an S3 Bucket Key is configured for SSE-KMS server-side encryption, a short-lived encryption key is created and stored and used to encrypt objects internally inside AWS S3 rather than utilize AWS KMS encryption processes. The S3 Bucket Key creates unique data keys for encrypting objects in the specific S3 bucket that has enabled the S3 Bucket Key option. The encryption process reduces AWS KMS requests for external encryption keys and can reduce encryption costs by 99%. The S3 Bucket Key is a worker process within the S3 bucket that enables you to perform encryption services without constant communication with KMS.

- **SSE-C:** You can use SSE with a customer-provided encryption key. With each request, the encryption key is provided to AWS, and Amazon S3 manages the encryption and decryption of S3 objects by using the supplied key. The same encryption key that was used to encrypt the object must be provided before the object can be decrypted (see Figure 5-13). After the encryption process is complete, the supplied encryption key is deleted from memory. To upload an object with an organization-provided encryption key (SSE-C), the AWS CLI, AWS SDK, or Amazon S3 REST API must be used.

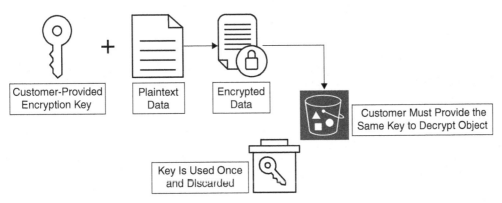

Figure 5-13 SSE-C Encryption Process

Amazon S3 Object Lock Policies

Amazon S3 buckets and Amazon S3 Glacier have data policies that can lock objects so they cannot be deleted or changed. Amazon S3 objects can be locked using a *write-once/read-many (WORM)* policy. Object lock policies enable you to set rules that restrict certain actions on objects, such as deleting or overwriting them, in order to protect objects and ensure they remain available and unaltered. Object lock policies are set at the S3 bucket level and apply to all objects in the bucket, or set on individual objects. This can be useful for complying with legal or regulatory requirements or protecting important or sensitive data. Apply a WORM policy, as shown in Figure 5-14, to stop an Amazon S3 object from being overwritten, or deleted for a fixed time period, or indefinitely. There are several options to WORM policies to understand. First is the *retention period*, which refers to a set number of days or years during which an object will remain locked, protected, and unable to be overwritten or deleted. There are two retention modes:

- **Governance mode:** An S3 object cannot have its lock settings overwritten and cannot itself be overwritten or deleted unless the user has unique permissions. To override governance mode retention settings, an IAM user must have the **s3: BypassGovernanceRetention** permission and **x-amz-bypass-governance-retention: true** applied.

- **Compliance mode:** A protected object in your AWS account cannot be overwritten or deleted by anyone, including the root user, for the entire retention period.

Figure 5-14   WORM Policy Settings

Legal Hold

An object lock allows you to place a legal hold on an S3 object. Legal hold provides the same protection as a previously discussed retention period but does not have an expiration date. expiration date. Once in force, a legal hold remains in place until it is removed. An object lock works on S3 buckets that have versioning already enabled. Legal hold can be applied to a single S3 object. A legal hold can be placed and removed by any user with the **s3:PutObjectLegalHold** permission applied to their IAM user or group account they are a member of.

NOTE   Object lock can only be enabled for new buckets when they are being created.

Amazon S3 Glacier Storage at Rest

Objects stored in Amazon S3 Glacier are automatically encrypted using SSE and AES-256 encryption. Amazon S3 Glacier Vault Lock enables you to deploy and enforce regulatory and required compliance controls by applying a Vault Lock policy on an Amazon S3 Glacier vault. Once a WORM policy has been applied to an S3 Glacier vault, the policy cannot be changed.

NOTE   Both EFS and FSx use AES-256 encryption to encrypt EFS data and metadata at rest. When your file system is mounted, you can also encrypt your EFS data in transit with TLS. FSx also supports the encryption of data in transit on file shares mapped on a computer instance that supports SMB Version 3.0 or newer. Encryption of data records at rest is automatically enabled when an FSx file system is created.

Data Backup and Replication

Amazon S3 object backups can be carried out with the services and utilities listed in Table 5-2. AWS Backup and AWS DataSync can back up additional AWS storage service data records.

Table 5-2   Data Backup and Replication Options

AWS Service	Use	Data Types
AWS Backup	Back up all AWS storage services	EBS volumes and snapshots, S3 buckets, EFS, FSx for Windows File Server, RDS, DynamoDB
Amazon S3 Same-Region Replication (SRR)	Replicate objects to an S3 bucket in the same AWS region	Objects and versioned objects
Amazon S3 Cross-Region Replication (CRR)	Replicate objects to an S3 bucket in a different AWS region	Objects and versioned objects
Amazon S3 Multi-Region Access Points	Replicate data sets across multiple AWS regions	Objects and versioned objects
AWS DataSync	Copy data to and from AWS storage services	Network File System (NFS) or Server Message Block (SMB) shares, Hadoop Distributed File Systems (HDFS), AWS Snowcone, S3 buckets, EFS, FSx for Windows File Server

AWS Key Management Service

AWS Key Management Service (KMS) lets organizations create, manage, and control cryptographic keys used to protect data records. AWS KMS integrates with AWS services that can encrypt data records (see Figure 5-15).

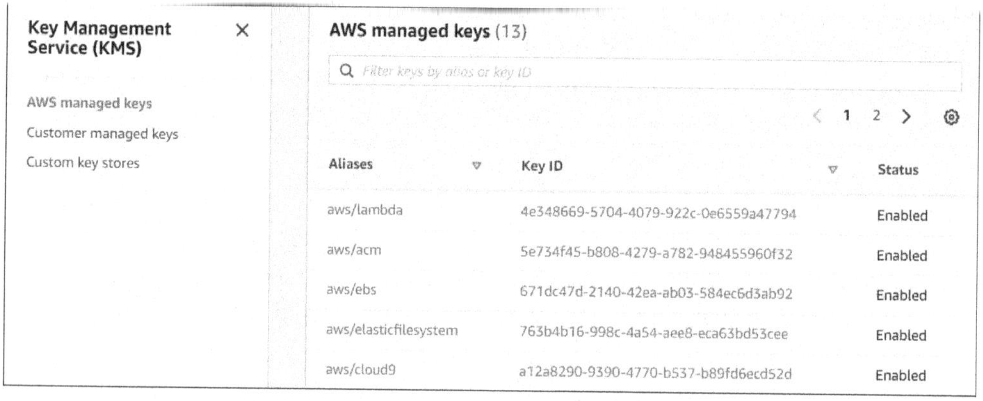

Key Management Service (KMS)	✕	AWS managed keys (13)		
		Q *Filter keys by alias or key ID*		
AWS managed keys				‹ 1 2 › ⚙
Customer managed keys				
Custom key stores		**Aliases** ▽	**Key ID** ▽	**Status**
		aws/lambda	4e348669-5704-4079-922c-0e6559a47794	Enabled
		aws/acm	5e734f45-b808-4279-a782-948455960f32	Enabled
		aws/ebs	671dc47d-2140-42ea-ab03-584ec6d3ab92	Enabled
		aws/elasticfilesystem	763b4b16-998c-4a54-aee8-eca63bd53cee	Enabled
		aws/cloud9	a12a8290-9390-4770-b537-b89fd6ecd52d	Enabled

Figure 5-15   KMS Console

Organizations do not have to directly interface with AWS KMS to enable data encryption; instead, they can use AWS KMS services through more than 100 integrated AWS services, such as Amazon EBS storage, Amazon RDS, Amazon S3, Amazon EFS, Amazon FSx for Windows File Server, Amazon Aurora, and Amazon DynamoDB. When you enable encryption services using AWS KMS, a CMK is automatically generated in your AWS account for data encryption and decryption services. Organizations can choose to create one or more CMKs and use them to match their security requirements. A custom CMK allows you to control each key's access control and usage policy; you can also grant permissions to other AWS accounts and services to use a specific custom CMK.

You can also choose to create symmetric CMKs, which use the same key to encrypt and decrypt data, or asymmetric CMKs, which use a public/private key pair (one for encrypting and one for decrypting).

The most common way to use KMS is to choose which AWS service will encrypt your data and select the CMK from within the AWS service itself; for example, you can encrypt an RDS database volume, as shown in Figure 5-16.

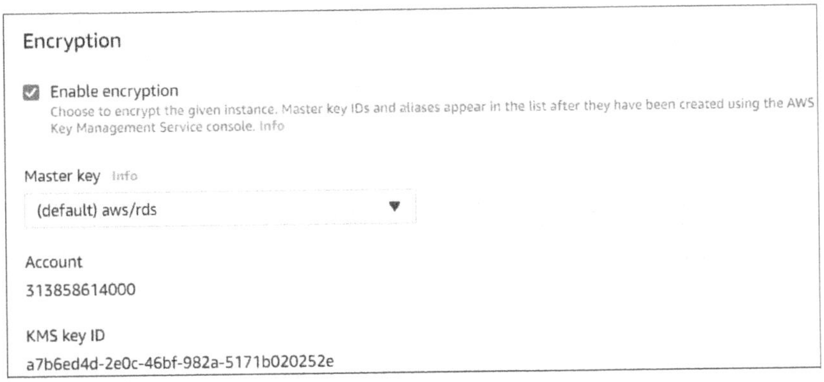

Encryption

☑ Enable encryption
   Choose to encrypt the given instance. Master key IDs and aliases appear in the list after they have been created using the AWS
   Key Management Service console. Info

Master key Info

(default) aws/rds   ▼

Account
313858614000

KMS key ID
a7b6ed4d-2e0c-46bf-982a-5171b020252e

Figure 5-16 Generating CMKs with KMS for an RDS Instance

Envelope Encryption

KMS uses a process called *envelope encryption* to encrypt data at rest. It involves two layers of encryption: the first layer encrypts the data using a key generated by the organization, and the second layer encrypts the customer-generated key using a key that is managed by the AWS Key Management Service (KMS). This process enables each organization to retain control over their encryption keys and also enables them to rotate and manage the keys as needed, while still benefitting from the security and reliability of using the KMS for encryption key management. When you need to encrypt data, KMS generates a data key that is used to encrypt the data locally within the AWS service or application. The data keys are also encrypted under the organization's CMK. When it's time to decrypt your data, a request is sent to KMS to decrypt the data key (that is, the data key copy that was stored with the encrypted data) using your CMK. The entire encryption or decryption process is logged in AWS CloudTrail for auditing purposes.

NOTE You can create up to 10,000 CMKs per AWS account per AWS region. Keys generated by AWS KMS can be enabled to be automatically rotated on an annual basis. However, automatic key rotation is not supported for external cryptographic keys imported into AWS KMS.

Organizations that choose to import 256-bit symmetric keys into AWS KMS for compliance requirements are responsible for managing the imported keys' expiration dates.

In addition to encrypting your data, AWS KMS provides other security features to help protect your encryption keys:

- **Key management:** As an administrator, you can create, rotate, disable, and delete the CMKs that are used to encrypt your data. You can also view the key policy for a CMK, which specifies who has access to the CMK and what actions they can perform with it.

- **Access control:** Organizations can use AWS IAM policies to control who has access to their CMKs and what actions can be performed with them. For example, users can be granted the ability to encrypt data using a specific CMK, but not to decrypt it or change the key policy.

- **Auditing:** AWS KMS logs all API calls to AWS CloudTrail so organizations can track who is using each CMK and for what purpose. Auditing can help ensure that encryption keys are being used securely and in accordance with an organization's security policies.

- **Key material:** KMS stores the key material for your CMKs in secure hardware devices called hardware security modules (HSMs). This helps protect the security of each organization's keys and ensures that they are only accessible to authorized users.

- **Key rotation:** CMKS can be configured to automatically be rotated on an annual basis, to help prevent security breaches.

 ### AWS KMS Cheat Sheet

For the AWS Certified Solutions Architect – Associate (SAA-C03) exam, you need to understand the following critical aspects of AWS KMS:

- AWS KMS can be used to create symmetric keys within a custom key store such as AWS CloudHSM.

- An organization's symmetric keys can be imported for use with AWS KMS.

- AWS KMS can create symmetric and asymmetric data key pairs for application use.

- CMKs can be automatically rotated annually.

- CMKs can be disabled and re-enabled.

- AWS KMS keys can be audited with AWS CloudTrail.

AWS CloudHSM

Instead of using the default AWS KMS store, you can create a custom key store using a VPC-hosted AWS CloudHSM cluster and authorize KMS to use it as its dedicated key store. AWS CloudHSM clusters are created using multiple single-tenant hardware devices (see Figure 5-17). Amazon maintains the AWS CloudHSM hardware and backs up its contents but never enters an AWS CloudHSM device. Organizations might use an AWS CloudHSM deployment if compliance rules explicitly require that encryption keys are protected in a single-tenant hardware device. AWS CloudHSM can operate as a complete stand-alone hardware device for your synchronous and asynchronous keys and provide you with Federal Information Processing Standard (FIPS) 140-2 Level 3 compliance.

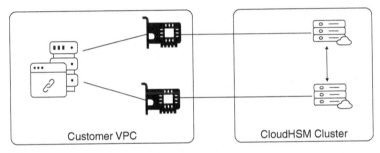

Figure 5-17 CloudHSM Design

AWS Certificate Manager

AWS Certificate Manager (ACM) is a managed service that allows you to provision, manage, and deploy public and private SSL/TLS certificates that can be used with your AWS services and AWS-hosted websites and applications. Certificates can also be deployed on ELB load balancers, CloudFront distributions, Elastic Beanstalk, and APIs hosted on Amazon API Gateway. There is no additional charge for provisioning public or private SSL/TLS certificates for use with AWS services. However, organizations will pay a fee for creating and operating a private *certificate authority (CA)* and for the private certificates that are issued by the private CA that is used by your internally hosted resources, such as application servers or appliances.

ACM can generate the following certificate types (see Figure 5-18):

- **Public certificates:** ELB port 443 traffic, CloudFront distributions, and public-facing APIs hosted by Amazon API Gateway all use public certificates. Use AWS Certificate Manager to request a public certificate for a domain name for your site. AWS Certificate Manager validates that you own or control the domain name in your certificate request. Validation options include DNS validation and email validation.

- **Private certificates:** Delegated private certificates are managed by an AWS Certificate Manager–hosted private CA, which can automatically renew and deploy certificates for private-facing Amazon ELB and Amazon API Gateway deployments. Private certificates can also secure Amazon EC2 instances, Amazon ECS containers, and IoT devices.

- **Imported certificates.** Third-party certificates can be imported into AWS Certificate Manager.

- **CA certificates:** Certificates can be issued for creating a private CA up to five levels deep, including a root CA, three levels of subordinate CAs, and a single issuing CA.

Figure 5-18   Certificate Choices in AWS Certificate Manager

Encryption in Transit

AWS uses HTTPS endpoints communication, providing encryption in transit for communicating with AWS APIs. AWS service endpoints can also be accessed using TLS version 1.2. Some AWS services offer endpoints that support the Federal Processing Standard (FIPS) 140-2 in some regions. Each endpoint is the URL of the entry point for each AWS service. AWS SDKs and the AWS Command Line Interface (AWS CLI) automatically use the default endpoint for each service per AWS Region, but an alternative endpoint can be specified for API requests. Most AWS services have regional endpoints that can be used to make requests. The format for a regional endpoint is *protocol://service-code.region-code*.amazonaws.com. AWS endpoints can be referenced here: https://docs.aws.amazon.com/general/latest/gr/aws-service-information.html.

Global endpoints are used for global services and services located in edge locations. The global AWS services are

- Amazon CloudFront

- AWS Global Accelerator

- AWS Identity and Access Management (IAM)

- AWS Organizations

- Amazon Route 53

- AWS Shield Advanced

- AWS WAF Classic

HTTP endpoints for domains and hosted workloads hosted at AWS can be be blocked with Security Groups and Network ACLs and can automatically be redirected to HTTPS endpoints when using Amazon CloudFront or an Amazon ELB.

Exam Preparation Tasks

As mentioned in the section "How to Use This Book" in the Introduction, you have a couple of choices for exam preparation: the exercises here, Chapter 16, "Final Preparation," and the exam simulation questions in the Pearson Test Prep software online.

Review All Key Topics

Review the most important topics in the chapter, noted with the Key Topic icon in the margin of the page. Table 5-3 lists these key topics and the page number on which each is found.

Table 5-3 Chapter 5 Key Topics

Key Topic Element	Description	Page Number
Figure 5-1	Encryption Choices at AWS	204
Section	Data Retention and Classification	207
Section	Infrastructure Security	209
Section	Detective Controls	210
Section	Amazon EBS Encryption	212
Figure 5-6	Enabling Key Rotation	213
Section	S3 Storage at Rest	220
Section	Amazon S3 Object Lock Policies	221
Section	Amazon S3 Glacier Storage at Rest	222

Key Topic Element	Description	Page Number
Section	AWS Key Management Service	224
Section	AWS KMS Cheat Sheet	226
Section	AWS CloudHSM	227
List	AWS Certificate Manager certificate types	227

Define Key Terms

Define the following key terms from this chapter and check your answers in the glossary:

Amazon Elastic Block Storage (EBS), symmetric key, access control list (ACL), bucket policy, write-once/read-many (WORM), AWS Key Management Service (KMS), certificate authority (CA)

Q&A

The answers to these questions appear in Appendix A. Use the Pearson Test Prep Software Online for more practice with exam format questions.

1. Which AWS storage service is available with AWS as a single-tenant storage design?

2. What is the default state of an S3 bucket regarding public access when the bucket is first created?

3. What is the security advantage of using SSE-C encryption with Amazon S3 buckets?

4. Describe the concept of envelope encryption that KMS uses.

5. What type of data stored at AWS is always automatically encrypted by default?

6. Why is AWS CloudHSM chosen by companies that must adhere to a high compliance standard?

7. How does AWS KMS carry out automatic key rotation for imported keys?

8. Where can private CAs created by AWS Certificate Manager be deployed?

This chapter covers the following topics:

- Scalable and Resilient Architecture
- Application Integration Services
- Amazon API Gateway
- Automating AWS Infrastructure
- AWS Elastic Beanstalk

This chapter covers content that's important to the following exam domain and task statement:

Domain 2: Design Resilient Architectures

Task Statement 1: Design scalable and loosely coupled architectures

CHAPTER 6

Designing Resilient Architecture

The AWS Certified Solutions Architect – Associate (SAA-C03) exam requires that you understand the AWS services that assist in developing workloads and applications hosted in the AWS cloud. The exam does not expect that you're a developer; however, it does expect that you can help advise developers and educate them on what services could be useful for creating stateless applications to run successfully in the AWS cloud.

Although the cloud can certainly host legacy monolithic applications, the SAA-C03 exam also tests your understanding of the purpose of AWS application integration services. Lifting and shifting an application from an on-premises location into AWS does work, but, in the long term, moving existing workloads to the cloud without re-architecting to take advantage of the features of AWS will not be a successful plan long-term.

This chapter begins by demystifying the terms *stateful* and *stateless* as they pertain to the AWS cloud. This chapter also looks at the Amazon API Gateway and automation strategies for deploying scalable architecture using AWS CloudFormation, AWS Service Catalog, and AWS Elastic Beanstalk.

"Do I Know This Already?"

The "Do I Know This Already?" quiz allows you to assess whether you should read this entire chapter thoroughly or jump to the "Exam Preparation Tasks" section. If you doubt your answers to these questions or your own assessment of your knowledge of the topics, read the entire chapter. Table 6-1 lists the major headings in this chapter and their corresponding "Do I Know This Already?" quiz questions. You can find the answers in Appendix A, "Answers to the 'Do I Know This Already?' Quizzes and Q&A Sections."

Table 6-1   "Do I Know This Already?" Section-to-Question Mapping

Foundation Topics Section	Questions
Scalable and Resilient Architecture	1, 2
Application Integration Services	3, 4
Amazon API Gateway	5, 6
Automating AWS Infrastructure	7, 8
AWS Elastic Beanstalk	9, 10

CAUTION   The goal of self-assessment is to gauge your mastery of the topics in this chapter. If you do not know the answer to a question or are only partially sure of the answer, you should mark that question as wrong for purposes of the self-assessment. Giving yourself credit for an answer you correctly guess skews your self-assessment results and might provide you with a false sense of security.

1. Which of the following AWS services is stateful?

    a. Security groups

    b. AWS SQS

    c. Amazon Route 53

    d. Availability zone

2. Which of the following terms would apply to a virtual server that saves data about each current client session?

    a. Stateless

    b. Stateful

    c. Primary

    d. Secondary

3. Which AWS service could be useful for storing application state for processing?

    a. AWS SNS

    b. AWS SQS

    c. Amazon S3 Glacier

    d. Amazon EBS

4. Which AWS service is used to send notifications about AWS service changes to both humans and services?

   a. Amazon SES

   b. AWS SNS

   c. Amazon Chime

   d. Amazon Kinesis

5. Which AWS service can be used to host and execute custom functions?

   a. Amazon EC2

   b. AWS Lambda

   c. Amazon IAM

   d. AWS SQS

6. What is the commercial charging model for AWS Lambda?

   a. Processing time

   b. RAM/CPU and processing time

   c. The number of functions executed per month per account

   d. RAM and CPU allocated per function

7. What is the purpose of using AWS CloudFormation?

   a. To recover from failures

   b. To automate the building of AWS infrastructure components

   c. To deploy applications with automation

   d. To document manual tasks

8. What AWS CloudFormation component is used to advise on deployment changes to existing deployed infrastructure?

   a. AWS CloudFormation template

   b. Stack

   c. Change set

   d. JSON script

9. What two components are deployed using AWS Elastic Beanstalk?

   a. Infrastructure and storage

   b. Application and infrastructure

   c. Compute and storage

   d. Containers and instances

10. What term defines application updates that are applied to a new set of EC2 instances?

    a. Rolling

    b. Immutable

    c. All at once

    d. Blue/green

Scalable and Resilient Architecture

Designing scalable and loosely coupled architecture allows organization workloads to automatically scale, meeting business and design requirements and increasing workload reliability.

Modern modular design can help create workloads constructed with many loosely coupled services integrated using a common set of APIs, creating a functional workload with micro-service architectures. Modular applications can be linked together using *serverless* services performing one or more specific tasks as an integrated workload service. The application shown in Figure 6-1 utilizes several AWS serverless services:

- **Amazon API Gateway:** The AWS API Gateway is located between your client applications and back-end services and routes requests from clients to the appropriate back end located at AWS, or on premises, returning information back to the client. API Gateway can also provide other useful features, such as authentication and caching of common API requests, to help improve the security and performance of the hosted API.

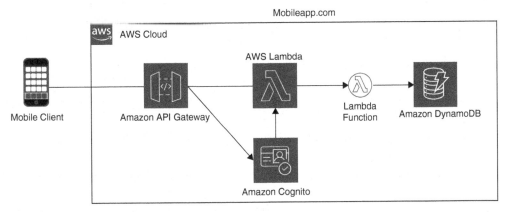

Figure 6-1 Complex Application Broken into Smaller Parts

- **Amazon Cognito:** Amazon Cognito provides authentication, authorization, and user management for mobile applications helping developers build applications that securely store and manage user data. Amazon Cognito can authenticate end-user requests authorizing access to API Gateway endpoints.

■ **AWS Lambda:** AWS Lambda executes custom functions in response to events within milliseconds of each request. The underlying compute resources that execute each function are automatically managed in the background. Custom functions can be written and hosted by AWS Lambda implementing the business logic for an API hosted at Amazon API Gateway.

■ **Amazon DynamoDB.** Amazon DynamoDB is a fully managed NoSQL database service that provides fast and predictable performance with seamless scalability. Amazon DynamoDB enables organizations to offload the administrative tasks of hardware provisioning, setup and configuration, replication, software patching, or cluster scaling. Amazon DynamoDB supports both document and key-value data models, enabling users to store and retrieve data for mobile, web, gaming, IoT, and applications that need low-latency access to its data.

Scalable Delivery from Edge Locations

Including Amazon CloudFront and edge locations as part of your application solution architecture allows regional workloads to scale globally, and reliably. Leveraging a CloudFront distribution can also help minimize DDoS attacks by protecting application data stored in Amazon S3 buckets. AWS WAF filters can provide additional application layer protection to help protect web applications from common web exploits that could affect application availability, compromise security, or consume excessive resources. The following workload designs will benefit from deploying Amazon CloudFront as a content delivery network (CDN):

■ **Static website content delivery:** Use an Amazon S3 bucket to host a web application and store static web assets and content. For example, host a React application and deliver requested content quickly across hundreds of AWS edge locations using an Amazon CloudFront distribution.

■ **Live streaming video:** CloudFront supports streaming of various types of media content, such as audio, video, and live events, using the HTTP Live Streaming (HLS) and Dynamic Adaptive Streaming over HTTP (DASH) protocols to any device caching media fragments at the edge location closest to the end user, ensuring delivery of live streaming fragments from origin. CloudFront streaming also integrates with other AWS services such as Amazon Elastic Transcoder and Amazon Kinesis Video Streams to provide solutions for streaming media content.

■ **Encrypting system fields:** Use an HTTPS connection with field-level encryption to encrypt specific fields, ensuring applications are restricted from viewing sensitive data fields. AWS Field Level Encryption enables you to encrypt sensitive data fields in your objects, such as credit card numbers or personally identifiable information (PII), before they are cached in a Cloud-Front distribution at an edge location. AWS Field Level Encryption ensures that the sensitive data is protected while in transit to and from CloudFront. Field Level Encryption is useful for e-commerce and financial services applications that handle large amounts of sensitive data.

- **Customize processing at edge locations:** AWS Lambda@Edge is a feature of Amazon Web Services (AWS) that enables you to run serverless functions in response to CloudFront requests to website data records. AWS Lambda@Edge functions execute at edge locations, providing fast and reliable performance for requests and queries. Technical details of Lambda@Edge include the following:

    - Lambda@Edge functions are written in JavaScript using the Node.js runtime.

    - Lambda@Edge can be triggered in response to four different types of CloudFront events: viewer request, viewer response, origin request, and origin response.

    - Lambda@Edge is executed at the edge location, which provides faster response times.

    - Lambda@Edge executed in the context of a specific CloudFront distribution can access information about request and response details, such as request headers and cookies.

Stateful Versus Stateless Application Design

Before the popularity of the public cloud, the application stack was stored locally on one server that contained application data and the end user accounts. The application also maintained a data store, to store information about each user session. The local server also had local logging services, and middleware required to support and run the application. Application performance was limited by the size and speed of the physical hardware components (CPU, RAM, and hard drive). This design of the application stack was *stateful*—all required application components are running on one server in the customer's local data center.

A stateless application design utilizes a software architecture where the application does not maintain information about user accounts or sessions.

When older applications are moved to the cloud, migration tools lift and shift on-premises applications currently running on local servers to AWS. An application server rehosted at AWS will have local dependencies replaced with cloud services, as illustrated in Figure 6-2. Due to the application integration cloud services available at AWS, stateful features are easily replicated in the cloud using highly available cloud services.

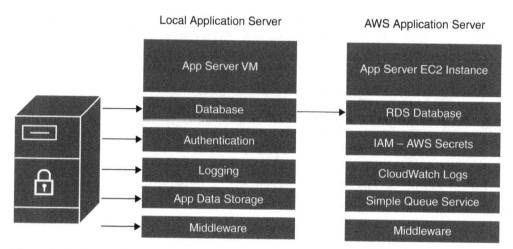

Figure 6-2   Locally Hosted Application Server Versus AWS Hosted Server

When a URL is clicked for an application hosted at AWS, end-user requests are typically sent to a load balancer and onto a targeted web or application server, as illustrated in Figure 6-3. At AWS, the load balancer service (Elastic Load Balancing) is part of a massive regional server farm composed of thousands of load balancers. If one load balancer instance fails, another one takes its place instantaneously. In addition, a load balancer is deployed to each availability zone. Each associated AWS cloud service provides resiliency, durability, failover, performance, and high availability to each hosted workload design. There are several advantages to using a stateless design for your application:

- **Scalability:** Because stateless web and application servers do not maintain user, session, or application data state, they can be easily scaled horizontally by simply adding more instances to handle additional traffic.

- **Fault tolerance:** Stateless workloads can continue to operate even if an individual instance fails. This can help improve the overall reliability and availability of the application.

- **Flexibility:** Stateless applications that don't maintain user and application state information can be deployed on any number of servers.

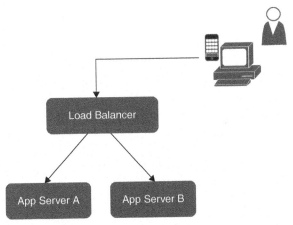

Figure 6-3 Adding a Load Balancer Adds High Availability to the Workload

Changing User State Location

A server that stores user session information is defined as *stateful*, because of the single location for storing the two data states—application data and user session data.

A properly designed workload hosted at AWS uses cloud services to store both the user and application data records as ***stateless*** data in separate highly available and resilient locations:

- The user authentication credentials could be stored in an AWS Identity and Access Management (IAM) database, AWS Managed Active Directory AD, or using the IAM Identity Center or Amazon Cognito. User account authentication information is stateful—credentials remain the same until changed by the end user.

- The application state (orders and requests, for example) is stored in a messaging queue, such as Amazon Simple Queue Service (SQS), discussed later in this chapter.

- The application data is stored in a database solution, with a primary and standby database design such as Amazon RDS or Amazon DynamoDB.

- User session information can be stored redundantly and durably in an Amazon ElastiCache for Memcached or Amazon ElastiCache for Redis in-memory key-value store.

Reviewing the communication, when ordering from Amazon.com, the essential data generated is a combination of stateful and stateless data (see Table 6-2). Stateless data is retained only as long as it is required; for example, for the duration of the authenticated user session, listening to online music, or playing online games. A typical online ordering process requires the following data:

- **Stateful data:** Data includes user account information, purchases, history, refunds, games played, high scores, music listened to, or music downloaded.

- **Stateless data:** Data includes user session information, such as information on browsing for products, browsing for games, reviewing account information, or searching for music.

Where does the application workload need to store the data? If data needs to be stored permanently, it should be stored in a database. From time to time, records will be updated and changed, but SQL and NoSQL databases are a persistent data store.

Data stored for a short or a long period of time but not permanently can be defined as stateless. Stateless data is discarded after it has been used; for example, user session information or items in a shopping cart. Review Table 6-2 for the various stateless options that could be used by a SaaS application.

Table 6-2 Workload Data Choices

Type of Data Stored	Stateful or Stateless	AWS Service
User account data	Stateful	AWS Managed Active Directory (AD), Amazon Cognito, IAM Identity Center, IAM users and roles
Session information data	Stateless	Amazon DynamoDB, Amazon ElastiCache for Redis, Amazon ElastiCache for Memcached
Load balancer	Stateless	ELB, sticky sessions, cookies
Database queries	Stateful	Amazon RDS database/read replicas, Amazon DynamoDB and DAX
Application state data	Stateless	Amazon SQS, Amazon MQ
Event notification data	Stateless	Amazon Simple Notification Service (SNS), AWS EventBridge

NOTE   For the AWS Certified Solutions Architect – Associate (SAA-C03) exam, it is important to understand the distinction between stateless and stateful data in the context of stateless and stateful applications and how they are different.

User Session Management

There are two common ways to manage AWS user sessions:

- *Sticky sessions*: When you deploy an application load balancer (ALB), you can enable sticky sessions by changing the default attributes on the target group of registered servers binding a user's session to a specific server. The term *sticky* means that once a user session is started with a specific application server, the session will continue with that application server until the user session has been completed. The drawback of sticky sessions is that if the application server fails, session information is lost. If an application creates its own session cookie, application-based stickiness can be selected. If an application does not generate a session cookie, duration-based stickiness can be selected, generating a load balancer session cookie.

- **Distributed session management:** Another way to address shared data storage for user sessions is to use an in-memory key-value store hosted by Amazon ElastiCache deploying either ElastiCache for Redis or ElastiCache for Memcached caching the user session state. For a simple deployment with no redundancy, you could choose to employ ElastiCache for Memcached, but this solution provides no replication of the in-memory nodes. Figure 6-4 shows the operation of a distributed cache with no built-in replication of the user cache. When an end user communicates with an application, the user session information is stored in an Amazon ElastiCache for Memcached cache. When Server A fails, the user session is continued on Server B because the user session information is stored in ElastiCache for Memcached instead of on an application server. For a redundant *distributed session* solution, you could deploy ElastiCache for Redis, which supports replicating user session information between multiple nodes across multiple availability zones (AZs), adding redundancy and durability to the cached user session information.

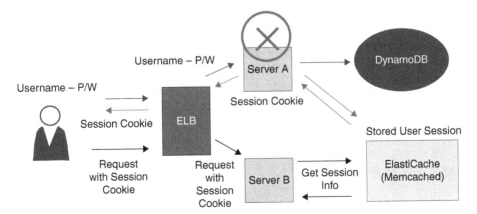

Figure 6-4   An ElastiCache for Redis Distributed User Session Cache

NOTE   The terms *stateless* and *stateful* have slightly different meanings when discussing network components such as security groups compared to network access control lists (NACLs). A security group is a firewall that controls each EC2 instance's incoming network traffic. Inbound rules control the incoming traffic, and outbound rules control the outgoing traffic. Any traffic allowed in by a security group is allowed back out. Security groups remember the incoming and outgoing network traffic flow state; they are stateful. In contrast, a NACL operates with a stateless mindset. An NACL is a subnet firewall that either allows or denies incoming and outgoing requests at the subnet level. The NACL decision-making process about what traffic is allowed in or out is not dependent on what traffic was previously allowed (in or out). Incoming and outgoing traffic decisions are determined solely by the independent inbound and outbound allow and deny rules.

Container Orchestration

Orchestration of container workloads at AWS can be carried out by an ever-increasing number of orchestration options, including Amazon Elastic Container Service (ECS) and the Amazon Elastic Kubernetes Service (EKS) control and data plane open-source deployments.

- **Amazon EKS:** Kubernetes control and data plane instances are located across three AZs, ensuring high availability. Amazon EKS can detect and replace unhealthy control plane instances.

- **Amazon ECS:** Docker containers are deployed across multiple AZs within an AWS region.

- **AWS Fargate:** Provision and manage containerized applications that are hosted on either Docker or Kubernetes deployments.

Other options for deploying and managing containerized workloads at AWS include AWS Copilot, AWS App Runner, AWS Lightsail, AWS App2Container (A2C), and AWS Elastic Beanstalk, as outlined in Table 6-3.

Table 6-3 Orchestration Options at AWS

	AWS Service	**Use Case**	**Details**
Container Orchestration	Amazon ECS	Docker applications or micro-services	Hybrid deployments and scale
	Amazon EKS	Manage Kubernetes container deployments (applications or micro-services)	Hybrid deployments and scale
Compute Options	Fargate	Manage ECS or EKS deployments	Manage containerized applications, not infrastructure, at AWS
	Amazon EC2 instances	Containers with full control	Bare-metal deployments at AWS, AWS Outposts
Container Tools	AWS Copilot	Manage containerized applications	CLI controlled deployments on ECS and Fargate
	Amazon Elastic Container Registry (ECR)	Storage and deploy containers	AWS hosted repository
	AWS App Mesh	Hybrid application-level networking service mesh	Use with Fargate, EC2, ECS, EKS, Kubernetes, AWS Outposts
	AWS Cloud Map	AWS cloud resource discovery service	Register AWS application resource services (databases, queues, microservices) with custom names; resource health is checked to ensure the location is up to date
	AWS Lambda	Integrate with many AWS services with custom functions	Package Lambda functions as container applications
	AWS App Runner	Run containerized web apps at AWS	Infrastructure and container orchestration is fully hidden
	Amazon ECS Anywhere	Run containers on customer-managed hardware	AWS supported hybrid deployments
	Amazon EKS Anywhere	Operate Kubernetes clusters on customer hardware	AWS supported hybrid deployments
	AWS Proton	Self-service portal for platform team infrastructure deployment tool templates	Deploy existing infrastructure-as-code tools using CloudFormation or Terraform
	Amazon Elastic Beanstalk	Deploy the app and AWS infrastructure	EC2 instances or Docker containers

Migrating Applications to Containers

AWS App2 Container (A2C) transforms existing applications running on-premises VMs or EC2 instances into containers. Applications supported include

- ASP.NET web apps running on Windows

- Java applications running on Linux JBoss and Apache Tomcat

A2C can create the containers using the following AWS services:

- ECS task definitions and Kubernetes deployment YAML files for integration with Amazon Elastic Container Registry, Elastic Container Service, and Elastic Kubernetes Service.

- CloudFormation templates to configure the required compute, network, and security infrastructure for the deployed containerized applications.

- Continuous integration/continuous delivery (CI/CD) pipelines for Amazon CodeBuild and CodeDeploy for building and deploying container builds.

Resilient Storage Options

The default for all AWS storage services is built on failover and resiliency. Additional storage resiliency can be created using the respective features of each storage service or the AWS utilities listed in Table 6-4.

Table 6-4   Resilient Storage Options

Storage Service	Resiliency	Additional Resiliency
Amazon EBS	Stored within AZ	EBS volumes copied across regions (AWS DataSync)
		Snapshots copied across regions (Amazon Data Lifecycle Manager)
		Multi-attach EBS volumes (io1)
Amazon EFS	Multi-AZ deployment Sync data across region/ on-prem; back up with AWS Backup	Transfer across AWS storage services (AWS DataSync), AWS Backup
Amazon FSx for Windows File Server	Multi-AZ deployment	AWS DataSync, AWS Backup
Amazon RDS	Single AZ	Multi-AZ, cluster (three AZs), read replicas

Storage Service	Resiliency	Additional Resiliency
Amazon Aurora	Six copies across three AZs	Global Database, read replicas
Amazon DynamoDB	Six copies across three AZs	Global Tables, DynamoDB Accelerator (DAX)
Amazon S3	Across three AZs minimum	Single-region replication, cross-region replication
Amazon Kinesis Data Streams	Multi-AZ	S3 storage
Amazon Kinesis Data Firehose	S3, Amazon Redshift	Analyze using Athena, EMR, and Redshift Spectrum
Amazon Redshift	Multi-AZ	Continual backup to S3
Amazon SQS	Multi-AZ, 1 minute to 14 days retention of messages	Dead letter queue, backup to S3 using Lambda function
Amazon SNS	Multi-AZ, push notifications	DynamoDB

Application Integration Services

The sections that follow cover the following application integration services:

- Amazon SNS

- Amazon SQS

- AWS Step Functions

- Amazon EventBridge

For the AWS Certified Solutions Architect – Associate (SAA-C03) exam, you need to understand the concepts of AWS application integration services (see Figure 6-5) that store stateless data for workloads.

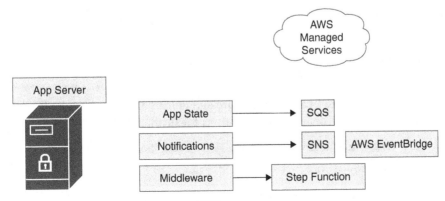

Figure 6-5   Data Store Options at AWS

Amazon Simple Notification Service

Amazon Simple Notification Service (SNS) enables applications, end users, and devices to send, store, and receive notifications from different applications, services, and servers. SNS has four main integrated components:

- **Publishers,** applications, or AWS services send messages to access points called topics.

- **Messages** can be application-to-application messaging for the following subscribers: Kinesis Data Firehose delivery streams, Lambda functions, SQS queues, and HTTP/S endpoints.

  Messages can also be application-to-person push notifications for mobile applications, phone numbers, and email addresses.

- **Topics** are the access points to which publishers send messages asynchronously.

- **Clients** subscribe to SNS topics to receive published messages.

Amazon SNS is integrated with Amazon CloudWatch. Utilizing SNS notifications as part of your workload design lets you decouple your application communications and react when changes occur to workloads or associated AWS services; for example, changes in a DynamoDB table being monitored by CloudWatch can trigger an alarm when data values increase or decrease.

SNS messages are redundantly stored across multiple servers in each region. Many AWS cloud services can communicate with SNS topics as a publisher, sending messages and notifications to SNS topics using CloudWatch alarms, Amazon EventBridge, or Amazon Pinpoint.

To receive notifications from Amazon SNS, the appropriate service or end user subscribes to the desired SNS topic. Each SNS topic can have a choice of subscribers, as shown in Figure 6-6, including these subscribers:

- **AWS Lambda:** An SNS notification can be linked to a function to carry out one or more tasks at AWS

- **Amazon SQS:** Queues can notify SNS topics that messages have been delivered

- **Amazon Kinesis Data Firehose:** Capture and upload data into Amazon S3, Amazon Redshift, or Elasticsearch data stores for further analysis

- **HTTP/S endpoints:** Deliver SNS notifications to a specific URL

- **Email:** Email subscribers using push notifications

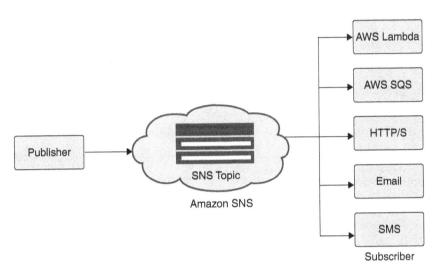

Figure 6-6   SNS Publisher and Subscriber Options

Amazon SNS can be used to send *event notifications* when AWS service failures occur. Event updates and notifications concerning inventory changes or shipment status can also be immediately delivered to subscribers. For example, when you order a product online, many SNS notifications are executed in the background to complete the ordering process:

Step 1.   You order a new set of dishes.

Step 2.   A notification is issued to check for stock.

Step 3.   After confirmation of inventory, the order is placed against your account.

Step 4.   Your credit card information is checked.

Step 5.   Taxes and relevant fees are added to the order.

Step 6.   Shipping is calculated.

Step 7.   An email is sent to your email account or device, thanking you for the order.

To use Amazon SNS, first create a topic and then associate the topic to a specific event type. Figure 6-7 illustrates the creation of a standard notification topic.

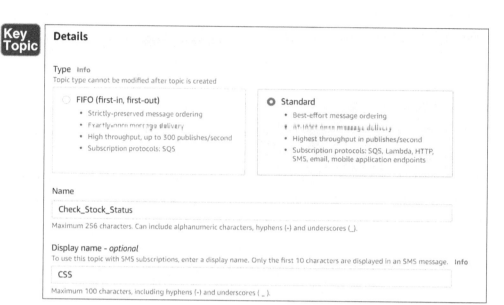

Figure 6-7   Creating a Notification Topic

Amazon SNS Cheat Sheet

For the AWS Certified Solutions Architect – Associate (SAA-C03) exam, you need to understand the following critical aspects of SNS:

- Amazon SNS provides push-based deliveries of messages.

- Messages are application-to-application or application-to-person.

- Application-to-application message delivery choices are HTTP/HTTPS via email, SQS queue endpoints, Kinesis Data Firehose, and AWS Lambda.

- Application-to-person message delivery choices are SMS, email, and push notifications.

- JSON is the supported data type for messages.

- Amazon SNS messages are stored redundantly across multiple AZs.

Amazon Simple Queue Service

Amazon Simple Queue Service (SQS) is a fully managed message queue that allows developers to decouple communications between distributed workload components such as applications and microservices. Amazon SQS allows messages to be sent, stored, and received between applications and cloud services. Use cases include system-to-system messaging and request offloading. Messages can be stored and retrieved at any volume.

In Amazon SQS, a *message* is a discrete unit of data stored in SQS queues. SQS provides different options for sending and receiving messages, including the ability to send and receive messages in batches, to specify the order in which messages are processed, and set the visibility timeout for them. SQS also supports the following features:

- Messages can be stored in SQS queues for up to 14 days; the default is 4 days.

- SQS messages can contain up to 256 KB of XML, JSON, and unformatted text.

- Messages larger than 256 KB can be sent to S3 buckets using the SQS Extended Client Library for Java.

- Applications can push messages into an SQS message queue, triggering a Lambda function that retrieves and stores the message into a storage service such as Amazon S3 or Amazon DynamoDB (see Figure 6-8).

- SQS queues can be used with applications hosted on EC2 instances and Elastic Container Services.

- All SQS message queues and messages are stored in a single AWS region across multiple AZs providing redundancy and failover.

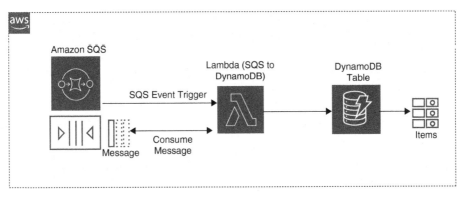

Figure 6-8   SQS and Triggered Lambda Function

SQS Components

Sender programs (SQS-configured applications) send messages into a queue, and *receiver programs* (SQS-configured applications or services) retrieve messages from the queue for processing; each stateless program runs independently without any knowledge of each other. SQS messages are stored in SQS queues until they are processed by a receiving application or service. The SQS API enables developers to interact with SQS queues and messages using various programming languages and tools. The API provides a set of operations that can be used to send, receive, and manage messages and queues. There are several main SQS components:

- **Standard queues:** This default queue type has the best-effort ordering of messages, and messages are delivered at least once. The order in which messages are received from a standard queue is not guaranteed to be the same as the order in which they were sent. Standard queues are suitable for a wide range of use cases, such as sending notifications, storing application state, or processing workloads in parallel. Standard queues are more cost-effective than FIFI queues.

- **FIFO (first-in, first-out) queues:** This queue type preserves the order in which messages are sent and received, and each message is delivered exactly once. FIFO queues should be used when the order of operations and events is important. Duplicate messages are not stored in a FIFO queue; instead, messages are grouped into distinct ordered bundles tagged with a message group ID. Messages are stored in the order in which they arrive and processed in order. FIFO queues are designed for use cases where message ordering and deduplication are important, such as financial transactions or communication between microservices. FIFO queues support a limited number of transactions per second and have higher costs compared to standard queues.

- **Message polling:** Applications can receive messages from an SQS queue using either the default short polling method or the long polling method. Communicating using a short polling method may return empty message responses. Long polling can help reduce the number of empty received message responses by allowing Amazon SQS to wait until messages are available in the queue before notifying a receiver program; the default polling wait time is 20 seconds for long polling.

- **Dead-letter queue (DLQ):** Messages can be stored in the optional dead-letter queue after the maximum number of processing attempts have completed successfully. Alarms linked to SNS notifications can be configured for any messages delivered to a DLQ. Messages can be moved from the DLQ back to the source queue for reprocessing.

- **Visibility timeout:** During the processing of each message, there is a period of time where a message being processed is not visible (see Figure 6-9). Once a message is successfully processed, a deletion request removes the processed message from the message queue.

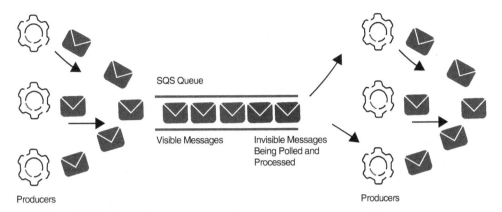

Figure 6-9 Visibility Timeouts

Amazon SQS can be used with the following AWS services:

- **Amazon DynamoDB:** You can use SQS to transfer messages to DynamoDB by using a Lambda function.

- **EC2 instances:** You can scale an Auto Scaling group out or in when messages in the SQS queue increase.

- **Amazon ECS:** Worker tasks within a container execute a script that polls for SQS messages and processes them as necessary.

- **Amazon RDS:** A lightweight daemon connects to an SQS queue and delivers messages to a SQL database.

- **AWS Lambda function:** SQS queues can be configured to trigger a Lambda function.

NOTE Amazon MQ supports several different messaging protocols, including JMS, NMS, and MQTT, and can be used to integrate different applications, services, and systems without having to rewrite the messaging code for migrated applications.

Amazon SQS Cheat Sheet

For the AWS Certified Solutions Architect – Associate (SAA-C03) exam, you need to understand the following critical aspects of SQS:

- SQS uses pull-based polling.

- The visibility timeout is the amount of time a message is unavailable after a message is being processed.

- If a message cannot be processed within the visibility timeout period, the message becomes available in the queue for processing.

- Each message is deleted after it is processed successfully within the visibility timeout period.

- The maximum visibility timeout period is 12 hours.

- Queues can be either standard or FIFO.

- FIFO preserves the exact order in which messages are sent and received.

- The maximum size of SQS messages is 256 KB.

- Queues can be encrypted with server-side encryption (SSE) using keys managed by AWS Key Management Service (KMS).

- Notifications can be published to an SNS topic with multiple subscribers to SQS queues from different AWS accounts.

AWS Step Functions

Step Functions provides a way to model and automate complex, multi-step processes and applications using a graphical workflow editor. AWS Step Functions is based on the concepts of tasks and state machines, and can track, monitor, and manage the execution of workflows. AWS Step Functions integrates with many other AWS services, including Amazon EC2, Amazon ECS, AWS Lambda, Amazon SQS, and Amazon SNS, and can be used to build scalable, reliable, and efficient applications and microservices. Step Functions enables you to orchestrate numerous Lambda functions and multiple AWS services into a serverless application process. Developers can create a *state machine* with multiple states. Each workflow has checkpoints that maintain each workflow throughout each defined stage. The output of each stage in the workflow is the starting point of the next stage. Defined steps within each state function execute in the precise order defined by the logic. At each stage, decisions are made based on the supplied input parameters, actions are performed, and the output is passed to the next stage, as shown in Figure 6-10.

AWS Step Functions has built-in application-level controls, including try/catch and retry and rollback capabilities, to help automatically deal with errors and exceptions. The following workflows are possible to design with AWS Step Functions:

- Consolidating data from multiple databases into a unified report

- Fulfilling orders or tracking inventory processes

- Implementing a user registration process

- Implementing a custom workflow

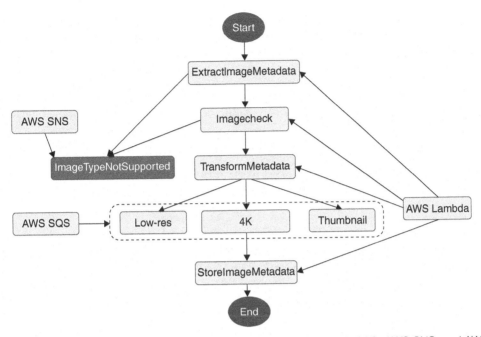

Figure 6-10 Step Function Logic: Create a Workflow Using AWS SQS, AWS SNS, and AWS Lambda

Activity and Service tasks can be used with state machine step functions:

- **Activity tasks:** Allow you to assign a specific step in your defined workflow to external software code. The external function polls the function associated with any required work requests; when required, it performs its work and returns the results. The activity task can run on any application that can make an HTTP connection from its location, such as an EC2 instance hosted at AWS, a mobile device, or an on-premises server.

- **Service tasks:** Allow you to connect steps in your defined workflow to a supported AWS service. In contrast to an activity task, a service task pushes requests to other AWS services; the service performs its action, reports to the workflow once the action is completed, and moves to the next step. Examples of service tasks include the following:

  - Running an Amazon ECS or Fargate task hosted in a VPC
  - Submitting an AWS Batch job and waiting for completion
  - Retrieving or placing a new item into an Amazon DynamoDB table

Step Functions integrate SNS notifications and SQS queues within a logical processing framework. The building blocks of Step Functions automate the relationship between SNS and SQS. SNS notifications can report when your workflow has completed. Workflow failure could trigger additional communications to developers indicating the problem and relevant error messages.

AWS Step Functions state machines are defined using JSON as the declarative language. You can create activity tasks by using any AWS SDK that supports code written in Node.js, Python, Go, or C#. There are two choices for creating workflows:

- **Express workflows:** Use express workflows for workloads with high event rates of more than 100,000 per second and short durations of less than 5 minutes.

- **Standard workflows:** Use standard workflows for long-running, durable, and auditable workflows, such as machine learning models, generating reports, and the processing of credit cards. Standard workflows guarantee one execution of each workflow step, with a maximum duration of 1 year. Developers can inspect a processed workflow during and after the workflow execution has been completed.

Table 6-5 compares the functions and use cases of SNS, SQS, and Step Functions.

Table 6-5   SNS, SQS, and Step Functions

Service	Function	Use Case
SNS	Sending notifications	Alert when services or applications have issues
Step Functions	Creating AWS service processing workflow	Visual workflow
SQS	Messaging queue	Decouple applications from application state

Amazon EventBridge

Another AWS service that can react to changes in AWS services, AWS applications, or SaaS applications is Amazon EventBridge. The selected source event can be linked in real time to an AWS target, such as AWS Lambda, Simple Notification Service, and Kinesis Data Firehose (see Figure 6-11). EventBridge automatically ingests, filters, and sends each event to the selected target. Each event includes the source of the event, the timestamp, and the AWS region. Events can be filtered by creating rules that match an incoming event to an event bus, routing the event to a specific target for processing. EventBridge rules can customize events before they are delivered to a target by adding a custom response.

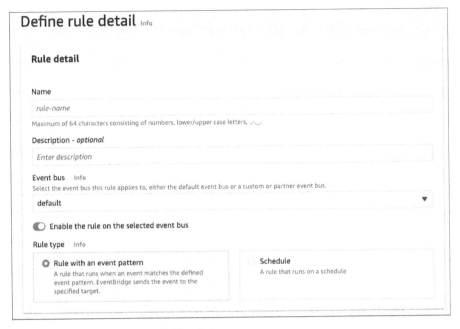

Figure 6-11   Amazon EventBridge Setup

CloudWatch rules and events have been spun off into Amazon EventBridge. Both Amazon EventBridge and Amazon CloudWatch use the same API and CloudWatch service infrastructure. However, Amazon EventBridge is recommended for ingesting data from SaaS applications due to Amazon EventBridge and the built-in SaaS integration with many popular SaaS applications.

Features of Amazon EventBridge include

- **Global endpoints:** Destinations for an Amazon EventBridge events can be replicated across primary and secondary regions for multi-region deployments.

- **API destinations:** Events can also be sent to on-premises SaaS applications for controlling application throughput and authentication.

- **Replay events:** Reprocess past events for analyzing application errors that have been fixed.

- **SaaS integration:** AWS EventBridge responds to events generated by well-known SaaS applications, including Shopify, Salesforce, SignalFx, and Zendesk (see Figure 6-12).

- **Event filtering:** Rules can match incoming events and route them to a specific target or AWS service for processing.

- **Targets:** Targets can be a single or multiple AWS accounts.

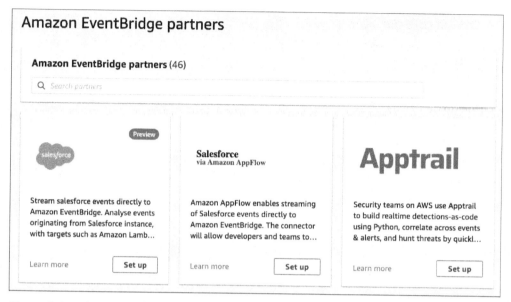

Figure 6-12   SaaS Integration with EventBridge

Amazon API Gateway

API Gateway is a service that makes it easy for developers to create, publish, maintain, and secure APIs that enable applications to access data and business logic from various AWS services, as well as from external sources. API Gateway provides features such as authentication and authorization, rate limiting, and caching, to help ensure that APIs are secure and scalable. It also provides tools for monitoring and analyzing API usage and performance. For a mobile application hosted on a smartphone, the backend API or APIs for the application could be hosted at API Gateway. An ***application programming interface (API)*** is a set of rules and protocols for building software applications. Let's expand the definition of API a bit more:

- The *A*, for *application*, could be a custom function, the entire app, or something in between.

- The *P* is related to the type of *programming* language or platform that created the API.

- The *I* is for *interface*, and API Gateway interfaces with HTTP/REST APIs and/or WebSocket APIs. Java API types can direct HTTP requests across the private AWS network. Hosted APIs are exposed publicly using HTTPS endpoints.

APIs are commonly made available by third-party companies for use with mobile and web applications. One example is the API for Google Maps. When you book a hotel room using a mobile app, the app is likely using the Google API to call Google Maps with a location request. APIs can be thought of as software plug-ins that allow integration from one system to another. The Google API is the public frontend that communicates with the backend Google Maps application.

NOTE   For an older example, think of an EXE file, which is matched up with a library of DLLs. The library file contains a number of functions that, if called by the EXE file, would execute to carry out a task. If the EXE were a word processor like Word.exe, the associated DLLs would contain the code for calling the spell check routine or other features.

If you're programming applications to be hosted at AWS, you should consider hosting your applications' APIs using Amazon API Gateway. Think of API Gateway as the front door that, with authentication, allows entry to the AWS cloud where the selected AWS service resides. Several methods are available for communicating with API Gateway, including public communications through an edge location via Amazon CloudFront, a *regional endpoint* from a specific AWS region, or from a service or micro-service running on an EC2 instance hosted in a VPC using a private interface endpoint for communicating with the API Gateway service (see Figure 6-13).

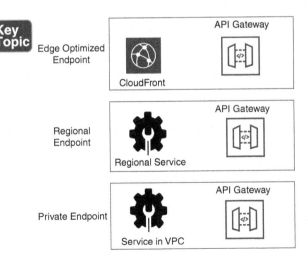

Figure 6-13   API Gateway Communication Options

API Gateway supports HTTP, REST, and WebSocket APIs (see Figure 6-14).

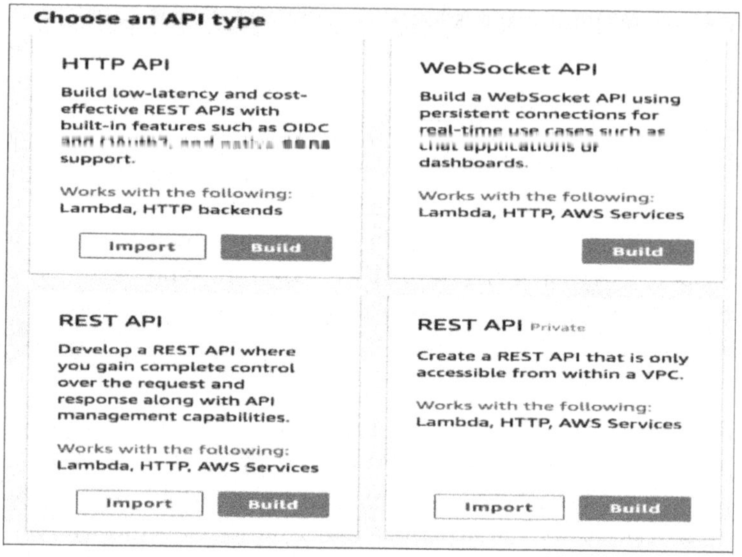

Choose an API type

HTTP API

Build low-latency and cost-effective REST APIs with built-in features such as OIDC and OAuth2, and native CORS support.

Works with the following:
Lambda, HTTP backends

Import   Build

WebSocket API

Build a WebSocket API using persistent connections for real-time use cases such as chat applications or dashboards.

Works with the following:
Lambda, HTTP, AWS Services

Build

REST API

Develop a REST API where you gain complete control over the request and response along with API management capabilities.

Works with the following:
Lambda, HTTP, AWS Services

Import   Build

REST API Private

Create a REST API that is only accessible from within a VPC.

Works with the following:
Lambda, HTTP, AWS Services

Import   Build

Figure 6-14 Choosing the API Protocol to Use

NOTE APIs hosted at API Gateway can also call custom AWS Lambda functions, EC2 instances in your AWS account, and HTTP endpoints that access Elastic Beanstalk deployments.

Amazon API Gateway has the following features:

- **Security:** API Gateway supports AWS IAM and Amazon Cognito for authorizing API access.

- **Traffic throttling:** It is possible to cache API responses for incoming requests; cached responses can be answered for an API call with the same query. The number of requests each API can receive can be defined, with usage plans defining an API's allowed level of traffic.

- **Multi-version support:** Multiple API versions can be hosted by API Gateway.

- **Metering:** Metering allows you to throttle and control desired access levels to a hosted API.

- **Authorized access:** When an AWS API is called, API Gateway checks whether authentication is required before the task that the API has requested is carried out. Authentication options are an AWS Lambda authorizer or

Amazon Cognito user pool (see Figure 6-15). API Gateway calls the selected authorizer, passing the incoming authorization token for verification. An Amazon Cognito user pool can be configured for authenticating the mobile application using various methods, including single sign-on (SSO), OAuth, or an email address to access the backend application components.

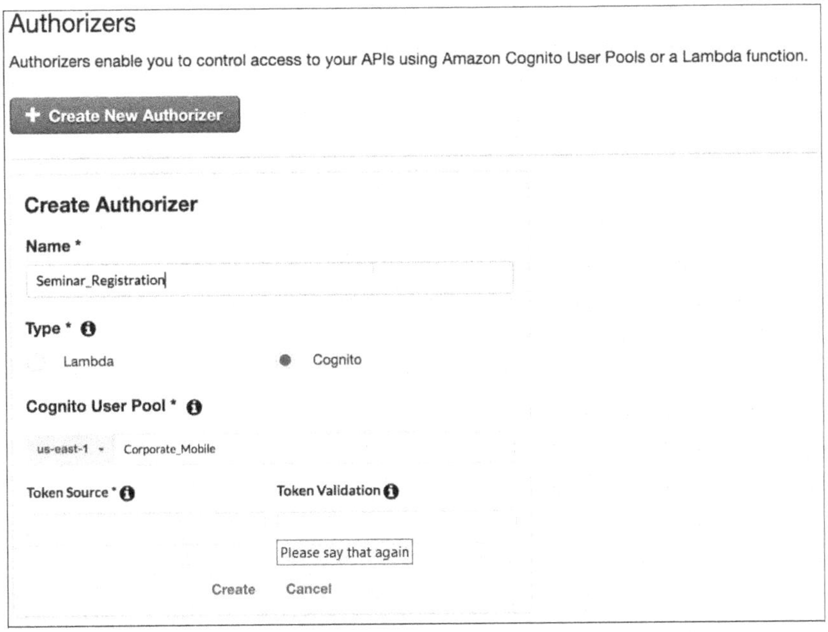

Authorizers

Authorizers enable you to control access to your APIs using Amazon Cognito User Pools or a Lambda function.

+ Create New Authorizer

Create Authorizer

Name *

Seminar_Registration

Type * ⓘ

    Lambda   ⬤ Cognito

Cognito User Pool * ⓘ

us-east-1 ▾   Corporate_Mobile

Token Source * ⓘ   **Token Validation** ⓘ

              Please say that again

      Create   Cancel

Figure 6-15 Selecting an Authorizer for the API Gateway

NOTE API Gateway can use client-side SSL certificates to verify that all requests made to your backend resources were sent by API Gateway.

API Gateway Cheat Sheet

For the AWS Certified Solutions Architect – Associate (SAA-C03) exam, you need to understand the following critical aspects of APIs:

- With API Gateway, developers can publish, maintain, and secure APIs at any scale.
- API Gateway can process hundreds of thousands of concurrent API calls.
- API Gateway works together with Lambda to create application-facing serverless infrastructure.

- Amazon CloudFront distributions can be used as a public endpoint for API Gateway requests.

- Edge-optimized APIs can be used for clients in different geographic locations. API requests are routed to the closest edge location.

- Regional API endpoints can be used by clients located in the same AWS region.

- Private API endpoints can be accessed from a VPC using an interface VPC endpoint.

- API Gateway can scale to any traffic level required.

- API Gateway logs track performance metrics for the backend, including API calls, latency, and error rates.

- API Gateway only charges when your hosted APIs are called. Charges are based on the amount of data that is transferred outbound.

- API requests can be throttled to prevent overloading your backend services.

Building a Serverless Web App

AWS Lambda and Amazon API Gateway can be used together to create a serverless application, such as an event website that allows users to register for a corporate function. For example, a simple web-based interface could allow users to register for a corporate function after registering as an attendee. Figure 6-16 illustrates this scenario, and the following sections describe the development process in more detail.

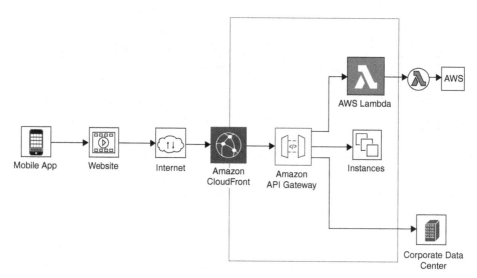

Figure 6-16   A Serverless Corporate Application

Step 1: Create a Static Website

The first step in building the serverless web app just described is to create a website that can be hosted in an Amazon S3 bucket (see Figure 6-17). Because the website will be hosted in an S3 bucket, it must be a static website with no dynamic assets. After you configure the S3 bucket for website hosting, all the HTML, Cascading Style Sheets (CSS), images, and web server files can be uploaded and stored.

Step 2: User Authentication

Create an Amazon Cognito user pool for the users registering for the conference (see Figure 6-18). Configure Cognito to send users who register on the conference website a standard confirmation email, including a verification code to confirm their identity. The corporate users will use their corporate email addresses to register as new users on the website.

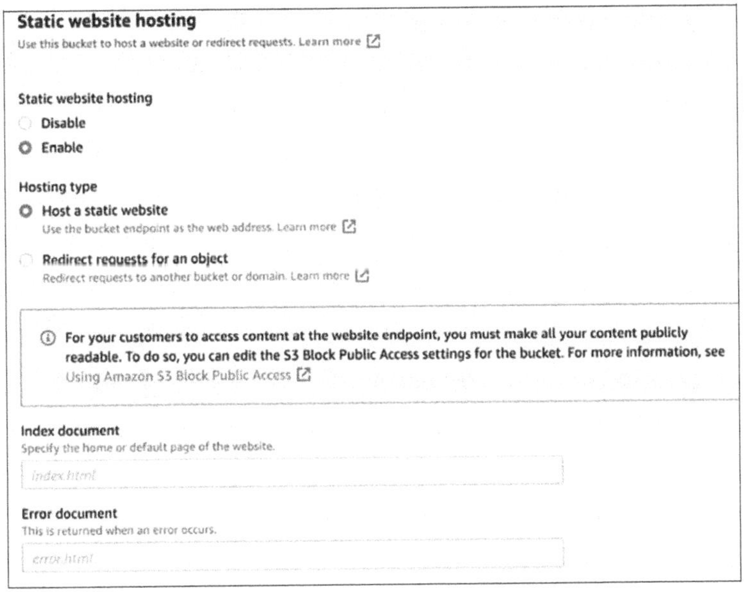

Figure 6-17   Using an S3 Bucket for Static Website Hosting

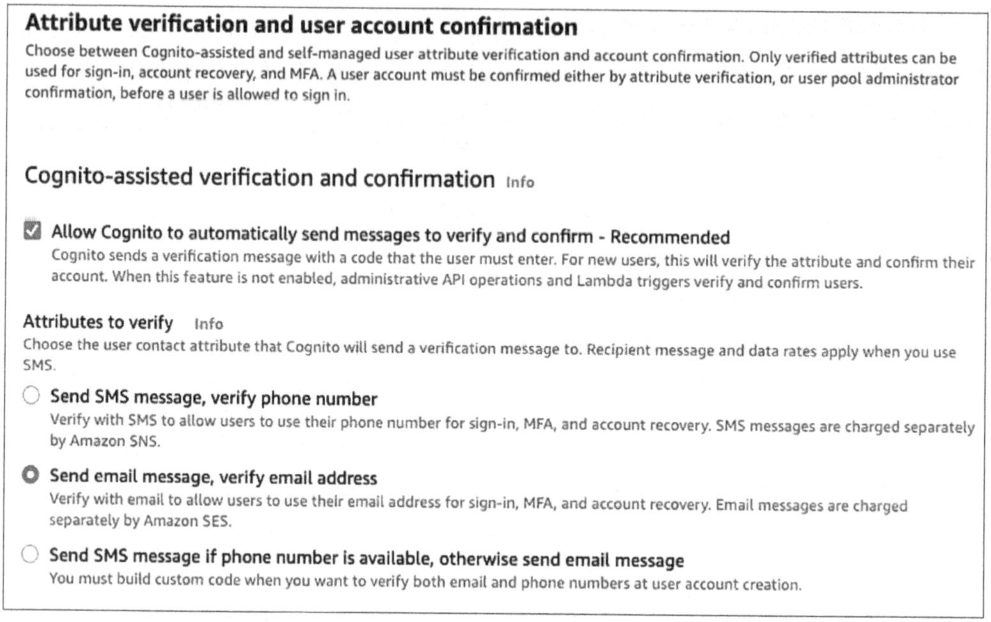

Attribute verification and user account confirmation

Choose between Cognito-assisted and self-managed user attribute verification and account confirmation. Only verified attributes can be used for sign-in, account recovery, and MFA. A user account must be confirmed either by attribute verification, or user pool administrator confirmation, before a user is allowed to sign in.

Cognito-assisted verification and confirmation Info

☑ **Allow Cognito to automatically send messages to verify and confirm - Recommended**
Cognito sends a verification message with a code that the user must enter. For new users, this will verify the attribute and confirm their account. When this feature is not enabled, administrative API operations and Lambda triggers verify and confirm users.

Attributes to verify Info
Choose the user contact attribute that Cognito will send a verification message to. Recipient message and data rates apply when you use SMS.

○ **Send SMS message, verify phone number**
Verify with SMS to allow users to use their phone number for sign-in, MFA, and account recovery. SMS messages are charged separately by Amazon SNS.

◉ **Send email message, verify email address**
Verify with email to allow users to use their email address for sign-in, MFA, and account recovery. Email messages are charged separately by Amazon SES.

○ **Send SMS message if phone number is available, otherwise send email message**
You must build custom code when you want to verify both email and phone numbers at user account creation.

Figure 6-18 Creating an Authentication Pool Using Cognito

After the users have successfully signed in to the website, a JavaScript function communicates with Cognito, authenticating them using the Secure Remote Password (SRP) protocol and returning a web token that will be used to identify users as they request access to the conference.

Step 3: Create the Serverless Backend Components

Create the Lambda function that registers users to the conference and sends them their attendance code. All registration requests are stored in a DynamoDB table (see Figure 6-19).

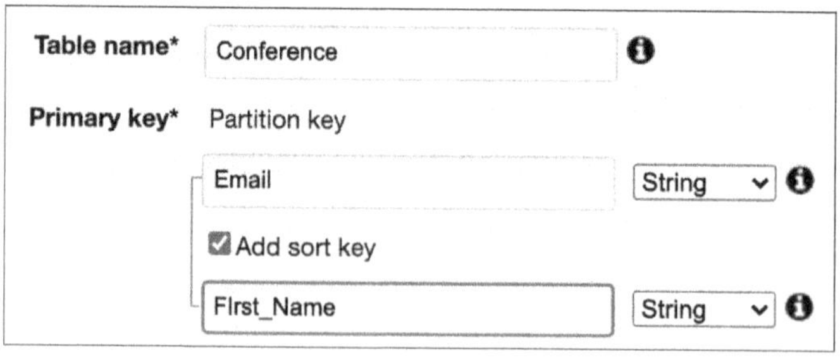

Table name* [Conference] ⓘ

Primary key* Partition key

[Email] [String ∨] ⓘ

☑ Add sort key

[First_Name] [String ∨] ⓘ

Figure 6-19 Creating a DynamoDB Table

Step 4: Set Up the API Gateway

The hosted API allows registered users to register for the conference. Registered users have already been approved through registration and verification by being a member of the Cognito user pool. Each registration request invokes the Lambda function, which is securely called from the user's browser to carry out the registration as a RESTful API call to API Gateway (see Figure 6-20).

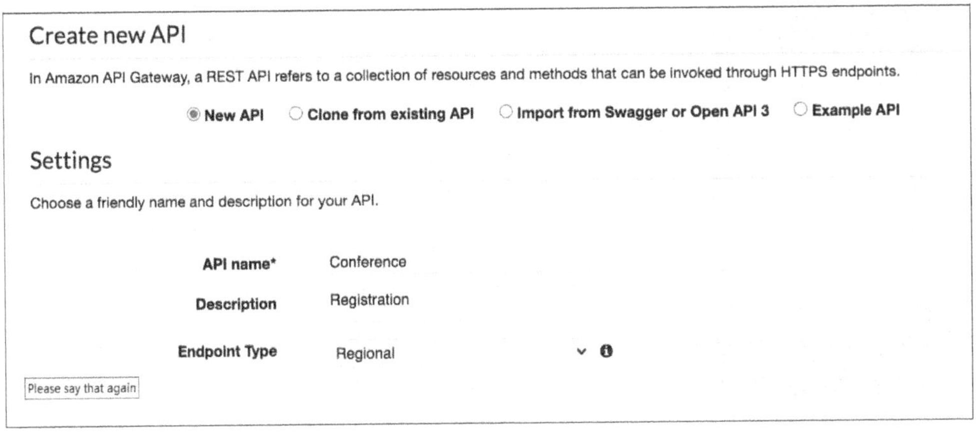

Create new API

In Amazon API Gateway, a REST API refers to a collection of resources and methods that can be invoked through HTTPS endpoints.

◉ **New API**   ○ **Clone from existing API**   ○ **Import from Swagger or Open API 3**   ○ **Example API**

Settings

Choose a friendly name and description for your API.

API name*	Conference
Description	Registration
Endpoint Type	Regional ⌄ ❶

Please say that again

Figure 6-20   Registering the RESTful API with the API Gateway

Representational State Transfer (REST) is a key authentication component of the AWS cloud, and RESTful APIs are the most common AWS API format. JavaScript runs in the background on user devices communicating with the publicly exposed API hosted by API Gateway carrying out each RESTful request. REST uses the following HTTP verbs to describe the type of each request:

- **GET:** Request a record

- **PUT:** Update a record

- **POST:** Create a record

- **DELETE:** Delete a record

A user who types a URL into a browser sends a **GET** request. Submitting a request for the conference is a **POST** request.

RESTful communication is stateless, meaning that all the information needed to process a RESTful request is self-contained within the actual request; the server doesn't need additional information to process each request. The beauty of this design is that only Lambda is required to host the required functions for the application's logic and the application request that the user carries out.

Step 5: Register for the Conference

The user sees none of the infrastructures described to this point; instead, they use the user interface to register for the conference, shown in Figure 6-21.

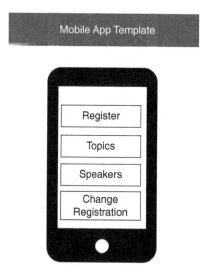

Mobile App Template

Register

Topics

Speakers

Change Registration

Figure 6-21   The Mobile Application on the User's Phone

Automating AWS Infrastructure

Automating infrastructure refers to the use of tools and processes to manage and provision the underlying hardware and software infrastructure of an organization in a repeatable and efficient manner. This can include tasks such as provisioning and configuring servers, storage, and networking resources, deploying and updating applications and services, and managing and scaling infrastructure based on demand. Automating infrastructure can help organizations save time and reduce the potential for errors, and it enables them to quickly and easily deploy new services and applications. Various tools and technologies are available for automating infrastructure, including infrastructure as code (IaC) tools, configuration management tools, and orchestration and deployment tools.

The one characteristic of AWS that stands above all others is the level of integrated automation used to deploy, manage, and recover AWS services. There is not a single AWS service offered that is not heavily automated for deployment and in its overall operation and management. When you order a virtual private network (VPN), it's created and available in seconds. If you order an Elastic Compute Cloud (EC2) instance through the AWS Management Console or the AWS command-line interface (CLI) tools, it's created and available in minutes. Automated processes provide the just-in-time response you want when you order cloud services.

AWS services are being changed, enhanced, and updated 24/7, with features and changes appearing daily. The AWS cloud is deployed and maintained using a combination of developer agility and automated processes.

AWS wasn't always so automated and controlled. In the early days, Amazon was a burgeoning online e-commerce bookseller. In 2006, organizations could order a virtual machine from a cloud provider and wait several days for an email that the requested service was ready to go. Over time, Amazon developed rules for developers and the development process at AWS. One of the most important rules developers follow is this: "Each underlying service that supported the Amazon store must be managed using a core set of shared APIs available to all developers built and maintained on the common core of AWS compute and storage resources."

Amazon developers built and continue to build its hosting environment using mandated internal processes, which can be described as a mixture of the following:

- **ITIL:** Information Technology Infrastructure Library (ITIL) is a framework of best practices for delivering IT services.

- **Scrum:** Scrum is a framework in which a development team works together to manage product development.

- **Agile:** Agile is a software development cycle in which developers plan, design, develop, test, and evaluate as a team with open communications.

- **DevOps:** DevOps is a continuation of the Agile framework that features full collaboration among the development and operations teams.

Many AWS developers work together effectively, making hundreds of changes to the AWS cloud every minute. In addition, all AWS services are being monitored, scaled, rebuilt, and logged through completely automated processes and services available to all organizations. Amazon avoids manual processes, and your long-term goal should be for your company to do the same.

Automation services will always manage your resources more effectively than you can manually. When resources are created using the AWS Management Console or the AWS CLI, the background automated processes finish the deployment and management of all AWS cloud resources.

There are several powerful tools in the AWS toolbox that can help you automate procedures:

- **AWS CloudFormation:** AWS CloudFormation enables developers to create, manage, and deploy infrastructure in the AWS cloud.

- **AWS Service Catalog:** AWS Service Catalog enables organizations to create, manage, and distribute a catalog of IT services that are approved for use on AWS built by CloudFormation templates.

- **AWS Elastic Beanstalk:** AWS Elastic Beanstalk enables developers to upload their application code and Elastic Beanstalk will automatically handle the deployment, scaling, and management of the underlying infrastructure.

AWS CloudFormation

Looking under the hood at any cloud service running at AWS, you'll find the deployment process largely driven by *JavaScript Object Notation (JSON)* scripts and AWS CloudFormation. AWS's extensive use of JSON is similar to Microsoft Azure's use of PowerShell. At AWS, JSON scripts are used internally for many tasks and processes; creating security policy with AWS IAM and working with AWS Cloud-Formation are two common examples.

AWS CloudFormation is an AWS-hosted orchestration engine that works with JSON and YAML templates to deploy AWS resources on demand and on predefined triggers (see Figure 6-22). AWS uses CloudFormation extensively, and AWS uses CloudFormation to manage the deployment of just about everything, including infrastructure workload deployments and updates. Each CloudFormation template declares the infrastructure stack to be created, and the CloudFormation engine automatically deploys and links the needed resources together as described. Control variables can be added to each CloudFormation template to manage and control the precise order of the installation of resources. If mistakes are found in a CloudFormation script during deployment, all changes that have been carried out will be rolled back and reversed.

Step 1 **Specify template**	**Create stack**
Step 2 Specify stack details	**Prerequisite - Prepare template**
Step 3 Configure stack options	Prepare template Every stack is based on a template. A template is a JSON or YAML file that contains configuration information about the AWS resources you want to include in the stack. ○ Template is ready ○ Use a sample template ○ Create template in Designer
Step 4 Review	**Specify template** A template is a JSON or YAML file that describes your stack's resources and properties. Template source Selecting a template generates an Amazon S3 URL where it will be stored. ○ Amazon S3 URL ○ Upload a template file

Figure 6-22   The CloudFormation Console

Consider the following differences between the manual AWS deployment process and the automated CloudFormation process:

- **Time spent:** In the past, maintaining manual processes such as building computer systems and stacks provided job security; these days, it's just not prudent to manually deploy production resources. Although every Cloud-Formation script takes time to craft, each CloudFormation deployment takes less time than a manual process; there are no wasted steps, and all steps are in the proper order. Over time, executing an automated process to build EC2 instances will save you hours or even weeks; the CloudFormation process runs in the background, allowing you to do something else. CloudFormation can also perform updates and deletions for existing AWS resources and workloads.

- **Security issues:** Humans make mistakes, and mistakes made during manual changes can introduce huge security issues, particularly where the changes lack oversight. CloudFormation templates can be secured and controlled for usage by specific IAM users and groups. Templates also carry out the same steps every time they are executed, preventing the fat-finger mistakes humans make. CloudFormation automation can also be locked down using a companion service called AWS Service Catalog, discussed later in this chapter, to ensure that only specific IAM users and groups can access and execute specific Cloud-Formation deployment tasks.

- **Documentation:** It is difficult to document manual processes if processes constantly change; CloudFormation templates are readable, and when you get used to the format, they reveal themselves to be self-documenting. When you create a CloudFormation stack, you use a template that defines the collection of AWS resources to deploy. The template includes all the required information; names and settings of the resources and any dependencies between them. Later, when changes are made to the stack, such as adding or removing resources, CloudFormation automatically updates the stack using a change set and manages the underlying infrastructure changes accordingly, ensuring that your infrastructure is always in the desired state and that changes are made in a controlled and predictable manner.

- **Repeatability:** Repeating your manual steps not only is prone to error but also a waste of time and effort. With a CloudFormation template, you can deploy and redeploy the listed AWS resources in multiple environments, such as separate VPC development, staging, and production environments. Every time a CloudFormation template is executed, it repeats the same steps.

CloudFormation Components

CloudFormation works with templates and change sets. A *CloudFormation template* is an AWS resource blueprint that can create a complete application stack or a simple stack, such as a VPC network complete with multiple subnets, Internet gateways, and NAT services, all automatically deployed and configured. You can also create a *change set template* to help visualize how proposed changes will affect AWS resources deployed by a CloudFormation template.

CloudFormation Templates

Each CloudFormation template follows either JSON or YAML formatting standards. Example 6-1 shows a CloudFormation template in JSON format deploying an EC2 instance, and Example 6-2 displays the same information in YAML format. It's a matter of personal preference which format you use. When creating CloudFormation templates, you might find YAML easier to read.

Example 6-1   CloudFormation Template in JSON Format

```
{
    "AWSTemplateFormatVersion" : "2022-09-09",
    "Description": "EC2 instance",
    "Resources": {
    "EC2Instance" : {
    "Type" : "AWS::EC2::Instance",
    "Properties": {
    "ImageId" : "ami-0ff8a91497e77f667",
    "InstanceType" : "t1.micro"
    }
    }
    }
}
```

Example 6-2   CloudFormation Template in YAML Format

```
AWSTemplateFormatVersion: '2022-09-09'
Description: EC2 instance
Resources:
EC2Instance:
Type: AWS::EC2::Instance
Properties:
ImageId: ami-0ff8a91497e77f667
```

CloudFormation templates can have multiple sections, as shown in Example 6-3. However, the only mandatory section is Resources. Using the Metadata section for comments is highly recommended to ensure that templates can be understood when troubleshooting. As with any other template or script, the better the detailed comments within the script, the more usable a CloudFormation template is—for the author and other individuals.

Example 6-3 Valid Sections in a CloudFormation Template

```
"AWSTemplateFormatVersion": "version date",
"AWSTemplateFormatVersion": "2022-09-09"
<TemplateFormatVersion: Defines the current CF template version>


"Description": "Here are the additional details about this template
and what it does",
<Description: Describes the template: must always follow the version
section>


"Metadata": {
   "Metadata" : {
   "Instances" :  {"Description : "Details about the instances"},
   "Databases": {"Description: "Details about the databases"}
  }
},
<Metadata: Additional information about the resources being deployed
by the template>


   "Parameters": {
   "InstanceTypeParameter" : {
       "Type": "String",
       "Default" : "t2.medium",
       "AllowedValues" : ["t2.medium", "m5.large", "m5.xlarge"],
       "Description" : "Enter t2.medium, m.5large, or m5.xlarge.
       Default is t2.medium."
   }
}
<Parameters: Defines the AWS resource values allowed to be selected
and used by your template>


"Mappings": {
    "RegionMap" : [
       "us-east-1          : { "HVM64 : "ami-0bb8a91508f77f868"},
       "us-west-1         : { "HVM64 : "ami-0cdb828fd58c52239"},
       "eu-west-1         : { "HVM64 : "ami-078bb4163c506cd88"},
       "us-southeast-1    : { "HVM64 : "ami-09999b978cc4dfc10"},
       "us-northeast-1    : { "HVM64 : "ami-06fd42961cd9f0d75"}
   }
 }
```

```
<Mappings: Defines conditional parameters defined by a "key"; in this
example, the AWS region and a set of AMI values to be used>

  "Conditions": {
  "CreateTestResources": {"Fn::Equals" : [{"Ref" : "EnvType"},
"test"]}
},
<Conditions: Defines dependencies between resources, such as the
order when resources are created or where resources are created. For
example, "test" deploys the stack in the test environment>
```

CloudFormation Stacks

AWS has many sample CloudFormation templates that you can download from online CloudFormation documentation, as shown in Figure 6-23, and deploy at AWS. A CloudFormation stack can be as simple as a single VPC or as complex as a complete three-tier application stack with the required network high availability infrastructure and associated cloud services.

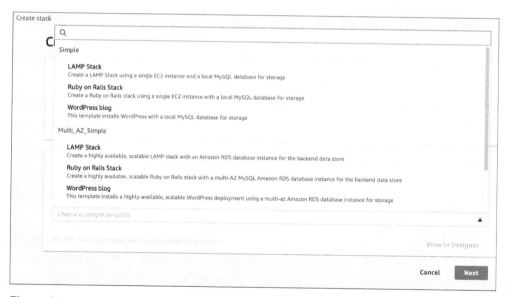

Figure 6-23   AWS Sample Stacks and CloudFormation Templates

CloudFormation can be useful for deploying infrastructure at AWS, including the following areas:

- **Network:** Define a baseline template for developers to ensure that their VPC network deployment matches company policy.

- **Frontend infrastructure:** Deploy Internet gateways, associated route table entries, or load balancers into existing or new AWS network infrastructure.

- **Backend infrastructure:** Create database infrastructure, including primary and alternate database instances, subnet groups, and associated security groups.

- **Multi-tier application:** Using a multi-tier CloudFormation script allows you to handle failures or disasters by enabling you to rebuild a complete application stack with required network and infrastructure components or to launch the application stack in another AWS region.

- **Windows Server Active Directory:** Deploy Active Directory on a Microsoft Windows Server 2022 instance in a VPC for a custom Microsoft SQL Server deployment.

- **Demo applications:** Define an application stack for demonstrations, allowing the sales team or end users to quickly create a working AWS infrastructure environment.

- **AWS managed services:** Use CloudFormation templates to automate the setup of any AWS managed services. For example, you can enable and set up AWS Config or Amazon Inspector using a CloudFormation template.

NOTE   There are many standardized CloudFormation templates, called AWS Blueprints, available from AWS (see https://aws.amazon.com/solutions/implementations/aws-blueprints/. AWS solution architects and trusted partners have built these templates to help you deploy complete solutions on AWS. These templates follow the current AWS best practices for security and high availability.

Creating an EC2 Instance

Example 6-4 provides a simple example that shows how to create an EC2 instance using a CloudFormation template. The template parameters are easily readable from top to bottom. Under Properties, the AMI ID, subnet ID, and EC2 instance type all must be present already in the AWS region where the template is executed; if not, the deployment will fail. The Ref statement is used in this template to attach the Elastic IP (EIP) address to the defined EC2 instance deployed and referenced under the resources listed as EC2 Machine.

NOTE Take a look at the AWS Quick Starts website https://aws.amazon.com/quickstart/ to see CloudFormation deployment options.

Example 6-4 CloudFormation Template for Creating an EC2 Instance

```
AWSTemplateFormatVersion: 2022-09-09
Description: EC2 Instance Template
"Resources": {
 "EC2Machine": {
 "Type": "AWS::EC2::Instance",
 "Properties": {
    "ImageId": "i-0ff407a7042afb0f0",
    "NetworkInterfaces": [{
    "DeviceIndex": "0",
    "DeleteOnTermination": "true",
    "SubnetId": "subnet-7c6dd651"
    }]
    "InstanceType": "t2.small"
    }
   }
},
"EIP": {
  "Type": "AWS::EC2::EIP",
  "Properties": {
  "Domain": "VPC"
  }
},
"VpcIPAssoc": {
"Type": "AWS::EC2::EIPAssociation",
  "Properties": {
  "InsanceID":  {
  "Ref": "EC2Machine"
  },
  "AllocationId": {
  "Fn::GetAtt": ["EIP",
  "AllocationId"]
  }
  }
}
```

Updating with Change Sets

A change set is a summary of changes that will be made to a stack in AWS Cloud-Formation. Change sets allow you to preview how your existing AWS resources will be modified when a deployed CloudFormation resource stack needs to be updated (see Figure 6-24). Select an original CloudFormation template to edit and input the desired set of changes. CloudFormation then analyzes your requested changes against the existing CloudFormation stack and produces a change set that you can review and approve or cancel.

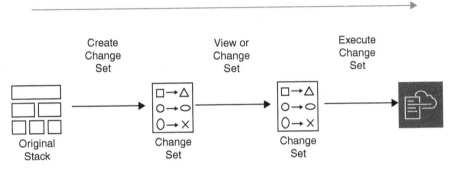

Figure 6-24   Using Change Sets with CloudFormation

Multiple change sets can be created for various comparison purposes. Once a change set is created, reviewed, and approved, CloudFormation updates your current resource stack. Several behaviors can be chosen when change set updates are approved:

- **Updates with No Interruption:** The resource is updated without disrupting the operation of the resource. For example, if you update any property on a CloudTrail resource, CloudFormation updates the trail without disruption.

- **Updates with Some Interruption:** The resource is updated with some interruption. For example, if you update certain properties on an EC2 instance resource, the instance might have some interruption while CloudFormation and EC2 reconfigure changes to the instance.

- **Replacement:** CloudFormation re-creates the resource during an update, which also generates a new physical ID. CloudFormation first creates the replacement resource, then changes references from other dependent resources to point to the replacement resource, and then the old resource is deleted. For example, if you update the Engine property of an Amazon RDS DBInstance resource type, CloudFormation creates a new resource and replaces the current DB instance resource with a new database instance.

CloudFormation Stack Sets

A stack set enables you to create a single CloudFormation template to deploy, update, or delete AWS infrastructure across multiple AWS regions and AWS accounts. When a CloudFormation template is deploying infrastructure across multiple AWS accounts, as shown in Figure 6-25, the AWS resources that the template references must be available in the AWS account and region. Region-specific resources must be copied to each AWS region where the CloudFormation template is executed. For example, EC2 instances, EBS volumes, AMIs, and key pairs are always created in a specific AWS region. It is also important to review global resources such as S3 buckets created by the CloudFormation template to make sure there are no naming conflicts during creation, as global resources such as S3 bucket names must be unique across all AWS regions.

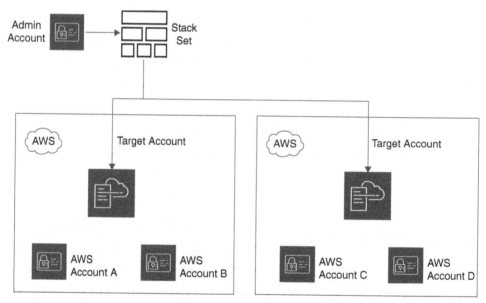

Figure 6-25   A Stack Set with Two AWS Target Accounts

Once a stack set is updated, all instances of the stack created are also updated. All corresponding stack sets are deleted if a stack set is deleted.

A stack set is first created in a single AWS account. Before additional stack instances can be created from the primary stack set, trust relationships using IAM roles must be created between the initial AWS administrator account and the administrators in the AWS target accounts.

For testing purposes, one example available in the AWS CloudFormation console is a sample stack set that allows you to enable AWS Config across selected AWS regions or accounts.

Third-Party Solutions

There are several third-party solutions, such as Chef, Puppet, Ansible, and Terra-Form, for performing automated deployments of compute infrastructure. CloudFormation is not a replacement for these third-party products but can be a useful tool for building automated solutions for your AWS infrastructure if you don't use one of the third-party orchestration tools. AWS has a managed service called OpsWorks that comes in three flavors and might be useful to your deployments at AWS if your company currently uses Chef or Puppet:

- **AWS OpsWorks Stacks:** Manage applications and services hosted at AWS and on premises by running Chef recipes, Bash, or PowerShell scripts.

- **AWS OpsWorks for Chef Automate:** Build a fully managed Chef Automate server that supports the latest versions of Chef server and Chef Automate, any community-based tools or cookbooks, and native Chef tools.

- **AWS OpsWorks for Puppet Enterprise:** A fully managed Puppet Enterprise environment that patches, updates, and backs up your existing Puppet environment and allows you to manage and administrate both Linux and Windows Server nodes hosted on EC2 instances and on premises.

AWS Service Catalog

AWS Service Catalog enables organizations to create, manage, and distribute a catalog of approved IT services installed with CloudFormation templates (see Figure 6-26). Service Catalog can help organizations maintain control over their IT environments by providing a central repository for approved cloud services and ensuring that only authorized services are deployed. With AWS Service Catalog, administrators can create and manage catalogs of AWS and third-party services, making them available to users within the organization. Users can access the catalog and launch services while AWS Service Catalog ensures that they are launched in the correct AWS accounts and with the appropriate permissions. To control who gets to deploy specific CloudFormation templates, AWS Service Catalog can be used to manage the distribution of CloudFormation templates portfolios to a single AWS account ID or an organizational unit contained within an AWS organization.

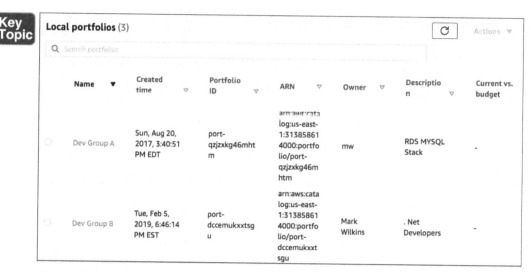

Key Topic

Figure 6-26   Portfolios in Service Catalog

When an approved product is selected, Service Catalog delivers a confirmation to CloudFormation, which executes the template and creates the product.

Each developer in an AWS account could be granted access to a Server Catalog portfolio of multiple approved products. Because products are built using common confirmation templates, any AWS infrastructure components, including EC2 instances and databases hosted privately in a VPC, can be deployed. Service Catalog also supports third-party products hosted in the AWS Marketplace, and software appliances are bundled with a CloudFormation template. VPC endpoints can access AWS Service Catalog and associated portfolios.

When you're creating a Service Catalog portfolio of products, you can use constraints with IAM roles to limit the level of administrative access to the resources contained in the stack being deployed (see Figure 6-27).

In addition, you can add rules that control any parameter values that developers enter during deployment. For example, you could mandate that specific subnets must be used for a stack deployment. You can also define rules that allow you to control which AWS account and region a product is allowed to launch.

Use CloudFormation and Service Catalog together to create a self-serve portal of portfolios and products.

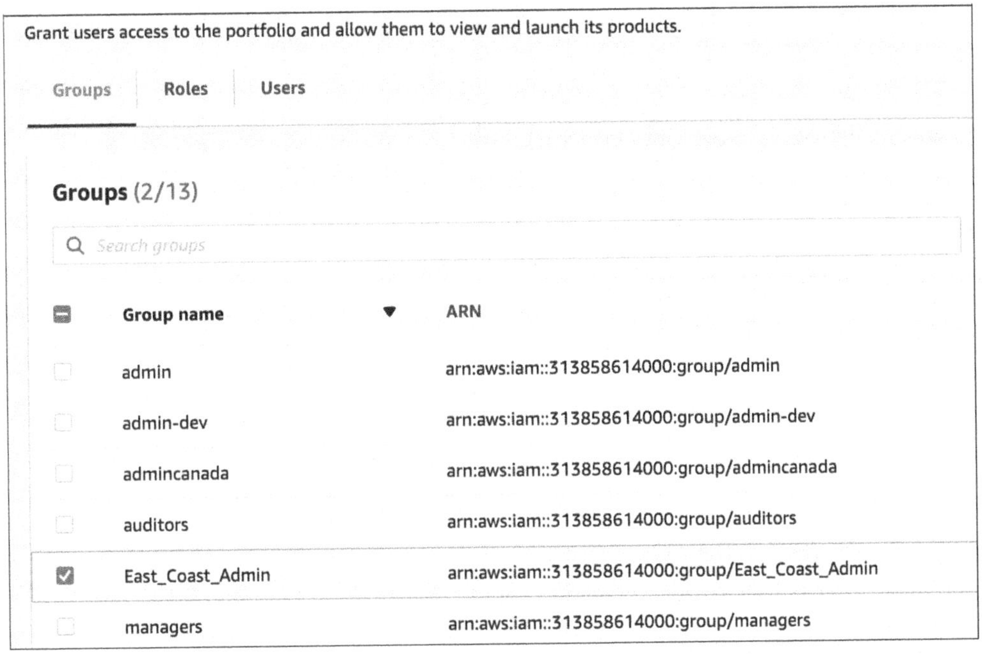

Grant users access to the portfolio and allow them to view and launch its products.

| Groups | Roles | Users |

Groups (2/13)

Q Search groups

	Group name ▼	ARN
☐	admin	arn:aws:iam::313858614000:group/admin
☐	admin-dev	arn:aws:iam::313858614000:group/admin-dev
☐	admincanada	arn:aws:iam::313858614000:group/admincanada
☐	auditors	arn:aws:iam::313858614000:group/auditors
☑	East_Coast_Admin	arn:aws:iam::313858614000:group/East_Coast_Admin
☐	managers	arn:aws:iam::313858614000:group/managers

Figure 6-27   IAM Group Constraints Controlled by Service Catalog

AWS Elastic Beanstalk

When moving to the AWS cloud, developers typically have little time and budget but must develop a web application or migrate an existing web app into the AWS cloud while adhering to the company's compliance standards. The web application needs to be reliable, able to scale, and easy to update. In such situations, Elastic Beanstalk can be of some help.

Elastic Beanstalk, which has been around since 2011, was launched to help enable developers to easily deploy web applications hosted on AWS Linux and Windows EC2 instances in the AWS cloud. Elastic Beanstalk automates both application deployment, as shown in Figure 6-28, and the infrastructure components required by the application, including single and multiple EC2 instances, load balancers, and EC2 Auto Scaling. Monitoring is carried out with CloudWatch metrics for monitoring the health of your application infrastructure. Elastic Beanstalk also integrates with AWS X-Ray, which can monitor and debug the internal operations of your hosted application.

Elastic Beanstalk > Create environment

Select environment tier

AWS Elastic Beanstalk has two types of environment tiers to support different types of web applications. Web servers are standard applications that listen for and then process HTTP requests, typically over port 80. Workers are specialized applications that have a background processing task that listens for messages on an Amazon SQS queue. Worker applications post those messages to your application by using HTTP.

○ **Web server environment**
    Run a website, web application, or web API that serves HTTP requests.
    Learn more [↗]

○ **Worker environment**
    Run a worker application that processes long-running workloads on demand or performs tasks on a schedule.
    Learn more [↗]

Cancel   **Select**

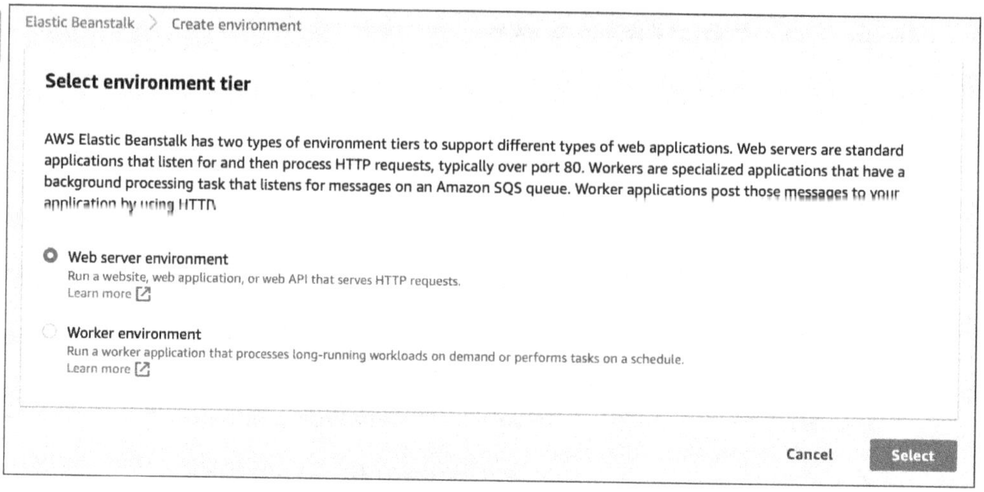

Figure 6-28   Elastic Beanstalk Creating Infrastructure

Elastic Beanstalk supports several development platforms, including Java (Apache HTTP or Tomcat) for PHP, Node.js (Nginx or Apache HTTP), Python (Apache HTTP), Ruby (Passenger), .NET (IIS), and the Go language. Elastic Beanstalk allows you to deploy different runtime environments across multiple technology stacks running on EC2 instances or Docker containers.

Developers can use Elastic Beanstalk to quickly deploy and test applications on defined infrastructure. After testing, the infrastructure can be quickly discarded at little cost. Keep in mind that Elastic Beanstalk is not a development environment (like Visual Studio). The application must be written before Elastic Beanstalk is useful. After an application has been written, create and upload a configuration file that details the infrastructure that needs to be built, and Elastic Beanstalk deploys the infrastructure and the application.

Elastic Beanstalk can help developers automate tasks and procedures previously carried out by administrators when applications were hosted in an on-premises data center. Elastic Beanstalk carries out the following tasks automatically:

- Provisions and configures EC2 instances, containers, and security groups using a CloudFormation template

- Configures an external database server environment

- Configures your load balancer and Auto Scaling

- Stores the application server's source code, associated logs, and artifacts in an S3 bucket

- Enables CloudWatch alarms that monitor the load of your application, triggering Auto Scaling for your infrastructure as necessary

- Routes access from the hosted application to a custom domain

- Performs blue/green deployments and immutable updates

Elastic Beanstalk is free of charge; you are charged only for the resources used for the deployment and hosting of your applications. The AWS resources that you use are provisioned within your AWS account, and you have full control of these resources. At any time, you can go into the Elastic Beanstalk configuration and make changes, as shown in Figure 6-29.

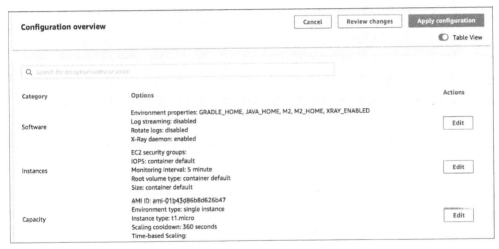

Figure 6-29   Modifying the Capacity of the Elastic Beanstalk Application Infrastructure

Applications supported by Elastic Beanstalk include simple HTTPS web applications and applications with worker nodes that can subscribe to Amazon SQS queues to carry out more complex, longer-running processes.

After an application has been deployed by Elastic Beanstalk, you can automatically update the selected application platform environment by enabling managed platform updates, which can be deployed during a defined maintenance window. These updates include minor platform version updates and security patching but not major platform updates to the web services used; major updates must be initiated manually.

Database support for Elastic Beanstalk includes any application installed on an EC2 instance, RDS database options, and DynamoDB. A database can be provisioned by Elastic Beanstalk during launch or can be exposed to the application through environmental variables.

Updating Elastic Beanstalk Applications

You can deploy new versions of the application to your Elastic Beanstalk environment, depending on the complexity of the application. During updates, Elastic Beanstalk archives the current application version in an S3 bucket. The methods available for updating Elastic Beanstalk applications include the following:

- **All at once:** The new application version is deployed to all EC2 instances simultaneously. The current application is unavailable while the deployment process is underway. To keep an older version of your application functioning until the new version is deployed, choose the immutable method or the blue/green update method.

- **Rolling:** The application is deployed in batches to a select number of EC2 instances defined in each batch configuration, as shown in Figure 6-30. As the batches of EC2 instances are being updated, they are deregistered from the load balancer queue. When the update is successful and the instances pass load-balancing health checks, the instances are registered to the load-balancing target group again.

- **Immutable:** The application update is only installed on new EC2 instances contained in a second Auto Scaling group launched in your environment. Only after the new environment passes health checks is the old application version removed. The new application servers are made available all at once. Because new EC2 instances and Auto Scaling groups are being deployed, the immutable update process takes longer.

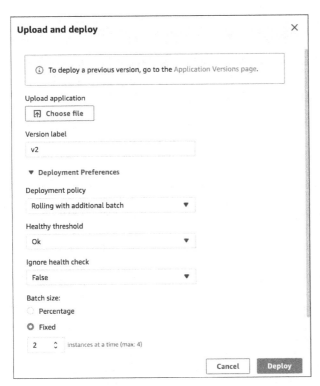

Figure 6-30   Apply Rolling Updates to an Elastic Beanstalk Application

- **Blue/green:** The new version of the application is deployed to a separate environment. When the new environment is healthy, the CNAMEs of the two environments are swapped, so traffic is redirected to the new application version. In this scenario, if a production database is to be used in the application design to maintain connectivity, the database must be installed separately from the Elastic Beanstalk deployment. Externally installed databases remain operational when the new Elastic Beanstalk application version is installed and swapped on the application's EC2 instances.

- **Traffic-splitting deployments:** Canary testing can also be included in your application deployment. Elastic Beanstalk can launch a set of new instances with a new version of the application; however, only a specific percentage of incoming traffic will initially be forwarded to the new application instances for a defined time. If the new application instances remain healthy during the evaluation period, Elastic Beanstalk then forwards traffic to the new instances and terminates the old instances. If the new instances don't pass their health checks, traffic is moved back to the current instances, and the new instances that were under evaluation are terminated, leaving the existing instances online with no service interruption.

Exam Preparation Tasks

As mentioned in the section "How to Use This Book" in the Introduction, you have a couple of choices for exam preparation: the exercises here, Chapter 16, "Final Preparation," and the exam simulation questions in the Pearson Test Prep Software Online.

Review All Key Topics

Review the most important topics in the chapter, noted with the Key Topic icon in the margin of the page. Table 6-6 lists these key topics and the page number on which each is found.

Table 6-6 Chapter 6 Key Topics

Key Topic Element	Description	Page Number
Section	Stateful Versus Stateless Application Design	239
Section	Changing User State Location	241
Table 6-2	Workload Data Choices	242
Section	User Session Management	243
Section	Container Orchestration	244
Section	Resilient Storage Options	246
Section	Amazon Simple Notification Service	248
Figure 6-7	Creating a Notification Topic	250
Section	Amazon SNS Cheat Sheet	250
Section	SQS Components	251
Section	Amazon SQS Cheat Sheet	253
Table 6-5	SNS, SQS, and Step Functions	256
List	Features of EventBridge	257
Figure 6-13	API Gateway Communication Options	259
List	API Gateway features	260
Section	API Gateway Cheat Sheet	261
Paragraph	CloudFormation as AWS-hosted orchestration engine	268
Section	CloudFormation Components	269

Key Topic Element	Description	Page Number
Section	CloudFormation Stacks	272
Section	CloudFormation Stack Sets	276
Figure 6-26	Portfolios in Service Catalog	278
Figure 6-28	Elastic Beanstalk Creating Infrastructure	280
Section	Updating Elastic Beanstalk Applications	282

Define Key Terms

Define the following key terms from this chapter and check your answers in the glossary:

serverless, stateful, stateless, sticky session, distributed session, event notification, application programming interface (API), regional endpoint

Q&A

The answers to these questions appear in Appendix A. Use the Pearson Test Prep Software Online for more practice with exam format questions.

1. What is the disadvantage of enabling sticky sessions?
2. What is the advantage of using a central location to store user state information?
3. What is the purpose of enabling notifications with Simple Notification Service?
4. How can Simple Notification Service and Simple Queue Service work together?
5. What is the advantage of using Step Functions?
6. What is the advantage of using Lambda to respond to SNS notifications?
7. Why would you use Lambda to create serverless applications?
8. How can Lambda be used with API Gateway?
9. What service allows you to deploy an architectural solution for an application that you have already written?

This chapter covers the following topics:

- High Availability and Fault Tolerance
- AWS Regions and Availability Zones
- Choosing an AWS Region
- Distributed Design Patterns
- Failover Strategies
- AWS Service Quotas
- Amazon Route 53

This chapter covers content that's important to the following exam domain and task statement:

Domain 2: Design Resilient Architectures

Task Statement 2: Design highly available and/or fault-tolerant architectures

CHAPTER 7

Designing Highly Available and Fault-Tolerant Architecture

When discussing the proper design of infrastructure for supporting customer workloads at AWS, terms used repeatedly in the AWS Well-Architected Framework documentation when describing proper workload design (covered in depth in Chapter 2, "The AWS Well-Architected Framework") are high availability, fault tolerance, and resilience. This chapter is focused on achieving workload reliability designing with high availability creating fault-tolerant workloads based on the recommendations of the Well-Architected Framework's Reliability pillar. To be reliable describes the capability of a workload to be able to recover successfully from an infrastructure or service disruption or network failure. Workload reliability also depends on the following well-architected framework pillars:

- **Operational Excellence pillar:** When problems occur, automation should be the solution when responding to failures, utilizing Amazon CloudWatch metrics and alarms, Amazon Simple Notification Service (SNS), AWS Lambda functions, and Amazon EventBridge rules and events.

- **Security pillar:** Workloads must be designed to restrict any harm to valuable data records or infrastructure. Options can include encryption at rest for all data records stored at AWS, AWS WAF filters for protecting workload or data, Elastic Load Balancing (ELB) providing high availability failover for web and application servers, Amazon Virtual Private Cloud (VPC) deployments across multiple availability zones, and deploying the Amazon Route 53 Resolver DNS Firewall, creating rules that filter outbound DNS traffic from a virtual private cloud (VPC).

- **Performance Efficiency pillar:** Performance efficiency refers to how well a system or process can achieve its desired output utilizing the available resources (CPU, memory, and storage) to complete tasks quickly and efficiently. A system or process that is highly performance-efficient can lead to cost savings and improved user experience.

- **Cost Optimization pillar:** The cost optimization pillar focuses on identifying and implementing strategies to reduce costs and optimize spending on AWS resources. Cost optimization strategies include right-sizing resources, using the best-managed service, and leveraging pricing discounts for compute resources. Scaling compute resources out horizontally can reduce workload costs for web apps, containerized apps, and database compute engines

High availability refers to hosted workloads being always available, regardless of the situation or circumstances that happen from time to time when running workloads in the cloud. In other words, a system with high availability can remain operational and accessible to end users even during failures or disruptions. The phrase "Everything fails" is a favorite saying of Amazon's CTO, Werner Vogels. How can workloads automatically respond to failure? If one web server, database, or storage array fails, there should be a backup web or database server or separate storage location available for automatic failover.

High availability ensures *fault tolerance*. Fault-tolerant cloud services and workloads are designed to continue operating when problems occur, without failing or experiencing a loss of data. Having multiple web servers or containers hosted in separate availability zones fronted by a highly available load-balancing service also deployed across multiple availability zones provides a high degree of fault tolerance, high availability, and resilience. A highly available workload environment typically has a defined level of uptime defined as a percentage, such as 99.9% uptime over a given year. Therefore, high availability refers to a workload that can operate for an extended period with minimal downtime. Adding fault tolerance services to a workload results in minimal service interruptions, with significantly higher operating costs as more resources have been utilized. Most organizations accept the higher operating costs of high availability and fault tolerance for mission-critical workloads hosted in the cloud, such as online stores or financial systems that must be available at all times.

Resiliency is the capability of a system or component to withstand external stresses such as sudden increases in load, attacks from malicious actors, or environmental factors such as extreme temperatures or natural disasters. A resilient system has been designed for high availability operation across multiple availability zones and can recover quickly from such stresses and continue to function without significant disruption. Resiliency is present because of high availability. All storage services available at AWS maintain multiple copies of stored data records stored across multiple physical locations in separate availability zones. Multiple web servers hosted in availability zones or across separate AWS regions provide high availability, fault tolerance, and a resiliency.

Each AWS Certified Solutions Architect – Associate (SAA-C03) exam question presents a current or proposed design that needs improvement. Always consider answers that present a solution that achieves high availability, fault tolerance, and resiliency.

Any workload running in the AWS cloud should be able to continue to operate when internal failures, latency, and unexpected problems occur. This chapter looks at the building blocks that AWS uses to build and host its cloud services and for customers to deploy their resilient workloads. By designing with regions, availability zones, and global cloud services, you can ensure workloads enjoy high availability, reliability, resilience, and fault tolerance.

"Do I Know This Already?"

The "Do I Know This Already?" quiz allows you to assess whether you should read this entire chapter thoroughly or jump to the "Exam Preparation Tasks" section. If you are in doubt about your answers to these questions or your own assessment of your knowledge of the topics, read the entire chapter. Table 7-1 lists the major headings in this chapter and their corresponding "Do I Know This Already?" quiz questions. You can find the answers in Appendix A, "Answers to the 'Do I Know This Already?' Quizzes and Q&A Sections."

Table 7-1   "Do I Know This Already?" Section-to-Question Mapping

Foundation Topics Section	Questions
High Availability and Fault Tolerance	1, 2
AWS Regions and Availability Zones	3, 4
Choosing an AWS Region	5, 6
Distributed Design Patterns	7, 8
Failover Strategies	9, 10
AWS Service Quotas	11, 12
Amazon Route 53	13, 14

CAUTION   The goal of self-assessment is to gauge your mastery of the topics in this chapter. If you do not know the answer to a question or are only partially sure of the answer, you should mark that question as wrong for purposes of the self-assessment. Giving yourself credit for an answer you correctly guess skews your self-assessment results and might provide you with a false sense of security.

1. Which of the following definitions describes the concept of a highly available workload?

   a. The workload remains available even when various issues occur to the infrastructure and to the managed services hosting the workload.

   b. The workload is available only during business hours.

   c. The workload remains available even under increased load.

   d. The workload is hosted in a single availability zone.

2. Which listed AWS service provides increased workload availability?

   a. ELB

   b. An EC2 instance

   c. Route table

   d. Web Application Firewall (WAF)

3. Which of the following does Amazon use to store multiple copies of objects stored in an S3 bucket?

   a. AWS Regions

   b. Availability zones

   c. Edge locations

   d. Data centers

4. How do multiple availability zones help increase workload reliability in an AWS region?

   a. By caching content for Amazon CloudFront

   b. By storing backup copies of EBS volumes

   c. Workloads are hosted across multiple subnets in different availability zones within an AWS region

   d. By locating workload servers closer to the end users' physical locations

5. What is the name of the compliance program that defines the available cloud services that can be accessed by federal agencies operating at AWS?

   a. HIPAA

   b. FERPA

   c. FISMA

   d. ITAR

6. Where are existing compliance reports hosted and made available for AWS customers?

    a. AWS Compliance website

    b. AWS IAM

    c. Artifact

    d. AWS Config

7. What benefit is gained by deploying workloads across multiple availability zones?

    a. Automatic scaling of resources on demand

    b. High availability

    c. Automatic backups

    d. Lower operating costs

8. What does the term immutable mean?

    a. Never changed or altered

    b. Always changes

    c. Rollback when failure occurs

    d. Highly scalable

9. What is a benefit of a pilot light disaster recovery scenario?

    a. Automatic failover

    b. Required services are kept up to date

    c. Disaster recovery site servers are smaller until needed

    d. RTO is very small

10. What is a benefit of a warm standby disaster recovery scenario?

    a. Disaster recovery site servers are smaller until needed.

    b. Automatic failover occurs.

    c. Disaster recovery site resources are online.

    d. RTO is longer than for a pilot light DR deployment.

11. What utility reports current service quota levels?

    a. AWS Inspector

    b. AWS Config

    c. AWS Control Tower

    d. AWS Trusted Advisor

12. Once you have created an AWS account, how does Amazon control the resources you're allowed to order?

    a. Allowable resources are based on the purchased support agreement.

    b. AWS applies hard and soft limits.

    c. Service quotas control resource amounts

    d. By AWS regional resources used.

13. What Route 53 DNS record provides redundancy for AWS services?

    a. Alias records

    b. Latency records

    c. Geoproximity records

    d. A records

14. What AWS service provides DNS services for both private and public queries?

    a. CloudFront

    b. Route 53

    c. Global Accelerator

    d. Traffic policies

Foundation Topics

High Availability and Fault Tolerance

Successful organizations achieve and maintain highly available and fault-tolerant workloads by deploying compute, database, and storage services based on the recommendations of the Well-Architected Framework. Decisions are based on taking into account the availability, reliability, and resilience required by each workload's business needs and requirements. Application security is a key component of workload availability and reliability. If a workload gets hacked and is not available, it's not very reliable. Ultimately, the terms high availability, fault tolerance, resilience, and reliability describe a properly designed workload.

Let's explore the meaning of these terms further in the context of hosting and operating workloads at AWS. In the context of AWS, the term *workload* refers to an application and the associated AWS cloud services. When you host a workload at AWS, there are a number of moving parts to consider within each workload that you design and deploy. Cloud hosted applications use what is sometimes called a managed service. A *managed service* is an AWS service that is built, maintained, and patched by AWS; every single cloud service offered by AWS has some level of AWS management. For example, Amazon CloudWatch is the monitoring service that is embedded into many AWS infrastructure services such as Amazon EC2, ELB, Amazon EBS, Amazon S3, and Amazon RDS, enabling customers to monitor each cloud service using metrics that can alert you when a cloud service is either working or not working as expected.

The Amazon mantra they follow when building the cloud services that we use and depend on is to design with security at all layers, ensuring each service is as reliable and dependable and as responsive and as fast as it can be performance-wise, without sacrificing any security or reliability requirements. This is the mindset you must assume when answering AWS Certified Solutions Architect – Associate (SAA-C03) exam questions, proving to Amazon that you're a competent cloud architect. Amazon does not expect you to have every single technical answer for each AWS service, but it does expect you to display a level of technical common sense and be able to implement Amazon's best practices for designing workloads that meet the stated business objectives and requirements and take into account security, reliability, performance, and cost.

High Availability in the Cloud

High availability becomes a little more complicated when there are numerous cloud services involved behind the scenes for each hosted workload. *Availability* refers to the proportion of time that a system, service, or resource is able to function and be accessed as a percentage, indicating the amount of time that a system, service, or resource is expected to be operational and accessible to end users. As previously mentioned, availability is usually defined as a percentage of uptime ranging from 99.9% to 100% over a defined period, typically per year. Table 7-2 lists some common examples of high availability and the maximum potential unavailability over a calendar year.

Table 7-2 Availability

Availability (%)	Potential Unavailability per Year	Use Case
99%	3 days, 15 hours	Batch processing, data transfer
99.9%	8 hours, 45 minutes	Project management
99.95%	4 hours, 22 minutes	Point of sale (POS), online retail
99.99%	52 minutes	Video delivery
99.999%	5 minutes	ATM transactions

AWS publishes service-level agreements (SLA) for many of its cloud services, including Amazon Elastic Compute Cloud (EC2), Elastic Block Store (EBS), and Elastic Container Service (ECS) with a stated availability of 99.99%, which means that the total downtime expected per year utilizing any of these services is 52 minutes per service, per year. However, there is no exact time when downtime will even actually occur. Perhaps your workloads hosted at AWS won't have any downtime!

Having a hosted workload that is expected to be always available—when the workload is created out of numerous independent cloud services—adds additional complexity to each workload design. Service-level agreements define the individual AWS service availability, not a workload's availability. Customers shouldn't host mission-critical workloads on a single EC2 instance; instead, multiple EC2 instances are typically deployed and hosted in separate availability zones within each AWS region, and in many cases across multiple AWS Regions.

The virtual hard drives created for boot drives and data volumes are EBS storage volumes. Multiple copies of each EBS volume are automatically created, providing an added measure of high availability, fault tolerance, and reliability. EBS volumes are designed to be highly reliable, with an average annual failure rate of less than

0.1%; EBS volumes are expected to experience an outage or failure less than once per year on average. The EBS service provides volume durability using data replication and backup within the availability zone where each volume is created, increasing the reliability of each EBS volume.

Snapshots are point-in-time backups of EBS volumes. EBS snapshots can be used to recover data in the event of data loss, corruption, or accidental deletion, or to create new EBS volumes with the same data as the original volume. EBS snapshots can also be used to migrate data from one AWS region to another, or to create a new EBS volume in a different Availability Zone or region for disaster recovery purposes.

EBS volumes are used when deploying Amazon RDS databases, which are designed to be highly reliable, with an average annual failure rate of less than 0.1%. RDS recommends Multi-AZ deployments, which automatically create one or more secondary copies of the database in multiple availability zones, providing additional protection against outages and data loss.

Reliability

Workload *reliability* is measured in terms of the availability of a system or service, and its capability to handle failures and disruptions without impacting the overall quality of the application. Organizations operating workloads at AWS need to design their workloads based on their own expectations and business requirements for each hosted workload. How much workload downtime is acceptable to your organization? How many failures can occur before the entire workload cannot be trusted to operate at an acceptable level?

The reliability of each workload can be affected by several factors, such as the design of the system, the quality of the cloud services used, and the level of maintenance and support. It is important to carefully evaluate the reliability of a workload before using it in critical applications, and to implement appropriate procedures to ensure that the workload remains reliable over time. When designing for reliability, consider the acceptable trade-off between the desired service level based on your business requirements and needs and the true cost of maintaining desired workload reliability.

You might be wondering why the cost has entered the discussion of reliability. If unlimited funds are available, workloads can be designed to rarely, if ever, fail. Having 1,000 workload servers hosted across six different availability zones will certainly guarantee success—but probably isn't affordable for most organizations. Thankfully, the AWS cloud is a pretty reliable entity on its own. However, it is each customer's responsibility to design their hosted workloads for the required availability and reliability.

Other concerns that can affect reliability are operational changes such as updates or patching that are carried out on your workload on a daily, weekly, and yearly cadence. Are these changes performed using automation and playbooks? Are you using multiple AWS VPCs to host separate test, development, and production environments? Well-architected designs must also include workload security and performance efficiencies. If workload security is lax, allowing harm to the workload or to the essential data records, overall reliability will be reduced. In the area of performance efficiencies, are you paying too much to ensure compute resources have high availability and stability 24-7, or should you automatically scale up the compute capacity as required? To achieve workload reliability, each of the six pillars of the Well-Architected Framework needs to be fully considered. As a reminder, Chapter 2 explores the AWS Well-Architected Framework design concepts in more detail.

The next section looks at how Amazon has designed its cloud services to be as available and reliable as possible—and how customers can use their online cloud services to design highly available, fault-tolerant, and reliable workloads.

AWS Regions and Availability Zones

It is important to understand where Amazon cloud services are located, why they are located in multiple physical locations, and how this design helps organizations in designing hosted workloads for high availability, reliability, and durability. Amazon cloud services are hosted in *regions* in populous areas of the world. Each AWS *region* is located in a specific geographic area of the world. Each region has, at a minimum, two availability zones. Each availability zone has a minimum of one data center for hosting customer workloads. Availability zones are spaced apart by a minimum of 10–15 miles and are powered by different electrical grids and external support services such as ISPs and third-party services. Additional data centers within each AWS region and availability zone locations host various AWS-managed cloud services for storage, databases, and managed services used by workloads. Each AWS region is completely isolated from other regions; problems that arise within one region remain localized to that one region and should not affect any other AWS region you also may be operating in.

Each customer with a standard AWS account can choose to work in any AWS region except for the GovCloud regions and several regions in China that require a special AWS GovCloud (US) account. Figure 7-1 shows the areas of the world where AWS regions are currently located.

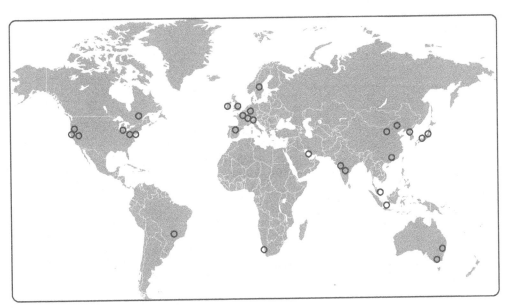

Figure 7-1   AWS Regions and Geographic Locations

Currently, there are at least 30 AWS regions worldwide. There may be additional regions online by the time you read this book because AWS is continuously expanding its cloud resources throughout the world.

NOTE   For information on current regions and availability zones, see https:// aws.amazon.com/about-aws/global-infrastructure/regions_az/.

Each AWS region is initially physically and securely separated from other regions, as shown in Figure 7-2.

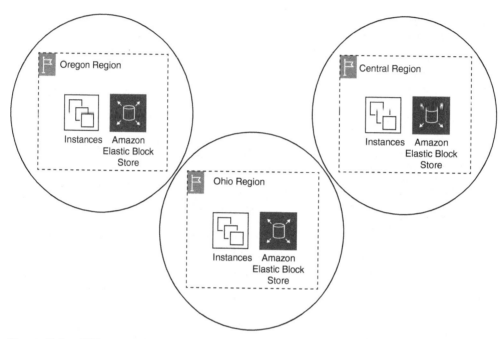

Figure 7-2 AWS Regions Starting Off as Isolated Entities

Isolating regions enables AWS to guarantee a level of operational compliance and data sovereignty. AWS recognizes that the industry that you work in might have strict rules and regulations regarding how your user data is managed and controlled. If your data is stored within a particular AWS region, that data will never leave its selected region unless you move it or specifically direct AWS to do so.

As mentioned, within each region, AWS offers a variety of cloud services that are designed not only to support customers' needs for storage, load balancing, DNS services, managed database services, and more but also to be highly available and fault tolerant with the ability to fail over to other service locations within the same AWS region when disaster strikes.

Various numbers of separate regional data centers support the offered AWS cloud resources and services; it's handy to visualize a sampling of strategically placed regional cloud services linked together with high-speed private networking across each availability zone and AWS region (see Figure 7-3). (Availability zones are discussed in the next section.) The AWS cloud services are designed for high availability, fault tolerance, and resilience. The failure of customer workloads located within each region does not affect and derail the operation of the AWS managed services because AWS managed services are located in their own regional data centers. For example, Amazon's S3 storage and Elastic Load Balancing (ELB) services are specifically designed to integrate with customer workloads within each AZ; however, each of these services is located in its own regional data center cluster.

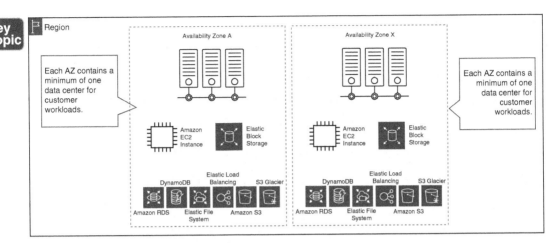

Figure 7-3 Visualizing Availability Zones and Regional Services

Depending on the scope and requirements of an organization's workload design, the AWS region that is chosen must meet all the required design needs and compliance requirements; there may be no need to operate in multiple AWS regions. For other use cases, you might have business requirements to host workloads spanning multiple AWS regions; for example, the use case for a public-facing software as a service (SaaS) workload requiring database synchronization across multiple regions to protect against a regional failure of the database service.

Amazon DynamoDB provides high availability and horizontal scaling of regional tables that can also be synchronized across multiple regions. Amazon Aurora is MySQL and PostgreSQL compatible, storing data records in clustered shared storage deployed across single or multiple AWS regions. A regional solution could be Amazon RDS MySQL, deployed using a cluster of primary and two standby databases utilizing multiple database instances across availability zones. AWS Route 53 DNS services and custom traffic policies can also be used to geographically load balance workloads that are hosted in different AWS regions.

NOTE You might not know much about databases at this point—and that is okay. For this discussion, you just need to be able to appreciate that each of the potential database options just mentioned provides a much higher level of availability and reliability than a single database running on a single virtual server with multiple virtual hard drives. Databases are covered in detail in Chapter 10, "Determining High-Performing Database Solutions." For now, we are concerned with the concept of high availability, fault tolerance, and reliability and the various cloud services provided by AWS that you might choose to use. Using multiple AWS regions can provide a very large measure of high availability, fault tolerance, and reliability for hosted workloads.

Availability Zones

AWS provides availability zones for reliability and high availability for the cloud services offered within each region and for your hosted workloads. *Availability zones (AZs)* are physical locations within a region where data centers are located. Each availability zone has at a minimum one data center dedicated to customer workloads. Each AZ is designed to be isolated from the others, with its own power, cooling, and networking infrastructure. This allows for the creation of highly available and fault-tolerant applications, because data can be stored and accessed from multiple availability zones, providing protection against outages or other disruptions in any single location. Most AWS regions have three AZs or more.

Each AZ is linked to the other AZs in the same region through private dedicated, redundant, low-latency fiber network connections that Amazon owns (see Figure 7-4). As an example of network speed, traffic between EC2 instances and S3 storage can utilize up to 100 Gbps of bandwidth to VPC endpoints and public IPs within the same region.

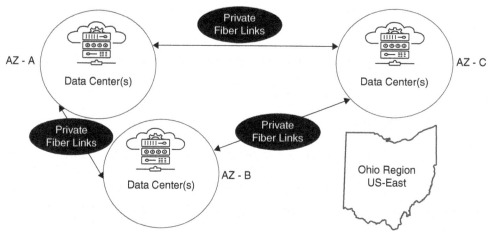

Figure 7-4   Availability Zones

To offer cloud services that are designed to adhere to the many compliance programs that AWS supports, including HIPAA and PDI DSS, Amazon owns the cloud service infrastructure.

Designing a workload to operate across multiple availability zones is one of the major concepts to understand for the AWS Certified Solutions Architect – Associate (SAA-C03) exam. Amazon S3 storage, DynamoDB, and Amazon Aurora deployments operate across three AZs.

AWS does not disclose whether an AZ has a single or multiple data centers; that's private information. It's important to keep in mind that the discussion of data centers within the AZ refers to the data centers dedicated to customer workloads. Amazon does not officially disclose infrastructure numbers; however, in its largest region, North Virginia, us-east-1, there are many data centers dedicated for customer workloads. When a customer selects a particular AZ to host servers or containers, the exact data center is not specifically identified, just the AZ, as shown in Figure 7-5. It is important to reiterate that no two AZs share the same single data center. Each data center in each AZ is a separate entity that is isolated from other data centers within the same and different AZs.

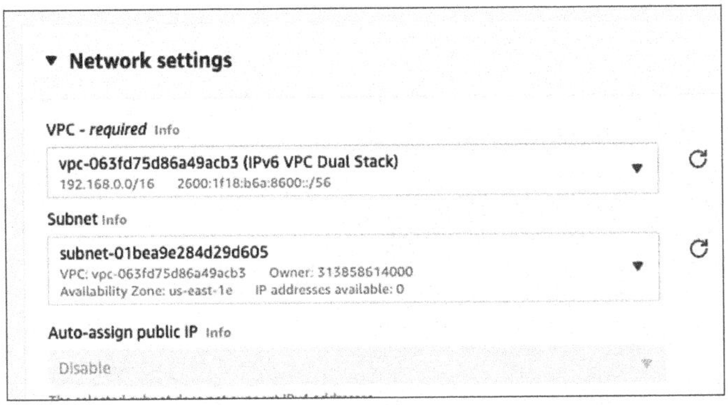

Figure 7-5   Availability Zone Selection

Throughout its tenure as a public cloud provider, AWS has had very limited failures of availability zones and regions. We need to keep perspective on AWS failures when they are reported by the media. Remember there are many data centers within each region that host the regional cloud services offered by AWS; there are also the many data centers that are provided for customer workloads. Separating cloud services and customer workloads into separate data centers ensures a very high level of reliability and uptime across the entire AWS cloud.

Availability Zone Distribution

It is also important to understand that AWS carries out balancing and distribution of customer resources that are hosted in availability zones. For example, if Mark logs in to his AWS account, selects the US-East Northern Virginia region, and creates a subnet in Availability Zone A, the physical data center location of Mark's subnet is probably not the same as the subnet for another Amazon customer, Julian, who has also selected the US-East Northern Virginia region creating a subnet in Availability Zone A. Both customers have created a subnet in Availability Zone A, but their subnets are most likely not in the same physical AZ. They are most likely in different physical data centers, as shown in Figure 7-6. What's important is the use of multiple availability zones within a region; the exact physical location of each AZ is not public information.

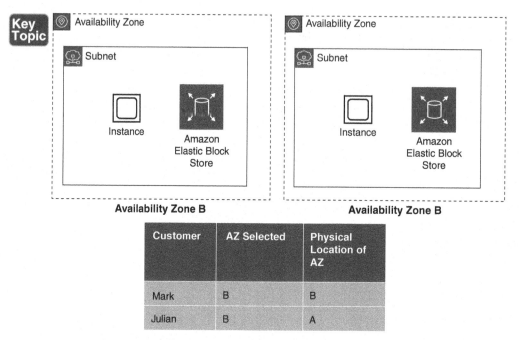

Figure 7-6 AZ Balancing and Distribution of Resources

Latency between AZs within an AWS region is also not an issue; average latency between AZs within a region is around a few milliseconds. Certainly, if you're concerned about network speeds, you can perform latency testing from one EC2 instance hosted in one AZ to an EC2 instance located in another AZ by using ping (local routing is enabled within a virtual private cloud). You could also deploy iPerf3 – SpeedTest Server on Ubuntu, available in the AWS Marketplace, which can determine the maximum achievable bandwidth across the AWS private network. You can also use the AWS Latency Monitoring tool at https://www.cloudping.co/grid to review the current latencies between AWS regions.

NOTE   Each AZ within each AWS region has a moniker based on the region it is hosted within as well as a letter code, such as us-west-1.

Within a single AZ, the data center private network connections are defined as intra-AZ connections, as they are local to the AZ, as shown in Figure 7-7. The wiring between the AZs is defined as inter-AZ connections, with additional private links connecting the regions. The primary reasons for using AZs in your infrastructure design are high availability with automatic workload failover and primary/standby/read replica database replication.

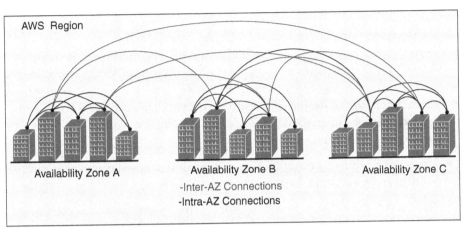

Figure 7-7 Private Network Wiring for AWS Regions and AZs

Customers that operate across a minimum of two AZs with independent redundant components, such as EC2 instances and multi-AZ RDS database deployments with an availability of 99.9%, will have an effective 99.9999% availability.

AWS services defined as global services are designed to operate outside of AWS regions located at the perimeter of the AWS cloud in *edge locations*. Edge services include the DNS service Amazon Route 53, Amazon CloudFront, AWS's CDN, and the AWS Web Application Firewall. You can find more about the edge services in Chapter 11, "High-Performing and Scalable Networking Architecture."

NOTE All data flowing across AWS regions across the AWS global network is automatically encrypted at the physical layer before it leaves AWS facilities. All network traffic between AZs is also encrypted.

Planning Network Topology

When deploying workloads at AWS, designing with multiple availability zones to provide high availability, fault tolerance, and reliability is an important concept to understand. The key infrastructure services offered by AWS are all designed to be deployed across multiple AZs, providing each customer with the ability to design their workload infrastructure with high availability, fault tolerance, and reliability with networking (Amazon VPC), load balancing services (ELB), virtual servers or containers (Amazon EC2 instances, Amazon EKS), Amazon RDS databases, Amazon DynamoDB, monitoring (Amazon CloudWatch), and Auto Scaling (designed to scale your compute resources based on demand).

Workloads can also be hosted across multiple AWS regions or be part of a hybrid design with existing on-premises data centers. Amazon Virtual Private Cloud (VPC) allows you to provision a private, isolated network utilizing multiple AZs within a single region. VPC endpoints allow private connections from VPC workloads hosted on subnets to AWS services across the AWS private network, allowing private network communication. Resiliency for private network connections at AWS, and from on-premises locations to AWS VPCs and AWS cloud services, can also be provided by the following cloud services:

- Using AWS Direct Connect (DX), a dedicated high-speed connection can connect an on-premises data center to the AWS cloud.

- Having redundant DX connections from multiple separate data centers or adding a second DX connection can provide additional high availability connections.

- Using AWS VPN connections can provide dedicated VPN connections at 1.25 Gbps throughput per VPN tunnel.

- Deploying AWS Marketplace appliances with high availability across multiple AZs on redundant EC2 instances.

High-availability endpoints for public network connections from end users to public-facing workloads and AWS resources are provided by the following:

- **Amazon CloudFront:** Delivers data through over 300 points of presence (PoPs) to edge location caches and regional edge caches.

- **AWS Global Accelerator:** Optimizes workload traffic requests to multiple edge location endpoints.

- **Amazon API Gateway:** Operates as a reverse proxy accepting API calls to hosted APIs; API Gateway is located between the end-use requests and the AWS backend services.

- **Elastic Load Balancing (ELB) service:** Provides load balancing across availability zones and integrates with EC2 Auto Scaling to provide high availability and self-healing infrastructure. Incoming traffic requests can be filtered using AWS WAF.

- **Amazon Route 53 (highly available DNS service):** Routes user requests to workloads and services running at AWS, edge locations, multi-region workload deployments, and outside of AWS to other external on-premises locations or other public clouds. The following are high-availability routing choices:

  - **Latency routing policy:** Routes end users to the AWS region that has the lowest latency

- **Failover routing policy:** Routes end users to resources that are available in an active-passive or active-active design across multiple regions

- **Geolocation routing policy:** Routes traffic based on the location of the end user

- **Geoproximity routing policy:** Routes traffic based on the location of your resources

- **Multivalue answer routing:** Includes health checks of resources, improving high availability

NOTE   As you've noticed, a number of Amazon services start with the word *Elastic* (for example, Elastic Compute Cloud and Elastic Block Store). A service that is defined as *elastic* allows the resource to change size and power after the initial creation. For example, an EC2 instance can be changed to increase resource size without having to start over, and EBS volumes' size and speed can also be changed whenever the need arises.

A few years ago, Amazon had issues in Australia. The media announced that "the Amazon cloud was down." This was true to a degree because an AZ in the Asia Pacific region had issues; however, not all the AZs within the Asia Pacific region had issues. If an organization's workload or website was hosted in the unavailable AZ, and the workload or website was not designed for automatic failover to another AZ, as shown in Figure 7-8, then workloads were potentially not available for a period of time.

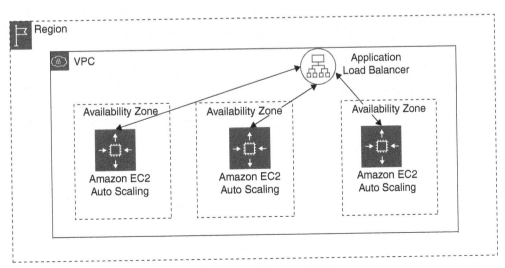

Figure 7-8   Failover Possibilities of Availability Zones for Workloads

Is a sudden lack of availability of a customer's hosted workload Amazon's fault? This is a fair question to consider; however, it most likely is the customer's fault for not utilizing proper cloud design standards for its hosted workloads. In fact, a customer that fails to design its workloads to properly fail over across multiple AZs violates the customer's SLA with AWS. If workload issues are due to an Amazon failure beyond the customer's control and the customer has designed its workload following best practices, the customer will get a credit on its bill for the downtime. The customer also needs to prove that the workload was down by providing relevant network traces. In some situations, a credit is automatically provided because an outage is obviously AWS's problem.

NOTE Hosting your workload in a single AZ is accepting a single point of failure.

Local Zones

Even with the rapid expansion of regional cloud resources carried out by AWS over the last few years, there are still many businesses specializing in real-time gaming, streaming, video productions, or virtual reality that haven't moved to the AWS public cloud because the speed of accessing cloud services is not fast enough for their needs. Local data residency requirements for sectors such as healthcare, financial services, and governments have also made moving to the public cloud an issue for some sectors. To solve these issues, Amazon has rolled out *Local Zones* to over 30 cities in 27 countries, as shown in Figure 7-9. Local Zones are deployments of AWS infrastructure in a single data center, including compute, storage, and database services, resulting in single-digit millisecond latency speeds for customers located in these locations. Local Zones for these use cases may help by

- Deploying workload stacks closer to the location of the business and end users that require low latency and high performance

- Migrating on-premises workloads to a nearby Local Zone and maintain low-latency requirements for hybrid designs

- Meeting data residency requirements for compliance with country or business regulations

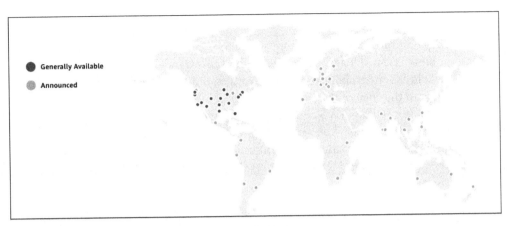

Figure 7-9   Local Zones Available in Many AWS Regions

A Local Zone contains cloud resources without any built-in redundancy; however, each Local Zone can be associated with an AWS region by linking the Local Zone with an organization's existing region's AWS VPC network infrastructure by including Local Zone subnets, as shown in Figure 7-10, providing additional redundancy and failover through connections to other AZs in the AWS region.

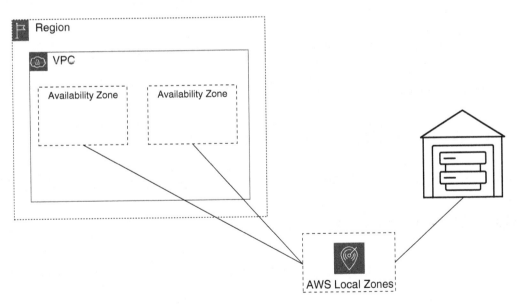

Figure 7-10   Local Zone Architecture

Wavelength Zones

As the 5G protocol becomes more commonplace across the world, the infrastructure that hosts 5G workloads for mobile applications is moving closer to the end user's handheld 5G smartphone or device. Workloads deployed in Wavelength Zones are moving to the edge of the cloud, as shown in Figure 7-11, and closer to the end user. Amazon is installing AWS compute and storage services in the telecommunications provider's data center. The workloads are developed and hosted in the telecommunications provider's own data center on AWS infrastructure, shortening the end users' distance to the 5G workload, resulting in ultra-low latency and increased performance.

Figure 7-11   Wavelength Zones Move the Workload Closer to the End User

AWS Services Use Cases

It is not expected or even possible that you will understand the complete details of every AWS service covered by the AWS Certified Solutions Architect – Associate (SAA-C03) exam. It is, however, important to have a conceptual use case in your mind for each AWS service that could be the focus of an exam question. When an AWS service is described in the cloud services FAQ, a use case is provided. For example, the service Amazon Comprehend is defined as "a natural language processing service that uses machine learning to find meaning and insights in text."

The suggested use cases for Amazon Comprehend are to analyze the "text" for key phrases and customer sentiment analysis. Developers looking to deploy natural learning language processing in workloads hosted at AWS can use this service. For the SAA-C03 exam, that's the amount of detail to know about Amazon Comprehend.

For many AWS cloud services, a short description is all you need to know for the SAA-C03 exam. Other cloud services covered by the exam require additional knowledge of deployment and design details. The knowledge level being tested of an AWS cloud architect is a competent understanding of the cloud services covered by the exam. During your preparation for the SAA-C03 exam, it is highly recommended to review the FAQs for the highly available (HA) and fault-tolerant (FT) services listed in Table 7-3, noting the use cases.

NOTE   AWS FAQs can be found at https://aws.amazon.com/faqs/.

Table 7-3   AWS Services Details

AWS Service	What is it?	FT and HA Use Case	Deployment	Considerations	Use Case
Amazon EC2	Virtual servers	Multiple AZs with ELB, EC2 Auto Scale	Requires Amazon Machine Image (AMI), VPC, security group	Reserved pricing, Savings Plans, Spot Instances	On-demand, GPU; web apps; databases; EBS optimized, General purpose, and Memory Optimized instances
Amazon ECS	Docker containers	A cluster of EC2 instances across AZs	Task Statement	AWS Fargate management	Hybrid environment, batch processing, microservices
Amazon EBS	Virtual hard drives	Multiple copies	Attach to EC2 instances	SSD, IOPS, Throughput optimized, EBS Block Express, Lifecycle Manager (Snapshots)	Boot and data drives, Multi-attach
EC2 Auto Scaling	Scale compute automatically	Across multiple AZs with ELB	Scheduled, step, simple, target tracking, Predictive scaling	Works with ELB and Elastic Beanstalk	Automatically scale compute

AWS Service	What is it?	FT and HA Use Case	Deployment	Considerations	Use Case
AWS Auto Scaling	Compute auto scaling	Across multiple AZs	Predictive scaling	Amazon EC2, Amazon ECS, Amazon DynamoDB, Amazon Aurora	Automatically scale workloads
Amazon CloudFront	CDN	Origin Shield	Edge locations, Regional edge caches, HTTPS, Field-Level Encryption	Caching static content, Lambda@Edge, AWS WAF, OAI	Live streaming, distribute static and dynamic content
Application Load Balancer (ALB)	HTTPS load balancing service	EC2 instance and Docker container failover, health checks	Supports operation across multiple AZs	Routing based on host name, path, query string parameter, HTTP headers, source IP address, or port number	Server Name Indication (SNI) support for serving multiple domain names, authentication support, WAF
Network Load Balancer (NLB)	TCP load balancing service	Workload failover, health checks, TLS end-to-end encryption	Supports operation across multiple AZs	TCP, UDP, and TCP connections encrypted with TLS	High performance, EIP support; supports targets outside of AWS

Choosing an AWS Region

Reasons to choose a specific AWS region depend on four interlinked conditions:

- **Compliance rules:** Where is your organization allowed to operate?

- **Latency issues:** How far away are your customers from the desired cloud service?

- **Services offered:** In what region is the cloud service that you require offered?

- **Pricing:** Are infrastructure costs the main driver for migrating to the cloud?

To make the decision about which AWS region to operate in, evaluate each of these conditions thoroughly. The following sections look at each of these conditions, starting with the most important condition: the compliance rules and regulations that your organization must follow.

Compliance Rules

Before your company begins hosting any workloads in the AWS cloud, it needs to analyze any rules and regulations that it is required to follow in its day-to-day business practices. For example, your organization must adhere to ISO 27001 standards. AWS maintains its data centers, networks, and shared infrastructure in accordance with a suite of ISO certifications that mandate a strict level of compliance with security management, information security controls, and best practices while operating in the public cloud. The security standards in this example are likely very close to AWS's own standards because AWS holds certification for compliance with the current ISO/IEC 27001, 27017, and 27018 certifications. The *AWS Artifact* utility is located in the AWS Management console and allows AWS customers to review the compliance standards supported by AWS, as shown in Figure 7-12.

Figure 7-12   Artifact Utility

Third-party ISO auditors audit the AWS cloud on a rigid schedule to ensure that AWS maintains and upholds its overall operations to the current ISO/IEC security management standards. Other third-party compliance auditors also ensure that AWS lives up to the many other compliance standards and assurance programs that AWS is also aligned with. When an organization signs on as an AWS customer, it has access to the compliance reports regarding the standards, certifications, and attestations that Amazon has achieved and maintains. Most compliance reports are available to all AWS customers upon request; for others, you must sign a nondisclosure agreement (NDA) with AWS.

The steps to get started with reviewing the available compliance and attestation reports at AWS are as follows:

Step 1.   Sign into your AWS account with root user account credentials.

Step 2.   In the AWS Management Console, search for Artifact. The available security and compliance documents are listed for all AWS customers.

Step 3.   Choose your compliance program and click Get This Artifact.

Step 4.   Download the selected document and review the services that are defined as being in scope, shown in Figure 7-13.

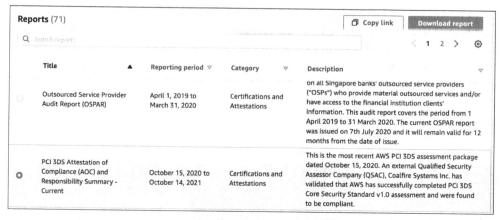

Figure 7-13   Reviewing Audit Reports Using AWS Artifact

Understanding Compliance Rules at AWS: Use Case

To begin to understand the compliance rules and regulations that AWS supports, follow these steps:

Step 1.   Visit the AWS Compliance Programs website at https://aws.amazon.com/compliance/programs/.

Step 2.   Review the IT standards that Amazon currently complies with.

Step 3.   Select a standard and review the following details:

    a. What level of certification does AWS hold?

    b. What services are in the scope of the selected compliance program?

    c. What does AWS's attestation of compliance cover?

    d. What controls is the customer responsible for?

    e. Do your organization's compliance needs match successfully with what AWS currently offers?

A detailed review of the scope of the IT standards that your organization must adhere to is the best first step to follow when analyzing what is possible in the AWS cloud. If you find that an AWS service you were thinking of using is not yet supported by your compliance rules, it's certainly better to know that before starting.

You might prefer to visit an AWS data center and perform your own auditing, but that is not possible. Random visitors to a data center adhering to a high level of compliance are just not allowed. Even Jeff Bezos would have trouble getting into an AWS data center unless he was cleared to perform data center–specific tasks.

For example, suppose you work for a company that wants to analyze AWS for its level of Payment Card Industry Data Security Standard (PCI DSS) compliance. Your company is designing a workload for customers to pay their bills online. AWS will be hosting the SaaS workload, and you are tasked with reviewing and understanding both your company's responsibilities and the responsibilities of AWS. The compute services for the SaaS workload are to be hosted on the shared EC2 infrastructure at AWS, if that's allowed. The workload must adhere to the rules of PCI DSS compliance in terms of the storage, processing, and transmission of the credit card information. Several vice presidents are sure that PCI compliance is not allowed in the AWS cloud, or, if it is allowed, bare-metal servers must be used. To get the most up-to-date answer about PCI DSS, follow these steps:

Step 1.   From AWS Artifact in the AWS Management Console, download the PCI DSS Attestation of Compliance (AoC) and Responsibility Summary.

Step 2.   Read the summary report and review the services that are within the scope of PCI DSS and determine whether the standard virtual environment for computing and storage at AWS is PCI compliant for both Amazon's and your responsibilities.

Step 3.   Visit https://aws.amazon.com/compliance/programs/ scroll down, and click PCI DSS Level 1.

Step 4.   Under PCI DSS Resources on the right side of the page, select the "Compliance Guide: PCI DSS 3.2.1 on AWS" and review requirements for Amazon, requirements for the cloud service provider (CSP), and the responsibilities of the client, as shown in Table 7-4.

Table 7-4 PCI Checklist for Compliance

PCI DSS Requirement	Details	Customer Responsibilities	AWS Responsibilities	AWS Solution
Install and maintain firewalls to protect cardholder data	Shared responsibility	Firewalls on instances, firewalls at the subnet levels	Firewalls at the cloud perimeter between AWS clients	Security groups and network ACLs
Don't use vendor defaults for passwords and security	Customer's responsibility	Workloads	Network devices	AWS Identity and Access Management (IAM)

PCI DSS Requirement	Details	Customer Responsibilities	AWS Responsibilities	AWS Solution
Protect stored cardholder data	Customer's responsibility	Encrypted data	Secured storage arrays	AWS Marketplace
Encrypt transmission of cardholder data across public networks	Customer's responsibility	Encrypted transmissions	Supplied security controls	VPN connections
Use and update antivirus software	Customer's responsibility	Third-party software	N/A	AWS Marketplace options
Develop and maintain secure systems	Shared responsibility	EC2 instance	Hypervisor security	Secure API calls and certificates
Develop and maintain secure workloads	Customer's responsibility	On the instance	Hypervisor security	AWS Marketplace options
Restrict access to cardholder data	Customer's responsibility	Access controls	Physical security	AWS IAM
Assign unique IDs to each person with computer access	Customer's responsibility	Access controls, password policy	Strong authentication	AWS IAM
Restrict physical access to cardholder data	Amazon's responsibility	N/A	Physical security	AWS responsibility
Track and monitor all access to network resources and cardholder data	Shared responsibility	Customer's virtual environment	Physical infrastructure and hypervisor	CloudTrail, CloudWatch, and AWS GuardDuty
Test security systems and processes regularly	Shared responsibility	Customer's virtual environment	Intrusion detection system/intrusion prevention system (IDS/IPS)	AWS Config and AWS Inspector
Define security policies for information security	Shared responsibility	Customer's security policy	ISO security policies	AWS IAM
Additional PCI DSS requirements for shared hosting providers	Amazon's responsibility	N/A	PCI DSS audits	N/A

AWS Compliance Standards

AWS supports several compliance programs for a variety of businesses running in regulated industries, including financial services, healthcare, and the U.S. government (see Table 7-5). AWS compliance programs support global standards and countries grouped by Americas, Asia Pacific and Europe, Middle East and Africa. For further details look here: https://aws.amazon.com/compliance/programs/.

Table 7-5   North American Compliance Frameworks

Compliance Framework	Details
CJIS Criminal Justice Information Services	Workloads for state and federal law enforcement agencies at AWS
Family Educational Rights and Privacy Act (FERPA)	Educational agencies and institutional storage of data records at AWS
Federal Financial Institutions Examination Council (FFIEC)	Rules for federal financial institutions on the use and security of AWS services at AWS
Federal Information Security Modernization Act (FISMA)	Security authorizations for government agencies using systems hosted at AWS, adhering to NIST 800-37 standards in AWS GovCloud
GxP	Rules and guidelines for food and medical products data hosted at AWS
HIPAA	Rules for processing, storing, and transmitting protected health information at AWS
International Traffic in Arms Regulations (ITAR)	Compliance with ITAR in AWS GovCloud
Motion Picture Association of America (MPAA)	Rules for securely storing, processing, and delivering protected media and content
NIST SP 800-53	Security controls applied to U.S. federal information systems to ensure confidentiality, integrity, and availability (CIA)
Voluntary Product Accessibility Template (VPAT)/Section 508	Rules for developing electronic and information technology for people with disabilities

In addition, AWS supports some well-known global compliance programs. The SOC 2 audit is a good place to start in reviewing available security controls at AWS (https://aws.amazon.com/compliance/soc-faqs/). All current compliance certifications that AWS is aligned with are audited and assessed on a regular schedule using independent third-party auditors.

HIPAA

If your business needs to comply with the 1996 Health Insurance Portability and Accountability Act (HIPAA), you must provide protections for what is defined as protected health information (PHI). Each healthcare provider—defined as the "covered entity" using AWS services to architect and host its workloads—is solely responsible for complying with the HIPAA rules and regulations. In HIPAA terminology, Amazon is defined as having a business associate role. HIPAA is applicable in the United States. Depending on where you live, there may be other compliance standards that are relevant to your country. Make sure to review the compliance standards and compliance certifications that AWS currently supports by visiting https://aws.amazon.com/compliance/programs/.

Since 2013, Amazon has provided a signed contract called a Business Associate Addendum (BAA). In this contract, Amazon promises to safeguard the stored healthcare information properly and lays out the rules and responsibilities that AWS is undertaking, including a list of the services and tasks that AWS will carry out on the customer's behalf. Each customer who enters a BAA with AWS must use only the defined HIPAA-eligible AWS services defined in the BAA.

Many common services available at AWS are now allowed by HIPAA regulations. However, to be sure, check the current AWS compliance documentation because certifications and regulations are constantly in flux. For example, the AWS Systems Manager Console and Resource Groups are currently not in scope for HIPAA. However, the VPC, encrypted EBS volumes, EC2 instances, and S3 storage are all supported under the HIPAA BAA; each customer decides how encryption is enabled for each service. A great place to start learning about compliance is by reviewing the AWS Services in Scope by Compliance Program (see https://aws.amazon.com/compliance/services-in-scope/).

NIST

Your business might align its compliance rules with the National Institute of Standards and Technology (NIST). In 2011, NIST presented preliminary documentation on what the public cloud industry was doing up to that point. The NIST definitions have morphed into a set of standards that many organizations, including the U.S. government, must achieve and maintain (https://nvlpubs.nist.gov/nistpubs/legacy/sp/nistspecialpublication800-145.pdf).

There is a wealth of NIST documentation to review at https://www.nist.gov that deals with cloud security, virtualization, operations, and many other areas of the public cloud. Even if you are not bound by a compliance standard, reviewing and following NIST recommendations can help you in developing your organization's required level of security in the AWS cloud. Visit this link for a summary of the features, benefits, risks, and recommendations for cloud computing for government agencies: https://www.nist.gov/publications/cloud-computing-review-features-benefits-and-risks-and-recommendations-secure-efficient.

AWS is compliant with the NIST 800-37 security controls, which allow U.S. government agencies to achieve and sustain compliance with FISMA. FISMA was passed into law in 2002 (and at the time stood for Federal Information Security Management Act) and required federal agencies to follow a set of standards when implementing their information security programs. FISMA focuses on properly managing and securing federal data records.

AWS has also obtained Federal Risk and Authorization Management Program (*FedRAMP*) authorization to operate its GovCloud regions. The U.S. federal government is using AWS to deliver some cloud services, and AWS must adhere to and demonstrate compliance with the FedRAMP standard, which is why the AWS GovCloud (US East/West) regions exist. The GovCloud region us-gov-west-1 is categorized as a high-impact level (Level 5); for comparison, public us-east-1 and us-west-2 regions are categorized as a moderate impact level (Level 2). Consider the following definitions:

- **NIST 800-53 Rev. 5:** This publication provides security guidance for security controls, including access control, auditing and accountability, configuration management, risk assessment, and incident response (https://csrc.nist.gov/publications/detail/sp/800-53/rev-5/archive/2020-09-23).

- **FedRAMP:** A defined methodology for security assessments, authorization, and continuous monitoring of cloud services and products.

- **High impact level:** Unclassified national security data.

- **Moderate impact level:** Publicly releasable data.

- **FISMA:** All data should be classified based on its sensitivity and automatically encrypted. If you work in the U.S. federal government or any state government, FISMA applies to you, and you must meet these requirements:

    - Maintain an up-to-date inventory of all information systems deployed

    - Categorize each information system's level of risk to the appropriate FISMA risk level

    - Create and maintain for your organization a security plan that details security policies and controls

    - Carry out risk assessments against your business processes, security risks at the organizational level, and risks at the information systems level

    - Conduct annual security audits

AWS GovCloud

AWS GovCloud is an isolated region that has been designed to match the regulatory compliance requirements of the U.S. government, federal and state agencies, and anybody else who works with the U.S. government (see Figure 7-14). It's important to note that all AWS regions and services have the same level of security. The differences with GovCloud follow:

- Vetted U.S. citizens manage the operations of GovCloud.

- AWS GovCloud is accessible only to U.S. citizens or green card root account holders.

- GovCloud is physically and logically isolated from all other AWS regions.

- GovCloud has provisional authorization for Department of Defense SRG Impact Level 2 (publicly releasable data), Impact Level 4 (unclassified sensitive data), and Impact Level 5 (unclassified national security data) workloads.

- GovCloud supports HIPAA, CJIS, and ITAR regulations.

- Certain AWS services, especially newly introduced services, will not be in scope for the GovCloud regions. New AWS services are reviewed for inclusion in GovCloud at both the moderate and the high impact levels.

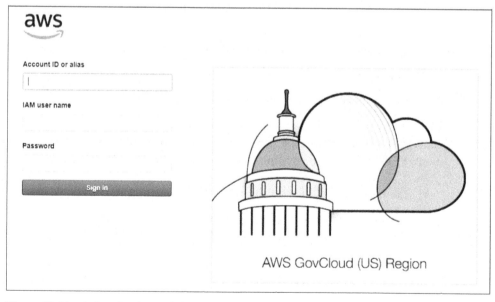

Figure 7-14 Authenticating to the GovCloud Region

Latency Concerns

Network latency, typically measured in milliseconds, tells you how much time a packet takes to travel from its source location to its destination. The interface between your end users and a hosted AWS workload is typically a browser or app interface that communicates with the hosted workload or website hosted at AWS. Latency in this example is how much time packets take to travel from your device to AWS and back to your location. Workloads and services hosted in the cloud will be influenced by latency. Connecting to workloads across the Internet is unpredictable because Internet speeds are unreliable. If any workload at AWS needs to query a database located in the corporate data center, latency can be an issue. Slow connection problems can be solved with faster private connection speeds such as AWS Direct Connect; however, the workload that you need to connect to may be available only across the Internet.

Because most, if not all, workload requests require some form of data transfer, using a content distribution network such as AWS CloudFront to cache data records or web pages can greatly help in speeding up workload access. For example:

- If you're accessing any workload hosted at AWS from a device such as a phone, computer, tablet, or watch, you will connect to your workload most likely across the Internet. In the background, Amazon's DNS service, Route 53, helps direct you to the public endpoint of the hosted workload at AWS.

- If you're planning to move workloads from your corporate data centers to the AWS cloud and are planning to operate in a hybrid model (with resources remaining in the corporate data center and some resources hosted in the cloud), the location of your data centers might influence the AWS region chosen and the types of network connections to use.

- For a public-facing SaaS workload, companies typically choose a region closest to where customers are located. Deploying Amazon's content delivery network (CDN), CloudFront, will help remediate latency concerns for customers located globally.

Latency can also be solved with the following AWS solutions:

- **Connecting to a hosted workload in another geographic location:** Connection speeds across the Internet to AWS are slower the farther away your user location is. AWS Global Accelerator can route your user traffic to a hosted workload at AWS using the closest edge location speeding up access.

- **Transferring data records to an S3 bucket:** Amazon S3 Transfer Acceleration speeds up content transfers to Amazon S3 storage location using Amazon

CloudFront edge as the ingress entry point onto the AWS private network, speeding up the transfer of files over long distances between the end user and the S3 bucket location.

■ **Replicating MySQL DB clusters:** Read replicas are read-only copies of the source database records. Read replicas can be geographically located in specific AWS regions to speed up queries for end users located in different geographical locations. Since read-replica updates are performed with asynchronous replication, replicas can contain stale information from time to time until replication has completed. Another solution is to deploy Amazon Aurora across multiple AWS regions. Replication from the primary DB cluster to all secondary read-only clusters is handled by the Aurora storage layer instead of the database engine, resulting in replicated changes in less than one second.

Services Offered in Each AWS Region

Not all AWS services are available in all regions; it can take a long time for a recently introduced cloud service to become available in every AWS region. *Generally available* is a term that AWS uses to indicate that a specific AWS service is operating in most, if not all, AWS regions. The core infrastructure services including EC2 instances, EC2 instances, RDS, ELB, S3 buckets, virtual private networking, and many others are available in every AWS region.

Each new AWS service is typically offered in a *preview mode*, where the service is initially available to a limited number of users that sign up to test the new service. Some services can take years to change from preview status to full online status. (For example, Amazon Elastic File System [EFS] was in preview mode for quite a long time before it became generally available across all AWS regions.)

The cloud services being offered in each AWS region might dictate what regions you choose. Whereas core compute, networking, and storage services are available everywhere, newer AWS services take time to become generally available in all regions. As a general rule, the newer the service, the longer it will take for the service to be deployed in all regions.

Your compliance rules and regulations may also determine your service availability. For example, if you are bound by FedRAMP rules and regulations, there will typically be several services and management tools that are not approved for use at this time—and that perhaps never will be.

Calculating Costs

It is important to understand costs when dealing with a cloud provider. The AWS mantra is to pay for what you use. AWS uses a consumption-based model; as you use a higher volume of AWS services, you pay more—but on a sliding scale. Some costs are bundled into the prices of services; for example, there's no charge to order an AWS VPC and add subnets. However, there are charges when EC2 instances are deployed, and there are additional costs for replicating compute instance traffic across availability zones. Adding additional EC2 when running workloads designed for high availability and failover will also increase overall costs.

AWS pricing depends on the region and AZs that you have selected to operate in; you can pay a little or a lot more for the same service in comparison to other AWS regions. An organization might have a limited choice of regions if compliance rules for your industry dictate where you can operate in the cloud. For example, choosing the AWS Canada Central region ca=central-1 means you are using AWS resources and AZs located in Canada, and depending on the currency exchange rate, pricing in Canada might be less than what you would pay in your home country. Is your company allowed to operate in Canada? During the planning and design phases of moving to the AWS cloud, it is important to carefully consider the compliance rules that your company may have to follow.

The biggest and least expensive AWS region is the us-east-1 (Northern Virginia) region, offering the largest number of availability zones and AWS services. Another region with comparable pricing and service availability to Northern Virginia is us-east-2 (Ohio). For the EU or São Paulo regions, you can expect pricing to be a few hundred percent more!

Don't forget that the monthly costs that customers pay for their workload infrastructure will increase as the requirements for high availability and improved reliability increase. Customers can greatly reduce their EC2 instance pricing by ordering Reserved Instances and saving on other compute costs with Savings Plans. (Chapters 12, 13, 14, and 15 provide detailed information about managing cloud costs.)

Distributed Design Patterns

Successful workloads hosted at AWS have high availability and fault tolerance baked into the underlying design. As you prepare for the AWS Certified Solutions Architect – Associate (SAA-C03) exam, you need to understand these concepts conceptually in conjunction with the services that can provide a higher level of redundancy and availability. After all, if a workload is designed to be highly available, it will have a higher level of redundancy and will continue to function at an acceptable working level when issues occur.

The same is true with a fault-tolerant design—if your workload is hosted on infrastructure that has been designed with tolerance for issues such as latency, performance, and durability issues, your workload will be able to operate most of the time successfully.

Designing for High Availability and Fault Tolerance

Imagine that your initial foray into the AWS cloud is to host a monolithic workload at AWS. Although this is possible using a "lift and shift" cloud migration tool that moves the virtual server from the on-premises data center to the AWS cloud, there will eventually be issues with availability. The single EC2 instance will eventually fail or need to be taken down for maintenance. A failure of the EC2 instance, as shown in Figure 7-15, impacts all clients. There are also design issues related to the workload state and data records stored on a single EC2 instance. The old-style monolithic workload will not function well on premises nor in the cloud.

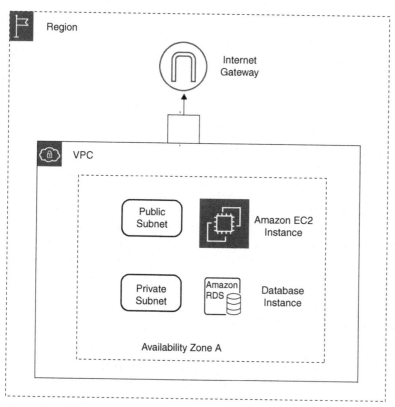

Figure 7-15   Starting AWS Infrastructure

To add high availability to this design, as a first step you could split the monolithic workload into a web tier with multiple EC2 instances hosted across multiple availability zones receiving workload requests from a load balancer, as shown in Figure 7-16, providing high availability and additional redundancy. Therefore, a database tier is also added, hosting the data records on at least two database servers. The primary database server replicates all changes to the secondary database using synchronous replication. The secondary database must communicate to the primary database that the data transferred has been successfully received and written before additional records will be sent.

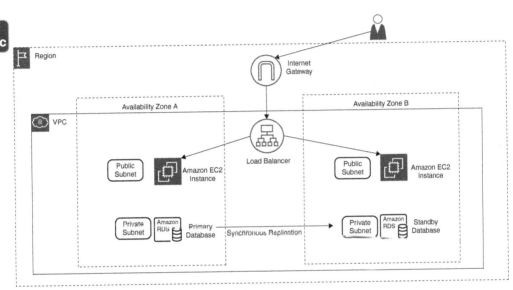

Figure 7-16   Hosting Across Multiple AZs to Increase Availability and Fault Tolerance

AWS data centers and AZs are built for deploying high-availability designs connected together with high-speed/low-latency links and are located far enough away from each other that a single natural disaster won't affect all of the AZs in each AWS region at the same time.

If the mandate for this workload is that it should be down for no more than 4.5 hours in any given year, this equates to 99.5% *uptime*. Internal reviews of the current infrastructure show that over the past year, the web server has 90% availability and the database server has 95% availability, resulting in total availability of 85.5%, as shown in Figure 7-17.

SLA Required: 99.5%

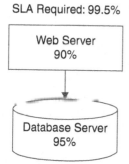

Total Availability: 0.9 × 0.95 = 85.5%

Figure 7-17   Availability Calculation for a Simple Hosted Workload

This amount of uptime and availability obviously needs to be increased to meet the availability mandate of the business requirements. Adding an additional web server to the design increases the overall availability to 94.5%, as shown in Figure 7-18.

SLA Required: 99.5%

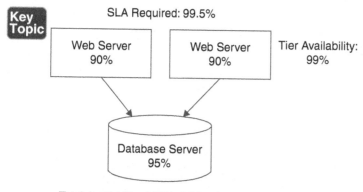

Total Availability: 0.95 × 0.99 = 94.5%

Figure 7-18   Increasing Workload Availability by Adding Compute Workload

The design now has some additional high availability and built-in fault tolerance for the web tier, so if one server fails, the workload will still be available. Next, the database tier availability needs to be increased. Adding two replica database servers to the existing database infrastructure in addition to adding a third web server to the web server tier results in both tiers achieving a total availability of 99.8%, exceeding the *SLA* goal, as shown in Figure 7-19.

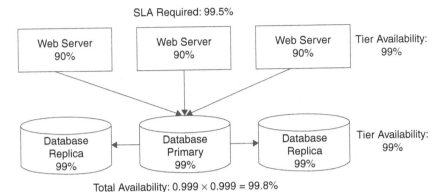

Figure 7-19 Adding Availability to Both Tiers

Removing Single Points of Failure

Eliminating as many single points of failure as possible in your workload design will greatly increase workload high availability and fault tolerance. A *single point of failure* is a critical component in a system that, if it fails, will cause the entire system to fail. Single points of failure are a major concern in system design because they can lead to significant disruptions and downtime. To avoid single points of failure, design with redundant components or backup systems in place, ensuring that the application remains operational even if a critical component fails. Take some time to review Table 7-6, which discusses possible mitigation plans for single points of failure.

Table 7-6 Avoiding Single Points of Failure

Possible Single Point of Failure	Mitigation Plan	Reason
On-premises DNS	Route 53 DNS	Anycast DNS services are hosted across all AWS regions and edge locations. Health checks and traffic patterns support workload failover.
Third-party load balancer	Elastic Load Balancing (ELB) services	ELB load-balancers are deployed per AZ. Elastic IP addresses provide fast failover.
Web workloads	ELB/Auto Scaling	Scale workload compute resources automatically up and down to meet demand.
RDS database servers	Redundant data nodes (primary/standby/ cluster)	Synchronized replication between primary and multiple standby nodes provides a minimum of three or more copies of data.

Possible Single Point of Failure	Mitigation Plan	Reason
EBS data volumes	Snapshots and retention schedule	Automatically copy snapshots across regions for additional redundancy using Lifecycle Manager.
Authentication problems	Redundant authentication nodes	Multiple Managed AD domain controllers provide alternate authentication options.
Data center failure	Multiple availability zones	Each region has multiple AZs providing high-availability and failover design options.
Regional disaster	Multi-region deployment with Route 53	Route 53 routing policy provides geo-redundancy for workloads hosted across AWS regions.

Table 7-7 lists AWS services that can be improved with high availability, fault tolerance, and redundancy.

Table 7-7 Planning for High Availability, Fault Tolerance, and Redundancy

AWS Service	High Availability	Fault Tolerance	Redundancy	Multi-Region
EC2 instance	Additional EC2 instance	Multiple availability zones	EC2 Auto Scaling	Route 53 health checks
EBS volume	Cluster design	Snapshots	AMI	Copy AMI/snapshot
Load balancer	Multiple AZs	Elastic IP addresses	Server farm	Route 53 geoproximity load balancing options
Containers	Elastic Container Service (ECS)	Fargate management	Workload load balancer/ Auto Scaling	Regional service not multi-region
RDS deployment	Multiple AZs	Synchronous replication	Snapshots/ backup EBS data volumes and transaction records	Regional service, not multi-region
Custom EC2 database	Multiple AZs and replicas	Asynchronous/ synchronous replication options	Snapshots/ backup EBS volumes	Custom high-availability and failover designs across regions with Route 53 Traffic Policies

AWS Service	High Availability	Fault Tolerance	Redundancy	Multi-Region
Aurora (MySQL/ PostgreSQL)	Six copies of data replicated across three AZs	Multiple writers	Clustered shared storage VSAN	Multi-region deployment database hosted and replicated across multiple AWS regions
DynamoDB (NoSQL)	Six copies of data replicated across three AZs	Multiple writers	Continuous backup to S3	Multi-region deployment across multiple AWS regions
Route 53	Health checks	Failover routing	Multi-value answer routing	Geolocation/ geoproximity routing
S3 bucket	Same-region replication	Built-in	Built-in	Cross-region replication

Immutable Infrastructure

Immutable architecture is a design in which select components of a workload, such as a web or application server, are replaced rather than modified or updated. When changes need to be made, the old components are discarded and new, updated components are put in their place. This approach has several advantages over mutable architecture, in which resources are modified in place. Because immutable architectures use new resources, they are not affected by changes that might have been made to the old resources. Because older components are discarded rather than modified, it is easier to revert to a previous version of the system if necessary. The term *immutable*, when applied to the AWS cloud, defines resources deployed to a production environment by replacing the existing version of the EC2 instance or image (AMI) with a new, updated version that should not change when they are deployed. For example, an EC2 instance, after being deployed, may get security updates from the Internet. Becaue of the updates there is no guarantee that the installed dependencies have not changed since the last deployment if immutable deployments are not the norm. With immutable servers, any changes result in new servers being deployed instead of updating the servers currently in production. Changes are not allowed in immutable infrastructure; therefore, the state of an immutable server is always known.

Creating an immutable server starts with an image called a golden image or golden AMI. Starting with the base image, all unnecessary software packages and tools are removed. Security patches and approved configurations are applied to harden the image. After the image is tested and approved, it is locked and ready for deployment in the production environment.

When workloads are deployed using immutable infrastructure, canary deployments should be used to minimize the risk of failure when new server versions are deployed into production. *Canary deployments* are a technique for releasing software updates, and the new version of the software is initially made available to a small subset of users. This enables the update to be tested in a production environment before it is made available to the larger user base. If the software update performs as expected and no issues are discovered, it is gradually rolled out to additional users. However, if any problems are found, the update can be quickly rolled back without affecting the entire user base.

Immutable deployments have no upgrades, because upgrades have been replaced with new deployments (see Figure 7-20). Administrative access is not required to production servers preventing undocumented manual changes and hotfixes. All servers (web, application, database) that are part of the same workload are version controlled.

Figure 7-20   Deploying Immutable Servers

Immutable infrastructure is supported by the following services at AWS:

- AWS CloudFormation can test deployed stacks to determine if any changes, called drift, have occurred on the deployed stack resources when compared to the initial stack template.

- AWS Elastic Beanstalk supports immutable deployments of EC2 instances and Docker containers.

- Amazon EC2 Auto Scaling supports instance refresh that enables automatic deployments of new workload versions using Auto Scaling Groups (ASG).

- ELB Application and Network Load Balancers supports A/B and canary deployments by routing requests to different weighted target groups based on listener rules, as shown in Figure 7-21. Developers can control the distribution of traffic to multiple versions of their workload using two target groups with weights of 80 and 20; the load balancer will route 80 percent of the traffic to the first target group and 20 percent to the second target group.

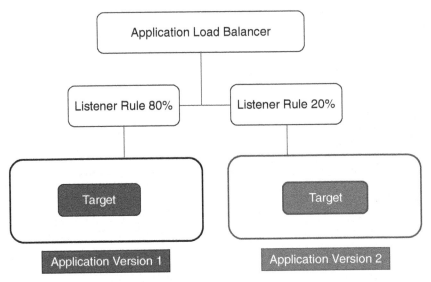

Figure 7-21 Weighted ALB Target Groups

- Multiple VPCs can be created for dev, test, and production environments.
- Amazon EC2 Image Builder, in conjunction with AWS CodePipeline, supports the building, testing, and deployment of virtual machine and container images for immutable deployments.

NOTE AWS X-Ray can be used to analyze workload behavior using end-to-end tracing identifying performance issues and errors for individual workload requests to workloads running on EC2 instances and Amazon ECS, AWS Lambda, Kinesis, DynamoDB, and AWS Elastic Beanstalk.

Storage Options and Characteristics

Storage services also utilize availability zones for their replicated data center storage locations. Each storage service listed in Table 7-8 can operate in a single AZ with redundancy and high availability or across multiple AZs within the chosen AWS region of deployment.

Table 7-8 Storage Service Characteristics

Storage	Durability	Replication
Amazon EBS	Multiple storage volumes, snapshots stored in Amazon S3	Replicated within each AZ across multiple servers
Amazon FSx	Multiple storage volumes, automatic backup to Amazon S3	Single or Multi-AZ deployments
Amazon EFS	Multiple storage volumes, automatic backup to Amazon S3	Single or Multi-AZ deployments
Amazon S3 Standard	Eleven 9s durability	Across three AZs or more depending on AWS Region
Amazon S3 One Zone	Eleven 9s durability	Single availability zone
Amazon S3 Glacier Deep Archive	Eleven 9s durability	Across three AZs
Amazon DynamoDB	SSD volumes on multiple servers	Across three AZs, or multiple AWS regions
Amazon RDS	EBS volumes	Across one, two, or three AZs
Amazon Aurora	SSD volumes cluster shared storage	Across three AZs, or multiple AWS regions
AWS Backup	Eleven 9s availability	Across three AZs

NOTE Use the EBS lifecycle service to schedule EBS and remove unneeded snapshots. Use S3 versioning and lifecycle policies to purge old object versions when they are no longer required.

Failover Strategies

Each customer must use the tools and services available at AWS to design their workload environment to be able to withstand failures when they occur. Workloads must be designed to be redundant and proper backups must be available to help restore the customer's workload when required. A disaster recovery (DR) strategy must be designed and implemented for workloads running at AWS.

High-availability designs deployed across multiple availability zones protect against disruptions in a single AZ, as the other AZs will continue to function, providing workload availability and no data loss. If failures must be prevented against larger potential disasters involving multiple AZs, backups of key services and data records can be stored in other regions, or multiple AWS regions can be used for active-passive or active-active deployments.

It's important to understand the published uptime figures for the AWS cloud. Published uptime figures are not guarantees; instead, they are what AWS strives for—and typically achieves. Route 53, AWS's DNS service, is designed for 100% uptime, but issues still may occur without warning.

Failures are going to happen. Disaster recovery procedures focus on carrying out the recovery steps after a disaster has occurred. For each workload, acceptable recovery objectives must be defined. There are two generally agreed-upon metrics that define how a disaster recovery process should be designed: What is the recovery objective when a disaster occurs? What is the acceptable amount of data that can be lost when a disaster occurs?

- **Recovery point objective (RPO):** *RPO* is defined as the maximum acceptable amount of time since the last data recovery point or the acceptable loss of data. If your RPO is defined as 5 minutes, then the disaster recovery process needs to be designed to restore the data records to within 5 minutes of when the disaster occurred.

- **Recovery time objective (RTO):** *RTO* is defined as the maximum acceptable delay between a service interruption and a return to normal service. If RTO is set to 1 hour, for example, the workload should be up and functional within that 1-hour timeframe.

Customers need to define acceptable values for RPO and RTO, defining a recovery strategy that meets the recovery objectives of each workload. Strategies chosen include active-passive (backup and restore, pilot light, or warm standby), or multi-site active-active (see Figure 7-22).

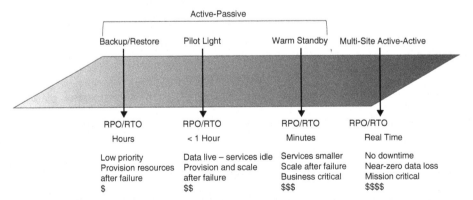

Figure 7-22 Disaster Strategies Compared

Backup and Restore

Backup and restore strategies back up data and workloads into a DR location. The DR location could be a separate AWS region, as shown in Figure 7-23, or an availability zone within a select AWS region. Using a Multi-AZ strategy within a single AWS region may be sufficient for some workloads; it will depend on the specific use case and business requirements. For an on-premises workload, a hybrid architecture could be deployed, allowing operation in both locations using AWS Direct Connect providing a dedicated high-speed connection.

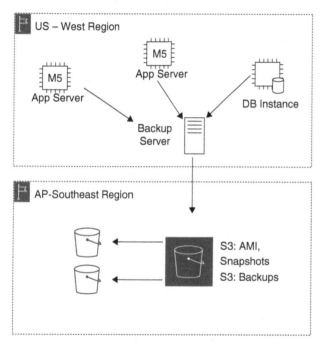

Figure 7-23 Multi-Region Backup and Restore

The following AWS services can help assist in creating a backup and restoration plan:

- **Amazon Machine Images:** Images can be manually copied to multiple regions for safekeeping. Amazon Data Lifecycle Manager and AWS EC2 Image Builder can automate the creation and retention of Amazon EBS-backed AMIs across multiple AWS regions and AWS accounts.

- **Amazon EBS Snapshots:** Snapshots can be manually copied to multiple regions for safekeeping. Amazon Data Lifecycle Manager can automatically copy snapshots on a schedule across up to three regions. The Data Lifecycle Manager also supports cross-account sharing, automatically sharing and copying snapshots across AWS accounts.

■ **Amazon Outposts:** Outposts allows customers to deploy Amazon RDS database engines as a hybrid cloud database deploying RDS to an on-premises data center accross a Direct Connect connection. Backups and snapshots are stored locally or in an AWS region.

Pilot Light

A disaster recovery pilot light is a disaster recovery strategy in which a minimal system is kept running at all times, ready to be expanded into a full-scale workload in the event of a disaster. *Pilot light* deployments could have synchronized database records and idle compute services. For example, a pilot light disaster recovery strategy has a defined online primary site where web and primary database servers are operating and are fully operational. The primary site could be on premises, as shown in Figure 7-24, an AWS availability zone or regional location, as shown in Figure 7-25. The standby web and application servers are ready to launch but are not powered on. The primary database server located in the primary site replicates data updates and changes to the standby database server. When planning the AWS location for your disaster recovery site, the compliance rules and regulations that your organization adheres to may dictate which region should be used. In addition, you might want the DR location to be as close as possible to your physical corporate location if latency is a concern.

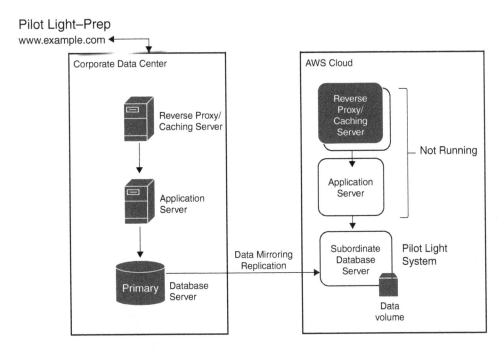

Figure 7-24   Pilot Light Setup

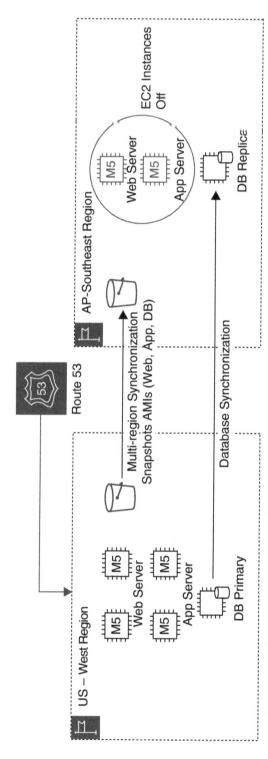

Figure 7-25   Multi-Region Pilot Light Setup

When a disaster occurs, the standby web and workload instances will need to be turned on or deployed using an Amazon Machine Images that were copied to the recovery site. The standby database server at the recovery site will need to be defined as the primary database server, and DNS services will have to redirect traffic to the AWS region disaster recovery site, as shown in the example for the on-premises pilot light response in Figure 7-26, and the multi-region responses shown in Figure 7-27. The RTO to execute a pilot light deployment is certainly faster than the backup and restoration scenario; there is no data loss, but there is also no access to the hosted workload at the recovery site until configuration and startup is complete.

Pilot Light Recovery

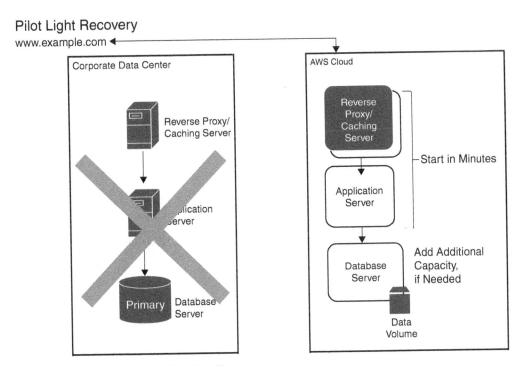

Figure 7-26   On Premises Pilot Light Response

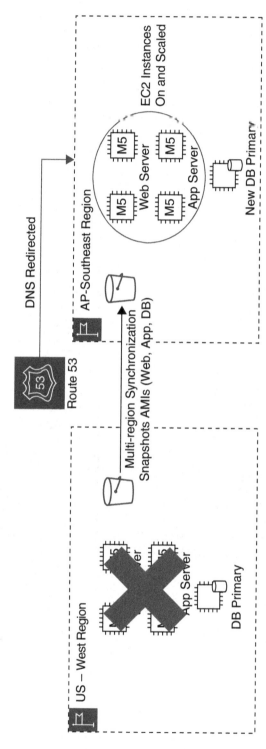

Figure 7-27 Multi-region Pilot Light Response

Another option for a faster pilot light DR deployment is to automate the configuration using CloudFormation templates, ensuring that DR infrastructure is built and ready to go as fast as possible.

AWS Backup can also assist you in designing a backup and restoration solution that is much more effective than the traditional DR design. AWS Backup can back up Amazon EC2 instances, Amazon EBS volumes, Amazon S3 buckets, RDS deployments, Amazon EFS, Amazon FSx for Windows File Server, Amazon DynamoDB tables, and VMware workloads on premises, on Amazon Outposts, and hosted in VMware Cloud on AWS.

Many third-party backup vendors also have built-in native connectors to directly write to Amazon S3 buckets as the storage target. Backups can be uploaded and written to S3 storage using a public Internet connection or using a private AWS Direct Connect or AWS VPN connection.

Warm Standby

A *warm standby* solution speeds up the recovery time because all the components in the warm standby location are already in active operation—hence the term *warm*—but at a smaller scale of operation when compared to the primary site.

The secondary system in the standby location is maintained and updated in a similar manner to the system's primary location, but it is not actively in use. In the event of a disaster, the warm standby can be quickly activated and replace the primary, enabling the organization to maintain critical operations and minimize downtime. Warm standby is more comprehensive than a disaster recovery pilot light, because the secondary system location is fully functional and ready for use instead of being a minimal recovery solution that needs to be turned on and scaled. Standby web and workload servers are online and in operation, as shown in the example shown in Figure 7-28. The database servers are also online and functional, and load balancing (ELB) and auto-scaling (EC2 Auto Scaling) have been deployed.

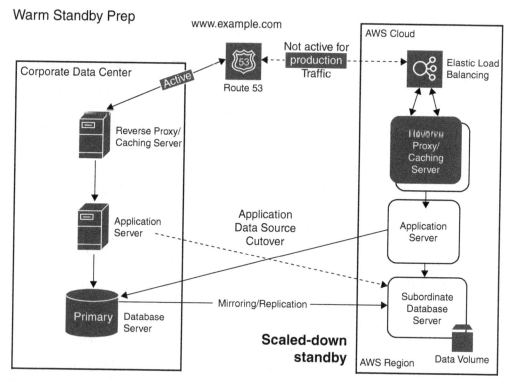

Figure 7-28 Warm Standby Setup

The key variable, when compared to a pilot light deployment, is that the warm standby workload is active; when a disaster occurs, the recovery site can handle some amount of traffic at once. The additional EC2 instances will need to be scaled, and Route 53 reroutes DNS traffic requests to the standby location, as shown in Figure 7-29. Because warm standby resources were already active, the recovery time is shorter than with a pilot light solution; however, a warm standby solution is more expensive than a pilot light option as additional standby resources are running 24/7.

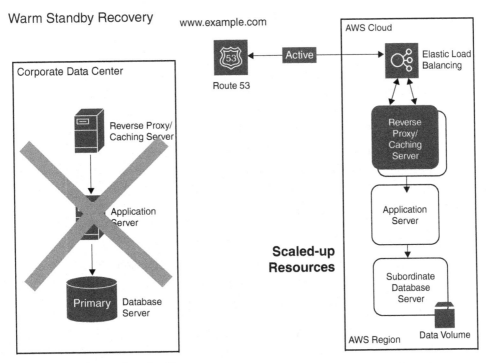

Figure 7-29 Warm Standby Response

NOTE AWS Elastic Disaster Recovery can be used by organizations to set up automated disaster recovery for on-premises physical or virtual server workloads and cloud-hosted applications to AWS.

Multi-Region Scenarios

Workloads designed for minimal downtime with no data loss can be deployed across two or more availability zones, or across multiple AWS regions. Use cases requiring this level of availability include critical business workloads such as finance or banking workloads. Deployment of a workload across multiple AWS regions adds an additional level of redundancy and availability but has additional costs because each region must host a complete copy of the workload. Multi-region scenarios can be active-passive, or active-active with a minimum of two AWS regions hosting both the primary and alternate locations. An active-passive scenario uses one region as a primary site and the other region as a warm standby. In each region there is a minimum of two AZs in each AWS region hosting both the primary and alternate locations.

Warm Standby with Amazon Aurora

In this example, the workload is deployed to each AWS region using the warm standby design, as shown in Figure 7-30. The passive site is scaled down, but data records are kept consistent. Data records are asynchronously replicated from the primary Aurora RDS cluster to the read replicas in the passive region with a global database solution providing strongly consistent data stores, keeping the workload data synchronized across multiple AWS regions.

Web and workload servers in both AWS regions are hosted using Workload Load Balancers integrated with EC2 Auto Scaling to automatically scale each workload to changes in workload demand. The ELB service is deployed to all AZs. Using an Auto Scale Group (ASG), the EC2 Auto-Scaling service operates across multiple AZs and mitigates availability zone failures by managing the required compute resources mandated by the ASG to the remaining AZs.

An Amazon Aurora global database has one primary region and can have up to five read-only secondary regions. Cross-region replication latency with Aurora is typically around 1 second. Amazon Aurora allows you to create up to 16 additional read-only database instances in each AWS region. If the Amazon Aurora primary region fails, one of the secondary regions can be promoted to take over the reading and writing responsibilities in less than 1 minute, with an effective RPO of 1 second and an RTO of less than 1 minute.

For a read-local/write-global strategy, an organization could define one region as the primary for all database writes. Data would be replicated for reads to the other AWS region. If the primary database region fails, failover to the secondary site occurs. Both workload tiers are online; when issues occur with one workload tier, traffic gets redirected automatically.

Amazon Route 53 can perform health checks to ensure each regional location remains available, routing requests to the other regional location when a resource becomes unhealthy.

NOTE AWS services that operate across multiple regions with continuous asynchronous replication include Amazon S3 Multi-region access points, Amazon RDS read replicas, and Amazon DynamoDB multi-region tables. Up-to-date versions of data are synchronized and available in each of your active regions.

Active-Active

Active-active failover refers to a scenario in which two or more systems are operating simultaneously and either system can take over if web, databases, or storage services fail or become unavailable. This type of failover allows for increased availability and reliability of the system because there is always a backup server ready to take over

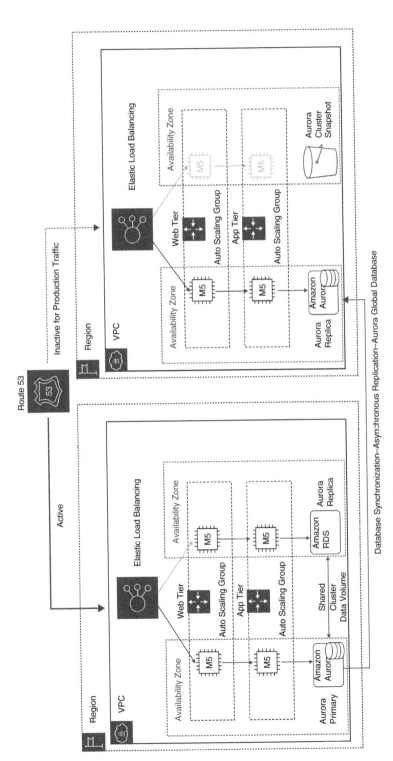

Figure 7-30 Warm Standby with Aurora Global Database

in the event of a failure. Therefore, at AWS with an ***active-active*** design, two or more AWS regions can accept requests. When a failure occurs, requests are rerouted from the region with issues to the other AWS region. Figure 7-31 shows Amazon DynamoDB deployed as a global deployment with a local DynamoDB table deployed in each region and synchronized across the two AWS regions. Each local DynamoDB table has data changes propagated to the local table in the other region within seconds.

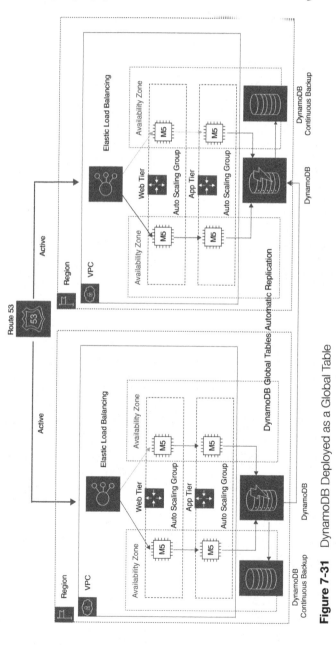

Figure 7-31 DynamoDB Deployed as a Global Table

NOTE Multi-region active-active deployments may have to consider possible data sovereignty requirements; if regions are hosted in the EU, data storage will be bound by the General Data Protection Regulation (GDPR).

Single and Multi-Region Recovery Cheat Sheet

Availability goals are typically defined as a percentage such as 99% or 99.9%. Recovery solutions could use availability zones within a single AWS region, or use multiple AWS regions, for failover and recovery. Table 7-9 summarizes the relevant tasks for each chosen scenario.

Table 7-9 Single or Multi-Region Scenario Tasks

Single AWS Region				Multi-Region
Task	99% Scenario	99.9% Scenario	99.99% Scenario	99.999% Scenario
Monitor resources	Monitor website OK status	Amazon CloudWatch metrics and alarms for web and DB tier issues	Amazon CloudWatch success and failure metrics with alerts for web and DB tier issues	Amazon CloudWatch metrics and alarms for all web, database, and region failure
Adapt to changes in demand with automated responses	Hardware failures, software updates	EC2 Auto-Scaling based on 70% CPU utilization	AWS Auto-Scaling and Amazon Aurora with regional read replicas	Auto-scaling and Amazon Aurora multi-region database with regional read replicas
Implement changes	CloudFormation stacks	CloudFormation stacks	Blue/green or canary deployments on schedule	Blue/green or canary deployments every month
Back up data	Back up to Amazon S3; enable Versioning; WORM policy	Amazon RDS backups (snapshots transaction logs); backup to Amazon S3; enable Versioning; WORM policy	RDS backups (snapshots, transaction logs); backup to Amazon S3; enable Versioning; WORM policy	RDS backups (snapshots, transaction logs); backup to Amazon S3; enable Versioning; WORM policy
Architect for resiliency	One region, one AZ	Two AZs; ELB; Auto Scaling; RDS Multi-AZ; ELB health checks	Three AZs; Amazon Aurora read replicas in each zone; Amazon CloudFront CDN	Three AZs; Amazon Aurora read replicas in each zone; Amazon CloudFront CDN; regional failover

Single AWS Region				Multi-Region
Task	99% Scenario	99.9% Scenario	99.99% Scenario	99.999% Scenario
Test resiliency	Limited testing of EC2 instances	Limited testing of EC2 instances	Game day testing	Game day testing
Disaster recovery	Redeploy in same or alternate AZ.	Recovery with runbooks	Recovery with runbooks using regional backups	Active-active multi-region deployment; workload and data operating in separate AWS regions
Availability	Recover from failure in 2 hours	Recover from failure in 1 hour	Recover in 15 minutes	Recover within 1 minute automatically

Disaster Recovery Cheat Sheet

Review the following cheat sheet statements to help solidify your knowledge of disaster recovery before taking the AWS Certified Solutions Architect – Associate (SAA-C03) exam:

- **Single region DR:** Multiple availability zones and Elastic Load Balancing provide high availability for Amazon EC2 instances and Amazon ECS.

- **Single region DR:** Multiple availability zones, Elastic Load Balancing, and EC2 Auto Scaling provide high availability, automatic scaling, and self-healing web and workload tiers.

- **Multi-region DR:** Route 53 health checks monitor the health and performance of web servers and are used to route traffic to healthy resources.

- **Multi-region DR:** Route 53 health checks monitor endpoints, other health checks, and CloudWatch alarms.

- **Multi-region DR:** Route 53 DNS active-active failover configurations are for scenarios where all resources are available. All records have the same record type and routing policy (for example, weighted, geoproximity, or latency policies).

- **Multi-region DR:** Route 53 DNS active-passive failover configurations use Failover as the routing policy. Scenarios are where the primary resource is available, with secondary resources on standby when primary resources become unavailable.

- **Multi-region DR:** Amazon Route 53 Workload Recovery Controller (ARC) is a special health check that determines when workloads and resources are ready for recovery and coordinates the failover process.

- **Single region DR:** Use AWS Backup to back up AWS data resources and hybrid VMware deployments to S3 storage.

- **Single/Multi-region DR:** AWS RDS can be deployed Multi-AZ or in a cluster (primary plus two standby DB replicas).

- **Single region DR:** Amazon Aurora can be deployed as a regional deployment across three AZs per region.

- **Single/Multi-region DR:** Amazon Aurora can also be deployed as a global database across multiple AWS regions.

- **Single/Multi-region DR:** Amazon DynamoDB can be deployed as a regional deployment across three AZs per region or as a global table across multiple AWS regions.

- **Single/Multi-region DR:** AWS CloudFormation can be used to define and deploy infrastructure across AWS Regions. AWS CloudFormation Stack Sets enables you to create and update CloudFormation stacks across multiple accounts and regions.

AWS Service Quotas

When resources are ordered in each AWS account, the number of resources that can be ordered is controlled by default *service quotas* (formerly called *service limits*) that are defined for over 100 AWS cloud services. Quotas control the availability of AWS resources and attempt to prevent customers from provisioning more resources than needed without careful thought. Customers can request quota increases using the AWS Service Quotas service, shown in Figure 7-32. Customers need to be aware of the assigned default quotas and the increases that are required for the deployment of workload architecture.

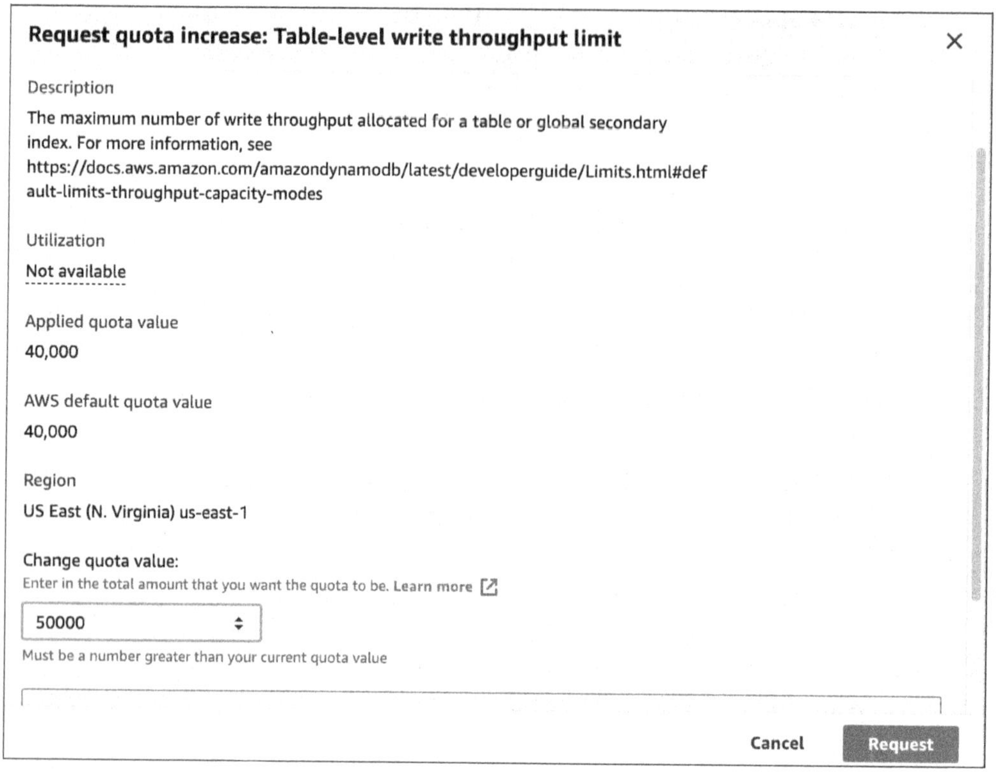

Request quota increase: Table-level write throughput limit   ✕

Description

The maximum number of write throughput allocated for a table or global secondary index. For more information, see https://docs.aws.amazon.com/amazondynamodb/latest/developerguide/Limits.html#def ault-limits-throughput-capacity-modes

Utilization

Not available

Applied quota value

40,000

AWS default quota value

40,000

Region

US East (N. Virginia) us-east-1

Change quota value:

Enter in the total amount that you want the quota to be. **Learn more** 🔗

| 50000 | ⇕ |

Must be a number greater than your current quota value

Cancel   **Request**

Figure 7-32 Requesting a Quota Increase (Attached)

Issues that could arise unexpectedly over time could include the number of VPCs that an AWS account can create per region, or the number of EC2 instances that can be launched per availability zone. If you want to scale the number of EC2 instances above your current service quota, for example, there is a possibility that you might not have the ability to add additional EC2 instances when you need them. The AWS Service Quotas utility can also centrally control quota limits for an AWS Organization, which manages a collection of AWS accounts in a tree-like design.

Organizations can use the AWS Service Quotas console to review and request increases for most AWS quotas. AWS Trusted Advisor can also review your current use of AWS resources and display current quota values for some services, as shown in Figure 7-33.

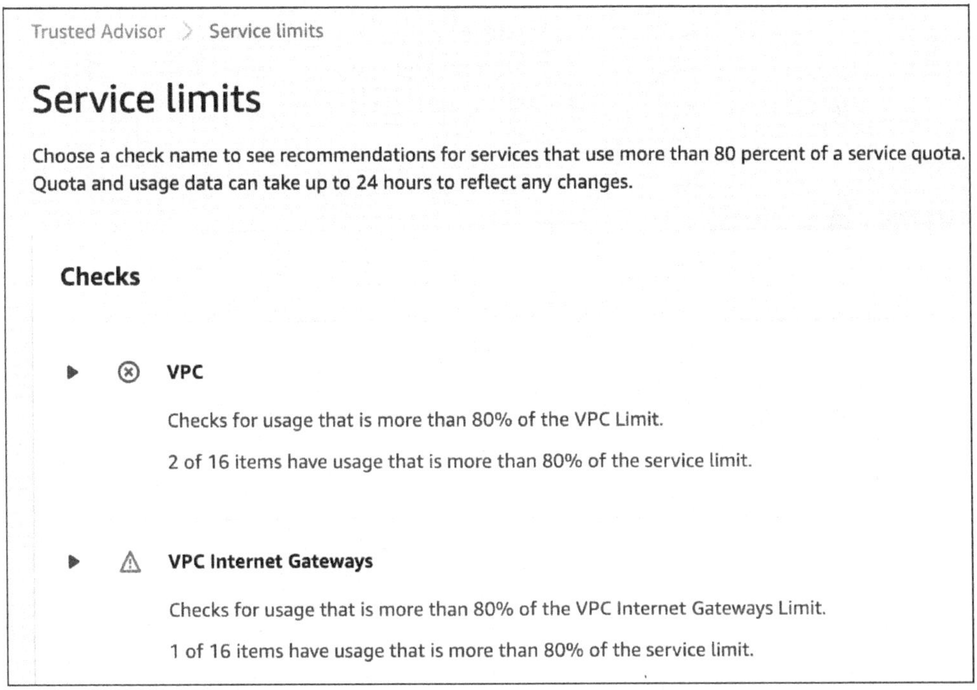

Trusted Advisor > Service limits

Service limits

Choose a check name to see recommendations for services that use more than 80 percent of a service quota. Quota and usage data can take up to 24 hours to reflect any changes.

Checks

▶ ⊗ **VPC**

   Checks for usage that is more than 80% of the VPC Limit.

   2 of 16 items have usage that is more than 80% of the service limit.

▶ ⚠ **VPC Internet Gateways**

   Checks for usage that is more than 80% of the VPC Internet Gateways Limit.

   1 of 16 items have usage that is more than 80% of the service limit.

Figure 7-33   Trusted Advisor Displays Current Quota Levels

Several AWS resources are also defined by specific constraints. For example, EBS volumes have maximum disk sizes, and EC2 instances have defined vCPU, RAM, storage, and network bandwidth constraints. Constraints can be changed for EBS volumes using the properties of each EBS volume to change the type, size, and network bandwidth; EC2 instances can be changed by type and family after the EC2 instance has been powered down.

AWS Service Quotas Cheat Sheet

Review the following cheat sheet statements to help solidify your knowledge before taking the AWS Certified Solutions Architect – Associate (SAA-C03) exam.

- AWS Service Quota manages usage across AWS accounts and regions where workloads are running.

- Service quotas are tracked per AWS account.

- Service quotas are region-specific.

NOTE   Most service quotas are specific to the AWS region where the service is located, as most AWS services are region-specific. You can also create CloudWatch alarms for a specific quota and be alerted when you are close to reaching your quota.

Amazon Route 53

Amazon's hosted DNS service, Route 53, is named for the standard DNS port number. Route 53 has a public side tuned to the public edge locations that accepts incoming customer requests and resolves each query to the requested AWS resource located on Route 53's private side, as shown in Figure 7-34. Route 53 knows about every resource created at AWS that is hosted on the private network. It supports both IPv4 and IPv6 address records, including the common A, AAAA, CA, CNAME, MX, NS, PTR, SOA, SRV, and TXT records.

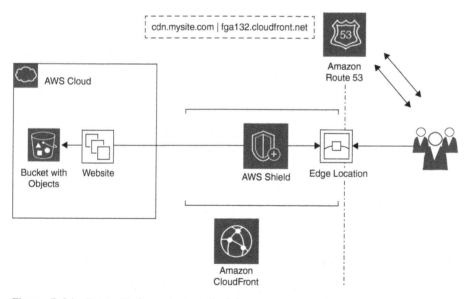

Figure 7-34   Route 53 Operations at the Edge

If a customer accesses an application hosted at AWS from a device, a DNS query is carried out to find the application's location and connect. You need an Internet connection or a private network connection to AWS for a device to begin communicating with the AWS cloud. HTTP and HTTPS endpoints are available to connect to an AWS service. Endpoints are regional and, in some cases, global (for global services such as Route 53).

DNS services, namely Amazon Route 53, need to be operational for the initial query to be successful. Operating in the AWS public cloud, the scope of DNS services has changed from local DNS services per corporation to worldwide redundant global

DNS services that are linked together with full knowledge of where the Amazon regions and availability zones are located and where each requested AWS service resides.

Amazon Route 53 is designed and operates using anycast DNS routing algorithms. Each destination AWS service location is known by the anycast DNS servers that are hosted across all the AWS regions and edge locations. The network location determines the edge location where Route 53 directs requests. When an application request reaches the selected edge location, the application request continues across Amazon's private network to the preferred AWS service location.

Route 53 offers the following services:

- **Domain name registration:** You use Route 53 to register the domain name for your website or application. After you choose a domain name and it is verified, the domain name is registered with Route 53. Route 53 DNS records can also be linked to an existing domain. When a domain has been registered with Route 53, it becomes the DNS service for the domain and creates a hosted zone for the domain. For redundancy, Route 53 assigns four name servers to the hosted zone; these name servers provide details about the location of your resources.

- **DNS resolution:** Route 53 routes Internet traffic to the resources for your domain both for public-facing resources and services and for AWS resources and services hosted at AWS. A public hosted zone is required for public-facing resources such as a company website. Private hosted zones are created to route traffic within a VPC. Each hosted zone has two records: a name server (NS) record and the start of authority (SOA) record. The name server record identifies the four name servers available to answer queries. The start of authority record indicates the authoritative location for answering queries for your domain.

- **Health checks:** Automated health checks can be delivered on a persistent schedule to cloud services and resources to confirm they are still available and functioning. When resources become unavailable, Route 53 routes requests from unhealthy resources to healthy resources.

Route 53 Health Checks

Health checks can monitor both the health and the performance of regional services including load balancers, web applications, and other external resources registered with Route 53. Each health check can monitor the following:

- **The health of resources:** Health checks can monitor selected endpoints based on their DNS name, IP address, or domain name to verify whether resources are reachable and functioning.

- **The status of other health checks:** Health checks can monitor multiple regional workloads to ensure that healthy resources are available across AWS regions or resources located on other public clouds or on premises.

- **The status of CloudWatch alarms:** Route 53 can monitor the same metrics being monitored by CloudWatch and make decisions without needing to communicate directly with the CloudWatch service.

Route 53 Routing Policies

When Route 53 receives a query, a routing policy determines the response. Table 7-10 lists routing policies supported by Route 53.

Table 7-10 Route 53 Routing Policies

Routing Policy	Function	Use Case
Simple	A simple DNS response matching the requested resource with the current IP address.	A single resource, such as a web server, that is serving content for a single domain
Failover	If the primary resource is not responding, the request is sent to the secondary location.	For active/passive failover design with multiple AWS regions
Geolocation	Choose resources based on the geographic locations of your users. Content can be localized based on the language of your users or to restrict where content can be distributed.	For routing traffic based on the physical location of the end user
Geoproximity	Route traffic to your resource based on the geographic locations of your users and requested resources. This routing requires you to create a defined Route 53 traffic policy.	For routing traffic based on the location of your AWS resources
Latency	Use for applications hosted in multiple AWS regions. Requests are sent to the resources at the closest location with the lowest-latency route.	
Multivalue answer	Using multiple IP addresses with health checks, Route 53 will return records for healthy resources that respond successfully to health checks.	For responding with up to eight healthy address records
Weighted	Associate multiple resources with a single domain name and choose how much traffic is routed to each resource stack. If a weight of 64 is assigned to one stack and a weight of 255 to the other, a weight of 64 would get 25% of the traffic requests.	For routing traffic to multiple resources at defined traffic levels

Route 53 Traffic Flow Policies

Route 53 traffic flow provides global traffic management services (GTMS) using traffic flow policies created using the traffic flow visual editor (see Figure 7-35). This editor enables you to create specific routing configurations for your resources.

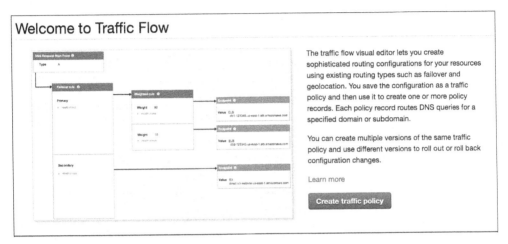

Figure 7-35   Route 53 Traffic Flow Policies

You can create traffic flow policies for situations involving geoproximity, endpoint health, overall application load, and latency (see Figure 7-36). For example, you might want to route traffic based on the locations or the languages of your end users. In addition, you might want to control the amount of traffic sent to resources by using a *bias*, which enables you to change the size of the geographic region from which traffic is routed to a resource.

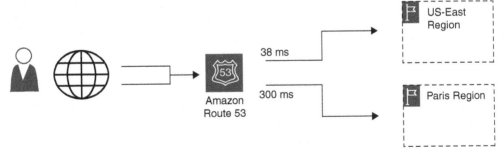

Figure 7-36   Route 53 Latency Records Defining the Fastest Paths to Access Resources

NOTE   With traffic policies, you can create a tree of alias records and routing policies.

Alias Records

Alias records provide additional workload redundancy as multiple records can be provided for requests for AWS resources. When Route 53 receives a query for an AWS resource using an alias record, one or more IP addresses can return pointing to redundant AWS service locations. Route 53 responds with multiple IP addresses; if one IP address doesn't work due to maintenance or failures, one of the other IP addresses will resolve the request. The following AWS services support alias records:

- **API gateway API request:** Route 53 provides one or more IP addresses for the requested API.

- **VPC interface endpoint:** Route 53 provides one or more IP addresses for the endpoint.

- **CloudFront distribution:** Route 53 provides one or more IP addresses for edge servers for servicing the request.

- **Elastic Beanstalk environment:** Route 53 provides one or more IP addresses for the environment.

- **ELB load balancer:** Route 53 provides one or more IP addresses for the load balancer.

- **Global accelerator:** Route 53 provides one or more IP addresses for each accelerator.

- **S3 bucket configured as a static website:** Route 53 provides one or more IP addresses for the S3 bucket.

Alias records also enable you to route traffic at the top node of a DNS namespace, known as the *zone apex*. For example, if the domain mydomain.com is registered with Route 53, the zone apex is mydomain.com. At AWS, a CNAME record cannot be created for mydomain.com; however, an alias record can be created to route traffic to mydomain.com.

Route 53 Resolver

When an organization creates a VPC to host application servers running on EC2 instances, the Route 53 resolver automatically answers DNS queries from the EC2 instance's VPC-specific DNS names and Route 53 private hosted zones.

If you have a hybrid need for communication between on-premises resources and your VPC resources at AWS or between other peered VPCs, communication can be initiated with forwarding rules, as shown in Figure 7-37. You first need to create resolver inbound and/or outbound endpoints. Inbound queries from the on-premises resource is provided by defining a Route 53 resolver endpoint that resolves to an

AWS-hosted domain and the IP addresses of the DNS resolvers to which you want to forward the queries.

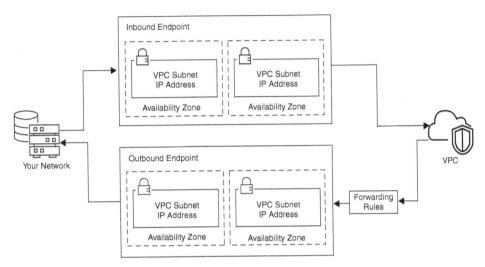

Figure 7-37   Forwarding Rules

You enable outbound DNS queries by using conditional forwarding rules, as shown in Figure 7-38.

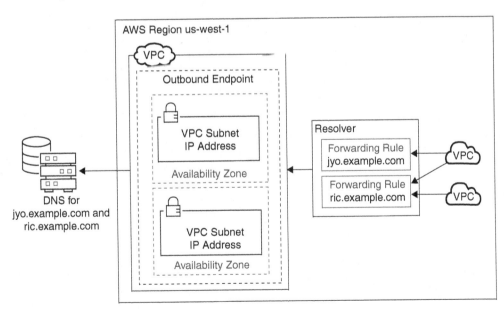

Figure 7-38   Conditional Forwarding Rules

Exam Preparation Tasks

As mentioned in the section "How to Use This Book" in the Introduction, you have a couple of choices for exam preparation: the exercises here, Chapter 16, "Final Preparation," and the exam simulation questions in the Pearson Test Prep Software Online.

Review All Key Topics

Review the most important topics in the chapter, noted with the Key Topic icon in the outer margin of the page. Table 7-11 lists these key topics and the page number on which each is found.

Table 7-11   Chapter 7 Key Topics

Key Topic Element	Description	Page Number
Section	High Availability in the Cloud	294
Section	Reliability	295
Figure 7-3	Visualizing Availability Zones and Regional Services	299
Section	Availability Zones	300
Figure 7-6	AZ Balancing and Distribution of Resources	302
Section	Planning Network Topology	303
Section	Local Zones	306
Section	AWS Services Use Case	308
Figure 7-12	Artifact Utility	311
Section	Latency Concerns	319
Section	Designing for High Availability and Fault Tolerance	322
Figure 7-16	Hosting Across Multiple AZs to Increase Availability and Fault Tolerance	323
Figure 7-18	Increasing Workload Availability by Adding Compute Workload	324
Table 7-6	Avoiding Single Points of Failure	325
Table 7-7	Planning for High Availability, Fault Tolerance, and Redundancy	326
Figure 7-20	Deploying Immutable Servers	328
Table 7-8	Storage Service Characteristics	330
Section	Failover Strategies	330

Key Topic Element	Description	Page Number
Section	Single and Multi-Region Recovery Cheat Sheet	343
Section	Disaster Recovery Cheat Sheet	344
Section	AWS Service Quotas	345
Section	AWS Service Quotas Cheat Sheet	347

Define Key Terms

Define the following key terms from this chapter and check your answers in the glossary:

availability, reliability, region, availability zone (AZ), Local Zones, AWS Artifact, FedRAMP, uptime, SLA, immutable, RTO, RPO, pilot light, warm standby, active-active, service quota

Q&A

The answers to these questions appear in Appendix A. For more practice with exam format questions, use the Pearson Test Prep Software Online.

1. First, you design with security, and then you make your workload as _____ and _____ as possible.

2. Problems with one AWS region remain _____ to that region and should not affect other regions.

3. Having multiple availability zones provides _____, _____, and _____.

4. Costs are different for each _____ where an organization hosts workloads and cloud services.

5. Artifact allows you to review _____ reports.

6. Amazon Aurora global database deployments are deployed across multiple AWS _____.

7. Amazon Route 53 routing provides global traffic management services using _____.

8. The AWS resources that can be ordered are controlled by a default _____.

This chapter covers the following topics:

- AWS Storage Options
- Amazon Elastic Block Store
- Amazon Elastic File System
- Amazon FSx for Windows File Server
- Amazon Simple Storage Service
- Amazon S3 Glacier
- AWS Data Lake

This chapter covers content that's important to the following exam domain and task statements:

Domain 3: Design High-Performance Architectures

Task Statement 1: Determine high-performing and/or scalable storage solutions

Task Statement 5: Determine high-performing data ingestion and transformation solutions

CHAPTER 8

High-Performing and Scalable Storage Solutions

The amount of public cloud storage utilized by public and private data records continues to grow, with no sign of stopping anytime soon. Workloads hosted at AWS consume a lot of data storage, and these out-of-sight data records become expensive to store. It's important to understand how each AWS storage service works and how cost savings and performance requirements can be achieved by picking the right storage solution.

According to https://raconteur.net, over 4 petabytes (PB) of data are created daily by Facebook users, 4 TIB of data are produced each day by connected cars, 65 billion messages are sent via WhatsApp daily, and wearable devices generate 28 PB of data. In addition, corporations and software as a service (SaaS) applications are using the cloud to store vast quantities of data, from Word and Excel files to machine learning, online gaming results, and, of course, cat pictures.

By 2025, over 463 exabytes (EB) of data will be created in the public cloud daily. That's 1,000,000,000,000,000,000 bytes! Any low advertised storage price becomes quite expensive over the long term as companies store data records for long periods of time.

NOTE For additional details on these figures on data storage, see https://www.raconteur.net/infographics/a-day-in-data/.

AWS has made great strides in providing "cloud" solutions for companies whose data records are still required to be stored on premises because of security concerns, rules, and regulations. (For example, some financial organizations are not allowed to move specific data resources to the cloud due to governance and security concerns.)

To combat compliance concerns AWS has launched AWS Outposts, which is designed to let customers run AWS services on premises, in their own data centers. AWS Outposts can be used for a variety of workloads, including data processing, machine learning, and low-latency applications, including compute and storage services (Amazon EC2, Amazon ECS/Amazon Kubernetes) and storage (Elastic Block Store [EBS] and Amazon Simple Storage Service [S3]). Organizations can now choose whether to operate in AWS public cloud regions or operate from an on-premises AWS Outposts deployment.

By the end of this chapter, you will understand the choices for storing your work-load data using AWS managed storage services. The AWS Certified Solutions Architect – Associate (SAA-C03) exam will expect you to be able to select the appropriate storage solution based on the use case presented in relevant exam questions. AWS storage services store many different types of data using the fol-lowing storage services:

- Amazon EBS stores files in persistent scalable block storage volumes that are attached to EC2 instances. Boot and data volumes are supported.

- Amazon S3 offers unlimited object cloud storage in buckets for any data type, including logging services, CloudWatch logs, CloudTrail trails, Amazon Machine Images (AMIs), EBS snapshots, AWS managed services data, database backups, and more.

- Amazon S3 Glacier Flexible Retrieval provides archive and vault storage for records that need to be archived for long periods of time and retrieved at no cost.

- Amazon S3 Glacier Instant Retrieval provides archive and vault storage at a very low cost, with millisecond retrieval speeds when retrieval is necessary.

- Amazon S3 Glacier Deep Archive is offline archival and vault storage with data retrieval speeds within 12 hours.

- Amazon EFS or FSx storage is available for both AWS-hosted and on-premises Linux and Windows workloads that require access to a shared file system.

"Do I Know This Already?"

The "Do I Know This Already?" quiz allows you to assess whether you should read this entire chapter thoroughly or jump to the "Exam Preparation Tasks" section. If you are in doubt about your answers to these questions or your own assessment of your knowledge of the topics, read the entire chapter. Table 8-1 lists the major headings in this chapter and their corresponding "Do I Know This Already?" quiz questions. You can find the answers in Appendix A, "Answers to the 'Do I Know This Already?' Quizzes and Q&A Sections."

Table 8-1 "Do I Know This Already?" Section-to-Question Mapping

Foundation Topics Section	Questions
AWS Storage Options	1, 2
Amazon Elastic Block Store	3, 4
Amazon Elastic File System	5, 6
Amazon FSx for Windows File Server	7, 8
Amazon Simple Storage Service	9, 10
Amazon S3 Glacier	11, 12
AWS Data Lake	13, 14

CAUTION The goal of self-assessment is to gauge your mastery of the topics in this chapter. If you do not know the answer to a question or are only partially sure of the answer, you should mark that question as wrong for purposes of the self-assessment. Giving yourself credit for an answer you correctly guess skews your self-assessment results and might provide you with a false sense of security.

1. What is the best AWS option for storing archival records?

    a. Amazon S3

    b. Amazon S3 Deep Archive

    c. Ephemeral storage

    d. Snapshots

2. What type of AWS storage allows storage of an unlimited number of objects?

    a. Amazon EFS

    b. Amazon S3

    c. Amazon FSx

    d. Amazon EBS

3. How can Amazon EBS storage volumes be publicly accessed from the Internet?

    a. Attach an Internet gateway.

    b. EBS volumes are private.

    c. Deploy Amazon Storage Gateway.

    d. Attach a virtual private gateway.

4. What does the term *elastic* signify with Elastic Block Store volumes?

   a. EBS volumes scale on demand.

   b. EBS volume size and type can be changed after creation.

   c. EBS volumes are replicated to multiple locations.

   d. EBS volumes can be shared across availability zones.

5. How can Amazon EFS be accessed by on-premises systems and applications?

   a. Internet Gateway connection

   b. NAT Gateway service connection

   c. Direct Connect connection

   d. Internet connection

6. What is the recommended performance mode of operation to select when starting with Amazon EFS?

   a. Max I/O

   b. General Purpose

   c. Bursting Throughput

   d. Provisioned Throughput

7. What Microsoft Windows Server file system feature does FSx support?

   a. NTFS

   b. Distributed File System (DFS)

   c. Services for NFS

   d. Active Directory Federated Service

8. What Windows service does AWS FSx for Windows File Server use to replicate FSx data?

   a. SMB 2.0

   b. Volume Shadow Copy Service

   c. SMB 3.0

   d. NTFS

9. How can you protect Amazon S3 objects from being deleted?

   a. Enable encryption

   b. Enable versioning

    c. Turn off public access

    d. Create a lifecycle rule

10. What storage class provides automatic movement of objects?

    a. Amazon S3 Glacier

    b. Intelligent-Tiering

    c. Reduced redundancy storage

    d. Standard IA

11. Where are files uploaded into Amazon S3 Glacier?

    a. Amazon S3 archives

    b. Amazon S3 Glacier archives

    c. Vaults

    d. Buckets

12. How can objects be moved automatically from Amazon S3 into Amazon Glacier?

    a. Lifecycle rule

    b. S3 transfer acceleration

    c. Versioning

    d. AWS Snow Family device

13. Where is data stored when deploying AWS Lake Formation?

    a. Amazon EMR

    b. Amazon S3

    c. Amazon S3 Glacier

    d. Amazon EFS

14. What AWS service creates metadata from existing source data records when creating a data lake?

    a. AWS Glue

    b. AWS Athena

    c. AWS Quicksight

    d. Amazon Kinesis Data Firehose

Foundation Topics

AWS Storage Options

AWS offers a wide breadth of storage options—for block, object, and file storage—that are similar to but not the same as your on-premises storage options. Figure 8-1 shows the available options, and the list that follows briefly describes the available options:

Figure 8-1 AWS Storage Options

- **Sharable file system for Linux environment using Amazon EFS:** EFS scales on-demand from gigabytes to petabytes accessed through using NFSv4 mount points from selected VPC/subnets by Amazon Elastic Compute Cloud (EC2) instances, Amazon Elastic Container Service (ECS), Amazon Elastic Kubernetes Services (EKS), or from on-premises servers.

- **Object:** *Object storage* at AWS is the Amazon Simple Storage Service (S3). Amazon S3 storage is accessed and managed through simple API (application programming interface) calls, such as **GET** and **PUT**. Each file stored in an S3 bucket is called an *object*, and each S3 object is identified and accessed by a unique key. The original design for S3 was for accessing content across the Internet. S3 is scalable, durable, and highly cost-effective object storage.

  When an object is stored in S3, the entire object is uploaded. Changes to existing objects result in updating the entire object. S3 buckets can host a website's static content and media files and static websites that do not require server-side processing. S3 provides storage for big data analytics and machine learning and EBS *snapshots*, Amazon CloudWatch logs, and AWS Backup backups.

- **Block storage:** Block storage volumes are provided by Amazon EBS for Windows, Linux, or macOS instances. Formatted block storage is accessed at the block level by the operating system and applications. AWS *block storage* describes Amazon EBS volumes, and *ephemeral storage* SSD storage volumes that are attached directly to the bare-metal servers that host EC2 instances.

Amazon EBS arrays use solid-state drives (SSDs) or hard disk drives (HDDs), providing persistent block storage only accessible across the private AWS network. Enabling direct public access to EBS storage volumes is not possible.

NOTE Many EC2 instance families also include direct-attached storage as local storage volumes called ephemeral storage (or instance storage). Ephemeral storage is located on the bare-metal server that hosts the EC2 instance; therefore, it's incredibly fast. However, ephemeral storage has no long-term durability; it is temporary storage. It can survive an EC2 instance reboot but is deleted when the EC2 instance is powered off or fails.

- **Sharable file system for Windows File Server:** Amazon FSx for Windows File Server provides fully managed native Microsoft Windows SSD or HDD storage accessible using Windows file shares. Amazon FSx for Windows File Server supports the *Server Message Block (SMB)* protocol.

NOTE Chapter 10, "Determining High-Performing Database Solutions," covers database storage offerings Amazon RDS, Amazon Aurora, Amazon DynamoDB, and Amazon ElastiCache.

Workload Storage Requirements

Before choosing an AWS storage solution, organizations need to review their current storage requirements carefully. Each workload dictates what storage solution or solutions are required. Consult Table 8-2 for reviewing storage requirements and the available storage solutions.

Table 8-2 Storage Requirements

Workload Requirements	Storage Solution
Operating system support	AWS supports the Linux, Windows, and macOS operating systems. Linux EC2, Windows, and macOS instances support EBS volumes and Amazon EFS shared storage and also can attach to FSx for Windows File Server shared storage.
File-sharing protocols	Amazon EFS supports the Network File System (NFSv4) versions 4.0 and 4.1, and Amazon FSx for Windows File Server supports the service message protocol SMB.

Workload Requirements	Storage Solution
Performance requirements	Shared storage solutions such as EFS and FSx provide baseline performance that can burst or scale up dramatically or be mapped to a defined throughput capacity. EBS General Purpose SSD 2 (gp2) volumes provide 3,000 IOPS and 125 MIB/s of consistent performance. EBS Io2 Block Express volumes offer sub-millisecond latency up to 256,000 IOPS and 4,000 MIB/s throughputs and up to 64 TiB in size for a single volume.
Compliance requirements	Cloud storage solutions at AWS support various levels of compliance. As discussed in Chapter 7, you might need to follow your organization's compliance requirements, such as PCI DSS, FedRAMP requirements, or internal rules and regulations. Use AWS Artifact in the AWS Management Console to review the currently supported compliance standards.
Capacity requirements	What are your daily, monthly, and yearly storage requirements? EBS volumes have capacity size limits ranging from 1 TiB up to 64 TiB.
Data encryption	What needs to be encrypted for compliance—data records at rest or data in transit across the network? All data storage options can be encrypted using AES 256-bit encryption; Amazon S3 and S3 Glacier storage is encrypted by default.
Concurrent access	Do virtual servers need to access shared storage? Amazon EFS and FSx for Windows File Server provide shared storage services.
Input/output (I/O) requirements	What is a workload's percentage of reading and writing files? Is it balanced or unbalanced? Provisioned input/output requirements are supported by EBS gp3, io1, and io2 volumes, and Amazon EFS and FSx for Windows File Server throughput modes.
I/O performance requirements	What input/output performance is required? EBS Block Express volumes offer up to 256,000 IOPS. Amazon EFS and FSx for Windows File Server offer adjustable performance modes.
Number of files	How many files will you be storing in the cloud daily, weekly, or for the long term? Amazon S3 offers unlimited storage. Amazon EFS and FSx for Windows File Server support petabyte storage.
File size per directory	What's the largest required file size? For example, EFS storage has a maximum file size of 49 TiB. Amazon EBS volumes using the third extended file system (efs3) and 4 KB block size have a maximum 2 TiB file size.
Throughput for on-premises storage	What are your average data throughput requirements on premises? Are you expecting these or higher levels of performance at AWS? Do your workloads have specific IOPS requirements? Amazon EBS Block Express volumes offer up to 256,000 IOPS. Amazon EFS and FSx for Windows File Server offer burst and adjustable throughput performance levels. Amazon EBS Throughput Optimized HDDs provide a baseline for the performance of 40 MIB per TiB of storage.

Workload Requirements	Storage Solution
Latency	What latency can your workload handle? Test workload latency using EC2 optimized instances with dedicated, high-bandwidth connections to EBS storage, which enables them to fully utilize the I/O capacity of the attached EBS volumes. This can significantly improve the performance of EBS-intensive workloads, such as databases, big data processing, and media processing.

NOTE The terms IOPS and PIOPS are often used in technical documentation related to storage in the cloud without any explanation. *IOPS* stands for *input/output operations per second*. The higher the number, the faster the HDD, SSD, or SAN. With provisioned IOPS (PIOPS), a specific amount of IOPS can be ordered or provisioned. AWS supports up to 256,000 IOPS for EBS Block Express volumes. Every hard drive has a particular measurement of performance that defines how quickly data can be stored (written) or retrieved (read).

Amazon Elastic Block Store

Amazon Elastic Block Store (EBS) is a block-level storage service for use with Amazon EC2 instances. It provides persistent storage, and it can be configured to deliver high levels of I/O performance. EBS volumes are attached to EC2 instances and are exposed as block devices. They can be used as raw block devices or can be formatted with a file system and used to store files. EBS volumes can also be backed up by creating snapshots of each EBS volume that are stored in Amazon S3 as a point-in-time backup.

The "E" in EBS defines the "elastic volumes" feature that enables you to increase your current volume capacity and performance or change your volume after an EBS volume has been created.

Amazon CloudWatch metrics and alarms can be used to define and monitor a desired baseline for each EBS volume. When baseline values for capacity or performance have been breached, Amazon CloudWatch alarms can alert the Simple Notification Service (SNS). SNS, in turn, can notify Amazon Lambda, which can execute a custom function to increase capacity and performance or carry out any specific task as required.

When an EBS volume is created, the blocks for the volume are spread across multiple storage arrays, providing a high level of redundancy and durability. EBS volumes are stored within the same availability zone (AZ) where your instances reside, as shown in Figure 8-2, providing 99.8% to 99.999% durability, depending on the type of EBS volume created.

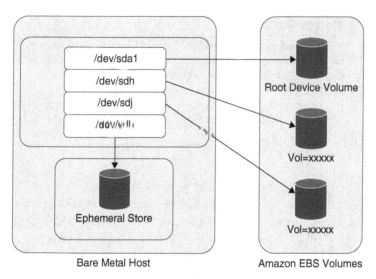

Figure 8-2 EBS Data Storage Architecture

Each EBS volume can be attached to any EC2 instance located in the AZ where the EBS volume resides. Multiple EBS volumes can also be attached to a single EC2 instance. A feature called Multi-attach allows up to 16 **Nitro**-backed EC2 instances to concurrently attach to a single EBS volume at the same time.

To use multi-attach, create a volume with the multi-attach attribute enabled, and then attach it to the desired EC2 instances. All instances will have read/write access to the volume, and any changes made to the volume by one instance will be visible to all other instances.

Multi-attach is only supported on Amazon EBS Provisioned IOPS SSD io1 and io2 volume types and is supported on a limited number of EC2 instance types.

Multi-attach can be useful in scenarios where you want to ensure high availability for your data using a cluster-aware file system such as Red Hat Global File System2 (GFS2).

NOTE Boot and data records should always be separated. Never store data records on the boot drive of an EC2 instance; boot volumes should only contain the operating system and the application. Storing data on separate EBS volumes allows you to back up (snapshot) the data volume as a separate process, making backup and restoration easier. Separating the boot and data volumes also makes it easier to plan the size, speed, and usage of your boot volumes. Separate EBS data volumes can have higher provisioned IOPS (for example, with database storage volumes).

EBS Volume Types

Several EBS volume types are available depending on the required use case and workload requirements (see Table 8-3). Different workloads will require different performance needs; for example, various volume types can be selected for database storage volumes, or data that is not accessed as frequently, as shown in Figure 8-3. For example, an EBS boot volume will not need to be as fast or as large as a high-performing EBS database volume.

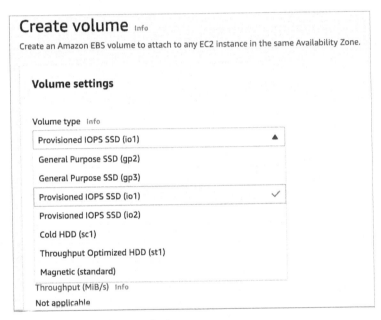

Figure 8-3   EBS Volume Options

The following EBS volumes can be chosen:

- General Purpose SSD gp2 volumes provide a baseline of 3 IOPS per GiB of volume storage with a minimum of 100 IOPS, burstable to 3000 IOPS with single-digit-millisecond latency and 99.8% to 99.9% durability. Volume sizes are Min: 1 GiB, Max: 16384 GiB.

- General Purpose SSD gp3 volumes also provide a minimum baseline of 3000 IOPS with a maximum of 16000 IOPS that can be selected with single-digit-millisecond latency, and 99.8% to 99.9% durability. Volume sizes are Min: 1 GiB, Max: 16384 GiB.

- Provisioned IOPS SSD io1 volumes can select IOPS from 100 to 4,950 IOPS with single-digit-millisecond latency, and 99.8% to 99.9% durability. Volume sizes are Min: 4 GiB, Max: 16384 GiB.

- Provisioned IOPS SSD io2 volumes can select from 100 IOPS up to a maximum 99,000 IOPS. Volume sizes are Min: 4 GiB, Max: 65536 GiB. Provisioned IOPS SSD (io2) volumes with a size greater than 16 TiB and IOPS greater than 64,000 are supported only with instance types that support io2 Block Express volumes.

- EBS io2 IOPS SSD Block Express volumes are designed to provide 4,000 MIB/s throughputs per volume, 256,000 IOPS/volume, up to 64 TiB storage capacity, and 99.999% durability with sub-millisecond latency. These increased speeds are due to the Nitro hypervisor and Nitro I/O card dedicated for EBS I/O, which is embedded on the bare-metal server hosting the Nitro hypervisor. Selecting EC2 R5b instances in the EC2 Dashboard allows you to select io2 Block Express volumes, as shown in Figure 8-4.

Step 4: Add Storage

Your instance will be launched with the following storage device settings. You can attach additional EBS volumes and instance store volumes to your instance, e edit the settings of the root volume. You can also attach additional EBS volumes after launching an instance, but not instance store volumes. Learn more about storage options in Amazon EC2.

Volume Type ⓘ	Device ⓘ	Snapshot ⓘ	Size (GiB) ⓘ	Volume Type ⓘ	IOPS ⓘ
Root	/dev/xvda	snap-08cbb15f1c8eb5387	8	✓ General Purpose SSD (gp2)	100 / 3000
ephemeral0	/dev/nvme0n1	N/A	900	General Purpose SSD (gp3)	N/A
ephemeral1	/dev/nvme1n1	N/A	900	Provisioned IOPS SSD (io1)	N/A
ephemeral2	/dev/nvme2n1	N/A	900	Provisioned IOPS SSD (io2)	N/A
ephemeral3	/dev/nvme3n1	N/A	900	Magnetic (standard)	N/A
				SSD (NVMe AMI required)	
				SSD (NVMe AMI required)	

Figure 8-4 Provisioned IOPS SSD (io2) Selection

- ***Throughput Optimized*** HDD volumes (st1) provide good throughput performance for sequential I/O with a set throughput/volume at 40 MiB/s per TiB. Volume sizes are Min: 4 GiB, Max: 16,384 GiB.

- Cold HHD (sc1) volumes have a max throughput/volume of 12 MiB/s per TiB of storage. Volume sizes are Min: 125 GiB, Max: 16,384 GiB.

- Magnetic HDD volumes average 100 IOPS. Volume sizes are Min: 1 GiB, Max: 1,024 GiB.

Table 8-3 Performance Specifications for EBS Volume Types

Parameter	EBS Provisioned IOPS SSD Block Express	io2	io1	gp3	gp2
Use case	SAP HANA	I/O-intensive NoSQL	I/O-intensive NoSQL	Virtual desktops	Single-instance databases
Durability	99.999%	99.999%	99.8%–99.9%	99.8%–99.9%	99.8%–99.9%
Size	4 GB–64 TiB	4 GB–16 TiB	4 GB–65 TiB	1 GB–16 TiB	500 GB–16 TiB
Max IOPS/ volume	256,000	64,000	64,000	16,000	16,000
Max IOPS/ instance	260,000	160,000	260,000	260,000	260,000
Max throughput/ volume	7,500 MiB/s	4,750 MiB/s	7,500 MiB/s	7,500 MiB/s	7,500 MiB/s

General Purpose SSD (gp2/gp3)

General Purpose SSD gp2 is designed with a minimum baseline of 3 IOPS per GiB with a minimum of 100 IOPS, burstable to 3,000 IOPS. Gp2 volumes come with a baseline level of I/O performance and a maximum burst threshold, and the burst capability of a gp2 volume is determined by the number of I/O credits it has available. If a gp2 volume runs out of I/O credits, its I/O performance will be limited to the baseline level until it earns more I/O credits. Bursting is designed for the use case where applications have periods of idle time followed by periods of high IOPS. The smallest gp2 drive can burst to 3,000 IOPS while maintaining a single-digit-millisecond latency with throughput up to 160 MiB/s.

All EBS General Purpose gp2 SSD storage volumes support bursting using a burst token bucket design, as shown in Figure 8-5. During quiet idle times, each volume accumulates burst tokens at 3 IOPS per gigabyte per second. When the driver needs additional performance using the acquired burst tokens, it can burst up to higher levels of IOPS. A larger storage volume is assigned additional *burst credits*, allowing the drive to burst for a longer time frame. For example, a 300-GB volume can burst up to 40 minutes, 500-GB volumes can burst for almost an hour, and even larger 900-GB volumes can burst for almost 10 hours.

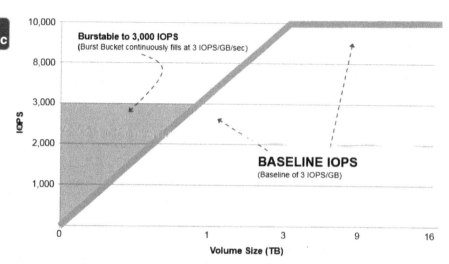

Figure 8-5   EBS Burst Credit Architecture

General Purpose SSD gp3 volumes do not support bursting but include 3000 IOPS per second and 125 MiB/s of consistent performance at no additional cost. EBS volumes created with the desired IOPS value meet their desired performance requirements 99.9% of the time.

For *cold storage* and Throughput-Optimized volumes, burst credits accumulate based on the size of the drive. A storage-optimized volume accumulates burst credits at 40 MiB/s per terabyte; a cold storage volume accumulates burst credits at 12 MiB per terabyte.

If you have a large sequential workload running for 3 hours on a Throughput-Optimized volume, approximately 5.4 TIB of data will be transferred. On the other hand, if your workload storage is random, using the same drive in the same working time frame of 3 hours, 87 GB of data will be transferred.

> **NOTE**   To carry out workload testing on a Linux system, you could use the utility **iostat**; for Windows systems, use the built-in **Perfmon**. Testing results are displayed in sectors. You then need to know the number of bytes you're using per sector and multiply the sectors by the number of bytes to calculate the current workload transfer rate.

Elastic EBS Volumes

Amazon EBS enables you to increase the current volume size and change the volume type, size, and, if applicable, change provisioned IOPS in near real time, as shown in Figure 8-6. There is no maintenance window required when manually scaling an EBS volume. Elastic volumes provide cost savings; organizations do not have to overprovision storage volumes by planning for future growth at the start. Amazon RDS MySQL and Microsoft SQL Server deployments support Storage autoscaling; EBS volumes can be set to a maximum storage threshold providing dynamic scaling support when additional storage is required. AWS CloudWatch can also monitor EBS volumes' read and write throughput and latency using Amazon CloudWatch metrics and send alarms to the AWS Simple Notification Service when issues arise. To monitor the free space on your EBS volumes using the CloudWatch Agent, you can configure the CloudWatch Agent to collect the VolumeFreeSpace metric for your EBS volumes. Next, set up a CloudWatch alarm to trigger an alert when the VolumeFreeSpace metric falls below a certain threshold.

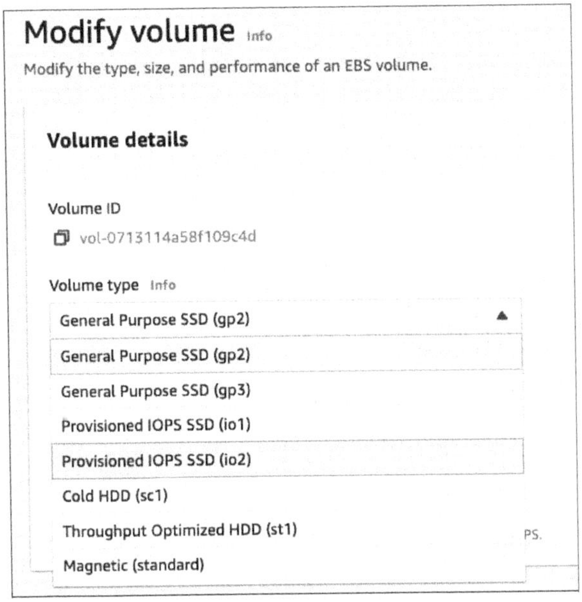

Modify volume Info

Modify the type, size, and performance of an EBS volume.

Volume details

Volume ID

vol-0713114a58f109c4d

Volume type Info

General Purpose SSD (gp2)	▲
General Purpose SSD (gp2)	
General Purpose SSD (gp3)	
Provisioned IOPS SSD (io1)	
Provisioned IOPS SSD (io2)	
Cold HDD (sc1)	
Throughput Optimized HDD (st1)	PS.
Magnetic (standard)	

Figure 8-6 Modifying EBS Volumes

Attaching an EBS Volume

When an EBS volume is attached to an EC2 instance, several background processes begin running, depending on the hypervisor being used to host the EC2 instance:

- **Instances hosted on the Xen hypervisor:** Instances are associated with a system component called an I/O domain. When an EBS volume is attached, it is attached to the I/O domain. Another system component, called a *shared memory segment*, is initiated at the hypervisor architecture level, acting as a queue to handle data access from the instance to the EBS volume.

When an instance wants to perform an I/O call, it first submits a system call to the kernel. Assuming that it's a read request, a data block is placed in the hypervisor queue. Next, the I/O domain takes the data from the hypervisor queue and sends it to the defined queue, which delivers the data blocks to the EBS volume.

- **Instances hosted on the Nitro hypervisor:** A PCI interface is used to directly interface with the Nitro card, which presents a direct storage interface to the EC2 instance. Storage requests in this design are submitted directly to the PCI interface; the Nitro hypervisor has no part to play in communicating with EBS storage volumes. The Nitro interface provides a huge performance boost with minimal latency to local instance storage hosted on the Xen hypervisor.

Amazon EBS Cheat Sheet

For the AWS Certified Solutions Architect – Associate (SAA-C03) exam, review the details for creating and managing EBS volumes:

- EBS volumes are network-attached storage volumes attached to an EC2 instance.

- There are eight volume types: Provisioned IOPS SSD (io2 Block Express, io2, io1), General Purpose SSD (gp2, gp3), Throughput Optimized (st1), and Cold HDD (sc1).

- EBS volumes support three storage categories: SSD storage for transactional workloads, HDD storage for cold storage and throughput optimized workloads, and magnetic hard drives.

- Multiple EBS volumes can be attached to a single EC2 instance.

- EBS volumes can be attached and detached from a running EC2 instance.

- EBS volumes must be in the same AZ where the EC2 instance is located to be attached.

- Use AWS Backup to back up your attached EBS volumes with EBS snapshots on a schedule.

- By default, root EBS volumes are set for deletion on termination.

- By default, non-boot volumes are not deleted on termination.

- EBS data volumes should have a snapshot schedule in place for backing up EBS data volumes as required.

- Don't store application data on your root EBS boot volumes.

- EC2 instances can be created with encrypted EBS boot and data volumes.

- EBS volumes allow volume size, volume type, and IOPS changes while online.

- Create separate EBS volumes for boot volumes.

- Ephemeral storage volumes are faster than EBS volumes for storing temporary files.

EBS Snapshots

An EBS snapshot is a point-in-time copy of an EBS volume. Snapshots are stored in controlled Amazon S3 object storage linked to your AWS account. *Controlled storage* means that AWS creates and manages the S3 storage location, but each customer has access to their snapshots through the EBS console or CLI.

The first time a snapshot of an EBS volume is taken, every block of the EBS volume is part of the primary snapshot captured and stored in controlled S3 storage. From this point forward, every additional snapshot is created as an incremental snapshot that records all the changes since the last snapshot. Only newly written and changed volume blocks are pushed to the incremental snapshot. When you delete a snapshot, only the data exclusive to the snapshot copy is retained. Each snapshot has a unique identifier, and new EBS volumes can be created from any snapshot.

Snapshots can be shared by modifying the permissions of the snapshot. Snapshots can be shared publicly or privately with other AWS accounts using the EC2 Dashboard, selecting Private or Public Snapshots.

NOTE   Deploying a daily snapshot schedule greatly reduces the possibility of data loss. AWS has three options for managing snapshots. First, the Data Lifecycle Manager allows you to schedule the creation and deletion of EBS snapshots. Second, AWS Backup allows you even more control of your storage by centrally managing EBS snapshots, including any Amazon RDS snapshots, Amazon Storage Gateway snapshots, Amazon EFS backups, and Amazon DynamoDB backups. The third option is to create a CloudWatch Event to trigger a custom Lambda function on a set schedule to carry out the snapshot process.

Taking a Snapshot from a Linux Instance

After you begin the snapshot process, the snapshot process continues in the background. If there are a small number of volume blocks to change, the snapshot will be created quickly; with many changes, the snapshot process will take longer to complete. Before beginning the snapshot process for an EBS boot volume, make sure to detach the volume to stop any ongoing I/O processes. After starting the snapshot process, as shown in Figure 8-7, the snapshot ID confirms that the snapshot is being created.

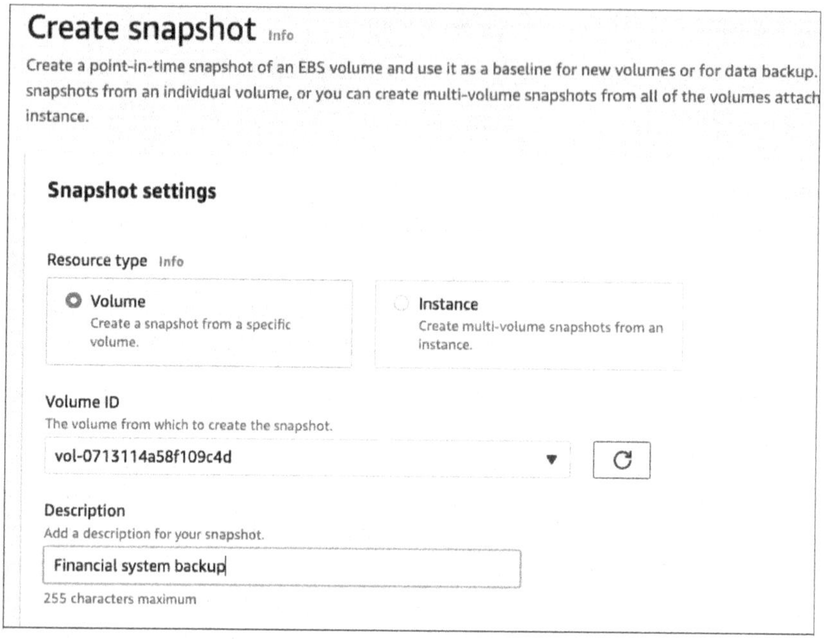

Create snapshot Info

Create a point-in-time snapshot of an EBS volume and use it as a baseline for new volumes or for data backup. snapshots from an individual volume, or you can create multi-volume snapshots from all of the volumes attach instance.

Snapshot settings

Resource type Info

◉ **Volume**
Create a snapshot from a specific volume.

○ **Instance**
Create multi-volume snapshots from an instance.

Volume ID
The volume from which to create the snapshot.

vol-0713114a58f109c4d ▾ ⟳

Description
Add a description for your snapshot.

Financial system backup

255 characters maximum

Figure 8-7   Creating a Snapshot

Taking a Snapshot from a Windows Instance

For Windows instances, the windows operating system uses the **sync** utility to *quiesce* the file system and create the snapshot. Windows Server has a built-in operating system service utility called the Volume Shadow Copy Service (VSS) for creating application-consistent snapshots. The AWS Systems Manager (SSM) can automate Windows VSS commands such as **ec2-creates snapshot** to schedule snapshots of Windows EC2 instances. Windows Server images AMI 2017.11.21 and higher include the SSM and VSS snapshot utilities.

Fast Snapshot Restore

Fast snapshot restore is a feature of Amazon EBS that enables you to quickly restore an EBS volume from a snapshot, creating a new volume from the snapshot and attaching it to an Amazon Elastic Compute Cloud (EC2) instance.

Fast snapshot restore enables you to skip the process of creating a new volume and then copying the data from the snapshot to the new volume. Instead, the new volume is created directly from the snapshot, which can save a significant amount of time.

Amazon EBS fast snapshot restore (FSR) enables you to speed up restoring data to multiple EBS volumes from a snapshot. FSR has been designed to help speed up the snapshot restore process for virtual desktop environments and custom AMIs.

Snapshot Administration

Various administrative tasks need to be considered when planning for disaster recovery, or creating EBS volumes from existing snapshots:

- **Within an AWS region:** Snapshots can be used to create an EBS volume within any AZ within the same region where the snapshot is stored.

- **To another AWS region:** By using the EBS copy utility via the AWS CLI or Amazon Data Lifecycle Manager, snapshots can be copied to multiple AWS regions.

- **Launching EC2 instances:** EBS boot volumes can be used to create a new EC2 instance.

- **Rebuilding a database:** AWS RDS database instance snapshots can be used to create a new database instance.

- **Creating volumes:** Existing snapshots can be used to create new EBS volumes.

Typically, snapshots are stored in the EBS Snapshot Standard tier, which supports incremental EBS snapshots. A new storage tier called Amazon EBS Snapshots Archive is available for low-cost, long-term storage of rarely accessed snapshots that do not require fast retrieval, as shown in Figure 8-8. Organizations can archive a snapshot for long-term storage using the Amazon EBS Snapshots Archive. The incremental snapshot is converted to a full snapshot and moved to the EBS Snapshots Archive tier. Amazon EBS Snapshots Archive storage has 75% lower snapshot storage costs for archived snapshots stored over 90 days. When an archived snapshot needs to be restored, it is moved from the archive tier to the standard tier and then restored.

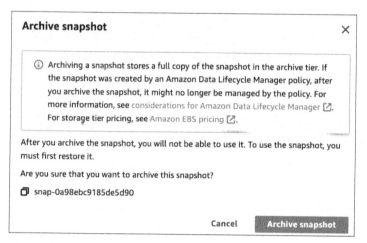

Archive snapshot   ✕

ⓘ Archiving a snapshot stores a full copy of the snapshot in the archive tier. If
   the snapshot was created by an Amazon Data Lifecycle Manager policy, after
   you archive the snapshot, it might no longer be managed by the policy. For
   more information, see considerations for Amazon Data Lifecycle Manager ☑.
   For storage tier pricing, see Amazon EBS pricing ☑.

After you archive the snapshot, you will not be able to use it. To use the snapshot, you
must first restore it.

Are you sure that you want to archive this snapshot?

⧉ snap-0a98ebc9185de5d90

                                              Cancel   **Archive snapshot**

Figure 8-8   EBS Snapshots Archive

EBS Recycle Bin

The Amazon EBS Recycle Bin feature enables you to recover EBS snapshots and volumes that were deleted within the past 90 days. When an EBS snapshot or volume is deleted, it is moved to the Recycle Bin, where it can be recovered if needed.

To use the EBS Recycle Bin, you must first enable the feature in the AWS Management Console. View and recover deleted snapshots and volumes by navigating to the EBS Dashboard and select the Recycle Bin, selecting the snapshots or volumes that you want to recover. Both tag-level and region-level retention rules are supported.

Snapshot Cheat Sheet

For the AWS Certified Solutions Architect – Associate (SAA-C03) exam, you need to understand these snapshots details:

- Snapshots are saved incrementally in Amazon S3 controlled storage.

- Snapshots are region-specific, whereas EBS volumes are AZ-specific.

- A snapshot can be copied to another AWS region.

- Snapshots can be archived for low-cost, long-term retention.

- When a snapshot is encrypted, encryption keys are created and managed by the AWS Key Management Service (KMS).

- Snapshots use AES-256 encryption.

- The Amazon Data Lifecycle Manager can be used to create a snapshot management schedule that controls the creation and deletion of snapshots.

- The Amazon Data Lifecycle Manager can be used to create a snapshot management schedule that stores snapshots across multiple AWS Regions.

- Snapshots that have accidently been deleted can be restored from the EBS Recycle Bin.

- EBS snapshots can be stored locally in a local AWS Outposts deployment.

Local EC2 Instance Storage Volumes

There are two main types of storage that EC2 instances can directly use: persistent EBS block storage volumes and temporary block storage (also called ephemeral storage).

An ephemeral storage volume is a hard drive (SSD/HDD) physically attached to the bare-metal server where the EC2 instance is hosted.

The local temporary block storage volume is shared between the hosted EC2 instances that support ephemeral storage. Depending on the EC2 instance type selected, there could be one or more SSD volumes exposed as ephemeral storage devices. Ephemeral storage volumes are numbered from 0 to 23 and are labeled as ephemeral 0 to ephemeral 23, as shown in Figure 8-9.

Volume Type ⓘ	Device ⓘ	Snapshot ⓘ	Size (GiB) ⓘ	Volume Type ⓘ	IOPS ⓘ
Root	/dev/xvda	snap-08cbb15f1c8eb5387	8	General Purpose SSD (gp2) ⌄	100 / 3000
ephemeral0	/dev/nvme0n1	N/A	7500	SSD (NVMe AMI required)	N/A
ephemeral1	/dev/nvme1n1	N/A	7500	SSD (NVMe AMI required)	N/A
ephemeral2	/dev/nvme2n1	N/A	7500	SSD (NVMe AMI required)	N/A
ephemeral3	/dev/nvme3n1	N/A	7500	SSD (NVMe AMI required)	N/A
ephemeral4	/dev/nvme4n1	N/A	7500	SSD (NVMe AMI required)	N/A
ephemeral5	/dev/nvme5n1	N/A	7500	SSD (NVMe AMI required)	N/A
ephemeral6	/dev/nvme6n1	N/A	7500	SSD (NVMe AMI required)	N/A
ephemeral7	/dev/nvme7n1	N/A	7500	SSD (NVMe AMI required)	N/A

Figure 8-9 Instance Storage

Ephemeral storage volumes can be useful for buffers and caches and for storing temporary data records. However, ephemeral storage volumes are *non-persistent data stores*; when an EC2 instance is turned off or terminated, the storage is discarded (however, it *does* survive a reboot). Ephemeral storage data records do not have any long-term durability because they are not automatically replicated to another location, and there is no integrated support with the existing EBS Snapshots service. A use case for choosing ephemeral storage for high-performance database storage could involve the following components:

- Choosing ephemeral storage—for example, an i2 EC2 instance for a large Microsoft SQL Server database—would provide incredible speed for the database records at the local storage level.

- For redundancy, additional EBS volumes designed for a further level of throughput optimization or IOPS could be added as volumes for full and partial backups of the ephemeral storage volumes and transaction logs.

- A third-party VSS-aware snapshot utility could be installed locally on the Microsoft SQL server EC2 instance performing backup from the ephemeral storage volumes to the additional EBS volumes.

- EBS snapshots could then be taken from the additional EBS volumes for safekeeping.

Testing has shown that EC2 NVMe instance storage is more than five times faster than EBS SSD general drives for the cached reads, and it is more than ten times faster for writes. (For specifications, see https://docs.aws.amazon.com/AWSEC2/latest/UserGuide/storage-optimized-instances.html.) EC2 instances with both EBS *and* ephemeral volumes deployed could provide some advantages:

- Boot drives could be EBS SSD volumes, providing fast boot times, and the ephemeral storage could be used to store cached data or logs of the hosted web application.

- Ephemeral storage could be considered for workloads where you do not need the data volumes and storage records to persist.

NOTE With proper planning, you may be able to take advantage of ephemeral storage volumes. And ephemeral storage, if available, is included in the computed price of each EC2 instance.

Amazon Elastic File System

Amazon Elastic File System (Amazon EFS) is a fully managed, elastic file storage service (see Figure 8-10) that scales on demand up to petabytes for Linux, Windows, and macOS instances. EFS removes the need to provision and attach EBS volumes for data storage, and operates as a shared storage service that allows you to concurrently serve EC2 instances hosted on subnets within select VPCs by using NFS *mount points*. The key features of EFS include the following:

- **Availability and durability:** Choose Regional to store data redundantly across multiple availability zones. Choose One Zone to store data redundantly within a single availability zone. Amazon EFS can store and share data access for Amazon EC2 instances, containerized applications, and on-premises servers.

- **No networking or file layer to manage:** There are no EBS drives to provision, manage, and pay for. Pay for the storage used and the level of performance.

- **Elastic:** The EFS file system automatically scales as you add and remove files; you do not need to select an initial storage size.

- **Scale:** EFS can scale to petabytes of capacity and performance can scale along with the increase in size.

- **Performance:** Two performance modes are available: General Purpose and Max I/O. Max I/O is designed for thousands of instances that need access to the same files at the same time.

- **Compatible:** Amazon EFS supports the Network File System (NFS) protocol supported by a wide range of applications and operating systems.

- **Lifecycle management:** Amazon EFS Intelligent-Tiering automatically transitions files in and out of Standard-infrequent Access storage based on a defined number of days since last access.

General

Name - optional
Name your file system

Graphics_Depot

Name must not be longer than 256 characters, and must only contain letters, numbers, and these characters: + - = . _ : /

Availability and durability
Choose Regional (recommended) to create a file system using regional storage classes. Choose One Zone to create a file system using One Zone storage cl

- ◉ **Regional**
  Stores data redundantly across multiple AZs

- ○ **One Zone**
  Stores data redundantly within a single AZ

Automatic backups
Automatically backup your file system data with AWS Backup using recommended settings. Additional pricing applies. Learn more ⧉

☑ Enable automatic backups

Lifecycle management
EFS Intelligent-Tiering uses Lifecycle Management to automatically achieve the right price and performance blend for your application by moving your file
Infrequent Access storage classes. Learn more ⧉

Transition into IA
Transition files from Standard to Standard-Infrequent Access.

30 days since last access ▼

Transition out of IA
Transition files from Standard-Infrequent Access to Standard.

On first access ▼

Performance mode
Set your file system's performance mode based on IOPS required. Learn more ⧉

- ◉ **General Purpose**
  Ideal for latency-sensitive use cases, like web serving environments and content management systems

- ○ **Max I/O**
  Scale to higher levels of aggregate throughput and operations per second

Figure 8-10   EFS Configuration Options

EFS Performance Modes

There are two EFS performance modes (shown in Figure 8-10):

- **General Purpose:** The general purpose mode is assigned a throughput performance profile that supports up to 7,000 operations per second per file system deployment; general purpose is recommended as the starting mode of operation. Amazon recommends that you continue to monitor each EFS file system using the CloudWatch metric PercentIOLimit; if the file system is operating close to 100%, choose Max I/O.

- **Max I/O:** Max I/O scales to a much higher level of throughput and operations per second and was designed for situations where thousands of EC2 instances are attached to a single EFS file system deployment, or for big data and data warehousing workloads.

To select a performance mode for an Amazon EFS file system, use the AWS Management Console or the AWS CLI. The performance mode of an existing EFS file system can be changed at any time.

EFS Throughput Modes

There are two EFS throughput modes:

- **Bursting:** In bursting mode, Amazon EFS automatically adjusts the throughput of the file system up or down in response to changes in demand, enabling you to burst to higher levels of throughput when required. With the default throughput mode selected, when the EFS file system throughput remains below the assigned baseline rate, it earns burst credits that are saved for future throughput requirements. When the file system requires additional throughput, the saved burst credits are utilized for read and write performance throughput above the current baseline. New file systems have an initial credit burst balance of 2.1 TiB.

   The overall throughput is designed to increase as the number of stored files increases. As files are added to the file system, the amount of throughput allowed is increased based on the allotted file size. For example, a 5-TiB EFS file system can burst to 500 MiB/s of throughput (5 TiB × 100 MiB/s per terabyte); a 10 TiB file system can burst to 1000 MiB/s of throughput. Using the CloudWatch metric BurstCreditBalance, you can monitor the current burst credit balance. Move up to the Provisioned throughput mode with a few mouse clicks, as shown in Figure 8-11.

- **Provisioned:** In provisioned mode, specify the desired level of throughput for the file system, and Amazon EFS will automatically provision the necessary resources to meet the requested throughput. Provisioned Throughput can scale up to 3 GiB/s for read operations and 1 GiB/s for write operations per file system deployment. Customers are billed for the EFS storage used and any throughput that has been provisioned above the baseline.

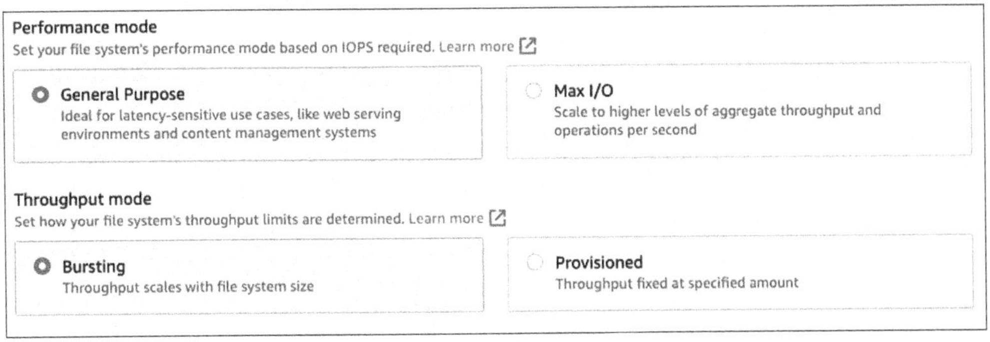

Performance mode
Set your file system's performance mode based on IOPS required. Learn more ☑

○ **General Purpose**
Ideal for latency-sensitive use cases, like web serving environments and content management systems

○ **Max I/O**
Scale to higher levels of aggregate throughput and operations per second

Throughput mode
Set how your file system's throughput limits are determined. Learn more ☑

○ **Bursting**
Throughput scales with file system size

○ **Provisioned**
Throughput fixed at specified amount

Figure 8-11   Selecting EFS Performance and Throughput

EFS Security

After creating an EFS file system and mount points from the selected VPC, you can use security groups to control the EC2 instance access to the EFS mount points (see Figure 8-12). Access to the EFS files and directories is controlled by application user and group permissions. All data stored within EFS can be encrypted at rest, and encryption keys are managed by AWS KMS.

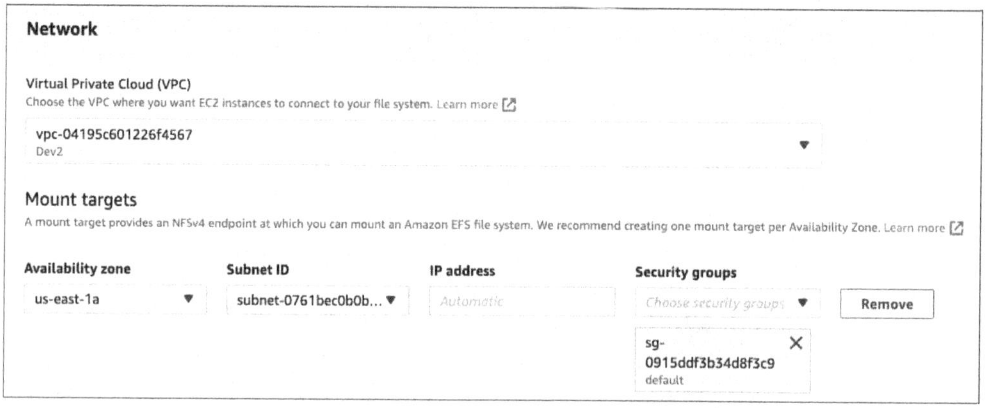

Network

Virtual Private Cloud (VPC)
Choose the VPC where you want EC2 instances to connect to your file system. Learn more

vpc-04195c601226f4567
Dev2

Mount targets

A mount target provides an NFSv4 endpoint at which you can mount an Amazon EFS file system. We recommend creating one mount target per Availability Zone. Learn more

Availability zone	Subnet ID	IP address	Security groups	
us-east-1a	subnet-0761bec0b0b...	Automatic	Choose security groups	Remove
			sg-0915ddf3b34d8f3c9 default ✕	

Figure 8-12 EFS Security

EFS Storage Classes

Amazon EFS supports three storage classes:

- **Standard:** The default storage class is selected by default.

- **Infrequent Access:** The infrequent storage (IA) storage class is for files that are accessed infrequently but require rapid access when needed. Transition into the IA tier can be set from 1 day to 90 days since the file was last accessed. The Infrequent Access tier provides a lower storage cost than the Standard storage tier, but has higher access fees.

- **One-Zone Infrequent Access:** This storage class is similar to the Infrequent Access storage class with the added benefit of being stored in a single availability zone. This can be useful for data that is not defined as critical; it provides a lower storage cost than Standard storage and Infrequent Access but has higher access fees.

EFS Lifecycle Management

EFS Lifecycle Management provides cost-effective file management. Files that have not been accessed for a defined period of time are moved to the Standard-Infrequent Access (IA) storage class from the Standard storage class. A *lifecycle policy* defines the period of time before lifecycle management transitions files into or out of Standard-Infrequent Access storage (see Figure 8-13). Lifecycle transitions into IA storage can be from 7 to 90 days since the file was last accessed. Files remain in IA storage and are transitioned out of IA storage when accessed once again.

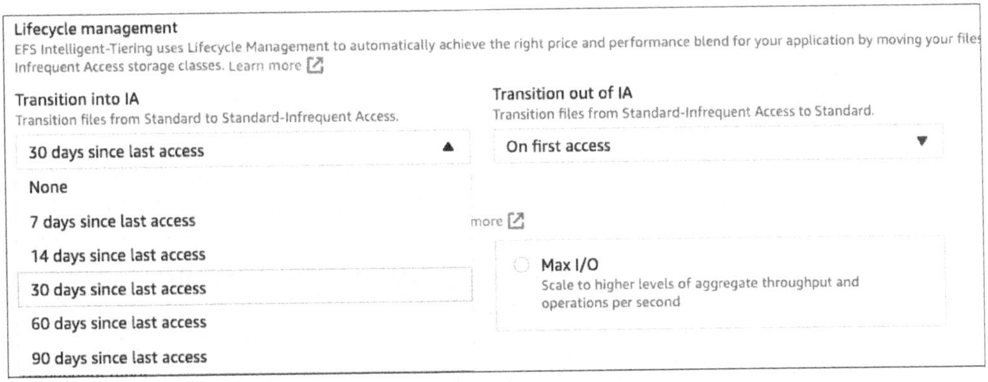

Lifecycle management
EFS Intelligent-Tiering uses Lifecycle Management to automatically achieve the right price and performance blend for your application by moving your files
Infrequent Access storage classes. Learn more

Transition into IA
Transition files from Standard to Standard-Infrequent Access.

| 30 days since last access | ▲ |

None

7 days since last access

14 days since last access

30 days since last access

60 days since last access

90 days since last access

Transition out of IA
Transition files from Standard-Infrequent Access to Standard.

| On first access | ▼ |

more

Max I/O
Scale to higher levels of aggregate throughput and operations per second

Figure 8-13   EFS Lifecycle Policy

Amazon EFS Cheat Sheet

For the AWS Certified Solutions Architect – Associate (SAA-C03) exam, you need to understand the following critical aspects of EFS:

- EFS storage is accessed using NFS mount points using the NFS protocol.

- Storage capacity is elastic; you pay for what you use.

- EFS storage can be attached from on-premises systems using a VPN connection or Direct Connect.

- Concurrent connections to an EFS file system can be made from multiple subnets.

- There are two EFS performance modes: General Purpose and Max I/O.

- Access to files and directories can be controlled with POSIX-compliant user and group-level permissions.

- AWS Key Management Service (KMS) manages encryption keys for encrypting and decrypting the EFS file system.

- Data encryption in transit uses TLS 1.3.

- EFS supports VMware ESXi.

- EFS supports AWS Outposts.

AWS DataSync

AWS DataSync enables you to sync data from an on-premises NFS storage array into EFS storage, as shown in Figure 8-14. AWS DataSync provides end-to-end security with encryption and integrity validation for in-transit and at-rest security. AWS DataSync is available as an installable agent that is installed to your AWS account. It also can be used to copy files from EFS file systems hosted in different AWS regions and to transfer data between AWS storage services with the exception of EBS volumes. AWS DataSync is much faster than standard Linux copy commands: uploads utilize encrypted parallel data transfer to the selected storage destination. AWS DataSync securely accesses AWS storage controlled by a service-linked IAM role. AWS DataSync supports connections to VPC endpoints, allowing the transfer of data using the private AWS network.

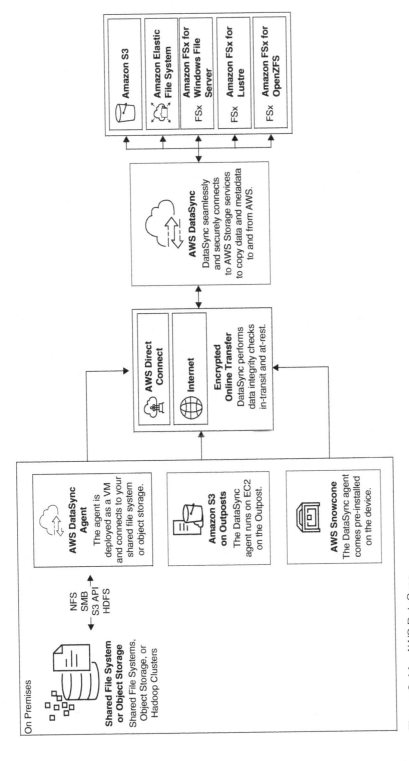

Figure 8-14 AWS DataSync

Amazon FSx for Windows File Server

Windows servers can use Amazon FSx for Windows File Server to set up a compatible Windows file system.

Amazon FSx for Windows File Server is supported by EC2 instances and containers, as well as Amazon WorkSpaces instances. FSx for Windows File Server also supports the use of the Distributed File System (DFS) namespace. Amazon FSx for Windows File Server integrates with on-premises Microsoft Active Directory and with AWS Managed Microsoft AD. Specify the level of redundancy for your FSx for the Windows File Server file system by selecting either a Single-AZ or Multi-AZ deployment.

Amazon FSx for Windows File Server file systems can be accessed from servers located in select VPCs or from an on-premises server using either a VPN or a Direct Connect connection. Amazon FSx for Windows File Server features include:

- **Single-AZ deployment:** Amazon FSx for Windows File Server automatically replicates data within the selected availability zone. Amazon FSx for Windows File Server uses the Windows Volume Shadow Copy Service to create daily backups stored in Amazon S3.

- **Multi-AZ deployment:** A Multi-AZ deployment, shown in Figure 8-15, provides continuous availability to your data when one AZ becomes unavailable; each AZ has a dedicated file server. All file changes are synchronously replicated to both file servers in each AZ. If an AZ becomes available, control is passed to the active file server, which services all read and write requests. When resources in the preferred AZ are once again available, Amazon FSx for Windows File Server falls back to the preferred file server in the preferred AZ; failover and recovery typically take less than 30 seconds. Automatic failover occurs when any of these situations occur:

  - Availability zone outage

  - The preferred file server is unavailable

  - The preferred file server is down due to maintenance

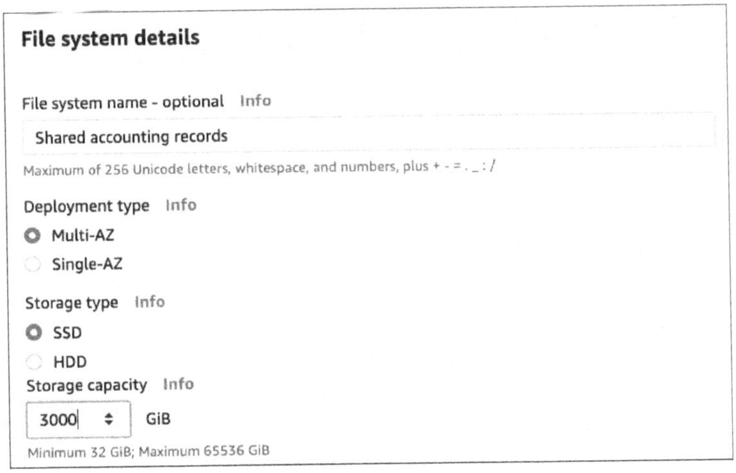

File system details

File system name - optional   Info

Shared accounting records

Maximum of 256 Unicode letters, whitespace, and numbers, plus + - = . _ : /

Deployment type   Info

○ Multi-AZ

○ Single-AZ

Storage type   Info

○ SSD

○ HDD

Storage capacity   Info

3000   ⇕   GiB

Minimum 32 GiB; Maximum 65536 GiB

Figure 8-15   FSx Deployment Options

- **Throughput:** Amazon FSx for Windows File Server file servers use an in-memory cache for accessing active files to maintain performance. Storage choices include SSD storage, which provides sub-millisecond file operations, or HDD storage, which provides single-digit-millisecond performance. FSx throughput capacity can be adjusted from 8 MiB/s to 2,048 MiB/s. Network baseline capacity ranges from 16 MiB/s to over 3,000 MiB/s.

  An Amazon FSx for Windows File Server file system configured with 2 TiB of hard disk drive storage capacity and 32 MiB/s throughput capacity has the following throughput parameters:

  - Network throughput of 32 MiB/s baselines and bursting up to 600 MiB/s when required

  - Disk throughput of 24 MiB/s baselines and 160 MiB/s when required

- **Windows shares:** Amazon FSx for Windows File Server is built using Windows file servers and accessed using SMB Version 2.0 to 3.11, allowing you to support older Windows 7 clients and Windows Server 2008 up to present-day versions.

- **File system:** Amazon FSx for Windows File Server file systems, built on SSDs, can be up to 64 TIB in size with more than 2 MIB/s of throughput. Multi-AZ support for Amazon FSx for Windows File Server allows you to use the Microsoft DFS namespace to replicate between multiple locations with up to 300 PB of storage.

- **Redundancy:** Amazon FSx for Windows File Server data is stored within a single AZ or multiple AZs. Incremental snapshots are automatically taken every day. Manual snapshots are supported for additional redundancy concerns.

- **Data deduplication:** Data deduplication can be enabled with compression to automatically reduce costs for redundant data records storing duplicated files.

- **Active Directory:** Existing Microsoft Windows environments can be integrated with Active Directory deployments and Amazon FSx for Windows File Server file systems; end users can use their existing identities for access to FSx resources. Your Active Directory deployment can be self-managed or hosted and deployed using Managed AD Directory Services for Microsoft Active Directory.

 Amazon FSx for Windows File Server Cheat Sheet

For the AWS Certified Solutions Architect – Associate (SAA-C03) exam, understand the following aspects of FSx:

- Amazon FSx for Windows File Server supports the SMB protocol, allowing connections to EC2 instances and ECs containers, VMware Cloud on AWS, and Linux and Windows applications.

- Amazon FSx for Windows File Server supports all Windows versions from Windows Server 2012 and Windows 7 forward.

- Amazon FSx for Windows File Server supports on-premises access via AWS Direct Connect or AWS VPN connections.

- Amazon FSx for Windows File Server supports access across multiple VPCs using VPC peering or AWS Transit Gateway connections.

- Amazon FSx for Windows File Server file systems are encrypted automatically at rest and in transit with keys managed by AWS Key Management Service.

- Daily backups are automatically stored in S3 storage.

- Amazon FSx for Windows File Server is integrated with the AWS Backup service.

Amazon Simple Storage Service

Amazon Simple Storage Service (S3) was one of the first AWS services offered, launched on March 14, 2006. Amazon S3 provides unlimited storage in a logical container called a *bucket* that can be made available publicly across the Internet or privately across Amazon's private network, as shown in Figure 8-16. AWS customers that use S3 storage can store any amount of data for many use cases, including data lakes, websites, mobile applications, backups, archived data, and big data analysis. Internally at AWS, almost every data component makes its way to S3 storage, including AMIs, EBS snapshots, and continuous backups from DynamoDB, Redshift, CloudWatch logs, and CloudTrail trails.

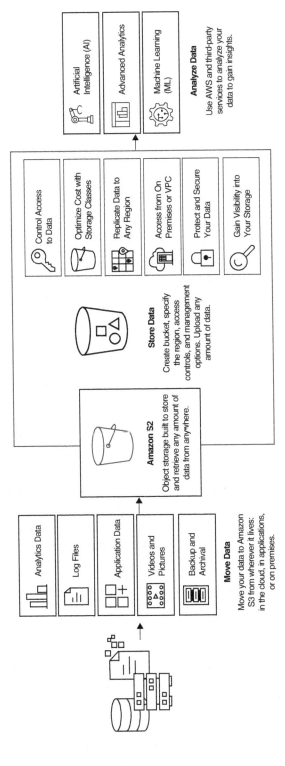

Figure 8-16   Amazon Simple Storage Service

Pricing for Amazon S3 storage is low at the start, but storage at AWS is assessed a monthly charge, plus a data transfer out fee that is applied when you retrieve, replicate, or download files from AWS storage. It's a great advantage to have unlimited storage, but organizations need to make sure they are getting the best bang for their money. When you have content stored at S3, charges are charged every month; fortunately, there are several storage classes designed to minimize S3 storage costs.

Amazon S3 storage can't be used as a boot drive, or as a hard drive location to install software applications. Amazon S3 is primarily designed for strong read after write consistency for both **PUT** and **DELETE** requests of stored objects. S3 provides read-after-write consistency for PUTS of new objects and eventual consistency for PUTS and DELETES. This ensures that when a new object is added to an Amazon S3 bucket, it is immediately available for reading. However, when an S3 object is overwritten or deleted, it can take some time for the updated version to be reflected when reading the object. S3 objects are replicated to multiple locations; eventually, all locations will be updated with the new or changed object. This replication process is defined as eventual consistency. Objects stored in Amazon S3 are also subjected to continuous integrity checks through checksums, from the source upload to the final bucket destination.

NOTE   In a single AWS region, the Amazon S3 service manages daily access peaks of over 60 TiB/s.

Amazon S3 Bucket Concepts

Following are the key terms and concepts to understand when working with Amazon S3 storage:

- *Buckets:* Buckets are the containers that store S3 objects. You can upload as many objects into an S3 bucket as you want; buckets do not have item or size limits. Use the multipart upload API to upload single objects larger than 5 MIB; once the upload is complete, the file components are combined into a single object.

- **Objects:** Each S3 object consists of the object data (the file itself) and associated metadata that describes the stored object, such as date and content type. Each object is identified within each S3 bucket by a unique key name.

- **Keys:** Each object key name uniquely identifies each object stored in an S3 bucket. For example, the object *cat.jpg*, stored in the Amazon S3 bucket *my-bucket*, stored in the us-west-2 region, can be addressed through the associated URL: https://my-bucket.s3.us-west-1.amazonaws.com/photos/mycat.jpg.

- **Access levels:** You can define public or private access levels to S3 buckets and objects with AWS Identity and Access Management (IAM) users and security policies, bucket policies, and access Control lists (ACLs).

- **Service quotas:** 100 Amazon S3 buckets can be created per AWS account; the default quota value can be increased using the Service Quota utility.

- **Object size limit:** There is no limit to the number of objects stored in a single S3 bucket; however, each individual object size is limited to 5 TiB.

- **AWS region:** Before selecting a particular AWS region for an S3 bucket, consider factors such as compliance, latency, and cost of the S3 service based on bucket/region location. As part of the S3 service-level agreement (SLA) with AWS, objects stored in a specified AWS region never leave the region unless you decide to transfer them to another location.

- **S3 bucket names:** All names for S3 buckets are Domain Name System (DNS) names stored in Amazon Route 53, AWS's global DNS service. S3 bucket names are therefore DNS names and must be globally unique across all AWS customers.

- **S3 object metadata:** Each object in an S3 bucket contains some mandatory components: the object itself and the associated metadata. Optionally, you can add additional custom metadata to each object when stored. Keep in mind that custom metadata is not encrypted. Review the mapping for each object with the bucket/key/version of objects, as shown in Figure 8-17.

Figure 8-17 S3 Object Details

Many options are available when you create an S3 bucket, as shown in Table 8-4. Understand these options for the AWS Certified Solutions Architect – Associate (SAA-C03) exam.

Table 8-4   S3 Bucket Configuration Options

S3 Feature	Details
AWS Region	The region where the Amazon S3 bucket is created.
S3 bucket policy	Bucket policies allow or deny requests to IAM users and groups and can grant cross-account access to other AWS accounts. Only the owner of the bucket can associate a bucket policy with an Amazon S3 bucket.
IAM policies	Create IAM users within your AWS account to grant access to Amazon S3 buckets and objects.
S3 Block Public Access	Block Public Access settings are enabled at the bucket level. There are three options that can be individually selected: Grant access with IAM identities, Bucket policies, or Buckets in a VPC setting.
S3 Access Points	Simplify data access for any AWS service or customer application that requires access to shared datasets stored in an S3 bucket. Separate S3 access points can be created and tailored for application accces or groups of IAM users. Access points can be configured to restrict access to a specific virtual private cloud (VPC).
Access Control Lists	ACLs can be used to grant read and write permissions to authorized users, groups, or AWS accounts for individual buckets and objects. AWS recommends that ACLs be disabled and to use the Bucket Owner Enforced setting for S3 object ownership.
Website hosting	An S3 bucket can be configured to host a static website that does not require service-side processing.
Logging	Track access requests to Amazon S3 buckets using Amazon CloudTrail, Amazon S3 Access Logs, AWS CloudWatch S3 metrics, or AWS GuardDuty analysis of S3 data events. Server access logging provides detailed records of requests made to an Amazon S3 bucket, assisting in security and access audits.
SNS notifications	Receive notifications when S3 bucket events (such as **GET**, **PUT**, and **DELETE**) occur.
S3 Versioning	Store multiple versions of the same object within a single Amazon S3 bucket. Versioning must be enabled for many other Amazon S3 features including Lifecycle policies and Bucket replication options.
Lifecycle policies	Create lifecycle rules for Amazon S3 controlling object retention and movement to other Amazon S3 storage classes to help manage storage costs.
Bucket replication	Automatically replicate objects to other Amazon S3 buckets hosted in the same region (Same Region Replication) or other Amazon S3 regions (Cross Region Replication) to help with disaster recovery. Replication can also be to another AWS account.

S3 Feature	Details
Server-Side Encryption (SSE)	As of January 5, 2003, all new object uploads to Amazon S3 will be automatically encrypted with Amazon S3 Managed keys (SSE-S3). Other choices are AWS-Key Management Service Keys (SSE-KMS) or SSE with customer provided keys (SSE-C).
Object tagging	Add up to ten tags to each Amazon S3 object to assist in controlling access with bucket or IAM policies. Tags can be used in lifecycle and replication policies. To ensure that the latest version of an object is always available for reading, S3 provides a mechanism called object tagging, which allows users to specify a version of an object to be the current version. This can be useful in scenarios where read-after-write consistency is required.
Requester pays	Charge the data transfer costs to the end user that requests the object.
Object lock	Enable write-once/read-many (WORM) policies on objects or buckets to manage compliance requirements. Define a "retain until date" or "legal hold" protection.
S3 Transfer acceleration	Speed up the transfer of larger Amazon S3 objects over long distances from the end user to the S3 bucket using CloudFront global edge locations and the AWS private network for uploads and downloads.
Multi-Region access point	Define a global endpoint to access data sets stored in Amazon S3 buckets located in multiple AWS regions. Multi-Region access uses the AWS Global Accelerator to select the S3 bucket with the lowest network latency.
AWS PrivateLink for Amazon S3	AWS PrivateLink for S3 provides private connectivity between Amazon S3 and on-premises locations using interface VPC endpoints for S3 in your VPC to connect your on-premises applications directly to S3 over AWS Direct Connect or AWS VPN.

NOTE   S3 Object Ownership is an S3 bucket-level setting used to disable ACLs and take ownership of all objects in your S3 bucket. S3 Object Ownership allows the owner of an S3 bucket to take control of all bucket objects.

Amazon S3 Data Consistency

Objects stored in an Amazon S3 bucket are replicated many times to at least three other separate physical storage locations (availability zones) within the AWS region where your Amazon S3 bucket is located, providing a high level of durability for each stored object. After a new object has been written to an Amazon S3 bucket, read requests retrieve the latest version of the object.

Working with multiple copies of data, replicating updates and deletions takes some time to complete. All S3 objects eventually in all linked storage locations will be the same.

Amazon S3 Storage Classes

When storing objects in Amazon S3 buckets, the available Amazon S3 storage classes have been designed for different use cases, as shown in Table 8-5.

Table 8-5   S3 Storage Classes

Storage Class	S3 Standard	S3 Intelligent-Tiering	S3 Standard IA (Infrequent Access)	S3 One Zone-IA	Glacier	Glacier Deep Archive
Access frequency	No restrictions	Automatically moves objects to the Standard-Infrequent Access tier after 30 days	Infrequent; minimum 30 days	30 days	90 days	180 days
Access speed	Milliseconds	Milliseconds	Milliseconds	Milliseconds	Instant Retrieval (milliseconds); Flexible Retrieval (minutes to hours)	Within 12 hours
Minimum Number of AZs	3	3	3	1	3	3
Retrieval cost	N/A	N/A	Per GB	Per GB	Per GB	Per GB
Minimum duration (days)	None	30	30	30	90	180
Availability	99.99%	99.9%	99.9%	99.5%	99.9%	99.9%
Minimum object size	N/A	N/A	128 KB	128 KB	40 KB	40 KB

There are six Amazon S3 storage classes to consider:

- **Amazon S3 Standard:** Designed for data regularly accessed by online cloud-hosted applications. It is designed for high performance and durability, offering eleven 9s durability and four 9s availability. Amazon states, "If you store 10,000 objects in S3, you may lose one object every 10 million years." Exact pricing depends on the amount you store and the Amazon S3 bucket's region. The first 50 TiB is charged at $0.023 per gigabyte per month; at 500 TiB of object storage, the price drops to $0.021 per gigabyte per month. Note that there are also charges for querying and retrieving objects. Amazon S3 Standard supports SSL for data in transit and data encryption can be enabled for objects at rest.

■ **Amazon S3 Intelligent-Tiering:** Rules for intelligent-tiering analyze and move less frequently accessed objects to lower-cost storage classes from Amazon S3 Standard to Amazon S3, Amazon S3-IA, One Zone-IA, or Amazon S3 Glacier (Instant Retrieval, Flexible Retrieval, or Deep Archive). S3 Intelligent-Tiering optimizes your storage costs by monitoring your access patterns at the object level, automating cost savings for your stored objects.

After 30 days of inactivity, your objects are automatically moved from the Frequent Access tier to the Infrequent Access tier on an object-by-object basis. If the infrequently accessed data objects begin to be accessed more frequently, they are moved back to the Frequent Access tier. Intelligent-Tiering might save organizations a great deal of money after deploying one of these use cases:

- ■ Moving all objects older than 90 days to Amazon S3-IA

- ■ Moving all objects after 180 days to Amazon S3 Glacier

- ■ Moving all objects over 365 days to Amazon S3 Glacier Deep Archive

■ **Amazon S3 Standard-Infrequent-Access (IA):** Designed for less frequently accessed data while maintaining eleven 9s durability. If you don't need to access your data frequently and object access is greater than 30 days, Amazon S3 Standard-IA is a cheaper option than Amazon S3 Standard.

■ **Amazon S3 One Zone-IA:** Designed for less frequently accessed data that could be re-created if necessary, Amazon S3 One Zone-IA provides less durability than Amazon S3 Standard-IA because the data is stored in a single AZ instead of across three or more AZs. The price point of Amazon S3 Standard-IA is 20% less than the price of Amazon S3-IA.

■ **Amazon S3 Glacier:** Long-term data archival storage stored in archives and vaults. If you need to access your archived data quickly, you can retrieve it within minutes—but you pay additional fees for the expedited access.

- ■ Glacier Instant Retrieval storage has a minimum storage requirement of 90 days. Retrievals are carried out in milliseconds and are allowed once a month for objects that might need to be accessed quickly, such as medical images or news media assets.

- Glacier Flexible Retrieval storage has a minimum storage requirement of 90 days. Retrievals are carried out in minutes of large archived datasets such as backup or disaster recovery records, or using free bulk retrievals, which take 5 to 12 hours.

- **S3 Glacier:** The concept of this archive storage option is to remove the need for on-premises long-term archiving vaults. It is the cheapest archive option at AWS: just $0.00099 per gigabyte per month with a minimum storage requirement of 180 days. Retrieval times are within 12 hours or less. Organizations can request faster retrieval times, but additional fees apply.

Amazon S3 Management

S3 buckets have a variety of powerful management controls to help manage your stored data:

- **S3 Batch Operations:** S3 Batch Operations can be used to perform operations on a large number of objects, making it an efficient way to manage data in S3. It can be particularly useful for scenarios where administrators need to perform the same operation on a large number of objects, such as migrating data between S3 buckets or applying data retention policies. To use S3 Batch Operations, create a job that specifies the operation to be performed, the objects to be affected, and any additional parameters. S3 Batch Operations can be initiated using the AWS Management Console, the AWS CLI, or using an AWS SDK.

- **S3 Object Lock:** Organizations can enforce retention policies based on defined "retain until" dates or legal hold dates. All storage classes can enable S3 Object Lock settings; however, versioning must also be enabled at the Amazon S3 bucket level before the Object Lock feature can be enforced.

Once Object Lock has been enabled, you can lock objects in that bucket. Object Lock can be deployed at the object level or Amazon S3 bucket level. For example, you could add a 3-year or a 5-year retention policy at the Amazon S3 bucket level; from that point forward, all objects placed in the specific Amazon S3 bucket would inherit the retention policy. S3 bucket level protection is especially for customers that need to adhere to SEC Rule 17-a 4(f), CFTC Regulation 1.3.1, and FINRA Rule 4511. There are two modes of protection available for locking Amazon S3 objects (see Figure 8-18):

- **Retention period:** Specifies a fixed period of time in which an S3 object remains locked. During this period, the object is WORM-protected and can't be overwritten or deleted.

- **Legal Hold:** Adds S3 Object Lock protection to an Amazon S3 object that remains until it is explicitly removed by an authorized administrator.

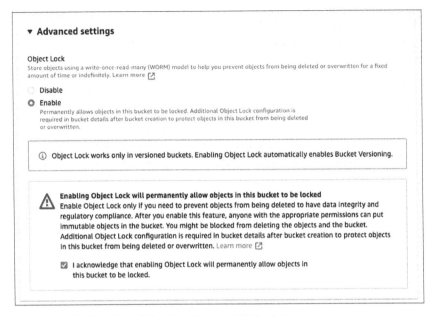

Figure 8-18 Enabling Object Lock on an S3 Bucket

- **S3 Replication:** This feature provides replication of objects between buckets within the same AWS region or across different AWS regions. Two-way replication between two or more buckets within the same or different AWS region is also supported. Predictable replication times can be accomplished by using Replication Time Control (RTC), which replicates objects in less than 15 minutes.

- **Cross-Region Replication (CRR):** This feature can be used from any AWS region to any other region to any Amazon S3 storage class and across AWS accounts. The replication process is carried out by enabling CCR at the source bucket for the entire bucket contents or by a prefix or tag, as shown in Figure 8-19. In addition, lifecycle rules control the replication of objects stored in Amazon S3 Standard to other Amazon S3 storage classes on the destination bucket or, optionally, to Amazon S3 Glacier. CCR replication is encrypted to maintain data security. The cost for using CRR is calculated based on the copy request and the inter-region data transfer charge for each replicated object.

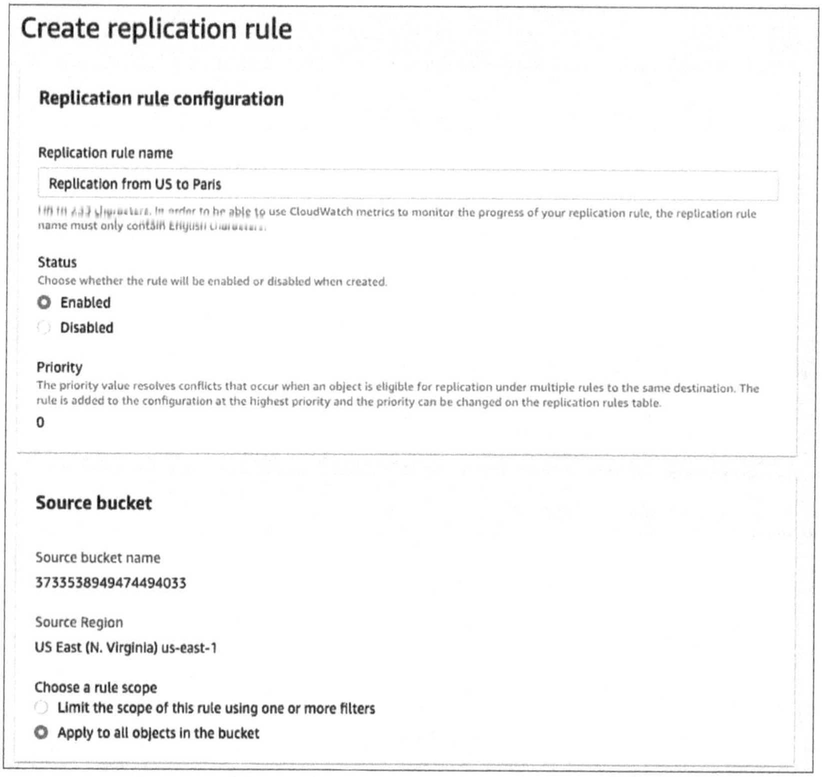

Create replication rule

Replication rule configuration

Replication rule name

Replication from US to Paris

In order to be able to use CloudWatch metrics to monitor the progress of your replication rule, the replication rule name must only contain English characters.

Status
Choose whether the rule will be enabled or disabled when created.

○ **Enabled**

○ Disabled

Priority
The priority value resolves conflicts that occur when an object is eligible for replication under multiple rules to the same destination. The rule is added to the configuration at the highest priority and the priority can be changed on the replication rules table.

0

Source bucket

Source bucket name
3733538949474494033

Source Region
US East (N. Virginia) us-east-1

Choose a rule scope
○ Limit the scope of this rule using one or more filters
○ Apply to all objects in the bucket

Figure 8-19   Enabling Cross-Region Replication

- **Same-Region Replication (SRR):** This feature allows you to achieve data compliance for storing your data in a separate AWS account within the same region as the original bucket contents. SRR can be used within any AWS region to any Amazon S3 storage class and across AWS accounts. The replication process enables SRR at the source bucket for the entire bucket contents or based on a prefix or tag. Configure lifecycle rules to replicate objects stored in Amazon S3 Standard to other Amazon S3 storage classes on the destination bucket or to Amazon S3 Glacier. To ensure data security, SRR replication is encrypted.

- **S3 Storage Lens:** This feature allows you to gain visibility into your Amazon S3 storage usage and activity across your entire AWS organization or AWS account. Amazon S3 Storage Lens provides recommendations to improve your cost efficiency and the data security of your stored objects.

- **S3 Inventory:** If you want to find details about your current object inventory in Amazon S3, you can run an inventory process using S3 Inventory, shown in Figure 8-20. After you select the source bucket for analysis, S3 Inventory creates a flat CSV file based on your query criteria and stores the inventory listing in a specified destination Amazon S3 bucket. The inventory listing encompasses current objects and their associated metadata, including the object's key name, version ID, encryption and replication status, retention date, storage class, object hold status, and object size. The inventory list file can be encrypted using S3-managed or KMS-managed keys.

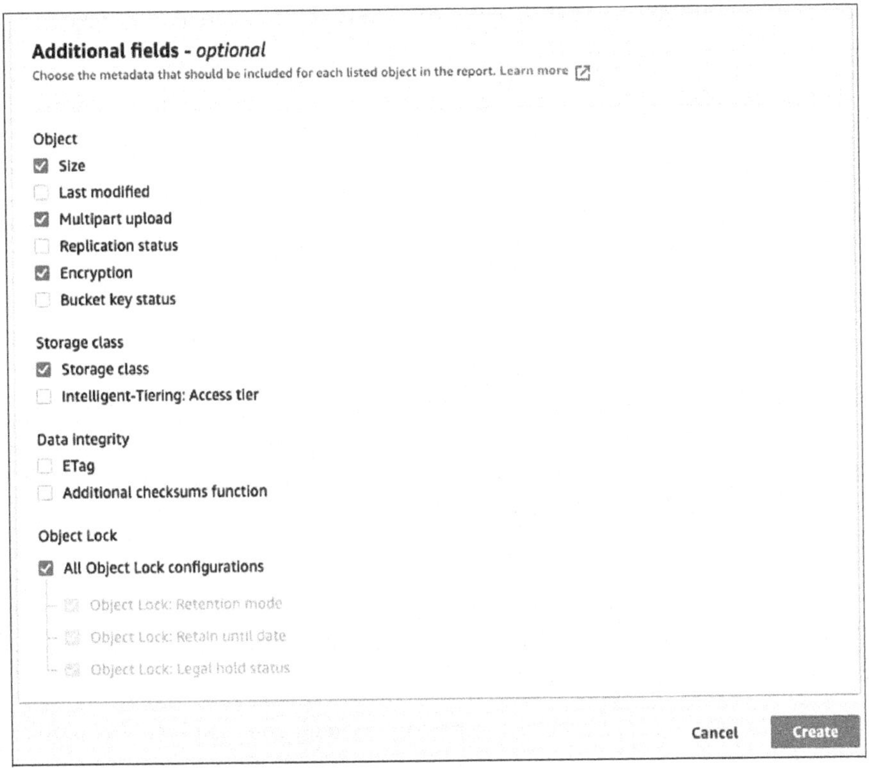

Figure 8-20 Creating an S3 Inventory Report

- **Storage Class Analytics:** Through machine learning processes, your Amazon S3 storage is categorized into groups of less frequently accessed data based on an analysis of retrievals against the stored objects. Analysis can also be performed based on Amazon S3 buckets or object tags.

- **Object tags:** Up to ten tags can be added to each Amazon S3 object. The following are some of the actions that can be performed based on the assigned S3 object tag:

    - **Searching and filtering:** S3 enables users to search for and filter objects based on their tags.

    - **Lifecycle management:** S3 enables users to define lifecycle policies that automatically transition objects to different storage classes or delete them based on the object's tags.

    - **Access control:** S3 enables users to specify access controls on objects based on the object's tags.

    - **Cost optimization:** S3 enables users to optimize storage costs by transitioning objects to different storage classes using lifecycle policies that are based on the object's tags.

    - **Auditing and compliance:** S3 enables users to use object tags to track and audit data access and usage.

S3 Bucket Versioning

Versioning can be enabled on each Amazon S3 bucket to further protect your objects from accidental deletion. As a best practice, versioning could be enabled before any objects are stored in an Amazon S3 bucket to ensure that all objects will be protected from deletion. Enabling versioning guarantees the following:

- Every new **PUT** of an existing object is created as a new object with a new version ID.

- The newest version is defined as the current version, and the previous versions are retained and not overwritten.

- When you request just the S3 key name of an object, you are presented with the current version of the versioned object.

After versioning has been enabled, additional lifecycle management rules for the versioned content can be created, as shown in Figure 8-21. These rules can define a lifecycle expiration policy that dictates the number of versions that you want to maintain. Lifecycle rules help you manage previous versions of objects by transitioning or expiring specific objects after a defined number of days.

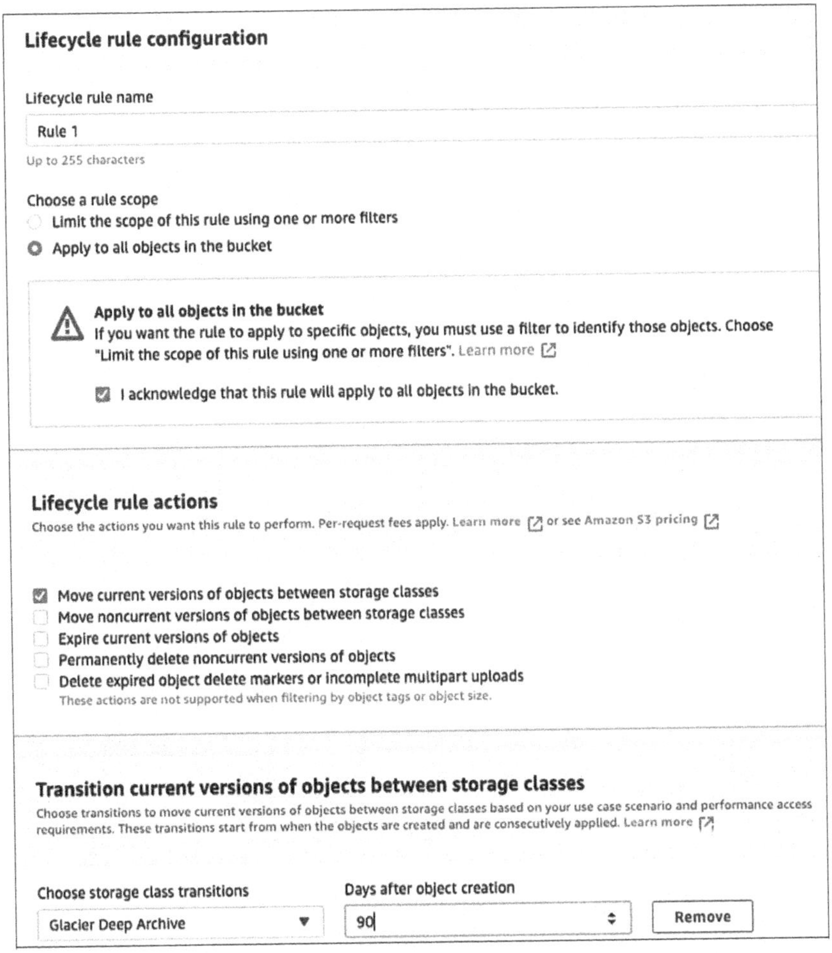

Lifecycle rule configuration

Lifecycle rule name

> Rule 1

Up to 255 characters

Choose a rule scope
- ○ Limit the scope of this rule using one or more filters
- ◉ Apply to all objects in the bucket

⚠ **Apply to all objects in the bucket**
If you want the rule to apply to specific objects, you must use a filter to identify those objects. Choose "Limit the scope of this rule using one or more filters". Learn more ⤴

☑ I acknowledge that this rule will apply to all objects in the bucket.

Lifecycle rule actions
Choose the actions you want this rule to perform. Per-request fees apply. Learn more ⤴ or see Amazon S3 pricing ⤴

- ☑ Move current versions of objects between storage classes
- ☐ Move noncurrent versions of objects between storage classes
- ☐ Expire current versions of objects
- ☐ Permanently delete noncurrent versions of objects
- ☐ Delete expired object delete markers or incomplete multipart uploads
  These actions are not supported when filtering by object tags or object size.

Transition current versions of objects between storage classes
Choose transitions to move current versions of objects between storage classes based on your use case scenario and performance access requirements. These transitions start from when the objects are created and are consecutively applied. Learn more ⤴

Choose storage class transitions	Days after object creation	
Glacier Deep Archive ▼	90 ⇕	Remove

Figure 8-21 Lifecycle Rules

NOTE Amazon S3 supports SNS notifications that can alert you at no additional cost when S3 object deletions occur. You can also enable multi-factor authentication (MFA) on S3 buckets that is activated when objects are selected to be deleted.

Amazon S3 Access Points

You can simplify access to objects stored in Amazon S3 buckets from multiple AWS locations by creating Amazon S3 access endpoints that are directly attached to specific Amazon S3 buckets, as shown in Figure 8-22. Each Amazon S3 access point can have different permissions and network controls for requests made through the access point. The following are key features of S3 access points:

- S3 access points can deploy an optional AWS IAM policy.

- Access points block public access by default.

- Access points can have permissions defined for IAM users and groups, and specific applications.

- Access points can be configured to accept requests only from a VPC.

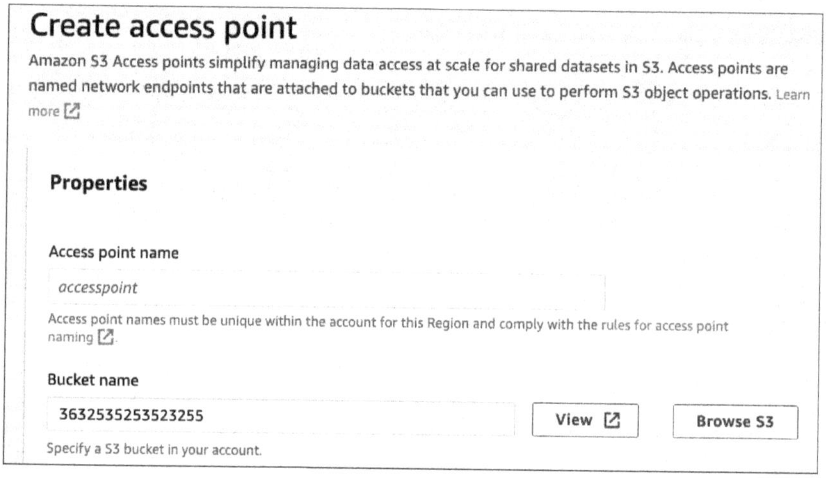

Create access point

Amazon S3 Access points simplify managing data access at scale for shared datasets in S3. Access points are named network endpoints that are attached to buckets that you can use to perform S3 object operations. Learn more 🗗

Properties

Access point name

accesspoint

Access point names must be unique within the account for this Region and comply with the rules for access point naming 🗗.

Bucket name

3632535253523255   View 🗗   Browse S3

Specify a S3 bucket in your account.

Figure 8-22   Amazon S3 Access Points Setup

S3 access can also be controlled using a VPC endpoint, which provides secure access using either a gateway or interface connection to an S3 bucket from applications running in a VPC without requiring an Internet Gateway or NAT gateway. Access to an S3 bucket using a VPC gateway endpoint connection is not charged.

Multi-Region Access Points

Multi-region S3 access points can also be created that provide a global endpoint, allowing applications to request content from S3 buckets located in multiple AWS regions.

When creating a S3 multi-region access point, multiple AWS regions are selected where the replicated S3 buckets will be served through a global endpoint. Application requests use the AWS Global Accelerator service to route requests across the private AWS global network to the S3 bucket with the lowest network latency.

Preselected URLs for S3 Objects

Amazon S3 allows the generation of preselected URLs for objects stored in the service. These URLs can be shared with others, enabling them to access the S3 object without the need for an AWS account or AWS IAM credentials.

There are several methods to generate preselected URLs for Amazon S3 objects:

- **Query String Authentication:** S3 Query String Authentication enables users to generate a time-limited URL for an object that includes a signature calculated using the user's AWS secret access key. This URL can be shared with others and used to access the object without the need for AWS credentials.

- **Presigned URLs:** S3 Presigned URLs enable users to generate a time-limited URL that can be used to access an object or perform an operation on the object, such as uploading or downloading it. Presigned URLs are signed using the user's AWS access key and secret access key.

- **Object URLs:** S3 Object URLs can be used to access objects stored in S3 using the S3 endpoint and the object's key. Object URLs can be accessed by anyone with the URL, but they do not include any security or access controls.

S3 Cheat Sheet

For the AWS Certified Solutions Architect – Associate (SAA-C03) exam, you need to understand the following aspects of Amazon S3 storage:

- An Amazon S3 bucket is a flat container that contains file objects.

- Amazon S3 buckets cannot be nested.

- Amazon S3 buckets are region-specific.

- Amazon S3 bucket names must be unique globally across the AWS cloud, as the S3 namespace is actually a DNS namespace hosted by Amazon Route 53.

- Objects stored in Amazon S3 storage can be addressed through a service endpoint, by bucket name, by object name, and by object version.

- There are five methods for controlling access to Amazon S3 storage: bucket policies, IAM policies, access control lists, presigned URLs, and query-string authentication.

- An Amazon S3 bucket owner can define cross-account permissions for controlling access from another AWS account.

- Membership in the Authenticated Users group allows S3 bucket access from any AWS account. By default, this group includes all AWS accounts.

- Membership in the All Users group allows anyone outside AWS to access the S3 Bucket. Requests can be signed or unsigned.

- *Multipart uploads* should be used for objects larger than 5 GB. Uploads occur synchronously and in parallel.

- Amazon S3 Transfer Acceleration uses edge locations to speed up transfers of files over long distances from the end user's location to the selected S3 bucket.

- An Amazon S3 bucket can be used to host a static website.

- A custom domain name can be used with a Route 53 alias record for an Amazon S3 bucket that is hosting a static website.

- *Versioning* stores all versions of an object and protects against accidental deletion or overwrites.

Amazon S3 Glacier

Amazon S3 Glacier is an extension of Amazon S3 storage that offers the lowest cost of any AWS storage services. S3 Glacier costs on average $0.004 per gigabyte per month, and S3 Glacier Deep Archive costs just $0.00099 per gigabyte per month.

The premise with Amazon S3 Glacier archival storage data is that customers don't require regular access to the content stored in S3 Glacier vaults and archives. Therefore, the minimum storage time is 90 days; accessing the Amazon S3 Glacier content sooner results in a financial penalty. Amazon S3 Glacier storage pricing is based on monthly storage capacity and the total number of lifecycle transition requests for moving data into Amazon S3 Glacier. Objects archived into Amazon S3 Glacier must remain a minimum of 90 days, or additional charges apply.

Amazon S3 Glacier has the same eleven 9s durability as S3 Standard storage. Amazon S3 Glacier data is stored in vaults and *archives*, set up through the Amazon S3 management console or using the AWS CLI. Amazon S3 Glacier automatically encrypts all stored objects. Content can be delivered to Amazon S3 Glacier by using the following methods:

- Amazon S3 Lifecycle or Intelligent-Tiering rules

- CLI commands

- Direct use of the REST API or AWS SDK

- AWS Storage Gateway: Tape Gateway, which integrates with S3 Glacier

- AWS Snowball, AWS Snowcone, and AWS Snowmobile devices, which can directly migrate data records into S3 storage

- A direct **PUT** stores objects directly in S3 Glacier using the S3 API

- Cross-Region Replication or Single-Region Replication can replicate objects into S3 Glacier storage

Vaults and Archives

You can store an unlimited number of archives within a single Amazon S3 Glacier vault: the term *archive* refers to the objects (such as documents, photos, or videos) that are stored in each archive. Amazon S3 Glacier archives can be from 1 byte up to 40 TiB; archives up to 4 GiB can be uploaded in a single operation. Archives from 100 MiB up to 40 TiB use the multipart upload API and are synchronously uploaded and stored in an Amazon S3 Glacier vault (see Figure 8-23) stored in your chosen AWS region. Each AWS customer can have up to 1,000 vaults per AWS region.

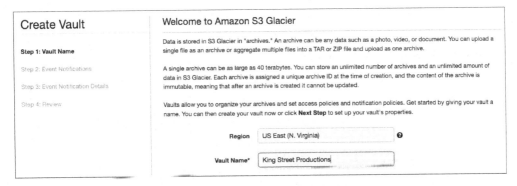

Figure 8-23 Creating S3 Glacier Vaults

S3 Glacier Retrieval Policies

To retrieve objects from S3 Glacier, create an archive retrieval job using the Management Console or the S3 API. The archive retrieval job is a separate temporary copy of your data placed in either Amazon S3 Reduced Redundancy Storage or Amazon Standard-IA storage, leaving the actual archived data in its original location in Amazon S3 Glacier. Temporary archived data is accessed using an Amazon S3 **GET** request. To retrieve an archive from S3 Glacier, use the AWS CLI to get the ID of the archive to retrieve. Next, initiate a job requesting Amazon S3 to prepare the archive request. Three retrieval options are available:

- **Expedited:** Retrieval is within 1 to 5 minutes for archives less than 250 MiB. Provisioned capacity can be purchased to ensure that expedited retrieval requests under all circumstances will be carried out.

- **Standard:** Retrieve any archive within several hours, typically 3 to 5 hours. This is the default option when retrieval options are not specified.

- **Bulk:** Retrieve any archive within 5 to 12 hours. Bulk retrievals are the lowest-cost S3 Glacier retrieval option.

S3 Glacier Deep Archive

If archive records are rarely viewed, organizations should consider using Amazon S3 Glacier Deep Archive, for which you are charged about $1 per terabyte per month for storage. Larger customers can move on-premises magnetic tape libraries into Amazon S3 Glacier Deep Archive and save money. Objects archived to Amazon S3 Glacier Deep Archive have a minimum storage requirement of 180 days. Amazon S3 Glacier Deep Archive data can be accessed by two retrieval processes. Free standard retrieval delivers your data within 12 hours. Bulk retrieval returns your data within 48 hours. Expedited data retrieval is not supported.

Amazon S3 Glacier Cheat Sheet

For the AWS Certified Solutions Architect – Associate (SAA-C03) exam, you need to understand the following critical aspects of S3 Glacier:

- Data in Amazon S3 Glacier is resilient even if one availability zone is unavailable.

- Archived objects are visible upon retrieval request through an Amazon S3 temporary storage location and not directly through Amazon S3 Glacier.

- Amazon S3 Glacier automatically encrypts all stored data at rest using AES 256-bit encryption.

- The Amazon S3 **PUT** API allows direct uploads to Amazon S3 Glacier.

- Amazon Glacier Deep Archive is lower cost than Amazon S3 Glacier but has longer retrieval times.

- Once an archive has been uploaded, it cannot be modified.

- Amazon Glacier Instant Retrievals can be expedited within milliseconds.

- Amazon Glacier Flexible Retrieval bulk retrievals are free of charge once a year.

- Amazon Glacier Flexible Retrieval bulk retrieval times are typically between 5 and 12 hours.

AWS Data Lake

A *data lake* is a central repository that enables you to store all your structured and unstructured data at any scale. Data records stored in a data lake come from a variety of sources, such as transactional databases, log files, sensors, and social media feeds. One of the key benefits of a data lake is that it enables organizations to store data in its native format, without the need to transform or structure it upfront. A data lake stores both structured and unstructured data records. Many different types of analytics can be performed on stored data, including data visualizations and dashboard views, big data processing, and machine learning. The following are key features of a data lake:

- **Multiple data sources:** Data is collected in real time from multiple sources, including relational databases, business applications, and nonrelational data types such as IoT devices, social media, and mobile applications (see Figure 8-24).

- **Catalog:** A centralized catalog presents data lake content built from analyzing, cataloging, and indexing data records in multiple locations.

- **Analysis:** Data scientists, developers, and analysts can access the data lake using a variety of analytic tools and frameworks such as Apache Hadoop, Apache Spark, and Presto.

- **Machine Learning:** Generate insights on historical data using models that can forecast outcomes.

- **Combine customer data:** Retail sales can be compared against incident tickets for additional customer insights.

- **Improve operational efficiencies:** Collect and analyze real-time data from connected IoT devices.

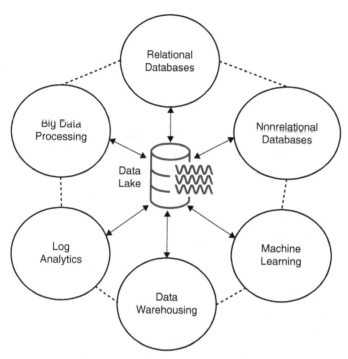

Figure 8-24 Corporate Data Sources

> **NOTE** Data lakes enable customers to run analytics without first having to move data records from their source locations.

Before data lakes, many larger customers used data warehouses, which stored data from a business's line of business applications, and the daily transactions between customers (CRM) and human resources (HRM). A data warehouse's data structure and schema were designed for efficient SQL queries that created reports and detailed analysis and provided a single source of truth for the company. A data warehouse can still be a component of a modern data lake, as detailed in Table 8-6.

Table 8-6 Amazon Redshift Compared to AWS Data Lake

Characteristics	Data Warehouse (Amazon Redshift)	AWS Data Lake
Data types	Relational data for transactional systems, databases, and LOB applications	Both relational and nonrelational (social media, mobile apps, websites, IoT devices)
Schema	Designed before deployment	Defined when analyzed

Characteristics	Data Warehouse (Amazon Redshift)	AWS Data Lake
Cost and performance	Fast queries require high IOPS storage	Fast queries use low-cost storage
Quality of data records	Central source of truth	Curated and noncurated (raw) data
End users	Business analysts	Data scientists, data developers, and business analysts
Analytics	Business intelligence (BI), batch reporting, data visualizations	Machine learning, predictive analysis

AWS Lake Formation

Today's modern data lake architecture enables customers to integrate an on-premises data lake, a data warehouse, and custom data stores into a unified data lake stored in Amazon S3. A data lake provides secure data access utilizing compliance and governance across an organization. Deploying AWS Lake Formation, data can be connected from external data silos into a data lake for analytics and machine learning analysis (see Figure 8-25).

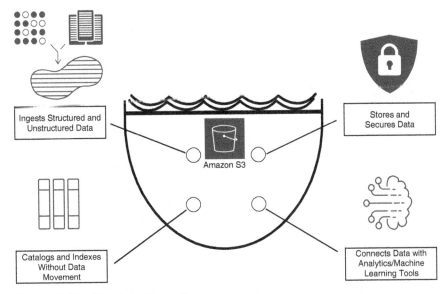

Figure 8-25   AWS Lake Formation

- AWS Lake Formation automates the creation of a secure centralized data lake that stores all customer data in its original format and is prepared for analysis.

■ AWS Lake Formation uses Amazon S3 storage to create the data lake, ensuring unlimited storage and durable storage across multiple availability zones.

■ AWS Lake Formation does the work of loading selected data from source locations, turning on encryption and key management, and reorganizing data into a columnar format for analysis by various analytical tools.

An AWS data lake is a central repository for storing a vast amount of raw data in its native format, which can then be used for various analytics and machine learning purposes. Data records that are part of a data lake are stored in both structured and unstructured data formats. AWS offers a range of services and tools for creating and managing data lakes, including AWS Glue, Amazon S3, Amazon Redshift, Amazon Kinesis, and Amazon EMR (see Figure 8-26). These services can be used to collect, process, and store data from a variety of organizational sources, including transactional systems, IoT devices, and social media platforms. Building a data lake involves the following steps:

1. Identify the organizational sources of data that will be included in the data lake, such as transactional systems, IoT devices, and social media platforms. Data is stored in two formats: structured and semi-structured.

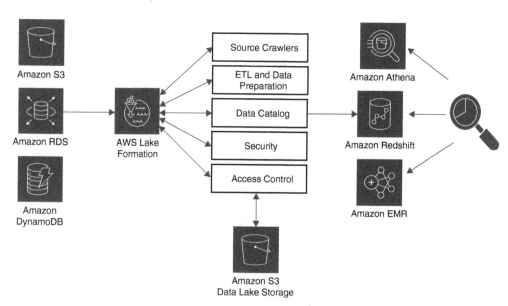

Figure 8-26   Data Lake Services

2. Extract the data from these sources and transform it into a format that is suitable for storage in the data lake. This may involve cleaning and normalizing the data and applying any necessary transformations to make it consistent and usable.

3. Load the data into the data lake, typically using Amazon S3.

4. Organize the data in the data lake by applying metadata tags and creating a logical structure that makes it easy to find and access the data.

5. Secure the data lake by implementing proper access controls and permissions using AWS IAM policies or service control policies. Policies include setting up authentication and authorization mechanisms as well as encrypting sensitive data. Authentication can be managed using Amazon Cognito. It is also important to monitor the data lake for any security threats or anomalies and to implement appropriate safeguards for protection.

6. Monitor the data lake for any security threats or anomalies, and implement appropriate safeguards to protect against them.

7. Use the data in the data lake for various analytics and machine learning purposes, using built-in AWS services or by integrating with third-party tools and services.

Structured and Unstructured Data

Structured data is organized in a specific format and is easy to search, process, and analyze. It is typically organized in a way that enables both humans and machines to easily interpret it. Examples of structured data storage AWS include databases, tables, and spreadsheets. Unstructured or semi-structured data is data that doesn't fit neatly into a predefined data model or doesn't follow a fixed format, such as data stored in text files or images. AWS provides a number of cloud services that can be used to store, process, and analyze unstructured data:

- **Amazon S3:** An object storage service that can be used to store unstructured data of any size, at any scale.

- **Amazon Textract:** A machine learning service used to extract text and data from scanned documents and images.

- **Amazon Comprehend:** A natural language processing (NLP) service used to extract insights from unstructured text data.

- **Amazon Rekognition:** A machine learning service used to analyze images and videos and extract insights.

Structured data storage services can be used individually or together to store, process, and analyze unstructured data. For example, a data scientist could use Amazon S3 to store images, Amazon Textract to extract text and data from the images, and Amazon Comprehend to extract insights from the extracted text data. AWS provides a number of services that can be used to store, process, and analyze structured data:

- **Amazon RDS:** Supports a variety of database engines, including MySQL, Microsoft SQL, PostgreSQL, and Oracle.

- **Amazon Redshift:** A data warehousing service that analyzes structured data using SQL and business intelligence tools.

- **Amazon DynamoDB:** A NoSQL database service that provides fast and predictable performance with seamless scalability.

- **Amazon EMR:** A big data processing service that supports a range of big data frameworks, such as Apache Spark and Hadoop.

Unstructured data storage services can be used individually or together to store, process, and analyze structured data. For example, you could use Amazon RDS to store structured data in a relational database, Amazon Redshift to analyze the data using SQL and business intelligence tools, and Amazon EMR to process the data using a big data framework.

Analytical Tools and Datasets

After the data lake has been created, administrators can set up access to existing datasets and analytical tools. End users access the centralized data catalog that lists the available datasets. Each dataset can then be used with a choice of analytics and machine learning services, listed in Table 8-7.

Table 8-7 Tools for Analytics, Data Movement, and AWS Data Lake

Category	Use Case	AWS Service
Analytics	Interactive analytics	Amazon Athena, Amazon Kinesis
	Big data	Amazon EMR
	Data warehouse	Amazon Redshift
	Operational analysis	Amazon OpenSearch Services
	Data visualizations	Amazon Quicksight
	Data preparation	AWS Glue DataBrew
Data movement	Real-time data movement	AWS Glue
		Amazon Managed Streaming for Apache Kafka (MSK)
		Amazon Kinesis Data Streams
		Amazon Kinesis Data Firehose
		Amazon Kinesis Video Streams
		Amazon Kinesis

Category	Use Case	AWS Service
AWS data lake	Object storage	Amazon S3
	Backup and archive	Amazon S3 Glacier, AWS Backup
	Data catalog	AWS Glue, AWS Lake Formation
	Third-party data	AWS Data Exchange
Predictive analysis and machine learning	Frameworks	AWS Deep Learning AMIs
	ML Service	Amazon SageMaker

AWS Glue

Amazon Glue is a fully managed extract, transform, and load (ETL) service that automatically discovers and profiles data, creates and updates metadata, and enables users to create and orchestrate ETL jobs using the AWS Glue console. AWS Glue also provides several useful features, such as data classification, data discovery, and data lineage, to help customers understand, cleanse, and transform their data. AWS Glue can also be used to move data between data stores, transform data, and process data for analysis. It is often used with Amazon Redshift, Amazon S3, and Amazon EMR, as well as other AWS data storage and analytics services. AWS Glue consists of several key components:

- **ETL jobs:** Python or Scala code that defines the ETL logic for extracting data from sources, transforming the data, and loading it into targets.

- **ETL libraries:** Customizable Apache Spark libraries for common ETL tasks such as reading and writing data, data type conversion, and data processing.

- **Data catalog:** A central repository for storing metadata about data sources and targets, as well as ETL jobs and development endpoints. The data catalog is used to access data sources and targets using AWS Glue ETL jobs and development endpoints.

- **Development endpoints:** Apache Spark environments used to develop, test, and run ETL jobs.

- **Triggers:** Start ETL jobs on a schedule, in response to an event, or on-demand.

- **Crawlers:** Discover data stored in data stores and populate the AWS Glue data catalog with metadata about the discovered data.

- **AWS Glue Studio:** A visual interface for creating, debugging, and managing ETL jobs and development endpoints.

- **Glue schema registry:** Validate and control streaming data using registered schemas for Apache Avro and JSON.

- **Glue DataBrew:** Clean and normalize data without having to write code.

- **Glue elastic views:** Use SQL queries to combine and replicate data to S3 buckets or Amazon Redshift.

The process of using AWS Glue to create and execute ETL jobs involves the following steps:

1. **Define source and target data stores:** Identify the data stores that contain the source data and the data stores that will receive the transformed data. Data sources include data stored in databases, data lakes, or file systems at AWS or on premises.

2. **Connect to the data stores:** Create connections in the AWS Glue data catalog to the source and target data stores, enabling AWS Glue to access the data and metadata stored in the data stores.

3. **Discover data and schema:** AWS Glue discovers the data and its schema by crawling through the data stored in the data stores and extracting metadata, for example data types and field names.

4. **Create an ETL job:** Use AWS Glue to create an ETL job. Each job is a defined set of ETL tasks that are executed on a schedule or on demand.

5. **Define the ETL process:** Define the ETL process using Python or Scala code using a development endpoint to extract data from the source data stores, transform the data as required, and load the transformed data into the target data stores.

6. **Execute the ETL job:** The ETL job can now be executed either on demand or on a schedule (see Figure 8-27). The ETL job will extract, transform, and load the transformed data into the target data stores.

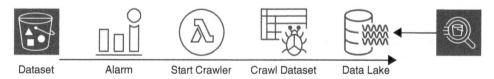

Dataset   Alarm   Start Crawler   Crawl Dataset   Data Lake

Figure 8-27   AWS Glue ETL Job Flow

7. **Monitor and maintain the ETL process:** While the ETL job is being executed use the AWS Glue console to monitor the job's progress, view the job's logs, and view the metadata for the transformed data. You can also edit, update, and maintain each ETL job as needed.

Analytic Services

Several analytic services analyze structured and unstructured data stored in a variety of storage locations at AWS and when working with AWS Lake Formation:

- **Amazon Athena:** A serverless query service that analyzes Amazon S3 data. Amazon Athena enables users to query data stored in Amazon S3 using SQL, without the need to set up any infrastructure or manage any databases. Queries can be performed in parallel in a variety of standards, including CSV, JSON, ORC, Avro, and Parquet, resulting in extremely high performance. Amazon Athena integrates with other AWS services such as Amazon Glue, providing a seamless way to analyze data from a variety of sources. Amazon Athena is easy to use, with a simple web-based interface and the capability to run ad-hoc queries or save and reuse commonly used queries.

- **Amazon OpenSearch Service:** Performs log analysis and real-time application monitoring, providing visibility into your workload performance. Find relevant data within applications, websites, and data lakes using SQL query syntax. Data can be read using CSV tables or JSON documents.

- **Amazon QuickSight:** Enables users to create dashboards and interactive reports using data from a variety of sources, including relational databases, data warehouses, and data lakes. Amazon QuickSight offers a range of visualization tools and features, including the ability to create custom charts and graphs and share dashboards and reports with others. Amazon QuickSight integrates with other AWS services, such as Amazon Redshift and Amazon Athena, making it easy to analyze and visualize data stored in those services and providing data visualizations and insights from an organization's data sources. Data records can be stored at AWS or stored in external locations, including on-premises SQL Server, MySQL, and PostgreSQL databases, or in Amazon Redshift, Amazon RDS, Amazon Aurora, and Amazon S3 storage.

- **Amazon Elastic Map Reduce (EMR):** A big data platform for data processing and analysis and machine learning using Apache Spark, Apache Hive, and Presto. Runs petabyte-scale analysis much cheaper than traditional on-premises solutions. EMR integrates with other AWS services, such as Amazon S3 and Amazon Kinesis, enabling users to easily move and analyze data stored in those services.

- **Amazon Managed Streaming for Apache Kafka (Amazon MSK):** Streaming data can be consumed using a full-managed Apache Kafka and Kafka Connect Clusters hosted at AWS, allowing Kafka applications and Kafka connectors to run at AWS without requiring expert knowledge in operating Apache Kafka. Amazon MSK can be used to build a real-time data pipeline that streams data between applications and data stores, or for building a real-time streaming application that can process and analyze data in real time. Amazon MSK used with other AWS services, such as Amazon S3, Amazon Redshift, and Amazon EMR, can build complete data architectures on AWS. Amazon MSK is built using Apache Kafka; an open-source distributed event streaming platform used for building real-time data pipelines and streaming applications.

- **AWS Data Exchange:** The secure exchange of third-party data files and data tables into AWS. Customers can use the AWS Data Exchange API to copy selected third-party data from AWS Data Exchange into S3 storage. Data Exchange third-party products include weather, healthcare, data sciences, geospatial, and mapping services.

- **AWS Data Pipeline:** Process and move data between different AWS compute and storage services and from on-premises siloed data sources, and transfer the results into S3 buckets, Amazon RDS, DynamoDB, and Amazon Elastic Map Reduce.

- **AWS DataSync:** A data transfer service for moving large amounts of data between on-premises storage and Amazon S3, Amazon EFS, or Amazon FSx for Windows File Server. AWS DataSync can transfer data between any NFS, SMIB, or Amazon S3-compatible storage, so you can use it to move data between a variety of different storage solutions.

- **Amazon Storage Gateway:** Connects an on-premises software appliance with cloud-based storage providing secure integration between an organization's on-premises IT environment and the AWS S3 storage. The Storage Gateway appliance is available in three different deployments:

  - File Gateway enables users to store files in Amazon S3, with local caching for low-latency access.

  - Volume Gateway provides block-level storage volumes that can be used as iSCSI targets, with local caching for low-latency access.

  - Tape Gateway emulates a tape library providing virtual tape infrastructure (VTI) that can be used with existing backup applications.

The Storage Gateway appliance is a virtual machine installed on premises that connects to the cloud via secure, encrypted channels using the Amazon S3 API for communication and supports data transfer rates of up to 100 MiBps.

Amazon Kinesis Data Streams

Amazon Kinesis is a fully managed, cloud-based service offered by AWS for real-time data processing and analysis. Kinesis makes it easy to collect, process, and analyze streaming data, providing the ability to build custom applications that can process and analyze large amounts of data in real time. Kinesis is highly scalable and can handle data streams of any size. It offers several different types of data streams, including the Amazon Kinesis Data Streams, Amazon Kinesis Data Firehose, Amazon Kinesis Video Streams, and Amazon Kinesis Data Analytics:

- Amazon Kinesis Data Streams enables users to collect, process, and analyze streaming data, providing the ability to build custom applications that can process and analyze large amounts of data in real time. Amazon Data Streams offers a flexible, scalable, and durable platform for streaming data, with the ability to process hundreds of thousands of data streams per second. Amazon Data Streams also integrates with other AWS services, such as Amazon S3, Amazon Redshift, and Amazon EMR, allowing users to easily move and analyze data stored in those services.

- Amazon Kinesis Data Firehose captures, transforms, and loads streaming data into services such as Amazon S3, Amazon Redshift, and Amazon Elasticsearch Service, without the need to write any custom code. It enables users to set up a data stream and specify a destination for the data, such as an S3 bucket or a Redshift cluster. Amazon Data Firehose will then automatically deliver the data to the specified destination, applying any necessary transformations or enrichments along the way.

- The Amazon Kinesis Video Streams SDK enables connected camera devices, such as phones, drones, and dashcams, to securely stream video to custom real-time or batch-oriented applications running on AWS EC2 instances. The video streams can also be stored and encrypted for further monitoring and analytics.

- Amazon Kinesis Data Analytics is a service offered by AWS for real-time analysis of streaming data. Amazon Data Analytics enables users to run SQL queries on streaming data, providing the ability to build applications that can analyze and process data in real time. Amazon Data Analytics also integrates with other AWS services, such as Amazon S3, Amazon Redshift, and Amazon EMR, allowing users to easily move and analyze data stored in those services.

Exam Preparation Tasks

As mentioned in the section "How to Use This Book" in the Introduction, you have a couple of choices for exam preparation: the exercises here, Chapter 16, "Final Preparation," and the exam simulation questions in the Pearson Test Prep Software Online.

Review All Key Topics

Review the most important topics in the chapter, noted with the Key Topic icon in the margin of the page. Table 8-8 lists these key topics and the page number on which each is found.

Table 8-8   Chapter 8 Key Topics

Key Topic Element	Description	Page Number
Figure 8-1	AWS Storage Options	362
Table 8-2	Storage Requirements	363
List	EBS volume choices	367
Table 8-3	Performance Specifications for EBS Volume Types	369
Figure 8-5	EBS Burst Credit Architecture	370
Section	Amazon EBS Cheat Sheet	372
Section	Fast Snapshot Restore	374
Section	Snapshot Administration	375
Section	Snapshot Cheat Sheet	376
Section	EFS Performance Modes	380
Section	EFS Throughput Modes	381
Section	Amazon EFS Cheat Sheet	383
Section	AWS DataSync	384
Section	Amazon FSx Cheat Sheet	388
Table 8-4	S3 Bucket Configuration Options	392
Table 8-5	S3 Storage Classes	394
Paragraph	S3 object lock	396
Paragraph	S3 replication	397

Key Topic Element	Description	Page Number
Section	S3 Bucket Versioning	400
Section	S3 Cheat Sheet	403
Section	S3 Glacier Retrieval Policies	405
Section	Amazon S3 Glacier Cheat Sheet	406

Define Key Terms

Define the following key terms from this chapter and check your answers in the glossary:

object storage, snapshot, block storage, ephemeral storage, Server Message Block (SMB), input/output operations per second (IOPS), Nitro, Throughput Optimized, burst credits, cold storage, mount point, lifecycle policy, bucket, multipart upload, versioning, archive

Q&A

The answers to these questions appear in Appendix A. For more practice with exam format questions, use the Pearson Test Prep Software Online.

1. What is the advantage of EFS shared storage over EBS volumes?

2. What is the difference between files stored in object storage and files stored using block storage?

3. What is the difference between EBS io2 and io1 volumes regarding attaching the volumes to instances?

4. What happens when an EBS snapshot is deleted in the background?

5. What is the fastest storage that can be ordered at AWS?

6. To use most management features of Amazon S3 storage, what must first be enabled?

7. How can S3 objects be shared with clients that do not have AWS credentials?

8. After a WORM policy has been applied to an Amazon S3 bucket in Compliance mode, when can the policy be removed?

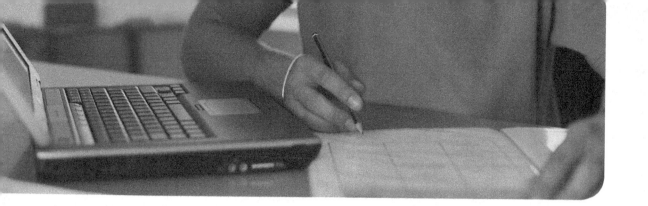

This chapter covers the following topics:

- AWS Compute Services
- AWS Lambda
- Amazon Container Services
- Monitoring with AWS CloudWatch
- Auto Scaling Options at AWS

This chapter covers content that's important to the following exam domain and task statement:

Domain 3: Design High-Performing Architectures

Task Statement 2: Design high-performing and elastic compute solutions

CHAPTER 9

Designing High-Performing and Elastic Compute Solutions

Designing and deploying high-performing computing resources for workloads involves Amazon Elastic Compute Cloud (EC2) instances and understanding which instance family and type to select. Web and application servers, databases, and containerized applications are hosted on EC2 instances. The compute service AWS Lambda is also covered in this chapter. AWS EC2 instances also host container deployments at AWS, including Amazon Elastic Container Service (ECS) and the Amazon Elastic Container Service for Kubernetes (EKS).

For the AWS Certified Solutions Architect – Associate (SAA-C03) exam, you also need to understand monitoring using AWS CloudWatch, the built-in monitoring service. AWS CloudWatch is a key component of AWS autoscaling services. Autoscaling compute resources at AWS is carried out using the EC2 Auto Scaling service, managing a workload's autoscaling resources using AWS Auto Scaling, which are both covered in this chapter.

"Do I Know This Already?"

The "Do I Know This Already?" quiz allows you to assess whether you should read this entire chapter thoroughly or jump to the "Exam Preparation Tasks" section. If you are in doubt about your answers to these questions or your own assessment of your knowledge of the topics, read the entire chapter. Table 9-1 lists the major headings in this chapter and their corresponding "Do I Know This Already?" quiz questions. You can find the answers in Appendix A, "Answers to the 'Do I Know This Already?' Quizzes and Q&A Sections."

Table 9-1 "Do I Know This Already?" Section-to-Question Mapping

Foundation Topics Section	Questions
AWS Compute Services	1, 2
AWS Lambda	3, 4
Amazon Container Services	5, 6
Monitoring with AWS CloudWatch	7, 8
Auto Scaling Options at AWS	9, 10

CAUTION   The goal of self-assessment is to gauge your mastery of the topics in this chapter. If you do not know the answer to a question or are only partially sure of the answer, you should mark that question as wrong for purposes of the self-assessment. Giving yourself credit for an answer you correctly guess skews your self-assessment results and might provide you with a false sense of security.

1. What compute service is designed for processing high volumes of batch jobs?

    a. Amazon Elastic Container Service

    b. Amazon EC2

    c. AWS Batch

    d. AWS Lambda

2. When an Amazon EC2 instance is ordered, what additional software component must be chosen?

    a. Security group

    b. AMI

    c. Enhanced Network Adapter

    d. Subnet

3. What type of service is AWS Lambda?

    a. Database service

    b. Storage service

    c. Management service

    d. Event-driven service

4. What is the main component of AWS Lambda?

   a. Automation

   b. Functions

   c. Monitoring

   d. Compliance

5. What AWW service supports Docker deployments?

   a. AWS EC2

   b. AWS ECS

   c. AWS S3

   d. AWS EKS

6. What is required to launch a container at AWS?

   a. Container registry

   b. Task definition

   c. Launch template

   d. Fargate

7. Which of the following does AWS CloudWatch use to monitor AWS resources for EC2 Auto Scaling?

   a. Alarms

   b. Alerts

   c. Metrics

   d. Rules

8. Where does AWS CloudWatch store monitoring records?

   a. Amazon S3 buckets

   b. Log group

   c. Trails

   d. Amazon DynamoDB table

9. How does EC2 Auto Scaling determine what type of EC2 instance to add to an Auto Scaling group?

   a. AWS CloudWatch

   b. Launch template

   c. Registration

   d. Deregistration

10. How does EC2 Auto Scaling maintain a defined level of compute capacity automatically?

    a. Scheduled scaling

    b. Target tracking

    c. Simple scaling

    d. Step scaling

Foundation Topics

AWS Compute Services

Planning and running well-architected applications at AWS requires designing, deploying, and managing workload compute resources. Tasks include

- **Provisioning compute infrastructure:** Compute choices include EC2 instances hosting virtual servers or containerized applications running in a virtual private cloud (VPC); database services such as the Amazon Relational Database Service or Amazon DynamoDB.

- **Configuring infrastructure:** Security, high availability, and performance efficiency (compute, database, network).

- **Automated management:** AWS Fargate for Docker or EKS container management, AWS Lambda custom functions for executing event-driven responses, or AWS Elastic Beanstalk for creating and maintaining application infrastructure for virtual server or containerized applications.

- **Scaling:** Auto-scaling services for EC2 instances (EC2 Auto Scaling) or workload auto-scaling (AWS Auto Scaling).

- **Monitoring:** Visibility into all cloud services that make up the application architecture tracking resource usage, deployment success and failure, workload health and automated responses using AWS CloudWatch *metrics* and alarms, Amazon EventBridge rules and alerts, Amazon Simple Notification Service (SNS) notifications, and AWS Lambda functions that carry out tasks in response to metric alarms or alerts.

Table 9-2 details the available AWS compute services and use cases.

Table 9-2 Compute Services and Use Cases

Compute Type	Compute Service	Use Case
EC2 instances (VMs)	Amazon EC2—resizable compute capacity with Intel, AMD, and Graviton processors	Web and application hosting, data processing, high-performance computing
Batch processing	AWS Batch—Dynamically run massive batch computing workloads based on the number and resource requirements of the batch job	Data processing, machine learning training, and financial modeling

Compute Type	Compute Service	Use Case
Scaling	Amazon EC2 Auto Scaling—add and remove compute capacity to match application demand	Scale EC2 instances and containers with dynamic and predictive scaling
Containers	Amazon Elastic Container Service (Amazon ECS)	Host Docker containers with AWS ECS
	Amazon Elastic Container Registry (Amazon ECR)	Store, manage, and deploy container images
	Amazon Elastic Kubernetes Service (Amazon EKS)	Fully managed Kubernetes service
	Amazon EKS Anywhere	Run Kubernetes containers on customer-managed on-premises infrastructure
	AWS Fargate	Serverless compute management for Docker and Kubernetes container deployments at AWS
	Amazon ECS Anywhere	Run Dockers containers on customer-managed on-premises infrastructure
	AWS App Runner	Configure applications and deploy to AWS using a Git repository or a Docker image, without having to set up the underlying infrastructure
Serverless	AWS Lambda	Run custom functions for event-driven solutions without having to provision or manage servers
Edge and hybrid	AWS Outposts	Bring native AWS services and infrastructure to your on-premises environments
	AWS Local Zones	Run latency-sensitive workloads closer to on-premises data centers
	AWS Wavelength Zones	AWS cloud services and infrastructure hosted in third-party telecommunication data centers for developing and hosting 5G workloads

Compute Type	Compute Service	Use Case
Capacity management	AWS Compute Optimizer	Recommend compute resources to improve workload performance and reduce costs
	AWS Elastic Beanstalk	Deploy web applications running on instances and containers on AWS infrastructure services
	Elastic Load Balancing (ELB)	Distribute requests to targeted EC2 instances and containers across multiple availability zones
	Amazon EC2 Auto Scaling	Scale workloads (web servers and databases) using dynamic and predictive scaling

AWS EC2 Instances

Amazon Elastic Compute Cloud EC2 instances are virtual servers that let you run applications in the AWS cloud. Each EC2 instance is a virtual server running Windows, Linux, or the macOS as a guest operating system hosted by the Xen or Nitro hypervisor. All new EC2 instances offered by AWS since 2017 are hosted on the Nitro hypervisor, called the Nitro System.

NOTE Additional details on EC2 instance types can be found in Chapter 13, "Designing Cost-Effective Compute Solutions."

Each EC2 instance is configured at launch with an allotted amount of RAM and virtual CPU (vCPU) cores, storage, and networking bandwidth. The Nitro System is designed to provide high performance, security, and reliability for EC2 instances using internal Nitro services.

The Nitro System (see Figure 9-1) consists of several key components:

- **Nitro Hypervisor:** A lightweight hypervisor designed to provide efficient resource isolation and high performance for EC2 and ECS instances at bare-metal speeds.

- **Nitro Security Chip:** Minimizes the attack surface for EC2 and ECS instances, protecting against physical attacks, and prohibits all administrative access, including AWS employees.

- **Nitro Controller:** Several what are called nitro cards offload I/O operations for increased performance, including the Nitro Card for VPC, Nitro Card for EBS, Nitro Card for Instance Storage, and the Nitro Security Chip.

- **Nitro TPM:** Provides cryptographic proof of EC2 instance integrity. The Trusted Platform Module (TPM) 2.0 helps migrate existing on-premises TPM workloads to EC2.

- **AWS Nitro Enclaves:** Enables organizations to create isolated and secure compute environments deploying EC2 instances deployed with hardware-based isolation and memory protection to securely process highly sensitive workloads such as financial transactions, healthcare data, and government applications.

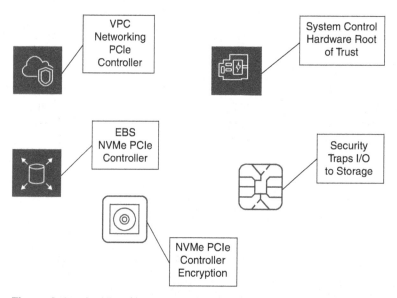

Figure 9-1 The Nitro System Architecture and Components

The following components are part of each EC2 configuration:

- *Amazon Machine Images (AMIs)*

- Authentication using a unique public/private key pair

- Amazon Elastic Block Store (EBS) and/or temporary storage volumes

- A mandatory firewall called a *security group* that protects each basic or elastic network interface

- Basic or elastic network interfaces (ENI)

- Multi-tenant, single-tenant, dedicated, or bare-metal instance deployment

Amazon Machine Images

An Amazon Machine Image (AMI) is a virtual machine image used to launch EC2 instances.

Organizations can create their own AMIs or use existing AMIs provided by AWS or third parties. An instance launched with a particular AMI creates a virtual machine that is identical to the selected AMI.

AWS provides a wide range of AMIs for various operating systems and applications, including Windows, Linux, macOS, and various open-source operating systems and application stacks (see Figure 9-2). Create custom AMIs using the EC2 Dashboard or the AWS command-line interface (CLI).

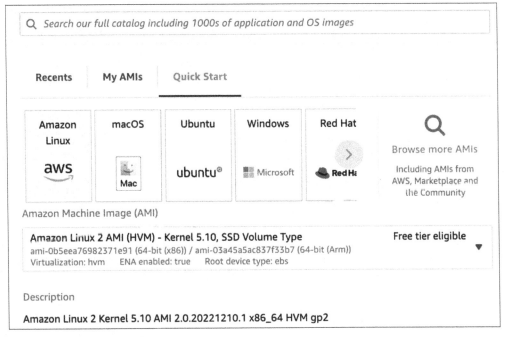

Figure 9-2 AMI Options at AWS

Each AMI is a template containing a software configuration including the operating system, application software, and any additional software or configuration required.

Each organization's needs and requirements will dictate which type of AMI to create and use; if you want super-fast block storage and your design works with temporary storage volumes, perhaps a local instance with ephemeral storage makes sense. If you require virtual hard disks, EBS-backed AMIs are widely available. You can also mix and match by deploying an EBS boot volume and additional EBS and ephemeral volumes. Each AMI includes the following components, described by an associated XML manifest:

- **Boot volume:** The root boot volume for an EC2 instance can be either an EBS boot volume created from a snapshot or a local instance storage volume copied from an Amazon S3 bucket.

- **Launch permissions:** Launch permissions define the AWS account permitted to use the AMI to launch instances. Default launch permissions are set to private, which means that only the AWS account where the AMI was created can use that AMI. Launch permissions can also define a select list of AWS accounts. Switching AMI launch permissions from private to public means any organization in the overall AWS cloud has access.

- **Volumes to attach:** Volumes attached to the EC2 instance at launch are contained in a block device mapping document. Local instance temporary volumes are listed as ephemeral0 to ephemeral23, depending on the number of instance store volumes created. Instance ephemeral volumes are SSD or NVMe drives.

- **Default region:** AMIs are stored in the local AWS region where they are created. After creation, AMIs can be manually copied or backed up to other AWS regions as necessary.

- **Operating system:** Choices are Linux, Windows, or macOS.

- **Root device storage:** Amazon EBS or an EC2 instance storage volume.

EBS boot volumes are created from EBS snapshots stored in AWS-controlled storage. An EC2 instance storage volume has the root volume created from a template is stored in S3 storage.

AWS Linux AMIs

Prebuilt AMIs supplied by Amazon include Amazon Linux 2 AMI, as shown in Figure 9-3, and Amazon Linux AMI. Amazon Linux 2 is the latest version of Amazon Linux; Amazon's Linux distribution is based on Red Hat Enterprise Linux (RHEL). The Amazon Linux 2 AMI supports EC2 instances, including EC2 bare-metal instances, and also supports Docker container deployments.

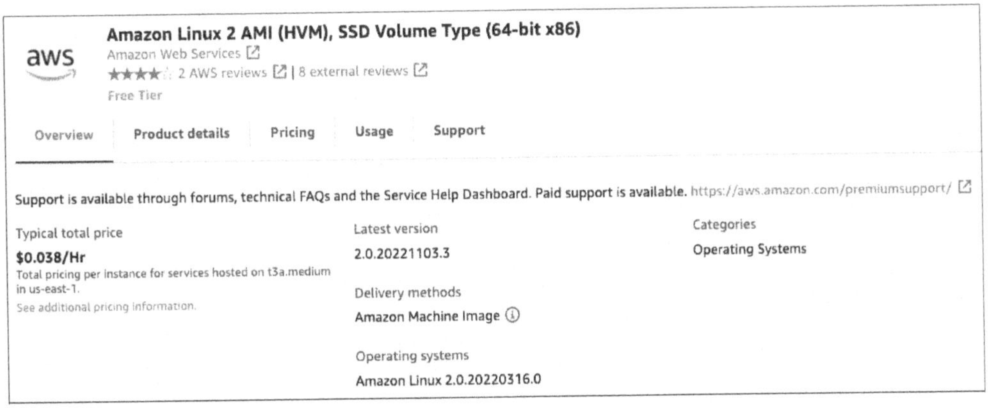

Figure 9-3 Amazon Linux 2 AMI in the EC2 Console

The Amazon Linux 2 AMI can be used on all EC2 instance types that support hardware virtual machine (HVM) AMIs. The Amazon Linux 2 AMI does not support paravirtualization functionality. Paravirtualization is an older virtualization technique that Linux supported to allow direct execution of user requests from the guest VM to the host computer; increasing the speed of the guest VM operating system calls for networking and storage. With advances in HVM architecture and the AWS Nitro hypervisor, paravirtualization AMIs have extremely limited support at AWS.

The Linux 2 AMI includes a variety of software packages and configurations that seamlessly integrate with many AWS services, such as Amazon CloudFront monitoring and AWS Systems Manager Patch Manager, the AWS CLI, and **cloud-init**, which is used for automating user data scripts at boot. AWS provides long-term support (5 years), including updates from a private repository stored in the AWS region where the instance is located.

Windows AMIs

Amazon has worked with Microsoft to make available a library of AMIs, including Windows Server versions from 2016 to 2022. Windows instances bundle the licensing fees in their cost (Windows Server and SQL Server licenses). AWS's Windows AMIs are, by default, patched within 5 days of Microsoft's "Patch Tuesday" release.

AWS AMIs

AWS Marketplace has thousands of AMI options (see Figure 9-4). Many third-party software appliances are available; for example, Cisco, Juniper, F5, and OpenVPN Access Server images. After selecting an AMI from the AWS Marketplace, decisions to be made include software license fees, the AWS region, and the EC2 instance type.

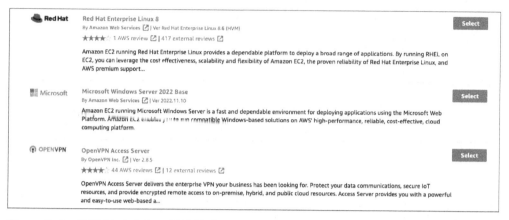

Figure 9-4 AWS Marketplace AMI Choices

Creating a Custom AMI

Creating a custom AMI enables you to create the desired software build for a specific workload.

Follow these steps to create a custom AMI:

1. Launch an EC2 instance and select the latest version of the Amazon Linux AMI. This initial deployment will be used as the base for a custom AMI.

2. Connect to the EC2 instance using SSH, and install and configure any software or applications to include in your custom AMI. Make any necessary changes to the configuration of the operating system or applications. Additional tasks to complete include defragmenting the attached hard drives for faster operation, deleting temporary files, and creating the desired user accounts and passwords.

3. Stop the EC2 instance. From the EC2 dashboard, select the stopped instance, then choose Create Image from the Actions menu (see Figure 9-5).

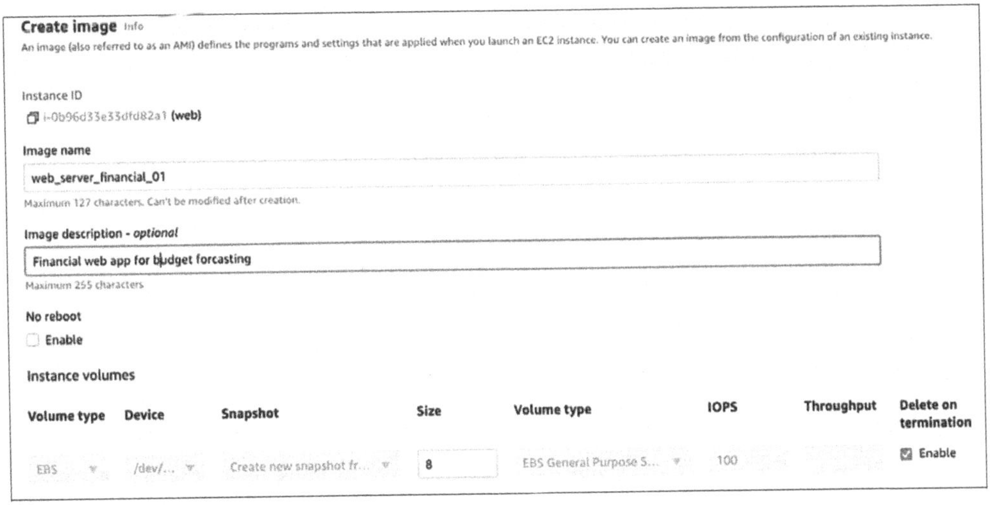

Create image Info

An image (also referred to as an AMI) defines the programs and settings that are applied when you launch an EC2 instance. You can create an image from the configuration of an existing instance.

Instance ID

i-0b96d33e33dfd82a1 **(web)**

Image name

web_server_financial_01

Maximum 127 characters. Can't be modified after creation.

Image description - *optional*

Financial web app for budget forcasting

Maximum 255 characters.

No reboot

☐ Enable

Instance volumes

Volume type	Device	Snapshot	Size	Volume type	IOPS	Throughput	Delete on termination
EBS ▾	/dev/... ▾	Create new snapshot fr... ▾	8	EBS General Purpose S... ▾	100		☑ Enable

Figure 9-5 AMI Creation

4. Enter a name and description for your custom AMI, and choose Create Image.

5. Wait for the AMI to be created. This process may take several minutes.

6. Once the AMI has been created, launch a new EC2 instance selecting the custom AMI.

During the creation of the AMI, snapshots of the EC2 instance's root volume and any other attached EBS volumes are created. After the AMI build process has been completed, the EC2 instance is rebooted to check the file system integrity of the snapshots and AMI that was just created. Once a custom AMI is created, tested, and finalized for production, it should be considered a *golden AMI*; the image should be as perfect as possible; customizations or changes should not be allowed to a finalized production AMI.

You can deploy Windows or Linux AMIs using any of the following options:

- **EC2 dashboard:** Create an EBS-backed AMI from an EBS-backed instance.

- **AWS CLI:** Use the **create-image** command to create an EBS-backed AMI from an EBS-backed instance.

- **Amazon Marketplace:** Many commercial Windows and Linux operating system images and third-party virtual software appliance images are available for deployment.

- **My AMIs:** This EC2 dashboard location stores custom AMIs created in your AWS account.

- **AWS Application Migration Service (AMS):** This service enables you to automate the migration of physical, virtual, and cloud-based servers to

Amazon EC2. The AWS Application Migration Service creates AMIs of your on-premises servers.

- **AWS Database Migration Service (DMS):** This service enables you to migrate databases to and from Amazon RDS and Amazon Redshift, and migrate on-premises database engines into AWS.

Custom Instance Store AMIs

Table 9-3 outlines the differences between instances backed by EBS volumes and instances using attached local instance stores.

Table 9-3   Differences in Instance Storage

Parameter	EBS Root Device	Instance Store Root Device
Boot time	Fast (under 1 minute)	Not so fast (approximately 5 minutes) because the root drive image must be copied from S3 storage at boot
Root drive	gp2, gp3, io1, io2 SSD drives	10 GB maximum
Volume type	EBS block storage	Local instance with block storage located on the bare-metal server hosting the instance
Data persistence	By default, EBS root volumes are deleted when the instance terminates	No persistence when the instance store root device is turned off or terminated
Backup	AMI, snapshot, Amazon Data Lifecycle Manager, AWS Backup	AMI storage in Amazon S3 storage
State	When the EBS instance is turned off, the root volume is persistently stored in Amazon EBS	Running or in a terminated state

NOTE   AMIs that support the Nitro hypervisor must be HVM in design and support enhanced networking, with the ability to boot from EBS storage using an NVMe interface. The latest AWS AMIs for Linux and Windows are HVM by design, as are the latest AMIs for Ubuntu, Debian, Red Hat Enterprise Linux, SUSE Enterprise Linux, CentOS, and FreeBSD.

AMI Build Considerations

Over time, you will develop a standardized procedure for building and maintaining AMIs. Consider the following questions when designing workload compute requirements:

- Are your EC2 instances in an Auto Scaling Group? The EC2 instance and AMI are documented in the Launch Template or Launch Configuration used by the Auto Scaling Group.

■ Are there any licensing requirements? AWS License Manager can help manage software licenses from third-party software vendors that are part of your AMI software build.

■ How often do you plan to update your AMIs? By default, AMIs supplied by AWS have security and maintenance updates applied to the repository for each supported AMI, such as Amazon Linux 2 and currently supported Microsoft Windows Server builds.

Amazon EC2 Image Builder

Amazon EC2 Image Builder helps organizations create, manage, and maintain customized AMIs. With EC2 Image Builder, you can automate the process of building, testing, and distributing AMIs. Here are some key features of EC2 Image Builder:

■ **AMI creation:** EC2 Image Builder provides prebuilt image pipelines that enable you to quickly create custom AMIs without having to write any code.

■ **Automated testing:** EC2 Image Builder includes built-in testing capabilities that allow a variety of supplied tests and custom tests to validate the functionality and security of your AMIs before they are distributed (see Figure 9-6).

■ **Image distribution:** EC2 Image Builder integrates with AWS IAM and Amazon S3 for secure distribution of AMIs to designated administrators and AWS accounts.

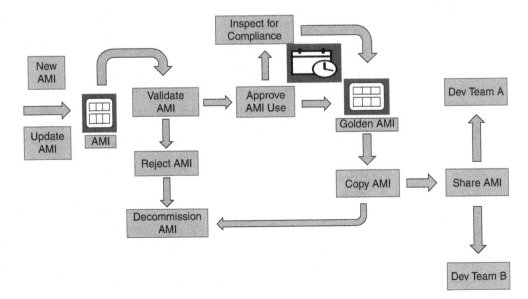

Figure 9-6 Building and Maintaining AMIs

Here are several considerations when creating an AMI for production:

- Don't embed passwords or security information in an AMI. Instead, use AWS Identity and Access Management (IAM) roles and AWS Secrets Manager.

- At a minimum, use a standard bootstrapping process with user data scripts to customize the initial boot process. User data scripts allow you to automate the initial boot of your instances with required updates and configurations.

- Properly tag your AMIs for identification purposes. Tags can be used for monitoring, automation, security, and creating custom cost and billing reports.

> **NOTE**   Amazon has released a golden AMI pipeline sample configuration that is available at https://github.com/aws-samples/aws-golden-ami-pipeline-sample. Here, you will find a readme file with step-by-step instructions, including cloud formation templates to help you set up a golden AMI pipeline for the creation and distribution of AMIs.

AWS Lambda

AWS Lambda is a serverless computing service that enables you to run custom functions in response to events or specific triggers. AWS Lambda provides compute processing power on demand, executing functions that you've either written or selected from a library of functions created by AWS. With AWS Lambda, you can create functions without the need to provision or maintain any infrastructure. Here are some key features of AWS Lambda:

- **Pay-per-use:** AWS Lambda charges you only for the time your code executes.

- **Event-driven:** AWS Lambda functions can be triggered by a wide range of events, such as object changes in an Amazon S3 bucket or an Amazon DynamoDB table, or from an HTTP request to an Amazon API Gateway endpoint.

- **AWS service integration:** AWS Lambda can communicate with other AWS services.

- **Execution environment:** AWS Lambda is compatible with code written in a variety of programming languages, including Node.js, Java, Python, and C#.

To use AWS Lambda, create a function and specify the trigger or event that will trigger your function (see Figure 9-7). AWS Lambda also provides monitoring and logging features to help you troubleshoot and debug each function's operation. Lambda supports two types of deployment packages: container images and .zip file archives. Container images are stored in the Amazon Elastic Container Registry. Zip archives are stored in an S3 bucket.

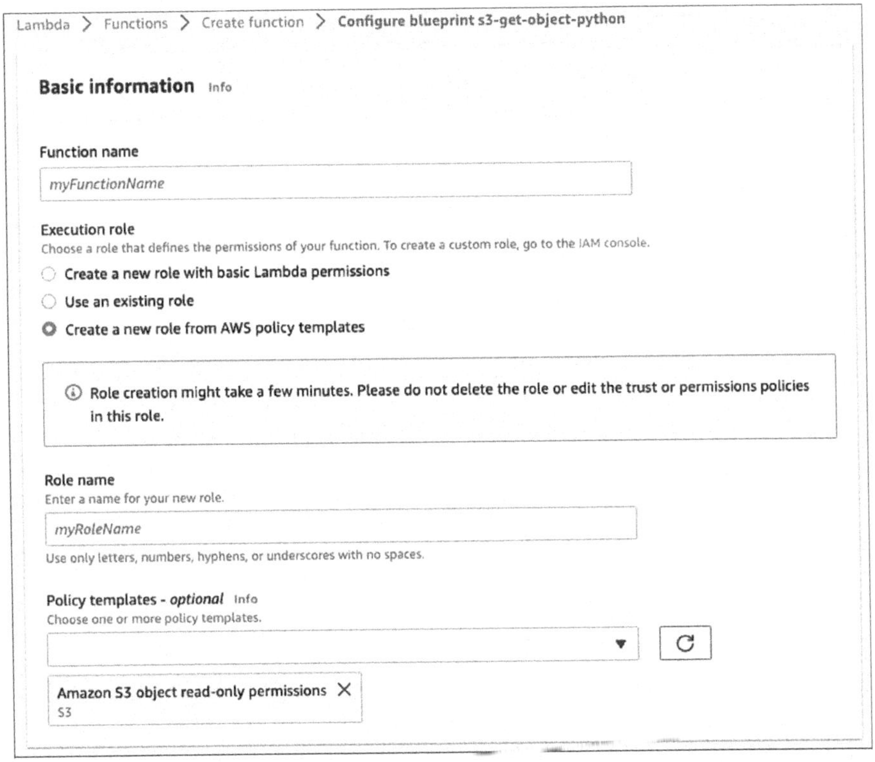

Lambda > Functions > Create function > **Configure blueprint s3-get-object-python**

Basic information Info

Function name

myFunctionName

Execution role
Choose a role that defines the permissions of your function. To create a custom role, go to the IAM console.
○ **Create a new role with basic Lambda permissions**
○ **Use an existing role**
◉ **Create a new role from AWS policy templates**

ⓘ Role creation might take a few minutes. Please do not delete the role or edit the trust or permissions policies in this role.

Role name
Enter a name for your new role.

myRoleName

Use only letters, numbers, hyphens, or underscores with no spaces.

Policy templates - *optional* Info
Choose one or more policy templates.

Amazon S3 object read-only permissions ✕
S3

Figure 9-7 Creating a Custom Lambda Function for a Specific Task

Every time a Lambda function executes, you are charged based on the RAM/CPU and processing time the function uses.

Lambda functions run in a specialized virtualization format called Firecracker hosted on EC2 instances. It was developed by Amazon and is used as the virtualization technology for AWS Lambda and AWS Fargate.

Firecracker uses a microVM architecture, creating a lightweight VM for each function that is executed. Firecracker microVMs are based on the Kernel-based Virtual Machine (KVM) hypervisor and are designed to be small, fast, and secure.

Firecracker utilizes a small footprint of approximately 5 MB of RAM (see Figure 9-8). Each Firecracker microVM is launched in less than 100 ms. To secure each AWS Lambda function during execution, each Firecracker VM runs in an isolated guest mode, using a network device for communication, a block I/O device to store the function code, and a programmable interval timer. The libraries required for execution are included in the local executable code; no outside libraries are required or allowed.

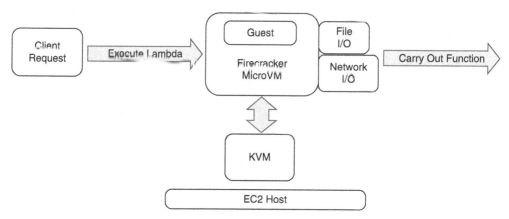

Figure 9-8   Firecracker Micro VM Architecture

AWS Lambda Integration

Many AWS management services have been integrated with Lambda functions:

- **S3 bucket:** AWS Lambda can be triggered when an object is uploaded to an S3 bucket. The uploaded object triggers a Lambda function that converts the object into three different resolutions storing the converted object in three different S3 buckets.

- **DynamoDB table:** AWS Lambda can be triggered when an entry is made in a DynamoDB table, triggering a Lambda function that performs a custom calculation.

- **Amazon Kinesis:** AWS Lambda can be triggered when data is added to an Amazon Kinesis stream. AWS Lambda functions can be executed to process, transform, or analyze real-time data streams.

- **Amazon SNS:** AWS Lambda can be triggered when a message is published to an SNS topic (see Figure 9-9).

- **Amazon Cognito:** AWS Lambda can be triggered when a user signs up or signs in to an Amazon Cognito user pool, customizing the user experience or sending confirmation emails.

- **Amazon API Gateway:** AWS Lambda can be integrated with Amazon API Gateway to build serverless backends for web, mobile, and IoT applications.

- **Amazon CloudWatch logs:** Content delivered to an AWS CloudWatch log triggers an SNS notification that calls an AWS Lambda function to carry out a specific task.

- **AWS Config:** AWS Config rules analyze whether resources created in an AWS account follow a company's deployment guidelines. When AWS resource deployments don't meet defined compliance requirements, an AWS Lambda function can be executed to delete the out-of-bounds resource.

- **Application Load Balancer (ALB):** Incoming mobile application requests can be directed to AWS Lambda functions hosted by a target group.

- **AWS Step Functions:** Step Functions can utilize Lambda functions as part of the state machine workflow.

- **CloudFront:** Both ingress and egress traffic flow to and from an edge location can be intercepted and queried using Lambda@Edge functions hosted at edge locations for a CloudFront CDN distribution.

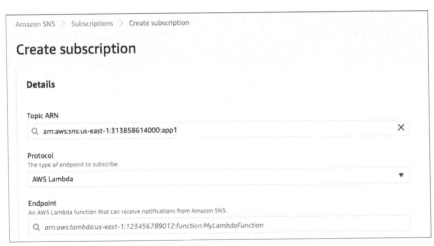

Figure 9-9   SNS Subscription and Lambda Function Executing Actions

Lambda Settings

When you create an AWS Lambda function, there are several basic settings that you must configure to specify how each function will operate:

- **Function name:** The function name must be unique within the region and account in which you are creating the function.

- **Runtime:** AWS Lambda supports a variety of runtimes, including Node.js, Python, Java, C#, and Go.

- **Role:** The AWS IAM role that defines the permissions that your function has to access other AWS resources or perform actions.

- **Memory:** Specify a value between 128 MB and 3,008 MB in 64 MB increments.

- **Timeout:** The maximum amount of time that your function is allowed to run before it is terminated. You can specify a value between 1 second and 15 minutes.

- **VPC:** Specify a VPC to give your function access to resources in a private network, such as an Amazon RDS database.

Once a Lambda function is created, the required amount of memory, ephemeral storage, and performance is allocated to your function (see Figure 9-10). The maximum execution CPU time is 15 minutes, and the minimal execution time is 1 second. Memory can be requested at 64 MB increments from 128 to 10.24 GB.

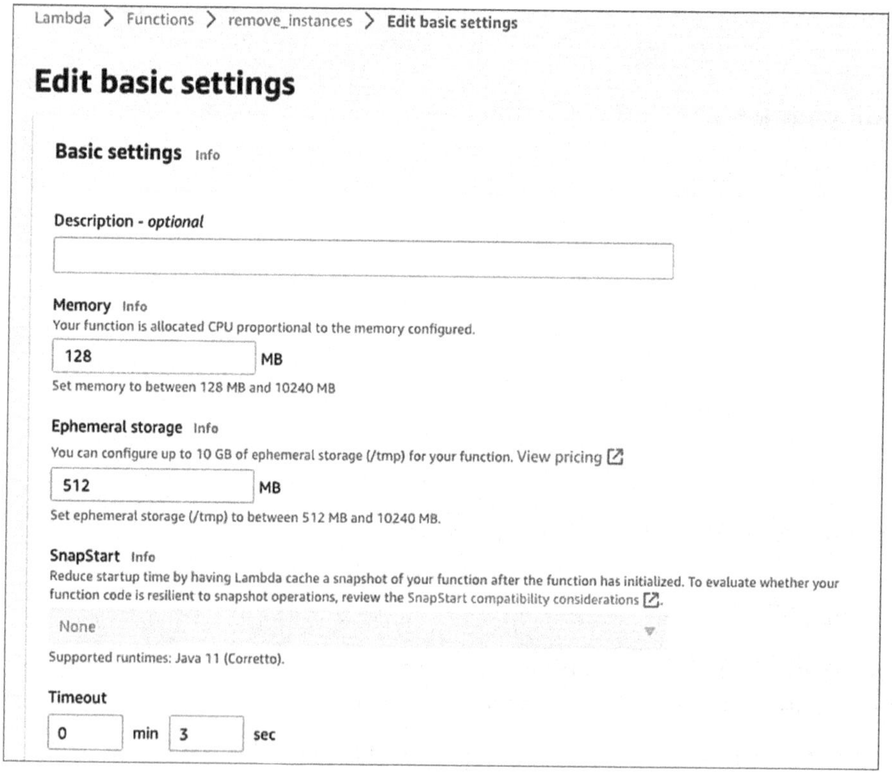

Lambda > Functions > remove_instances > **Edit basic settings**

Edit basic settings

Basic settings Info

Description - *optional*

Memory Info
Your function is allocated CPU proportional to the memory configured.

| 128 | MB |

Set memory to between 128 MB and 10240 MB

Ephemeral storage Info
You can configure up to 10 GB of ephemeral storage (/tmp) for your function. View pricing ⧉

| 512 | MB |

Set ephemeral storage (/tmp) to between 512 MB and 10240 MB.

SnapStart Info
Reduce startup time by having Lambda cache a snapshot of your function after the function has initialized. To evaluate whether your function code is resilient to snapshot operations, review the SnapStart compatibility considerations ⧉.

None   ▼

Supported runtimes: Java 11 (Corretto).

Timeout

| 0 | min | 3 | sec |

Figure 9-10   Lambda Function Basic Settings

AWS Lambda Cheat Sheet

For the AWS Certified Solutions Architect – Associate (SAA-C03) exam, you need to understand the following critical aspects of AWS Lambda:

- AWS Lambda allows you to run code as custom functions without having to provision servers to host and execute the function.

- AWS Lambda manages the required vCPU/RAM, storage, and execution of Lambda functions.

- AWS Lambda functions consist of programming code and any associated dependencies.

- Firecracker runs AWS Lambda functions in a lightweight virtual machine (microVM).

- Uploaded AWS Lambda code is stored in an S3 bucket or the Elastic Container Registry.

- Each AWS Lambda function receives 500 MB of temporary disk space for use during execution.

- AWS Lambda monitors executing functions using real-time Amazon CloudWatch metrics.

- A Savings Plan can reduce the cost of running AWS Lambda functions.

Amazon Container Services

Another way of running applications at AWS is by using containers. Using containers involves changing the underlying virtualization from a complete emulation of a computer system to just the virtualization of the operating system components required for communication: the necessary runtime, libraries, and system tools. A container shares the host operating system's kernel and its system libraries using a Kubernetes control plane or the Docker engine. Containerized applications have read-only access to the host operating system's file system and network stack, as shown in Figure 9-11. When compared to virtual machine deployments, there is less duplication of operating system components when running applications or micro-systems in containers.

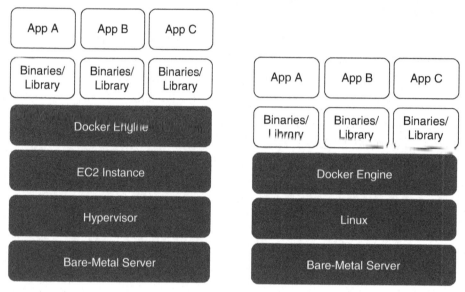

Figure 9-11 Container Architecture Options

The operating system that hosts the Docker or Kubernetes container deployments could run on a bare-metal server or on EV2 instances, providing flexibility in how containers can be hosted at AWS. Organizations could choose a bare-metal instance, a large on-demand or reserved instance hosted within a VPC, to install a custom Docker or Kubernetes environment. When you compare the operating concepts of containers and EC2 instances, containers offer interesting advantages, as detailed in Table 9-4.

Table 9-4 VMs Versus Containers

Parameter	VMs/Instances	Containers
Stack components	Full application stack	Lightweight—just the application
Isolation	Each app has its own VM	Containers share the host OS kernel
Startup	Startup in minutes	Startup in seconds
Size	Gigabytes in size	Megabytes in size
Security	FIPS 140-2 Approved	FIPS 140-2 validation

Containerized applications are moving to the forefront for most public cloud providers due to the interest in multi-cloud—the ability to run an application across different cloud providers. Whether or not you accept or embrace the multi-cloud model, AWS supports Dockers and Kubernetes container environments, which can run in multi-cloud environments hosted by AWS, Microsoft Azure, or Google Cloud.

AWS, Google, and Microsoft Azure also all have multi-cloud container solutions. AWS has AWS Outposts, which focuses on on-premises deployments using hardware and infrastructure services provided by AWS. Google offers Anthos, a managed application platform that extends the management of containerized applications that are running at Google, AWS, and Azure and on-premises locations. Microsoft Azure has Azure Arc, which can leverage containerized applications on premises, in the Azure cloud, or on a competitor's cloud.

Amazon Elastic Container Service

Amazon Elastic Container Service (Amazon ECS) is a fully managed container orchestration service that makes it easy to deploy, run, and scale containerized applications on AWS running Docker containers running on a managed cluster across multiple availability zones (AZs) within an AWS region. Here are the key features of AWS ECS:

- **Container orchestration:** Amazon ECS enables you to easily deploy and manage your containers across a fleet of Amazon EC2 instances.

- **Auto Scaling:** Amazon ECS automatically scales your containers using Amazon EC2 Auto Scaling to automatically scale your EC2 instances and Docker container workloads.

- **Task Definition:** Specify the desired state of your containerized applications and AWS ECS or Fargate automatically schedules tasks to meet requirements.

- **Monitoring and Logging:** AWS ECS is integrated with the following AWS services: AWS IAM, Amazon EC2 Auto Scaling, ELB Application Load Balancer, Amazon RDS, and the Amazon Elastic Container Registry (ECR).

AWS ECS Task Definition Choices

An Amazon Elastic Container Service (ECS) task definition is a blueprint that describes the containers that make up an ECS task. It specifies the container image, CPU and memory requirements, networking settings, and other information needed to run a containerized application. The management of the container infrastructure that your tasks and services are hosted on is determined by the launch type selected (see Figure 9-12).

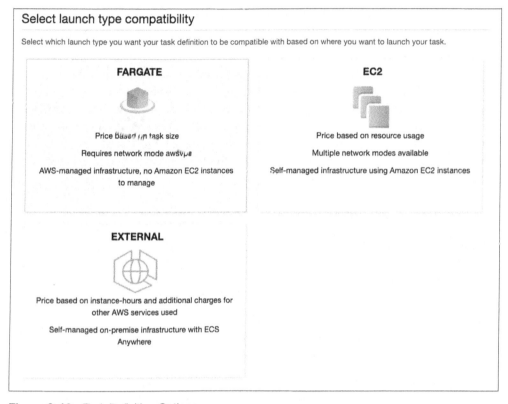

Figure 9-12   Task Definition Options

- **AWS Fargate launch type:** Fargate is a container management service you can select when creating a task definition when running ECS. Fargate relieves you of having to manage the underlying instances and clusters. When you select Fargate, you have the option to specify the container image and memory and CPU requirements by using an ECS task definition. Fargate then takes over scheduling the orchestration, management, and placement of the containers throughout the cluster, providing a highly available operation environment. Optionally, you can still launch your container environment using manual EC2 launch patterns using the ECS service.

AWS Fargate with ECS can also be used to run containers without having to manage (provision, configure, or scale) your clusters of EC2 instances. Applications launched by Fargate are packaged in containers with the defined CPU, memory at the task level, networking, and security policies. AWS Fargate supports Amazon Linux 2 and Microsoft Windows Server 2019 and 2022 Full and Core editions.

EKS running Kubernetes pods can be also managed by Fargate. Fargate profiles control which pods use Fargate management when launched. Each Fargate profile defines the pod's execution role, subnets where pods will be launched, and namespace.

- **EC2 launch type:** Run containerized applications that are hosted on a cluster of EC2 instances that you manage. Task definitions are created that define the container images that will run across your clusters. Direct fine-grained control can be run using the EC2 launch type that deploys EC2 instances in your cluster. ECS follows what is called a *task placement strategy* and uses a defined task definition when launching your containers. For example, your strategy might be to spread the containers across multiple EC2 instances and across multiple AZs. Task placement strategies might include running a task per EC2 instance or running your own custom-designed tasks. ECS monitors all running tasks and restarts tasks as a service restart when failure occurs.

- **External launch type:** Self-managed ECS on-premises deployments on an organization's own hardware resources.

NOTE   Amazon ECR is Amazon's own private container registry store for storing and deploying containers both publicly and privately.

Each ECS *task definition* must define the following criteria:

- The container image to be pulled from the private registry to create the containerized application.

- Container definitions, each of which includes the container image, the command to run when the container starts, the CPU and memory requirements, and other settings.

- The launch type to use for your task: AWS Fargate, EC2, or ECS Anywhere deployments on premises.

- The task execution role, which is the IAM role the ECS agent uses to perform tasks on your behalf.

- Links that need to be established between containers.

- Volumes, which can be used to store data that is persisted across container restarts or to share data between containers.

- Network and port settings. ECS supports several networking modes, including bridge mode, host mode, and awsvpc mode.

NOTE   ECS supports both rolling updates and blue/green deployments using AWS CodeDeploy.

Amazon Elastic Kubernetes Service

Another container management service supported by AWS is Amazon Elastic Kubernetes Service (EKS). EKS can be used to run Kubernetes at AWS without having to install and maintain your own Kubernetes control plane. EKS clusters have two main components: the Kubernetes control plane and clusters of EKS EC2 instances. EKS clusters contain pods that contain one or more containers. Pods can be deployed as self-managed nodes, EKS-managed node groups, or using AWS Fargate.

The EKS control plane has a minimum of two highly available API server instances. The API server is the primary point of interaction for users and other components of the Kubernetes system, and it is responsible for handling requests to create, update, and delete resources within the cluster. There are also three etcd instances hosted across three availability zones within each AWS region. The etcd instances communicate with each other to form a distributed system that can be used to store and retrieve configuration data. EKS automatically scales the control plane instances based on load, detects and replaces unhealthy instances, and automatically patches and updates control plane instances. Amazon EKS is integrated with AWS services such as Amazon CloudWatch, EC2 Auto Scaling groups, IAM, and ELB Application Load Balancers:

- Amazon CloudWatch logs are directly updated from the EKS control plane audit and diagnostic logs.

- EC2 Auto Scaling communicates with the Kubernetes Cluster Autoscaler with Auto Scaling groups and Launch templates.

- The AWS Load Balancer Controller manages AWS ELB Load Balancers for each Kubernetes cluster.

- AWS IAM security creates IAM roles for role-based access control (RBAC). Access to an EKS cluster using IAM entities is enabled by the AWS Authenticator for Kubernetes, which allows authentication to a Kubernetes cluster.

Amazon EKS can be deployed via the following methods:

- **Amazon EKS:** Deploy managed EKS control plane and nodes managed by AWS.

- **EKS on AWS Outposts:** AWS Outposts allows the running of EKS and other AWS infrastructure services in on-premises locations.

- **Amazon EKS Anywhere:** Deploy and manage Kubernetes clusters on premises supported by AWS using customer hardware and VMware vSphere.

- **EKS Distro:** Deploy open-source deployment of Kubernetes clusters on premises using customer hardware *and* customer support.

EKS workload clusters can be deployed on any type of EC2 instance. Currently, EKS supports Kubernetes clusters, with support for versions up to 1.23.14.

EKS has been certified Kubernetes conformant, so any third-party plug-ins or tools that you are using or have developed can be migrated to AWS for use in Kubernetes deployments.

Monitoring with AWS CloudWatch

Amazon CloudWatch is a monitoring service provided by AWS that enables you to monitor and manage various resources and more than 70 cloud services in the AWS cloud. With CloudWatch, you can monitor metrics, set alarms, and automatically react to changes in your resources.

Amazon CloudWatch provides data and operational insights for various AWS resources, such as Amazon Elastic Compute Cloud (Amazon EC2) instances and Amazon Relational Database Service (Amazon RDS) instances. You can use Amazon CloudWatch to collect and track metrics, shown in Figure 9-13, which are variables you can measure for your resources and applications. You can also use Amazon CloudWatch to set metric alarms, which enable you to receive notifications or automatically make changes to the resources you are monitoring when a threshold is breached.

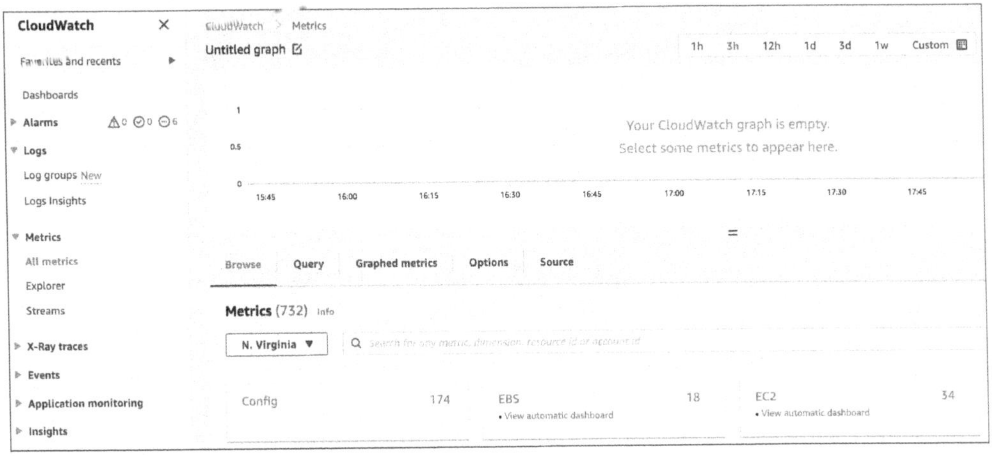

Figure 9-13 CloudWatch Metrics

You don't *have* to use CloudWatch; you might have specific needs and requirements that CloudWatch can't match. However, if you're using hosted AWS resources that employ EC2 instances or containers hosting applications—or database servers hosted by Amazon Relational Database Service (RDS)—and you don't have another monitoring solution, then you should consider using CloudWatch monitoring because AWS service metrics are already integrated into the CloudWatch monitoring service. You may already have a monitoring solution, such as Loggly, Service Now, or Datadog, that can integrate with CloudWatch data points using the CloudWatch application programming interface (API) with your third-party monitoring solution.

The following are useful features of CloudWatch to know:

- *Auto Scaling* **and CloudWatch metrics and alarms:** You can automatically adjust your application's compute power as needed with EC2 Auto Scaling and EC2 metrics linked to Amazon CloudWatch alarms.

- **Log filtering with metric filters and alerts:** You can arrange to be notified when specific data patterns occur in your logs and act accordingly using Amazon CloudWatch alarms and Amazon SNS notifications that call AWS Lambda to run custom functions providing automated solutions.

- **Billing Alerts:** You can monitor and control AWS cloud costs by using Billing Alerts and SNS notifications.

- **Logging of CloudTrail API calls to CloudWatch logs:** You can use Cloud-Trail to log all the API calls made to your AWS resources and send the logs to CloudWatch Logs for storage and monitoring. This can be useful for a variety of purposes, such as auditing and compliance, debugging, and security analysis.

NOTE Any third-party monitoring service you use today, such as Splunk, Datadog, or New Relic, supports integration with AWS CloudWatch data records and S3 buckets using RESTful APIs.

CloudWatch Basic Monitoring

Basic monitoring provided by CloudWatch is free of charge and, depending on the AWS service, a select number of basic metrics are available for monitoring the operation of the service. Metrics, once enabled, report to Amazon CloudWatch on a set schedule. For example, for EC2 instances and containers (ECS), metric data is sent to CloudWatch every 5 minutes. For RDS and Elastic Load Balancing (ELB), a selection of metric data is sent to CloudWatch every 60 seconds. EC2 instances can also enable detailed monitoring, which increases the reporting period to every 60 seconds; however, detailed monitoring is not free.

Make sure to check what basic metrics are available for each service in the AWS documentation; new metrics are being added to CloudWatch all the time to further enhance its monitoring ability. With every AWS service, there are additional metrics you can choose to enable to assist in monitoring. For example, Figure 9-14 shows the current CloudWatch metrics that are available.

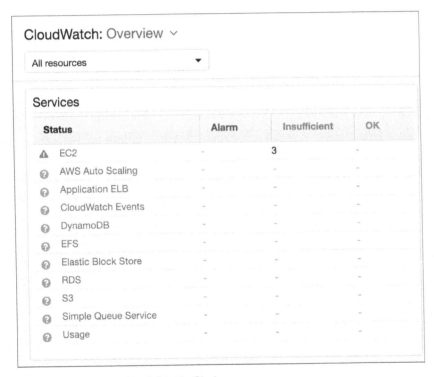

Figure 9-14   CloudWatch Metric Choices

CloudWatch Logs

Amazon CloudWatch allows you to send your event data from AWS CloudTrail custom trails to CloudWatch log groups. This enables Amazon CloudWatch to analyze and search for any specific patterns, such as errors or system issues to analyze further (see Figure 9-15).

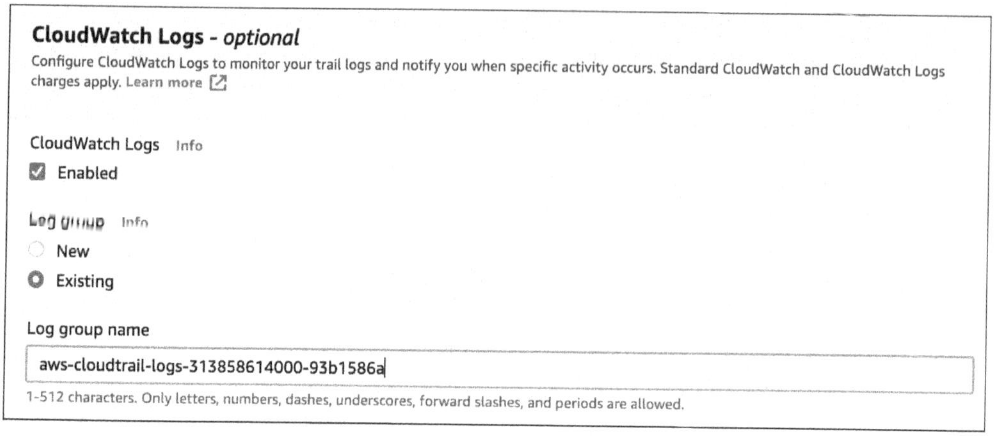

CloudWatch Logs - *optional*

Configure CloudWatch Logs to monitor your trail logs and notify you when specific activity occurs. Standard CloudWatch and CloudWatch Logs charges apply. Learn more

CloudWatch Logs Info
☑ Enabled

Log group Info
◯ New
🔘 Existing

Log group name

aws-cloudtrail-logs-313858614000-93b1586a

1-512 characters. Only letters, numbers, dashes, underscores, forward slashes, and periods are allowed.

Figure 9-15 CloudTrail Event Logging to CloudWatch Logs

The CloudTrail service tracks all API calls and authentications made to each AWS account. Stored CloudWatch log data can be reviewed by creating a metric filter that looks for specific events or patterns.

VPC flow logs also store network traffic log data in ***CloudWatch log groups***. Network traffic across a VPC, subnet, or elastic network adapter can be captured and stored in a CloudWatch log group for analysis. Collected data stored in a CloudWatch log can also be analyzed by one of the following options (see Figure 9-16):

- **Export Data to Amazon S3:** Log information for a defined date range can be exported to an S3 bucket for analysis by any third-party monitoring application.

- **Create an AWS Lambda subscription filter:** When a log event matches a specific filter, AWS Lambda functions can execute a custom task based on the event type generated.

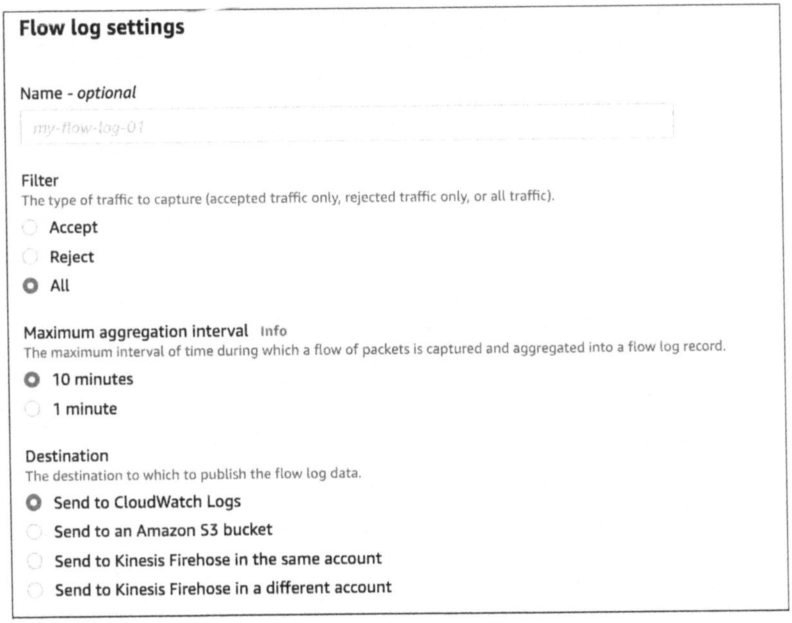

Flow log settings

Name - *optional*

    my-flow-log-01

Filter
The type of traffic to capture (accepted traffic only, rejected traffic only, or all traffic).

○ Accept

○ Reject

◉ All

Maximum aggregation interval   Info
The maximum interval of time during which a flow of packets is captured and aggregated into a flow log record.

◉ 10 minutes

○ 1 minute

Destination
The destination to which to publish the flow log data.

◉ Send to CloudWatch Logs

○ Send to an Amazon S3 bucket

○ Send to Kinesis Firehose in the same account

○ Send to Kinesis Firehose in a different account

Figure 9-16 CloudWatch Log Data Export Options

Developers can use CloudWatch logs to analyze network traffic captured in a VPC flow log; company auditors can analyze AWS CloudTrail API calls made to any of the company's AWS accounts.

NOTE Retention time for CloudWatch logs is forever; however, you can choose a retention time frame of up to 10 years. Retention of records stored in S3 buckets can be managed with lifecycle rules.

Collecting Data with the CloudWatch Agent

Amazon CloudWatch receives and stores metrics or log data from the CloudWatch agent installed on each EC2 instance or, optionally, on servers located on premises. AMIs have the CloudWatch agent installed by default.

The CloudWatch agent installation steps for on-premises servers are

Step 1. At the AWS CLI command prompt download the CloudWatch Agent installer package using this command syntax:

```
curl https://s3.amazonaws.com/amazoncloudwatch-agent/amazon_
linux/amd64/latest/amazon-cloudwatch-agent.rpm - O
```

Step 2.   Install the CloudWatch Agent using the AWS CLI:

```
sudo yum install -y ./amazon-cloudwatch-agent.rpm
```

Step 3.   Configure the CloudWatch agent using the AWS CLI:

```
sudo /opt/aws/amazon-cloudwatch-agent/bin/
amazon-cloudwatch-agent-config-wizard
```

This command will start the CloudWatch Agent configuration wizard, which will guide you through the process of configuring the CloudWatch Agent to collect and send metrics and log data to CloudWatch. You can also use the CloudWatch Agent configuration file to specify the metrics and log files that you want to collect and send to CloudWatch.

Planning for Monitoring

When you are operating in the cloud, monitoring helps you know when your AWS applications and associated services are operating properly, or there are issues that need to be adressed. You are ultimately monitoring to be kept abreast of potential problems before they occur, and to learn when and why problems occur. Monitoring allows you to be proactive in solving problems. Using CloudWatch, customers can monitor application services and compute resources, including the following variables:

- **Performance:** Monitoring your application's compute speed (database, application, or web server) over time allows you to develop an initial baseline of operation and what you deem to be an acceptable level of performance. For example, by monitoring an application server over a relatively long time period, such as multiple weeks or months, you will get valuable data insights about when EC2 instances, ECS containers, and RDS instances get busy, which times are quieter, and when systems get overloaded, such as at the end of the month or at certain times of each day.

- **Instance resources:** The initial components to monitor with regard to compute performance are CPU, memory, storage, and networking.

- **CPU and RAM utilization:** On EC2 instances running Windows Server, the CloudWatch agent can collect all counters supported by Performance Monitor. Linux instances collect system information using CloudWatch metrics for CPU, disk, memory, and networking.

- **Available disk space:** EBS volumes have disk performance and disk read and write operation metrics, and the CloudWatch agent can report on total disk space, used space, percentage of total disk space, and many other metrics.

- **IOPS:** CloudWatch has metrics for EBS volumes, as shown in Figure 9-17. In addition, you can monitor the overall read and write performance of EBS volumes and input/output operations per second (IOPS) performance.

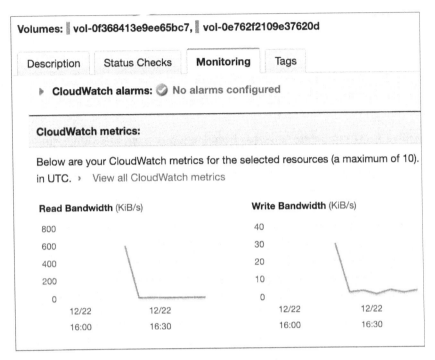

Figure 9-17   EBS CloudWatch Metrics

- **Network traffic:** Traffic can include subnet traffic and load-balancing traffic and VPN and Direct Connect connections. CloudWatch metrics are available for the ELB service, the network address translation (NAT) gateway, the transit gateway, and VPN connections. VPC flow logs also capture pertinent network information that is stored in CloudWatch. Additional metrics are available for EC2 instance networking.

NOTE   At AWS, you can set up notifications that are emailed, texted, or sent to an SQS queue, an SNS topic, or AWS Lambda, which could carry out an automated solution using a custom function.

Amazon CloudWatch Integration

The following are some of the infrastructure cloud AWS services that are embedded with CloudWatch metrics:

- **Amazon SNS:** SNS is used to send alerts when CloudWatch metric alarms are triggered.

- **Elastic Load Balancing (ELB):** Load-balancing metrics available include active connection count, request count, healthy host count, Transport Layer Security (TLS) connection errors, HTTP responses, and errors.

- **Amazon S3:** Storage metrics detail the number of objects and bucket size; request metrics include all requests, **GET** requests, bytes uploaded and downloaded, and 4xx and 5xx errors.

- **Amazon EC2:** Once an instance has been launched, from the Monitoring tab, 14 metrics are displayed, including options for CPU utilization, disk read and write operations, network traffic and packet flow, and status checks (see Figure 9-18).

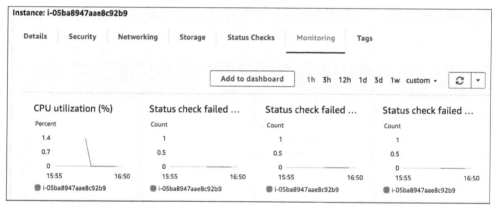

Figure 9-18 EC2 Instance Metrics

- **EC2 Auto Scaling:** Launch or terminate instances using CloudWatch metrics and alarms that trigger EC2 Auto Scale Groups.

- **AWS CloudTrail:** After a custom trail has been created, CloudWatch can be configured to write all API calls and authentications in your AWS account to a CloudWatch log file.

- **AWS Config:** Rules that discover resources that are out of compliance can invoke a custom AWS Lambda function to perform remediation.

- **Amazon RDS:** Metrics include database connections, disk queue length, free storage space, read and write throughput, SSD burst balance, and CPU credit usage.

- **AWS IAM:** All authentication attempts, both successful and unsuccessful, can be monitored with Amazon CloudWatch. SNS notifications can notify humans and automated subscribers.

Amazon CloudWatch Terminology

Amazon CloudWatch has its own specific terms and definitions. For each alarm, you set a *threshold*. You can choose whether the alarm will trigger when the value is greater than (>), greater than or equal to (>=), less than (<), or less than or equal to (<=) the defined statistic. You need to understand the following common terms when using CloudWatch and for the AWS Certified Solutions Architect – Associate (SAA-C03) exam:

- **Namespace:** Each AWS service stores its CloudWatch metrics and associated data in its own container. At this writing, there are more than 74 AWS services that use CloudWatch metrics.

- **Metrics:** Each metric is a variable within an AWS service. Each monitored variable produces a data set that is collected over a time period, resulting in a graph defined by data points. The data points represent the metric data received from the variable being monitored at an exact point in time, based on the range of times selected. For example, with EC2 instances, you can monitor the metric CPU usage. You can see in Figure 9-19 on the x-axis (which represents time) that the data points represent the data collected over the past hour, in 5-minute increments. The y-axis shows the percentage of CPU utilization.

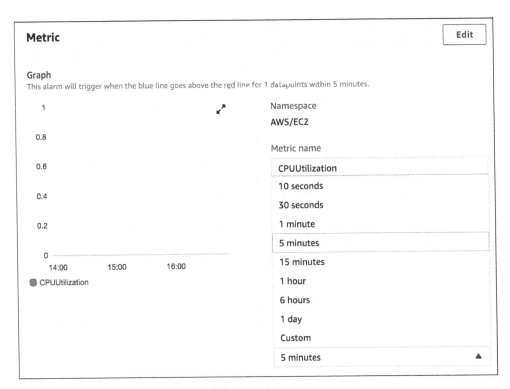

Figure 9-19   Data Points Summarized Every 5 Minutes

- **Statistics:** Each metric that you select for analysis collects data based on a defined time period. Graphed data is categorized statistically using some of the following terms:

  - **Minimum:** The lowest value seen during the specified time period

  - **Maximum:** The highest value seen during the specified time period

  - **Sum:** All values added together, based on a specific time period

  - **SampleCount:** The number of data points over a specific time period

  - **Average:** Calculated from Sum divided by SampleCount, based on the time period

- **Dimensions:** A dimension describes the metric and what data it stores. Multiple dimensions can be multiple instances assigned to the metric CPU utilization.

- **Units of measurement:** Statistics are defined by bytes, seconds, counts, or percentages.

- **Timestamp:** Each metric is stamped with a timestamp that references the exact time when data was received. Each timestamp includes the date, hours, minutes, and seconds based on the current time in UTC format.

- **Time range (period):** This is the length of time data is collected based on a metric calculated on the defined statistical value. Periods of time can be set from 1 minute up to 15 months. The number of periods determines the number of data points presented on the graph.

- **Alarms:** An *alarm* starts an action based on the state of the metric's data over the defined time period. Alarms can trigger notifications using SNS topics, an EC2 action, or an Auto Scaling action. You can also analyze the data output for each of the CloudWatch metrics against a custom baseline of defined measurement; if the data is below a defined threshold, all is well. However, once the metric's results cross or exceed the baseline for a defined time period, the CloudWatch alarm fires, notifying you of potential issues. CloudWatch can also alert an AWS Lambda function and the problem can be fixed—automatically. Once an alarm has been enabled, there are three possible states:

  - **OK:** This means that the data collected and evaluated by CloudWatch still fits within the defined alarm *threshold*. For example, you may have defined the CPU utilization at 60%. CloudWatch's analysis of the metric's data points over a defined evaluation period indicates that CPU utilization is currently at 52%; therefore, everything is still okay.

- **ALARM:** The metric's data indicates that the established baseline of acceptable CPU utilization has been breached.

- **INSUFFICIENT DATA:** There is not enough evaluated data to make a definitive analysis.

- **Events:** CloudWatch provides a near-real-time stream of system events for most AWS services based on a defined pattern, such as API calls indicating root account usage within the AWS account or any IAM API calls. Events can be stored in a CloudTrail log group and tracked using a metric filter, as shown in Figure 9-20. CloudTrail typically delivers events to the configured log group within 15 minutes of the API call. The target that is notified when the event rule fires can be one of several AWS services, including an SNS topic, a Lambda function, or an SQS queue.

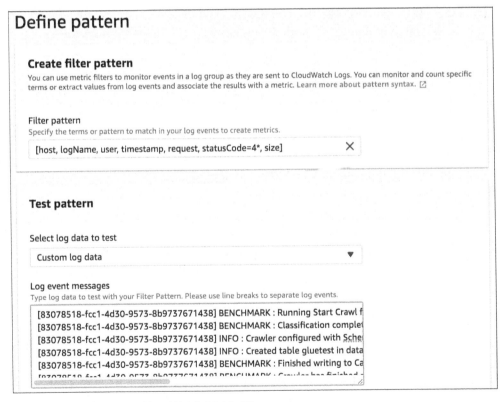

Figure 9-20   Defining a CloudWatch Metric Filter

All metric data is stored with timestamps referencing specific points in time; at AWS, these timestamps are defined as data points. By default, metrics are defined as standard resolution—that is, a resolution of 1 minute. Changing the resolution of a data point from 1 minute to 1 second will provide a much more granular distribution of data points. Data stored in a high-resolution format can be retrieved in periods ranging from 1 second up to multiple minutes.

> **NOTE**   Pricing for CloudWatch is based on the type of metric, the number of dashboards, and the number of alarms that fire. The first 5 GiB of CloudWatch log data storage is free; additional storage is charged. The AWS services that are integrated with CloudWatch send their associated basic metric information to the default CloudWatch dashboard at no additional charge.

One of the best examples of AWS service integration and automated problem solving is the relationship between the three essential AWS services, Amazon CloudWatch, EC2 Auto Scaling, and Elastic Load Balancers (ELB), which work together as a team. Here's how these cloud services work together:

Step 1.   EC2 instances hosted on subnets in different AZs could be hosted on private subnets and targeted by a public-facing load balancer. EC2 instances can be monitored by Amazon CloudWatch on a select metric such as NetworkPacketsIn or CPUUtilization, as shown in Figure 9-21.

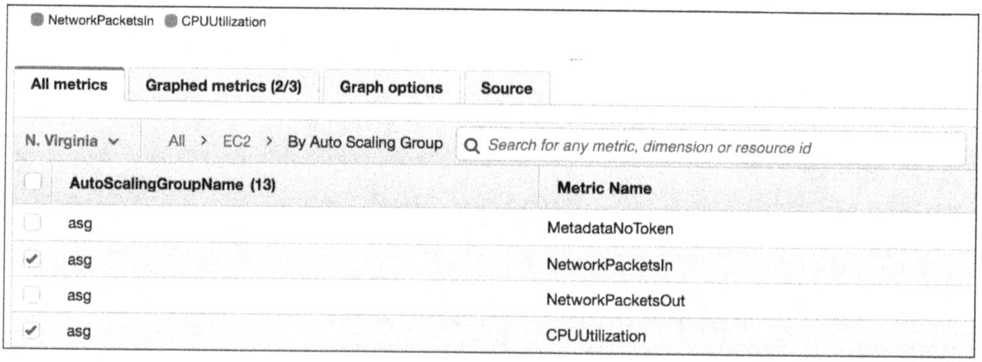

Figure 9-21   CloudWatch and EC2 Auto Scaling

Step 2.   Once the selected metric on the instances has exceeded the defined performance threshold for a defined time period—such as 75% for 5 minutes—CloudWatch can fire an alarm that calls the EC2 Auto Scaling service.

Step 3.   EC2 Auto Scaling starts the build of an additional EC2 instance; when it is ready, the instance is added to the pool of instances targeted by the load balancer. The performance problem is automatically solved without human intervention.

Creating a CloudWatch Alarm

When creating a CloudWatch alarm, the first task is to choose the metric that you want to link with an alarm function. You then need to define the threshold that, when breached, fires the alarm. To create a CloudWatch alarm, follow these steps:

Step 1.   From the CloudWatch console, choose Alarms. Choose Create Alarm and then Select Metric.

Step 2.   From the service namespace (for example, EC2), choose your metric or metrics.

Step 3.   Select the Graphed metrics tab, as shown in Figure 9-22, and set the following options:

- **Statistics:** Choose Minimum, Maximum, Sum, or Average.
- **Period:** Choose the time frame that data is sampled, such as 1 minute.

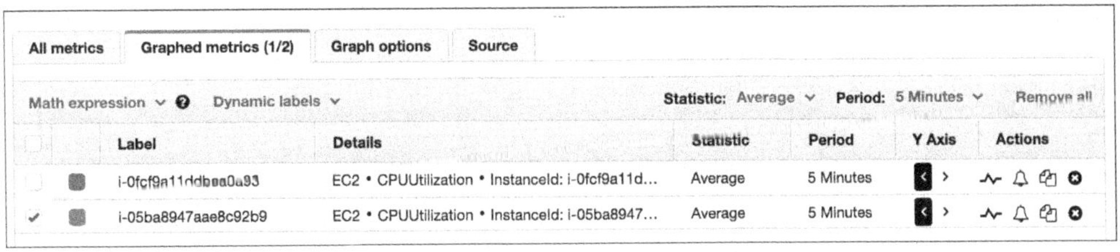

All metrics	Graphed metrics (1/2)	Graph options	Source				
Math expression ∨ ❓ Dynamic labels ∨				Statistic: Average ∨	Period: 5 Minutes ∨		Remove all
	Label	Details		Statistic	Period	Y Axis	Actions
	i-0fcf9a11ddbea0a93	EC2 • CPUUtilization • InstanceId: i-0fcf9a11d...		Average	5 Minutes	❮ ❯	∿ 🔔 🗂 ✖
✓	i-05ba8947aae8c92b9	EC2 • CPUUtilization • InstanceId: i-05ba8947...		Average	5 Minutes	❮ ❯	∿ 🔔 🗂 ✖

Figure 9-22   Defining Metric Behaviors

Step 4.   Define the alarm with a name and the threshold at which the alarm should fire (see Figure 9-23):

- **Whenever:** Define the metric, which in this example is CPUUtilization.
- **Is:** This can be defined as greater than (>), less than (<), or greater than or equal to (>=).
- **For:** This is the number of data points and the number of sampling periods (in this case, three data points).

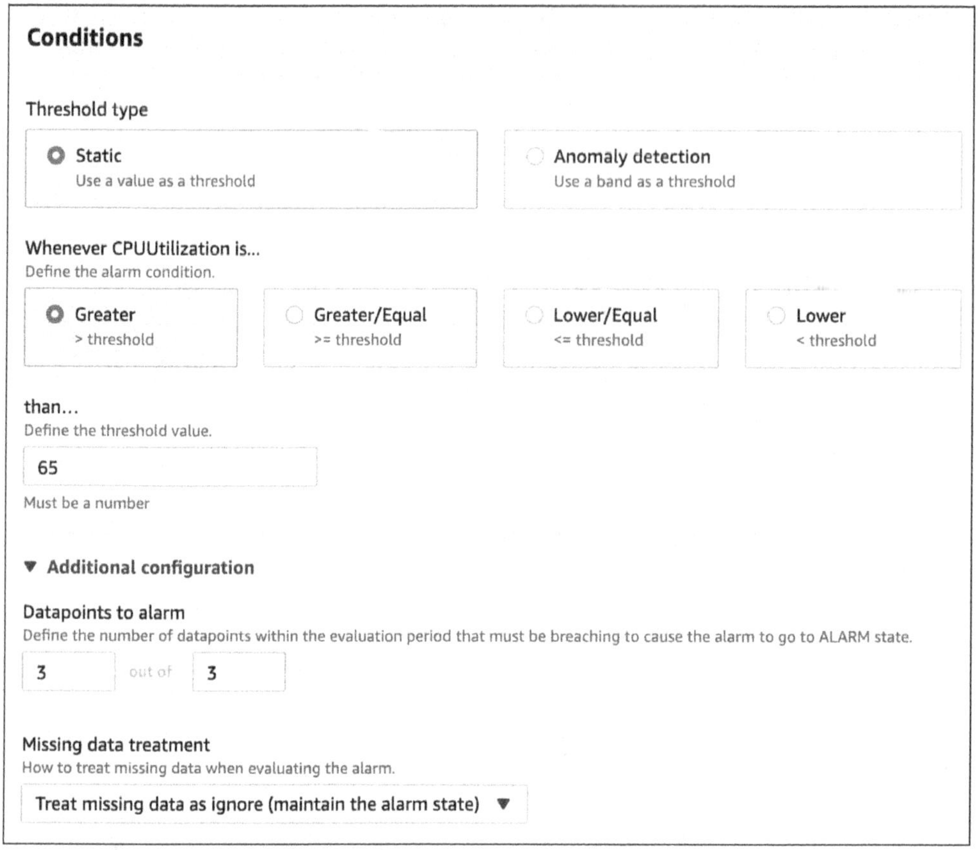

Conditions

Threshold type

○ **Static**
Use a value as a threshold

○ **Anomaly detection**
Use a band as a threshold

Whenever CPUUtilization is...
Define the alarm condition.

○ **Greater**
> threshold

○ **Greater/Equal**
>= threshold

○ **Lower/Equal**
<= threshold

○ **Lower**
< threshold

than...
Define the threshold value.

65

Must be a number

▼ **Additional configuration**

Datapoints to alarm
Define the number of datapoints within the evaluation period that must be breaching to cause the alarm to go to ALARM state.

3   out of   3

Missing data treatment
How to treat missing data when evaluating the alarm.

Treat missing data as ignore (maintain the alarm state) ▼

Figure 9-23 Setting CloudWatch Alarm Details

Additional Alarm and Action Settings

There are some complicated settings that can define how the stream of metric data is handled when it is stored in CloudWatch. Say that an instance runs into problems and doesn't send data; in this case, the default setting "Missing" means that the alarm doesn't worry about any missing data points in its evaluation of whether to change the state from OK to ALARM. In other words, the missing data isn't considered critical.

You could also choose to treat the missing data points as being within the defined threshold; in this case, you would choose Not Breaching. Or you could choose to treat the missing data points as reaching the threshold, in which case you would choose Breaching. Our example uses Breaching under the assumption that if data points are not being delivered to CloudWatch, there's a problem with the EC2 instance; as a result, the missing data points are critical.

Amazon SNS actions define the type of notification used when an alarm fires. For EC2 instance metrics, you have several choices:

- Send an SNS notification via email or text.

- Choose an Auto Scaling action that adds additional instances to be added, reducing the CPU utilization.

Amazon CloudWatch Cheat Sheet

For the AWS Certified Solutions Architect – Associate (SAA-C03) exam, you need to understand the following critical aspects of CloudWatch:

- Amazon CloudWatch monitors resources such as EC2 instances, EBS volumes, and RDS instances.

- Amazon CloudWatch monitors custom metrics and log files generated by hosted applications.

- Amazon CloudWatch monitors application performance and operational health.

- Amazon CloudWatch logs allow you to monitor and troubleshoot systems and applications.

- Amazon CloudWatch logs allow you to store log files from EC2, AWS CloudTrail, ELB, and Amazon Route 53 and other third-party logs.

Auto Scaling Options at AWS

Imagine that you have a web application designed and operating on EC2 instances; you have followed best practices and have the application load spread across multiple AZs on multiple instances. The application works well with adequate performance for about 4,000 users. But last week the application was made available to 1,000 additional users, and the application performance started to slow down. Developers added some additional instances, and everyone was happy once again.

This type of manual solution does work, and if the application in question is going to have additional users in the future, why not just add a few more instances into the mix when required? Users won't complain. Or will they? Performing a manual analysis of the existing EC2 instances and waiting for complaints from the end users is not a proactive approach. Another issue is cost; if more compute instances are running 24/7, the cost of hosting the application increases.

Amazon faced exactly this problem in its early days of running the Amazon.com website. Running excessive compute capacity was expensive. Amazon solved this problem with EC2 Auto Scaling.

Scaling is the secret sauce for all public cloud providers; all public clouds offer a version of auto scaling. Every application that you use on your smartphone or tablet is controlled by some elements of compute scale. If your application is slow, perhaps it's because there are too many users currently accessing the application. If your application has decent performance, the odds are that the application is being carefully monitored, and resources are being added or removed based on demand.

Perhaps you're watching a movie on Netflix. If it is a popular movie, the odds are that other people are also watching it. When Netflix can scale or increase the resources that host the movie based on user demand, it has happy customers. When you shop online, you have probably experienced slow page loads and slow response time. The odds are that this rarely happens at Amazon.com because of AWS's ability to scale its cloud resources based on demand.

In Chapter 1, "Understanding the Foundations of AWS Architecture," we looked at the definition of the public cloud based on the National Institute of Standards and Technology (NIST) definitions and characteristics of the public cloud. One of the NIST characteristics of the public cloud is *rapid elasticity*, defined as follows in NIST SP 800-145: "capabilities can be elastically provisioned and released, in some cases automatically, to scale rapidly outward and inward commensurate with demand."

Amazon.com, which is powered by the AWS cloud, relies on auto-scaling. On Black Friday events or during the holiday season, one could reasonably expect additional web and application servers to be required to handle the unknown number of customers who will be buying goods on Amazon.com. However, in the initial years of operation of the Amazon.com store, the number of servers running was based on expectations; Amazon tried to have enough resources available when there were lots of customers. It was a proactive but very expensive design.

Running too many underutilized resources costs Amazon a lot of money, and this practice will cost your organization a lot of money running hosted resources online and available but not fully utilized. The Amazon online retail store uses monitoring and automation to horizontally scale out its web and application compute resources (adding more compute power) and scaling in (removing compute power) based on the demand. Running just the right number of servers, based on current demand, and dynamically scaling out and in as required, greatly improves workload cost utilization.

NOTE The automatic scaling of compute resources at AWS is dependent on monitoring the compute resources that need to scale using CloudWatch metrics and alarms.

AWS uses CloudWatch monitoring, ELB load balancing, and Auto Scaling services to run its managed cloud services at the required scale.

EC2 Auto Scaling

The Amazon EC2 Auto Scaling service enables you to automatically scale your Amazon EC2 resources in response to changes in demand for your application. It helps you ensure that you have the right number of Amazon EC2 instances available to meet the needs of your application, without having to manually create or terminate instances. Here are some key technical details about Amazon EC2 Auto Scaling:

- **Policies:** Amazon EC2 Auto Scaling uses scaling policies to determine when to scale your Amazon EC2 resources up or down. You can create simple scaling policies based on a single metric, such as CPU utilization, or you can create more complex policies that use multiple metrics based on the size of your Amazon EC2 fleet of instances.

- **Scaling actions:** When a scaling policy is triggered, Amazon EC2 Auto Scaling takes a scaling action to either launch or terminate Amazon EC2 instances. The number of instances to launch or terminate can be defined, or you can use a percentage to scale the number of instances relative to the size of your Amazon EC2 fleet.

- **Scaling groups:** Amazon EC2 Auto Scaling groups are logical collections of Amazon EC2 instances that are managed as a single entity. Multiple scaling groups can be created with their own scaling policies and configurations.

- *Health checks:* Amazon EC2 Auto Scaling uses *health checks* to ensure that only healthy Amazon EC2 instances are used to serve traffic. If an instance fails a health check, it is terminated and replaced with a new instance.

- **CloudWatch alarms:** Amazon EC2 Auto Scaling uses CloudWatch alarms and SNS notifications to trigger scaling actions based on metrics with defined thresholds linked to alarms. For example, an alarm can send an SNS notification when the CPU utilization of your Amazon EC2 instances exceeds a certain threshold, triggering a scaling action to launch additional instances.

EC2 Auto Scaling Operation

EC2 Auto Scaling works with three main components: a launch template or launch configuration, an Auto Scaling group, and a defined *scaling policy*.

Launch Configuration

A launch configuration is a simple template used by an ASG to launch EC2 instances. The process of creating a launch configuration is much like the process you would follow to manually launch an EC2 instance from the AWS Management Console. The launch configuration contains the installation details for the EC2 instances that will be built by the ASG. Each launch configuration is associated with one ASG. A launch configuration includes numerous system components, including the instance ID of the AMI, the instance type to build, the key pair for authentication, the desired security groups, and a block storage device. Launch configurations are slowly being superseded by the launch template, which has many additional settings that can be used when deploying instances.

Launch Templates

A *launch template* is similar to a launch configuration, with added features related to versioning an existing template, so you can make changes. In addition, launch templates support all new AWS features related to EC2 instances and Auto Scaling, whereas launch configurations do not. A default launch template can be created as a source template; then, other versions of the template can be created and saved. AWS recommends that you use launch templates rather than launch configurations because a launch template has many deployment options when compared to a launch template (see Figure 9-24).

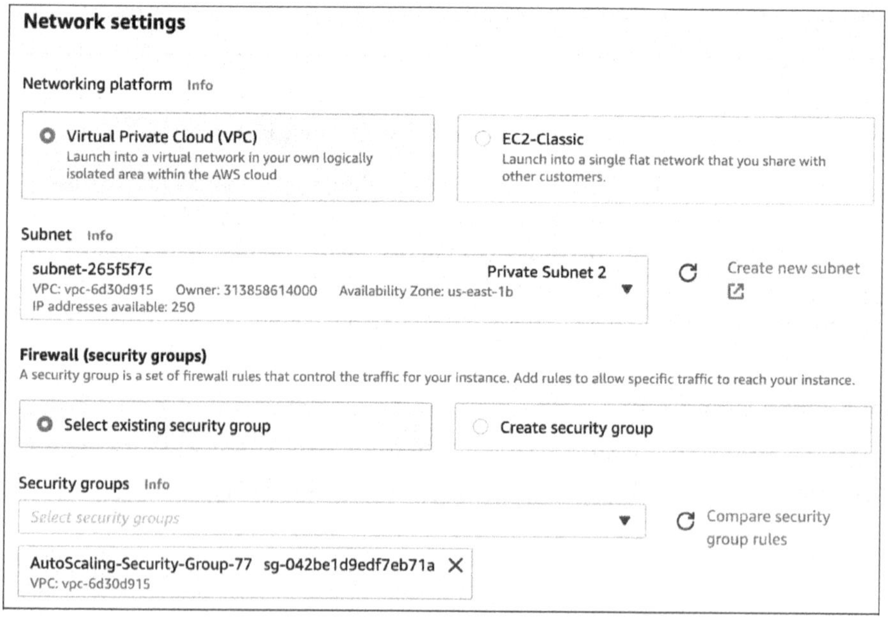

Figure 9-24   Launch Template Network Settings

Auto Scaling Groups

An Auto Scaling group (ASG) is built from a collection of EC2 instances that have been generated from the associated launch configuration or launch template. Each ASG launches instances, following the parameters of the launch template, to meet the defined scaling policy. An ASG can function independently or be associated with a load balancer, as shown in Figure 9-25.

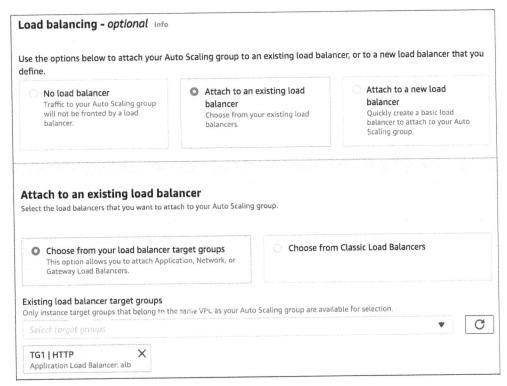

Figure 9-25 Auto Scaling Group Settings and Options

Scaling policies are attached to ASGs, which automatically increase or decrease the number of EC2 instances based on CloudWatch alarms and notifications.

The EC2 instance types that can be added to an ASG include on-demand, spot, or reserved instances across multiple AZs. You can also define the percentage of on-demand and spot instances to deploy for additional cost savings.

An ASG performs health checks on instances added to the ASG; ELB health checks can also be chosen. EC2 Auto Scaling performs health checks for recently launched EC2 instances using the EC2 status check (see Figure 9-26). If instances added to an

ASG fail their status checks after boot, they are considered unhealthy, and EC2 Auto Scaling terminates, relaunches, and re-adds them to the ASG.

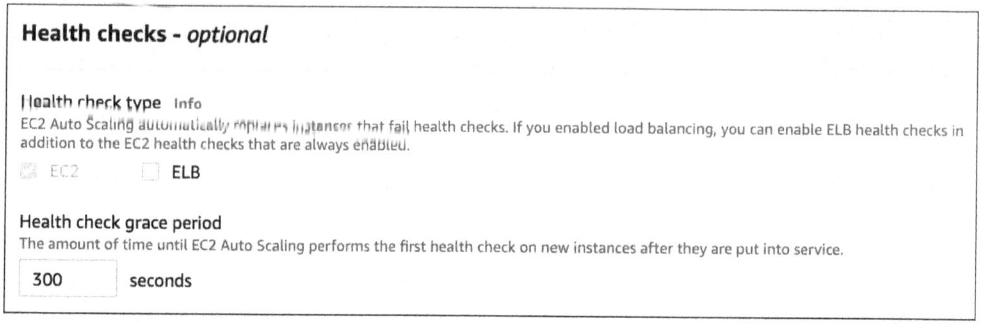

Health checks - *optional*

Health check type Info
EC2 Auto Scaling automatically replaces instances that fail health checks. If you enabled load balancing, you can enable ELB health checks in addition to the EC2 health checks that are always enabled.

☑ EC2   ☐ ELB

Health check grace period
The amount of time until EC2 Auto Scaling performs the first health check on new instances after they are put into service.

300   seconds

Figure 9-26   Health Check Options

ELB health checks are a little more rigorous than Auto Scaling health checks, and ASGs can and should be configured to also use ELB health checks. If an ASG or ELB health check fails, the unhealthy instances are terminated and relaunched.

NOTE   If an ASG is not associated with a load balancer, the ASG status health checks of each EC2 instance are used to determine the health of the new instance.

Scaling Options for Auto Scaling Groups

For the AWS Certified Solutions Architect – Associate (SAA-C03) exam, you need to understand several scaling options for deploying Auto Scaling groups:

- **Target tracking scaling policy:** You can select the metric type and target value to maintain the desired capacity (see Figure 9-27) and automatically have any instances that are determined to be unhealthy (by the Auto Scaling health check or the load-balancing health check) replaced.

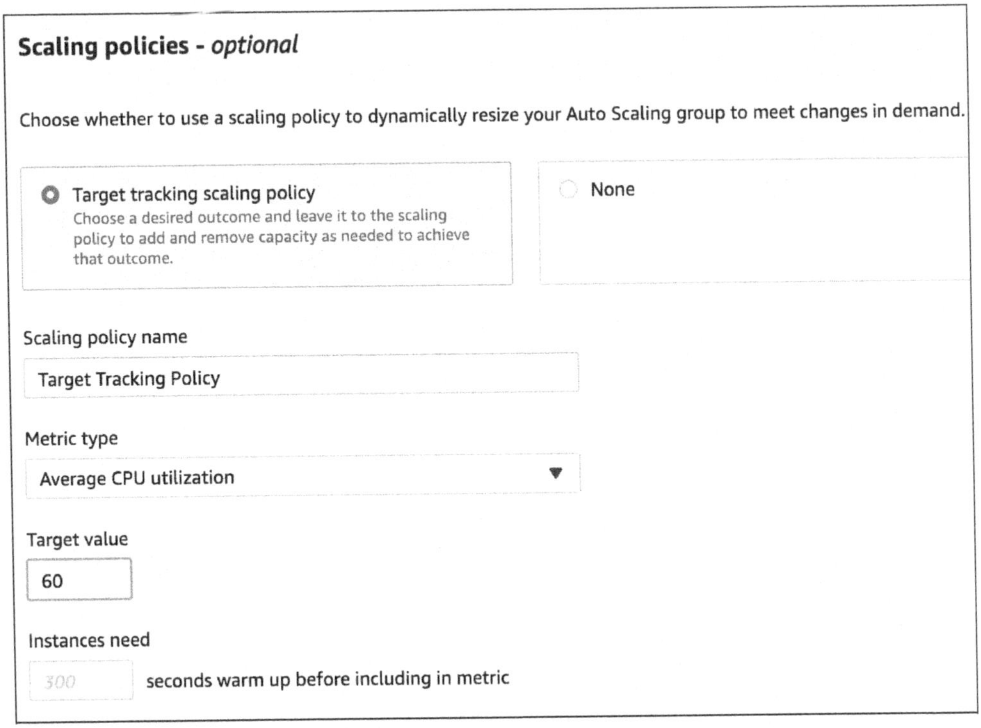

Scaling policies - *optional*

Choose whether to use a scaling policy to dynamically resize your Auto Scaling group to meet changes in demand.

⦿ **Target tracking scaling policy**
Choose a desired outcome and leave it to the scaling
policy to add and remove capacity as needed to achieve
that outcome.

◯ None

Scaling policy name

Target Tracking Policy

Metric type

Average CPU utilization ▼

Target value

60

Instances need

300   seconds warm up before including in metric

Figure 9-27   Target Tracking Variables for Increasing Group Size

- **Simple scaling:** You can increase and decrease the size of an ASG based on a single metric and automatically manage the size of the EC2 instances in the Auto Scaling group. An Auto Scaling group has three key parameters that determine the size and capacity of the group: minimum size, maximum size, and desired capacity.

- **Minimum size:** The minimum size is the minimum number of Amazon EC2 instances that you want to have running in your Auto Scaling group at any given time. The minimum size cannot be set to a value lower than the current size of the group.

- **Maximum size:** The maximum size is the maximum number of Amazon EC2 instances that you want to have running in your Auto Scaling group at any given time. The maximum size cannot be set to a value higher than the current size of the group.

- **Desired capacity:** The desired capacity is the number of Amazon EC2 instances that you want to have running in your Auto Scaling group at a given time. The desired capacity can be any integer value between the minimum size and the maximum size, inclusive. The minimum size, maximum size, and desired capacity of an Auto Scaling group determine the range of values that Amazon EC2 Auto Scaling can use to scale your Amazon EC2 fleet.

You can select from EC2 instance metrics, such as CPU utilization, to support target tracking. Setting CPUUtilization to 60% results in instances being added to or removed from the Auto Scaling group as required to maintain the desired CPU utilization (see Figure 9-28). Slightly more instances may be added than necessary when maintaining the desired CPU utilization because the math behind the scaling calculations rounds up the number of instances to add or remove.

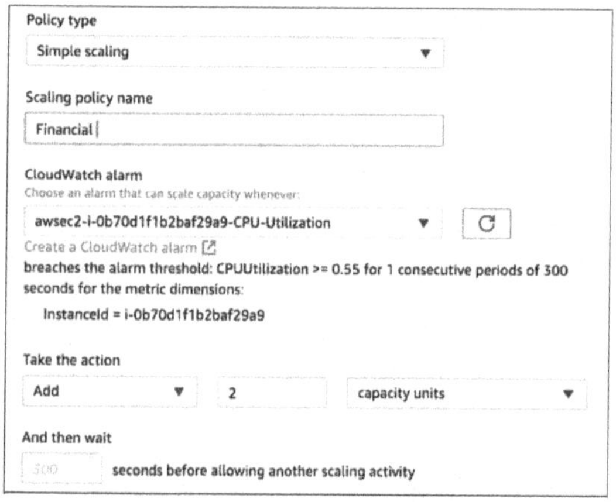

Figure 9-28   Simple Scaling Parameters

Simple scaling allows the use of a single custom metric that determines the scaling out and in of your defined fleet of EC2 instances. Multiple policies can be attached to an ASG that can control the scaling out and in. Multiple scaling policies can provide scaling control. For example, a scaling policy might react to the Cloud-Watch metric Network Utilization and scale out when network traffic is greater than (>) a certain percentage. Or a scaling policy could measure the depth of messages in an SQS queue and scale out when the number of messages is over a certain value. Both simple scaling and step scaling, discussed next, support the following parameters for scaling instances:

- **ChangeInCapacity:** This parameter increases or decreases the capacity of the ASG by the defined number of instances.

- **ExactCapacity:** This parameter defines the capacity of the ASG based on a defined number. For example, if the current capacity is four instances and an adjustment to the ASG is three instances, the capacity is set to seven instances.

- **PercentChangeInCapacity:** This parameter changes the capacity of the ASG by either a positive or a negative percentage value.

NOTE Amazon recommends that metrics used for target tracking should be set for a 1-minute frequency to ensure faster response time. Detailed monitoring must be enabled to use 1-minute intervals.

- *Step scaling*: A step scaling policy enables you to define a series of steps, or thresholds, for a metric, and specify a different number of Amazon EC2 instances or capacity units to launch or terminate for each step. For example, you could specify that if the average CPU utilization of your Amazon EC2 instances exceeds 70%, Amazon EC2 Auto Scaling should launch two additional instances, and if the average CPU utilization falls below 50%, it should terminate two instances. Step scaling enables you to define lower and upper boundaries for the metric being used and to define the amount by which to scale in or scale out the instances, as shown in Figure 9-29, with incremental steps in or out:

    - A first instance is added when CPU utilization is between 40% and 50%.

    - The next step adds two instances when CPU utilization is between 50% and 70%.

    - In the third step, three instances are added when CPU utilization is between 70% and 90%.

    - When CPU utilization is greater than 90%, a further four instances are added.

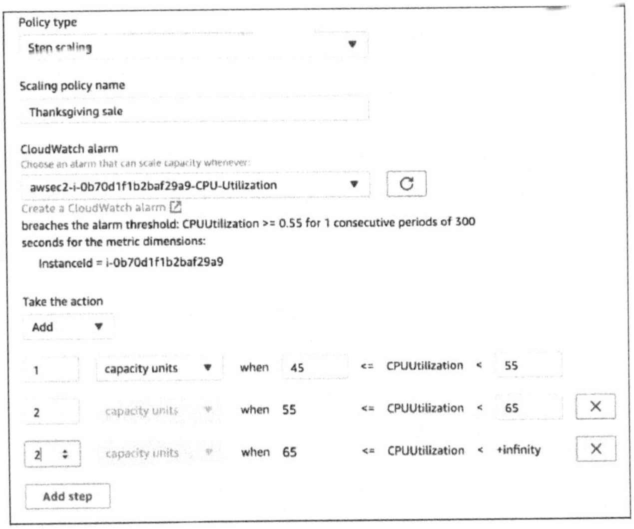

Figure 9-29 Step Scaling Parameters

The step scaling policy also defines a warmup period. This is a period of time that you can specify during which Amazon EC2 Auto Scaling will not take any scaling actions in response to a trigger to add additional instances. The warm-up period gives EC2 instances time to start up and become fully operational before they start serving traffic. Keep in mind that newly launched EC2 instances might need to apply updates, finish configuration, and pass health checks before they are operational. Defined scale-down steps are carried out when scaling in.

When you create or update an Auto Scaling group, you can specify the desired capacity in terms of Amazon EC2 instances or in terms of capacity units. A capacity unit is a unit of capacity that represents the number of Amazon EC2 instances that you want to have running in your Auto Scaling group.

By using capacity units, you can specify the desired capacity of your Auto Scaling group in a more flexible and granular way. For example, you can specify that you want to have two capacity units of a particular instance type, which would equate to two Amazon EC2 instances of that type. This enables you to specify the desired capacity of your Auto Scaling group in a way that is independent of the specific instance type that you are using.

- **Scale based on a schedule:** Scaling can be defined based on time and date values that instruct Auto Scaling to scale up or down at a specific time. The start time and the minimum, maximum, and desired sizes can be set for recurring actions.

Management Options for Auto Scaling Groups

There are several options available for managing ASGs, including Predictive scaling, Warm pools, and Instance replace.

- **Predictive scaling:** A feature called predictive scaling uses machine learning models to analyze the deployed application and traffic pattern history to forecast recommended scaling. In the case of a workload that has high usage during normal business hours and lower usage overnight, predictive scaling can add capacity before an increase in daily traffic occurs.

- **Warm pools:** Having the ability to scale quickly in response to real-time application demand is sometimes hard to manage due to the latency that occurs when the EC2 instance or container is initialized at startup. Latency can sometimes be several minutes or longer until the instance is ready to be added to an Auto Scaling group. EC2 Auto Scale warm pools allow you to reduce scale-out latency by maintaining a pool of pre-warmed EC2 instances ready to be immediately placed into service when a scale-out event is issued.

■ **Instance refresh:** Instance refresh can be used to update the instances currently in an ASG instead of replacing the instances one at a time. Instance refresh can be useful to deploy a new AMI or new user data script. Instances can also be replaced by specifying the maximum amount of time an instance can be in service before it is terminated and replaced. A minimum instance refresh value of at least 1 day must be initially set.

NOTE You can make manual changes to your ASGs at any time by changing the maximum, minimum, or desired state values to start capacity changes.

Cooldown Period

Simple scaling policies are bound to a ***cooldown period***. Let's look at an example of where a cooldown period is useful. Suppose that your company has a three-tier application running in test mode on AWS, consisting of web servers, application servers, and the AWS RDS database tier. Separate ASGs are created for the web tier and for the application tier. Each tier uses CloudWatch alarms to scale out whenever the CPU utilization for each tier exceeds 70%. The triggering of the CloudWatch alarm instructs the ASG to launch and configure additional instances.

For this example, the EC2 instances are using a user data script for installing updates at first boot. These additional tasks can take time—perhaps 4 or 5 minutes. When an instance has finished updating and is ready for use and marked as "healthy," it enters the *InService* state.

While the new EC2 instance is being readied, if an unexpected increase in CPU utilization occurs to the web tier, the CloudWatch alarm may trigger once again, ordering the ASG to launch another EC2 instance. However, because a cooldown period is in force, even after the ASG is directed to launch an EC2 instance on a scale-out request, all scaling requests are ignored until the cooldown period finishes. The default cooldown period is 300 seconds; you can change this value when creating an ASG or at a later point if you wish to make modifications.

Termination Policy

When a scale-in event occurs, defined default termination policies control which EC2 instances are first terminated. The default termination policy is designed to ensure that your instances are evenly spaced across the availability zones to maintain high availability. Termination of unhealthy instances occurs first; then Auto Scaling attempts to launch new instances to replace the terminated instances.

Other termination options that can be chosen for a custom termination policy include the following:

- **Oldest launch template:** Remove instances that are using an older launch template.

- **Oldest launch configuration:** Remove instances that are using an older launch configuration.

- **Closest to next instance hour:** Terminate instances that are closest to the next billing hour.

- **Newest Instance:** Terminate the newest instance in the ASG.

- **Oldest Instance:** Terminate the oldest instance in the ASG.

- **Allocation strategy:** Terminate instances based on on-demand or spot instance strategies.

NOTE   The scale-out setting defines which instances are launched by the defined scaling policy. The scale-in setting defines which instances are terminated by the scaling policy.

Lifecycle Hooks

You can create custom actions that are carried out on instances that an ASG launches or terminates. With such an action, an instance is placed into a wait state and held from becoming registered in the ASG or from being terminated for a period of time. While it is being held in the wait state, custom actions can be performed on the instance. Think of a wait state as an opportunity to perform any task you want on an EC2 instance before it is added to or removed from the ASG. An instance can be held in a wait state for a maximum of 48 hours. During the wait time, the following custom actions are allowed:

- Call an AWS Lambda function to perform a specific task.

- Send a message to a defined SNS notification.

- Execute a script as the instance starts and remains in the defined wait state.

- Add a *lifecycle hook* to an ASG by using AWS CLI commands that populate the user data location in a launch template, as shown here:

```
AWS autoscaling put-lifecycle-hook --lifecycle-hook-name <lifecycle
code> --auto-scaling-group-name <ASG here > --lifecycle-transition
autoscaling:EC2_INSTANCE_LAUNCHING
```

EC2 Auto Scaling Cheat Sheet

For the AWS Certified Solutions Architect – Associate (SAA-C03) exam, you need to understand the following critical aspects of EC2 Auto Scaling:

- EC2 Auto Scaling ensures that you have the correct amount of compute power required by an application at all times.

- An Auto Scaling group is a collection of EC2 instances that can provide horizontal scaling across multiple AZs.

- An Auto Scaling group requires an attached Auto Scaling policy.

- EC2 Auto Scaling can be integrated with ELB target groups and Amazon CloudWatch metrics and alarms.

- A launch template is a template used by Auto Scaling to create additional EC2 instances as required.

- Application Load Balancers, Network Load Balancers, and Gateway Load Balancers can be attached to an Auto Scaling group.

- Load balancers must be deployed in the same region as the Auto Scaling deployment.

 AWS Auto Scaling

You now know about EC2 Auto Scaling, but there's another scaling option called AWS Auto Scaling. What's the difference? AWS Auto Scaling can manage auto scaling for the following AWS workload after they have been deployed using a scaling plan. Organizations can use AWS Auto Scaling to manage scaling for these AWS resources.

- **Amazon Aurora:** Increase or decrease the number of read replicas that have been provisioned for an Aurora DB cluster.

- **EC2 Auto Scaling:** Increase or decrease the number of EC2 instances in an Auto Scaling group.

- **Elastic Container Service:** Increase or decrease the desired task count in ECS.

- **DynamoDB:** Increase or decrease the provisioned read and write capacity of a DynamoDB table or global secondary index.

- **Spot fleet:** Increase or decrease the target capacity of a spot fleet. A spot fleet enables you to launch a desired number of instances, called a *fleet* of instances, based on the desired price and number of spot instance types.

A scaling plan tells AWS Auto Scaling how to optimize the utilization of supported AWS resources defined in your scaling plan. You can optimize for availability, for cost, or a balance of both options. AWS Auto Scaling can also be used to create predictive scaling for EC2 instances that are members of a target tracking EC2 auto scaling group. Predictive scaling looks at historic traffic patterns and forecasts and schedules changes in the number of EC2 instances running at the appropriate time.

Exam Preparation Tasks

As mentioned in the section "How to Use This Book" in the Introduction, you have a couple of choices for exam preparation: the exercises here, Chapter 16, "Final Preparation," and the exam simulation questions in the Pearson Test Prep Software Online.

Review All Key Topics

Review the most important topics in the chapter, noted with the Key Topic icon in the margin of the page. Table 9-5 lists these key topics and the page number on which each is found.

Table 9-5   Chapter 9 Key Topics

Key Topic Element	Description	Page Numbers
Table 9-2	Compute Services and Use Cases	425
Section	Amazon Machine Images	429
Section	Creating a Custom AMI	432
Section	AWS Lambda	436
Section	AWS Lambda Integration	438
Section	AWS Lambda Cheat Sheet	441
Section	Amazon Elastic Container Service	443
Section	Amazon Elastic Kubernetes Service	446
List	Useful features of CloudWatch	448
Section	CloudWatch Logs	449
Section	Collecting Data with the CloudWatch Agent	451
Section	CloudWatch Integration	453
Section	Additional Alarm and Action Settings	460
Section	CloudWatch Cheat Sheet	461
Section	EC2 Auto Scaling Operation	463

Key Topic Element	Description	Page Numbers
Section	Scaling Options for Auto Scaling Groups	466
Section	Management Options for Auto Scaling Groups	470
Section	Termination Policy	471
Section	Lifecycle Hooks	472
Section	EC2 Auto Scaling Cheat Sheet	473
Section	AWS Auto Scaling	473

Define Key Terms

Define the following key terms from this chapter and check your answers in the glossary:

metric, Amazon Machine Image (AMI), task definition, Auto Scaling, Cloud-Watch log group, alarm, health check, scaling policy, launch template, simple scaling, step scaling, cooldown period, lifecycle hook

Q&A

The answers to these questions appear in Appendix A. For more practice with exam format questions, use the Pearson Test Prep Software Online.

1. Each AMI is a _____ containing the desired software configuration.

2. What is the best reason for creating golden AMIs for your web and application servers?

3. Every time a Lambda function executes, you are charged based on the _____ and _____ the function uses.

4. What would be a good reason to consider customizing the CloudWatch agent?

5. When planning an Auto Scaling deployment, should you use a launch configuration or a launch template?

6. What is the recommended EC2 Auto Scaling policy setting to start with?

7. When should simple scaling policies be deployed to help improve application performance?

8. How do step scaling policies help you save additional money on compute?

This chapter covers the following topics:

- AWS Cloud Databases
- Amazon Relational Database Service
- Amazon Aurora
- Amazon DynamoDB
- Amazon ElastiCache
- Amazon Redshift

This chapter covers content that's important to the following exam domain and task statement:

Domain 3: Design High-Performing Architectures

Task Statement 3: Determine high-performing database solutions

CHAPTER 10

Determining High-Performing Database Solutions

Just as it's likely that you're using networking services at AWS, you are almost certainly using one or more databases for your workload data records. I can't think of a single application that's hosted in the cloud or on premises that doesn't have a backend database. As the saying goes, "If you have data, it should be stored in a database."

SQL databases have been around for decades, but there are other database choices available for consideration. There are a number of NoSQL databases, such as Amazon DynamoDB service, for customers who need databases that provide single-digit-millisecond performance with unlimited throughput and storage, and automatic multi-region replication if desired. In order to pass the AWS Certified Solutions Architect – Associate (SAA-C03) exam, you need to know about the architecture of the database offerings at AWS, how they are deployed, and how they are constructed for durability and failover. You don't have to be a database administrator, but you need to be able to provide basic technical advice about the available AWS database offerings.

"Do I Know This Already?"

The "Do I Know This Already?" quiz allows you to assess whether you should read this entire chapter thoroughly or jump to the "Exam Preparation Tasks" section. If you are in doubt about your answers to these questions or your own assessment of your knowledge of the topics, read the entire chapter. Table 10-1 lists the major headings in this chapter and their corresponding "Do I Know This Already?" quiz questions. You can find the answers in Appendix A, "Answers to the 'Do I Know This Already?' Quizzes and Q&A Sections."

Table 10-1   "Do I Know This Already?" Section-to-Question Mapping

Foundation Topics Section	Questions
AWS Cloud Databases	1, 2
Amazon Relational Database Service	3, 4
Amazon Aurora	5, 6
Amazon DynamoDB	7, 8
Amazon ElastiCache	9, 10
Amazon Redshift	11, 12

CAUTION   The goal of self-assessment is to gauge your mastery of the topics in this chapter. If you do not know the answer to a question or are only partially sure of the answer, you should mark that question as wrong for purposes of the self-assessment. Giving yourself credit for an answer you correctly guess skews your self-assessment results and might provide you with a false sense of security.

1. What is Amazon's key database offering that supports key-value tables?

   a. Amazon ElastiCache for Memcached

   b. RDS

   c. Amazon DynamoDB

   d. Amazon Keyspaces

2. Which cloud database is suggested for storing user session information?

   a. Amazon DynamoDB

   b. Amazon DocumentDB

   c. Amazon RDS

   d. Amazon ElastiCache for Memcached

3. After ordering and configuring Amazon Relational Database Service, which of the following is true regarding the ongoing maintenance of the database infrastructure?

   a. Each customer must perform all the maintenance.

   b. AWS performs all maintenance and failover management.

   c. The customer is responsible for making manual snapshots of the database instances.

   d. The customer is responsible for changing the size of the database instances.

4. Which of the following is a suggested best practice when deploying Amazon RDS?

   a. Use a single availability zone.

   b. Use just a single primary database instance.

   c. Use multiple primary database instances.

   d. Use multiple availability zones.

5. What type of storage is used by Amazon Aurora?

   a. EBS storage arrays

   b. A virtual SSD cluster storage volume

   c. Ephemeral storage

   d. SSDs

6. How many copies of data does Amazon Aurora maintain?

   a. Four copies stored in multiple availability zones

   b. Multiple copies stored in Amazon S3 storage

   c. Six copies stored across three availability zones

   d. A single copy

7. Amazon DynamoDB performance is defined using what type of units?

   a. Read units

   b. Capacity units

   c. Write units

   d. Read and write units

8. What type of Amazon DynamoDB table can you create to span multiple AWS regions?

   a. Regional table

   b. Multi-region table

   c. Global table

   d. Amazon DynamoDB table

9. Why is Amazon ElastiCache operationally fast?

   a. It performs execution in RAM.

   b. It executes using SSDs.

    c. The size of the instances selected for the cluster is optimal.

    d. It uses SSDs with maximum IOPS.

10. Which of the following deployments of ElastiCache is not persistent?

    a. Memcached

    b. DAX

    c. Amazon Redis

    d. Amazon DynamoDB

11. Where do Amazon for Redshift continuous backups get stored?

    a. Local hard drives

    b. Leader nodes

    c. Compute nodes

    d. Amazon S3 storage

12. What type of queries can be performed on an Amazon for Redshift cluster?

    a. Python queries

    b. SQL queries

    c. JSON queries

    d. Complex queries

Foundation Topics

AWS Cloud Databases

Amazon offers over 15 database engines to support a variety of data models, including relational, key-value, document, in-memory, graph, time-series, wide-column, and ledger databases. AWS fully managed database services are continually monitored, have self-healing storage, and in many cases offer automated scaling solutions. Databases can be deployed across multiple availability zones and multiple regions. Table 10-2 summarizes the available database types and services at AWS.

Table 10-2   Database Choices at AWS

Database Type	Use Case	AWS Service
Relational	E-commerce, traditional applications, ERP, CRM	Amazon Aurora, Amazon RDS, Amazon Redshift
Key-value	High-performance web applications, e-commerce, gaming systems	Amazon DynamoDB
In-memory	Caching, user session management, gaming leaderboards	Amazon ElastiCache for Memcached, Amazon ElastiCache for Redis, Amazon MemoryDB for Redis
Document	Content management, user profiles	Amazon DocumentDB (with MongoDB compatibility)
Wide-column	Equipment maintenance, fleet management	Amazon Keyspace
Graph	Social networking, recommendation engines	Amazon Neptune
Time-series	IoT applications, DevOps	Amazon Timestream
Ledger	System of record, supply chain, banking transactions	Amazon Ledger Database Services (QLDB)

Amazon Relational Database Service

Databases at AWS can be hosted by several managed database services, the most popular of which is Amazon Relational Database Service (RDS). Amazon RDS hosts a variety of popular relational database engines, as shown in Table 10-3. RDS is a completely managed database service. Focus on your data records and leave the running, monitoring, backup, and failover of your database instances to AWS. If you want to maintain complete control, however, you can build your own EC2 database instances and manage every aspect of your database infrastructure as a self-managed infrastructure as a service (IaaS) deployment by deploying RDS Custom.

Table 10-3 RDS Database Engines

Database Engine	Data Recovery Support	SSL/TLS Support	Replication	Encryption	Real-Time Monitoring	Compliance Support
MariaDB 10.0.1–10.0.6	InnoDB Version 10.2 and XtraDB Versions 10.0 and 10.1	yaSSL, Open SSL, or TLS	Point-in-time restoration	AES-256	Yes	HIPAA
MySQL 5.5–8.0	InnoDB	yaSSL, Open SSL, or TLS	Point-in-time restoration	AES-256	Yes for 5.5 or later	HIPAA, PCI DSS, FedRAMP
SQL Server 2008–2019	All versions support data recovery	SSL	SQL Server database mirroring, SQL Server AlwaysOn	AES-256, TDE	Yes	N/A
Oracle Database 12c and 11g	All versions support data recovery	SSL or NNE	Point-in-time restoration	AES-256, TDE	Yes	N/A
PostgreSQL 9.6, 10–14	All versions support data recovery	SSL	AWS synchronous replication	AES-256	Yes	HIPAA, PHI DSS; FedRAMP
RDS Custom	The Amazon RDS database service supports customization of the underlying operating system and database environment. Customers deploying RDS Custom have access to the database and underlying operating system to configure settings, install patches, and enable native features to meet their organization's applications' requirements. RDS Custom supports the Oracle and SQL Server database engines.					

Thousands of AWS customers have decided that they need databases but don't want to manage the database infrastructure anymore. The essential component that makes up the relational database service hosted by RDS and managed by AWS includes the complete management of the instances hosting your data, automatic backups, synchronous replication from the *primary database* instance to the *standby database* instance, and automatic failover and recovery, as required.

Amazon RDS Database Instances

Under the hood of all Amazon RDS deployments is a familiar compute component: the EC2 instance. When you order an RDS database instance, you order the CPU, memory, storage, and required storage performance (input/output operations per second [IOPS]). These initial selections can also be resized later. RDS supports a variety of standard, memory-optimized, and burstable performance EC2 instances that support Intel hyper-threading technology, which allows multiple threads to run concurrently on a single vCPU core. Threads connect the physical processor on the bare-metal server to the virtual CPUs (vCPUs). AWS RDS pricing supports on-demand and RDS Reserved Instance (RI) pricing. The odds are that you want to use RI pricing because it provides price breaks up to 70%.

Amazon RDS database instance data is stored on Amazon Elastic Block Store (EBS) volumes, which are automatically striped to provide additional performance. EBS volume types can be either general-purpose SSDs, provisioned IOPS SSDs, or magnetic hard drives.

NOTE   Magnetic drives, which are limited to 4 TB, are available for backward compatibility because some customers still use them. For production databases, Amazon does not recommend using magnetic drives.

MySQL, MariaDB, Oracle, and PostgreSQL volumes can be from 20 GB to 64 TiB in size. Microsoft SQL Server is limited to a maximum of 16-TiB EBS storage volumes. General-purpose SSD storage EBS volume uses burst credits, which provide sustained burst performance depending on the size of the volume. Customers can deploy up to 40 Amazon RDS database instances for hosting MySQL, MariaDB, or PostgreSQL databases; these numbers are defined by your AWS account service quota limits and can be increased upon request. For typical production databases, the recommendation is to use EBS data storage volumes with provisioned IOPS, which can be set from 1,000 to 256,000 IOPS, depending on the database engine.

NOTE   For production databases, use Multi-AZ deployments with provisioned IOPS for the primary and standby databases and *read replicas*.

As mentioned earlier, as needs change, you can vertically scale the size of your RDS database compute and resources and also change the size, type, and IOPS of your storage volumes, as shown in Figure 10-1. While changes are being made to a database instance, the database instance being resized is unavailable. Since RDS database instances are hosted and maintained by the Amazon RDS service, there is no direct access to a database instance; AWS carries out the backup, patching, monitoring, and recovery of each RDS instance.

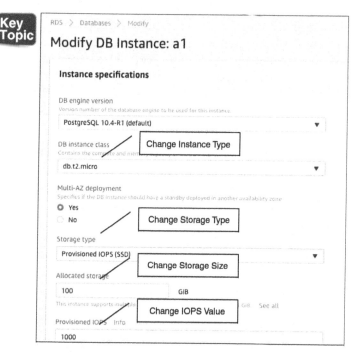

Figure 10-1   Changing Database Instance Parameters

Amazon RDS supports MySQL, MariaDB, PostgreSQL, Oracle, and Microsoft SQL Server database engines. Note that not every version of a supported database engines is supported by Amazon RDS. You must carefully check out the database engine versions that are currently supported and decide whether Amazon RDS suits your requirements.

If you do decide to build and maintain your own database instances, you will have to provision the desired EC2 instance size, attach the appropriate EBS volumes and provisioned IOPS, and define and maintain your own backup and DR schedule. For custom database deployments customers are also responsible for monitoring the database instances and carrying out all the required maintenance, including failover and recovery when required.

Database Instance Class Types

The database instance class you choose determines the amount of compute, memory, and network speed assigned to the RDS instance. Amazon RDS supports three types of instance classes:

- **Standard:** These instance classes range from general-purpose instances optimized for low latency and high random I/O performance and high sequential read throughput. A good modern example to start testing with would be the general-purpose m5 instance, which is hosted by the Nitro hypervisor supporting local NVME SSD storage up to 3.6 TiB with network speeds up to 100 Gbps.

- **Memory optimized:** These instance classes are designed for memory-intensive databases. For example, the r5b instance is powered by the Nitro hypervisor and can deliver up to 60-Gbps bandwidth and 260,000 IOPS of EBS performance.

- **Burstable performance:** These instance classes provide a baseline of performance with the ability to burst to full CPU usage when required. These general-purpose instances may be useful for initial testing purposes.

NOTE   You can review the full specifications for RDS instance classes at https://docs.aws.amazon.com/AmazonRDS/latest/UserGuide/Concepts.DBInstanceClass.html.

High-Availability Design for RDS

Production databases can and should at a minimum utilize Multi-AZ deployments, which provide automatic failover support with the primary database instance located in one AZ and the standby database instance, or instances located in another AZ. The technology used for RDS failover from the primary to a standby instance depends on the database engine that is deployed. Most Amazon RDS deployments use AWS's failover technology; however, Microsoft SQL Server uses SQL Server mirroring to perform failover. Note that Amazon RDS failover design is an active-passive design that will typically take 30–40 seconds to complete the failover process once enabled.

When you order a Multi-AZ RDS deployment, Amazon provisions and maintains the primary and standby replicas in different AZs, as shown in Figure 10-2. The primary database instance data records and any changes are automatically synchronously replicated to the standby replica, ensuring that there are always two copies of up-to-date database data records and data redundancy. The transaction logs are also backed up every 5 minutes. The process of synchronous data replication between the Amazon RDS database instances creates increased write and commit latencies between the primary and the standby instances. Therefore, your Amazon RDS database instances and volumes must be properly sized with the required computer power to be able to perform synchronous replication quickly and reliably without affecting the overall performance required for your database.

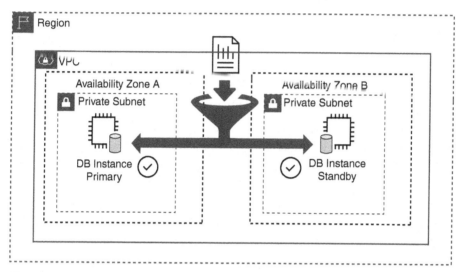

Figure 10-2 RDS Multi-AZ Synchronous Replication

Careful monitoring of both Amazon RDS database instances utilizing CloudWatch metrics such as CPU Utilization, Read Latency, Write Latency, and FreeableMemory help indicate when the existing database instances may need to be resized. Each Amazon RDS metric can be associated to an alarm; for example, an alarm that signals when the database instance CPU utilization exceeds 65%. The Amazon Simple Notification Service (SNS) can notify when a defined alarm threshold is exceeded.

It is important to choose a database instance with adequate storage and speed: either general-purpose SSDs or provisioned IOPS, depending on your production requirements. (IOPS represents how fast your hard drive can read and write per second.) A starting point might be CPU, RAM, and storage values equal to what the database is currently using while running on premises. When deploying Amazon RDS in production, make sure you have allocated enough RAM to each database instance, ensuring that your working data set can reside completely in memory. To test whether your working data set can operate while being completely contained in memory, use the RDS metrics ReadIOPS and WriteIOPS. When your Amazon RDS database instances are under load, both metric values should be less than the allocated IOPS. For further details, check out the RDS documentation, which will help you fine-tune requirements based on the RDS engine you are considering deploying:

https://docs.aws.amazon.com/AmazonRDS/latest/UserGuide/CHAP_
BestPractices.html#CHAP_BestPractices.DiskPerformance

NOTE   For RDS deployments, the standby database instance is treated as a true standby and is not used for any query requests.

The standby database records are kept up to date through synchronous replication from the primary database instance. The standby DB is kept up to date and ready to take over as the primary database when problems occur. To help improve the performance of database queries, additional read replicas can be created for MariaDB, MySQL, Oracle, PostgreSQL, and Microsoft SQL Server engines using AWS RDS. Deploy the read replicas if necessary in a specific AWS region to support additional query requests, and make sure to size the read replica instances the required compute power and storage size. Read replicas can be located in the same AWS region or in a different region from where the primary database is located, depending on your requirements.

A single AZ, two AZs, or a Multi-AZ DB cluster can be selected for deploying the MariaDB, MySQL, Oracle, PostgreSQL, and Microsoft SQL Server engines. Selecting the Multi-AZ cluster option creates a DB cluster with a primary DB instance and at least one standby DB instance deployed in a different AZ. Amazon Aurora is deployed across three AZs per region or as a global database across multiple AWS regions.

The automated Amazon RDS database failover process swings into action when problems occur, such as a failure of the primary database instance or an AZ failure. Failover can also occur when maintenance is being performed, such as when the primary and secondary database instance types are resized, or software patching is required.

When failure occurs, during the failover process, RDS automatically switches over to the standby replica, as shown in Figure 10-3. The standby replica database instance becomes the primary database instance. Route 53, the AWS DNS service, modifies the Amazon RDS *endpoint* to point end users to the new primary database instance (formerly the standby replica); this process should happen quickly, typically within a few minutes. Re-establishing the availability of a new standby database instance might take a bit more time because the standby EC2 instance has to be built and backups (snapshots) will have to be restored. After the new standby replica is re-created, to ensure that all changes have propagated from the primary database to the standby database, Amazon replays the *redo log* from the last database checkpoint, making sure all changes have been applied before the new standby database instance is available. AWS recommends that the time to live (TTL) for the CNAME record of 30 seconds be set at the end user location to ensure a timely failover.

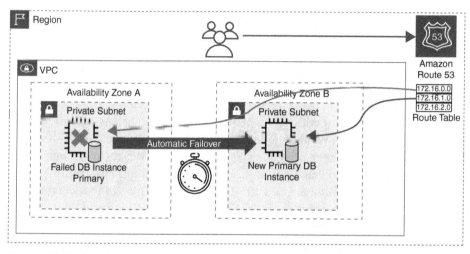

Figure 10-3   RDS Failover

The failover and recovery process isn't magic. It's simply an automated recovery process that Amazon carries out on your behalf. Other real-world issues might also be happening across the network; Amazon Route53 updates or database restorations may result in a longer recovery time than expected.

> **NOTE**   You can create database SNS notifications so that you are notified via text or email when a failover or recovery is under way. In addition, you can configure your Amazon RDS database backups to automatically replicate the associated snapshots and transaction logs to a specific AWS region for safekeeping.

Multi-AZ RDS Deployments

An Amazon RDS Multi-AZ deployment provides additional availability and durability for your data records; after all, with such a deployment, there are at least two database instances running in separate AZs with separate EBS storage volumes. When you order a Multi-AZ database deployment, after the primary database instance is created, Amazon RDS takes a snapshot of the primary database instance's EBS volume and restores it on a newly created standby database replica located in another AZ and then synchronizes the two database instances' database volumes.

Big-Picture RDS Installation Steps

The process for installing a database using Amazon RDS is similar for all the supported database engine types except for Amazon Aurora. After you select the database engine to deploy, choose the database instance details. Table 10-4 details the initial options depending on the database engine selected.

Table 10-4   Initial Amazon RDS Setup Options

Database Instance Setting	Details
License model	Bring your own license (BYOL) or general-purpose license included in the price
Database engine version	Select desired version to deploy
Database instance	Standard, memory-optimized, or burstable performance
Multi-AZ deployment	Synchronous AWS replication service; Native Mirroring or Always On for SQL Server
Multi-AZ DB cluster	DB cluster with a primary DB instance and two readable standby DB instances in different availability zones.
Storage type	SSD, provisioned IOPS, or HDD volumes
Amount of storage to allocate	1–64 TB (based on EBS volume types chosen)
Database instance identifier	Unique identifier, if required by database engine
Primary username and password	For database authentication and access

Table 10-5 shows the advanced database instance options you can configure.

Table 10-5   Advanced Amazon RDS Setup Options

Advanced Database Instance Setting	Details
Database port	The database engine default value
VPC	The virtual private cloud (VPC) to host/link to the database instances
Database subnet group	A predefined subnet for the database instance
Public accessibility	Private by default
Availability zone	The number of AZs to use
Security group	Firewall settings for controlling access to a database instance
Database name	A unique database name
Database port	The default access port of the database engine
Parameter group	A predefined group with a defined database engine, database instance specs, and allocated EBS storage
Option group	Additional features for the database engine, such as encryption

Advanced Database Instance Setting	Details
Copy tags to snapshot	Tags to be added to database snapshots
Encryption	The encryption type, which depends on the database engine deployed
Backup retention	The number of days automatic backups of the database are retained
Backup window	The specific time for database backup
Enhanced monitoring	Gathering of metrics in real time
Log exports	Select logs published to CloudWatch log groups
Auto minor version upgrade	Minor database engine version upgrades that occur automatically
Maintenance window	Defined window to apply database engine modifications

Monitoring Database Performance

Once your Amazon RDS database has been deployed, establish an Amazon Cloud-Watch baseline using AWS RDS metrics to monitor the ongoing performance of the database at different times of the day to establish an acceptable level of operation. You can use the RDS Management Console to select a variety of metrics that allow you to monitor the number of connections to the database instance, read and write operations, and the amount of storage, memory, and CPU being utilized. Table 10-6 lists some of the CloudWatch metrics that can be linked with alarms alerting you when issues occur.

Table 10-6   CloudWatch RDS Metrics

Metric	Description	Reporting	Values
Read I/O per second and write I/O per second	Input and output operations per second	Average read/write per second	IOPS
Read and write latency	Time it took from request to completion	1-minute interval	IOPS
Throughput	Bytes transferred to or from the database volume	1-minute interval	Megabytes per second
Queue depth	I/O requests waiting to be carried out	1-minute interval	From zero to several hundred queue entries

Best Practices for RDS

For the AWS Certified Solutions Architect – Associate (SAA-C03) exam, you need to be aware of a number of best practices related to AWS RDS deployment:

> **NOTE** For real-world deployments, be sure to check the best practices for each database engine by reviewing the documentation from each vendor.

- Define scaling storage capacity limits that allow your MySQL database instance storage to *scale out* as required.

- Match provisioned IOPS storage with the desired EC2 instance for the best performance.

- Monitor your infrastructure with CloudWatch metrics and alarms to ensure that you are notified when you are about to overload your capacity.

- Monitor AWS RDS database performance to define what is acceptable as normal operation. Define baselines for the minimum, maximum, and average values at defined intervals (hourly, one-half day, 7 days, 1 week, and 2 weeks) to create a normal baseline.

- Evaluate performance metrics such as CPU utilization, available memory, amount of free storage space, read/write metrics (IOPS, latency, throughput), network receive and transmit throughput, database connections, high CPU or RAM consumption, and disk space consumption.

- For the best performance, ensure that each AWS RDS database instance has enough allocated RAM so that the working set of the database resides in memory.

- Use AWS Identity and Access Management (IAM) users and groups to control access to AWS RDS resources.

- Use AWS RDS metrics to monitor your memory, CPU, replica lag, and storage usage.

- Enable automatic backups and define the backup window, picking a time when backups will be least disruptive (for example, in the middle of the night).

- For client applications caching the DNS data records of your AWS RDS DB instance, set a TTL value of less than 30 seconds to ensure faster connectivity after a failover has occurred.

- Test the failover process for your AWS RDS DB instances and document how long the failover process takes. Also confirm that the application that regularly accesses your database can automatically connect to the new database instance after failover has occurred.

Amazon Relational Database Service Proxy

Amazon Relational Database Service (RDS) Proxy is a fully managed, highly available database proxy for Amazon RDS that makes it easier to connect to your database from your applications. RDS Proxy can improve the reliability and performance of your database-driven applications by automatically routing connections to the appropriate RDS DB instance, based on connection and workload patterns. It also helps you scale your applications more easily by automatically distributing connections among multiple RDS DB instances. Here are some key benefits of using RDS Proxy:

- **Application availability:** It can automatically failover to a standby RDS DB instance if the primary instance becomes unavailable, ensuring that your application remains available even if the database fails.

- **Better connection performance:** It can cache connections and reuse them for subsequent requests, reducing the overhead of establishing new connections.

- **Application scaling:** It can distribute connections among multiple RDS DB instances, helping you scale your application more easily as demand increases.

- **Enhanced security:** It supports SSL/TLS encryption for connections to your RDS DB instances, helping you protect sensitive data.

To use Amazon RDS Proxy, configure your application to connect to the RDS Proxy endpoint instead of the RDS DB instance (see Figure 10-4). RDS Proxy then routes connections to the appropriate backend RDS DB instance based on the configured routing rules.

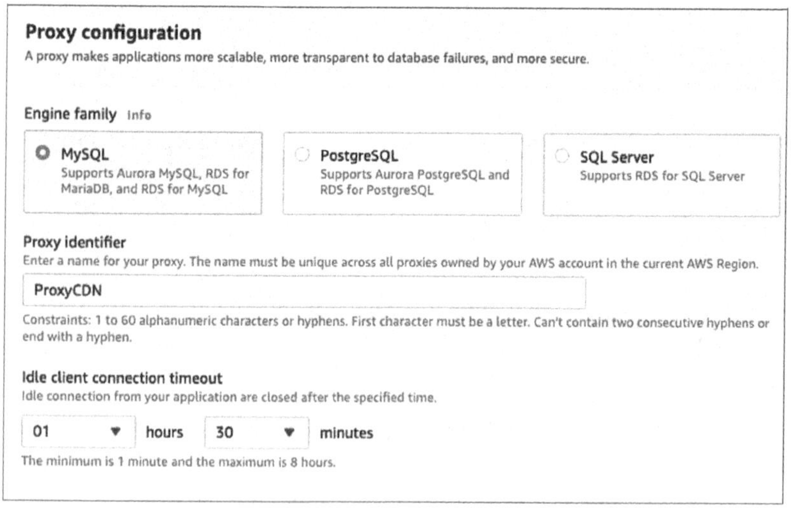

Figure 10-4 RDS Proxy Configuration

Amazon RDS Cheat Sheet

For the AWS Certified Solutions Architect – Associate (SAA-C03) exam, you need to understand the following critical aspects of RDS:

- A database subnet group is a collection of subnets designated for database instance deployment.

- When using encryption at rest, database snapshots, backups, and read replicas are all encrypted.

- With Multi-AZ deployments, you are not charged for synchronous database data replication from the primary database to the standby database in a single AZ or across multiple AZs.

- Changing the DB instance class or adding additional storage can be set to be applied during the specified maintenance window.

- During failover, configuration information, including the updated DNS primary location, is updated to point to the new primary database instance.

- You can have five read replicas for MySQL, Maria, PostgreSQL, and SQL.

- A read replica can be manually promoted to become a primary database instance.

- A restored database is a separate new RDS instance with a new DNS endpoint.

- The AWS Database Migration Service migrates the most widely used commercial and open-source databases to RDS.

Amazon Aurora

Another SQL-type database is Amazon Aurora, a fully compatible MySQL- or PostgreSQL-managed database as a service (DBaaS) solution. If you are currently using either MySQL or PostgreSQL on premises and are considering moving your database to the AWS cloud, Aurora is well worth evaluating. Amazon Aurora provides much faster performance than Amazon RDS MySQL deployments. Amazon Aurora has performance increases of up to five times the throughput of AWS RDS MySQL and three times the throughput of Amazon RDS PostgreSQL. Amazon Aurora achieves this performance by using an SSD virtual SAN cluster storage array that is replicated across three AZs maintaining six copies of data.

The following are features to know about the Amazon Aurora DB engine:

- **Backtracking:** Return the state of an Amazon Aurora cluster to a specific point in time within seconds without having to restore data from a backup.

- **Amazon Aurora Global Database:** A single database consisting of a primary DB cluster in one region and up to five secondary DB clusters in different regions, enabling very low latency reads and recovery from regional outages.

- **Machine learning (ML):** Machine learning models are exposed as SQL functions, using standard SQL queries to build applications that call ML models.

- **Parallel queries:** Parallel queries can speed up queries while maintaining a very high transactional throughput.

- **Aurora Serverless:** Automatically start up, shut down, and scale capacity as required by your application.

When deploying Aurora (see Figure 10-5), there are four choices:

- **Aurora Provisioned:** This is the standard deployment, where the customer defines the database engine (MySQL or PostgreSQL), instance class, and the advanced details of placement, accessibility, encryption, backup, and failover required.

- **Aurora versions that support the parallel query feature:** A single query can be distributed across all the available CPUs in the storage layer to greatly speed up analytical queries. More than 200 SQL functions, equijoins, and projections can run in parallel format.

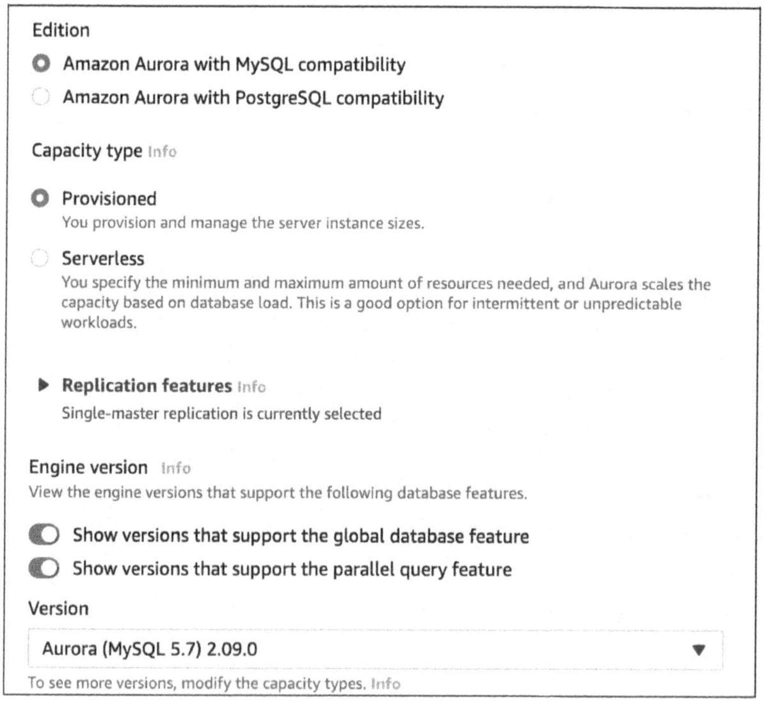

Edition

○ Amazon Aurora with MySQL compatibility

○ Amazon Aurora with PostgreSQL compatibility

Capacity type Info

● Provisioned
You provision and manage the server instance sizes.

○ Serverless
You specify the minimum and maximum amount of resources needed, and Aurora scales the capacity based on database load. This is a good option for intermittent or unpredictable workloads.

▶ **Replication features** Info
Single-master replication is currently selected

Engine version Info
View the engine versions that support the following database features.

⬤ Show versions that support the global database feature

⬤ Show versions that support the parallel query feature

Version

| Aurora (MySQL 5.7) 2.09.0 ▼ |

To see more versions, modify the capacity types. Info

Figure 10-5 Aurora Deployment Options

- **Serverless:** This deployment option supports the MySQL- and PostgreSQL-compatible edition of Amazon Aurora. As mentioned, when a serverless Aurora database cluster is deployed, it operates, and scales based on the minimum and maximum performance requirements that have been defined at creation. When your application enters a period of light or minimal activity, the associated Amazon Aurora database is scaled down to the minimum allocated size but remains online and continues to service application requests, scaling back out as required. When no activity is detected for a prescribed period of time, the Amazon Aurora database is paused, and you are not charged for the inactivity.

Rather than define the database instance class size for the Serverless option, you set the minimum and maximum capacity required. Behind the scenes, the database endpoint points to a fleet of resources that are automatically scaled based on your minimum and maximum requirements. Amazon Aurora Serverless scales up when monitoring reveals capacity constraints at any of the processing or database connections. For example, your serverless database cluster could be defined to scale up if the CPU utilization rises above 60%, or the connections are at more than 80% of the available connections. The Aurora cluster could also scale down if the application load is below 25% utilization and fewer than 30% of the connections are used. Consider a retail environment with multiple branch locations using a centralized point-of-sale system. As more customers enter the store and begin purchasing, the Amazon Aurora database scales up and down based on demand. After hours, after a defined period of inactivity, the Aurora database is paused until the next day. When database connections are requested after an Amazon Aurora database has been paused, resuming the cluster operation will take a few seconds or more. To speed up operations, Amazon Aurora preloads the buffer pool with pages for known common queries stored in an in-memory page cache.

- **Global deployments:** Amazon Aurora deployments are for globally distributed Aurora deployments across multiple AWS regions. Amazon Aurora storage-based replication typically has latency of less than 1 second. In the case of a regional outage, a secondary region can be promoted to read/write capability in less than 1 minute. Typical use cases include financial, travel, or gaming applications that have strict uptime requirements. Up to 16 database instances can be deployed in each AWS region of a globally deployed Amazon Aurora database. Deploying Amazon Aurora as a global database has the following advantages:

  - **Global reads with local latency:** A global deployment keeps the main database updated in the primary AWS region. Users in other regions access the database records from their own secondary cluster hosted in their own AWS region.

■ **Scalable secondary Amazon Aurora DB clusters:** Secondary clusters can be scaled by adding more read-only instances to the secondary AWS region.

Amazon Aurora Storage

When comparing Amazon Aurora to a standard RDS deployment of MySQL, with Aurora deployments there is no need to provision storage in advance for future growth. The internal design of the Amazon Aurora storage engine allows for the automatic scaling of its distributed storage architecture from a starting point of 10 GB up to 64 TB, in 10-GB increments; this storage is spread across multiple SSDs across multiple AZs (see Figure 10-6). As previously mentioned, Amazon Aurora replicates six copies of its data records across three AZs, providing enhanced durability and greater than 99.99% availability.

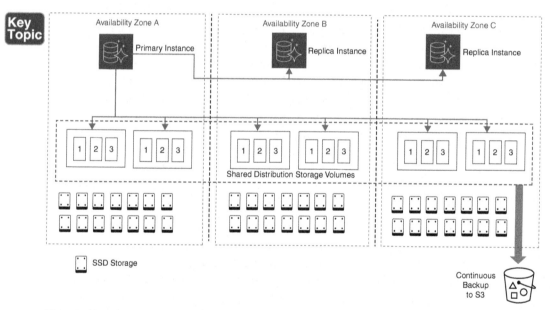

Figure 10-6   Aurora Data Storage Architecture

Amazon Aurora data is stored in a cluster volume, a single virtual volume supported by SSD drives.

Amazon Aurora data records are stored in a shared cluster storage volume of data stored on multiple SSDs across multiple AZs. The cluster quorum deployed across the three AZs includes the six data nodes; the write set is four nodes, and the read set is the two remaining nodes spread across the three AZs. As a result, each AZ has a current copy of the database cluster data.

Aurora performance enhancements are due to the design of the storage plane, which is an SSD-backed virtualized storage array. Aurora has at a minimum a primary database instance DB, and can have up to 15 additional Amazon Aurora DB replicas. To boost the storage durability, the data transaction logs are continuously backed up to Amazon S3 storage.

Amazon Aurora is designed so that the underlying SSD storage nodes that make up Amazon Aurora's shared storage volume are deployed in a cell-like design spread across the three AZs, which helps to limit the size of the blast radius when failures occur. Reads only require three out of six nodes to be available; writes require four out of six nodes to be available. A failure of a single AZ results in four storage volumes still being available to carry out database operations.

Amazon Aurora's cluster design has the primary and replica database instances connecting to the same storage plane. The primary database DB instance carries out the write operations to the cluster volumes in each AZ and offloads the read operations to the available replica database DB instances, as shown in Figure 10-7. This design is different from standard RDS MySQL or PostgreSQL deployments, where standby database instances do not perform read requests.

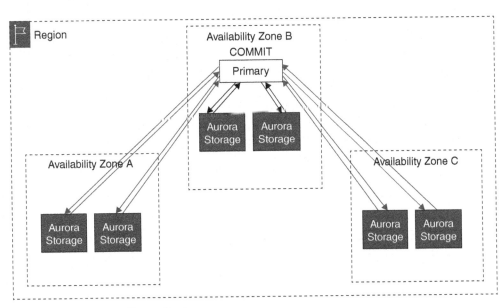

Figure 10-7 Aurora Cluster Design

The Amazon Aurora shared storage architecture results in data records being independent from the DB instances in the cluster; therefore, computation capacity is separated from the storage array. Adding an Amazon Aurora DB instance results in the new DB instance connecting to the shared storage volume that already contains the existing data records. Removing an Amazon Aurora DB instance from the cluster does not remove any existing data from the cluster. Data records remain in the cluster until the entire cluster is deleted.

Amazon Aurora Replication

Each Amazon Aurora DB cluster has automatic built-in replication between the multiple DB instances located in the same cluster. Replication can also be set up with an Amazon Aurora cluster as either the source or the target of the replication.

As you create additional DB instances in an Aurora provisioned DB cluster, replication is automatically set up from the writer DB instance to all the other DB instances in the cluster. These additional DB instances are read-only and are defined as Amazon Aurora Replicas, as reader instances. Amazon Aurora Replicas are fully dedicated to performing read operations, write operations are managed by the primary instance to the cluster volume.

Amazon Aurora Replicas are used for queries that have been issued from the reader endpoint of the cluster, spreading the query load across the available Aurora Replicas in the cluster. If a writer instance in a cluster becomes unavailable, one of the reader instances is automatically promoted to take its place as a writer instance. An Amazon Aurora DB cluster can contain up to 15 Amazon Aurora Replicas, which are distributed across the AZs within a single AWS region. An Auto Scaling policy can be created to automatically add or remove Amazon Aurora Replicas based on the following metrics: Average CPU Utilization or Average Connections of the current Amazon Aurora Replicas.

NOTE To increase the availability of your Amazon Aurora DB cluster, it is recommended that you create at least one or more Amazon Aurora Replicas in two or more availability zones.

The data contained in the Aurora DB cluster volume had its own high-availability and reliability design completely independent from the DB instances in the cluster. The DB cluster volume is physically made up of multiple copies of the data for the cluster; the primary instance and the Amazon Aurora Replicas in the DB cluster see the data in the cluster volume as a single logical volume. As a result, queries have minimal replica lag, usually less than 100 ms after data records have been updated.

If the primary database instance becomes unavailable, there is automatic failover to an Amazon Aurora Replica. You can also define the failover priority for the available Amazon Aurora Replicas.

When failover occurs, the failover process usually takes seconds; the canonical name record (CNAME) is changed to point to the Amazon Aurora replica that has been promoted to be the new primary database.

With Amazon Aurora, you can lose access to two copies of data without affecting the writing process, and you can lose up to three copies of data without affecting the ability to read your data. In the background, Amazon Aurora constantly checks and rechecks the data blocks and discs, performing repairs when necessary, automatically using validated data records from the other volumes in the cluster. Amazon Aurora Replicas can also be created in different AWS regions. The first Amazon Aurora Replica created in a different region acts as the primary Amazon Aurora replica DB in the new region. You can also add Amazon Aurora Replicas in different AWS regions that will then share the same storage plane.

NOTE   Amazon Aurora can also operate with multiple read/write primary database instances deployed across multiple AZs, improving Aurora's high-availability design. If one of the primary database instances fails, other instances in the cluster can take over immediately, maintaining both read and write availability for the cluster.

Communicating with Amazon Aurora

Communication with an Aurora cluster is performed with specific endpoints, as shown in Figure 10-8:

- **Cluster endpoint:** This endpoint to the Amazon Aurora database cluster is a single URL containing a host address and a port address to simplify connectivity to the primary database instance (M in Figure 10-7) for all writes, including insertions, updates, deletions, and changes. When failover occurs, the cluster endpoint automatically points to the new primary database instance.

- **Reader endpoint:** This endpoint connects to one of the available Aurora Replicas (R in Figure 10-8) for the database cluster; if there are multiple Amazon Aurora Replicas, the endpoint uses load balancing to support the read requests. If your Amazon Aurora deployment is small, containing a single primary instance, the reader endpoint services all read requests from the primary database instance.

- **Instance endpoint:** This endpoint points to the current primary database instance (M in Figure 10-8) of the database cluster.

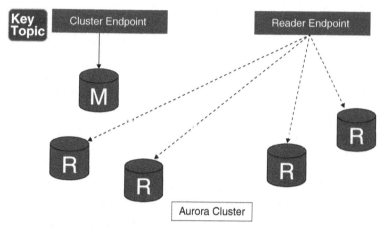

Figure 10-8 Aurora Endpoints

Endpoints can be used to map each connection desired to a specific DB instance. For write statements, directly connect to the primary instance DB. To perform queries, connect to the reader endpoint. Amazon Aurora will automatically load balance the queries among the available Aurora Replicas. Custom endpoints can also be created to connect to a specific instance endpoint (for example, for diagnostics testing).

> **NOTE**   Dow Jones used the AWS Data Migration service to migrate its legacy environment to Amazon Aurora (see https://aws.amazon.com/solutions/case-studies/dow-jones/). It uses a 1-TiB Amazon Aurora cluster that can handle 200 transactions per second. Alfresco used Aurora to scale to more than 1 billion documents with throughput of 3 million transactions per hour.

Amazon Aurora Cheat Sheet

For the AWS Certified Solutions Architect – Associate (SAA-C02) exam, you need to understand the following critical aspects of Amazon Aurora:

- Each Amazon Aurora cluster has a set of compute nodes and a copy of the shared storage volume.

- The storage volume consists of six storage nodes located across three availability zones.

- Each database node in a cluster is also a writer node and can execute read and write statements.

- A database change carried out by a writer node is written to six storage nodes and three availability zones.

- Amazon Aurora scales storage up in 10-GB increments.

- Amazon Aurora can lose two copies of data without affecting database writes.

- Amazon Aurora can have up to 15 read replicas per region.

- Amazon Aurora Serverless is an on-demand auto-scaling Aurora deployment.

- Aurora Serverless scales up and down based on the database requirements.

- Automated backups are stored in S3 storage.

- Amazon Aurora does not support Local Zones.

Amazon DynamoDB

Another popular database service offered by AWS is Amazon DynamoDB. Amazon developed Amazon DynamoDB internally in 2006 and initially started using it to host the familiar shopping cart in the online Amazon store. Amazon DynamoDB was publicly launched as a *NoSQL* database service in 2012, designed for Internet performance at scale for applications hosted at AWS. Today, the Amazon e-commerce store is mostly backed by Amazon DynamoDB and Amazon Aurora. Amazon DynamoDB is a fully managed NoSQL database service providing fast and predictable performance with horizontal scalability across availability zones and regions. Amazon DynamoDB tables can be created for storing and retrieving any amount of data with a very high number of requests. The following are the major Amazon DynamoDB features to know for the AWS Certified Solutions Architect – Associate (SAA-C03) exam:

- **Key-value and document data models:** These data models enable a flexible schema. Each row can have any number of columns at any point in time, allowing customers to easily adapt their table design when requirements change.

- **Amazon DynamoDB Accelerator (DAX):** In-memory cache provides fast read performance for Amazon DynamoDB tables, improving table performance from milliseconds to microseconds at millions of read requests per second.

- **Global tables:** Replicate Amazon DynamoDB table data automatically across multiple AWS regions scaling capacity to match workload requirements, providing single digit millisecond read and write performance within each AWS region.

- **Supports streaming applications:** Capture item-level changes in an Amazon DynamoDB table as a Kinesis data stream. Kinesis Data Streams and Amazon DynamoDB can work together to store and process large amounts of streaming data from Amazon Kinesis in near-real time.

- **Read/write capacity modes:** On-demand capacity modes can manage capacity automatically, or provision capacity with automatic scaling of throughput and storage based on defined capacity limits.

- **Track item data with triggers:** Integrate with AWS Lambda functions with custom triggers when item-level changes are detected.

- **ACID transactions:** Amazon DynamoDB has native service-side support for transactions for multiple items within and across tables. (ACID is described in the section "ACID and Amazon DynamoDB" later in this chapter.)

- **Encryption at rest:** All data is encrypted at rest by default with encryption keys stored in the AWS Key Management service.

- **Point-in-time recovery (PITR):** Continual backups of Amazon DynamoDB table data to Amazon S3 allows organizations to restore table data at any point in time, up to the second, during the preceding 35 days.

- **On-demand backup and restore:** Create full backups of Amazon DynamoDB tables for data archiving of any size.

NOTE For older applications that are designed to use a SQL database, there may be no reason to make any database design changes. AWS has use cases for customers using SQL databases with millions of customers. For newer applications with no legacy concerns or requirements, a nonrelational database such as Amazon DynamoDB might be a consideration.

Amazon DynamoDB has been designed as a NoSQL database service that doesn't follow the same rules as a standard SQL database, as outlined in Table 10-7.

Table 10-7 SQL and Amazon DynamoDB Comparison

Feature	SQL Server	Amazon DynamoDB
Database type	Relational database management system (RDBMS)	NoSQL database management system
Structure	Tables with rows and columns	Collection of JavaScript Object Notation (JSON) documents (key/value pairs)
Schema	Predefined	Dynamic
Scale	Vertical	Horizontal
Language	SQL structured	JavaScript

Feature	SQL Server	Amazon DynamoDB
Performance	Good for online analytical processing (OLAP)	Built for online transaction processing (OLTP) at scale
Optimization	Optimized for storage	Optimized for read/write
Query type	Real-time ad hoc queries	Simple queries

With an SQL database, there is a defined set of data rules, called the *schema*, which could be one or more interlinked tables, columns, data types, views, procedures, relationships, or primary keys. With SQL, the database rules are defined *before* any data is entered into the rows and columns of the relational databases table, according to the rules of **Structured Query Language (SQL)**.

In contrast, Amazon DynamoDB stores its data in tables but doesn't follow the same rules as a relational database. First, its data is stored in structured JSON key/value data values. There's more to Amazon DynamoDB than just a simple table, but before we get to those details, let's first think about databases and why we store data there. Databases keep our precious data safe, secure, and reliable. Relational databases have stored and secured our data reliably for years. And some relational databases at AWS can now automatically scale their compute performance and data storage; for example, Aurora Serverless can scale on demand, and all versions of Aurora scale data records automatically. At AWS, some of the infrastructure architecture designs between Amazon Aurora and Amazon DynamoDB are similar, even if the use cases are different.

NOTE   When Amazon looked at how its data operations on its internal Oracle databases were being carried out internally at AWS, it found the following:

- 70% of the queries were single SQL queries against the primary key of a single table with a single row of information being delivered.
- 20% of the queries were queries against multiple rows of a single table.
- 10% of the queries were complex relational queries.

This information helped Amazon realize that Amazon DynamoDB could completely replace its Oracle databases—a task that it mostly completed in 2019.

Amazon DynamoDB Tables

An Amazon DynamoDB table stores data as groups of attributes, also known as *items*. This concept is similar to the rows and columns found in other relational databases. Each item stored in an Amazon DynamoDB database can be stored and retrieved using a primary key that uniquely identifies each item in the table.

When you construct a table in Amazon DynamoDB, you must define a primary key. In Figure 10-9, the primary key is station_id. A hash value is computed for the primary key, and the data in the table is divided into multiple partitions, each linked to the primary key hash for the table; in this case, it's station_id. You can also choose to have a secondary index, such as LastName.

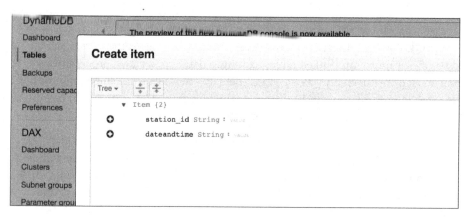

Figure 10-9   An Amazon DynamoDB Table

Provisioning Table Capacity

Amazon DynamoDB performance is defined in terms of *capacity unit* sizes:

- A single read capacity unit (RCU) means a strongly consistent read per second, or two eventually consistent reads per second for items up to 4 KB in size.

- A single write capacity unit (WCU) means a strongly consistent write per second for items up to 1 KB in size.

Amazon DynamoDB table design has a default level of read and write capacity units, as shown in Figure 10-10. A design might require only a defined amount of read and write performance because your tables could initially be small. The default provision capacity is five RCUs and five WCUs. However, over time, your design needs might change, and you might have to—or wish to—scale your table performance to a much higher level. With Amazon DynamoDB, you can make changes to the read and write capacity units for your table by switching from the default provisioned read/write capacity to on-demand and quickly adjusting the amount of scale that your application and, therefore, your Amazon DynamoDB table, require.

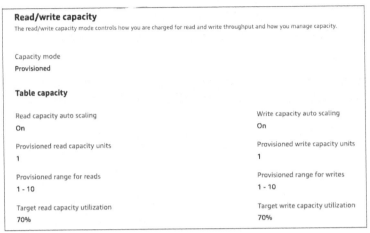

Read/write capacity

The read/write capacity mode controls how you are charged for read and write throughput and how you manage capacity.

Capacity mode
Provisioned

Table capacity

Read capacity auto scaling	Write capacity auto scaling
On	On
Provisioned read capacity units	Provisioned write capacity units
1	1
Provisioned range for reads	Provisioned range for writes
1 - 10	1 - 10
Target read capacity utilization	Target write capacity utilization
70%	70%

Figure 10-10 Adjusting Table Capacity

With Amazon DynamoDB, you can define both RCUs and WCUs for a table; the RCU value indicates how many reads you need per second for your table, and the WCU value indicates how many writes you need per second. A single read allows you to read up to 4 KB of data. If your object is under 4 KB, then a single read allows you to gather all the information; a 20-KB object would need 5 RCUs to perform the full read of the object. The same math applies to WCUs.

If you provision 300 RCUs for a table, Amazon DynamoDB splits up the reads across the three storage partitions. RCUs work on a system using the available tokens for the required read performance. Each token bucket has a *fill rate* that matches the defined RCUs. Say that the token bucket is refilled at the RCU rate of 100 tokens per second, ensuring that the table has enough tokens for the requested performance. Tokens are emptied from the token bucket at the rate of one token per read request. The number of tokens deducted from the bucket depends on the number of read requests and the size of the item read. The larger the item, the more tokens that are required to read the entire item.

When a read request is performed, if there are no tokens left in the token bucket, the read request is throttled. To get around this problem, the token bucket also has a burst token added to your bucket, which is calculated based on the rate of the number of provisioned RCUs multiplied by 300. This equals 5 minutes of additional performance at your defined RCU baseline; for spikes in read and write traffic to your table, you have up to 5 minutes of performance credits available to handle the increased load. When your Amazon DynamoDB table is not being read or written to, burst tokens are being added to your token bucket, up to a maximum of 30,000 tokens.

If you need to exceed read and write capacity throughput units higher than the maximum of 40,000, you can contact Amazon directly to request the desired unit increase.

Adaptive Capacity

To solve the problem of a table being throttled when it runs out of burst credits, Amazon DynamoDB has introduced a feature called *adaptive capacity* that increases the fill rate to the token bucket based on several parameters: the traffic to the table, the provisioned RCU capacity, the throttling rate, and the current multiplier. Adaptive capacity also provides additional burst tokens, so you have a longer period for bursting and don't run out of tokens as quickly as you would if adaptive capacity were not enabled. There are still limits to how many burst credits you get, which is why Amazon DynamoDB introduced Auto scaling.

Auto scaling, as shown in Figure 10-11, allows you to set lower and upper limits of performance capacity and a desired level of utilization. Amazon DynamoDB metrics for monitoring table performance and alarms are defined to alert Auto scaling when additional or less performance capacity is required for table reads and writes.

Figure 10-11 Amazon DynamoDB Auto Scaling Settings

Let's consider an example of a gaming company that uses Amazon DynamoDB as its database for millions of gamers. The information pieces that are being stored (such as game scores) are small, but potentially millions of scores need to be stored at scale. Data is stored in Amazon DynamoDB by first issuing a **PUT** request that is sent to a request router, which checks with the authentication services to see if the requested task is allowed. If everything checks out with security, the request is sent to the Amazon DynamoDB storage services, which determine where to first write the items to disk and then replicate to the other storage nodes. Amazon DynamoDB employs hundreds of thousands of request routers and storage nodes, following a cell-based architecture design, to limit when failures occur by storing request routers and storage nodes in multiple partitions and AZs throughout the AWS region, as shown in Figure 10-12.

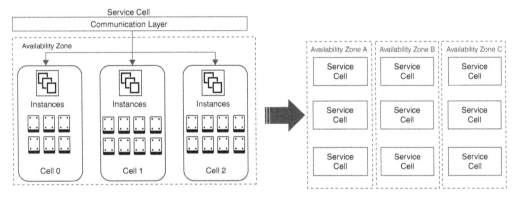

Figure 10-12   Amazon DynamoDB Cell-Based Design

Data Consistency

Because data is written into three partition locations across each AZ, data is not initially consistent in all storage partitions; however, after some time, all data locations across all AZs will be consistent. With Amazon DynamoDB, you have a choice of how consistent you want your data to be:

- **Strongly consistent:** If you want your data to be strongly consistent, a strongly consistent read produces a result from the storage nodes that performed a successful write of the information being requested.

- **Eventually consistent:** If you want your data to be eventually consistent, the leader node makes a random decision about which of the storage nodes that are hosting the partition to read from.

The odds are that you will get a consistent read even with eventual consistency because two storage partitions out of the three will always contain up-to-date data. Typically, the single storage node that is not consistent with the other two nodes is only milliseconds away from being up to date. One of the associated storage nodes will be assigned as the leader node—that is, the node that performs the first data write.

Once two of the associated storage nodes have acknowledged a successful write process, the leader storage node communicates with the request router that the write process is successful, and that router passes that information back to the application and the end user.

Each **PUT** request talks to the leader node first. Then the data is distributed across the AZs, as shown in Figure 10-13. The leader node is always up to date, as is one of the other storage nodes because there must be an acknowledgment that the **PUT** is successful in storage locations for a write process to be successful.

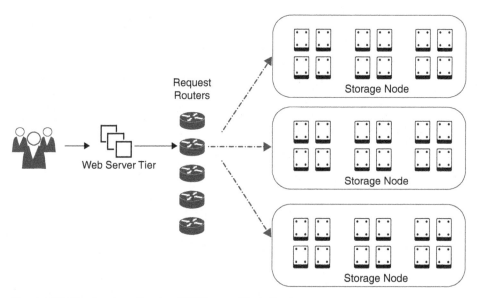

Figure 10-13   Amazon DynamoDB Storage Node Design

Paxos is the defined technical method to get the multiple storage systems to agree on a particular leader for the peer storage nodes. The leader storage node is always up to date. The leader and the peer storage nodes are also joined with a heartbeat that fires every 1.5 seconds with the associated storage peers. If the peer storage nodes fall out of sync with the leader storage node, an election is performed, and one of the peer storage nodes becomes the new leader node.

The request routers are themselves stateless devices; any selected request router communicates with the leader node of the associated storage partition where your database is located.

As your Amazon DynamoDB database table scales in size, the internal design ensures predictable performance through a process called ***burst capacity***. When partitions start to get overloaded, the partition is automatically split into multiple partitions so that the current read and write capacity units are spread across the available partitions to be able to better serve the required reads and writes of the Amazon DynamoDB table.

ACID and Amazon DynamoDB

Relational databases promise and deliver great reliability in the exact content of the data being stored. Relational database transactions achieve extremely high levels of storage consistency due to design principles such as ACID, which states that your database transactions have a high level of validity due to the properties of atomicity, consistency, isolation, and durability. The *ACID* standard has been adopted for years by relational database engines such as Oracle, MySQL, PostgreSQL, and SQL Server. Transactions follow the ACID principles as a single process with four conditional variables:

- *Atomicity:* Each database transaction completes successfully, or it's not accepted.

- **Consistency:** Database transactions are successfully written to disk and validated.

- *Isolation:* Database transactions are isolated and secure during processing.

- **Durability:** Database transactions are committed to persistent storage and logged.

Amazon DynamoDB also supports ACID across tables hosted within a single or multiple AWS regions. Two internal Amazon DynamoDB operations handle these transactions:

- **TransactWriteItems:** A batch write operation with multiple **PUT**, **UPDATE**, and **DELETE** item operations that check for specific conditions that must be satisfied before updates are approved.

- **TransactGetItems:** A batch read operation with one or more **GET** item operations. If a **GET** item request collides with an active write transaction of the same item type, the read transactions are canceled.

With replicated Amazon DynamoDB data, the records must also be exact copies stored on the primary and standby database instances. The process of data replication *can* be fast, but updating replicated data records always takes some time, and the process of verification takes additional time.

Global Tables

An Amazon DynamoDB global table is multiple synchronized copies of a local Amazon DynamoDB table with the same data records replicated across multiple AWS regions, as shown in Figure 10-14. Data is transferred from one AWS region to another using a synchronized replication engine in the source and destination AWS regions. AWS IAM service-linked roles ensure that the proper level of security is enforced when writing records to the global Amazon DynamoDB table partitions.

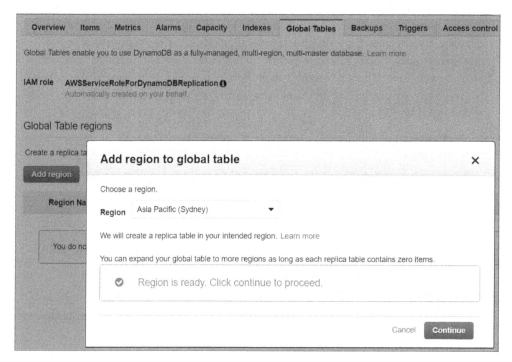

Figure 10-14   Amazon DynamoDB Global Tables

This can be useful for a variety of reasons, such as reducing latency for users in different regions, improving the availability of your data in the event of a region-wide outage, and enabling disaster recovery.

To set up global tables, first create a table in a primary region and then specify one or more secondary regions. Once the global table is set up, DynamoDB automatically replicates updates made to the table in the primary region to the secondary regions.

First, the local replication engine compiles all the **PUT**, **UPDATE**, and **DELETE** items in the local copy of the primary Amazon DynamoDB table. Next, the local changes are replicated across the private AWS network to the secondary Amazon

DynamoDB table in the destination AWS region. Global tables are replicated and updated in all region locations; updates first performed in one region are then updated in the other AWS regions. The outbound and inbound replication engines determine what updates are local, what updates need to be shipped outbound to the other linked copies of the Amazon DynamoDB table, and what updates need to be accepted inbound from other regions. Inbound replicated updates are compared using version numbers and millisecond timestamps to ensure *data consistency* is maintained across the Amazon DynamoDB global table, using a process called last-write conflict resolution; if the timestamps are the same, the local AWS region where changes were last initiated is proclaimed the winner. The data in the secondary regions is eventually consistent with the primary region, which means that it may take some time for the data to be fully replicated.

Amazon DynamoDB Accelerator

You can increase Amazon DynamoDB response times to eventually consistent data levels with microsecond latency by adding an in-memory cache to the design. E-commerce online sales, applications with read-intensive needs, and applications performing in-depth analysis over a long-term time frame are some of the use cases that can take advantage of Amazon DynamoDB Accelerator (DAX). Your DAX cluster, once provisioned, will be hosted in the VPC of your choice. Applications can use the DAX cluster after the DAX client is installed on the EC2 instances hosting the associated application.

DAX can be designed to be highly available, with multiple DAX nodes hosted across multiple AZs within an AWS region, and can scale out up to ten replicas. Read operations that DAX responds to include **GetItem**, **BatchGetItem**, **Query**, and **Scan** API calls. Write operations are first written to the table and then to the DAX cluster. Write operations include **BatchWriteItem**, **UpdateItem**, **DeleteItem**, and **PutItem** API calls.

Backup and Restoration

Amazon DynamoDB provides several options for backing up and restoring table data, allowing organizations to protect their data from accidental deletion or corruption and recover from data loss or data corruption. There are two options for Amazon DynamoDB backup:

- **Point-in-time recovery (PITR) backup:** This option allows you to restore your Amazon DynamoDB table to any point in time up to 35 days. This is a fixed maximum value of retention and cannot be changed. A point-in-time restore point can be chosen up to 1 second before the current time. Once PITR has been enabled for Amazon DynamoDB, continuous backups are performed to controlled S3 storage.

■ **On-demand backup:** This option allows you to create full backups of Amazon DynamoDB tables for long-term storage. An on-demand backup is created asynchronously, applying all changes that are made to a snapshot stored in S3 storage. Each on-demand backup backs up the entire Amazon DynamoDB table data each time.

A restored table, regardless of the backup type, includes local and global secondary indexes, encryption settings, and the provisioned read and write capacity of the source table at the time of restoration. After a table has been restored you must manually re-create any Auto scaling policies, IAM policies, tags, and TTL settings that were previously applied to the backed-up table.

 Amazon DynamoDB Cheat Sheet

For the AWS Certified Solutions Architect – Associate (SAA-C03) exam, you need to understand the following critical aspects of Amazon DynamoDB:

- Amazon DynamoDB supports both key/value and document data models.

- Amazon DynamoDB Global tables replicate your data across AWS regions.

- Amazon DynamoDB automatically scales capacity to match your workload demands.

- Amazon Kinesis Data Streams can capture item-level changes in your Amazon DynamoDB table as a Kinesis data stream.

- Amazon DynamoDB has two capacity modes: On-demand and Provisioned.

- Amazon DynamoDB performs automatic scaling of throughput and storage.

- Amazon DynamoDB triggers integrate with AWS Lambda functions when item-level changes occur in an Amazon DynamoDB table.

- Amazon DynamoDB supports ACID transactions.

- Amazon DynamoDB encrypts data at rest by default.

- Amazon DynamoDB supports point-time recovery up to the second, up to 35 days.

Amazon ElastiCache

To improve the performance of existing applications and supported databases, you can deploy **Amazon ElastiCache**, a fully managed in-memory caching service supporting Amazon ElastiCache for Redis, Amazon ElastiCache for Redis—Global Datastore, and Amazon ElastiCache for Memcached.

Amazon ElastiCache is designed to improve application performance by reducing the reads and writes to persistent storage and directing the traffic to an in-memory cache. Common uses include deploying ElastiCache as a read-only database replica or storage queue or as an in-memory read/write NoSQL database.

Amazon ElastiCache for Memcached

ElastiCache for Memcached is a Memcached-compatible in-memory key-value store service that can be used as either a cache or a data store:

- As a cache, ElastiCache for Memcached helps increase throughput and decrease access latency from RDS deployments or NoSQL databases such as Amazon DynamoDB.

- As a session store, ElastiCache for Memcached can be deployed using the Memcached hash table, which can be distributed across multiple nodes.

ElastiCache for Memcached use cases include application caching for database performance as an in-memory cache and session stores. ElastiCache for Memcached uses EC2 instances as nodes, and each node utilizes a fixed chunk of secure network-attached RAM running as an instance of Memcached deployment. ElastiCache for Memcached nodes are deployed in clusters, and each cluster is a collection of one single node or up to 40 nodes. For additional fault tolerance, place your Memcached nodes in select AZs across the AWS region. Features of ElastiCache for Memcached include the following:

- Automatic recovery from cache node failures

- Automatic discovery of nodes added or removed within a cluster

- Availability zone placement of nodes and clusters

One of the key features of ElastiCache for Memcached is the ability to deploy cache clusters across multiple AZs within a region (see Figure 10-15). Deploying a cache cluster across multiple AZs can improve the availability and durability of the cache. If one AZ becomes unavailable due to a failure or maintenance event, the cache cluster can continue to operate from the remaining AZs. This can help ensure that your application remains available and responsive even in the event of an infrastructure failure.

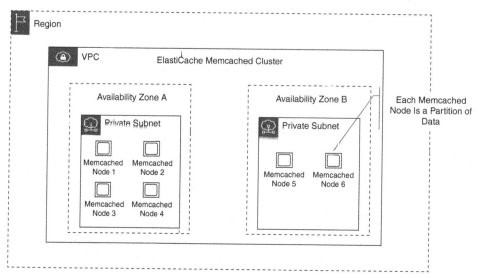

Figure 10-15   ElastiCache for Memcached Cluster

Amazon ElastiCache for Memcached Cheat Sheet

For the AWS Certified Solutions Architect – Associate (SAA-C03) exam, you need to understand the following critical aspects of ElastiCache for Memcached caches:

- ElastiCache for Memcached does not provide persistent data storage.

- Each node represents a partition of data.

- ElastiCache for Memcached cannot be used as a data store.

- ElastiCache for Memcached scales out and in through the addition and removal of nodes.

- ElastiCache for Memcached can be deployed as a read replica for RDS and Amazon DynamoDB databases.

- ElastiCache for Memcached is useful for storing users' session state.

- ElastiCache for Memcached does not support multi-region failover or replication.

- Local Zones are supported for ElastiCache clusters.

Amazon ElastiCache for Redis

Amazon ElastiCache for Redis is a fully managed in-memory cache service that makes it easy to deploy and operate a distributed cache environment in the cloud.

It is based on the popular open-source Redis cache engine and enables you to store and retrieve data from memory using the Redis data model.

ElastiCache for Redis is well suited for use cases that require fast data access and low latencies, such as real-time analytics, gaming, and social media. It can be used to cache frequently accessed data in memory, which can significantly improve the performance of applications that rely on databases or other persistent storage systems.

ElastiCache for Redis would be a good choice for storing user state session state for a user session; the user session information needs to be stored, but not for the long term, as shown in Figure 10-16. Rather than storing the user session information on the web instance that the user is connecting to, you store the user information in an in-memory cache; if the web instance fails, when the user is routed to another web instance, the user session information is still held in the memory cache and remains available for the duration of the user session.

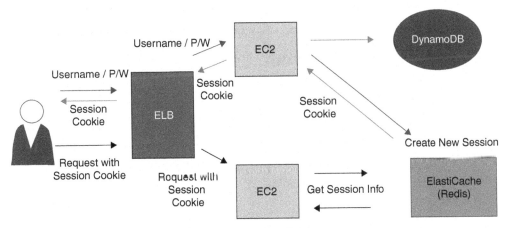

Figure 10-16 User State Information Stored in ElastiCache

Features of ElastiCache for Redis include the following:

- ElastiCache for Redis has automatic recovery from cache node failures.

- Multi-AZ deployment is supported for ElastiCache for Redis cluster nodes.

- ElastiCache for Redis cache data can be partitioned up to 500 shards.

- ElastiCache for Redis supports encryption in transit and encryption at rest, with authentication for HIPAA-compliant workloads.

- ElastiCache for Redis manages backups, software patching, failure detection, and recovery.

Amazon ElastiCache for Redis Cheat Sheet

For the AWS Certified Solutions Architect – Associate (SAA-C03) exam, you need to understand the following critical aspects of ElastiCache for Redis caches:

- Redis is widely adopted as an in-memory data store for use as a database, cache, message broker, or queue.

- The ElastiCache for Redis data store is persistent.

- ElastiCache for Redis can be used as a data store.

- ElastiCache for Redis scales through the addition of shards, which is a grouping of one to six related nodes.

- Each multiple-node shard has one read–write primary node and one to five replica nodes.

- Nodes are charged on a pay-as-you-go basis or reserved nodes.

- ElastiCache for Redis supports automatic and manual backups to S3.

- Maximum backup retention limit is 35 days.

- ElastiCache for Redis supports automatic detection and recovery from cache node failures.

- ElastiCache for Redis autoscaling allows you to increase or decrease the desired shards or replicas automatically.

- Redis Version 3.2 and later supports encryption in transit and at rest for HIPAA-compliant applications.

ElastiCache for Redis: Global Datastore

ElastiCache for Redis provides a fast and secure cross-region replication designed for real-time applications such as media streaming, real-time analytics, and gaming operating with a global footprint across multiple AWS regions. The Global Datastore supports cross-region replication latency under 1 second between primary and secondary clusters. A multiple-region deployment of the Global Datastore provides geo-local reads closer for end users operating in each AWS region. The global data store consists of a primary active cluster which accepts writes that are then replicated to all secondary clusters within the defined Global Datastore, as shown in Figure 10-17. The primary cluster also accepts read requests.

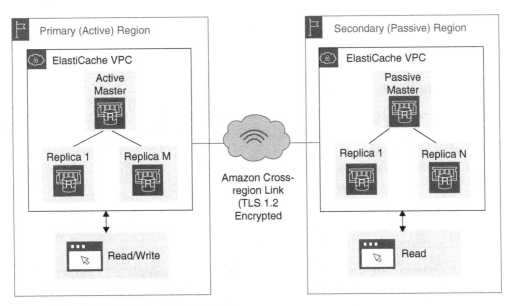

Figure 10-17   ElastiCache Global Data Store

A secondary cluster accepts only read requests and replicated data updates from the associated primary active cluster. Secondary clusters must be located in a different AWS region than the primary cluster; data records are replicated from the primary active cluster to the secondary cluster using automatic asynchronous replication. Designs using remote replica clusters in other AWS regions with synchronized data records help reduce data latency by serving geo-local reads across each region.

Amazon Redshift

Amazon Redshift is a SQL-based data warehouse service that allows you to analyze your data by using standard SQL and business intelligence (BI) tools and standard Microsoft Open Database Connectivity (ODBC) and Java Database Connectivity (JDBC) connections. Redshift is designed as an online analytical processing (OLAP) database service that allows you to run complex analytical queries against petabytes of data.

An organization might use Redshift when you need to pull data sets together from many different sources, such as inventory, financial, and retail systems. In comparison, Amazon EMR is designed for the processing of extremely large data sets, such as for machine learning or streaming data, using data processing frameworks such as Spark or Hadoop.

Redshift uses *columnar data storage*, where data records are stored sequentially in columns instead of rows; this makes it ideal for data warehousing storage and analytics. This format of data storage allows a very high level of parallel processing across all data stores, resulting in enhanced query performance. Less storage space is required due to the high level of compression of the data stores.

Data storage and queries are distributed across all nodes, which are high-performance local disks attached to the supported EC2 instance nodes shown in Figure 10-18. Each Redshift node is a minimum of 128 TB of managed storage across a two-node cluster. Depending on the instance size chosen, clusters range from 160 GB up to 5 PB. Choices for instances include the following options:

- **RA3 nodes:** Data is stored in a separate storage layer that can be scaled independently of compute. The data warehouse is sized based on the query performance required.

- **Dense Compute (DC):** High-performance requirements for less than 500 GB of data can utilize fast CPUs, large amounts of RAM, and SSD drives.

- **Dense Storage (DS2):** Create large data warehouses with a lower price point using HDDs with three-year-term reserved instances (RIs).

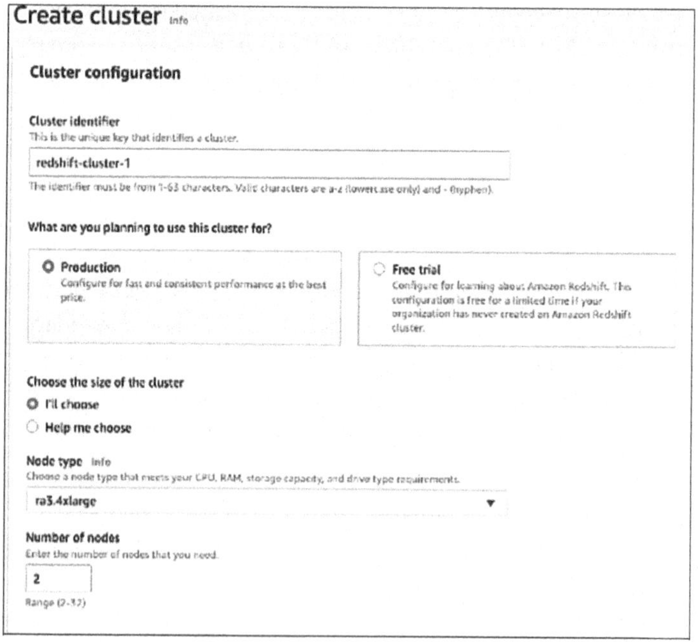

Figure 10-18   Creating a Redshift Cluster

The multimode design of a Redshift cluster includes both leader and compute nodes:

- **Leader nodes:** These nodes manage client connections and receive and coordinate the execution of queries. However, the queries themselves are performed by the compute nodes.

- **Compute nodes:** These nodes store all data records and perform all queries under the direction of the leader nodes. All compute work is performed in parallel, including queries, data ingestion, backups, and restores.

The size of a cluster can be automated using a feature called Concurrency Scaling, where Redshift adds additional cluster capacity as required to support an unlimited number of concurrent users and queries.

Redshift supports identity federation and SAML single sign-on, multifactor authentication, and additional security by hosting the Redshift cluster in an AWS VPC. Data encryption is supported using AWS Key Management Service (KMS).

To ensure data availability, Redshift replicates your data within your defined data warehouse cluster and continually backs up your data to Amazon S3 using snapshots. Redshift maintains three copies of your data:

- The original copy of data

- A replica copy that is stored on compute nodes in the cluster

- A backup copy that is stored in Amazon S3 and can be retained for 1 to 35 days

Redshift also supports SSL/TLS encryption in transit from the client application to the Redshift warehouse cluster.

NOTE   The Amazon Redshift Spectrum feature allows you to run SQL queries directly against exabytes of unstructured data stored in S3 data lakes.

Amazon Redshift Cheat Sheet

For the AWS Certified Solutions Architect – Associate (SAA-C03) exam, you need to understand the following critical aspects of Amazon Redshift:

- Redshift ML can use SQL statements to train Amazon SageMaker models on data stored in Redshift.

- Advanced Query Accelerator (AQUA) allows Redshift to run up to ten times faster.

- RedShift Spectrum can be used to run queries against petabytes of stored Redshift data in S3.

- Redshift supports end-to-end encryption.

- Redshift can be hosted inside a VPC to isolate your data warehouse cluster in your own virtual network.

- Redshift can be integrated with AWS Lake Formation, which allows you to set up a secure data lake to store your data both in its original form and prepared for analysis.

Exam Preparation Tasks

As mentioned in the section "How to Use This Book" in the Introduction, you have a couple of choices for exam preparation: the exercises here, Chapter 16, "Final Preparation," and the exam simulation questions in the Pearson Test Prep Software Online.

Review All Key Topics

Review the most important topics in the chapter, noted with the Key Topic icon in the margin of the page. Table 10-8 lists these key topics and the page number on which each is found.

Table 10-8   Chapter 10 Key Topics

Key Topic Element	Description	Page Number
Table 10-2	Database Choices at AWS	481
Figure 10-1	Changing Database Instance Parameters	484
Section	High-Availability Design for RDS	485
Table 10-4	Initial Amazon RDS Setup Options	489
Section	Best Practices for RDS	491
Section	Amazon RDS Cheat Sheet	493
Figure 10-6	Aurora Data Storage Architecture	496
Figure 10-8	Aurora Endpoints	500
Section	Amazon Aurora Cheat Sheet	500
Table 10-7	SQL and Amazon DynamoDB Comparison	502
Figure 10-10	Adjusting Table Capacity	505

Key Topic Element	Description	Page Number
Figure 10-11	Amazon DynamoDB Auto Scaling Settings	506
Section	Amazon DynamoDB Cheat sheet	512
Section	Amazon ElastiCache for Memcached Cheat Sheet	514
Section	Amazon ElastiCache for Redis Cheat Sheet	516
List	Leader nodes and compute nodes	519
Section	Amazon Redshift Cheat Sheet	519

Define Key Terms

Define the following key terms from this chapter and check your answers in the glossary:

primary database, standby database, read replica, endpoint, scale out, NoSQL, Structured Query Language (SQL), capacity units, burst capacity, ACID, data consistency, Amazon ElastiCache

Q&A

The answers to these questions appear in Appendix A. For more practice with exam format questions, use the Pearson Test Prep Software Online.

1. What is the advantage of using Amazon RDS to set up a database?

2. What is the disadvantage of using Amazon RDS to set up a database?

3. How can read replicas help improve database performance?

4. What two options are available at AWS for hosted databases with global multi-region solutions?

5. What is the difference between eventual consistency and strong consistency?

6. How does Amazon Aurora have an advantage over a standard MySQL deployment with Amazon RDS?

7. Where are continuous backups stored for all AWS database servers?

8. What is an advantage of using Amazon ElastiCache for Redis to store user state?

This chapter covers the following topics:

- Amazon CloudFront
- AWS Global Accelerator
- Elastic Load Balancing Service
- AWS VPC Networking
- Subnets
- IP Address Types
- Connectivity Options

This chapter covers content that's important to the following exam domain and task statement:

Domain 3: Design High-Performing Architectures

> Task Statement 4: Determine high-performing and/or scalable network architectures

CHAPTER 11

High-Performing and Scalable Networking Architecture

Domain 3 focuses on designing high-performing and scalable networking solutions for a workload. The network services that support hosted workloads that can adapt and scale include Amazon CloudFront, Amazon's content delivery network (CDN) service, designed to deliver high performance to end users across the globe in milliseconds. The AWS Global Accelerator provides improved application performance and availability using edge locations and the AWS global network. The Elastic Load Balancing (ELB) service also assists in delivering applications to end users with high availability and automatic scaling built in. Connectivity options for clients connecting to AWS include AWS Virtual Private Network connections, AWS Client VPN, or high-speed connections using AWS Direct Connect direct connections. Finally, all hosted workloads will reside on a logically isolated virtual private network (VPN); subnet options, IP addresses, and virtual private cloud (VPC) connectivity options are also covered in this chapter.

NOTE Network connection options, Direct Connect, and AWS VPN connections are covered in Chapter 4, "Designing Secure Workloads and Applications," which covers Domain 1, "Design Secure Architectures," Task Statement 2, "Design secure workloads and applications."

"Do I Know This Already?"

The "Do I Know This Already?" quiz enables you to assess whether you should read this entire chapter thoroughly or jump to the "Exam Preparation Tasks" section. If you doubt your answers to these questions or your own assessment of your knowledge of the topics, read the entire chapter. Table 11-1 lists the major headings in this chapter and their corresponding "Do I Know This Already?" quiz questions. You can find the answers in Appendix A, "Answers to the 'Do I Know This Already?' Quizzes and Q&A Sections."

Table 11-1   "Do I Know This Already?" Section-to-Question Mapping

Foundation Topics Section	Questions
Amazon CloudFront	1, 2
AWS Global Accelerator	3, 4
Elastic Load Balancing Service	5, 6
AWS VPC Networking	7, 8
Subnets	9, 10
IP Address Types	11, 12
Connectivity Options	13, 14

CAUTION   The goal of self-assessment is to gauge your mastery of the topics in this chapter. If you do not know the answer to a question or are only partially sure of the answer, you should mark that question as wrong for purposes of the self-assessment. Giving yourself credit for an answer you correctly guess skews your self-assessment results and might provide you with a false sense of security.

1. What is the purpose of deploying Amazon CloudFront?

    a. To speed up video compression

    b. To deliver shared data files to multiple servers

    c. To cache data files close to end users

    d. To secure data access

2. What special user makes content accessible only from CloudFront?

    a. AWS IAM user

    b. AWS account Root user

    c. Origin Access Identity (OAI)

    d. AWS IAM role

3. What network is utilized by AWS Global Accelerator to speed up application access?

    a. The public Internet

    b. AWS private network

    c. AWS Direct Connect

    d. AWS VPN connection

4. What kind of static IP addresses are assigned by AWS Global Accelerator?

    a. Elastic IP addresses

    b. Global IP addresses

    c. Private IP addresses

    d. IPv6 addresses

5. Which of the following ELB load balancer components determines what application traffic is accepted?

    a. Target group

    b. Listener

    c. Health check

    d. Access log

6. What is the standard methodology utilized by the EBS Application Load Balancer for delivering incoming traffic to registered instances?

    a. Connection draining

    b. SSL termination

    c. Round robin

    d. Sticky session

7. Once created, what does each AWS VPC span?

    a. Subnets

    b. Internet gateway

    c. Virtual private gateway

    d. Availability zones

8. Which type of networking is utilized by a VPC?

    a. Layer 2

    b. Layer 3

    c. VLAN

    d. MPLS

9. Where are the subnets hosted at AWS?

   a. In availability zones

   b. In regions

   c. Across availability zones

   d. Across regions

10. What type of IP address is automatically associated with every EC2 instance at creation?

    a. Non-routable IP address

    b. Elastic IP address

    c. Public IP address

    d. Private IP address

11. What type of IP address is not auto-assigned by default?

    a. Bring-your-own IP address

    b. Private IP address

    c. Elastic IP address

    d. Public IP address

12. Which of the following options can be used to connect VPCs?

    a. With an Internet gateway

    b. With route tables

    c. With security groups

    d. With peering connections

13. Which of the following does an endpoint provide?

    a. Public connections to AWS services

    b. Private connections to AWS services

    c. Private connections to the AWS Marketplace

    d. Public connections to the Internet

14. What does a gateway connection require to function?

    a. A VPC

    b. Route table entry

    c. Subnet

    d. EC2 instance

Foundation Topics

Amazon CloudFront

As previously mentioned, *Amazon CloudFront* is AWS's global CDN service. It is located at each edge location data center that optimizes the delivery of both static and dynamic web content, such as website images, videos, media files, and updates. (Details on AWS edge locations can be found in Chapter 4.) When the *viewer* (which is the end user in CloudFront terminology) requests content that is served by CloudFront, the viewer's request is sent to the closest edge location with the lowest latency, ensuring the requested content is delivered to the viewer with the best performance possible.

How Amazon CloudFront Works

Amazon CloudFront delivers content using the following steps:

Step 1. A viewer (user) makes a request to a website or application configured with CloudFront.

Step 2. The DNS service (Route 53) routes the viewer's request to the CloudFront edge location closest to the viewer.

Step 3. If the requested content is already in the edge location cache, it is delivered quickly to the viewer.

Step 4. If the requested content is not in the regional edge cache or edge location cache, CloudFront requests the content from the origin location and delivers the request.

Step 5. Copies of the delivered content are stored in multiple edge locations, providing redundancy and availability (see Figure 11-1). Persistent connections to each origin service location are kept open by CloudFront to fetch requested objects from the origin locations as quickly as possible. Deploying a CloudFront distribution also provides increased resiliency for your applications, as multiple edge locations are available for accessing the requested content. In addition, Amazon Route 53 records are stored redundantly in each region to ensure the reliability of the AWS global DNS service.

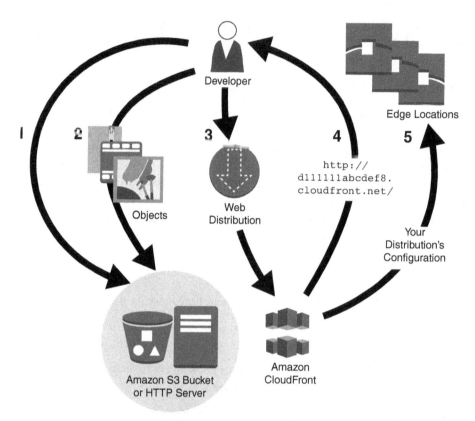

Figure 11-1   CloudFront Operation

Regional Edge Caches

A *regional edge cache* is an additional caching location within select AWS regions with a large amount of additional cache resources to ensure that more objects remain cached. A regional edge cache is located between the origin (Amazon S3 bucket or web server) and the edge location and helps speed up access to frequently accessed content by keeping cached content as close as possible to the end user. A simple request for content that is available is served by the regional edge cache; RESTful API methods such as **PUT**, **POST**, and **DELETE** are sent directly to the edge location and do not proxy through regional edge cache locations.

Requests served from the regional edge cache don't go back to the edge cache or to the origin location (see Figure 11-2).

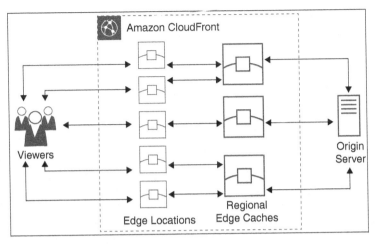

Figure 11-2   Regional Edge Location Placement

CloudFront Use Cases

You should be aware of the following use cases for the AWS Certified Solutions Architect – Associate (SAA-C03) exam regarding CloudFront distributions:

- **Speeding up static website content delivery:** This is the number-one reason for deploying a CloudFront distribution. Static content includes images, videos, CSS style sheets, and JavaScript files.

- **Providing video-on-demand or live streaming video:** Video on-demand options can stream formats such as MPEG DASH, Apple HLS, Microsoft Smooth Streaming, and CMAF to any network-enabled device. Live streaming supports the caching of media fragments at the edge location; the proper order to stream the media fragments is documented in the associated manifest file.

- **Encrypting content:** You can add field-level encryption to protect specific data fields against tampering during system processing. This ensures that only select applications can view the encrypted data fields.

- **Customized requests:** Using CloudFront functions or Lambda@Edge functions allows for customization of both ingress and egress requests with custom functions. Details on CloudFront Functions and Lambda@Edge functions are provided later in this chapter. Details on AWS Lambda are provided in Chapter 9, "Designing High-Performing and Elastic Compute Solutions."

HTTPS Access

CloudFront can be configured to require the use of the HTTPS protocol to request content, ensuring that all connections remain encrypted. CloudFront is configured from the properties of each distribution. Selecting HTTPS ensures that communication remains encrypted for both ingress and egress data transfer. The steps taken in the HTTPS communication process are as follows:

Step 1.   A request for content using HTTPS is submitted to CloudFront in an encrypted format.

Step 2.   If the object is present in the regional edge cache (if present) or the CloudFront edge cache, it is encrypted and returned to the viewer. If the object is not in either of the cache locations, CloudFront communicates with the origin via SSL/TLS, receiving the requested content from the origin location and sending the encrypted content to the viewer.

Step 3.   The object is saved in the edge cache and, if present, in the regional edge cache.

Serving Private Content

There are two methods available for securing the distribution of CloudFront private content to select viewers:

- Use signed URLs or signed cookies. You can create a signed URL or signed cookie that grants temporary access to a private file.

- Use an origin access identifier (OAI) to grant CloudFront permission to access your Amazon S3 bucket or custom origin and serve your private content.

Using Signed URLs

Using signed URLs and/or signed cookies helps you distribute private content across the Internet to a select pool of viewers. When you create a signed URL or cookie, the content is signed using the private key from the associated public/private key pair. When access to the content is requested, CloudFront compares the signed and unsigned portions of the signed URL or cookie. If the public/private keys match, the content is served; if the keys don't match, the content is not served. To use signed URLs with CloudFront, you must set up a trusted signer, which is an AWS account or an IAM user in your AWS account that has permission to create signed URLs and signed cookies. You also must configure your CloudFront distribution to use signed URLs as an additional layer of security. When creating signed URLs and/or signed cookies, conditions for accessing the URL are dictated by a JSON policy statement like the example shown in Example 11-1, which mandates which of the following restrictions are to be enforced:

- The date and time after which the URL is accessible

- The date and time after which the URL is no longer accessible

- The IP address range of devices that can access content

CloudFront checks the expiration date and time for signed URLs at the time of the viewer request.

Example 11-1   Accessing a File from a Range of Trusted IP Addresses

```
{
        "Statement": [
            {
                "Resource": "http://*",
                "Condition": {
                    "IpAddress": {
                        "AWS:Sourcelp": "192.0.4.0/32"
                    },
                    " DateGreaterThan": {
                        "AWS:EpochTime": 1367034400
                    },
                    "DateLessThan": {
                        "AWS:EpochTime": 1367120800
                    }
                }
            }
        ]
    }
```

Using an Origin Access Identifier

If the CloudFront origin is an S3 bucket, direct access to the S3 bucket can be restricted using a special CloudFront user called an ***origin access identity (OAI)*** that is associated with your CloudFront distribution, as shown in Figure 11-3. Configuring S3 bucket permissions allows the OAI to access the requested objects from the S3 bucket for CloudFront serving the objects to the viewer. The OAI is a special AWS Identity and Access Management (IAM) user associated with your CloudFront distribution. Once the OAI is created, only the OAI user can directly access objects in the S3 bucket origin; permissions need to be configured to allow only the OAI to access the bucket.

Figure 11-3   Ordering an Origin Access Identity

Restricting Distribution of Content

When an end user requests content from CloudFront, the content is served regardless of the physical location of the end user. To allow users only from approved countries to access cached content, geo-restrictions can be enabled by defining CloudFront access lists, as shown in Figure 11-4.

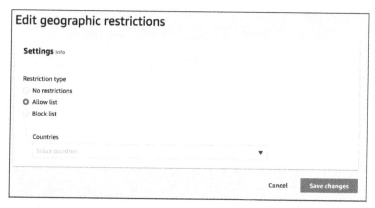

Figure 11-4   CloudFront Geographic Restrictions

CloudFront Origin Failover

CloudFront also has an additional option to assist with data reliability and resiliency called *origin failover*.

To set up origin failover, create a CloudFront distribution with at least two origins in place and define cache behavior to use the primary origin group for content requests, as shown in Figure 11-5. Next, in the CloudFront distribution origin group, define the HTTP status codes to be used as failover criteria to the secondary origin; for example, 500, 502, 503, or 504 codes.

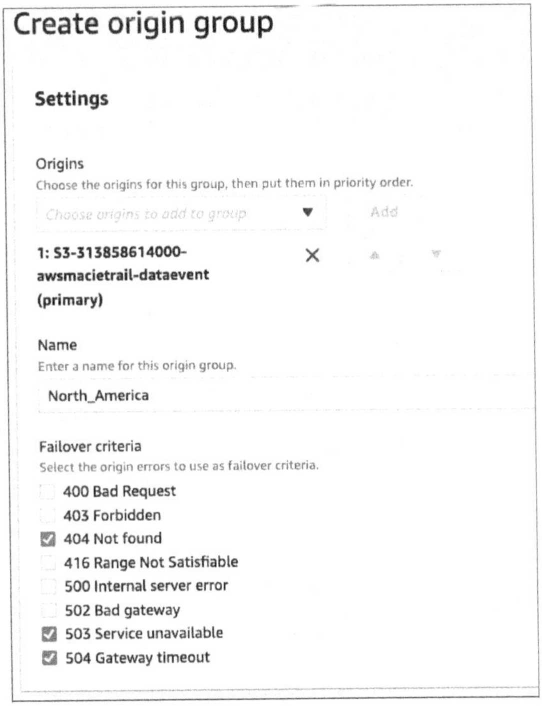

Create origin group

Settings

Origins
Choose the origins for this group, then put them in priority order.

| Choose origins to add to group ▼ | Add |

1: S3-313858614000-
awsmacietrail-dataevent
(primary)   ✕

Name
Enter a name for this origin group.

North_America

Failover criteria
Select the origin errors to use as failover criteria.
- ☐ 400 Bad Request
- ☐ 403 Forbidden
- ☑ 404 Not found
- ☐ 416 Range Not Satisfiable
- ☐ 500 Internal server error
- ☐ 502 Bad gateway
- ☑ 503 Service unavailable
- ☑ 504 Gateway timeout

Figure 11-5 Origin Failover Setup

With origin failover enabled, CloudFront operates normally and relies on the primary origin. When one of the specified HTTP status codes is received, failover to the secondary origin occurs if present. The speed of failover can be controlled by adjusting the Origin Connection Timeout and the Origin Connection Attempts default values for the respective CloudFront distribution.

Video-on-Demand and Live Streaming Support

CloudFront can deliver video on demand (VOD) or live streaming video from any HTTP origin. Video content must be packaged together with a supported encoder (MPEG DASH, Apple HLS, CMAF) before CloudFront can distribute the streaming content. CloudFront and AWS Media Services can be used together to deliver live streaming video.

- **Video on demand:** Content is stored on a server and can be watched at any time. Content can be formatted and packaged using AWS Elemental Media-Convert. After content is packaged, it can be stored in Amazon S3 and delivered upon request using CloudFront.

- **Live streaming video:** AWS Elemental MediaConvert can be used to compress and format the live streaming video delivered by CloudFront to end users.

Key Topic

Edge Functions

Serverless custom functions called *edge functions* can be written to customize how a CloudFront distribution processes HTTP viewer requests and responses. Edge functions can be written using CloudFront functions and Lambda@Edge functions.

CloudFront Functions

JavaScript can be used to create what are called "lightweight" functions to monitor viewer requests and responses for customizations. CloudFront Functions must finish executing within sub-milliseconds. Use cases include

- **Modifying the HTTP request from the viewer:** Return the modified request to CloudFront for processing. Headers, query strings, and URL paths can be modified.

- **Header manipulation:** Insert, modify, or delete HTTP headers for the viewer request or response.

- **URL redirects:** Redirect viewers to other pages based on information contained in the request, as shown in Figure 11-6.

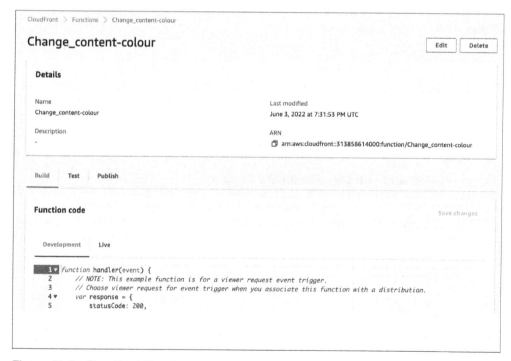

Figure 11-6 CloudFront Functions

Lambda@Edge Functions

Lambda@Edge is a managed AWS service that allows you to craft custom functions to carry out any task written in a variety of programming languages, including Python, Go, C#, Node.js, or Java. Lambda@Edge sits in the middle of the ingress and egress communication paths. Lambda@Edge could send specific content to users sending requests from a smartphone and send different specific content to users sending requests from a traditional computer. Lambda functions can be executed when the following requests occur:

- When CloudFront receives a request for content from a viewer

- When CloudFront forwards a request to the origin server (S3 bucket or web server)

- When CloudFront receives a response from the origin server (S3 bucket or web server)

- When CloudFront sends back a response to the viewer

Lambda@Edge Use Cases

AWS Certified Solutions Architect – Associate (SAA-C03) exam questions are based on scenarios, and some of the scenarios expect that you know the use cases for the services being considered by the question's solution. Lambda@Edge use cases include the following:

- You could return different objects to viewers based on the devices they're using. In this case, the Lambda@Edge function could read the User-Agent header, which provides information about a viewer's device.

- Perhaps you're selling clothing in different sizes. You could use cookies to indicate which size the end user selected when looking at clothing choices. The Lambda@Edge function could show the image of the clothing in the selected color and size.

- A Lambda@Edge function could inspect and confirm the validity of authorization tokens to help control access to your content.

- A Lambda@Edge function could be used to confirm viewer credentials to external sources.

CloudFront Cheat Sheet

For the AWS Certified Solutions Architect – Associate (SAA-C03) exam, you need to understand the following critical aspects of CloudFront:

- Control access to your public-facing content by mandating access via HTTPS endpoints using TLS 1.3.

- Origins include S3 buckets, AWS Elemental MediaStore container, an Application Load Balancer, a Lambda function URL, or a custom origin web server.

- Securing content access by using signed URLs and cookies.

- Use origin access identity (OAI) to restrict direct access to S3 bucket access, making it only accessible from CloudFront.

- Origin failover automatically serves content from the secondary origin when the primary origin is not available.

- Lambda@Edge functions support customizations that take from milliseconds to seconds to execute.

- CloudFront functions are lightweight functions that take less than one millisecond to execute.

AWS Global Accelerator

The Amazon Global Accelerator service routes traffic over the AWS private network to the closest available edge location endpoint that is closest to the end user. End user traffic enters the closest edge location and the Global Accelerator routes traffic to the closest application endpoint. The application outbound traffic returns over the AW private network back to the end user using the optimal endpoint (edge location). Application endpoints can be created in single or multiple AWS regions. Global Accelerator uses accelerators to improve the performance of applications for local and global users.

The Global Accelerator uses listeners to process inbound connection requests from end users based on the TCP port or port range specified for a single or multiple listeners. Each listener has one or more endpoint groups associated with it. Endpoint groups use endpoints in the defined AWS region (see Figure 11-7), and traffic is forwarded to the available endpoints in one of the groups. Both listener and endpoint ports can also be remapped to custom ports using port overrides.

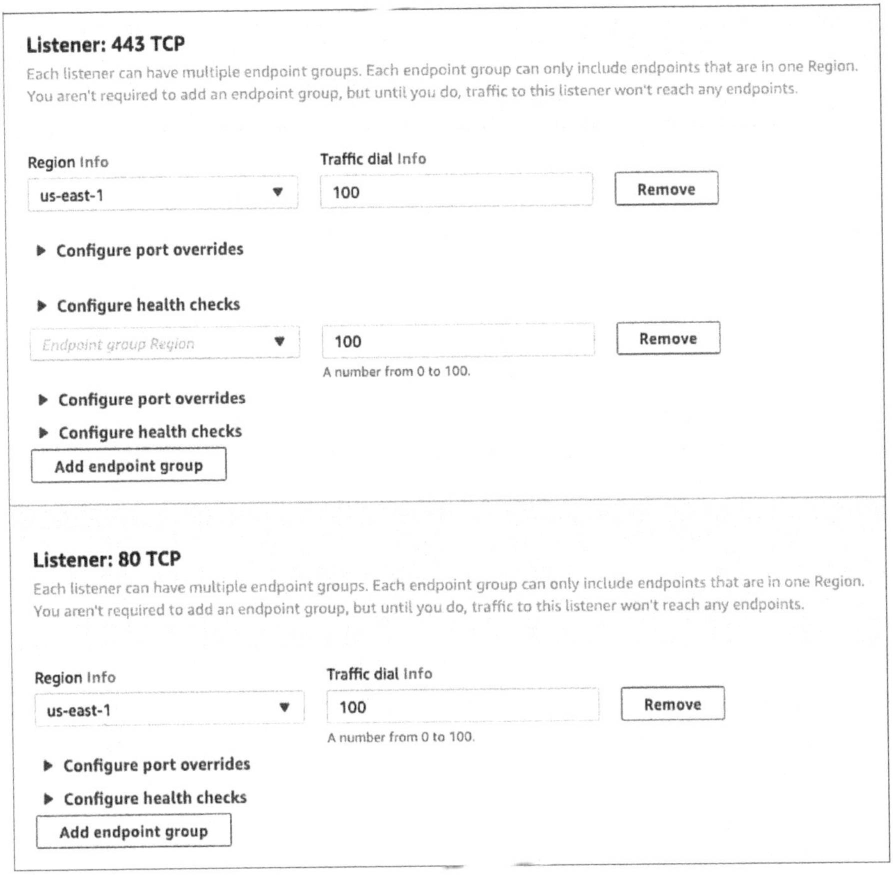

Listener: 443 TCP

Each listener can have multiple endpoint groups. Each endpoint group can only include endpoints that are in one Region. You aren't required to add an endpoint group, but until you do, traffic to this listener won't reach any endpoints.

Region Info   Traffic dial Info

| us-east-1 ▼ | 100 | Remove |

▶ **Configure port overrides**

▶ **Configure health checks**

| Endpoint group Region ▼ | 100 | Remove |

A number from 0 to 100.

▶ **Configure port overrides**

▶ **Configure health checks**

Add endpoint group

Listener: 80 TCP

Each listener can have multiple endpoint groups. Each endpoint group can only include endpoints that are in one Region. You aren't required to add an endpoint group, but until you do, traffic to this listener won't reach any endpoints.

Region Info   Traffic dial Info

| us-east-1 ▼ | 100 | Remove |

A number from 0 to 100.

▶ **Configure port overrides**

▶ **Configure health checks**

Add endpoint group

Figure 11-7 Adding Listeners to Accelerator

Two types of accelerators can be deployed:

- **Standard accelerator:** A standard accelerator automatically routes traffic to the optimal AWS region with the lowest latency, using static Anycast IP addresses that are globally unique and do not change. For a standard accelerator with IPv4 addresses, endpoints can be Network Load Balancers, Application Load Balancers, EC2 instances, or Elastic IP addresses. With dual-stack addresses (IPv4/IPv6), only Application Load Balancer endpoints that have been configured to support dual-stack are supported. The use case for a standard accelerator is for applications that require a consistent, low-latency connection, such as web applications, mobile applications, and gaming applications. Each listener created in a standard accelerator can include one or more endpoint groups; each listener has a Traffic dial (see Figure 11-7) that can be used to increase or decrease traffic to each endpoint in the selected AWS region.

- **Custom accelerator:** A custom routing accelerator maps listener port ranges to a specific Amazon EC2 private IP address and port destination in an AWS VPC and subnet. A custom accelerator can logically map one or more end users to a specific destination, such as a gaming application with multiple players or a training application that needs to assign multiple end users to a specific server for video training sessions. A custom accelerator is mapped to an AWS VPC endpoint with a destination port range that maps the incoming client connections.

The AWS Global Accelerator Speed Comparison Tool can also be used to review Global Accelerator download speeds compared to Internet downloads across AWS regions.

There are several additional use cases to know for the AWS Certified Solutions Architect – Associate (SAA-C03) exam:

- **Single-region applications:** End users' traffic is sent over 90 global edge locations onto Amazon's private network and sent to your application origin.

- **Multi-region applications:** Static IPs can be mapped to multiple application endpoints across AWS regions, as shown in Figure 11-8.

- **Multi-region storage:** S3 Multi-Region Access Points rely on the AWS Global Accelerator for accessing data sets stored in S3 buckets across multiple AWS regions.

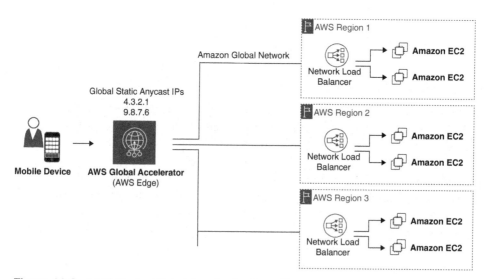

Figure 11-8   Multi-Region Global Accelerator Operation

Elastic Load Balancing Service

Amazon Elastic Load Balancer (Amazon ELB) is a load balancing service that distributes incoming application traffic across Amazon EC2 instances, Amazon ECS containers, AWS Lambda functions, and IP addresses.

ELB helps to ensure that your application is highly available and scalable by distributing incoming traffic across multiple resources. It can also help to improve the performance of your application by evenly distributing traffic across your resources and automatically scaling them to meet demand. The Elastic Load Balancing Service (ELB) provides the Application Load Balancer for HTTP/HTTPS workloads and the Network Load Balancer for TCP/UDP workloads. The Gateway Load Balancer can deploy and manage third-party load balancer virtual appliances such as Nginx, Cisco, and Broadcom (see Figure 11-9).

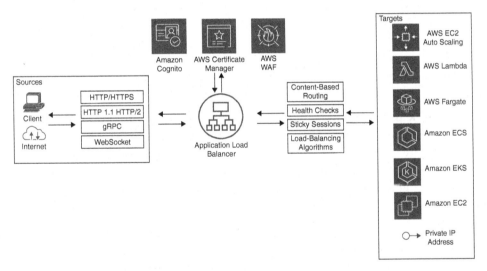

Figure 11-9 Application Load Balancer Targets

Each load balancer ordered is assigned a traffic profile with a prescribed amount of throughput capacity. The ELB service monitors the performance and requirements of each online load balancer and scales the performance and capacity required based on the incoming user requests.

For each load balancer ordered, you are charged a small monthly fee, plus data transfer charges based on the number of Load Balancer Capacity Units (LCUs) used every hour. The LCU is the hourly aggregate total of incoming traffic requests based on new and active connections, consumed bandwidth, and the number of *listener* rules evaluated.

Application Load Balancer Features

Application load balancers have features used to manage and route incoming public traffic from the Internet:

- **SSL/TLS traffic decryption:** Application load balancers deploy SSL offloading performing decryption on the incoming connection request; SSL traffic is terminated on the load balancer sending the decrypted request to the registered target.

- **Server Name Indication (SNI):** Application load balancers support hosting multiple certificates per ALB, enabling multiple websites with separate domains to be hosted by a single ALB. Up to 25 certificates can be attached per ALB. SNI enables the assignment of the correct SSL/TLS certificate to the associated server; the ALB sends the website's or domain's public key to the end user to establish a secure connection with the load balancer. ALB supports classic Rivest-Shamir-Adleman (RSA), the industry standard in asymmetric keys, and the newer Elliptic Curve Digital Signature Algorithm (ECDSA) for elliptic-curve cryptography. When ECDSA is compared to RSA with regard to the TLS handshake, ECDSA communication is nine times faster. ECDSA has become popular because it is used by Bitcoin, the Apple iOS, and iMessage.

- **Dynamic port mapping:** Application load balancers support load-balancing containers running the same service on the same EC2 instance where the containers are hosted. When Amazon EC2 Container Service (ECS) task definitions are launched multiple times on the same EC2 instance, the containers are running duplicates of the same service; dynamic port mapping process assigns a random port to each container task.

- **Connection draining:** When an EC2 instance that is registered with a load balancer is tagged as unhealthy by failing its health checks, the connections to the instance are closed through a process called *connection draining*. From the point of view of the load balancer, the connection draining process keeps existing connections open until the client closes them but prevents new requests from being sent to the instances that are tagged as unhealthy.

Connection draining removes select EC2 instances from a load balancer target group when maintenance is required—for example, when it's time to update a healthy EC2 instance with a new Amazon Machine Image (AMI). Performing the deregistration process on an EC2 instance (see Figure 11-10) starts the connection draining process, keeping the existing connections open to provide enough time to complete all ongoing requests. An EC2 instance that is in the process of deregistering will not accept new connection requests.

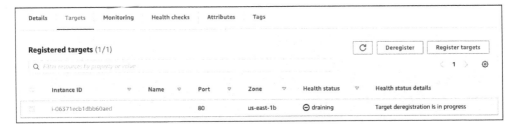

Figure 11-10 Connection Draining to Deregister Instances from Target Groups

- **Cross-zone load balancing:** The nodes for the load balancers distribute incoming traffic requests evenly across the registered targets in the enabled availability zones. If cross-zone load balancing is disabled, each load balancer node distributes traffic across the registered targets in its assigned AZ. Cross-zone load balancing can be disabled at the target group level; it is enabled by default for ALBs and disabled by default for NLBs.

- **User authentication:** Application Load Balancer allows you to offload the authentication process so the load balancer can authenticate users as they request access to cloud applications. ALB integrates with AWS Cognito, which allows both web-based and enterprise identity providers to authenticate through the ALB.

- **HTTP/2 and gRPC Support:** HTTP/2 allows multiple requests to be sent across the same connection. ALB can load balance gRPC traffic between microservices and gRPC-enabled clients and services. gRPC uses HTTP/2 for routing communications for microservice architectures.

NOTE If you're deploying an ALB, you can also add a Web Application Firewall (WAF) ACL for additional protection against malicious incoming public traffic.

Application Load Balancer Deployment

When ordering an Application Load Balancer, choose whether the load balancer accepts public inbound traffic (Internet-facing) or private inbound traffic (internal), as shown in Figure 11-11. Also select the IP address type to be used: IPv4 or Dual-stack (IPv4 and IPv6).

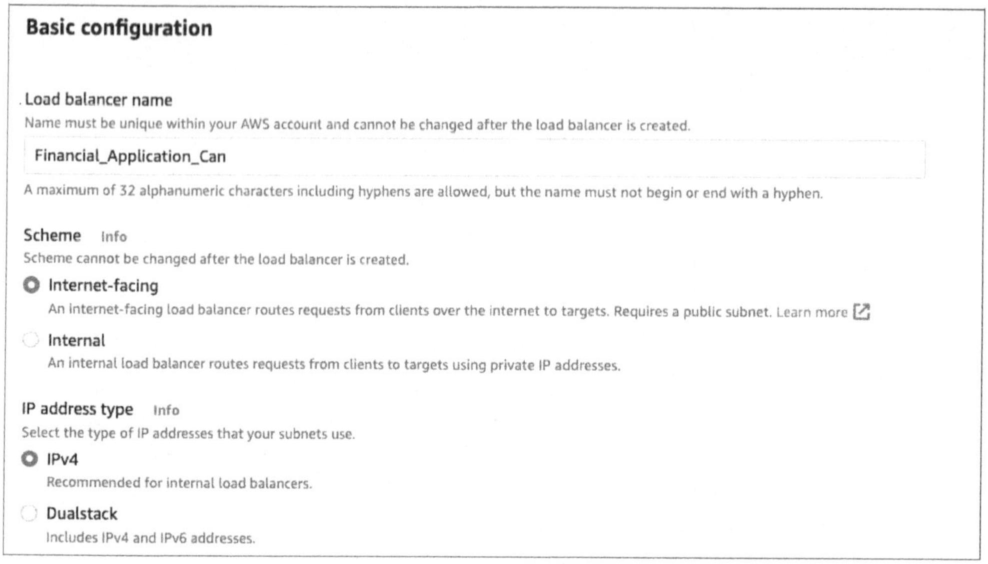

Basic configuration

. Load balancer name
Name must be unique within your AWS account and cannot be changed after the load balancer is created.

Financial_Application_Can

A maximum of 32 alphanumeric characters including hyphens are allowed, but the name must not begin or end with a hyphen.

Scheme   Info
Scheme cannot be changed after the load balancer is created.
◉ Internet-facing
   An internet-facing load balancer routes requests from clients over the internet to targets. Requires a public subnet. Learn more
○ Internal
   An internal load balancer routes requests from clients to targets using private IP addresses.

IP address type   Info
Select the type of IP addresses that your subnets use.
◉ IPv4
   Recommended for internal load balancers.
○ Dualstack
   Includes IPv4 and IPv6 addresses.

Figure 11-11   Initial Configuration of ALB

Next, select the VPC, availability zone(s), and the subnets the Application Load Balancer will be linked to. The ALB is always hosted in public subnets for Internet-facing applications. Public-facing load balancer deployments also require that an Internet gateway be attached to the VPC where the load balancer is being installed. When you enable an AZ for an ALB, the ELB service creates an ALB node in each AZ. For ALB deployments, at least two AZs are required, ensuring that if one AZ becomes unavailable or has no healthy targets, the ALB will route traffic to the healthy targets hosted in another AZ (see Figure 11-12).

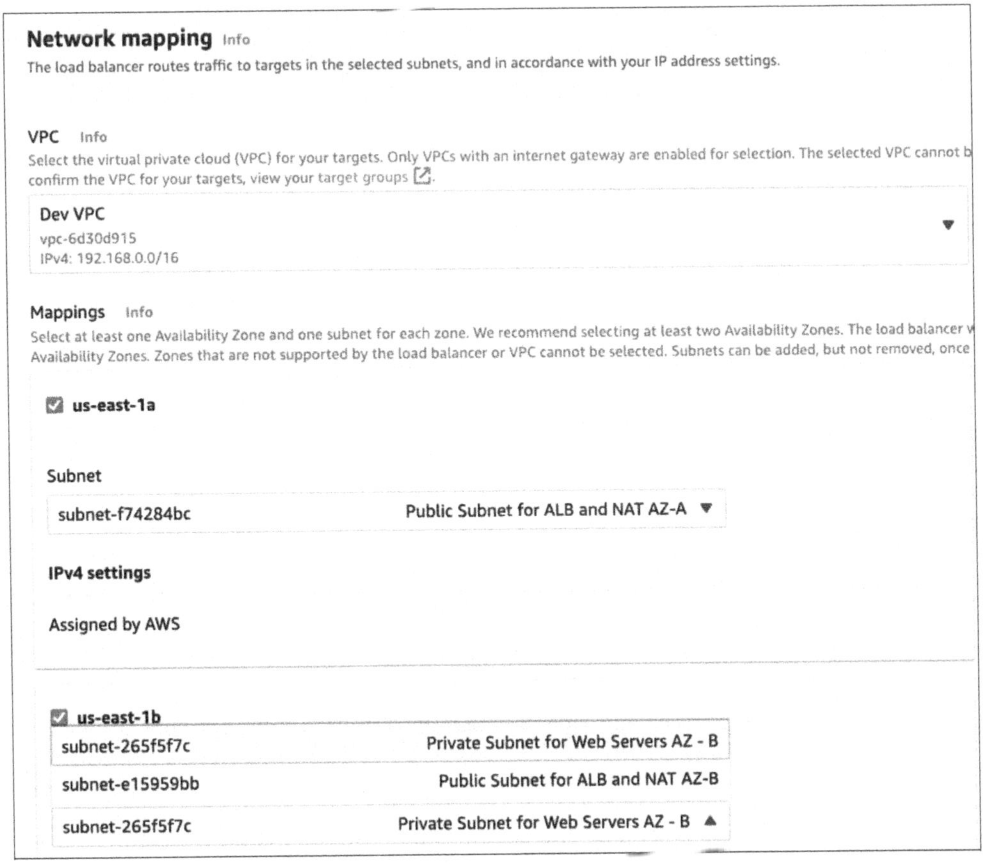

Network mapping Info

The load balancer routes traffic to targets in the selected subnets, and in accordance with your IP address settings.

VPC Info

Select the virtual private cloud (VPC) for your targets. Only VPCs with an internet gateway are enabled for selection. The selected VPC cannot b
confirm the VPC for your targets, view your target groups 🔗.

Dev VPC
vpc-6d30d915
IPv4: 192.168.0.0/16   ▼

Mappings Info

Select at least one Availability Zone and one subnet for each zone. We recommend selecting at least two Availability Zones. The load balancer w
Availability Zones. Zones that are not supported by the load balancer or VPC cannot be selected. Subnets can be added, but not removed, once

☑ **us-east-1a**

Subnet

| subnet-f74284bc | Public Subnet for ALB and NAT AZ-A ▼ |

IPv4 settings

Assigned by AWS

☑ **us-east-1b**

subnet-265f5f7c	Private Subnet for Web Servers AZ - B
subnet-e15959bb	Public Subnet for ALB and NAT AZ-B
subnet-265f5f7c	Private Subnet for Web Servers AZ - B ▲

Figure 11-12 Choosing AZs and Subnets

A security group must be created or selected to allow traffic requests from clients to the ALB. Allowed client traffic and health check traffic is sent to the respective target groups on the listener port—for example, port 80 or port 443. The security group for the ALB controls the traffic that is allowed to reach the load balancer; it does not affect the traffic that is forwarded to the targets in the target group. The ALB must be able to communicate with registered targets on both the listener port and the defined health check port, both inbound and outbound.

Listeners and Routing

A *listener* continuously checks for incoming connection requests based on the defined ports and protocols configured. Incoming connection requests that match are forwarded to a target group. Common protocol options are port 80 and port 443 (see Figure 11-13). An ALB listener supports HTTP/HTTPS and ports from

1-65535. Redirect actions can also be deployed to redirect client requests from one URL to another, such as HTTP to HTTPS, or HTTP to HTTP.

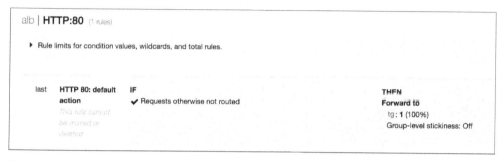

Figure 11-13   ALB Listener Setup

After an initial listener has been configured and the ALB has been launched successfully, additional listeners can be added by editing the ALB properties. ALB HTTPS listeners use a feature called SSL offload, which supports encrypted traffic between the client and the load balancer and decrypts traffic sent from the load balancer to registered targets. To ensure that registered targets decrypt HTTPS traffic instead of the ALB, create a Network Load Balancer with a TCP listener on port 443. With a TCP listener, the load balancer passes encrypted traffic directly to the targets without decrypting it first.

Elastic Load Balancing uses security policy to negotiate SSL connections between a client and the load balancer. For HTTPS listeners listening on port 443, an X.509 certificate must also be associated with the secure listener. Use AWS Certificate Manager (ACM) to first upload your organization's SSL/TLS website or domain certificate; then select the certificate and select a security policy that is applied to all frontend connections. Uploading a custom security policy to secure the back-end communications is not allowed. Each request accepted by the listener uses two connections:

- **A frontend connection between the client and the load balancer:** Organizations choose the security policy for frontend connections. During the connection negotiation between the client and the ALB, a set of ciphers and protocols is presented by the client and ALB and a cipher is selected for the secure connection.

- **A backend connection between the load balancer and the associated target:** The ELBSecurityPolicy-2016-08 security policy is always used for securing backend connections. Application Load Balancers do not support custom security policies.

By default, when frontend or backend load balancing connections have not processed data for 60 seconds, the connections are closed. Connections can be left open
for a longer time by editing the default attributes of the load balancer.

NOTE Certificates uploaded to the ALB from Certificate Manager are automatically
renewed by the Certificate Manager service.

Rules, Conditions, and Actions

A *rule* consists of a set of conditions and an action. When the ALB receives a
request, it evaluates the conditions in the rule to determine whether the action
should be taken. If the conditions are met, the action is performed and the request
is routed to the specified target group. If the conditions are not met, the next rule
is evaluated. Each listener has at least one default rule and action defined for routing traffic to a target group (see Figure 11-14). Default rules don't have conditions.
Additional rules can be created with defined conditions; if the conditions are met,
the rules' actions are performed; if the conditions are not met, the default rule is
used instead. With multiple rules, the rules are evaluated in priority from the lowest to the highest value. Multiple rules can be created for an ALB, and each rule
can have multiple conditions. The order of the rules is important because the ALB
evaluates the rules in the order in which they are specified. You can specify the order
of the rules being processed using the priority field.

Listeners and routing Info

A listener is a process that checks for connection requests, using the protocol and port you configure. Traffic received by the listener is then routed per your specification. You can specify
multiple rules and multiple certificates per listener after the load balancer is created.

▼ Listener **HTTPS:443**   Remove

Protocol	Port	Default action Info
HTTPS ▼	: 443	Forward to **tg**
	1-65535	Target type: Instance, IPv4
		Create target group 🗗

HTTP ▼   ⟳

Add listener

Secure listener settings Info

These settings will apply to all of your secure listeners. Once created, you can manage these settings per listener if desired.

	From ACM
	From IAM
Security policy	Import
Your load balancer uses a Secure Socket Layer (SSL) negotiation configuration, known as a security policy, to negotiate SSL connections with clients.	From ACM ▲ Select a certificate ▼ ⟳
ELBSecurityPolicy-FS-1-2-Res-2020-10 ▼	
Compare security policies 🗗	Request new ACM certificate 🗗

t connects without SNI protocol, or if there are no matching
ill automatically be added to your listener certificate list.

Figure 11-14 ALB Listener and Routing Setup

Each rule must include one of the following actions; the action with the lowest defined value is performed first:

- **forward:** This routing option forwards the request to a specific target group.

- **redirect:** This routing option redirects the request from one URL to another. Usable components include the protocol (HTTP to HTTP, HTTP to HTTPS, and HTTPS to HTTPS), hostname, port, or path.

- **fixed-response:** This routing option sends a custom HTTP response to the end user.

The following routing conditions are supported for rules:

- **host-header:** This routing option forwards requests to a target group based on the domain name contained in the host header. When the hostname in the host header matches the hostname in the listener rule, the request is routed. Wildcard characters can be used in the first part of the hostname but not in the part of the name after the period (*name*.com). For example, requests to a.example.com could be sent to one target group, and requests to b.example.com could be sent to another target group. Rules can be created that combine the path and host-based routing, allowing you to route requests to a specific path, such as /productiondocs.

- **http-header:** This routing option uses the HTTP headers (for example, Chrome or Safari).

- **path-pattern:** This routing option is based on the path pattern of the URL (for example, /images/*). If the path in the URL matches the path pattern defined in the listener's rule, as shown in Figure 11-15, the request is routed. Instead of just the root domain used as the path to send requests, endpoints can be defined at the ALB, directing the traffic requests. Both path and host-based routing allow you to control the compute environment where the requests are being directed. Certain requests, such as API calls, could be directed to be processed on a target group of compute-optimized EC2 instances; other requests could be directed to another target group containing memory-optimized EC2 instances.

- **query-string:** This routing option is based on key/value pairs or values in the query name configuration.

- **source-ip:** This routing option is based on the source IP address for each request.

Figure 11-15   Host- and Path-Based Rules Defined for Precise Traffic Flow

There are also authentication actions for authenticating users using Cognito (**authenticate-cognito**) or a compliant OpenID Connect identity provider (**authenticate-oidc**).

Target Groups

A *target group* routes requests to one or more registered targets. Once a registered target has passed its health checks, the load balancer will route connection requests to the target. There are four choices for target groups, as shown in Figure 11-16:

- **EC2 Instances:** EC2 instances that are located in the AWS VPC defined by the target group. Load balancers that are linked to an Auto Scaling group use EC2 instances that are defined by instance ID.

- **IP addresses:** IPv4 or IPv6 addresses for cloud hosted EC2 instances or on-premises servers.

- **Lambda function:** Register a Lambda function as targets and configure a listener rule forwarding requests to the target group for the Lambda function.

- **Application Load Balancer:** Associate an ALB as the target for NLB traffic.

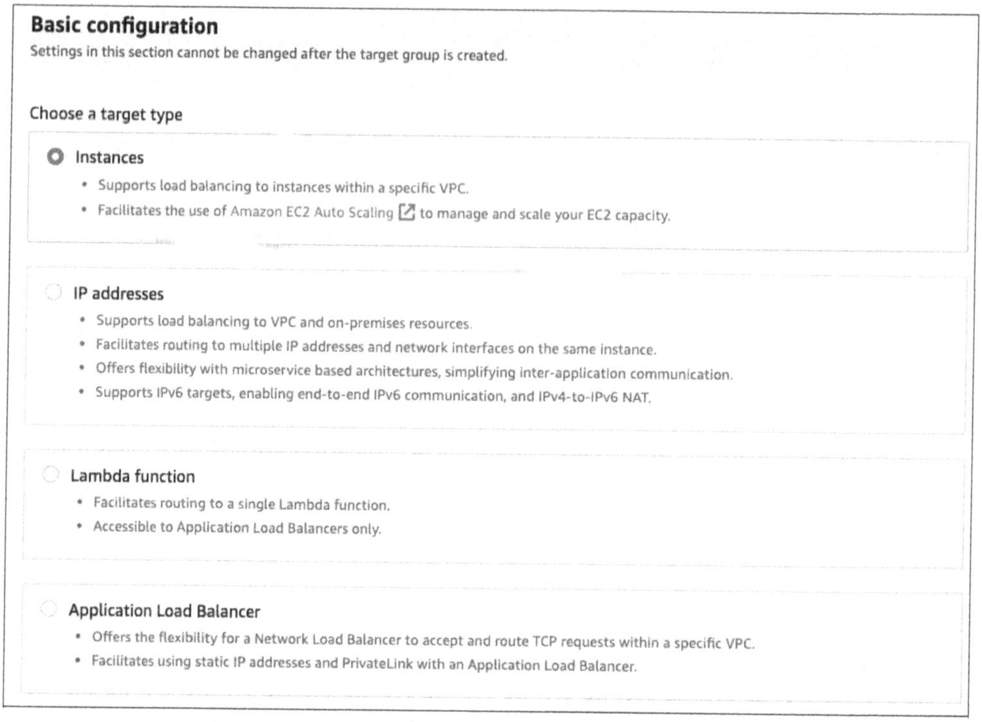

Basic configuration

Settings in this section cannot be changed after the target group is created.

Choose a target type

⦿ **Instances**
- Supports load balancing to instances within a specific VPC.
- Facilitates the use of Amazon EC2 Auto Scaling ☑ to manage and scale your EC2 capacity.

○ **IP addresses**
- Supports load balancing to VPC and on-premises resources.
- Facilitates routing to multiple IP addresses and network interfaces on the same instance.
- Offers flexibility with microservice based architectures, simplifying inter-application communication.
- Supports IPv6 targets, enabling end-to-end IPv6 communication, and IPv4-to-IPv6 NAT.

○ **Lambda function**
- Facilitates routing to a single Lambda function.
- Accessible to Application Load Balancers only.

○ **Application Load Balancer**
- Offers the flexibility for a Network Load Balancer to accept and route TCP requests within a specific VPC.
- Facilitates using static IP addresses and PrivateLink with an Application Load Balancer.

Figure 11-16 Adding a Target Group to ALB

Health Checks

Health checks are used to monitor the status of targets in a load balancer's target group. Requests for online availability status are sent to registered targets at a configured interval to verify that registered targets are available to serve traffic. If a target fails a health check, it is removed from the target group and will not receive traffic until it is deemed healthy again.

The frequency and nature of the health checks depend on the protocol and type of target group. For HTTP and HTTPS target groups, the load balancer sends a request to the target and expects a response using a certain status code. For TCP target groups, the load balancer establishes a connection to the target and verifies that it can send and receive traffic.

The *health check* settings for a target group can be customized to define the ping target, the interval between health checks, and the number of consecutive failures required before marking a target as unhealthy (see Figure 11-17). You can also specify a healthy threshold and an unhealthy threshold, which determine the number of successful or unsuccessful health checks required before marking a target as healthy or unhealthy.

Figure 11-17   Load Balancer Health Check Settings

If the EC2 instance responds within the defined response timeout period, the load balancer marks the EC2 instance as in service, and incoming user requests are routed to the healthy targets. Both the ALB and NLB perform health checks against all registered EC2 instances at specific intervals. Health checks are configured during the load balancer setup and configuration and can be changed at any time. The following language is used to describe health checks:

- A registered target is typically defined as *healthy* or *unhealthy*.

- A target newly added to the target group is defined as *initial*; once its health check is successful, the target is defined as *healthy*.

- When a registered target is being removed and connection draining is underway, the target is marked as *draining*.

Table 11-2 lists the options that can be defined to customize advanced health checks Health checks can be defined or modified for each target group by selecting the health check tab.

Table 11-2   Health Check Settings

Health Check Setting	Description
Health Check Protocol	Either HTTP or HTTPS.
Health Check Port	The port used for performing health checks on targets. The default is the communications protocol port, which is either 80 or 443.
Health Check Path	The destination ping path on the target. The default is /.
Health Check Timeout Seconds	The amount of time (from 2–60 seconds) after which a health check is considered failed.
Health Check Interval Seconds	The time between health checks (in the range of 5–300 seconds).

Health Check Setting	Description
Healthy Threshold Count	The number of consecutive health checks required from an unhealthy target before the target is considered healthy.
Unhealthy Threshold Account	The number of consecutive failed health checks that result in an unhealthy target.
Status code	The HTTP code (in the range 200–499) that indicates a healthy target.

Resilient workloads use health checks to ensure that resources placed behind load balancers (ALB/NLB) are available. EC2 Auto Scaling can also monitor ELB health checks when EC2 instances are automatically scaled using Auto Scaling groups. Chapter 9 provides additional details on EC2 Auto Scaling.

Target Group Attributes

Each EC2 instance or target group's operation can be controlled by modifying the target group attributes, as shown in Table 11-3.

Table 11-3 ALB Target Group Attributes for Instance or IP Targets

Attribute	Description
Deregistration delay	How much time before a target (instance or IP address) is deregistered. The default is 300 seconds.
Slow start duration	The time before a new target is sent a gradually increasing number of connection requests. It can be set to up to 15 minutes, and there is no default setting.
Round-robin load-balancing algorithm	Enabled or disabled.
Least-outstanding requests load-balancing algorithm	Enabled or disabled.
Stickiness	Enabled or disabled.

Configure health checks for each target group shown in Figure 11-18 by editing the target group health checks attributes.

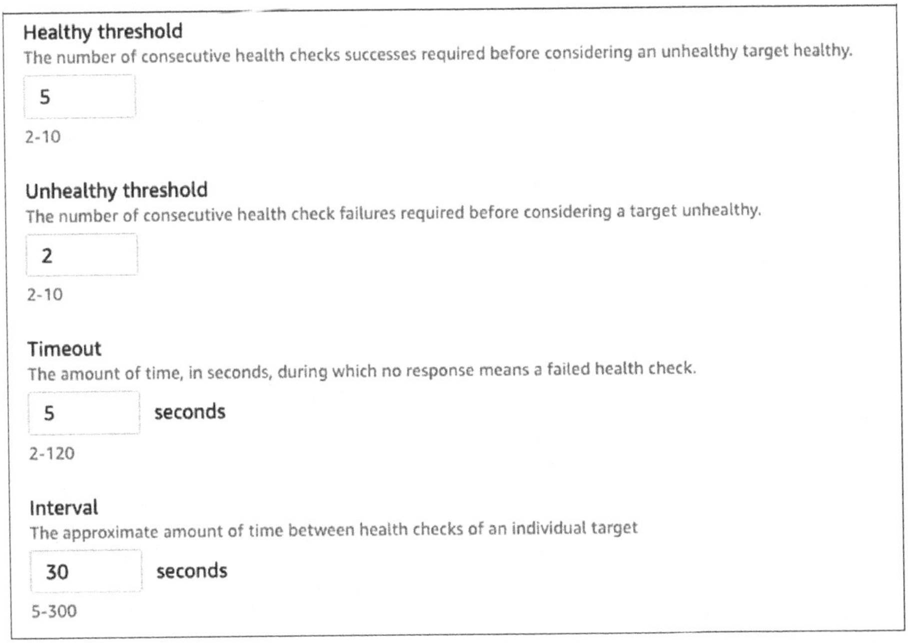

Healthy threshold
The number of consecutive health checks successes required before considering an unhealthy target healthy.

5

2-10

Unhealthy threshold
The number of consecutive health check failures required before considering a target unhealthy.

2

2-10

Timeout
The amount of time, in seconds, during which no response means a failed health check.

5   seconds

2-120

Interval
The approximate amount of time between health checks of an individual target

30   seconds

5-300

Figure 11-18   Configuring Health Checks

Sticky Session Support

If a load balancer is supporting an application that is providing generic information, maintaining a specific user session might not be required. However, for applications where the end user begins communication with an initial server, maintaining the session between the end user and the backend resource is important. If you are buying something online, you expect your session to begin and end properly, without problems.

An ALB supports *sticky sessions*, which allow the load balancer to bind the user's active session to a specific EC2 instance. With sticky sessions enabled on a load balancer, after a request is routed to a target, a cookie is generated by the load balancer or application and returned to the client, ensuring that requests are sent to the EC2 instance where the user session is located. All requests from the client to the load balancer include the identifying cookie, ensuring that all requests are routed to the same backend server. The enabling of sticky sessions and the parameters for the stickiness of the cookie are defined by editing the target group attributes tab, as shown in Figure 11-19.

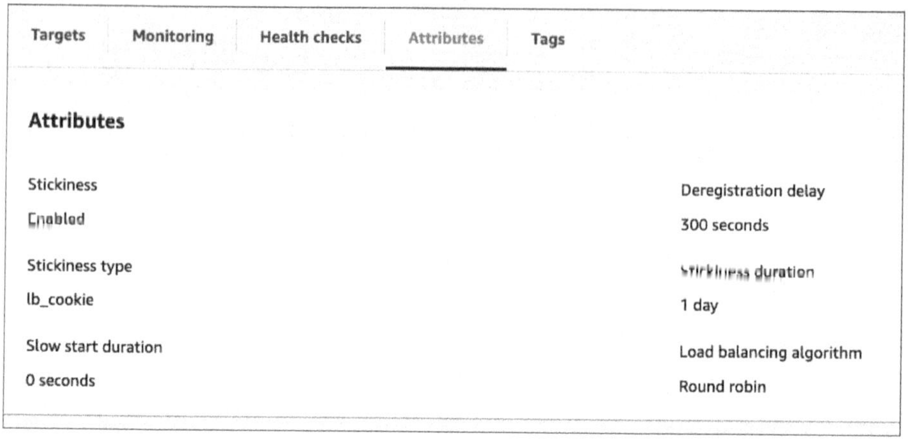

Targets	Monitoring	Health checks	Attributes	Tags

Attributes

Stickiness Enabled	Deregistration delay 300 seconds
Stickiness type lb_cookie	Stickiness duration 1 day
Slow start duration 0 seconds	Load balancing algorithm Round robin

Figure 11-19 Target Group Attributes

You can enable sticky sessions for an ALB by specifying a duration for the stickiness period. The stickiness period is the length of time that the ALB should route requests from the same user to the same target.

To enable sticky sessions you must define a stickiness policy when you create a target group. A stickiness policy defines the method that the ALB should use to bind a user's session to a target. The available stickiness policies are

- **Source IP:** This policy uses the client's IP address to bind the session to a target.

- **Application-based cookies:** This policy uses a cookie to bind the session to a target. You can specify the name and duration of the cookie.

What happens when the backend server that the user is connected to fails and is no longer available? The load balancer automatically chooses a new healthy EC2 instance and moves the user to a new server for the remainder of the session, even if the old instance becomes available. Sticky sessions are useful when everything works, but they're not useful when servers fail, as the new EC2 instance knows nothing about the user's previous session.

Instead of enabling sticky sessions, consider using a central storage location for user session information, for example a hosted ElastiCache for Redis cluster or ElastiCache for Memcached nodes. For applications with a large number of concurrent user sessions, one of these choices will be a better option to provide resilient storage for user session information.

Access Logs

You can choose to enable access logs, which provide detailed information about all incoming requests sent to the load balancer. Once access logs are enabled, ELB captures the logging details and stores them in the desired Amazon S3 bucket. Additional security can be provided by enabling server-side encryption on the bucket to encrypt each access log file. Use S3 managed encryption keys to ensure that each log file is encrypted with a unique Amazon S3 managed key. Automatic key rotation is carried out by the Key Management Service (KMS) service.

Log files are published every 5 minutes. Log details include the type of request or connection (that is, HTTP, HTTPS, HTTP2, WebSocket, or WebSocket over SSL/TLS) and the timestamp, client port, target port, request and target processing time, and sent and received bytes. Details provided by CloudWatch logging can also be provided by access logs for a fraction of the cost of using CloudWatch metrics and alarms.

ALB Cheat Sheet

For the AWS Certified Solutions Architect – Associate (SAA-C03) exam, you need to understand the following critical aspects of ALB:

- ALB operates at Layer 7, routing traffic to registered targets—EC2 instances, containers, and IP addresses—based on the content of the incoming request.

- ALB supports HTTP/HTTPS applications and HTTPS termination between the client and the load balancer.

- ALB supports HTTP/2, which allows multiple requests to be sent on the same connection.

- SSL/TLS certificates are managed using AWS Certificate Manager.

- Server Name Indication (SNI) enables you to secure multiple websites using a single secure listener.

- ALB supports IPv4 and IPv6 for Internet-facing load balancers; for internal load balancers, it supports only IPv4.

- ALB can be integrated with Amazon Cognito to provide end-user authentication.

- ALB uses either round-robin or a least-available-request algorithm for targeting registered EC2 instances.

- ALB supports AWS Outposts.

- AWS Certificate Manager or AWS IAM can be used to manage server certificates.

Network Load Balancer

ELB Network Load Balancer (NLB) is a load balancing service that distributes incoming traffic across multiple targets, such as Amazon EC2 instances, containers, and IP addresses, in one or more AZ. Network Load Balancer provides TCP and UDP load balancing at Layer 4 of the OSI stack. NLB uses a flow-based algorithm to distribute traffic to the targets in a target group. This means it distributes traffic based on the number of connections rather than on the amount of data transferred. The NLB can scale to handle millions of requests per second at very low latencies. It can also integrate with EC2 Auto Scaling, Amazon ECS, and AWS ACM. NLB supports end-to-end encryption using TLS.

You should know the following NLB features for the AWS Certified Solutions Architect – Associate (SSA-C03) exam:

- **TLS offloading:** Client TLS session termination is supported, allowing TLS termination tasks to be carried out by the load balancer.

- **Server Name Indication (SNI):** Serves multiple websites using a single TLS listener.

- **AWS Certificate Manager:** Manages server certificates.

- **Sticky sessions:** Can be defined per target session.

- **Preserve client-side source IP address:** Backend servers can see the IP address of the client.

- **Static IP address:** A static IP address is provided per AZ.

- **EIP support:** An Elastic IP address can be assigned for each AZ.

- **DNS fail-over:** If there are no healthy targets available, Route 53 directs traffic to load balancer nodes in other AZs.

- **Route 53 integration:** Route 53 can route traffic to an alternate NLB in another AWS region.

- **Zonal isolation:** The NLB can be enabled in a single AZ, supporting applications that require zonal isolation.

NLB Cheat Sheet

For the AWS Certified Solutions Architect – Associate (SAA-C03) exam, you need to understand the following critical aspects of NLB:

- The NLB can load balance applications hosted at AWS and on premises using IPv4/IPv6 addresses.

- The NLB supports connections across peered VPCs in different AWS regions.

- The NLB supports long-running connections, which are ideal for WebSocket applications.

- The NLB supports failover across AWS regions, using Route 53 health checks.

- With the NLB, the source IP addresses of the clients that are connecting are preserved.

- Each NLB allows for extremely high throughput; an NLB can scale and handle millions of requests per second.

- The NLB flow-based algorithm is ideal for latency-sensitive TCP/UDP applications.

- The NLB provides "end-to-end security" with TLS termination performed by the NLB.

Multi-Region Failover

An NLB supports failover across AWS regions using Amazon Route 53 health checks, allowing organizations to create a highly available, globally distributed load balancing solution that can route traffic to the optimal region based on the health of the targets in each region.

An NLB must be created in each AWS region where traffic will be load balanced. Then create a target group in each region that contains the regional targets to which to route traffic. Enable cross-zone load balancing for each NLB so traffic is distributed across the targets in each AZ.

Next, create an Amazon Route 53 health check for each target group. You can use the default health check configuration or customize the health check settings to meet your specific requirements.

Finally, create a Route 53 record set that points to the NLB in each AWS region. Choices are a weighted record set, or a latency-based record set to specify the routing policy for the record set. With a weighted record set the proportion of traffic that should be routed to each region is controlled based on the weights assigned to the record set. With a latency-based record set, Route 53 routes traffic to the region that provides the lowest latency for the end user.

CloudWatch Metrics

CloudWatch metrics for ELB can be used to monitor and ensure that a workload is performing as expected. Table 11-4 lists several metrics that provide operating details based on the sum of the totals.

Table 11-4 CloudWatch Metrics for ELB

ELB Metric	Description
ActiveConnectionCount	The number of concurrent TCP frontend and backend connections
ConsumedLCUs	The number of Load Balancer Capacity Units used
NewConnectionCount	The total number of TCP connections from clients to the load balancer to targets
ProcessedBytes	The total number of bytes processed by the load balancer
RequestCount	The number of requests processed with responses from a target
HealthyHostCount	The number of targets that are healthy
UnhealthyHostCount	The number of targets that are unhealthy
RequestCountPerTarget	The average number of requests received by each target in a group

AWS VPC Networking

The networking layer at AWS is called a *virtual private cloud (VPC)*. Each customer's EC2 instances and containers and EBS storage must be deployed in a VPC (see Figure 11-20). Elastic Cloud Compute instances are always hosted within an AWS VPC. Software that runs on a Windows or Linux virtual server as web servers or application servers, databases, third-party virtual appliances, and AWS ECS or AWS EKS deployments also run on EC2 instances hosted in AWS VPCs.

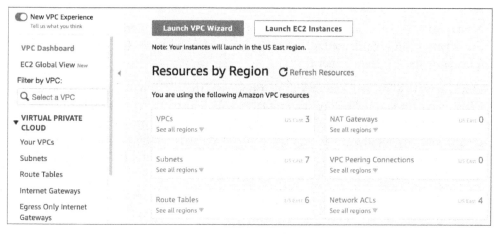

Figure 11-20 VPC Dashboard

When you create a VPC, AWS secures your VPC as a private, isolated software data center linked to your AWS account. AWS provisions, hosts, and secures each VPC; the remaining configuration is your responsibility. Amazon is responsible for safeguarding and protecting all VPC networks; Amazon must ensure the continued separation of your VPC from those of all other AWS customers. As described in the next section, the shared responsibility model specifies that AWS is responsible for the security *of* the cloud; each organization is responsible for maintaining workload security *in* the cloud.

There are lots of moving parts and pieces at AWS, which I like to describe as a large toolbox containing a variety of tools and attachments that you can snap together in any way that suits your design needs. Within the VPC toolbox are many configurable options, including route tables, public and private subnets, VPN connections, gateways, and private endpoints. In addition, there are multiple security choices available at every network level, allowing you to fully protect your EC2 instances and containers; choices include the AWS Network Firewall, the DNS Firewall, security groups (SGs), *network access control lists (NACLs)*, and more.

A VPC also has public and multiple private connectivity options, allowing you to connect your VPC to the Internet, to a private data center, or to other VPCs within or outside your region. Every cloud service that you order and deploy at AWS is hosted on the AWS network. It's up to you to plan where you want a service to be deployed, keeping in mind the goal of creating reliable, highly available, and secure workloads.

The Shared Security Model

When you host your applications in the Amazon public cloud, you have implicitly agreed to work in partnership with AWS in what is typically defined as a *shared security model*, as shown in Figure 11-21. AWS has responsibilities for building and securing its cloud infrastructure; this is typically referred to as *security of the cloud*. Your responsibility as an AWS customer is to design acceptable security provisions for your applications and data hosted on the AWS cloud. The level of acceptable security provisions is entirely your choice. Customers are therefore responsible for maintaining their *security in the cloud*. After AWS carries out the creation of a custom VPC, each customer makes the remaining design choices and security decisions.

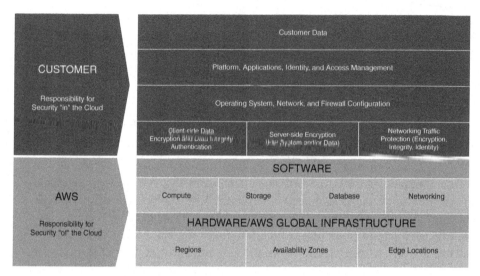

Figure 11-21   Shared Security Model

Within each VPC, EC2 compute instances are hosted on subnets that are created in selected AZs within the AWS region in which you have chosen to operate.

AWS Networking Terminology

Some of the AWS networking terms defined in this chapter may be new to you, whereas the names of other networking components and services that are used at AWS likely will sound familiar—for example, subnets, public and private IP addresses, and route tables. The networking services that are exposed to each customer at AWS are not the same network hardware devices that are deployed in customer data centers. Hosting hundreds of thousands of customers in a massive, shared networking environment requires networking services that will be different from your on-premises networking services due to the size and scope of Amazon's overall operations.

The first major concept of networking at AWS is that within each VPC, the networking exposed to each customer is designed and managed at the subnet level—specifically, the Layer 3 subnet address space contained within each availability zone. That's as deep as we're going to get in the network stack at AWS.

Your on-premises networking environment is probably composed of virtual local area networks (VLANs), Layer 2 networks, and Multiprotocol Label Switching (MPLS) connections. Why does a customer's exposure to the AWS network then start and end at Layer 3? Because thousands of customers running on a massively shared network infrastructure at AWS is at a scale that far exceeds the scale utilized within your own data centers. As a result, the internal network design offered to each customer needs to be different as well.

AWS does not deploy VLANs on the internal private AWS network because they cannot scale to the number of customers that Amazon hosts. A VPC also doesn't use MPLS for communication; however, you may be utilizing MPLS connections when connecting to a VPC using an external AWS Direct Connect or AWS Transit Gateway connection from your on-premises network.

Each VPC is a software-defined network built with Amazon's own code and custom network hardware developed by AWS to match its required scale of network operations. The underlying physical network at AWS would be quite recognizable at the component level; however, AWS customers don't have access to the physical network—that's restricted to the folks at AWS and it's their job to maintain it.

EC2 instances run on a hypervisor installed on custom-designed bare-metal servers (see Figure 11-22). For a number of years, the standard hypervisor that AWS used was a customized version of Xen, but many changes have happening at AWS. All new EC2 instance types since late 2017 are deployed on the Nitro System, a customized version of the KVM hypervisor with a published benchmark of less than 1% differential when comparing virtual EC2 instance performance to bare-metal system performance. The Nitro System uses Nitro chipsets that monitor the firmware and hardware at boot and support enhanced networking and EBS storage access and NVMe high-speed local SSD storage across a PCI bus.

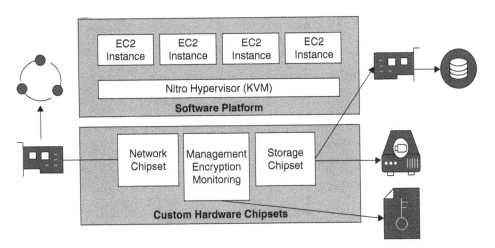

Figure 11-22 Instance Hosting by the Nitro Hypervisor

VPC Cheat Sheet

For the AWS Certified Solutions Architect – Associate (SAA-C03) exam, you need to understand the following critical aspects of VPCs:

- You can create private IP addresses from any private address range that adheres to RFC 1918 address allocation rules.

- You can expand your VPC by adding additional CIDR ranges.

- You can create both private and public subnets.

- It is possible to control both inbound and outbound subnet traffic by using NACLs.

- You can access most AWS services privately from your VPC by using private VPC endpoints and gateway connections.

- You can privately connect to third-party services hosted at AWS using a PrivateLink connection.

- You can connect on-premises resources privately with a VPC with a site-to-site connection.

- You create VPN connections to your VPC only after a virtual private gateway (VPG) has been installed.

- You can use VPC flow logs to log network traffic information to CloudWatch logs or S3 buckets for further analysis.

- With a VPC, you can deploy both IPv4 and IPv6 addressing.

- You can connect a VPC with another VPC by using a peering connection.

- You can assign Elastic IP addresses to EC2 instances for public Internet access.

- You can assign multiple elastic network interfaces to EC2 instances.

- You can protect access to EC2 instances by using one or more security groups.

- The Network Firewall is a managed service that provides network intrusion protection for VPCs using stateful firewall rules.

- The DNS Firewall allows the filtering and protection of DNS queries to public domain names from EC2 instances hosted in a VPC.

- The VPC Reachability Analyzer performs connectivity testing between a source and destination resource hosted in a VPC providing hop-by-hop details and the blocking component.

- The Network Access Analyzer helps identify network configurations that have security issues through testing current ingress and egress paths.

- You can control subnet traffic flow by defining custom route tables and route table entries.

- You can customize DHCP options to suit your needs by using DHCP options sets.

- You can enable private subnets to get updates by using *NAT gateway services* or NAT EC2 instances.

- You can protect IPv6 EC2 instances from direct communication from the Internet by deploying an *egress-only Internet gateway (EOIG)*.

- You can connect thousands of VPCs, attachments, and gateway connections together in a custom network deployment by using transit gateways, transit gateway peering, and transit gateway route tables.

- You can route multicast traffic between attached VPCs by creating a transit gateway multicast domain.

- You can capture and mirror network traffic for select EC2 instances by using VPC traffic mirroring.

Creating a VPC

The initial creation of a VPC is either a very simple process or a slightly more complex process, depending on the options you choose to deploy using the Create VPC wizard from the VPC Dashboard. You can also use the Amazon command-line interface (CLI) and enter a simple command line string to create a VPC.

Using the Create VPC Wizard

For this example, you begin by clicking the Your VPCs link on the VPC Dashboard. Here are the steps in creating a VPC by using the Create VPC wizard:

Step 1.   In the AWS Management Console, click Services, and under Networking and Content Delivery, select VPC. The VPC Dashboard appears.

Step 2.   In the VPC Dashboard, under Virtual Private Cloud, select Your VPCs.

Step 3.   Click the Create VPC button.

Step 4.   The selected resources to create are VPC only.

Step 5.   In the Name tag text box (see Figure 11-23), enter the name (tag) of your VPC.

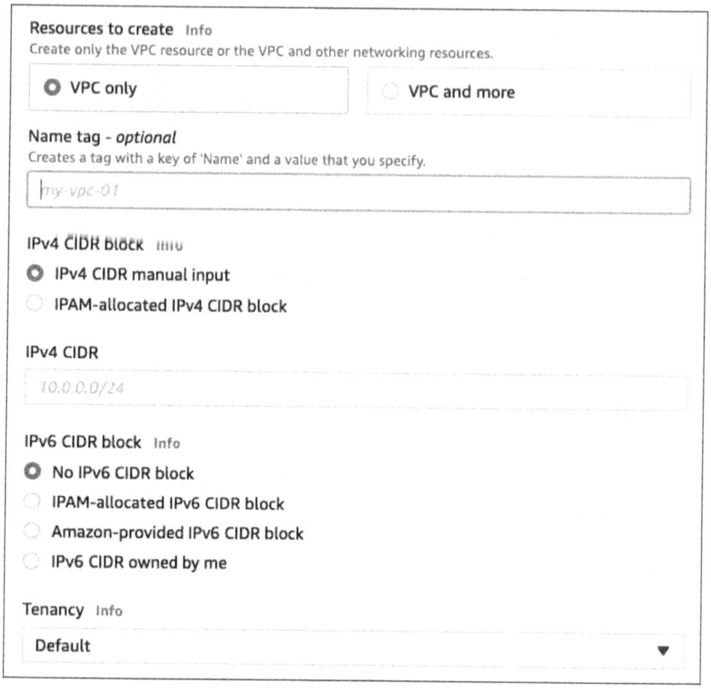

Resources to create Info
Create only the VPC resource or the VPC and other networking resources.

○ VPC only   ○ VPC and more

Name tag - *optional*
Creates a tag with a key of 'Name' and a value that you specify.

[my-vpc-01]

IPv4 CIDR block Info
◉ IPv4 CIDR manual input
○ IPAM-allocated IPv4 CIDR block

IPv4 CIDR

[10.0.0.0/24]

IPv6 CIDR block Info
◉ No IPv6 CIDR block
○ IPAM-allocated IPv6 CIDR block
○ Amazon-provided IPv6 CIDR block
○ IPv6 CIDR owned by me

Tenancy Info

[Default   ▼]

Figure 11-23   Using the Create VPC Wizard

Step 6.   Select the IPv4 CIDR manual input option and manually enter the desired IPv4 CIDR range. For example, entering 192.168.0.0/16 would allow you to create subnets within the VPC that could total approximately 65,530 possible hosts. The valid CIDR ranges supported by AWS are /16 to /28. For further details, see https://tools.ietf.org/html/rfc1519.

Step 7.   If required, in the IPv6 CIDR block section, select either IPAM-allocated IPv6 CIDR block, Amazon-provided IPv6 CIDR block, or IPv6 CIDR owned by me.

Step 8.   Optionally, change the Tenancy setting from Default (for shared tenancy) to Dedicated. Shared tenancy allows you to host EC2 instances that use default shared tenancy. Choosing dedicated tenancy mandates that all EC2 instances hosted in this VPC are dedicated EC2 instances.

Step 9.   Looking again at the top of Figure 11-23, if you choose the VPC and More radio button under Resources to Create, you can select IPv4 and IPv6 CIDR blocks up to two public subnets, up to three private subnets, associated route tables, up to three AZs, NAT gateways, S3 gateway endpoints, and custom DNS options, as shown in Figure 11-24. This figure is an excellent study guide for VPC network options.

Figure 11-24 VPC Starting Design Choices

NOTE Hosting EC2 instances at AWS in a VPC means other AWS customers will also be sharing the underlying bare-metal server hardware and hypervisor with you. You will not know which customers you are sharing AWS resources with. Selecting dedicated tenancy allows you to run your EC2 instances within a VPC designated as dedicated on single-tenant hardware where you are the only tenant or customer. This might be an important consideration if your organization is bound by strict governance rules that require it to operate with dedicated compute EC2 instances when operating in the AWS cloud.

Running dedicated EC2 instances at AWS is more expensive than multi-tenancy operations; a $2 charge per hour is added when dedicated EC2 instances are leveraged.

Using the AWS CLI to Create a VPC

The Create VPC wizard provides a starting point for creating a VPC network. You can also choose to use AWS CLI commands to create a VPC, as shown in Figure 11-25.

```
# Create a VPC with a /16 network and enable DNS hostnames
aws ec2 create-vpc --cidr-block 10.0.0.0/16 --enable-dns-hostnames

# Create two subnets in each Availability Zone
aws ec2 create-subnet --vpc-id <vpc-id> --cidr-block 10.0.0.0/24 --
availability-zone us-east-1a
aws ec2 create-subnet --vpc-id <vpc-id> --cidr-block 10.0.1.0/24 --
availability-zone us-east-1a
aws ec2 create-subnet --vpc-id <vpc-id> --cidr-block 10.0.2.0/24 --
availability-zone us-east-1b
aws ec2 create-subnet --vpc-id <vpc-id> --cidr-block 10.0.3.0/24 --
availability-zone us-east-1b
```

Figure 11-25   Creating a VPC by Using the AWS CLI

How Many VPCs Does Your Organization Need?

Depending on the creation process you have used, your new custom VPC might contain the required IPv4 or IPv6 CIDR blocks, or you might have fleshed out your design by choosing public and private subnets and associated network connectivity services. Now is a good time to pause and think about how many VPCs are required for your workload in total. Your company may have many developers creating their own set of VPCs without regard for other developers who are also creating VPCs. How much growth will you need over the next 2 years or more?

For example, suppose that your company is creating a custom human resources application; therefore, one VPC is required for the production workload. Will a separate VPC be useful for development? Perhaps an additional VPC could test for quality control. What if your company decides to operate in multiple AWS regions? What if multiple developers with multiple AWS accounts work on the development of the human resources system in different countries and with separate AWS accounts? Hopefully, you appreciate how complicated network decisions can become.

There are initial AWS service quotas on the number of VPCs that you can create. The number of VPCs each AWS account can create is a maximum of five VPCs per AWS account per AWS region. The Service Quotas utility is used for requesting the ability to create additional AWS resources including additional VPCs. Each AWS service has an initially defined quota limit assigned. Check the AWS documentation for each AWS service that you are planning to deploy to find the current and maximum quota limits and plan accordingly.

NOTE   Service quotas are per AWS account per region. With 30 regions available at AWS, a single AWS account could create 150 VPCs—5 per AWS region.

Consider these criteria for calculating the number of VPCs required:

- Your organization wants to extend, or burst, into the cloud, using resources in the corporate data center and cloud services when necessary at AWS. The primary need is to deploy additional compute resources at certain times of the month when additional performance is required. For this scenario, one VPC could be enough. A single VPC can host many subnets and EC2 instances with private connectivity back to a corporate data center.

- You are an independent developer creating a SaaS application that will be available across the Internet to users around the world. You have no corporate data center. You require a separate development, testing, and production workspace—three VPCs within a single region would be a good starting point.

- You are an administrator who has been tasked with leveraging cloud storage at AWS. You need unlimited storage, and you don't know the upper limit of your storage requirements. Your solution doesn't require a VPC. You need storage—perhaps S3 object storage or S3 Glacier archiving. The AWS S3 storage service does not reside within a VPC.

- You work for a large company that must follow specific compliance rules that dictate that workload resources must always remain separated. Separate VPCs for each workload must be created for development, testing, and production.

Creating the VPC CIDR Block

A VPC created using either an AWS CLI command or the Create VPC wizard is a blank slate except for the primary IPv4 Classless Inter-Domain Routing (CIDR) block and the local main routing table. Here are some CIDR details to be aware of:

- Both IPv4 and IPv6 subnets are supported within a VPC; however, a VPC or a subnet must have an initial IPv4 CIDR block defined first.

- IPv6 CIDR blocks can be associated with your VPC, but only after an initial IPv4 CIDR block has been created.

- Only IPv6 subnets can be created in a dual-stack (IPv4/IPV6 CIDR) VPC.

- CIDR blocks can't overlap with any existing CIDR blocks associated with another VPC connected with a peering connection. Overlapping CIDR blocks are to be avoided unless it's a deliberate decision to ensure that a VPC cannot connect to another VPC, regardless of the situation.

- The size of an existing CIDR block cannot be increased or decreased; it is locked after creation.

An Amazon-provided IPv6 CIDR block is a range of IPv6 addresses that can be used to create an IPv6 VPC and assign IPv6 addresses to your resources, such as EC2 instances and ELBs. When you create an IPv6 VPC, you can choose to use an Amazon-provided IPv6 CIDR block or specify your own IPv6 CIDR block. If you choose to use an Amazon-provided IPv6 CIDR block, AWS will automatically assign a range of IPv6 addresses to your VPC. Amazon-provided IPv6 CIDR blocks have the following characteristics:

- They are unique and globally routable, meaning they can be used to communicate with resources on the Internet.

- They are associated with your AWS account and are not transferable.

- They are automatically assigned when you create an IPv6 VPC, and you cannot specify the range of addresses that will be assigned.

Planning Your Primary VPC CIDR Block

There are many questions and many possible answers when planning IP addressing for your VPC. I can't stress it enough that if you are not the prime networking expert at your company, you should talk to your networking team and get advice on what IP address ranges you should use at AWS. Two or three years down the road, you might want to connect your network hosted at AWS to your corporate network, and you might find out that the IP address ranges selected were not the best choices. Meeting with your network team at the start of your cloud deployment will save you hours of future rework and prevent a serious meltdown. Without proper planning, your initial IP addressing choices could come back to haunt you.

NOTE   The primary IPv4 CIDR block and network mask that you choose for your VPC determines the number and size of IPv4 addresses that can be assigned to the subnets created within the VPC. Think of the CIDR block as a large bucket of IP addresses; the total number of addresses represents the number of EC2 instances, endpoints, AWS Lambda functions, and VPC connections that could be hosted on your VPC. The initial CIDR blocks that were added when you first created the VPC can't be changed; however, you have the option of adding additional four secondary CIDR blocks to an existing VPC.

Organizations can specify a range of IPv4 addresses for each VPC using a Classless Inter-Domain Routing (CIDR) block.

CIDR notation is a standard syntax for representing IP addresses and their associated routing prefix. It consists of an IP address and a prefix size, separated by a slash (/) character. The prefix size specifies the number of bits in the routing prefix, which determines the number of addresses in the range.

For example, the CIDR block 10.0.0.0/16 specifies a range of 256 IP addresses starting with 10.0.0.0 and ending with 10.0.255.255. The /16 prefix size indicates that the first 16 bits of the address are used for the routing prefix, and the remaining bits are used for host addresses.

For a VPC's starting CIDR address, choosing 192.168.0.0 with a /16 network mask determines the number of possible hosts that can be contained on subnets within this single VPC (see Figure 11-26.)

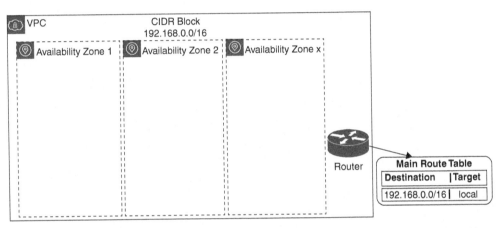

Figure 11-26 The Basic VPC Infrastructure Components

Table 11-5 lists sample address ranges from which you should be able to find an acceptable range of hosts and addresses to match your project. When in doubt, increase the subnet CIDR block size to allow the accommodation of additional hosts.

Table 11-5 VPC CIDR Block Examples

CIDR	Subnet Mask	Number of Hosts
/16	255.255.0.0	65,536
/17	255.255.128.0	32,768
/18	255.255.192.0	16,384
/19	255.255.224.0	8192
/20	255.255.240.0	4096
/21	255.255.248.0	2048
/22	255.255.252.0	1024

CIDR	Subnet Mask	Number of Hosts
/23	255.255.254.0	512
/24	255.255.255.0	256
/25	255.255.255.128	128
/26	255.255.255.192	64
/27	255.255.255.224	32
/28	255.255.255.240	16

As discussed earlier, during the creation of a VPC, an IPv4 CIDR block must be assigned to each VPC, even if you're planning to use IPv6 addresses. VPCs can also operate with just IPv6 addressing or in a dual-stack mode, communicating over both IPv4 and IPv6 protocols. The subnet CIDR block for IPv6 addresses that are assigned by AWS is fixed at /64. During or after VPC creation, you can choose to associate an IPv6 CIDR block to your VPC.

NOTE The first four IP addresses (0, 1, 2, and 3) and the last IP address (255) in each subnet's CIDR block are reserved for Amazon's use. Using /22 as a standard netmask for all subnets, the maximum number of hosts is 1,019. If you're creating a subnet for hosting thousands of clients using a VDI solution, you may need to pick a larger range for future expansion.

 Adding a Secondary CIDR Block

Up to four secondary IPv4 CIDR blocks can be associated with an existing VPC. After you add an additional CIDR block, the new route is automatically added to the VPC's main route tables, enabling the additional local routes throughout the VPC. Routing table details are discussed later in this chapter.

NOTE Keep in mind that the additional secondary CIDR block cannot be larger than the initial primary CIDR block. For example, if you associate a primary CIDR block of 10.0.0.0/24, an additional CIDR block of the same range or larger is not allowed. However, a CIDR block of 10.0.0.0/25 is allowed because it's a smaller range. The higher the CIDR number, the smaller the range of IP addresses available.

The primary advantage of being able to add additional secondary CIDR blocks to an existing VPC is for future expansion when necessary. If the initial primary CIDR block faces address space limitations over time, additional secondary CIDR blocks can be added in order to increase the number of IP addresses that can be assigned to subnets within the VPC. Each VPC can have up to 64,000 network access units (NAU) by default. You can request a service quota increase of up to 256,000.

The Default VPC

A default VPC is created in each AWS region, with each availability zone containing a public subnet. The default VPC is available within each AWS region and is created with the IPv4 CIDR block 172.30.0.0/16, which provides up to 65,531 private IPv4 addresses. In addition, an *Internet gateway (IG)* is created and attached to the default VPC with a route table entry that sends all IP traffic intended for the Internet to the attached Internet gateway. A default security group and default network ACL are also associated with the default VPC. An EC2 instance placed on the default public subnet within the default VPC receives both a public and a private IPv4 address and public and private DNS hostnames. EC2 instances deployed into the default VPC automatically have Internet access.

AWS provides the prebuilt default networking VPC environment to enable you to start working with AWS quickly, even if you have limited network knowledge. The default VPC can be handy if you want to do a quick demo and don't want to bother setting up subnets and Internet connectivity or have to think about any CIDR decisions; these networking decisions have already been carried out for the default VPC.

Perhaps having a separate demo AWS account using the default VPC for demonstrations would be useful. However, the default VPC can easily cause deployment issues; the default VPC may be preselected, as shown in Figure 11-27, and if you're not paying attention, using the default VPC can be trouble. For example, you might not want Internet access that has been defined for the public subnets of the default VPC by default. I recommend deleting the default VPC from every AWS region in your AWS account. This means you must set up all your AWS networking from scratch. But perhaps in the longer term, you'll be happier knowing there's no default VPC with Internet access provided to unsuspecting developers and administrators.

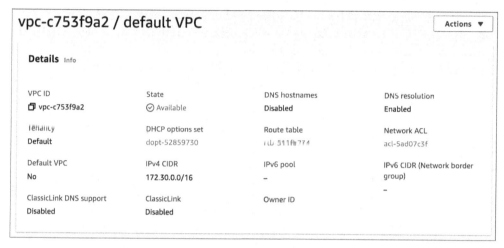

Figure 11-27   The Default VPC

NOTE   You cannot assign an existing VPC to become a default VPC, but you can delete the default VPC. If you want to re-create the default VPC, you can run an AWS-provided AWS CLI script.

Subnets

A *subnet* is a range of IPv4 or IPv6 addresses within a VPC that is associated with a specific availability zone. When you create a subnet, you specify the CIDR block for the subnet, which determines the range of IPv4 and IPv6 addresses that are available for use in the subnet.

You can create multiple subnets within a VPC, and each subnet can span one or more AZs. You can also specify a different CIDR block for each subnet.

When creating an IPv6 subnet, you will need to specify the IPv6 network range for the subnet and the number of IPv6 addresses that the subnet will contain. AWS uses a slash notation to specify the network range, similar to how IPv4 subnets are specified. For example, a subnet with a network range of 2001:db8:1234:5578::/64 would contain 64 IPv6 addresses.

Once an IPv6 subnet has been created, you can assign IPv6 addresses to resources within the subnet, such as EC2 instances, ELBs, and other resources. You can also create route tables and security groups to control inbound and outbound traffic for the IPv6 subnet.

There are several benefits to creating subnets within a VPC:

- **Network security:** Subnets can help you segment your network and isolate resources from each other, which can improve security and reduce the risk of unauthorized access.

- **Network management:** Subnets can help you organize and manage your network more efficiently, by allowing you to group resources based on their purpose or location.

- **Control traffic flow:** Subnets can help you control the flow of traffic between resources within the VPC and between the VPC and the Internet, by allowing you to specify different routing rules for different subnets.

The AZs that you select for subnet location are already available within the region where the VPC is created. It's usually stated that a VPC spans "all of the availability zones within its region," and certainly there is the potential to include all the AZs within a VPC if your design includes subnets for each AZ. However, AZs don't show up automatically in each VPC; instead, they are added during subnet creation when selecting each subnet's VPC and AZ location.

Each subnet that you create resides within its assigned AZ, as shown in Figure 11-28. If you choose to design your applications for resiliency and high availability, you'll want to design your workload to operate across at least two AZs.

Figure 11-28   Physical Locations of Network Components

Every subnet you create begins life as a private subnet with no connectivity outside of the VPC where it is hosted. To create a subnet with Internet access, you must complete several steps:

Step 1.   Order an Internet gateway (IGW).

Step 2.   Associate the IGW with a VPC.

Step 3.   Add a route table entry for the IGW to the subnet's route table that requires Internet access.

After you have completed these steps, you have created a public subnet.

Subnets are defined by the entries in the attached subnet route table:

- **Public subnet:** If a subnet's associated route table forwards traffic to the Internet through an Internet gateway, the subnet is defined as a public subnet.

- **Private subnet:** If a subnet's associated route table has no gateway or endpoint to direct traffic to, it is a private subnet, as traffic remains on the local subnet with no external connectivity. A subnet with no external gateway connectivity is a private subnet.

- **Protected subnet:** Protected subnets are often used to host resources that need to be isolated from the public Internet for security or compliance reasons, such as database servers or application servers. The subnet's route table allows inbound and outbound traffic only to and from resources within the subnet.

Most public-facing workloads or SaaS workloads will require the following subnet types:

- Public subnets for hosting public-facing load balancers and NAT services for private subnets

- Private subnets for web servers, application servers, or containers

- Protected subnets for database servers

 Subnet Cheat Sheet

For the AWS Certified Solutions Architect – Associate (SAA-C03) exam, you need to understand the following critical aspects of subnets:

- Subnets are contained within an AZ.

- IPv4 or IPv6 subnets can be created.

- IPv6-only subnets can be created.

- Subnets host EC2 instances.

- Public subnets have access to the Internet.

- Public subnets are for hosting infrastructure resources such as load balancers or NAT services.

- Private subnets are private, with no direct Internet access, although NAT services can provide indirect Internet access.

- A subnet cannot span multiple availability zones.

- If a subnet's traffic is routed to an Internet gateway, the subnet is a public subnet because there is a defined path to the Internet.

- If a subnet does not have a route to the Internet gateway, the subnet is a private subnet with no external destination defined.

- If a subnet has a route table entry that routes traffic to a virtual private gateway, the subnet is known as a VPN-only subnet, and it can be connected by using an external VPN connection.

IP Address Types

AWS supports both public and private IP address ranges that are assigned to public and private subnets and to the EC2 instances that are hosted on each subnet. Amazon, by default, handles the assigning of IP addresses using DHCP services. This section looks at the IP address options available at AWS, starting with private IPv4 addresses.

Private IPv4 Addresses

When a new EC2 instance is created and launched, by default, AWS assigns a primary private IP address to the default elastic network interface card (eth0) from the range of available IP subnet addresses. Network interfaces attached to EC2 instances are defined at AWS as elastic network interfaces (ENIs). Private IP addresses only communicate across the private network at AWS. A private DNS hostname that points to the associated private IPv4 address is also assigned to each EC2 instance. Private IP addresses are defined as addresses that are not routable over the Internet, regardless of whether they are used at AWS or on premises. If you choose to manually assign a primary private IP address, the private IP address chosen must be available in the subnet IP address range where the EC2 instance will reside. You can assign any private IP address in the assigned subnet range to an EC2 instance if it is not currently in use or reserved by AWS for its communication needs.

NOTE   Once a primary private IP address is assigned, the EC2 instance retains the address for the lifetime of the EC2 instance.

Additional (secondary) private IP addresses can also be assigned to ENIs of an EC2 instance, and these addresses can be unassigned and moved to other EC2 instances that reside on the same subnet at any time.

> **NOTE**   Cost is a factor here. Communication between EC2 instances residing on the same subnet using their private IP addresses is free of charge. However, EC2 instances using private IP addresses located on subnets in different AZs are charged an outbound data transfer fee for communicating with each other.
>
> The Simple Monthly Calculator (http://calculator.s3.amazonaws.com/index.html) is useful for carrying out detailed pricing scenarios.

Private IPv4 Address Summary

A private IP address is assigned by default to every EC2 instance on both public and private subnets. Here are some other criteria to remember:

- EC2 instances don't need to use public IP addresses; however, an EC2 instance is always assigned a private IP address.

- A private IP address is assigned for the life of each EC2 instance. The IP address remains attached until the EC2 instance is terminated.

Public IPv4 Addresses

Public IP addresses are used to access resources that have been placed in a public subnet, which is a subnet that is configured to allow inbound and outbound traffic to and from the Internet. A public IP address is typically assigned from AWS's pool of public IP addresses, as shown in Figure 11-29. Public IP addresses from AWS's own pool are managed and controlled by AWS and are therefore not permanently assigned to an EC2 instance. Instances in a public subnet can be assigned a public IP address automatically when they are launched. These public IP addresses are dynamic and are associated with the instance until it is stopped or terminated. Whether or not your EC2 instance receives a public IP address during creation is dependent on how the public IP addressing attribute has been defined on the subnet where the EC2 instance is to be hosted. At the subnet attribute level of any subnet you have created, the IPv4 public addressing attribute is initially set to false, which means no public IPv4 address will be assigned to any EC2 instance at creation.

```
 ● ● ●      🌐 https://ip-ranges.amazonaws.   ×   +

 ←  →  C  ⌂      🔒 ip-ranges.amazonaws.com/ip-ranges.json

{
 "syncToken": "1614269053",
 "createDate": "2021-02-25-16-04-13",
 "prefixes": [
    {
      "ip_prefix": "3.5.140.0/22",
      "region": "ap-northeast-2",
      "service": "AMAZON",
      "network_border_group": "ap-northeast-2"
    },
    {
      "ip_prefix": "15.230.56.104/31",
      "region": "us-east-1",
      "service": "AMAZON",
      "network_border_group": "us-east-1"
    },
    {
      "ip_prefix": "35.180.0.0/16",
      "region": "eu-west-3",
      "service": "AMAZON",
      "network_border_group": "eu-west-3"
    },
    {
      "ip_prefix": "52.93.153.170/32",
      "region": "eu-west-2",
      "service": "AMAZON",
      "network_border_group": "eu-west-2"
    },
    {
      "ip_prefix": "52.93.178.234/32",
      "region": "us-west-1",
      "service": "AMAZON",
      "network_border_group": "us-west-1"
    },
```

Figure 11-29 The AWS Public IP Address Pool

You can enable the public IP addressing attribute during the creation of an EC2 instance; if you do, an AWS-controlled public IP address is assigned, overruling the default state of the subnet's public IP address attribute.

Elastic IP Addresses

An *Elastic IP (EIP) address* is a static public IPv4 address that is created and assigned to your AWS account and can be easily remapped to any EC2 instance or elastic network interface in your AWS account. They are useful for EC2 instances or services, such as NAT gateway services that need to be reachable from the Internet and require a consistent, static IP address. Requesting an EIP address is simple: Request an EIP address, as shown in Figure 11-30, and it's added to your AWS account from the regional pool of available EIP addresses. EIPs are unassigned; you need to first assign an EIP to the desired VPC and then to the desired EC2 instance.

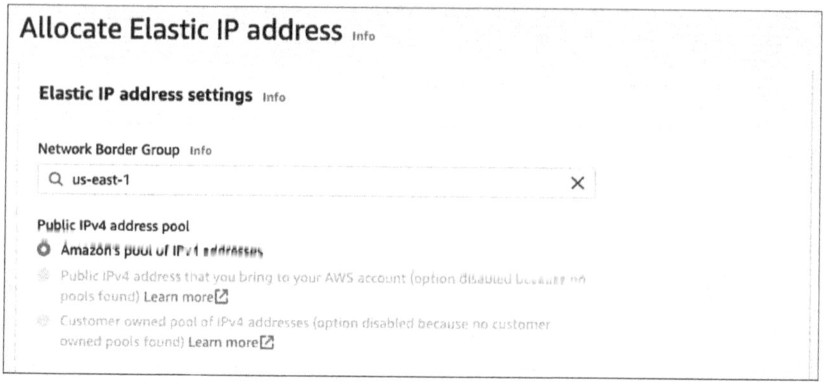

Figure 11-30   Elastic IP Addresses

AWS advertises each regional pool of its EIPs across the public Internet and to all other AWS regions. Because of this advertising, EIPs hosted at AWS can be located across the public Internet and within the public AWS address space.

> **NOTE**   A public listing of all available AWS EIP addresses is available at https://docs.aws.amazon.com/general/latest/gr/aws-ip-ranges.html.

When an EC2 instance has been assigned an EIP address, turning the EC2 instance off and back on is not an issue. The EIP address remains attached because it's assigned to your AWS account and to the EC2 instance. And there's no additional charge for ordering and assigning a single EIP address to an EC2 instance. However, if you order but don't assign an EIP address, AWS charges you because EIPs are in limited supply.

At AWS, there are four public pools of IP addresses to consider:

- **Dynamically assigned public IPv4 addresses:** Assigned to EC2 instances and returned to the common public pool of AWS addresses when an EC2 instance shuts down, releasing its dynamically assigned public IPv4 address.

- **Elastic IP addresses:** Elastic IP addresses are static, public IP addresses that are allocated to your AWS account.

- **BYOIP public IPv4 and IPv6 addresses:** Detailed in the upcoming section "Bring-Your-Own IP (BYOIP)."

- **Global unicast IPv6 addresses:** These addresses are unique, globally routable addresses that are assigned to VPCs and subnets. They are used to communicate with resources on the Internet and can be assigned to instances, ELBs, and other resources in a VPC.

The public IPv4 address is displayed as an attribute of the network interface when viewed through the AWS EC2 dashboard, but the internal wiring is a little more complicated. On an EC2 instance with a public IP address, this address is internally mapped to the EC2 instance's primary private IPv4 address using NAT services. When a public IP address is assigned to an EC2 instance, the inbound traffic is directed to your EC2 instance's private internal IP address.

If your EC2 instance is directly accessible from the Internet, when someone wants to directly reach your EC2 instance, the inbound destination is the public IP address. When the EC2 instance needs to communicate outbound across the Internet, the source address is its public IP address. Queries on the private network of the EC2 instance always use the private address of the EC2 instance. The takeaway from this example is that AWS attempts to use the private IP address, whenever possible, for network communication with an EC2 instance.

Each EC2 instance that receives a public IP address at AWS is also provided with an external DNS hostname. As a result, the external DNS hostname is resolved to the public IP address of the EC2 instance when queries are external to AWS, as shown in Figure 11-31.

Figure 11-31   Assigned IP Addresses and DNS Hostnames

Public IPv4 Address Cheat Sheet

For the AWS Certified Solutions Architect – Associate (SAA-C03) exam, you need to understand the following critical aspects of public IPv4 addresses:

- You can use EIP addresses for NAT EC2 instances or custom public-facing appliances.

- You can use EIP addresses for public-facing load balancers.

- You can use EIP addresses for public-facing EC2 instances.

- You must use EIP addresses for the NAT gateway services.

- Public IP addresses are not necessary for EC2 instances.

Inbound and Outbound Traffic Charges

It's important to realize that you are billed differently for public traffic and private traffic at AWS. Your AWS outbound traffic costs can become extremely high if you don't pay attention. For example, you will be charged more for public traffic sent to a public IP address traveling across the Internet than for private IP address traffic. Private traffic traveling within AWS data centers is always cheaper than traffic on a public subnet (see Figure 11-32); therefore, whenever possible, AWS uses the private network for communication.

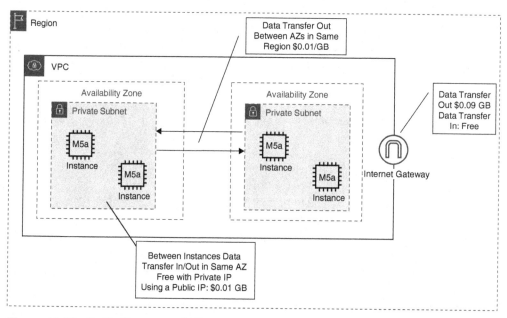

Figure 11-32 Traffic Charges at AWS

Private traffic that stays within a single subnet incurs no additional charges, whereas private traffic that travels across multiple private subnets that are hosted by different AZs incurs an egress charge of $.01 per gigabyte. However, RDS database replication across separate availability zones is free for the synchronous replication of your data from the primary database EC2 instance to the secondary database EC2 instance. One task to carry out is a detailed cost optimization of your production workload traffic patterns, including the costs for replication across AZs, load balancer traffic, and outbound traffic flow.

NOTE All inbound communication traffic that an EC2 instance receives is free, regardless of whether it comes from inside AWS or from the public Internet. However, EC2 instance replication traffic across multiple AZs, with the exception of RDS deployments, is charged a data transfer fee.

Bring-Your-Own IP

Bring-Your-Own IP (BYOIP) is a feature offered by AWS that enables you to bring your own public IPv4 or IPv6 addresses to AWS and use them with your AWS resources. This can be useful if you want to use a specific range of IP addresses for your resources or if you want to migrate your existing IP addresses to AWS. If you own a publicly routable public IPv4 or IPv6 address range, you can move part or all of a public IP address from your on-premises network to AWS. Each organization still owns their public IP range; however, AWS hosts and advertises the public IP address range hosted at AWS across the Internet and AWS regions for you. The public address range must be registered with your Regional Internet Registry (RIR)—for example, the American Registry for Internet Numbers (ARIN)—and must also be registered to a business or institution, not to an individual person. Bringing your own public IPv4 or IPv6 address space to AWS allows you to accomplish the following:

- Maintain your public IP address reputation.

- Avoid any changes to public IP addresses that have been whitelisted.

- Avoid changing IP addresses that legacy applications still use.

- Use a public IP address as a hot standby failover for on-premises resources.

The following are some examples of situations in which you might want to control your own public address space in the AWS cloud:

- You want to keep a recognizable public IP address but have the service assigned to that address hosted on AWS.

- You have 10,000 hard-coded lottery machines, and you want to change the hardware devices to virtual ones at AWS with your public IP addresses.

- You have 2,000 hard-coded public IP addresses within your data center, and you want to change the physical location of your data center to AWS but keep the same public IP addresses.

- You have legacy workloads—or older applications that rely on specific fixed public IP addresses—and want to move these addresses to AWS.

NOTE   The specific prefix supported by BYOIP at AWS for IPv4 public addresses is /24. The specific prefix for IPv6 addresses is /48 for CIDRs that are publicly advertised, and /56 for CIDRs that are not publicly advertised.

The BYOIP Process

These are the basic steps for allocating BYOIP addresses to AWS:

Step 1.   Import the public IP address, or the range of public IP addresses, into AWS. AWS creates a pool of these addresses and assigns the address pool to you.

After AWS has analyzed and accepted the range of public IP addresses, the state of the public address range to be hosted at AWS changes to "provisioned," indicating that the IP address request has been accepted. At this point, you can use these public IP addresses, but they have not yet been advertised across the Internet or to the peering partners of AWS.

Step 2.   Advertise the public address range to all the peering partners of AWS. When the advertising process has been accepted and started at AWS, it's time to stop the advertising of the same public IP addresses to avoid any strange duplication routing conflicts.

Step 3.   Allocate EIP addresses from your AWS-hosted pool of public IP addresses.

When using the hosted pool of addresses at AWS to allocate EIP addresses, you can select a random IP address from the hosted pool or select a specific IP address.

If in the future you decide you don't want AWS to advertise and host your pool of public IP addresses, you can execute a "withdraw" command to change the state of the public IP addresses from advertised back to an unadvertised state. At this point, AWS no longer advertises your public IP addresses. The last step is to run the deprovisioning command to remove the assigned EIP addresses.

IPv6 Addresses

Even though IPv6 addresses are fully supported within a VPC, an IPv4 CIDR block must be created first. The allowable format for IPv6 addresses is 128 bits, with a fixed CIDR block size of /56. Amazon is in control of IPv6 addressing at AWS; you cannot select your own IPv6 CIDR range. At AWS, IPv6 addresses are globally unique addresses and can be configured to remain private or reachable across the Internet.

Amazon VPC has built-in support for address assignment via DHCP for both IPv4 and IPv6 addresses. If your EC2 instance is configured to receive an IPv6 address at launch, the address will be associated with the primary network interface (eth0). Assigned IPv6 addresses are also persistent; you can stop and start your EC2 instance, and the IPv6 addresses remain assigned. Access to the Internet using an IPv6 address can be controlled by using the egress-only Internet gateway (EOIG), route tables, and, optionally, network access controls. Here is a short summary of the steps for providing IPv6 Internet access:

Step 1.   Associate the AWS-provided IPv6 CIDR block with your VPC.

Step 2.   Create and attach an Internet gateway to the VPC and add a route table entry to the subnet that will communicate with the IGW.

Step 3.   Create an egress-only Internet gateway. This allows your private subnet to enable outbound communications to the Internet using IPv6; the EOIG allows outbound communication and prevents any inbound communication.

Step 4.   Update your route tables to route your IPv6 traffic to the EOIG:

- **For EC2 instances hosted on IPv6 public subnets:** Add a route that directs all IPv6 traffic from the subnet to the Internet gateway. Note that this is the regular Internet gateway and not the EOIG; the EOIG is controlling private outbound communication from the private subnet and stopping any inbound connections from the Internet.

- **For EC2 instances on IPv6 private subnets:** Create a route that directs all Internet-bound IPv6 traffic to the EOIG.

Step 5.   Review and, if necessary, update your network access controls.

NOTE   EC2 instances launched in IPv6-only subnets and ENIs attached to them are assigned IPv6 addresses through the DHCPv6 options set from the IPv6 CIDR block of your subnet. When EC2 instances are launched in IPv6-only subnets, resource-based naming (RBN) is used automatically; the EC2 instance ID is included in the hostname of the instance.

VPC Flow Logs

Network traffic can be captured for analysis or to diagnose communication problems at the level of the elastic network interface, subnet, or entire VPC. AWS does not charge you for creating a flow log, but it will impose charges for data storage. When each flow log is created, you define the type of traffic that will be captured—either accepted traffic only, rejected traffic only, or all traffic, as shown in Figure 11-33.

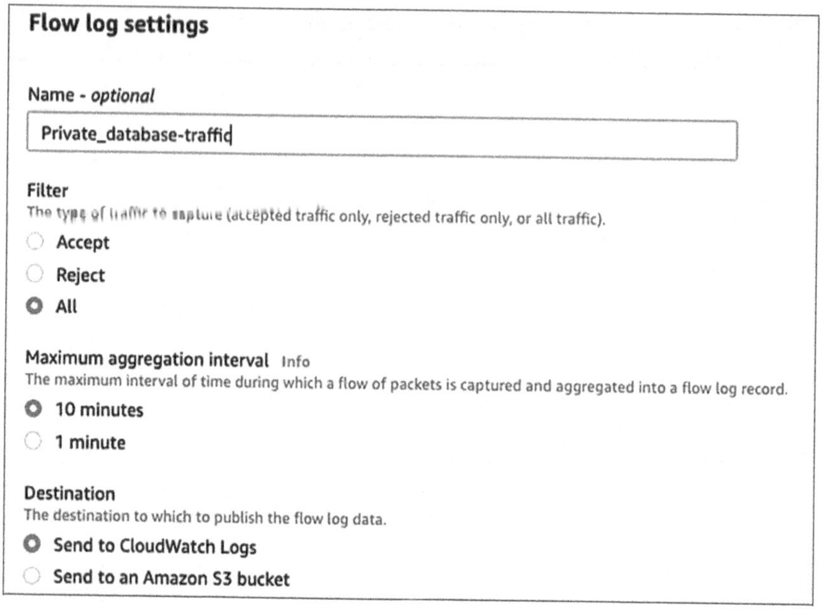

Flow log settings

Name - *optional*

Private_database-traffic

Filter
The type of traffic to capture (accepted traffic only, rejected traffic only, or all traffic).

○ Accept

○ Reject

◉ All

Maximum aggregation interval Info
The maximum interval of time during which a flow of packets is captured and aggregated into a flow log record.

◉ 10 minutes

○ 1 minute

Destination
The destination to which to publish the flow log data.

◉ Send to CloudWatch Logs

○ Send to an Amazon S3 bucket

Figure 11-33 Flow Log Storage Location Choices

Flow logs can be stored either in a CloudWatch log group or directly in an Amazon S3 bucket for storage, also shown in Figure 11-33. If VPC flow logs are stored as a CloudWatch log group, IAM roles must be created that define the permissions for the CloudWatch monitoring service to publish the flow log data to the CloudWatch log group. Once the log group has been created, you can publish multiple flow logs to the same log group.

Creating a flow log for a subnet or a VPC, each network interface present in the VPC, or subnet is then monitored. Launching additional EC2 instances into a subnet with an attached flow log results in new log streams for each new network interface and any network traffic flows.

Not all network traffic is logged in a flow log. Examples of traffic that is not logged in flow logs include AWS DNS server traffic, Windows license activation traffic, instant metadata requests, Amazon Time Sync Service traffic, reserved IP address traffic, DHCP traffic, and traffic across a PrivateLink interface.

Any AWS service that uses EC2 instances with network interfaces can take advantage of flow logs. Supporting services also include ELB, Amazon RDS, Amazon ElastiCache, Amazon Redshift, Amazon EMR, and Amazon WorkSpaces. Each of these services is hosted on an EC2 instance with network interfaces.

Connectivity Options

There are several methods of connecting resources in VPCs across the AWS private network, as summarized in Table 11-6.

Table 11-6 VPC Private Connectivity Options

Option	Details
Peering VPC connections	Connect two VPCs together with a private network connection
Gateway endpoints	Connect a VPC to S3 buckets or a DynamoDB table across the AWS private network
Interface endpoints	Connect a VPC to most AWS services across the AWS private network
Transit gateway	The *transit gateway* is a network transit hub used to interconnect VPCs and on-premises networks privately. Traffic is encrypted automatically. Connect VPCs, Direct Connect gateways, VPN connections, and peering connections.

VPC Peering

VPC peering enables you to connect two VPCs in the same or different regions and communicate with each other as if they were on the same network, using private IP addresses. It's quite common to find that a single company has many AWS accounts and multiple VPCs. This can be a management nightmare, especially if separate AWS accounts and separate VPCs might need to be connected to share resources or common services, such as monitoring or authentication. Thankfully, you can create networking connections between VPCs through a process called *peering*, which enables you to route traffic between two VPCs that have been peered together. Route tables, security groups, and NACLs control which subnets or EC2 instances are able to connect using the peered connection with an AWS region.

A *peering connection* is not the same as a gateway connection or a VPN connection. Instead, peering is set up by first sending an invitation from one VPC to another VPC; the invitation must be accepted before the peering connection is established. Peering within the same AWS account involves using each VPC's ID for identification. Peering VPCs between different AWS accounts requires both AWS account IDs and the VPC IDs.

Peering occurs between a VPC in one AWS account or between a VPC in another AWS account. Peered VPCs can also reside in completely different AWS regions. Data traffic between VPCs peered in different regions is encrypted using *AEAD encryption*, which uses the Authenticated Encryption with Associated Data protocol. With AEAD encryption, AWS manages the entire encryption process and supplies and rotates the encryption keys.

Establishing a Peering Connection

The VPC that starts the peering process is called the *requester VPC*; it defines the owner of the VPC that would like to establish a peering connection. The *accepter VPC* is the VPC and account owner that needs to accept the request to establish a peer (see Figure 11-34). Here are the basic steps involved in peering:

Step 1.   The owner of the requester VPC sends a request to the owner of the accepter VPC.

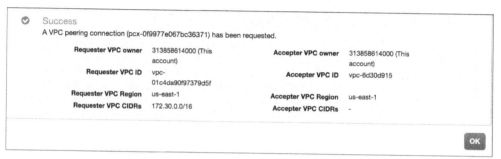

Figure 11-34   Peering Traffic Flow

Step 2.   The owner of the accepter VPC accepts the VPC peering connection request.

Step 3.   The peering connection is activated.

Step 4.   Security group rules are updated within each VPC to ensure proper traffic routing to and from the VPCs that have been peered together.

Step 5.   Route tables are updated with entries to allow the flow of traffic to enable communications between the two VPCs.

The accepter VPC might be a VPC that is in your AWS account and therefore one of your own, or it could be another AWS account's VPC. This relationship flexibility is important because single companies can have many developers with VPCs created within their AWS accounts. A VPC could also be from a third-party service provider that has developed an application that's entirely hosted in a separate private VPC infrastructure, such as a monitoring service or a disaster recovery service.

The following are some additional considerations for VPC peering:

■ VPC peering connections cannot be created between VPCs that have matching or overlapping IPv4 or IPv6 CIDR blocks.

■ More than one VPC peering connection between the same two VPCs is not allowed.

The following are some inter-region VPC peering limitations to be aware of:

- Public IPv4 DNS hostnames cannot be resolved from EC2 instances on one side of the peered connection to a private IPv4 address on the other side of the peered connection.

- VPC peering supports both IPv4 and IPv6 addresses, enabling you to connect VPCs that use either protocol.

- The maximum transmission unit (MTU) across the VPC peering connection is 1500 bytes; jumbo frames are not supported.

- Security group rules cannot reference a VPC security group across a peered connection; directing outbound traffic from one side of a peered connection to a security group on the other side of the peered connection is not allowed. A VPN or a Direct Connect connection to a corporate network across a peered connection is not allowed.

- An Internet connection from a private subnet to a NAT device in a public subnet cannot travel across a peered connection to an AWS service such as DynamoDB or S3. For example, VPC A is connected to the corporate network using a Direct Connect connection. Users at the head office cannot connect through the Direct Connect connection to VPC A and across the peered connection to VPC B.

- A VPC peering connection is always a one-to-one relationship between two VPCs. Transitive peering relationships are not supported.

- A VPC can have multiple peering relationships with other VPCs, but each peering relationship is always a direct, one-to-one relationship.

VPC Endpoints

Endpoints enable you to create a private connection between your VPC and another AWS service without the need for an Internet gateway, a NAT gateway, or a VPN connection. VPC endpoints are used to enable communication among resources in your VPC and other AWS services using private IP addresses, which can improve the security and performance of your applications. The majority of endpoint connections are interface VPC endpoints; however, there is a gateway endpoint for accessing Amazon DynamoDB.

VPC Gateway Endpoints

VPC Gateway endpoints are attached to your VPC and use a route in the associated subnet's route table to connect to the target service. They can be used to connect to Amazon S3 and DynamoDB, as shown in Figure 11-35. VPC Gateway endpoints are not charged for creation and data transfer.

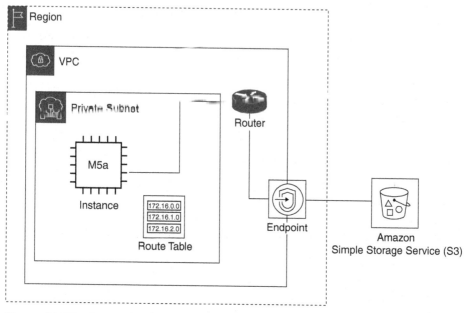

Figure 11-35   Gateway Endpoint Access to S3

To create a gateway endpoint, you need to follow these steps:

Step 1.   From the VPC Dashboard, select the Endpoints tab on the left and click Create Endpoint.

Step 2.   Select the gateway endpoint for DynamoDB.

Step 3.   Select the VPC and subnets where access is required.

Step 4.   Modify the default endpoint policy to match your security needs.

Step 5.   Update the security groups and network ACLs as necessary.

Endpoint policies can be deployed to further define the endpoint access rules. The default policy allows full access to the service; this default policy should be evaluated and changed if necessary. Custom endpoint policies control access from the VPC through the gateway endpoint to the service from the EC2 instance.

VPC Interface Endpoints

The newest form of a VPC endpoint supported by AWS is an *interface endpoint* powered by a technology called PrivateLink. The "interface" is a network adapter designated with a private IP address. AWS services are not all accessible through interface endpoint connections; however, many AWS services are accessible through private interface endpoints.

AWS resources with an interface connection are accessed using a private IP address from the selected VPC subnet. If AWS resources are connected with multiple sub-nets, multiple private IP addresses will be used—one IP address per availability zone subnet. If you are using AWS Direct Connect to link your on-premises data center with AWS resources, there is also a bonus: You can access AWS-hosted data records and AWS services from your on-premises network.

For example, a developer is sitting in an office, working on developing applications using the AWS Cloud9 IDE. The developer accesses the development portal privately across the high-speed fiber Direct Connect connection, and VPC interface connnection shown in Figure 11-36. When the application is finished and deployed in production, the application can continue to be accessed privately through the Direct Connect connection from the head office.

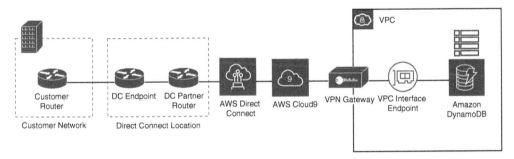

Figure 11-36 Using Interface VPC Endpoints

Many large corporations considering a move to the cloud remain cautious of having corporate data records stored in the cloud. For these situations, endpoint connections combined with high-speed 100-Gbps Direct Connect connections deliver speed, security, and AWS services across a totally private environment.

With no public connectivity, the AWS services that are being accessed using an interface or gateway endpoint are fully protected from any Internet-facing attacks, including DDoS attacks, because the private interface endpoints simply cannot be reached from the Internet. When you create an endpoint inside your VPC, service names are protected; Route 53 DNS services send you to the private endpoint loca-tion and ignore any public routes that also may be advertised. Private endpoints also have regional zonal names designed for keeping traffic within the region, allowing customers to isolate traffic, if necessary, to a specific AZ. These zonal endpoints could also potentially save you additional data transfer charges and latency issues.

The hardware powering interface endpoints is publicly called PrivateLink, but internally, AWS calls this network hardware Hyperplane. Hyperplane is a massively scalable, fault-tolerant distributed system that is designed for managing VPC network connections. It resides in the fabric of the VPC networking layer, where AWS's software-defined networking is deployed; it can make transactional decisions in microseconds. When a VPC interface endpoint is created, it is associated with several virtual Hyperplane nodes that intercept network communications at the VPC networking layer and quickly decide what to do with each request. If a request is made to a private endpoint, the transactional decision and the shared state are applied in milliseconds. Interface VPC endpoints only accept TCP traffic, and each endpoint supports a bandwidth of up to 10 Gbps per availability zone. It also automatically scales up to 100Gbps.

Endpoint Services

Using the PrivateLink technology, AWS hopes to help provide private SaaS services to corporations that are currently using AWS services, as shown in Figure 11-37. The owner of a private SaaS service hosted at AWS is called a *service provider*, and the owner of an interface endpoint is called a *service consumer* because it is the consumer of the service. Private SaaS services could include monitoring services and disaster recovery services.

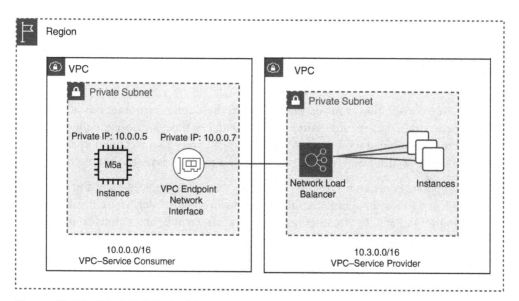

Figure 11-37   PrivateLink Endpoints

A customer who wants to access the third-party SaaS service creates a VPC gateway or interface endpoint connecting to the service provider's endpoint service.

To handle network access to the subscribed service, behind the "interface" connection is a private NLB positioned at the entrance to the hosted SaaS service.

Third-party microservice architectures could also be hosted within the third party's private VPC. The service provider VPC can follow the same best practices as recommended by AWS for creating fault-tolerant applications hosted in a VPC. Amazon uses this process to provide network load-balancing services to multiple customers within each region. Applications can be designed with availability targets located across multiple AZs.

Depending on the tenancy requirements of the customer, for a single-tenant mode of operation, a private NLB could be created for every client customer. Multi-tenant designs could allow multiple customers to use the same NLB service. There are several additional choices available to separate endpoint traffic from VPCs in a multi-tenant design:

- Use separate account/password security tokens at the application level.

- Use separate NLBs and different listener ports.

- Use the Proxy Protocol V2 preamble, which adds a header to each connection that lists the ID of the destination endpoint.

NOTE The costs for PrivateLink are split between the provider and the customer. The provider side pays for the NLB costs. The client side pays for the PrivateLink endpoint costs.

The steps for creating a PrivateLink interface endpoint are as follows:

Step 1. From the VPC Dashboard, select Endpoint from the menu and click Create Endpoint.

Step 2. Select the PrivateLink Ready partner service.

Step 3. Select the VPC and subnets where access is required.

Step 4. Select Enable Private DNS Name, if required.

Step 5. Select Security Group.

Step 6. Update route tables, security groups, and network ACLs as necessary.

Exam Preparation Tasks

As mentioned in the section "How to Use This Book" in the Introduction, you have a couple of choices for exam preparation: the exercises here, Chapter 16, "Final Preparation," and the exam simulation questions in the Pearson Test Prep Software Online.

Review All Key Topics

Review the most important topics in the chapter, noted with the Key Topic icon in the margin of the page. Table 11-7 lists these key topics and the page number on which each is found.

Table 11-7   Chapter 11 Key Topics

Key Topic Element	Description	Page
Section	CloudFront Use Cases	529
Section	Serving Private Content	530
Section	Using an Origin Access Identifier	531
Section	CloudFront Origin Failover	532
Section	Edge Functions	534
Section	CloudFront Cheat Sheet	536
List	Standard and custom accelerators	537
Section	Rules, Conditions, and Actions	545
Section	Target Groups	547
Section	Target Group Attributes	550
Section	ALB Cheat Sheet	553
List	NLB features	554
Section	NLB Cheat Sheet	554
Section	The Shared Security Model	557
Section	VPC Cheat Sheet	560
Figure 11-24	VPC Starting Design Choices	563
Section	Adding a Secondary CIDR Block	568
Section	Subnet Cheat Sheet	572
Section	Private IPv4 Address Summary	574

Key Topic Element	Description	Page
Section	IPv6 Addresses	580
Section	VPC Flow Logs	581
Table 11-6	VPC Private Connectivity Options	583
Section	Establishing a Peering Connection	584
Section	VPC Endpoints	585
Section	Endpoint Services	588

Define Key Terms

Define the following key terms from this chapter and check your answers in the glossary:

Amazon CloudFront, regional edge cache, origin access identity (OAI), origin failover, Lambda@Edge, listener, connection draining, target group, health check, sticky session, virtual private cloud (VPC), network access control list (NACL), NAT gateway service, egress-only Internet gateway (EOIG), Internet gateway (IG), subnet, Elastic IP (EIP) address, peering connection, endpoint

Q&A

The answers to these questions appear in Appendix A. For more practice with exam format questions, use the Pearson Test Prep Software Online.

1. How does deploying CloudFront help globalize your data records?

2. Can you manage third-party load balancers with an ELB service?

3. What CIDR address range should you use for your VPC?

4. Why would organizations require more than one VPC?

5. Why should you avoid using public subnets for your web servers?

6. How can you move your existing public IP addresses to AWS?

7. What AWS networking services can replace existing hardware devices?

8. What can network ACLs do that a security group cannot do?

9. Why would you use Elastic IP addresses?

10. How does deploying endpoints help secure VPC hosted workloads?

This chapter covers the following topics:

- Calculating AWS Costs
- Cost Management Tools
- Storage Types and Costs
- AWS Backup
- Data Transfer Options
- AWS Storage Gateway

This chapter covers content that's important to the following exam domain and task statement:

Domain 4: Design Cost-Optimized Architectures

Task Statement 1: Design cost-optimized storage solutions

CHAPTER 12

Designing Cost-Optimized Storage Solutions

Hosting applications at AWS is supposed to save you money, or so goes the common assumption. Moving to the cloud can help you save money, but you need to review AWS's pricing structure in depth to understand how AWS charges for using its cloud services. Pricing at AWS is complicated; someday, there will probably be a university degree focusing on AWS pricing. The AWS Certified Solutions Architect – Associate (SAA-C03) exam has been revised to include an expanded knowledge domain on costs. You must understand how to manage storage costs.

Recall from Chapter 2, "The AWS Well-Architected Framework," that Cost Optimization is one of the six pillars of the AWS Well-Architected Framework. The AWS document "Cost Optimization Pillar" (see https:// docs.aws.amazon.com/wellarchitected/latest/cost-optimization-pillar/ wellarchitected-cost-optimization-pillar.pdf) provides additional details to help you understand how to manage costs at AWS. Additionally, there are cost-optimization labs at https://wellarchitectedlabs.com/cost/ to assist you in developing hands-on skills in the management of AWS cloud costs. To help study for the SAA-C03 exam, make sure to sign up for an AWS Free Tier account; most of the Well-Architected Labs can be completed at little to no cost (https://aws.amazon.com/free).

"Do I Know This Already?"

The "Do I Know This Already?" quiz enables you to assess whether you should read this entire chapter thoroughly or jump to the "Exam Preparation Tasks" section. If you are in doubt about your answers to these questions or your own assessment of your knowledge of the topics, read the entire chapter. Table 12-1 lists the major headings in this chapter and their corresponding "Do I Know This Already?" quiz questions. You can find the answers in Appendix A, "Answers to the 'Do I Know This Already?' Quizzes and Q&A Sections."

Table 12-1 "Do I Know This Already?" Section-to-Question Mapping

Foundation Topics Section	Questions
Calculating AWS Costs	1, 2
Cost Management Tools	3, 4
Storage Types and Costs	5, 6
AWS Backup	7, 8
Data Transfer Options	9, 10
AWS Storage Gateway	11, 12

CAUTION   The goal of self-assessment is to gauge your mastery of the topics in this chapter. If you do not know the answer to a question or are only partially sure of the answer, you should mark that question as wrong for purposes of the self-assessment. Giving yourself credit for an answer you correctly guess skews your self-assessment results and might provide you with a false sense of security.

1. How are costs charged at AWS?

   a. Per AZ

   b. Per AWS region

   c. Per report

   d. Included in the price

2. How are Elastic Load Balancing (ELB) charges calculated?

   a. Number of connections

   b. Inbound traffic levels

   c. Load balancer capacity units

   d. Amount of outgoing data transferred

3. How do you access the cost management tools at AWS?

   a. AWS Cost Explorer

   b. AWS Billing Dashboard

   c. AWS Budgets

   d. AWS Cost and Usage Reports

4. How is the tracking of your AWS costs initiated?

   a. AWS Budgets

   b. AWS Cost and Usage Reports

   c. Enable data collection with Cost Explorer

   d. Enable rightsizing recommendations in Cost Explorer

5. How are Amazon S3 storage costs calculated ?

   a. By gigabytes per month stored

   b. Tiered pricing

   c. By storage class

   d. Based on AWS region

6. What are the most expensive Amazon EBS volume types?

   a. SSD volumes

   b. Throughput-optimized volumes

   c. PIOPS volumes

   d. Cold storage volumes

7. What two storage tiers are maintained by AWS Backup?

   a. Hot and cold tiers

   b. Standard and infrequent access tiers

   c. On-demand and continuous tiers

   d. Warm and cold storage tiers

8. What AWS Backup plan feature manages warm and cold storage tiers?

   a. Backup window

   b. Tags

   c. Lifecycle rules

   d. Regional copies

9. What service automates the movement of data from on-premises locations to either Amazon S3 buckets or EFS storage?

   a. AWS SFTP

   b. AWS FTP

   c. AWS Snow Family

   d. AWS DataSync

10. What is the smallest member of the AWS Snow Family?

   a. Snowball

   b. Snowmobile

   c. Snowcone

   d. Snowball Edge

11. Which AWS Storage Gateway storage option supports virtual tape backups?

   a. Tape Gateway

   b. File Gateway

   c. Volume Gateway

   d. Amazon S3 Glacier gateway

12. What type of storage is supported by AWS Storage Gateway?

   a. Cloud storage

   b. Amazon S3 storage

   c. Amazon FSx for Windows File Server storage

   d. Hybrid storage

Foundation Topics

Calculating AWS Costs

AWS costs are based on what is called a "consumption model," where customers pay for the cloud services ordered per AWS account by the second for compute resources and monthly for storage resources. The price of each AWS service is different in each AWS region. For example, choosing the Central AWS region means the AWS resources are located in Canada and, depending on the currency exchange rate of your country, pricing in Canada may be more or less than pricing in your home country. If you are restricted to operating in the European Union (EU) or South America (São Paulo), you can expect pricing to be a few hundred percent more than in Canada! Keep in mind, however, that you might not have the option to operate in a cheaper AWS region if compliance requirements dictate where your organization is allowed to operate.

It's just a fact that costs are higher in some areas of the world for all public cloud providers. The biggest and cheapest AWS region to operate in is us-east-1 (Northern Virginia), which also has the largest number of availability zones (AZs) and AWS cloud services. Other AWS regions with comparable pricing to Northern Virginia include Ohio, located in us-east-2, and Ireland (eu).

The purchase price of compute resources can be significantly reduced in many cases by purchasing Reserved Instances. For example, a human resources system deployed at AWS requires an average of ten t2.medium EC2 compute instances placed behind an ELB Application Load Balancer. Although there are many variables when analyzing pricing, there are some general trends, such as widely differing regional costs. For example, as shown in Figure 12-1, comparing the us-east Northern Virginia region costs to the São Paulo region costs for a load balancer results in an 80% price difference.

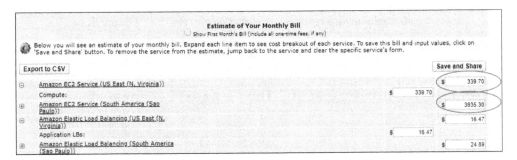

Figure 12-1   Comparing Regional Prices

> **NOTE**   Many costs are included in the price of AWS services. For example, there is no charge to spin up a VPC and add subnets.

Cloud Service Costs

Using a managed AWS cloud service for storage, database deployments, or monitoring removes the cost of managing, maintaining, updating, and administering a customer-built service. For example, when storing objects in S3 buckets, customers create buckets and manage their stored objects, but they don't have to maintain and update the S3 storage array. Overall, costs are reduced when you use AWS cloud services as part of your workload.

How AWS charges for cloud services that are used can be broken down by component, as shown in Table 12-2. This breakdown of costs is the same in every AWS region.

Table 12-2   Cloud Service Charges at AWS

Service	Charges	Components	Examples
Management tools	Number of times service performs selected tasks; tiered pricing after the minimum is reached	Compute, storage, notification, and automation charges	AWS Config, AWS Lambda, AWS CloudWatch, Amazon GuardDuty, Amazon Macie
Compute	By the hour or second	Compute hours plus *data transfer* charges	EC2 instance, ECS, RDS
Storage	Monthly per gigabyte stored; tiered pricing after the minimum is reached	Storage, data transfer, and, optionally, encryption or notification and automation charges	Amazon EBS, S3 Glacier, EFS, FSx, EBS snapshots, server logs
Amazon CloudWatch	By alarm, metrics, and analysis; tiered pricing after minimum is reached	Compute, storage, notification, and automation charges	Alerts/Alarms, CloudWatch logs, Events/Rules
Amazon SNS	Per notification; tiered pricing after minimum quota is reached	Compute, storage, notification, and automation charges	Notifications
Data transfer	Per gigabyte transferred	Data transfer out	Across AZs, regions, edge locations outgoing data

Tiered Pricing at AWS

Many AWS management services and data transfer costs offer *tiered pricing*. With tiered pricing, a customer uses a particular AWS service until their usage of the service exceeds a defined default value; then, the customer's costs scale based on a sliding price point. The more usage, the smaller the charges. After usage increases to the next tiered level, AWS provides another price break until the next checkpoint. For example, charges for data transfer out from EC2 instances to the Internet start at $0.09/gigabyte until you reach 10 TiB. Then, additional discounts apply, as shown in Table 12-3. The charge for region-to-region traffic is currently set at $0.02/gigabyte, but in the case of us-east-1 and us-east-2, it's $0.01/gigabyte. The prices presented here may change by the time you read this, because AWS changes prices from time to time.

Table 12-3 Tiered Storage Costs for Data Transfer Out from EC2 Instance to the Internet

Storage Amount	Price per Month
Up to 100 GiB	Free
Up to 9.999 TiB	$0.09 per gigabyte
Up to 40 TiB	$0.085 per gigabyte
Up to 100 TiB	$0.07 per gigabyte
Greater than 150 TiB	$0.05 per gigabyte
Greater than 500 TiB	Call AWS

A typical web application hosted at AWS will also most likely be using the following services. Each service has specific charges based on its operation.

- **Amazon CloudFront:** The first 1 TiB of data transfer, the first 10 million HTTP/S requests, and the first 2 million CloudFront Functions invocations are free.

- **Amazon CloudWatch:** Up to the first 10,000 custom metrics are charged $0.30 per month. The next 240,000 metrics are charged at $0.10 per month.

- **AWS CloudTrail:** The first copy of management events stored in S3 is free, then $2.00 per 100,000 management events delivered.

- **EC2 instance traffic:** EC2 traffic between different AZs hosted within the region costs the same as region-to-region data transfer. ELB to EC2 traffic is free of charge within the AZ.

- **ELB:** ELB charges are calculated by *Load Balancer Capacity Units (LCUs)* for Application Load Balancer and Network Load Balancer. The regional location of your load balancer is also considered when calculating the LCU price. The LCU measures the *dimensions* of your traffic, which include new connections, active connections, the amount of bandwidth, and the number of rules processed by the load balancer. Whichever LCU dimension is highest per ALB/NLB-hour (or partial hour) is the one charged.

- **Amazon S3 Standard:** First 50 TiB/month $0.023 per GiB; next 450 TiB/month $0.022 per GiB.

Management Tool Pricing Example: AWS Config

As an example of management pricing, AWS Config enables customers to monitor the configuration of their IaaS resources, such as compute, networking, and monitoring resources, against a set of managed and customer-defined rules that capture any changes to the resource's configuration. For AWS Config to operate, it needs to execute its review of resources in the AWS account. AWS Config then stores the results in S3 storage.

AWS charges you for the number of configuration items being monitored by AWS Config in your AWS account for each AWS region (see Figure 12-2). AWS Config managed rules are predefined rules created and managed by AWS and are organized into categories, such as compliance, security, and networking. An example of a Config managed rule is **encrypted-volumes**, which, once enabled, continually checks that all boot volumes attached to EC2 instances are encrypted. The management charges for AWS Config operation are as follows:

- AWS Config compares the **encrypted-volumes** rule against all boot volumes in your AWS account; the rule is defined as an "active rule" because the rule was processed by the Config management service. The first ten AWS Config managed rules are charged a flat rate of $2.00 per AWS Config rule per region per month. There are additional charges for executing custom rules.

- The next 40 managed rules have a slightly lower price per month: $1.50 per processed rule. When you reach 50 rules or more, the price drops further, to $1.00 per processed rule. Actual prices might increase or decrease over time. Examples provided throughout this book are used to demonstrate the pricing models used by AWS; actual pricing rates change over time.

AWS Config rules evaluations	Price
First 100,000 rule evaluations	$0.001 per rule evaluation per region
Next 400,000 rule evaluations (100,001-500,000)	$0.0008 per rule evaluation per region
500,001 and more rule evaluations	$0.0005 per rule evaluation per region

Figure 12-2 AWS Config Rules Pricing

AWS Config's data gathering is carried out using AWS Lambda functions. Lambda is an AWS-managed service that runs functions that can be created using several programming languages, including Python, C#, Node.js, and Java. When AWS Config rules are processed, additional AWS Lambda charges are applied for each AWS Config custom rule. Lambda charges are based on the amount of CPU, RAM, and time taken to complete the execution of each function.

AWS Config Results

The results gathered by AWS Config are stored in an Amazon S3 bucket. Charges for S3 storage depend on the size of the storage results. For example, S3 storage pricing is $0.023 per gigabyte for the first 50 TiB per month. AWS Config is also integrated with the monitoring service Amazon CloudWatch and sends detailed information about all configuration changes and notifications to AWS Simple Notification Server events.

Using AWS Config, customers can be alerted if their infrastructure components are found to be out of compliance. For example, if a developer creates an unencrypted boot volume, AWS Config alerts could use the Simple Notification Service (SNS) to call an AWS Lambda function. The first 1 million SNS requests per month are free; after that, they are charged $0.050 per 1 million SNS requests.

For this example, if a custom AWS Config rule discovers an unencrypted boot volume, an SNS event could trigger a custom AWS Lambda function to perform a snapshot of the unencrypted boot volume, and then delete the out-of-compliance EC2 instance and unencrypted volume.

Consider a scenario where you have 500 configuration items in your AWS account that are checked by AWS Config each month with 30 active AWS management rules in the us-east-1 (Northern Virginia) region. Your monthly charges would be as follows:

AWS Config costs: $500 \times \$0.003 = \$1.50$

AWS Config rules: $2.00 per active rule for the first ten active config rules = $20.00

$1.50 for each of the next ten active Config rules = $15.00

Total AWS Config monthly charges = $36.50

If resource configurations were found not to be in compliance with a defined AWS Config rule, notifications and alerts would be generated by AWS Config, resulting in additional SNS and AWS Lambda charges.

AWS pricing usually involves more than a single charge. Calculating costs at AWS is complicated because there are many moving parts in each managed service.

Cost Management Tools

To access cost management tools for your AWS account, select My Billing Dashboard from the AWS Management Console, as shown in Figure 12-3. The root account of your AWS account has full access to the Billing Dashboard. Using AWS IAM, access can be delegated to specific IAM users or IAM roles for accessing billing and cost management data for the AWS account by activating access to the Billing Dashboard and then attaching the desired IAM policy. The AWS Cost Explorer API is the engine powering the Cost Explorer; it can also be directly accessed by customers who wish to query cost and usage data programmatically or from the AWS CLI.

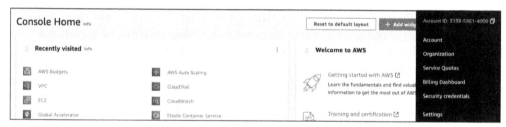

Figure 12-3   Accessing the Billing Dashboard and Cost Management

The cost management tools available at AWS for financial management are listed in Table 12-4 by use case, by Cost Management feature, and Billing Dashboard feature, along with associated AWS services.

Table 12-4   Cost Management Tools by Use Case

Use Case	Details	Cost Management Feature	Billing Dashboard Feature	Associated AWS Service
Organize	Define a tagging policy	—	Cost categories Cost allocation tags	Tag Editor, AWS CLI, Resource groups
Report	Default and custom cost reports	Cost Explorer	Cost and Usage Reports	CSV files Cost explorer API

Use Case	Details	Cost Management Feature	Billing Dashboard Feature	Associated AWS Service
Access	Track costs across AWS Organizations	—	Consolidated Billing Purchase Order Management AWS Credits	AWS Organizations Billing Dashboard and Cost Management
Control	—	Cost Anomaly Detection	—	SNS Topic, AWS Chatbot configuration
Forecast	—	Cost Explorer Budgets reports	—	Cost explorer API
Budget	Budget threshold and alert notifications to control spend	Budgets Budgets actions	—	Simple Notification Service Lambda functions
Purchase	Discounts for compute usage	Savings Plans Reserved Instances		Simple Notification Service
Rightsizing Recommendations	Match Reserved Instance allocation to current workload needs	Rightsizing recommendations	—	Amazon EC2, Amazon RDS, ElastiCache, OpenSearch Service, and Amazon Redshift
Inspect	Current resource deployment and costs	Cost Explorer	—	AWS Organizations

NOTE AWS Resource Groups can be used to manage a collection of tagged AWS resources that reside in the same region. Supported AWS resources include Amazon S3 buckets, Amazon SNS, Service Quotas, AWS Secrets Manager, Amazon SageMaker, Amazon Route 53, Amazon RDS, Amazon Redshift, AWS Organizations, Lambda functions, AWS IAM, AWS Config, Amazon DynamoDB, AWS CloudTrail, AWS CloudWatch, Amazon CloudFront, Amazon FSx for Windows File Server, ELB, EFS, ECS, and EC2 instances.

AWS Cost Explorer

Cost Explorer helps customers analyze AWS account costs and overall usage with free reports. Default reports include a breakdown of the AWS services that are incurring the most costs, including overall EC2 usage and Reserved Instance utilization. Optionally, an organization can carry out a deep-dive cost analysis, filtering with numerous dimensions; for example, by AWS service and region. AWS accounts that are members of an AWS Organization can take advantage of consolidated billing and review the charges generated by all member accounts. Using Cost Explorer (see Figure 12-4), you can filter AWS costs based on the following:

- **API operation:** Requests and tasks performed by each AWS service
- **Availability zone:** Charges per availability zone
- **All costs:** Costs per AWS account
- **Linked accounts:** Member accounts in an AWS organization
- **AWS region:** Where operations and AWS services operated
- **AWS service:** AWS services used
- **Tags:** Cost allocation tags assigned to the selected service
- **Tenancy:** Multi- or single-tenancy EC2 instances
- **Usage type:** Amounts of AWS service data (compute hours, data transfer in or out, CloudWatch metrics, I/O requests, and data storage)

Figure 12-4 Cost Explorer

To enable tracking of your costs with Cost Explorer, you need to sign in to the AWS Management Console and enable data collection by opening the Billing Dashboard and Cost Management and launching the Cost Explorer. After the initialization of Cost Explorer, costs are displayed for the current month and will be forecast for the next 12 months; updates will be made to the current spend every 24 hours. Cost Explorer can also display historical cost data, costs for the current month, and trends and forecasts. The following are the default Cost Explorer reports:

- **AWS Marketplace:** Costs for the products you've ordered through AWS Marketplace.

- **Daily Costs:** How much you spent over the past 6 months and projected costs over the next month.

- **Monthly Costs by Linked Account:** Costs for linked accounts in an AWS organization.

- **Monthly Costs by Service:** Costs over the past 6 months highlighted by the top five services' costs.

- **Monthly EC2 Running Hours Costs and Usage:** The amount spent on active reserved instances (RIs).

- **Reserved Instance Utilization Report:** Reserved instances used, including any overspending and net savings from using reserved instances.

- **Reserved Instance Coverage Report:** Details on how many EC2 instance hours have been covered by reserved instances, how much was spent on the on-demand instance, and how much could be saved by purchasing reserved instances. Compute services that can use EC2 reserved instances include Amazon Redshift, Amazon RDS, Elasticsearch clusters, and Amazon ElastiCache. Filters include the specific AZ, EC2 instance type, linked AWS account, operating system platform, AWS region, and compute tenancy. In addition, detailed information for each reservation can be downloaded as a CSV file.

- **Rightsizing Recommendations:** Cost Explorer recommendations for improving the use of reserved instances and AWS resources (see Figure 12-5).

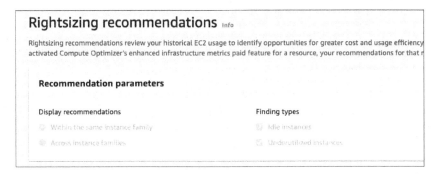

Figure 12-5 Cost Explorer Recommendations

Cost Explorer provides costing reports for daily and monthly charges based on the AWS services that you subscribe to (see Figure 12-6). The reports offered include information on the following:

- Monthly costs by service (view costs and usage over the last 12 months)

- Daily costs by service

- Monthly costs by linked account (view the monthly spend for paying accounts in an AWS organization)

- Services ordered by AWS Marketplace

- Monthly EC2 instance running hours cost and usage

- Reservation utilization report, and Reservation coverage help analyze purchases and savings

- Savings Plans utilization report and Savings Plans coverage help analyze purchases and savings

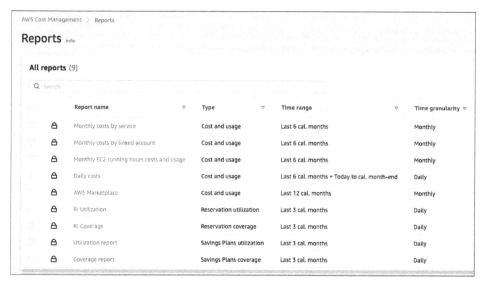

Figure 12-6   Cost Explorer Details

Customers can review the past 13 months of operation and forecast the potential bill for the next 3 months based on the current costs. Forecasts can be created for future AWS charges based on a custom time frame, filtering and grouping costs using several parameters, including:

- **Availability zone:** Where resources are located

- **Instance type:** The type of reserved instance used to launch EC2 and RDS instances

- **Purchase option:** On-demand, reserved, spot, or scheduled reserved pricing

- **AWS services ordered and used:** AWS service usage

- **Tenancy:** Dedicated or multi-tenant reserved EC2 instances

■ **Cost allocation tags:** Generate hourly and monthly cost allocation reports based on tagged resources

Additional features of the Billing Dashboard and Cost Management that can be useful include analyzing current and future costs with Cost Explorer graphs, and receiving email notifications when charges reach a defined cost threshold by enabling billing alerts (see Figure 12-7). Companies using Reserved Instances can create a budget to track the current spend and expected spend. Each budget defines a start and end date and a budgeted amount to track costs against. Budgets can also include AWS costs related to specific AWS services, associated tags, purchase options, instance types, region, and AZ locations. When a budget forecast hits the defined threshold (a percentage of a budgeted amount or a dollar figure), alerts and notifications can be sent to email accounts and an Amazon SNS topic.

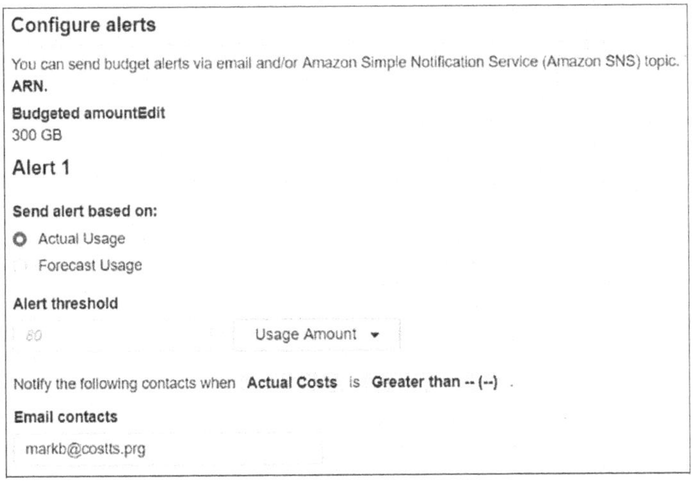

Configure alerts

You can send budget alerts via email and/or Amazon Simple Notification Service (Amazon SNS) topic.
ARN.

Budgeted amountEdit
300 GB

Alert 1

Send alert based on:
◉ Actual Usage
　Forecast Usage

Alert threshold

| 80 | | Usage Amount ▾ | |

Notify the following contacts when **Actual Costs** is **Greater than -- (--)** .

Email contacts

markb@costts.prg

Figure 12-7   Enabling Billing Alerts

NOTE   Cost Explorer can review EC2 instance memory utilization if the CloudWatch agent has been enabled. To enable the agent for Linux instances, use **mem_used_percent**; for Windows instances, use **% Committed Bytes In Use**.

AWS Budgets

AWS Budgets tracks AWS costs and can use billing alerts (refer to Figure 12-7) to alert organizations when costs are outside defined budget guidelines. Budget information is updated every 8 hours. Budgets can also be created to monitor the overall utilization and coverage of your existing reserved instances or savings plans. Alert notifications can be sent to an Amazon SNS topic and up to ten email addresses.

The following types of budgets can be created using Budgets (see Figure 12-8):

- **Cost budgets:** Define how much to spend on a particular AWS service (for example, EC2 instances).

- **Usage budgets:** Define how much to spend on one or more AWS services.

- **RI utilization budgets:** Define the expected usage level of purchased Reserved Instances and get alerted if RI usage falls below the defined usage threshold.

- **RI coverage budgets:** Define the expected coverage level of purchased Reserved Instances and get alerted if RI coverage of EC2 instances falls below the defined threshold number of hours.

- **Savings Plans utilization budgets:** Define the expected usage level of EC2 instances, Fargate, and AWS Lambda functions and get alerted when your savings plan falls below the defined threshold.

- **Savings Plans coverage budgets:** Define the expected coverage level of EC2 instances, Fargate, and AWS Lambda functions and get alerted when your savings plan falls below the defined threshold.

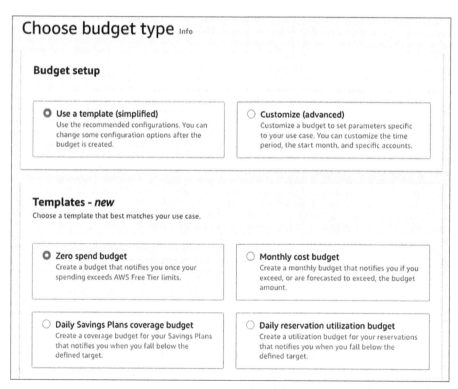

Figure 12-8 Budget Choices

You can also create custom budgets with predefined templates such as:

- Define a zero spend budget that notifies you when spending exceeds the AWS Free Tier limits.

- Define a budget with monthly costs, with fixed targets tracking all costs associated with an AWS account. Alerts could be defined for both actual and forecasted spending.

- Define a budget with escalating monthly spending costs, with notifications alerting when funds are spent in excess of the allowable increases.

- Define a budget with a fixed usage amount, with notifications alerting when the budget spend is close to being exceeded.

NOTE   Budget notifications use Amazon SNS to send alerts. Alerts are sent to defined SNS topics, and automated actions can be performed using AWS Lambda functions. Notifications can also alert via email or text message.

AWS Cost and Usage Reports

Cost and Usage Reports (CUR) provide a comprehensive overview of the monthly costs and usage of AWS services per AWS account or AWS organization (see Figure 12-9), showing hourly, daily, or monthly expenses based on products and resources used or based on resource tags that have already been defined. From the Billing Dashboard and Cost Management, select Cost and Usage Reports, and click Create Report. Resource IDs can be used to create individual line items for each AWS resource used. An Amazon S3 bucket must be chosen as the location for storing requested reports.

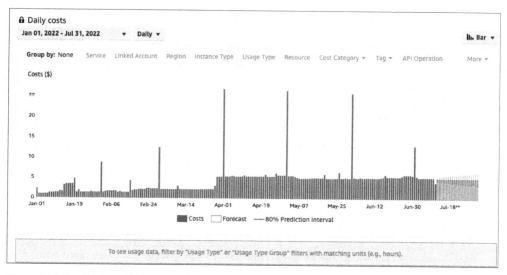

Figure 12-9   Cost and Usage Report

Reports can also be viewed directly from the Cost and Usage Reports console; a CSV usage report can also be downloaded. Optionally, you can use Amazon Athena with standard SQL queries, or load CUR data to an Amazon Redshift deployment, or use Amazon QuickSight for additional analysis.

Managing Costs Cheat Sheet

For the AWS Certified Solutions Architect – Associate (SAA-C03) exam, you need to understand the following critical aspects of managing costs:

- Track your costs and usage against defined budgets by using AWS Budgets.

- Use AWS Cost Explorer to review current costs and usage by creating a Cost and Usage Report.

- Create tags for your AWS resources and then activate the tags to add information to a Cost and Usage Report.

- Use AWS Cost Explorer to perform forecasting for your costs and overall usage for the upcoming month or year.

- Use AWS Organizations to take advantage of consolidated Billing Dashboard, with one bill for multiple accounts.

- Combine resource usage across all AWS accounts contained in an AWS organization, resulting in the sharing of volume pricing discounts.

- Use AWS Budgets to define a monthly budget for your AWS costs and usage and discounts for savings plans or reserved instances.

- Use AWS Config to review the inventory of your AWS resources and configuration within your AWS account or across your AWS organization.

- Use AWS Systems Manager to get a detailed inventory of your EC2 assets.

- Use tag policies in AWS Organizations defining rules for how tags must be used on AWS resources across your AWS accounts in the organization.

Tagging AWS Resources

One essential task to consider is the creation of tags when you create AWS resources. Each tag is a key/value pair, and 50 individual tags can typically be created for each AWS resource. Tags can be used for automation, analysis, reporting, compliance checks, and with the Billing Dashboard. Custom tags can be used for many reasons, including the following examples:

- **Tags on creation:** Tags can be created for EBS volumes at the time of creation.

- **Cost allocation tags:** These tags allow you to have visibility into your actual snapshot storage costs. In the Billing Dashboard and Cost Management, you can select Cost Allocation Tags and then select and activate tags that can be used for the Billing Dashboard process (see Figure 12-10).

- **Enforced tags:** AWS IAM security policies can enforce the use of specific tags on EBS volumes and control who can create tags.

Cost allocation tags Info

Cost allocation tags activated: 9

| User-defined cost allocation tags | AWS generated cost allocation tags |

User-defined cost allocation tags (16) Info   Undo

Q Search for a tag key | All statuses ▾ |

	Tag key	▲	Status
☐	apache		⊗ Inactive
☐	aws-control-tower		⊗ Inactive
☐	Default		⊘ Active
☐	Description		⊗ Inactive
☐	elasticbeanstalk		⊗ Inactive
☐	elasticbeanstalk:environment-id		⊘ Active
☐	elasticbeanstalk:environment-name		⊘ Active
☐	graphic dept		⊗ Inactive
☐	interface		⊘ Active

Figure 12-10   Activate Cost Allocation Tags

Using Cost Allocation Tags

Cost allocation tags can be created and deployed to track your AWS costs via cost allocation reports, which make it easier for you to track and categorize your existing AWS costs. There are two types of *cost allocation tags*: AWS-generated tags and user-defined tags. Each tag contains a key and a linked value. For example, user-defined tags might be **Mark=Developer** and **Costs** (see Figure 12-11). An example of an AWS-generated tag is the **createdBy** tag, which tracks who created the resource. The name of user-generated tags could include Cost Management and Stack.

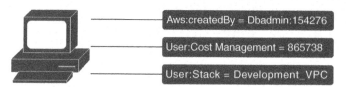

Figure 12-11   Cost Allocation Tags Example

AWS has defined the **createdBy** tag for use with selected AWS resources for cost allocation tracking. AWS-generated tags must be activated in the Billing Dashboard and Cost Management before they can be used. The **createdBy** tag is supported by the following AWS services: AWS CloudFormation, Amazon Redshift, Amazon Route 53, Amazon S3 storage, AWS Storage Gateway, and Amazon EC2 instances and networking components, including VPCs, security groups, snapshots, subnets, and Internet gateways.

As mentioned, once tags have been created and applied to an AWS resource, you can activate the tags in the Billing Dashboard and Cost Management, which then generates a cost allocation report in a CSV file that has your usage and costs grouped by the assigned active tags. AWS Cost Explorer and AWS Cost and Usage Reports can break down AWS costs by tags.

NOTE   Tag policies can be created to standardize tags across AWS Organizations, allowing customers to label resources using key/value pairs. Tag policies help Cost Explorer to identify resources by dimensions such as owner, cost center, or environment, helping identify and break out the cost of AWS.

Storage Types and Costs

Storage costs at AWS depend on the storage service being used—whether it's EBS storage volumes, shared file storage using Amazon EFS or Amazon FSx for Windows File Server, Amazon S3 object storage, or archival storage using Amazon S3 Glacier. The following list describes these AWS storage options and storage and data transfer costs:

- **Amazon S3 buckets:** An S3 bucket has monthly storage and retrieval costs based on the storage class and location of the request. Other costs are based on the frequency of operation. **PUT**, **COPY**, **POST**, and **LIST** requests per 1,000 requests for S3 Standard is $0.005. **GET**, **SELECT**, and all other requests per 1,000 requests for S3 Standard is $0.004. S3 lifecycle and data transfer requests are charged per 1,000 requests. There are no data transfer charges for storing and retrieving objects from an S3 bucket located in the same region where the EC2 instance is located.

  Optional Amazon S3 features such as S3 Lifecycle transitions, data transfer (outbound directly to the Internet or to Amazon CloudFront), S3 Transfer acceleration, and Cross-Region replication to another S3 bucket all have separate and additional costs. Amazon S3 bucket replication within or across AWS regions also has specific bundled costs:

  - **S3 Same-Region Replication (SRR):** Amazon S3 charges for storage in the selected destination Amazon S3 storage class, the primary copy, replication **PUT** request, and if applicable, an infrequent access storage retrieval charge.

  - **S3 Cross-Region Replication (CRR):** S3 charges for storage in the selected destination S3 storage class, the primary copy, replication **PUT** requests, and if applicable, an infrequent access storage retrieval charge, and inter-region data transfer out to the selected region.

As an example, storing 500 TiB of standard storage in the us-east-1 (Northern Virginia) region would cost you roughly $12,407.14 per month (see Figure 12-12). It would include 5,000 **PUT/COPY/POST/LIST** requests and 30,000 **GET** requests.

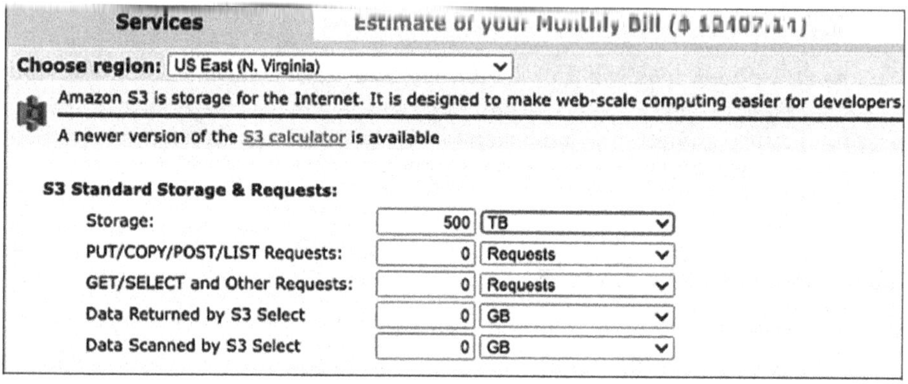

Services	Estimate of your Monthly Bill ($ 12407.14)

Choose region: US East (N. Virginia) ▼

Amazon S3 is storage for the Internet. It is designed to make web-scale computing easier for developers

A newer version of the S3 calculator is available

S3 Standard Storage & Requests:

Storage:	500	TB ▼
PUT/COPY/POST/LIST Requests:	0	Requests ▼
GET/SELECT and Other Requests:	0	Requests ▼
Data Returned by S3 Select	0	GB ▼
Data Scanned by S3 Select	0	GB ▼

Figure 12-12 S3 Storage Pricing

- **Amazon S3 Glacier:** S3 Glacier archive storage ranges from $0.04 to under $0.01 for archival storage in S3 Glacier Deep Archive:

  - S3 Glacier Instant Retrieval storage costs $0.004 per GiB when accessed every 90 days

  - Amazon S3 Glacier Flexible Retrieval storage with retrieval from 1 minute to 12 hours ($0.0036 per GiB)

  - Amazon S3 Glacier Deep Archive storage that is accessed once or twice a year and is restored within 12 hours ($0.004 per GiB)

Amazon S3 Glacier storage is also subject to storage and retrieval pricing that is based on the speed of the data retrieval required. In addition, it is subject to outbound data transfer pricing, which varies based on the destination (for example, outbound directly to the Internet or to CloudFront). A recommended practice is to archive infrequently used data in S3 Glacier Flexible Retrieval and move long-term archived data to Glacier Deep Archive. Storing 100 TiB of archived records in the US-East (Northern Virginia) region with data retrieval of 10 GiB per month and an average of 20 requests per month would cost roughly $411.92.

- **EBS volumes:** Virtual hard drives can be ordered in several flavors: SSDs, SSDs with provisioned IOPS, throughput-optimized drives, or cold HDDs (infrequently accessed hard drive storage). You are also charged for snapshot storage in Amazon S3 for EBS volume snapshots.

For example, a single general-purpose SSD sized at 16,384 GiB hosted in the US-East-1 (Northern Virginia) region would cost you roughly $1,798 per month. A provisioned IOPS SSD io1 volume sized at 8,000 GiB with 16,000 IOPS hosted in the US-East-1 (Northern Virginia) region would cost you $2,244.50 per month, as shown in Figure 12-13. Note that all prices quoted are subject to change over time.

Services	Estimate of your Monthly Bill ($ 2244.50)				

Choose region: US East (N. Virginia) ▾   Inbound Data Transfer is Free and Outbound Data

Amazon Elastic Compute Cloud (Amazon EC2) is a web service that provides resizable compute capacity in the cloud. computing easier for developers. Amazon Elastic Block Store (EBS) provides persistent storage to Amazon EC2 instan

Compute: Amazon EC2 Instances:

Description	Instances	Usage	Type	
⊕ Add New Row				

Compute: Amazon EC2 Dedicated Hosts:

Description	Number of Hosts	Usage	Type	Billing Option
⊕ Add New Row				

Storage: Amazon EBS Volumes:

Description	Volumes	Volume Type	Storage	IOPS	Baseline Throughput
⊖	1	Provisioned IOPS SSD (io1) ▾	8000 GB	16000	500 MBs/sec
⊕ Add New Row					

Figure 12-13   EBS Price Calculations

- **Snapshot storage:** Snapshot storage costs can be extremely high if snapshots that are no longer required are not deleted. Amazon Data Lifecycle Manager, which is found in the EBS section of the EC2 console, allows you to schedule and manage the creation and deletion of EBS snapshots.

- **Shared storage (EFS/FSx for Windows File Server):** Amazon EFS and Amazon FSx for Windows File Server are shared file storage services. At a minimum, you pay for the total amount of storage used per month. EFS Infrequent Access storage is priced based on the amount of storage used and the amount of data accessed. You can also optionally pay for faster-provisioned throughput in megabytes per month, depending on your performance requirements. FSx for Windows File Server usage is prorated by the hour, and customers are billed for the average usage each month, paying for the storage and throughput capacity specified and for any backups performed. FSx for Windows File Server customers pay for data transferred across availability zones or peering connections in the same region and for data transferred out to other AWS regions.

As an example for EFS, suppose a file system hosted in the US-East-1 (Northern Virginia) region uses 300 GiB of storage for 20 days for a single month. The charges would be as follows: total usage (GiB-hours) = 300 GiB × 20 days × (24 hours/day) = 144,000 GiB-hours. The total charge equates to $43.20 per GiB-month. Moving your files to the EFS Infrequent Access storage tier would reduce your EFS storage costs by up to 92%.

Table 12-5 provides a comparison of S3, EBS, EFS, and FSx storage services, including costs of storage, how to reduce storage costs, and the associated backup tools for each service.

Table 12-5   Amazon S3, EBS, EFS, and FSx for Windows File Server Comparison

Feature	Simple Storage Service (S3)	Elastic Block Store (EBS)	Elastic File System (EFS)	FSx for Windows File Server
Costs of storage	Scaled cost based on the first 50 TiB of storage used and the number of requests made (**POST, GET**) Data transfer per GiB out of S3	General-purpose SSD: $0.8 per GiB per month Provisioned IOPS SSD: $0.125 per GiB per month; $0.065 per provisioned IOPS per month Throughput-optimized HDD: $0.045 per GiB per month Cold HDD: $0.015 per GiB per month	Standard storage: $0.03 per GiB per month Infrequent access storage: $0.045 per GiB per month Infrequent Access requests: $0.01 per GiB transferred	SSD storage: $0.230 per GiB per month HDD storage: $0.025 per GiB per month Throughput capacity: $4.500 per MiBps per month
Storage size	No limit	Maximum storage size 65 GiB	Petabytes	Petabytes
Storage classes	Standard, Intelligent-Tiering, Standard IA, One Zone IA, Glacier Instant/Flexible Retrieval/Deep Archive	General-purpose SSD, Provisioned IOPS SSD io1, io2, Throughput optimized HDD volumes, Cold HDD volumes	EFS Standard or Infrequent Access and EFS One Zone or One Zone Infrequent Access	Single AZ and Multi-AZ deployment options

Feature	Simple Storage Service (S3)	Elastic Block Store (EBS)	Elastic File System (EFS)	FSx for Windows File Server
File size	5 TiB	64 TiB maximum volume size	47.9 TiB single file	47.9 TiB single file
How to reduce storage costs	Intelligent-Tiering, One Zone-Infrequent Access	Reduce volume size and type, reduce IOPS	Provisioned throughput, EFS Infrequent Access (EFS Standard-IA or EFS One Zone-IA)	HDD and SSD storage options, data deduplication, user quotas
Backup Tools	Cross-Region and Same-Region Replication	Snapshots, Data Lifecycle Manager	EFS Lifecycle Management, EFS Intelligent-Tiering	Automated backups to S3
Associated AWS service	AWS Backup, Snow Family	AWS Backup, EFS to EFS, or S3 backup with Lambda function	AWS Backup	AWS Backup
Data location	Data stays within the region or requested AZ	Data stays within the same AZ	Data stored within AZs of region	Data stored within AZs of region
Data access options	Public (HTTP, HTTPS) or private network endpoints (Gateway)	Private AWS network from an EC2 instance	Private network from multiple instances or from on-premises locations	Private network from multiple instances or from on-premises locations
Encryption	SSE: Amazon S3, AWS-KMS, SSE-C	AWS and KMS: managed (CMK) with AES 256-bit encryption	AWS and KMS: managed CMK with AES 256-bit encryption	AWS and KMS: managed CMK with AES 256-bit encryption
Availability	Four 9s; can survive the loss of two facilities	EBS volumes unavailable during AZ failure	Stored across multiple AZs	Stored across multiple AZs
Use Case	Static files	Boot drives, database instances SQL, NoSQL	Big data analytics, media workflows (media editing, studio production), or home directories	Big data analytics, media workflows (media editing, studio production), or home directories

AWS Backup

AWS Backup is a centralized backup service for managing data backups across multiple AWS regions for AWS compute, storage services, and database services (see Figure 12-14). Backups can be on-demand, scheduled, or continuous. A continuous backup includes a continuous backup of Amazon RDS database instances and continuous backup of the transaction logs. Continuous backups can restore RDS deployments with a point-in-time recovery (PITR) within 5 minutes of activity within a defined 35-day time period. Amazon S3 buckets can be restored within 15 minutes of recent activity. Backups can also be automated per EC2 instance with crash-consistent backups of attached EBS volumes. AWS Backup also integrates with AWS Organizations.

Figure 12-14 AWS Backup

The following AWS services can be backed up with AWS Backup:

- EBS volumes

- EC2 instances and Windows applications (including Windows Server, Microsoft SQL Server, and Microsoft Exchange Server)

- Amazon RDS databases (including Amazon Aurora clusters)

- Amazon DynamoDB tables

- Amazon Elastic File System file systems

- Amazon FSx for Windows File Server file systems

- Amazon FSx for Lustre, ONTAP, and OpenZFS file systems

- Neptune and DocumentDB clusters

- AWS Storage Gateway – Volume Gateway

- Amazon S3 buckets, objects, tags, and custom metadata

- Amazon Outposts, VMware Cloud on AWS, and on-premises VMware virtual machines (require AWS Backup gateway software to be installed on each VMware VM)

You can select templates when creating a backup plan with AWS Backup, or create a new backup plan (see Figure 12-15). When you assign a storage resource to a backup plan, the selected resource is backed up automatically on a defined schedule. A backup plan requires the following information:

- **Backup schedule:** Every hour (cron expression), 12 hours, daily, weekly, monthly

- **Backup window:** Starting time and duration

- **Lifecycle rules**: When a backup is transitioned to cold storage and when the backup expires

- **A backup vault:** For storing encrypted backups with KMS encryption keys

- **Regional copies:** Backup copies in another AWS region

- **Tags:** Associating multiple resources with tag-based backup policies

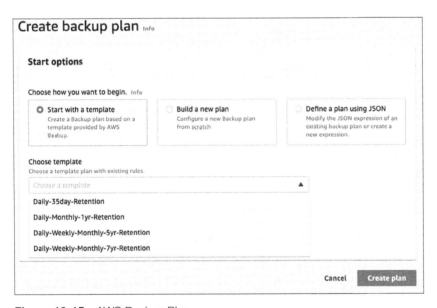

Figure 12-15   AWS Backup Plan

Lifecycle Rules

AWS Backup can be stored in either a warm or cold storage tier. *Lifecycle rules* allow customers to transition backups that are stored in warm storage to cheaper cold storage. In us-east-1, warm storage is $0.05 per GiB; cold storage is $0.01 per GiB. The defined lifecycle in each backup plan defines when a backup will transition into cold storage. Each backup stored in cold storage is a full backup. Backups that have transitioned to cold storage must remain in cold storage for 90 days. In Figure 12-16, transition rules have been set to transition the monthly backup to cold storage after 8 days and retain the backup for 1 year.

Backup rule name

Monthly

Backup rule name is case sensitive. Must contain from 1 to 50 alphanumeric or '-_' characters.

Backup vault Info

Default ▼   Create new Backup vault

Backup frequency Info

Monthly ▼

on   Day ▼   1 ▼

☐ Enable continuous backups for point-in-time recovery (PITR) Info
Available for RDS and S3 resources.

Backup window

○ Use backup window defaults - *recommended* Info
5 AM UTC, starts within 8 hours.

○ Customize backup window

Transition to cold storage Info

Days ▼   8

Retention period Info

Years ▼   1

Copy to destination Info

Choose a Region ▼

▶ Tags added to recovery points
AWS Backup copies tags from the protected resource to the recovery point upon creation. You can specify additional tags to add to the recovery point.

Figure 12-16 Lifecycle Settings

AWS Backup Cheat Sheet

For the AWS Certified Solutions Architect – Associate (SAA-C03) exam, you need to understand the following critical aspects of AWS Backup:

- A backup of an EC2 instance includes snapshots of all volumes and launch configuration.

- A continuous backup allows you to restore RDS deployments any point in time within 35 days within 5 minutes of activity

- Periodic backups retain data for the specified duration.

- On-demand backups back up the selected resource type at once.

- Backup plans create incremental backups.

- Incremental backups are lower cost than an on-demand or periodic backup.

- The first backup is always a full backup; subsequent backups are incremental.

- When an EFS file system is created, automatic backups with AWS Backup are turned on.

- AWS Backups are stored in vaults.

- AWS Backup vaults are encrypted with KMS encryption keys.

- AWS Backup Vault Lock enforces a write-once, read-many (WORM) setting for all backups stored in a backup vault.

- AWS Backup Audit Manager audits the compliance of your AWS Backup policies.

- Amazon S3 backups require versioning to be enabled.

- AWS Backup charges by the GiB-month depending on the amount of resource type stored and restored per month.

- The AWS Backup lifecycle feature automatically transitions your recovery points from a warm storage tier to a lower-cost cold storage tier for backups of Amazon EFS file systems, Amazon DynamoDB tables, and VMware virtual machines.

- Individual files can also be restored without having to restore the entire file system.

Data Transfer Costs

There is no charge for inbound data transfer into AWS from the Internet, from an edge location, or Direct Connect connection.

- When data is transferred to the Internet from an AWS service, data transfer charges apply based on the service and the AWS region where the service is located.

- Data transfers across the Internet are billed at AWS region-specific and tiered data transfer rates.

- Data transferred into and out from Amazon EC2, Amazon RDS, Amazon Redshift, Amazon DynamoDB, Amazon ElastiCache instances, an Elastic Network Adapter, or VPC peering connections across availability zones in the same AWS region is charged at $0.01/GiB in each direction.

- Data transferred across regional endpoints between Amazon S3, Amazon S3 Glacier, Amazon DynamoDB, Amazon Simple Queue Service (SQS), Amazon Kinesis, Amazon Elastic Container Registry (ECR), Amazon SNS, and Amazon EC2 instances in the same AWS region is free of charge. However, if data is transferred across a PrivateLink connection, VPC endpoint, AWS NAT Gateway Service, or AWS Transit Gateway, data transfer charges will apply.

The AWS Certified Solutions Architect – Associate (SAA-C03) exam will require an understanding of the available solutions for transferring data records into AWS. Regardless of the location of your data, an ever-increasing number of tools and services are available to move your data from on-premises locations into the AWS cloud. Tables 12-6, 12-7, 12-8, and 12-9 pose questions and details for data transfer options that are covered on the SAA-C03 exam.

Table 12-6   What Type of Data Do You Need to Transfer from On Premises to AWS?

Data Type	Transfer Option	Costs
Virtual server images	AWS Application Migration Service, AWS Server Migration Service (SMS)	Free for the first 90 days for each server migrated. EC2 and EBS charges.
Database	AWS Database Migration Service (DMS)	Data transfer into AWS DMS is free. Data transferred between DMS and databases in RDS and EC2 instances in the same AZ is free.
Bulk storage files	AWS Transfer Family (SFTP, FTPS, and FTP)	$0.30 per hour for enabled service. $0.04 per gigabyte for the amount of data uploaded/downloaded.

Table 12-7   Where Will On-Premises Data Be Stored at AWS?

Data Usage	Storage Options
Daily use at AWS	Amazon S3, Amazon EFS, or FSx for Windows File Server
Archived storage	Amazon S3 Glacier
Stored long-term	Amazon S3 Glacier Deep Archive

Table 12-8   How Much Data Needs to Be Transferred?

Data Size	Data Transfer Option
Gigabytes	AWS Transfer Family
Terabytes	AWS Snowball, AWS Snowcone, or AWS Snowball Edge
Exabytes	AWS Snowmobile

Table 12-9   What Data Transfer Method and Hybrid Solution Could You Choose?

Private Network Connection to AWS	AWS Direct Connect
Edge location transfer	S3 Transfer Acceleration
Internet transfer	AWS DataSync or AWS Transfer for SFTP
Offline data transfer	AWS Snowball, AWS Snowball Edge, or AWS Snowmobile
Hybrid storage	AWS Storage Gateway

Options for moving data records from on-premises locations into the AWS cloud are as follows:

- **AWS Direct Connect:** AWS Direct Connect allows you to create a private single-mode fiber connection from your on-premises data center or a co-location into AWS; a connection can be partitioned into up to 50 private virtual interfaces connecting to public and VPC resources at AWS.

- **AWS DataSync:** AWS DataSync can automate the movement of large amounts of data from on-premises locations to either Amazon S3 buckets or Amazon EFS storage across the Internet, or with an AWS Direct Connect or AWS VPN connection. Both one-time and continuous data transfers are supported using the NFSv4 protocol. Parallel processing creates fast data transfers using an AWS DataSync virtual machine agent downloaded and installed on your network. The first step is to create a data transfer task from your on-premises data source (NAS or file system) to the selected AWS destination, and then start the transfer. Data integrity verification is continually checked during the data transfer; data records are encrypted using Transport Layer Security (TLS). AWS DataSync supports both PCI DSS and HIPPA data transfers.

- **The AWS Snow Family:** The Snow family includes AWS Snowcone, AWS Snowball, and AWS Snowball Edge network-attached devices, or an AWS Snowmobile truck with a 40-foot storage container. Configuration involves logging in to the Snowball dashboard to create a job, selecting the parameters of the *Snow device* you wish to order, and select the S3 bucket that will store the locations of the Snow device once it is shipped back to AWS. When data has been moved to the selected S3 bucket and verified, the Snow device is securely erased and sanitized, removing all customer information. AWS Snow pricing is based on data transfer job fees, the commitment period, data transfer, and storage and shipping fees. Data transfer into Amazon S3 from an external location is free. The following Snow Family options are available:

  - **AWS Snowcone:** This is the smallest member of the Snow Family, with two vCPUs, 4 GiB of memory, and 8 TiB of object or block storage. It also has wired network access and USB-C power.

  - **AWS Snowball:** Petabyte data transfer is possible using multiple Snowball devices; each device can hold either 42 TiB or 80 TiB of object or block storage. After you create a job request, as shown in Figure 12-17, a Snowball device will be shipped to you via UPS. When you receive the device, hook it up to your network using an RJ-45 connection. The Snowball client software must be installed, and predefined security information must be entered before data transfer begins. After the data is transferred into the Snowball device, the device is shipped back to AWS and the device's data is deposited into an S3 bucket. This process can also be reversed, transferring object data from AWS back to your on-premises location. All data that is transferred to Snowball is encrypted with 256-bit encryption keys defined using AWS Key Management Service (KMS). The following use case options are available for Snowball devices:

- **Compute-optimized Snowball:** 42-TiB GPU option for machine learning or advanced video analysis use cases ($1,200 to $1,600 per job)

- **Storage-optimized Snowball:** Large data transfers and local storage ($300 to $500 per job)

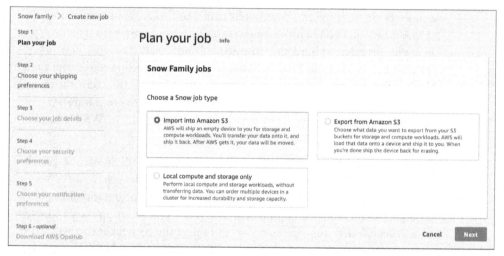

Figure 12-17   Creating a Snowball Job

- **AWS Snowball Edge:** The Snowball Edge device supports the installation of a local instance to carry out the local processing duties that can be built from your AMIs. Snowball Edge compute options are designed for local data processing within the device with storage for processing or analysis before being stored back at AWS.

- **AWS Snowmobile:** Move up to 100 PB of data with an AWS Snowmobile truck. AWS employees show up with a transport truck containing a 45-foot shipping container and attach it to your data center. After the shipping container is filled with data, it is carefully driven back to AWS accompanied by an escort vehicle for safety, and the data is uploaded into S3 storage.

- **AWS Transfer Family:** Transfer files into and out of S3 buckets using the SSH File Transfer Protocol (SFTP). Connect existing SFTP software to the SFTP endpoint at AWS, set up user authentication, select an S3 bucket, assign IAM access roles, and transfer data records to AWS.

AWS Storage Gateway

AWS Storage Gateway is a hybrid storage solution that allows you to integrate your on-premises network with AWS storage and allows your on-premises applications and utilities to seamlessly store data records to Amazon S3, Amazon S3 Glacier, and FSx or Windows Fire Server storage. AWS Storage Gateway can be used for backing up and archiving documents, storage migration, and storing on-premises tiered storage at AWS as a background process. The actual AWS Storage Gateway gateway device can be a hardware device such as a Dell EMC PowerEdge server with Storage Gateway preloaded, or a virtual machine image that can be downloaded and installed in VMware or Hyper-V environments. There are four configuration choices available for deploying AWS Storage Gateway:

- **Amazon S3 File Gateway:** File Gateway interfaces directly into Amazon S3 storage and allows you to store and retrieve files using either NFS or SMB, as shown in Figure 12-18. Access S3 storage from EC2 instances or from on premises.

- **File Gateway—Amazon FSx for Windows File Server:** Begin Windows file-based storage migration to AWS for data that is frequently accessed. Supports the SMB protocol.

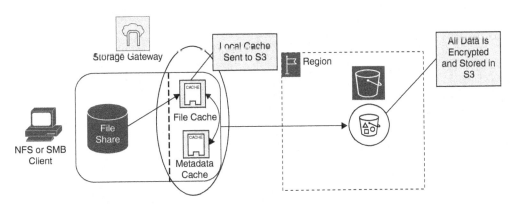

Figure 12-18   Storage Gateway: File Gateway Architecture

- **Volume Gateway:** Volume Gateway provides Amazon S3 cloud storage that can be mounted as an on-premises iSCSI device. Data is stored in Amazon S3 with a copy of frequently accessed data cached locally with the iSCSI volumes asynchronously backed up to Amazon S3 using incremental snapshots, as shown in Figure 12-19.

- **Tape Gateway:** Tape Gateway is a virtual tape drive that supports a wide variety of third-party backup applications and allows you to store and archive virtual tapes in Amazon S3 storage using the iSCSI protocol. Virtual tape backups can also be moved to Amazon S3 Glacier using lifecycle rules.

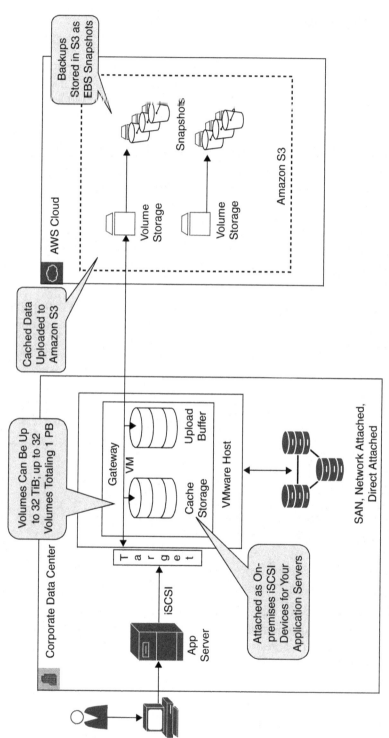

Figure 12-19   Storage Gateway: Volume Gateway Architecture

AWS Storage Gateway Cheat Sheet

For the AWS Certified Solutions Architect – Associate (SAA-C03) exam, you need to understand the following critical aspects of AWS Storage Gateway:

- AWS Storage Gateway provides hybrid storage between on-premises environments and AWS.

- AWS Storage Gateway stores frequently accessed content on premises while storing data securely and durably in S3 storage.

- AWS Storage Gateway is useful for on-premises disaster recovery solutions.

- AWS Storage Gateway is useful for cloud migrations of data records.

- AWS Storage Gateway supports three storage interfaces: File Gateway, Volume Gateway, and Tape Gateway.

- AWS File Gateway allows on-premises servers to store content in S3 buckets using NFSv4 or SMB mount points.

- AWS File Gateway allows on-premises servers to store content in FSx for Windows File Server.

- AWS Volume Gateway Stored mode provides asynchronous replication of on-premises data to Amazon S3.

- AWS Volume Gateway Cached mode stores your primary data in Amazon S3; frequently used data is cached locally.

- Tape Gateway allows you to use your existing tape software and store backups in Amazon S3 storage.

- With AWS Storage Gateway, data transfer is encrypted with SSL/TLS.

- With AWS Storage Gateway, data storage is encrypted with server-side encryption keys (SSE-S3).

- Storage Gateway pricing includes request, data transfer, and storage charges.

Exam Preparation Tasks

As mentioned in the section "How to Use This Book" in the Introduction, you have a couple of choices for exam preparation: the exercises here, Chapter 16, "Final Preparation," and the exam simulation questions in the Pearson Test Prep Software Online.

Review All Key Topics

Review the most important topics in the chapter, noted with the Key Topic icon in the margin of the page. Table 12-10 lists these key topics and the page number on which each is found.

Table 12-10   Chapter 12 Key Topics

Key Topic Element	Description	Page Number
Table 12-2	Management Service Charges at AWS	598
Section	Tiered Pricing at AWS	599
Table 12-4	Cost Management Tools by Use Case	602
Section	AWS Cost Explorer	604
Section	AWS Budgets	607
Section	AWS Cost and Usage Reports	609
Section	Managing Costs Cheat Sheet	610
Section	Using Cost Allocation Tags	612
Table 12-5	Amazon S3, EBS, EFS, and FSx for Windows File Server Comparison	616
Section	AWS Backup	618
Section	Lifecycle Rules	619
Section	AWS Backup Cheat Sheet	620
Table 12-6	What Type of Data Do You Need to Transfer from On Premises to AWS?	622
List	Options for moving data from on-premises locations into the AWS cloud	623
Section	AWS Storage Gateway	625
Section	AWS Storage Gateway Cheat Sheet	627

Define Key Terms

Define the following key terms from this chapter and check your answers in the glossary:

data transfer, tiered pricing, Load Balancer Capacity Unit (LCU), Cost and Usage Report (CUR), cost allocation tags, lifecycle rules, Snow device

Q&A

The answers to these questions appear in Appendix A. For more practice with exam format questions, use the Pearson Test Prep Software Online.

1. What are the two main components of calculating management service costs at AWS that are applied to every service cost?

2. How are data transfer costs incurred at AWS?

3. What type of pricing at AWS is calculated based on the usage of the service or resource?

4. What are additional components of storage charges other than data transfer charges?

5. What is the purpose of creating and enabling cost allocation tags?

6. What is the difference between an S3 lifecycle rule and an AWS Backup lifecycle management policy?

7. Where can AWS backups be copied to?

8. What is the difference between an AWS Storage Gateway Volume Gateway and File Gateway?

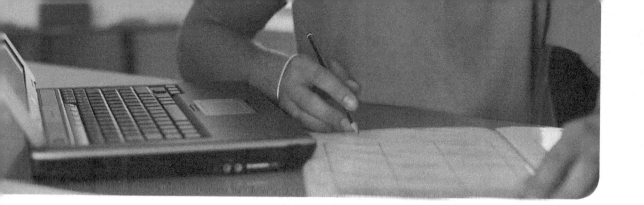

This chapter covers the following topics:

- EC2 Instance Types
- EC2 Instance Purchasing Options
- Strategies for Optimizing Compute

This chapter covers content that's important to the following exam domain and task statement:

Domain 4: Design Cost-Optimized Architectures

Task Statement 2: Design cost-optimized compute solutions

CHAPTER 13

Designing Cost-Effective Compute Solutions

There are hundreds of Amazon Elastic Compute Cloud (EC2) instances to consider deploying for a wide variety of workloads. EC2 instances also have a variety of pricing options to consider when deploying compute resources at AWS. EC2 instances can be deployed at AWS and on premises for hybrid deployments. Recall from Chapter 2, "The AWS Well-Architected Framework," that Cost Optimization is one of the six pillars of the AWS Well-Architected Framework. It's an excellent idea to download the AWS document "Cost Optimization Pillar" (see https://docs.aws.amazon.com/wellarchitected/latest/cost-optimization-pillar/wellarchitected-cost-optimization-pillar.pdf) and read it thoroughly; doing so will help you greatly in understanding how to manage costs at AWS.

"Do I Know This Already?"

The "Do I Know This Already?" quiz enables you to assess whether you should read this entire chapter thoroughly or jump to the "Exam Preparation Tasks" section. If you doubt your answers to these questions or your own assessment of your knowledge of the topics, read the entire chapter. Table 13-1 lists the major headings in this chapter and their corresponding "Do I Know This Already?" quiz questions. You can find the answers in Appendix A, "Answers to the 'Do I Know This Already?' Quizzes and Q&A Sections."

Table 13-1 "Do I Know This Already?" Section-to-Question Mapping

Foundation Topics Section	Questions
EC2 Instance Types	1, 2
EC2 Instance Purchasing Options	3, 4
Strategies for Optimizing Compute	5, 6

CAUTION The goal of self-assessment is to gauge your mastery of the topics in this chapter. If you do not know the answer to a question or are only partially sure of the answer, you should mark that question as wrong for purposes of the self-assessment. Giving yourself credit for an answer you correctly guess skews your self-assessment results and might provide you with a false sense of security.

1. What type of EC2 instance provides single tenant protection?

   a. C instances

   b. Dedicated instances

   c. Bare Metal instance

   d. Micro instances

2. How can network performance be improved for an EC2 instance?

   a. Add a second network adapter

   b. Change to an EC2 instance type that supports enhanced networking

   c. Install enhanced networking drivers

   d. Change to a general-purpose instance

3. What Reserved instance pricing is the least expensive?

   a. Convertible reservation with upfront 3-year payment

   b. Standard reservation with upfront payment for 3 years

   c. Spot instance pricing

   d. Capacity reservation

4. What type of compute instance pricing is the lowest cost?

   a. Micro instances

   b. Spot instances

   c. Reserved instances

   d. On-demand

5. What type of zone supports on-premises deployments?

   a. Local Zone

   b. Availability zone

   c. Wavelength Zone

   d. AWS Outposts

6. For companies requiring stringent data residency requirements, what is the best deployment choice?

   a. Multi-AZ deployment

   b. Multi AWS region deployment

   c. AWS Outposts deployment

   d. Local Zone deployment

Foundation Topics

EC2 Instance Types

EC2 instances are members of several *compute families* grouped and defined using a name and generation designation. In each instance's name, the first letter indicates the family that the instance belongs to (see Figure 13-1); the family dictates the resources allocated to the instance and the workloads that the instance is best suited for. The letter *c* stands for compute, *r* for RAM, and *i* for input/output operations per second (IOPS).

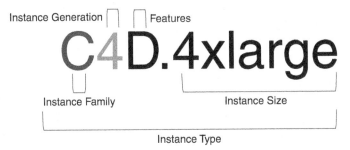

Figure 13-1 Decoding an Instance's Name

The next number in the instance name is the generation number. This number is very much like a software version number, so a c5 instance is newer than a c4 instance, and so on. (And, interestingly, a newer c5 instance is cheaper than the older c4 instance.)

The next letter, if present, indicates additional features that define the special characteristics of the instance. For example, in c4d, the "d" denotes solid-state drives (SSDs), for instance storage. The last component of the instance's name deals with the size of the instance; this is sometimes called a *T-shirt size*. Sizes range from small up to 32 times larger than the smallest size. (The size of an instance is based on the number of vCPU cores, the amount of RAM, and the amount of allocated network bandwidth.) For example, c4.8xlarge is eight times larger than c4.Large in terms of vCPU cores, RAM, and network bandwidth. Note that this example does not have an additional number or letter that would indicate additional features.

When you run a smaller instance at AWS, a smaller portion of the physical server's resources are allocated to the EC2 instance. When you run an x32-sized instance, you could possibly have all the resources assigned. Regardless of the instance type ordered, the allotted memory, vCPU cores, storage, and network bandwidth are isolated for each AWS instance. Customers are virtually isolated from each other, and this isolation is a key element of cloud security.

What Is a vCPU?

AWS defines the amount of CPU power assigned to each instance as a virtual CPU (vCPU). A vCPU is a part of a physical CPU core. A process called *hyperthreading* associates two virtual threads to each physical core—an *a* thread and a *b* thread working in a multitasking mode (see Figure 13-2). You can think of each physical core as a brain that can be split into two logical brains; a thread is a communication channel that links each instance to a specific amount of processing power. Linux and Windows process these virtual threads differently: The Linux operating system enumerates the first group of "*a*" threads before the second group of "*b*" threads. The Windows operating system interleaves the threads, selecting the "a" thread and then the "b" thread. Dividing the vCPU count shows the actual physical core count, which might be important if the licensing for your software requires a physical core count (for example, an Oracle database).

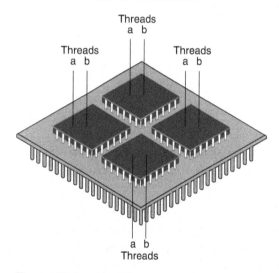

Figure 13-2   Virtual Cores

> **NOTE**   For further details on core counts, visit https://aws.amazon.com/ec2/virtualcores.

EC2 Instance Choices

The EC2 Dashboard has many instance types to choose from. There are at least 300 types grouped into an ever-increasing number of EC2 instance families, from general-purpose instances to EC2 instance families designed for compute, storage, and memory-optimized workloads (see Figure 13-3). There are even bare-metal instances available to order. (You do not have to memorize the EC2 instance types and families for the AWS Certified Solutions Architect – Associate [SAA-C03] exam.) When selecting an EC2 instance for a given workload, select the instance family that matches the required vCPU, memory and networking needs at the lowest cost.

Compare instance types

Amazon EC2 provides a wide selection of instance types optimized to fit different use cases. Instances are virtual servers that can run applications. They have varying combinations of CPU, memory, storage, and net you the flexibility to choose the appropriate mix of resources for your applications. Learn more about Instance types and how they can meet your computing needs.

Currently selected: t2.micro

Instance types (1/606)

Instance type ▽	vCPUs ▼	Architecture ▽	Memor... ▽	Storag... ▽	Stor... ▽	Network ... ▽	On-Demand Linux ... ▽	On-Demand Windows pricing
u-12tb1.112xl...	448	x86_64	12288	-	-	100 Gigabit	109.2 USD per Hour	129.808 USD per Hour
u-18tb1.112xl...	448	x86_64	18432	-	-	100 Gigabit	163.8 USD per Hour	184.408 USD per Hour
u-24tb1.112xl...	448	x86_64	24576	-	-	100 Gigabit	218.4 USD per Hour	239.008 USD per Hour
u-6tb1.112xlar...	448	x86_64	6144	-	-	100 Gigabit	54.6 USD per Hour	75.208 USD per Hour
u-9tb1.112xlar...	448	x86_64	9216	-	-	100 Gigabit	81.9 USD per Hour	102.508 USD per Hour
u-3tb1.56xlarge	224	x86_64	3072	-	-	50 Gigabit	27.3 USD per Hour	37.604 USD per Hour
u-6tb1.56xlarge	224	x86_64	6144	-	-	100 Gigabit	46.40391 USD per Hour	56.70791 USD per Hour

Figure 13-3 AWS Instance Choices

When you use the EC2 Dashboard to choose an instance, the initially available choices are defined as the "current generation" instance types. Organizations can still order the original m1 instance that AWS offered in 2006, but it's not recommended to do so as there are many more powerful and cost-effective options available.

NOTE The type of image (AMI) that you use at AWS to deploy your instance is also important to consider. Linux instance types defined as current generation do not support the older paravirtual (PV) images. If you require older PV images, at AWS, you are limited to a smaller number of EC2 instances (c1, c3, hs1, m1, m2, m3, and t1) and a limited number of regions that support PV AMIs, including Tokyo, Singapore, Sydney, Frankfurt, Ireland, São Paulo, North Virginia, Northern California, and Oregon. Windows AMIs support only hardware virtual machine (HVM) images.

An abundance of detailed documentation is available at AWS for EC2 instances at https://aws.amazon.com/ec2/instance-types. Here are some common EC2 instance types:

- **General purpose:** General purpose instance types are well suited for a wide range of workloads, including web and application servers, development, and test environments, and small to medium-sized databases. Examples include the m4, m5, and t3 instance types.

- **Compute optimized:** Compute optimized instance types are designed for compute-intensive workloads, such as batch processing, scientific simulations, and high-performance computing (HPC) applications. Examples include the c5, c6g, and c7g instance types.

- **Memory optimized:** Memory optimized instance types are designed for workloads that require high memory-to-vCPU ratios, such as in-memory databases and real-time processing of large data sets. Examples include the r5 and x1e instance types.

- **Storage optimized:** Storage optimized instance types are designed for workloads that require high I/O performance or large amounts of local storage, such as data warehousing, Hadoop, and NoSQL databases. Examples include the d2 and h1 instance types.

- **GPU instances:** GPU instances are designed for workloads that require graphics processing units (GPUs) for tasks such as video transcoding, machine learning, and scientific simulations. Examples include the p2 and g4 instance types.

- **Bare-Metal instances:** For developers who like to host databases on bare-metal servers for maximum performance, a bare-metal server might be an acceptable option to consider. Bare-metal instances were first created for VMware to be able to host ESXi deployments at AWS. Examples include the m5.metal and zlb.metal.

NOTE The selected EC2 instance size directly affects your overall network throughput. The larger the EC2 instance, the larger the associated EBS storage and network bandwidth.

Dedicated Host

A Dedicated Host is a physical server with Amazon EC2 instance capacity dedicated to a single customer. A Dedicated Host enables you to use your own existing software licenses—for example, Windows Server or Microsoft SQL Server—and to meet compliance requirements. A Dedicated Host also allows you to control the *affinity*, or placement of your EC2 instances, on the Dedicated Host. Dedicated Hosts support per-socket, per-core, or per-VM software licenses. Here are some benefits to deploying Dedicated Hosts:

- **Cost savings:** Dedicated Hosts can be a cost-effective option for organizations that have many EC2 instances and can take advantage of volume pricing discounts.

- **License compliance:** Dedicated Hosts can help meet licensing requirements for software that requires a specific underlying hardware configuration.

- **Improved security:** Dedicated Hosts can provide an additional layer of security by isolating your instances on physical hardware that is dedicated to your use.

There are some AWS limitations and restrictions when ordering and using Dedicated Hosts:

- The instance size and type of instance placed on a Dedicated Host must be the same type.

- To run RHEL, SUSE Linux, and Microsoft SQL Server on Dedicated Hosts, AMIs must be provided by each customer. RHEL, SUSE Linux, and SQL Server AMIs provided by AWS on AWS Marketplace can't be used with Dedicated Hosts.

- EC2 instances hosted on a Dedicated Host must be launched in a VPC with single tenancy enabled.

- Amazon Relational Database Service (RDS), placement groups, and EC2 Auto Scaling groups are not supported.

- Billing charges are just the hourly charge for each active, dedicated server host; you're not billed for the hosted instances on the dedicated host. Pricing is based on the on-demand dedicated host price or Reserved instance pricing.

NOTE A dedicated host is not the same as a bare-metal server; there is a hypervisor installed on a dedicated host.

Dedicated Hosts Cheat Sheet

For the AWS Certified Solutions Architect – Associate (SAA-C03) exam, you need to understand the following critical aspects of dedicated hosts:

- Dedicated hosts are physical servers dedicated completely to your usage and targeting of instances.

- Dedicated hosts are useful for server licenses that require per-core, per-socket, or per-VM metrics.

- Each dedicated host can run one EC2 instance type.

- Billing is per dedicated host.

Dedicated Instances

Organizations may choose to use a dedicated instance if compliance rules and regulations require complete compute instance isolation for a single virtual server. Each dedicated instance runs in a VPC on hardware resources dedicated to the customer. Dedicated instances have the same performance and security as instances hosted on a dedicated host but also have some limitations to be aware of, including the following:

- No access or control of the sockets and physical cores of the physical host is allowed.

- EBS volumes that are attached to a dedicated instance are standard EBS volumes.

Placement Groups

Amazon EC2 placement groups are logical groupings of EC2 instances within a single AZ. Placement groups are used to ensure that instances are physically isolated from each other within the same AZ.

There are three types of placement groups:

- **Cluster placement groups:** Cluster placement groups group instances that require low network latency and high network throughput. Cluster placement groups are recommended for applications such as HPC, big data, and other applications that require high-performance networking.

- **Spread placement groups:** Spread placement groups are used to distribute instances evenly across distinct hardware. Spread placement groups are recommended for applications that have a small number of critical instances that should be kept separate from each other, such as database masters.

- **Partition placement groups:** Partition placement groups are used to group instances across logical partitions so groups of instances in one partition do not share the underlying hardware with groups of instances located in different partitions. Recommended for large, distributed workloads, such as Kafka and Cassandra.

EC2 Instance Purchasing Options

Compute costs (think EC2 instances) are, by default, defined as on-demand or pay-as-you-go (PAYG) and are charged based on the instance's size and AWS region. Compute pricing can be significantly reduced by prepaying compute costs by ordering *Reserved instances*. There are also pricing considerations for dedicated or single-tenancy instances. EC2 instances can also be reserved based on a recurring schedule. There are several other pricing considerations for EC2 instances. For example, there are data transfer pricing differences for using public versus private IP addresses for communication. There are also pricing differences between instances located within the same AZ on the same subnet and communicating across different AZs.

Selecting an EC2 instance for your workload requirements at the lowest possible cost is the overall goal. Let's consider an example:

A new AWS customer has started initial development and testing in the AWS cloud, matching the EC2 instance size at AWS as closely as possible to the virtual machine size used on premises. However, the virtual machine used on premises is quite large, with many vCPU cores and gigabytes of RAM. The following considerations are important to consider for this scenario:

- Moving to the AWS cloud, the single EC2 instance size at AWS can be smaller because multiple EC2 instances can be deployed on subnets located across multiple AZs hosted behind an ELB load balancer, matching the required compute power with multiple instances and providing high availability and failover.

- Preliminary testing confirms the overall performance of the application stack under a steady-state load with a constant number of users accessing the application hosted on multiple EC2 instances.

- During the initial testing period, compute resources will not be scaled up and down.

- During initial testing and in production, the compute workload environment can be turned off after-hours, or scaled in, when it's not being heavily utilized, reducing compute and data transfer charges.

- Once the application moves from testing to production and requires higher utilization, Reserved instances pricing or Savings Plans could help reduce the compute price up to 70%.

- Once the application is running as a production application, the application load will change from a small number of users to a much larger number of users.

- Include elasticity in the design of the application stack by deploying EC2 Auto Scaling. Automatically scale out or in compute instances based on current user demand. Auto scaled EC2 instances match the end user requirements at any given time, providing the lowest compute costs and the required performance.

- Amazon RDS, and optionally, Amazon Aurora Serverless, has the ability to pause database operation after a defined period of inactivity.

Operating in the AWS cloud and running all resources 24/7 is not cost-effective. Therefore, each customer needs to decide what services should remain on 24/7 and what services should be turned off or reduced in operating size when not under high demand. Table 13-2 outlines options for what services need to always be online and what can possibly be turned off for additional cost savings.

Table 13-2 Service Uptime

AWS Service	On-Premises Operation	At AWS	Cost Savings	Redundancy
DNS servers	24/7	Use Amazon Route 53	Use managed DNS servers; no servers to manage and administrate	DNS records replicated across multiple edge locations
Development/ testing environments	24/7	Turn off when not being used	14 hours per day cost savings	Deployed across AZs
Applications	24/7	EC2 Auto Scaling or Amazon Auto Scaling	Minimize compute resources used	Instances managed by ASG and ELB health checks
Databases	24/7	Amazon Aurora, Amazon DynamoDB are supported by AWS Auto Scaling; Amazon Aurora Serverless	14 hours per day cost savings	Data records stored across three AZs
Storage arrays	24/7	Amazon EFS, FSx for Windows File Server, Amazon S3, Amazon EBS	No storage arrays to administrate and manage	Data records stored across multiple AZs

EC2 Pricing—On-demand

When you first start with AWS, you will use on-demand pricing for your instances. Over time, as you move into production, you will consider a variety of compute pricing options. On-demand pricing involves no long-term contract and requires no upfront payments, but it can be the most expensive pricing option if your EC2 instances are always running. Each EC2 instance also has a specific billing cycle:

- An EC2 instance that is turned on and assigned to your account is billed a compute charge while it is powered on.

■ When an EC2 instance is turned off, the billing cycle finishes, and there is no further compute charge. The only additional charges that will be associated with an EC2 instance are for the attached EBS storage volumes and any snapshots or AMIs that have been created. Storage charges at AWS are per month per gigabyte of EBS or S3 storage.

NOTE There is no separate charge for EC2 instances with ephemeral storage. The cost for temporary local block storage is included in the price of the EC2 instance.

With on-demand pricing, you pay a flat rate for using resources, and there is no long-term commitment. This model is charged based on an hourly rate, but the increments might be as low as 1 second (for example, for RDS deployments or Linux EC2 instances). For testing purposes or for very short-term usage— perhaps for a 4-hour training class—or for customers first starting out in the AWS cloud, on-demand pricing is fine. The following are other pricing options to consider at AWS:

■ On-demand pricing might be best for workloads only running during business hours.

■ If you require compute power for applications under constant usage and the application will be running for at least a year, then Reserved instances are a better option than on-demand instances because you will save up to 72%.

■ If your application can run any time, spot instances might be a consideration.

■ It is also possible to configure a Spot Fleet that uses a combination of on-demand, Spot requests, and Reserved instance pricing. Reserved instances and Spot instances are covered later in this chapter.

On-demand Instance Service Quotas

Once customers have signed up for AWS, they typically think they can spin up as many EC2 instances as desired; however, for every AWS service, there is a default service quota. On-demand EC2 instance quotas are based on the number of vCPUs that on-demand instances have deployed. There are several on-demand instance default service quotas outlined in Table 13-3.

Table 13-3   On-demand Limits Based on vCPUs

On-demand EC2 Instance Type	Default Quota
Running on-demand all standard (a, c, d, h, i, m, r, t, z) instances	1152 vCPUs
Running on-demand all f instances	128 vCPUs
Running on-demand all g instances	128 vCPUs
Running on-demand all inf instances	128 vCPUs
Running on-demand all p instances	128 vCPUs
Running on-demand all x instances	128 vCPUs

At first, the EC2 instance model might seem complicated, but it's rather simple; the default quota is the amount of compute power (vCPU) you are using. Instead of planning limits based on the instance types, you can plan your EC2 instance limits based on the total number of vCPUs used in your workload and AWS account.

For example, with the standard instance quota of 256 vCPUs, you could launch 16 c5.4xlarge instances or any combination of standard instance types and sizes that adds up to 256 vCPUs. It's important to note that current quotas can usually be increased using the Service Quotas utility from the AWS Management Console (see Figure 13-4).

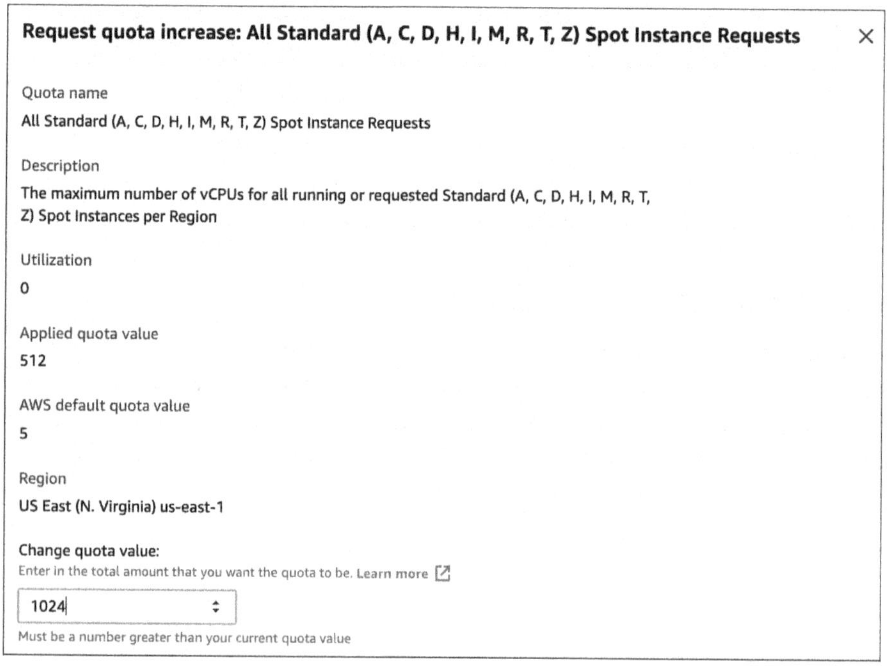

Request quota increase: All Standard (A, C, D, H, I, M, R, T, Z) Spot Instance Requests   ✕

Quota name
All Standard (A, C, D, H, I, M, R, T, Z) Spot Instance Requests

Description
The maximum number of vCPUs for all running or requested Standard (A, C, D, H, I, M, R, T, Z) Spot Instances per Region

Utilization
0

Applied quota value
512

AWS default quota value
5

Region
US East (N. Virginia) us-east-1

Change quota value:
Enter in the total amount that you want the quota to be. Learn more 🔗

> 1024| ↕

Must be a number greater than your current quota value

Figure 13-4   Requesting a Quota Change

If you have never communicated with AWS support, how are they going to know what resources you require in the AWS cloud? If you call your on-premises data center staff and request 100 virtual machines, the answer might be, "We can't right now; we don't have the capacity." The same difficulty will arise at AWS: They might not have the capacity or the types of instances that are required. Amazon has a handy calculator called the Limits Calculator that can help you figure out the number of vCPU views you need (see Figure 13-5). Open the EC2 dashboard, select an AWS region, and from the menu on the left select Limits. You can enter the following information in the Limits Calculator:

- **Instance type:** The instance type details
- **Instance count:** The number of instances you need

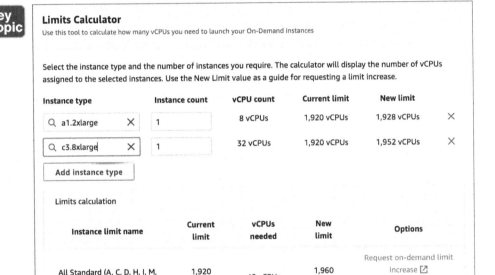

Figure 13-5   The Limits Calculator

The vCPU count column of the Limits Calculator shows the number of CPUs that correspond to the instance count entered in the Limits Calculator.

After calculations are finished, use the links at the bottom right of the Limits Calculator to request a limit increase. If running production workloads need to scale up at a moment's notice, you should guarantee that the EC2 instances you need are available when required.

Reserved Instances

Reserved instances (RI) are a cost-saving offering that enables you to reserve capacity for your Amazon EC2 instances in exchange for a discounted hourly rate. Reserved instances are automatically applied to running on-demand instances provided that the specifications match.

Once a Reserved instance is ordered, you will be charged the discounted hourly rate, which can be significantly lower than the on-demand rate. With Reserved instances, you pay for the entire term regardless of actual usage. You will be billed for the reserved term whether you run an instance that matches your reservation or not.

For EC2 instances or specific compute-related AWS services that are constantly in use, Reserved instance pricing will save a great deal of money. Organizations need to consider several variables when ordering Reserved instance pricing; for example, the AWS region they are operating in and the specific availability zone location. Note that a c5a.8xlarge EC2 instance is not available in each AZ in the Northern Virginia region, which has six AZs (see Figure 13-6). Reserved instance pricing can be ordered for standard 1-year or 3-year durations. A Reserved instance reservation provides a billing discount that applies to EC2 instances hosted in a specific AZ or region. The billing discount could be as high as 72% compared to the standard on-demand hourly rate. Each RI is defined by the following attributes:

- **Instance type:** The instance family and the size of the instance
- **Scope:** The AWS region or availability zone location of the Reserved instance
- **Regional:** The AWS region location of the Reserved instance
- *Zonal:* The AWS availability zone location of the Reserved instance
- **Tenancy:** Shared default hardware or single-tenant, dedicated hardware
- **Platform:** Windows or Linux

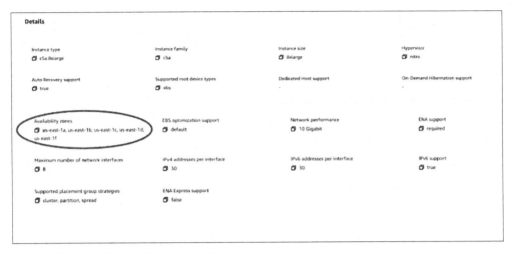

Figure 13-6 Availability Zone Availability

Once a purchased RI matches the attributes of a running EC2 instance in your AWS account, the RI is applied immediately. To reiterate: An RI is a billing discount; it is not an EC2 instance; rather, it is a billing discount that you have purchased for a type of EC2 instance.

For applications or web servers that are online and operational 24/7, RI pricing is essential. For example, selecting a c5a.8xlarge instance, the RI discount shown in Figure 13-7 could be as high as 75% when compared to the on-demand instance price.

Purchase Reserved Instances										✕

◯ Only show offerings that reserve capacity

Platform		Availability Zone		Tenancy		Offering class	
Linux/UNIX	▼	Any	▼	Default	▼	Standard	▼

Instance type		Term		Payment option		
c5ad.12xlarge	▼	1 month to 12 months	▼	All upfront	▼	Search

Seller ▽	Term ▽	Effective rate ▽	Upfront price ▽	Hourly rate ▽	Availability Zone ▼	Payment option ▽	Offering class ▽	Quantity available ▽	Desired quantity	
AWS	12 months	$1.214	$10,631.00	$0.000	us-east-1f	All upfront	Standard	Unlimited	1	Add to cart
AWS	12 months	$1.214	$10,631.00	$0.000	us-east-1d	All upfront	Standard	Unlimited	1	Add to cart

Figure 13-7 Reserved Instance Pricing

Term Commitment

A Reserved instance can be purchased for a 1-year or 3-year commitment; the 3-year commitment provides a larger discount.

Payment Options

Reserved instance pricing has several options to consider. Paying all monies upfront results in the biggest discount (refer to Figure 13-7).

- **All upfront:** Full payment at the start of the term; no other costs or charges will be incurred for the term.

- **Partial upfront:** A portion of the cost must be paid upfront, and the remaining hours in the term are billed at a discounted hourly rate—*regardless of whether the Reserved instance is being used.*

- **No upfront:** A discounted hourly rate is billed for every hour within the term—*regardless of whether the Reserved instances are being used.*

EC2 Reserved Instance Types

There are two flavors of Reserved instances:

- **Standard Reserved instance:** A standard Reserved instance gives you the biggest discount and can be purchased as repeatable 1-year terms or as a 3-year term. After you've purchased a standard Reserved instance, you can make some changes to your reservation: You can change the AZ where the instance will be hosted, the instance size, and the networking type. What happens if your needs don't match the reservation that was purchased? You can register and try to sell your standard Reserved instance reservation through the Reserved Instance Marketplace.

- **Convertible Reserved instance:** If you may have to change instance types, operating systems, or switch from multi-tenancy to single-tenancy compute operation—then you should consider a convertible Reserved instance reservation. The convertible reserved discount could be over 50%, and the term is a 1- or a 3-year term. A convertible Reserved instance reservation has more flexibility than a standard Reserved instance reservation because of the additional changes that can be made during the convertible Reserved instances term. However, you cannot sell a convertible reservation in the Reserved Instance Marketplace.

NOTE   Reserved instance pricing reservations, once expired, do not automatically renew. Billing alerts can be created in the Billing Dashboard to warn when any pricing reservations are due to expire.

Scheduled Reserved EC2 Instances

A scheduled RI reservation allows you to buy capacity reservations for a daily, weekly, or monthly term. The specific length of reservation time that can be requested is a maximum of 1 year. Once instances have been reserved as scheduled, you pay for the reserved compute time, regardless of whether the instances are used. You also can't modify or resell a scheduled instance reservation.

NOTE Scheduled instances are supported by c3, c4, c5, m4, and r3 instance types.

Regional and Zonal Reserved Instances

Scope is the important caveat related to the purchase of Reserved instances: The *scope* of the Reserved instance request is regional or zonal.

A Reserved instance for a region is a regional reservation that can be used anywhere in the region.

A zonal Reserved instance involves a discount for a specific AZ within an AWS region. A zonal reservation is also a *capacity reservation* for the selected AZ, in addition to the discounted RI price. Therefore, by purchasing zonal Reserved instances, the capacity—that is, the number of instances you wish to run in a specific AZ is defined.

The Reserved instance price is based on the AWS region in which the instances will be hosted.

- A zonal reservation provides you with a capacity guarantee per AZ as well as a discounted price.

- A regional reservation does not provide you with a capacity reservation; however, it provides flexibility to use the EC2 instances in any AZ.

Table 13-4 lists key differences between regional and zonal Reserved instances.

Table 13-4 Regional Versus Zonal Reserved Instance Reservations

Factor	Regional RI	Zonal RI
Availability zone flexibility	A discount applies to instance usage in any AZ in the region.	A discount applies to instance usage in the specified AZ only.
Reserve capacity	A regional RI does not reserve capacity.	A zonal RI reserves capacity in the specified AZ.
Instance size flexibility	A discount applies to any instance within the selected instance family, regardless of size, for Linux instances using default shared tenancy.	A discount applies to instance usage for the specified instance type and size only.
Queuing purchases	Regional RIs can be ordered for a future date and time to ensure that RI coverage continues at the regional level.	RIs cannot be pre-purchased for zonal reservations; zonal reservations apply immediately after purchase.

You can also view your organization's current RI and Savings Plans charges by opening the Billing Dashboard from the AWS Management Console. To review your current and estimated monthly total, select Bill Details by Service, expand the Elastic Compute Cloud section, and select the AWS region to review current service charges about instances for your AWS account or AWS organization. Costs can also be reviewed by viewing the AWS Cost and Usage Report, and optionally downloading its information in CSV file format.

When purchasing EC2 instances, you need to consider the following factors:

- What AWS region are you going to be operating in?

- How many AZs are you going to use?

- How many EC2 instances do you want to run in each AZ?

- What size of EC2 instance are you planning to run?

- How many EC2 instances need to be running 24/7?

- What are your AWS account limits for each on-demand EC2 instance type required per AWS region?

- Do you need to request a service quota increase for each EC2 instance type to match your needs?

- Do you require a Reserved Instance Standard or Convertible reservation?

Reserved instance pricing provides pricing discounts for many AWS Services that use on-demand instances by default at AWS. Table 13-5 shows the compute choices where RI can be applied.

Table 13-5   Reserved Pricing Choices with AWS

Reserved Instance Pricing Option	Details
Amazon RDS	Managed database instances
Amazon EMR	Hadoop cluster instances
Amazon ElastiCache	Memcached or Redis clusters
Amazon Redshift	Data warehouse clusters
EC2 instances	On-demand instances

NOTE You can also request a capacity reservation for reserving EC2 capacity if you need to guarantee that on-demand instances are always available for use in a specific AZ. This option is not a Reserved instance discount; it is another pricing option. It's important to remember that after you've created a capacity reservation, you will be charged for the capacity reservation whether you actually use the instances or not. However, there are no long-term commitments for a capacity reservation, and the limits can be modified or canceled at any time.

Savings Plans

Savings Plans are a cost savings option that provides discounts on Amazon EC2, AWS Fargate, and AWS Lambda usage in exchange for a commitment to a consistent amount of usage (measured in dollars per hour) for a one- or three-year term. You will be charged the discounted Savings plan price for your use of resources up to your defined commitment. For example, if you've committed to $50 of compute usage per hour, the savings plan price for that usage will be charged the commitment amount every hour; any computer usage beyond the defined commitment will be charged the current on-demand rate.

Three types of Savings Plans are available:

- **Compute:** Compute Savings Plans provide discounts on EC2 instance usage across all instance families, sizes, and regions, and on Fargate usage for all regions and AWS compute platforms.

- **EC2 Instance:** EC2 Instance Savings Plans provides savings up to 72% in exchange for a 1- to 3-year commitment to usage of EC2 instance families in a specific AWS region, regardless of availability zone, EC2 instance size, operating system, or tenancy. Customers can change instance sizes if staying within the selected EC2 instance family. EC2 instance usage will be automatically charged at the discounted price; compute usage beyond the per hour commitment will be charged at the current on-demand instance rate. Payment options are all upfront (which provides the best price break), partial upfront, and no upfront. A savings plan also works with AWS Organizations; benefits are applicable to all AWS accounts within an AWS organization.

- **SageMaker:** SageMaker Savings Plans helps you reduce SageMaker costs by up to 64% regardless of instance family, size, or AWS region.

NOTE With consolidated billing, AWS treats all AWS Organization accounts as one account with regard to consolidated pricing. Usage data is combined from all AWS accounts belonging to the AWS organization, applying the relevant volume pricing tier providing the lowest total price on the consolidated resources.

Spot Instances

A *spot instance* is spare compute capacity that AWS is not currently using that is available for much less than Reserved instance pricing. Organizations can potentially save up to 90% of their compute purchase price. However, if and when AWS takes your spot instance back, it only provides a 2-minute warning, and then—poof—your spot instance is gone. Spot instance pricing is based on EC2 availability, and as just mentioned, a spot instance is available until AWS reclaims it. Spot instances are not guaranteed to always be available; however, they are useful in these use cases:

- **Batch processing:** Spot instances can be used to run batch processing workloads, such as data analysis, machine learning, and video rendering. These types of workloads can be easily interrupted and are often time-sensitive, making spot instances a good choice.

- **Test and development environments:** Spot instances can be used to create test and development environments, where you can test new applications or perform experimentation.

- **High-performance computing (HPC) workloads:** Spot instances can be used to run HPC workloads, such as simulations and modeling, that require a large number of compute resources for a short period of time.

- **Web servers and application hosting:** Spot instances can be used to host web servers and applications, as long as the workload can tolerate the potential for interruption.

> **NOTE** Spot instances can be used with EC2 Auto Scaling groups, Elastic Map-Reduce instances (EMR), the Elastic Container Service (ECS), and AWS Batch.

Several terms are used when requesting spot instances:

- **Spot instance pool:** The EC2 instances of the same instance type, operating system, and AZ location that are currently unused.

- **Spot price:** The current per-hour price of a spot instance.

- **Spot instance request:** Request for a spot instance, includes the maximum price you're willing to pay. If you don't specify a maximum price, the default maximum price is the on-demand price. When your maximum spot price is higher than Amazon's current spot price, as long as capacity is available, your spot request will be fulfilled. You can request a spot instance request as a one-time purchase, or as a persistent request; when a spot instance is terminated, Amazon EC2 automatically resubmits a persistent spot instance request, which will remain queued until spot capacity becomes available once again.

■ **Spot instances:** The Spot Fleet service evaluates your spot instances request and selects a number of spot instance pools, using available instance types that meet or exceed your needs and launching enough spot instances to meet the desired target capacity (see Figure 13-8). Spot Fleets maintain the requested target capacity by default by launching replacement instances after spot instances in the current Spot Fleets are terminated. Note that a Spot Fleet can also include on-demand instances if requested; if your requested criteria cannot be met, on-demand instances should be launched to reach the desired target capacity. If on-demand instances used in the Spot Fleet deployment match a current RI billing discount, the discount is applied to the on-demand instances when they are running.

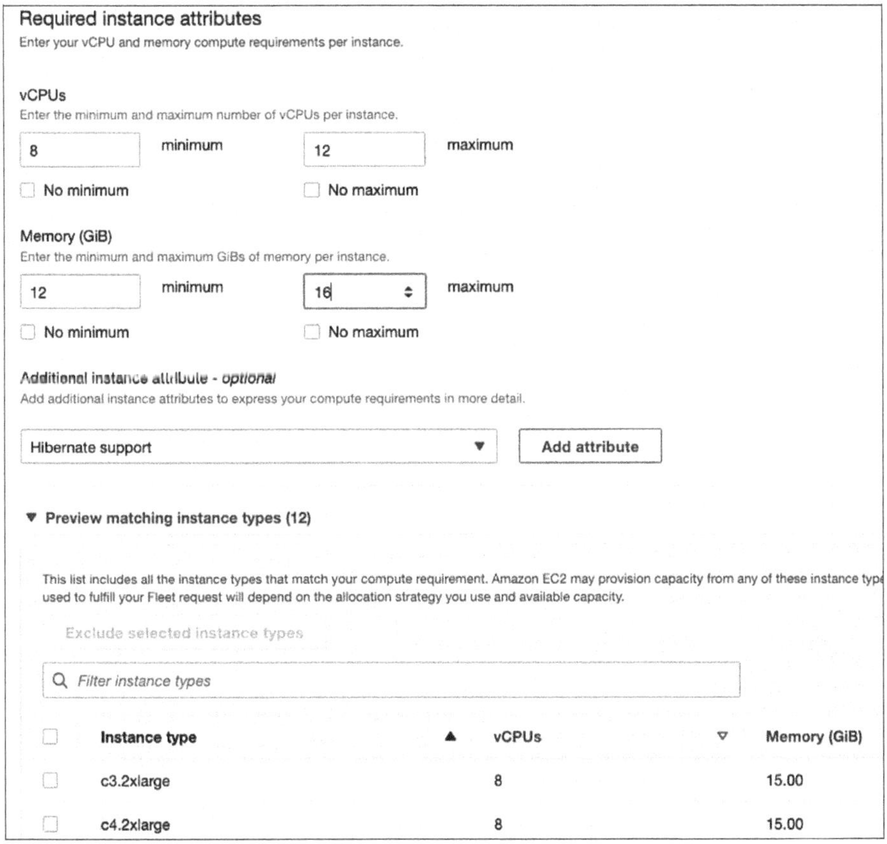

Required instance attributes
Enter your vCPU and memory compute requirements per instance.

vCPUs
Enter the minimum and maximum number of vCPUs per instance.

| 8 | minimum | 12 | maximum |

☐ No minimum   ☐ No maximum

Memory (GiB)
Enter the minimum and maximum GiBs of memory per instance.

| 12 | minimum | 16 ⬍ | maximum |

☐ No minimum   ☐ No maximum

Additional instance attribute - *optional*
Add additional instance attributes to express your compute requirements in more detail.

| Hibernate support ▼ | **Add attribute** |

▼ **Preview matching instance types (12)**

This list includes all the instance types that match your compute requirement. Amazon EC2 may provision capacity from any of these instance type used to fulfill your Fleet request will depend on the allocation strategy you use and available capacity.

Exclude selected instance types

Q *Filter instance types*

	Instance type ▲	**vCPUs** ▽	**Memory (GiB)**
☐	c3.2xlarge	8	15.00
☐	c4.2xlarge	8	15.00

Figure 13-8 Selecting Spot Instance Attributes

■ **Spot Fleet:** A Spot Fleet is a group of EC2 instances, created from a single request, that share a common set of options. To use a Spot Fleet, you specify the number and type of instances you want, as well as the maximum price you are willing to pay for each instance type. The Spot Fleet then uses this information to launch the optimal mix of instances to meet your capacity needs at the lowest possible cost. You can also use a Spot Fleet to specify the number of instances you want to maintain in each AZ, enabling you to distribute your workloads across multiple AZs for increased fault tolerance. A Spot Fleet could be helpful if you want to launch a certain number of instances for a distributed application, a long-running batch-processing job, or a Hadoop cluster.

- **Spot Fleet request:** When making a Spot Fleet request, first define the desired total target capacity of your desired fleet and whether you want to use a combination of on-demand and spot instances, or just spot instances. Using on-demand instances provides protection for your workload and ensures that you always have a set amount of capacity available. In Figure 13-9, the Spot Fleet request has, by default, a fleet allocation strategy of maintain target capacity.

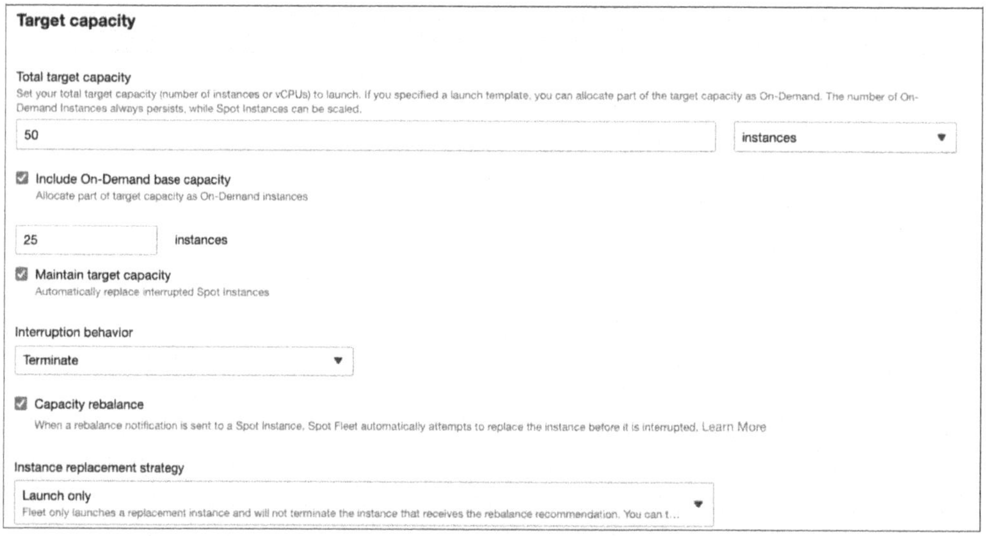

Figure 13-9   Spot Fleet Target Capacity

You can also include multiple launch specifications in the launch template and can further define a number of variables, including the EC2 instance type, AMI, AZ, and subnet to be used. The Spot Fleet service then attempts to select a variety of available spot instances to fulfill your overall capacity request based on your specifications.

NOTE   The number of spot instances that you can request depends on your defined account spot service quota limit for the AWS region in which you are operating.

Spot Fleet Optimization Strategies

To optimize the costs of using spot instances, you can deploy several allocation strategies:

- **Lowest price:** This strategy involves deploying the least expensive combination of instance types and availability zones based on the current spot price. This is the default Spot Fleet optimization strategy.

- **Diversified:** This strategy involves distributing spot instances across all available spot pools.

- **Capacity optimized:** This strategy involves provisioning from the most available spot instance pools.

- **Capacity rebalancing:** This strategy involves allowing the Spot Fleet service to replace spot instances that are at risk of interruption with new spot instances.

- **Instance pools to use:** This strategy involves distributing spot instances across the spot pools that you specify.

For Spot Fleets that run for a short period of time, you probably want to choose the lowest price strategy. For Spot Fleets that run for an extended period, you likely want to distribute spot instance services across multiple spot pools. For example, if your Spot Fleet request specifies five pools and a target capacity of 50 instances, the Spot Fleet service launches ten spot instances in each pool. If the spot price for one of the spot pools exceeds your maximum price for this pool, only 20% of your entire fleet is affected.

NOTE Spot instances can also be provisioned for other AWS services, including EC2 Auto Scaling and EMR, as well as through the use of CloudFormation templates.

Spot Capacity Pools

To design resiliency with spot instances, you can create spot capacity pools, as shown in Figure 13-10. Each pool is a set of unused EC2 instances that has the same instance type, operating system, and network platform.

Your fleet request at a glance

Total target capacity	Instance configuration	Fleet strength	Estimated price
200 instances	template1, v.1	Strong	~$24.427/hr
	2 vCPUs, 3 GiB (min) | 2 Availability Zones	12 instance pools	at target capacity
			36% savings
			compared to On-Demand

Figure 13-10   Spot Capacity Pools

To ensure that you always have the desired capacity available, even if some of your spot instances are suddenly removed, you can direct the Spot Fleet service to maintain your desired compute capacity by using on-demand instances if there are not enough spot instances available that match your launch specifications. The Spot Fleet service attempts to save you money by launching the lowest-priced instance type it can find—either a spot instance or an on-demand instance. Therefore, your spot capacity pools could contain both spot and on-demand instances, depending on what spot instances are available at the time of your request.

After your fleet is launched, the Spot Fleet service can maintain the desired target compute capacity when there are changes in the spot price or available capacity. The allocation strategy for your defined spot instances is based on Capacity Optimized. Other choices include Price Capacity Optimized or Lowest Price. You can also choose to distribute the available spot instances across the spot instance pools by selecting Diversified Across All Pools.

Each spot capacity pool can also have a different price point. The built-in automation engine helps you find the most cost-effective capacity across multiple spot capacity pools when requesting a Spot Fleet. Both Linux and Windows operating system instances are available as spot instances. Remember that Spot Fleets operate within the defined service quota limits of your AWS account, which include the number of Spot Fleets per region, the number of launch specifications per fleet, and Spot Fleet target capacity.

Although spot instances can be terminated after a 2-minute warning, according to Amazon's analysis, most spot instance interruptions are due to customers terminating their spot instances when work is completed.

NOTE   A Spot Fleet cannot span different subnets within the same AZ.

You can choose to have a spot instance hibernated or stopped when it is interrupted instead of just having it terminated. When your spot instances are hibernated, the data held in RAM is stored on the root EBS drive of the hibernated instance, and your private IP address is held. Spot hibernation is not supported for all instance types and AMIs, so make sure to check the current support levels for hibernated spot instances.

EC2 Pricing Cheat Sheet

For the AWS Certified Solutions Architect – Associate (SAA-C03) exam, you need to understand the following critical aspects of EC2 pricing:

- On-demand instances require no long-term commitments but have the highest price.

- On-demand capacity reservations allow you to guarantee that compute capacity is available when you need it. However, you pay for the reservation 24/7 whether you use it or not.

- Reserved instances offer up to 75% savings because you prepay for capacity.

- Zonal Reserved instances have capacity guarantees.

- Regional Reserved instances do not have capacity guarantees.

- A Savings Plan enables you to set a baseline hourly price that you are willing to pay.

- Savings Plans used for EC2 instances have increased flexibility and reduced operational costs.

- Spot instances requests run on spare compute capacity in AWS data centers and can save you up to 80%.

- To obtain a spot instance, you create a spot instance request.

- Spot Fleets can be created specifying the desired number of spot instances to launch to fulfill the capacity request.

- Spot requests can be one-time or persistent requests.

- Spot Fleets attempt to maintain the desired compute instance capacity.

- A Spot Fleet is a collection of different spot instance types and, optionally, on-demand instances.

Compute Tools and Utilities

For the AWS Certified Solutions Architect – Associate (SAA-C03) exam, you need to understand the following AWS tools and utilities for assisting in evaluating compute costs and EC2 instance usage:

- **AWS CloudWatch:** Continuous monitoring of EC2 instances using CPU utilization, network throughput, and disk I/O metrics allows customers to observe peak values of each metric to help select the most efficient and cheapest instance type.

- **AWS Cost Explorer:** EC2 Usage Reports are updated several times each day, providing in-depth usage details for all your running EC2 instances.

- **AWS Operations Conductor:** Use recommendations from Cost Explorer to automatically resize EC2 instance.

- **AWS Trusted Advisor:** Inspect and identify underutilized EC2 instances.

- **AWS Compute Optimizer:** AWS Compute Optimizer uses machine learning to recommend optimal AWS resources for your workloads to reduce costs and improve performance. Compute Optimizer helps you choose optimal configurations for EC2 instance types, EBS volumes, and Lambda functions.

- Compute-optimized instances with CPU usage and memory usage less than 40% usage over a one-month period should be rightsized to reduce operating costs.

- Storage-optimized instances IOPS settings should be monitored to make sure EC2 instances are not overprovisioned IOPS-wise.

- Amazon RDS instance performance baselines should be created and monitored using the RDS metrics Average CPU utilization, Maximum CPU utilization, Minimum available RAM, and Average number of bytes written and read to and from disk per second.

- Steady-state workloads that operate at a constant level over time should be switched to Savings Plans.

- Temporary workloads with flexible start and stop times should be deployed using spot instances instead of On-demand instances.

- Use spot instances for workloads that don't require high reliability.

- Schedule EC2 instances to ensure they run only during business hours using the AWS Instance Scheduler.

Strategies for Optimizing Compute

AWS has greatly increased its hybrid compute options to include AWS Local Zones, Wavelength Zones, and AWS Outposts (see Table 13-6) to allow customers to run AWS infrastructure and services anywhere.

Table 13-6   Distributed Compute Strategies Processing at the Edge

	CloudFront	Wavelength Zones	AWS Local Zones	AWS Outposts
Location	Edge cache for static and dynamic data	Hosted 5G applications in third-party data centers	AWS compute, storage, database, and services closer to customers	On-premises racks or servers running AWS infrastructure and services
Latency	Edge location close to the customer	Single-digit ms	Single-digit ms	Fastest
Use Case	Web servers, S3 static data	5G gaming, video streaming from the telco data center	High-bandwidth and secure connections between local workloads and AWS	Local applications running on AWS Services, VMware, Amazon EKS Anywhere
Performance	Better	Faster	Fast	Fastest

Customers that still remain cautious about moving to the cloud due to latency concerns or compliance regulations may find that AWS Local Zones, AWS Wavelength Zones, or AWS Outposts matches their requirements:

- **AWS Local Zones:** AWS infrastructure including compute, storage, and database services closer to customers in a single data center that can be linked to an existing VPC within an AWS region. Currently, EC2, VPC, EBS, Amazon FSx, Elastic Load Balancing, Amazon EMR, and RDS services can be deployed in a Local Zone, allowing local applications running in on-premises data centers to have high-speed connections into the AWS cloud.

- **AWS Wavelength Zones:** AWS compute and storage services infrastructure deployed into third-party telecommunication providers' data centers located at the edge of the 5G network (see Figure 13-11). Applications deployed in a Wavelength Zone data center can locally connect to application servers without leaving the Wavelength Zone. Use cases include gaming, live video streaming, and machine learning.

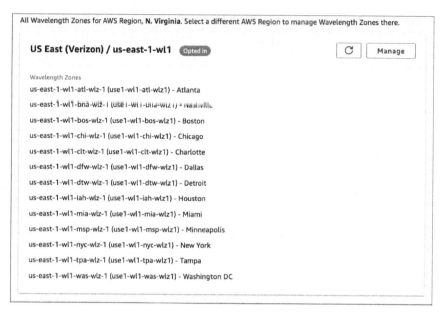

All Wavelength Zones for AWS Region, **N. Virginia.** Select a different AWS Region to manage Wavelength Zones there.

US East (Verizon) / us-east-1-wl1   Opted in   C   Manage

Wavelength Zones

us-east-1-wl1-atl-wlz-1 (use1-wl1-atl-wlz1) - Atlanta

us-east-1-wl1-bna-wlz-1 (use1-wl1-bna-wlz1) - Nashville

us-east-1-wl1-bos-wlz-1 (use1-wl1-bos-wlz1) - Boston

us-east-1-wl1-chi-wlz-1 (use1-wl1-chi-wlz1) - Chicago

us-east-1-wl1-clt-wlz-1 (use1-wl1-clt-wlz1) - Charlotte

us-east-1-wl1-dfw-wlz-1 (use1-wl1-dfw-wlz1) - Dallas

us-east-1-wl1-dtw-wlz-1 (use1-wl1-dtw-wlz1) - Detroit

us-east-1-wl1-iah-wlz-1 (use1-wl1-iah-wlz1) - Houston

us-east-1-wl1-mia-wlz-1 (use1-wl1-mia-wlz1) - Miami

us-east-1-wl1-msp-wlz-1 (use1-wl1-msp-wlz1) - Minneapolis

us-east-1-wl1-nyc-wlz-1 (use1-wl1-nyc-wlz1) - New York

us-east-1-wl1-tpa-wlz-1 (use1-wl1-tpa-wlz1) - Tampa

us-east-1-wl1-was-wlz-1 (use1-wl1-was-wlz1) - Washington DC

Figure 13-11   Wavelength Zones in US-East-1 (Northern Virginia)

- **AWS Outposts:** AWS Outposts allows companies to run AWS infrastructure services on premises or at co-locations. Available server form factors are 1U/2U Outpost servers on 42U Outpost racks (see Figure 13-12). A custom VPC can be extended to include an on-premises AWS Outposts location running AWS services locally. Customers can run workloads on Outpost racks or Outpost servers on premises and connect to any required cloud services hosted at AWS.

    - **AWS Outpost racks support the following AWS services locally:** Amazon Elastic Compute Cloud (EC2), Amazon Elastic Container Service (ECS), Amazon Elastic Kubernetes Service (EKS), Amazon Elastic Block Store (EBS), Amazon EBS Snapshots, Amazon Simple Storage Service (S3), Amazon Relational Database Service (RDS), Amazon Elasti-Cache, Amazon EMR, Application Load Balancer (ALB), CloudEndure, and VMware Cloud.

    - **AWS Outpost servers support the following AWS services locally:** Amazon EC2, Amazon ECS, AWS IoT Greengrass, or Amazon Sage-Maker Edge Manager.

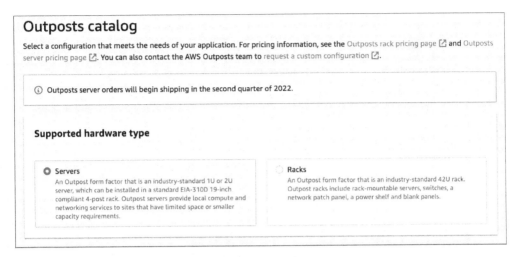

Figure 13-12   AWS Outposts Options

Matching Compute Utilization with Requirements

AWS has an ever-increasing expansion of compute services for a variety of customer workloads. EC2 instances power the many container offerings available from AWS (see Table 13-7), or you can choose to deploy bare-metal servers at AWS or on premises.

Table 13-7 Optimization of Compute Workloads

	EC2 Instance	Elastic Container Service	ECS Anywhere	Amazon EKS Anywhere	Amazon Elastic Kubernetes	AWS App Runner	Outposts
Pricing	On-demand, RI, Spot Instances, Savings Plans	On-demand, RI, spot instances, Savings Plans, Fargate Launch Type Model	$0.01025 per hour for each managed ECS Anywhere on-premises instance	No upfront commitments or fees to use Amazon EKS Anywhere	$0.10 per hour for each Amazon EKS cluster that you create	Compute and memory resources used by the app	Custom rack and server pricing
Placement	Per EC2 instance, Placement groups, Auto Scaling groups	Manual Task Scheduling, AWS Fargate, Auto Scaling groups	AWS Fargate with any VM VMware, Microsoft Hyper-V, or OpenStack	Run on existing on-premises hardware	EKS Cluster on EC2 instances, AWS Fargate	No infrastructure or container orchestration required	Secure, low latency, data residency
Location	AZs, Local Zones, AWS Outposts	AZs, Local Zones, AWS Outposts	AZs, Local Zones, AWS Outposts	AWS Outposts	AZs, Local Zones, AWS Outposts	AWS Cloud	On-premises, co-locations

Compute Scaling Strategies

Depending on the workload being deployed, both vertical or horizontal scaling and hibernation can also be an option (see Table 13-8):

- Every EC2 instance can be vertically scaled to a larger size EC2 instance, improving the available RAM, storage size and IOPS, and network speeds.

- Auto Scaling groups provide automatic scaling of EC2 instances and containers, minimizing costs while providing the desired performance.

- Spot instances can be set to hibernate when the EC2 service takes back a spot instance.

- Amazon Aurora Serverless deployments can scale up and down and also hibernate after a defined period of inactivity.

Table 13-8 Compute Scaling Strategies

	Vertical Scaling	Hibernation	Auto Scaling	EC2 Auto Scaling
EC2 Instances	Yes	No		
Containers	No	No		Yes
Spot Instances	No	Yes		Yes
Amazon Aurora Serverless v1/v2		Yes	Yes	Yes

NOTE Amazon EKS Anywhere allows customers to create and operate Kubernetes clusters on on-premises infrastructure using VMware vSphere.

NOTE Amazon Compute Optimizer will identify EC2 instance types, EBS volume configurations, and Amazon Lambda function memory sizes, using machine learning to analyze historical utilization metrics. AWS Compute Optimizer also integrates with AWS Organizations for recommendations within the organization.

Exam Preparation Tasks

As mentioned in the section "How to Use This Book" in the Introduction, you have a couple of choices for exam preparation: the exercises here, Chapter 16, "Final Preparation," compute resources at AWS, and the exam simulation questions in the Pearson Test Prep Software Online.

Review All Key Topics

Review the most important topics in the chapter, noted with the Key Topic icon in the margin of the page. Table 13-9 lists these key topics and the page number on which each is found.

Table 13-9   Chapter 13 Key Topics

Key Topic Element	Description	Page Number
Table 13-3	On-demand Limits Based on vCPUs	642
Figure 13-5	The Limits Calculator	643
Section	EC2 Reserved Instance Types	646
Table 13-4	Regional Versus Zonal Reserved Instance Reservations	647
Table 13-5	Reserved Pricing Choices with AWS	648
Section	Savings Plans	649
Section	Spot Instances	650
Section	Spot Fleet Optimization Strategies	653
Section	EC2 Pricing Cheat Sheet	655
Section	Compute Tools and Utilities	655

Define Key Terms

Define the following key terms from this chapter and check your answers in the glossary:

EC2, Reserved instance, zonal

Q&A

The answers to these questions appear in Appendix A. For more practice with exam format questions, use the Pearson Test Prep Software Online.

1. AWS defines the amount of CPU power assigned to each instance as a
_____.

2. A Dedicated Host is a physical server with _____ capacity dedicated to a single customer.

3. Dedicated hosts support per-socket, per-core, or _____ software licenses.

4. An EC2 instance that is turned on and assigned to your account is billed a _____ while it is powered on.

5. Reserved instance pricing and Savings Plan pricing provide _____ for the on-demand instances.

6. A scheduled RI reservation allows you to buy _____ for a daily, weekly, or monthly term.

7. A Reserved instance for a region is a _____ that can be used _____ in the region.

8. A zonal Reserved instance involves a discount for a specific _____ within an AWS region.

This chapter covers the following topics:

- Database Design Choices
- Database Data Transfer Costs
- Data Retention Policies

This chapter covers content that's important to the following exam domain and task statement:

Domain 4: Design Cost-Optimized Architectures

Task Statement 3: Design cost-optimized database solutions

CHAPTER 14

Designing Cost-Effective Database Solutions

Relational database choices provided by AWS include the Amazon Relational Database Service (RDS), which includes a database engine for deploying Oracle, MySQL, Microsoft SQL Server, PostgreSQL, MariaDB, and Amazon Aurora on EC2 instances. Each supported database engine has a predefined schema for the table of rows and columns and a key that uniquely identifies each row in the table. Each database is launched within a controlled VPC and typically hosted on private subnets. Storage is provided by Amazon Elastic Block Store (EBS) SSD volumes (gp2, io1, or io) with a defined amount of IOPS.

Amazon Web Services (AWS) offers a number of nonrelational databases that can be used to store and manage data. Some examples include Amazon DynamoDB, a fast and flexible NoSQL database service that can be used to store and retrieve any amount of data; Amazon DocumentDB, a fast, scalable, and fully managed document database service that is compatible with the MongoDB API—it allows you to store, retrieve, and manage document-oriented data; Amazon Neptune, a fully managed graph database service that makes it easy to build and run applications that work with highly connected data.

"Do I Know This Already?"

The "Do I Know This Already?" quiz allows you to assess whether you should read this entire chapter thoroughly or jump to the "Exam Preparation Tasks" section. If you are in doubt about your answers to these questions or your own assessment of your knowledge of the topics, read the entire chapter. Table 14-1 lists the major headings in this chapter and their corresponding "Do I Know This Already?" quiz questions. You can find the answers in Appendix A, "Answers to the 'Do I Know This Already?' Quizzes and Q&A Sections."

Table 14-1   "Do I Know This Already?" Section-to-Question Mapping

Foundation Topics Section	Questions
Database Design Choices	1, 2
Database Data Transfer Costs	3, 4
Data Retention Policies	5, 6

CAUTION   The goal of self-assessment is to gauge your mastery of the topics in this chapter. If you do not know the answer to a question or are only partially sure of the answer, you should mark that question as wrong for purposes of the self-assessment. Giving yourself credit for an answer you correctly guess skews your self-assessment results and might provide you with a false sense of security.

1. Which of the following is the most expensive SQL database deployment scenario?

   a. RDS Oracle

   b. Manual SQL deployment across multiple AZs

   c. RDS MySQL

   d. RDS PostgreSQL

2. What RDS database engine can be deployed as a multi-region global datastore?

   a. Microsoft SQL Server

   b. Oracle

   c. Amazon Aurora

   d. Amazon DynamoDB

3. A Multi-AZ custom-deployed Microsoft SQL database is charged for what type of data transfer cost?

   a. Snapshot backup

   b. Read replica queries within the AZ

   c. Updates to the primary database instance

   d. Database replication across AZs

4. What data transfer cost is always free?

    a. Communication within an availability zone

    b. Data transfer from the Internet to AWS

    c. Replication across AWS regions

    d. Replication within a region

5. RDS automatic snapshot retention policies can be set up for how many days?

    a. 7 days

    b. 14 days

    c. 21 days

    d. 35 days

6. Point-in-time recoveries can restore data to what degree of precision?

    a. To the second

    b. To the minute

    c. To the hour

    d. To the day

Foundation Topics

Database Design Choices

Production databases should be designed with a minimum of two database servers running in separate availability zones within the same AWS region.

However, when operating in the cloud, customers should always plan to deploy and maintain at least three separate copies of data. When using Amazon RDS as the database solution, at a minimum a primary database and a standby database are both kept up to date with synchronous replication. RDS disaster recovery is managed through scheduling automatic snapshots, and transaction logs are backed up every 5 minutes. Customers must make decisions about the desired resiliency, failover, and recovery of their database records and manage the overall costs of their database operations.

RDS Deployments

As mentioned, Amazon RDS deployments are SQL deployments that can be deployed in a single region or across multiple regions. The engine of RDS deployments, excluding Aurora Serverless, is defined by EC2 instances. DB instance classes supported by RDS include general-purpose and memory-optimized instances. Deployment options for RDS instances are on-demand instances with either Reserved Instance reservation or Savings Plan. Microsoft SQL licensing is bundled with the RDS database instance cost; customers that want to bring their own Microsoft SQL license to AWS must build a custom RDS SQL deployment. RDS Oracle deployments also have a BYOL option for On-demand DB instances. Table 14-2 compares the available RDS deployment options, Amazon Redshift, and Amazon ElastiCache deployment options including workload use cases, performance, backup options, and cost management.

Table 14-2 AWS Database Service Comparison

Database Engine	Amazon RDS	Amazon Aurora	Amazon Aurora Serverless 1	Amazon Aurora Serverless 2	Amazon Redshift	Amazon ElastiCache
Compute	EC2 instances	EC2 instances	Serverless	Serverless	Provisioned EC2-leader and compute nodes, Serverless	EC2 instances
Replication	Multi-AZ cluster deployment of one primary and two read replicas	Across three AZs	Across three AZs	Across three AZs	Single AZ deployment, cross-region sharing	Single AZ, multi-AZ cluster
Data type	SQL	PostgreSQL, MySQL	PostgreSQL, MySQL	PostgreSQL, MySQL	PostgreSQL	Redis, Memcached
Read replicas	5	Up to 15	Up to 15	Up to 15	—	—
Workload	Transactional (Simple)	Analytical (simple/parallel queries)	Infrequently used applications, Test DB deployments	Demanding business-critical applications	Online analytical processing (OLAP)	In-memory caching Redis: complex applications; Memcached: read replicas
Regional	Yes	Yes	Yes	Yes	Yes	Yes
Multi-region	No	Global Datastore, storage-based replication (< 1 second), secondary region	No	Global Datastore	No	Redis – Global Datastore
Performance	EC2 instance, EBS volume size	Five times of RDS, parallel query	Scaled transactions to match requirements	Scaled transactions to match requirements	Dense compute (DC) clusters, parallel processing	EC2 instance size, EBS volumes

Database Engine	Amazon RDS	Amazon Aurora	Amazon Aurora Serverless 1	Amazon Aurora Serverless 2	Amazon Redshift	Amazon ElastiCache
Auto Scaling Storage	Yes	In 10-GB chunks	In 10-GB chunks	In 10-GB chunks	Elastic resize, Redshift managed storage	No
Auto Scaling Compute	No. Manual compute sizing	Yes	Yes	Yes	Manual, automatic	No
Backup options	Snapshots, manual snapshots	Automatic, continuous, incremental, S3, point-in-time restore, manual snapshots, Backtrack	Automatic, continuous, incremental, S3, point-in-time restore, manual	Automatic, continuous, incremental, S3, point-in-time restore, manual	Automatic backup to S3 or another region	Redis—automatic backup
Cost management	On-demand, Reserved Instances, Savings Plans, data transfer costs	Provisioned on-demand, reserved instances, database storage and I/O charges, data transfer costs, globally replicated read-writes	Serverless Aurora Capacity Units (ACUs)	Serverless Aurora Capacity Units (ACUs)	On-demand, RA3 nodes with managed storage and automatic backup to S3, DC2 nodes with local storage (Best Price), Serverless (Base–Max), Data transfer costs	On-demand, reserved instances, data transfer costs

RDS Costs Cheat Sheet

For the AWS Certified Solutions Architect – Associate (SAA-C03) exam, you need to understand the following about RDS EC2 instance usage, EBS storage and IOPS, scheduled backups, and data transfer costs:

- PostgreSQL, MySQL, and MariaDB have similar costs for storage, provisioned IOPS, and data transfer costs.

- AWS RDS costs are specific to the AWS region of deployment.

- Oracle and Microsoft SQL Server deployments can be double the price due to licensing fees.

- Amazon Aurora can be deployed using provisioned EC2 instances or serverless compute.

- Amazon Aurora can be deployed as a multi-region Global Datastore.

- AWS RDS instance pricing includes vCPU, RAM, and network speeds per chosen RDS database instances.

- AWS RDS Reserved instances can save up to 60% in compute costs for 1 to 3 years.

- Auto-provisioning with a defined Amazon Aurora storage maximum is for unpredictable storage needs.

- AWS RDS snapshot backups are free and are performed every day.

- AWS RDS retention periods determine how many automatic backups are kept. The default is 7 days; the maximum is 35 days.

- AWS RDS Multi-AZ deployments create a standby database instance with a separate replicated database instance.

- On-demand RDS instances can be stopped for 7 days, during which time compute is not charged but EBS storage volumes are still charged.

- Data transfer costs are charged when data exits the source location and enters the target location, AZ-to-AZ, or Region-to-Region.

- The amount of retained backup storage can be lessened by reducing the backup retention period.

- Manual snapshots created by customers are never removed from storage.

NOTE CloudWatch metrics for RDS that can help monitor database instance costs include network usage, CPU utilization, and memory utilization.

RDS Database Design Solutions

Consider these design possibilities when choosing a managed database design solution:

- **Reserved instance pricing:** RDS deployments and provisioned versions of Amazon Aurora where customers choose the compute size can be powered by reserved instances to save money. On demand and spot instances should not be used for database instances that are always online; on-demand instances may be too expensive for 24/7 operation, and spot instances are not guaranteed to be always available.

- **RDS Cluster deployment:** Creates a DB cluster with a primary DB instance and two readable standby DB instances (see Figure 14-1). RDS DB instances are located in different AZs, providing high availability, data redundancy, and increased query capacity.

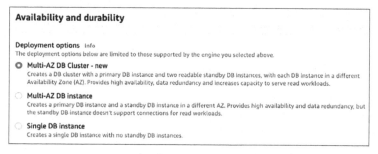

Figure 14-1   RDS Cluster Deployment Choices

- **RDS across multiple availability zones:** RDS high-availability and failover designs are especially effective for database deployments. In addition, durability can be provided by keeping primary and alternate database instances up to date with synchronous replication. When you deploy RDS solutions, AWS does not charge for replication between database instances located in different AZs (see Figure 14-2); when you deploy custom EC2 instances across multiple AZs with a custom database design, there will be data transfer charges for the replication between the primary and alternate database instances across separate AZs and regions.

- **RDS in a single availability zone:** A single AZ does not have any high-availability or failover options because the single database server is on a single subnet. High availability or failover might not be a concern due to prudent planning and backup procedures. Perhaps hourly snapshots and transaction logs are automatically created on a schedule and backed up into multiple S3 buckets hosted in different AWS regions. If your recovery time objective (RTO) allows you to be down for a longer period of time (for example, 6 hours), a single AZ deployment may be more economical than a multi-AZ design.

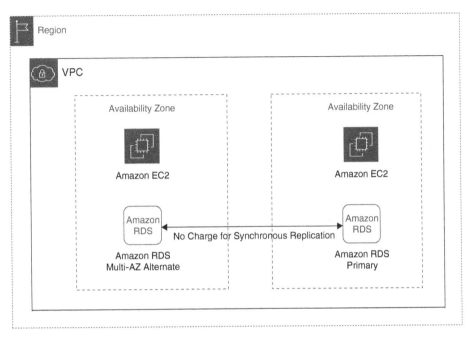

Figure 14-2 RDS Multi-AZ Deployment

- **Manual snapshots:** Snapshots can be created from RDS EBS volumes at any time. RDS deployments automate snapshots created based on a schedule; however, manual snapshots can also be created and stored in other AWS regions for safekeeping, allowing you to rebuild any EC2 instance (web, application, database, or software appliance).

- **Managing snapshots:** Without any long-term management, long-term storage of snapshots is expensive. The Amazon Data Lifecycle Manager allows you to create lifecycle policies to schedule the creation and deletion of EBS snapshots.

- **Read replicas:** A *read replica* is a copy of the primary database that is kept up to date with asynchronous (rather than synchronous) replication. Read replicas can be promoted to a standalone RDS instance as part of a manual disaster recovery solution if the primary RDS database fails (see Figure 14-3). MySQL, MariaDB, Oracle, and Microsoft SQL Server read replicas can be promoted and made writable, whereas a PostgreSQL read replica cannot be made writable. Read replicas provide the ability to scale read traffic horizontally and also provide additional durability for the database tier.

Figure 14-3 Promoting Read Replicas

- **Amazon Aurora Serverless:** Deploying Aurora Serverless allows you to pay for only the minimum capacity database resources (LCU and database storage) that you consume. You can choose either of two serverless versions:

    - Version 1 is for a single-region database deployment of a MySQL- or PostgreSQL-compatible engine. The term *capacity unit* refers to the amount of compute and memory resources assigned. Read or write capacity units (RCU/WCU) can be set from 1 capacity unit, which selects a minimum capacity of 2 GB of RAM, up to 256 capacity units, which selects 488 GB of RAM. Based on the minimum and maximum capacity unit settings, auto-scale compute capacity read/write rules are defined for the required CPU utilization, the number of connections, and required memory. When the workload for a serverless Amazon Aurora database drops below the maximum defined capacity unit threshold, Amazon Aurora automatically reduces the CPU and RAM resources made available for the database cluster.

    - Amazon Aurora version 2 can scale from hundreds to thousands of transactions completed in milliseconds both within and across AWS regions. In the background, the auto scaling service uses step scaling to ensure the proper sizing of database resources at any given time.

    - Serverless deployments of Amazon Aurora v2 can be paused after a defined period of activity (see Figure 14-4). There are no charges for an Amazon Aurora database instance when it is not running, potentially saving a high percentage of your database costs when compared to a provisioned deployment of Amazon Aurora.

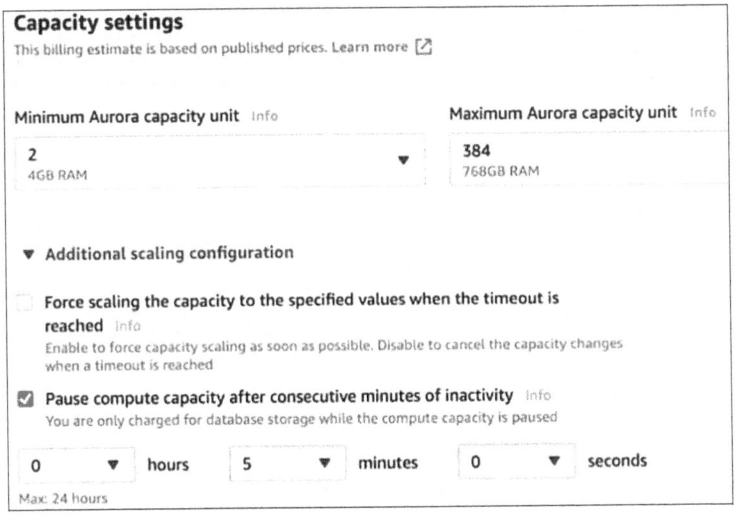

Figure 14-4 Pausing Amazon Aurora Deployments

NoSQL Deployments

NoSQL databases have several advantages when compared to SQL databases, including horizontal scaling to a cluster of servers, built-in high availability, and support for several flexible data structures:

- **Key-value stores:** Data is defined as a collection of *key-value* pairs with an attribute name and an associated value, for example, *<company name-location>*. Use cases include gaming applications and high-traffic applications.

The most popular NoSQL deployment at AWS is DynamoDB, which supports both document and key-value data structures for both regional and global deployments for IoT, mobile, web, and gaming workloads. The main features of DynamoDB are single-digit millisecond data access, serverless deployment with no servers to manage, auto-scaling to handle any spikes, and automatic data encryption by default. DynamoDB has two pricing models:

- **On-demand capacity:** Charges on a per request basis for reading and writing requests to the associated DynamoDB table.

- **Provisioned capacity:** Billing is charged hourly for utilized read and write capacity units and the maximum amount of resources required by each database table. Provisioned capacity should be selected when your workload's application traffic is consistent and the maximum workload for your application is known. Table 14-3 compares the available NoSQL deployment options, including workload use cases, performance, backup options, and managing costs.

- **Graph:** Graph data is composed of a set of nodes and a set of edges connecting the nodes. For example, *mammal*, the node and *shark*, the edge relationship would be defined as "is a type of fish." Use cases include fraud detection and recommendation engines. AWS service: Amazon Neptune.

- **Wide column:** Uses tables and rows and columns just like a relational database; however, the names and the format of each column can vary from row to row within the same table. Use cases include written optimization and fleet management. AWS Service: Amazon Keyspaces (for Apache Cassandra).

- **Document:** Data is stored in a document using a standard encoding such as JSON, XML, or YAML. Use cases include user profiles and content management. AWS services: DynamoDB, DocumentDB.

- **Times series:** Data is stored in time-ordered streams. Nodes contain individual data values; edges are the relationships between the data values. Use cases include social networking and recommendation engines. AWS service: Amazon Timestream.

- **Ledger:** Based on logs that record events that are related to specific data values. Ledger logs can be verified cryptographically, proving the authenticity and integrity of the data. Use cases for ledger databases include banking systems, supply chains, and blockchain. AWS service: Amazon Quantum Ledger Database (QLDB).

NoSQL Costs Cheat Sheet

For the AWS Certified Solutions Architect – Associate (SAA-C03) exam, you need to understand the following about determining database costs for NoSQL deployments:

- For managing consistent workload usage, choose provisioned mode DynamoDB tables with auto scaling enabled to handle expected changes in demand.

- An on-demand DynamoDB table costs more than provisioned tables.

- A DynamoDB table uses auto scaling to manage the read and write capacity units assigned to each table (see Figure 14-5). Each scaling policy defines what should be scaled—read or write capacity or both—and the maximum provisioned capacity unit settings for the DynamoDB table. The defined auto scaling policy also defines a target utilization; default utilization is set at 70% target utilization, and utilization values can be defined between 20% and 90% for both read and write capacity units.

Table 14-3 AWS NoSQL Database Service Comparisons

Database Engine	Amazon DynamoDB	Amazon S3	Amazon Keyspaces	Amazon DocumentDB	Amazon Neptune	Amazon TimeStream
Compute	Serverless	Serverless storage array	Serverless	EC2 Cluster	On-demand EC2, memory optimized	Serverless
Datatype	Transactional Key-Value/ Document store supports ACID transactions	Key-Value Hybrid backup, Database backup, Tape backup (Storage Gateway)	PostgreSQL	JSON	Apache TinkerPop; Gremlin; SPARQL— supports ACID transactions	Store and retrieve trillions of events in real time
Use case	Mobile applications	Object storage	Route optimization	Mongo compatible	Fraud detection	Analytics
Read replicas/ cache	ElastiCache, DynamoDB Accelerator (DAX)	—	—	Up to 15 read replicas	Up to 15 read replicas	—
Regional	Across three AZs	Across three AZs	Across three AZs	Yes	Across three AZs	Across three AZs
Multi-region	Yes	Yes	No	Global Clusters	No	No
Performance	Scale to 10 trillion requests per day over petabytes of storage	First-byte latency retrieval in ms	On-demand/ provisioned, AWS Keyspace tables scale to match application traffic	Manually scale memory/vCPU	Manually scale memory/vCPU	Data ingest and query auto-scale based on workload
Scaled storage	Yes	Yes	Provisioned capacity	Up to 64 TB	Up to 64 TB	Memory store (recent data) and read-optimized HDD (queries)

Key Topic

678   AWS Certified Solutions Architect – Associate (SAA-C03) Cert Guide

Database Engine	Amazon DynamoDB	Amazon S3	Amazon Keyspaces	Amazon DocumentDB	Amazon Neptune	Amazon TimeStream
Scaled compute	Provisioned throughput	Yes	Provisioned throughput	Automatic	Manual scaling	Automatic
Backups	On-demand backups, AWS Backup, point-in-time recovery—restore to any given second	AWS Backup	Point-in-time recovery—restore to any given second	Automatic/manual snapshots, point-in-time backup to S3	Manual snapshots, automatic, continuous, incremental, and point-in-time backup to S3	Data retention policies from memory to HDD storage
Pricing	Standard table, standard Infrequent access On-demand capacity (data read/writes charged) Provisioned capacity, data transfer costs	Storage classes, S3 Intelligent-tiering, S3 Glacier (instant, flexible), Deep archive, data transfer costs	Write requests units/read requests units, data transfer out costs	Four dimensions: on-demand instances, database I/O, database storage, backup storage, data transfer costs	EC2 instance, database I/O, backup, data transfer costs	Data writes, data stored, queries, data transfer costs

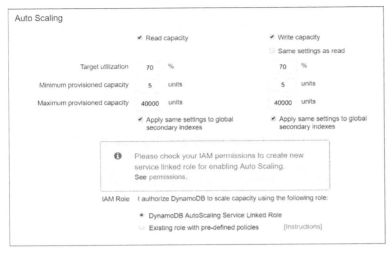

Figure 14-5   DynamoDB Scaling Policy

- Provisioned capacity deployments with a high amount of read and write capacity units should purchase reserved capacity for one or three years.

- Automatic DynamoDB backups use additional write capacity units, raising costs, but backups provide valuable high availability.

- One *read capacity unit (RCU)* performs one strongly consistent read request per second for items up to 4 KB in size, and two eventually consistent read requests. Transactional read requests require two RCUs.

- One *write capacity unit (WCU)* performs one standard rate request per second of items up to 1 KB in size. Transactional write requests require two WCUs.

- Replicated WCUs are used with global tables. Replicated write requests are automatically written to multiple AWS regions.

- To reduce workload costs, host DynamoDB deployments in AWS regions with the lowest operating cost if possible.

- Unnecessary data can be purged using the Time to Live (TTL) feature.

- Queries for data stored in DynamoDB use the primary or index key and only charge for RCUs for the items returned.

- Scans for data stored in a DynamoDB table are much more expensive as you are charged for all rows scanned regardless of how many items are returned.

- Store infrequently accessed data in standard infrequent access DynamoDB tables.

- Use DynamoDB metrics and CloudWatch to monitor usage and storage trends.

- Use the Trusted Advisor Amazon RDS Idle DB instances check to identify DB instances with no connection over the last seven days.

Migrating Databases

Database migration can be carried out using AWS Database Migration Service (DMS). DMS performs a live migration into AWS with little to no downtime. Databases to be migrated can be hosted on an EC2 or RDS instance or located on premises. The DMS server is an EC2 instance hosted in the AWS cloud running replication/migration software. Source and target connections inform DMS where to extract the source database from, and where to deploy the migrated database (see Table 14-4). Scheduled tasks run on the DMS server and replicate the database from the source to the destination server location. DMS can also create database tables and associated primary keys if these items don't exist on the target instance.

Table 14-4   Database Migration Service Source and Destination Migrations

DMS On Premises, EC2 Instances, Third-Party Cloud	DMS Target (On Premises/EC2 Database Instances)
Oracle Database 10.2 up to 11g and up to 12.2, 18c, and 19c Enterprise, Standard, Standard One, Standard Two editions	Oracle Database 10g, 11g, 12c, 18c, and 19c Enterprise, Standard, Standard One, Standard Two editions
Microsoft SQL Server 2005–2019 Enterprise, Standard, Workgroup, and Developer Editions	Microsoft SQL Server versions 2005, 2008, 2008R2, 2012, 2014, 2016, 2017, and 2019 Enterprise, Standard, Workgroup, and Developer editions (Web and Express editions not supported)
MySQL versions 5.5, 5.6, 5.7, and 8.0	MySQL versions 5.5, 5.6, 5.7, and 8.0
PostgreSQL version 9.4 and for versions 9.x, 10.x, 11.x, 12.x, 13.x and 14.0	PostgreSQL version 9.4 and later (for versions 9.x), 10.x, 11.x, 12.x, 13.x, and 14.0
MongoDB versions 3.x, 4.0, 4.2, and 4.4.	DynamoDB
SAP Adaptive Server Enterprise (ASE) versions 12.5, 15, 15.5, 15.7, 16, and later	SAP Adaptive Server Enterprise (ASE) versions 15, 15.5, 15.7, 16, and later
IBM Db2 z/OS for Linux, UNIX, and Windows	Aurora MySQL, Aurora PostgreSQL, MySQL, and PostgreSQL
Microsoft Azure SQL Database	Microsoft SQL Server versions 2005, 2008, 2008R2, 2012, 2014, 2016, 2017, and 2019 Enterprise, Standard, Workgroup, and Developer editions (Web and Express editions not supported)
Google Cloud for MySQL	MySQL versions 5.6, 5.7, and 8.0
RDS instance databases (Oracle, Microsoft SQL Server, MySQL, PostgreSQL, MariaDB), Amazon Aurora (PostgreSQL/MySQL)	Amazon RDS instance databases Amazon Redshift, Amazon DynamoDB, Amazon S3, Amazon OpenSearch Service, Amazon ElastiCache for Redis, Amazon Kinesis Data Streams, Amazon DocumentDB, Amazon Neptune, and Apache Kafka
Amazon DocumentDB	Amazon DocumentDB
Amazon Redis, Microsoft SQL, NoSQL	Amazon Redis

NOTE   AWS Database Migration Service charges for the compute resources used by the replication instance during the migration. Ingress data transfer into AWS is free of charge. Migrating from a supported target to Amazon Aurora, Amazon Redshift, Amazon DynamoDB, and Amazon DocumentDB is free for up to six months.

AWS Schema Conversion Tool

The AWS Schema Conversion Tool (AWS SCT) converts an existing database schema from one database engine to another (see Figure 14-6). The converted schema can be used with the following Relational Database Service engines: MySQL, MariaDB, Oracle, SQL Server, PostgreSQL DB, Amazon Aurora DB cluster, or Amazon Redshift cluster. The AWS SCT can convert tables, indexes, and application code to the target database engine. After a schema is converted, it is not immediately applied to the target database. Within the AWS SCT project, you can review and make changes to the converted schema before applying the converted schema to the target database.

Figure 14-6   AWS Schema Conversion Tool

Database Data Transfer Costs

Data transfer costs are calculated differently for the various managed database services that can be deployed at AWS. As a reminder, there is no charge for inbound data transfer for all services in all regions at AWS (see Figure 14-7). Transferring data from an Amazon resource across the Internet results in charges for each AWS service based on the region where the service is hosted. Outbound data transfer is currently charged at $0.09 per GB.

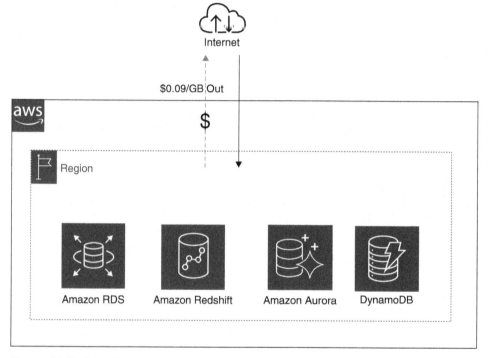

Figure 14-7   Data Transfer to the Internet

Data Transfer Costs and RDS

Workloads that use RDS deployments utilize EC2 instances and the EBS volumes. With multi-AZ deployment of primary and secondary database instances, read replicas will not have any charges for data transfer to and from any EC2 and RDS instances located in the same AWS region, availability zone, and virtual private cloud. Data charges apply as follows for data transfers (see Figure 14-8) between instances:

- EC2 and RDS instances that are located across AZs within the same VPC are charged $0.01 per GB ingress and egress.

- EC2 and RDS instances that are located across AZs and across different VPCs are charged $0.01 per GB ingress and egress.

- EC2 and RDS instances that are located across AWS regions are charged on both sides of the data transfer from the EC2 instance to the RDS instance and vice versa at $0.02 per GB ingress and egress.

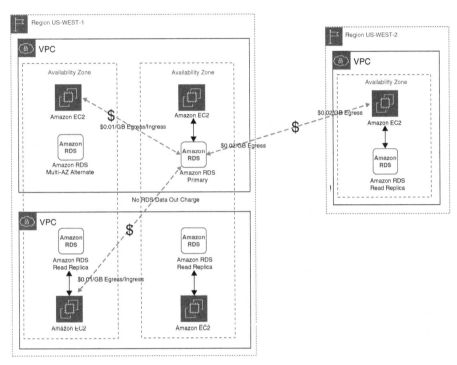

Figure 14-8   EC2 and RDS Data Transfer Across VPCs with Multiple AWS Regions

There are no data transfer charges for data replication in a multi-AZ deployment, or to any read replicas located within the same AWS region. There will also not be charges for the transfer of snapshots to the S3 bucket used for backup storage in the same AWS region. However, there will be data transfer charges for asynchronous data updates to read replicas that are located across different regions at $0.02 per GB egress. There will also be charges for any regional transfers for RDS snapshot copies or any automated cross-region backups at $0.02 per GB egress.

Data Transfer Costs with DynamoDB

Workloads that use DynamoDB and DynamoDB Accelerator (DAX) will not have data transfer charges for:

- Inbound data transfers to DynamoDB

■ Any data transfers between DynamoDB and EC2 instances located in the same region

■ Any data transfers between EC2 instances and DAX in the same AZ (see Figure 14-9)

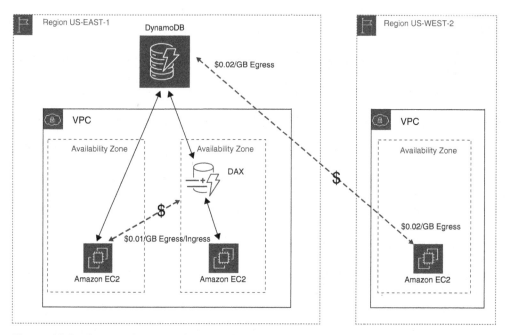

Figure 14-9   Amazon Aurora and Data Transfer Costs

For DynamoDB global table deployments, as shown in Figure 14-10, the following data transfer charges will apply:

■ Data transfer charges are charged between DynamoDB and a DAX deployment located in a different AZ.

■ Global tables for cross-region replication charged at the source region rate of $0.02 per GB egress.

■ Any data transfers between DynamoDB and EC2 instances located in different AWS regions are charged on both sides of the data transfer at $0.02 per GB egress.

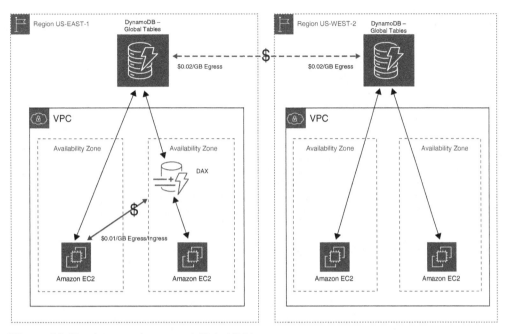

Figure 14-10 Amazon Aurora and Global Tables

Data Transfer Costs with Amazon Redshift

Workloads that use Amazon Redshift can analyze data stores using standard SQL queries and common business intelligence tools. For an ODBC application connecting to Redshift across multiple AWS regions, there are data transfer costs. For communication within the same availability zone and any data transfers to S3 storage in the same AWS region for backup and restore, there are no data charges. For deployments utilizing multiple AWS regions, as shown in Figure 14-11, the following data transfer charges will apply:

- EC2 and RDS instances that are located across AZs and across different VPCs are charged $0.01 per GB ingress and egress.

- EC2 and RDS instances that are located across AWS regions are charged on both sides of the data transfer from the EC2 instance to the RDS instance and vice versa at $0.02 per GB ingress and egress.

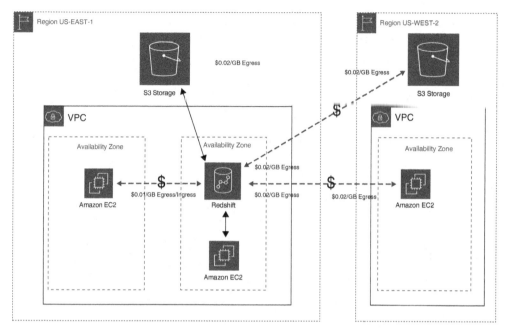

Figure 14-11   Amazon Redshift Data Transfer Costs

Data Transfer Costs with DocumentDB

Workloads that use DocumentDB are using a database service with MongoDB compatibility. An application using an EC2 instance using DocumentDB deployed as a global cluster as the data store across two AWS regions with cross-region replication will have data transfer charges (see Figure 14-12). However, read replicas in multiple AZs will have no data transfer charges for communication between any EC2 and DocumentDB instance located in the same AZ, or for data transferred between DocumentDB instances within the same AWS region. There will also be data transfer charges for:

- EC2 instance and DynamoDB communication across availability zones

- Cross-region replication between the DocumentDB primary and secondary instances

Data Transfer Costs Cheat Sheet

When designing database deployments, consider the following options:

- Calculate data transfer charges on both sides of the communication channel. "data transfer in" to a destination is also "data transfer out" from the source.

- Use regional read replicas and alternate replicas to reduce the amount of cross-availability zone or cross-region traffic.

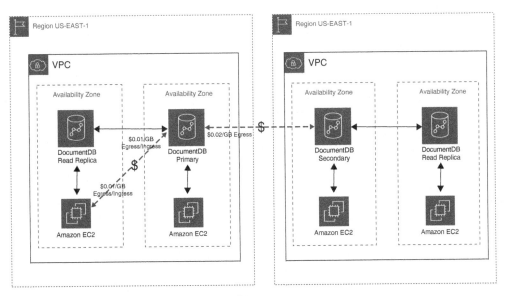

Figure 14-12   DocumentDB Data Transfer Charges

- Use data transfer tiered pricing when estimating workload pricing for data transferred out to the Internet across EC2 and RDS instances, Redshift, DynamoDB, and S3 buckets.

- Backup and snapshot requirements and how data transfer charges may apply.

- AWS offers various purpose-built, managed database offerings. Selecting the right database service for your workload can help optimize performance and cost.

- Review your application and how queries are designed, looking to reduce the amount of data transferred between your application and its data store.

Database Retention Policies

Database retention policies refer to the length of time that database backups are retained. During the defined backup window of each RDS deployment (see Figure 14-13), automatic backups of your DB instances are created and saved in controlled S3 storage. RDS creates a storage volume snapshot of the standby database; the automated backups of the RDS instance are saved according to the defined backup retention period currently specified. The automated backup contains a complete system backup, including a full database backup, transaction logs, and the DB instance properties. DynamoDB, Neptune, and DocumentDB also support continuous backup with point-in-time restoration.

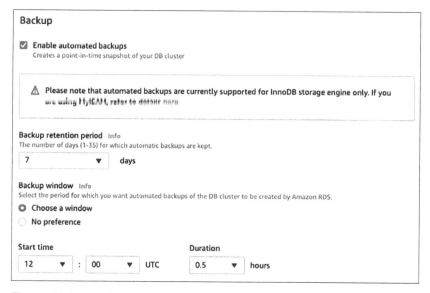

Figure 14-13   RDS Backup Windows

 Database Backup Policies Cheat Sheet

For the AWS Certified Solutions Architect – Associate (SAA-C03) exam, you need to understand the following about database backup policies:

- The first DB snapshot contains all the data for the complete DB instance.

- Subsequent snapshots of the same DB instance are incremental; only the data that has changed after the most recent snapshot will be saved.

- Databases can be recovered at any point in time during the backup retention period.

- RDS retains backup DB instances for a default retention period of 7 days.

- Retention periods can be set to up to 35 days.

- Point-in-time restores can specify any second during your retention period up to the latest restorable time.

- The preferred backup window is the period of time during which your DB instance is backed up.

- Amazon Aurora backs up your cluster volume automatically and retains the restored data for the length of the defined backup retention period.

- Amazon Document DB and Amazon Neptune back up your cluster volume continuously and retain the restored data for the length of the defined retention period.

- Amazon DynamoDB enables you to back up your table data continuously by using point-in-time recovery (PITR), backing up your table data automatically with per-second granularity allowing restores to any given second in the preceding 35 days.

- On-demand backups of DynamoDB can be performed using the DynamoDB service or AWS Backup.

- Amazon DocumentDB (with MongoDB compatibility) continuously backs up your data to S3 storage, allowing restoration to any point within the backup retention period of 1 to 35 days.

- Multi-AZ DB cluster deployments can be backed up with a Multi-AZ DB snapshot.

- RDS can replicate snapshots and transaction logs to another AWS region for Oracle version 12 and higher, PostgreSQL 9.6 and higher, and Microsoft SQL Server 2012 and higher.

- Manual snapshots can also be created at any time. Manual snapshots are not automatically deleted.

- Customers can have up to 100 manual snapshots per AWS region.

- Backups of RDS DB instances can be managed using AWS Backup. Resource tagging must be used to associate your DB instance with a backup plan.

- RDS snapshots can be exported to an S3 bucket from automated, manual, and AWS Backup snapshots.

- When a DB instance is deleted, a final DB snapshot can be created before deletion; the final DB snapshot can be used to restore the deleted DB instance later.

Exam Preparation Tasks

As mentioned in the section "How to Use This Book" in the Introduction, you have a couple of choices for exam preparation: the exercises here, Chapter 16, "Final Preparation," and the exam simulation questions in the Pearson Test Prep Software Online.

Review All Key Topics

Review the most important topics in the chapter, noted with the Key Topic icon in the margin of the page. Table 14-5 lists these key topics and the page number on which each is found.

Table 14-5   Chapter 14 Key Topics

Key Topic Element	Description	Page Number
Table 14-2	AWS Database Service Comparison	669
Section	RDS Costs Cheat Sheet	671
Section	NoSQL Costs Cheat Sheet	676
Table 14-3	AWS NoSQL Database Service Comparisons	677
Section	Migrating Databases	680
Section	AWS Schema Conversion Tool	681
Section	Data Transfer Costs and RDS	682
Section	Data Transfer Costs Cheat Sheet	686
Section	Database Backup Policies Cheat Sheet	688

Define Key Terms

Define the following key terms from this chapter and check your answers in the glossary:

key-value, read capacity unit (RCU), write capacity unit (WCU)

Q&A

The answers to these questions appear in Appendix A. For more practice with exam format questions, use the Pearson Test Prep Software Online.

1. On-demand capacity mode charges _____ for reading and writes requests.

2. Provisioned capacity mode charges _____ for read and write capacity units.

3. AWS SCT converts an existing _____ from one database engine to another.

4. Workloads that use Amazon Redshift can analyze data stores using _____.

5. Workloads that use DocumentDB are using a database service with _____.

6. Database retention policies refer to the _____ that database backups are retained.

7. Subsequent snapshots of the same DB instance are _____.

8. Backups of RDS DB instances can be managed using _____.

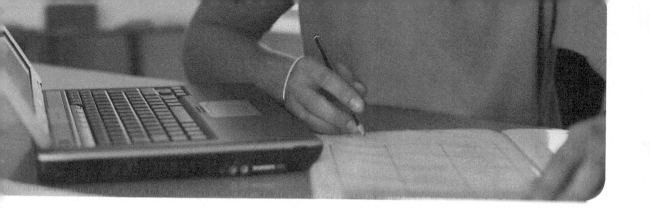

This chapter covers the following topics:

- Networking Services and Connectivity Costs
- Data Transfer Costs

This chapter covers content that's important to the following exam domain and task statement:

Domain 4: Design Cost-Optimized Architectures

Task Statement 4: Design cost-optimized network solutions

CHAPTER 15

Designing Cost-Effective Network Architectures

Network services and all types of communication at AWS use the AWS private network and Internet connections to transfer vast quantities of data inbound (ingress) and outbound (egress). Egress packet flow is charged a *data transfer cost*. Data transfer costs may be zero (free of charge), minimal, or sometimes very expensive. In preparing for the AWS Certified Solutions Architect – Associate (SAA-C03) exam, students require a good understanding of data transfer costs.

Recall Chapter 2, "The Well-Architected Framework," that one of the six pillars of the AWS Well-Architected Framework is Cost Optimization. As I mentioned in previous chapters, it's a really good idea to download the AWS document "Cost Optimization Pillar" (see https://docs.aws.amazon.com/wellarchitected/latest/cost-optimization-pillar/wellarchitected-cost-optimization-pillar.pdf) and read it thoroughly, which will help in understanding how to manage costs at AWS.

"Do I Know This Already?"

The "Do I Know This Already?" quiz allows you to assess whether you should read this entire chapter thoroughly or jump to the "Exam Preparation Tasks" section. If you are in doubt about your answers to these questions or your own assessment of your knowledge of the topics, read the entire chapter. Table 15-1 lists the major headings in this chapter and their corresponding "Do I Know This Already?" quiz questions. You can find the answers in Appendix A, "Answers to the 'Do I Know This Already?' Quizzes and Q&A Sections."

Table 15-1 "Do I Know This Already?" Section-to-Question Mapping

Foundation Topics Section	Questions
Networking Services and Connectivity Costs	1, 2
Data Transfer Costs	3, 4

CAUTION   The goal of self-assessment is to gauge your mastery of the topics in this chapter. If you do not know the answer to a question or are only partially sure of the answer, you should mark that question as wrong for purposes of the self-assessment. Giving yourself credit for an answer you correctly guess skews your self-assessment results and might provide you with a false sense of security.

1. Data transfer costs are charged based on what type of network traffic?

    a. Egress network data transfer

    b. Ingress network data transfer

    c. All inbound and outbound data flow

    d. None of these

2. What is the charge for incoming data traffic to AWS services?

    a. Incoming data is charged a tiered rate.

    b. Incoming data is free.

    c. Incoming data is charged a flat rate.

    d. Incoming data is charged at $0.01 per GiB.

3. How are Elastic Load Balancer (ELB) deployments charged?

    a. GIB of data and LCU

    b. By GIB of ingress data

    c. Service charge and LCU

    d. By GIB of egress data

4. How can NAT services be deployed as a highly available service?

    a. A NAT gateway service per availability zone.

    b. An EC2 instance NAT service per availability zone.

    c. NAT can't be deployed as a HA service.

    d. A NAT gateway service per AWS region.

Foundation Topics

Networking Services and Connectivity Costs

The typical network services used by workloads hosted at AWS include an Internet Gateway, a Virtual Private Gateway, Elastic Load Balancers (Application, Network, and Gateway), Amazon CloudFront, NAT services, and VPC networks and endpoint connections. Each service has a variety of operating costs, including an hourly charge for each service, and data transfer charges for data sent outbound.

Elastic Load Balancing Deployments

ELB charges are for each hour or partial hour that an ELB load balancer (NLB, ALB, or GWLB) is running, including the number of Load Balancer Capacity Units (LCUs) used per hour by each deployed load balancer. Each LCU offers

- 25 new connections per second
- 3,000 active connections per minute
- 1 GiB of processed bytes per second
- 1,000 rules evaluated per second

A Gateway Load Balancer allows organizations to centrally manage a target group of third-party load balancers distributing all incoming traffic to the virtual appliances (see Figure 15-1). Gateway Load Balancers use a virtual private cloud (VPC) endpoint called a Gateway Load Balancer endpoint (GWLB endpoint) powered by AWS PrivateLink, allowing traffic across the GWLB endpoint. Each GWLB endpoint is priced per VPC attachment and per GiB of data processed through the endpoint. The supported protocol is GENEVE and the port is 6061.

NOTE A *Load Balancer Capacity Unit (LCU)* measures the hourly characteristics and the capacity of network traffic processed by each deployed load balancer. You are charged based on the dimension with the highest hourly usage. The four dimensions are as follows:

- **New connections:** The number of newly established connections per second
- **Active connections:** The number of active connections per minute
- **Processed bytes:** The number of bytes processed by the load balancer in GiBps
- **Rule evaluations:** The number of listener rules processed by the load balancer

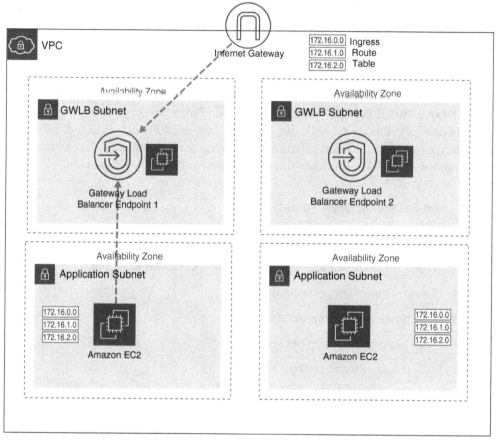

Figure 15-1 Gateway Load Balancer Deployment

NAT Devices

NAT devices relay packets between EC2 instances hosted on private subnets and Internet locations, returning responses back to the EC2 instance that sent the original request. There are hourly charges for each NAT gateway deployed and data processing charges for the GiBs of data transferred.

There are several use cases to consider when deploying NAT services at AWS:

- **NAT gateway instance use case:** An EC2 instance that has deployed a NAT AMI. Customers that choose this option must also manage updates and scale each NAT instance when more performance is required. The performance of the NAT instance will be determined by the EC2 instance type chosen. Network performance can be increased by choosing a different EC2 instance.

Many EC2 instances have up to 5 GiBps bandwidth; for example, an m5n.xl instance has 50 GiBps of network bandwidth.

■ **NAT gateway instance high availability:** For high-availability deployments, multiple NAT gateway instances can be deployed per availability zone (see Figure 15-2), but costs will be higher. The NAT gateway service can scale throughput up to 50 GiBps. Multiple NAT gateway service deployments per AZ provide high availability.

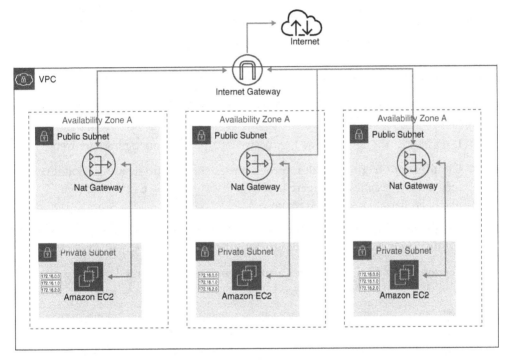

Figure 15-2 NAT Gateway Service HA Deployment

Costs can be reduced for NAT services by doing the following:

■ Enable NAT gateway instances during defined maintenance windows for required updates.

■ Create NAT gateways in the same AZ as the instances requiring Internet access to reduce cross-AZ data transfer charges.

■ If most traffic through the NAT service is to AWS services that support VPC interface endpoints, create an Interface endpoint for each service.

■ If the majority of NAT service charges are to Amazon S3 or Amazon DynamoDB, set up gateway VPC endpoints. There are no charges for using a gateway VPC endpoint.

AWS CloudFront

Amazon CloudFront delivers web and media content stored in S3 buckets to clients worldwide using one of the hundreds of edge locations. If the requested content is already cached at the edge location, it is delivered to the viewer (end user) quickly. Delivery costs are billed per GiB transferred from an edge location server to the viewer; customers are charged per 10,000 HTTP requests. The billing rate for serving data ranges from $0.085 per GiB to $0.170 per GiB and is determined by where the viewer request originates from. Any data transferred out to an edge location from an EC2 instance, S3 bucket, or an Elastic Load Balancer has no additional data transfer charges from each AWS service, just CloudFront charges (see Figure 15-3). Customers can save up to 30% in delivery costs and 10% off AWS WAF service charges by subscribing to a CloudFront Security Savings Bundle. Amazon CloudFront costs increase (see Table 15-2) as additional features are enabled:

- **Encryption:** Although there is a charge for encryption, less data will be sent; therefore, data transfer costs will be reduced.

- **Logging:** Enabling real-time logs costs $0.01 per million log lines written.

- **CloudFront Origin Shield:** Improves the cache hit ratio by using CloudFront regional edge caches, which are hosted across three AZs. Enabling Origin Shield is charged per 10,000 requests.

- **CloudFront functions and Lambda@Edge functions:** Charged per request and duration.

- **Custom SSL/TLS certificates and domain names:** Charged monthly.

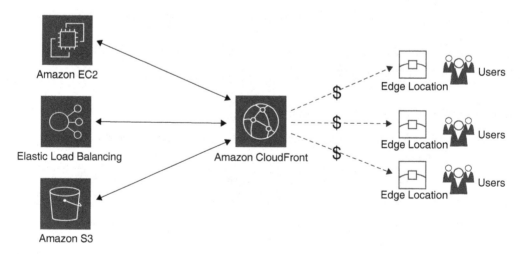

Figure 15-3 Data Transfer Charges Minimized

Table 15-2 Cost Comparison for CloudFront Costs

Data Type	Pricing	Details
CloudFront to the Internet/viewer	$0.085–$0.120 per GiB (first 10 TB)	Data transferred from edge location to viewer location
CloudFront to data or server origin	$0.020–$0.160 per GiB	Data requests to origin (**POST** and **PUT**)
HTTP/HTTPS requests	$0.0075–$0.0120 per 10,000 requests	Charges for HTTP and HTTPS requests
Origin shield requests	$0.0075–$0.0090 per 10,000 requests	Requests to origin shield cache layer
File invalidation requests	$0–$0.005 per path requested	Remove files from edge location before TTL expires
Lambda Functions requests	$0.60 per million requests/$0.00005001 per GiBps execution time	Charged per request and execution time
Field-Level Encryption requests	$0.02 per 10,000 requests	Encrypt specific fields in HTTP form
Real-time log requests	$0.01–$0.01 for every 1 million log lines written	Log requests to distribution
Custom SSL Certificate	$600 per month per certificate	Used when content is delivered to browsers that don't support Server Name Indication (SNI)

CloudFront Pricing Cheat Sheet

For the AWS Certified Solutions Architect – Associate (SAA-C03) exam, you need to understand the following important cost considerations before deploying CloudFront:

- S3 transfers under 1 GiB are free per month; however, Amazon CloudFront delivery could be faster depending on the location of the end user.

- Transfers of data over 50 GiB per month from Amazon S3 or EC2 instances will be cheaper using an Amazon CloudFront distribution.

- If applications exclusively serve **GET** requests, direct requests to the S3 bucket are cheaper.

- Applications using both **GET** and **POST** requests will be cheaper to access using an Amazon CloudFront distribution.

- HTTP requests for data are cheaper than HTTPS requests.

- By default, all files cached at an Amazon CloudFront edge location expire after 24 hours.

■ Change the minimum, maximum, and default *time to live (TTL)* values on all cached objects in the distribution to extend the cache storage time. Each object in the CloudFront cache is identified by a unique cache key. When a viewer requests an object that is stored in the edge location cache, this is defined as a cache "hit," which reduces the load on the origin server and reduces the latency of the object delivery to the viewer. To improve the cache hit ratio, include only the minimum values in the cache key (see Figure 15-4) for each object. The default cache key includes the domain name of the Cloud-Front distribution and the URL path of the requested object. Other cache values, HTTP headers, and cookies can be defined with a cache policy.

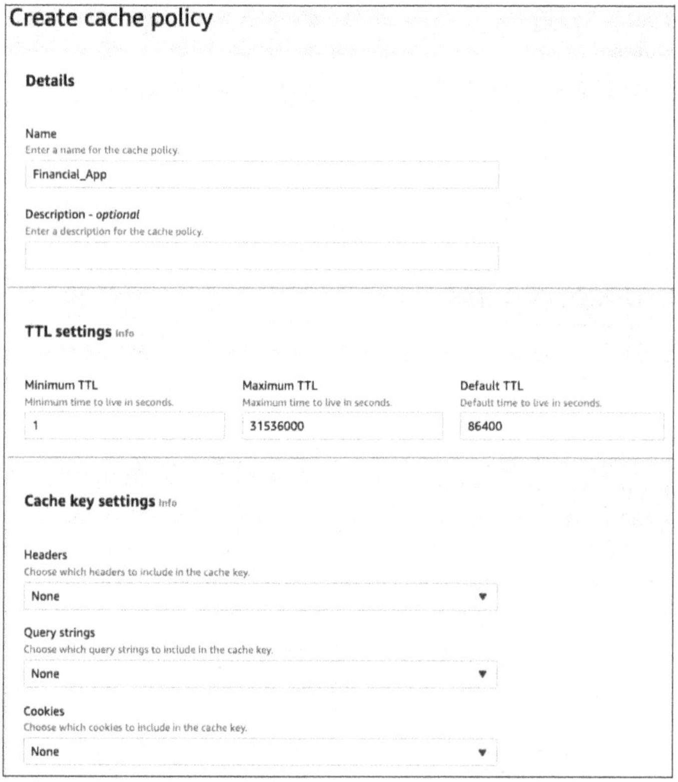

Create cache policy

Details

Name
Enter a name for the cache policy.

Financial_App

Description - *optional*
Enter a description for the cache policy.

TTL settings Info

Minimum TTL	Maximum TTL	Default TTL
Minimum time to live in seconds.	Maximum time to live in seconds.	Default time to live in seconds.
1	31536000	86400

Cache key settings Info

Headers
Choose which headers to include in the cache key.

None ▼

Query strings
Choose which query strings to include in the cache key.

None ▼

Cookies
Choose which cookies to include in the cache key.

None ▼

Figure 15-4 Cache Key Settings

■ For cache content that will rarely or never change, setting the Cache-Control HTTP headers on the origin server will set the cache rate at the client's browser and at the edge location.

■ Enabling compression will reduce data transfer costs.

■ Reserve capacity a year in advance.

■ Opt out of more expensive regions/edge locations to reduce data transfer costs.

VPC Endpoints

Endpoint services allow access to most AWS services across the private AWS network, providing security and speed:

■ **AWS PrivateLink:** AWS PrivateLink provides private connectivity between VPCs and on-premises locations to third-party services hosted at AWS. PrivateLink endpoints can also be accessed over VPC peering, VPN, and AWS Direct Connect connections.

■ **VPC endpoints:** VPC interface endpoints use elastic network interfaces (ENIs) provisioned from the selected subnet in your VPC to a supported AWS service such as Amazon Elastic Container Registry (ECR) (see Figure 15-5). Communicating from a VPC directly to an AWS service across the AWS private network does not require an Internet gateway, NAT gateway services, or AWS VPN connections, thereby saving costs. VPC gateway endpoints route traffic to Amazon DynamoDB and Amazon S3 buckets. There are no processing charges when using a VPC gateway endpoint.

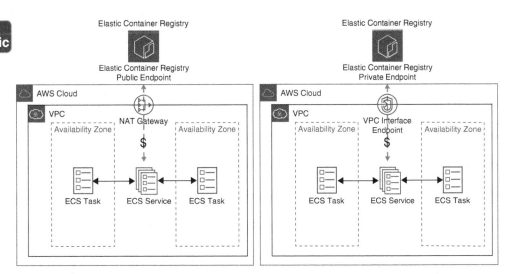

Figure 15-5   Accessing Elastic Container Registry Using an Interface Endpoint

For example, using the NAT Gateway Service to pull down images from the Amazon Elastic Container Registry is five times more expensive than using a VPC interface endpoint. VPC interface endpoints are used by AWS resources within the VPC and from on-premises locations using an AWS Direct Connect or VPN connection. VPC interface endpoint pricing is $0.01 per connection hour and $0.01 per GiB processed. Table 15-3 compares the data transfer costs for the NAT gateway and VPC endpoints processing 100 TB of data in a 500-hour timeframe.

Table 15-3 NAT Gateway and VPC Endpoint Charges Comparison (100 TB/500 Hours)

Processing Costs by AWS Service	NAT Gateway Service	VPC Interface Endpoint	VPC Gateway Endpoint
NAT gateway charge ($0.045) per hour	$45.00	$45.00	$45.00
NAT gateway processing ($0.045) GiB	$4,626.00	—	—
Gateway endpoint charge ($0.00) per hour	—	—	$0.00
Gateway endpoint processing ($0.045) GiB	—	—	$0.00
Interface endpoint charge ($0.00) per hour	—	$10.00	—
Interface endpoint processing ($0.045) GiB	—	$1,028.00	—
	$4,671.00	$1,083.00	$45.00

- **VPC peering:** Point-to-point connectivity provides full bidirectional direct connectivity between two VPCs. VPC peering costs are charged only when network traffic crosses the peering connection. Best practice is to peer fewer than ten VPCs together. VPC peering has the lowest cost when compared to an AWS Transit Gateway deployment and peering has no hourly infrastructure cost. VPC peering costs are discussed in the next section, "Data Transfer Costs."

- **AWS Transit Gateway:** Hub and spoke designs can connect thousands of VPCs within the same AWS region and on-premises networks. Both VPN and AWS Direct Connect and Direct Connect gateways can be attached to a single

AWS Transit Gateway deployment. AWS Transit Gateway peering allows peering Transit AWS Transit Gateway deployments within or across multiple AWS regions.

NOTE Use VPC peering and/or AWS Transit Gateway for Layer 3 IP connectivity between VPCs.

■ **VPC sharing:** The owner of a VPC can share a subnet and the resource hosted on the subnet to be shared, such as a database, with other participant AWS accounts. VPC sharing does not require VPC peering. There are no data transfer charges when sharing subnet resources between AWS accounts within the same availability zone. VPC sharing is enabled using AWS Resource Access Manager.

Network Services from On-Premises Locations

Workloads hosted at AWS requiring access to on-premises data centers will incur data transfer charges when connecting using an AWS Site-to-Site VPN connection or an AWS Direct Connect connection:

■ **Data transferred using an AWS Site-to-Site VPN connection:** Each AWS Site-to-Site VPN deployed will include an hourly charge for each connection and charges for data transferred from AWS across the connection (see Figure 15-6).

■ **Data transferred using an AWS Direct Connect connection:** Direct Connect provides a high-speed single-mode fiber connection for connecting on-premises networks to AWS. Direct Connect connections are charged a fee for each hour the connection port is utilized and a data transfer charge for data flowing out of AWS (see Figure 15-7). All data flowing into AWS is free ($0.00). Data transfer charges will depend on the source AWS region and the third-party AWS Direct Connect provider location. AWS Direct Connect can also connect to an AWS Transit Gateway instance using an AWS Direct Connect gateway (see Figure 15-8), allowing multiple VPCs to be connected together.

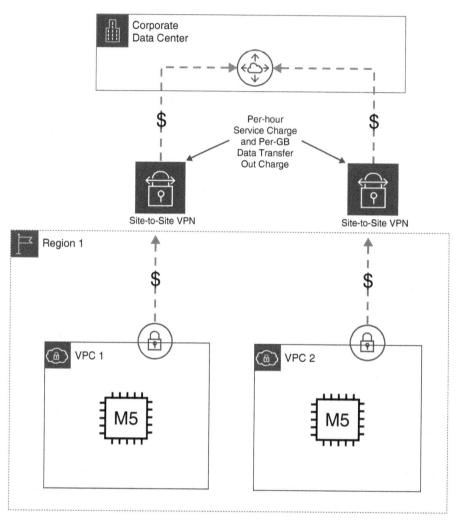

Figure 15-6   Traffic Charges for AWS Site-to-Site VPN Connections

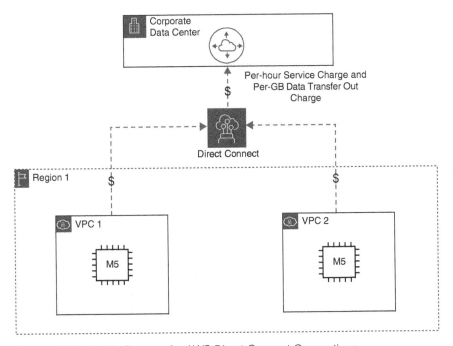

Figure 15-7   Traffic Charges for AWS Direct Connect Connections

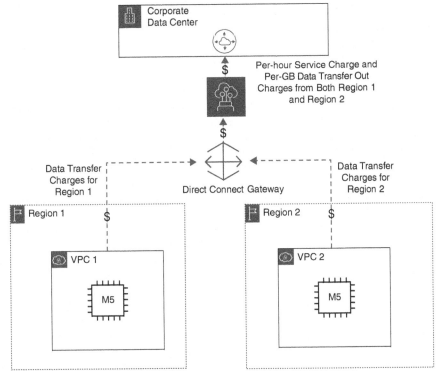

Figure 15-8   Traffic Charges for AWS Direct Connect Gateway Connections

Data Transfer Costs

To reduce networking costs, you need to look at network traffic flows—both egress and ingress. Data transfer costs are charges for egress (outgoing) network traffic across the AWS cloud, and when exiting the AWS cloud. AWS charges you for outbound network traffic to the Internet, across availability zones or regions, or across a peered network connection. Regional data transfer costs that include networking are NAT gateway services, VPN connections, and ELB deployments. There are no data transfer costs within a single AZ. There are data transfer costs when a workload spans multiple AZs.

Your first monthly AWS bill will contain a few data transfer charge surprises. Data transfer costs are generally higher for data transfer between AWS regions than for intra-region data transfer between AZs within the same region.

> **NOTE** It's a good idea to subscribe to the Amazon pricing notification service to receive alerts when prices for AWS services change (which happens all the time). See https://docs.aws.amazon.com/awsaccountbilling/latest/aboutv2/price-notification. html.

Sometimes, a link to a cost calculator is present when you order AWS services, but data transfer costs will need to be calculated. Data transfer costs can be expanded into the following breakdowns:

- Data transfer costs across AZs within a region. There are no data transfer costs for data transfer within a single AZ

- Data transfer costs between AWS regions

- Data transfer costs by service for egress data sent outbound

When you transfer data into an AWS region from any service from any other AWS region, it's free. As a rule, incoming data transfers are free for all public cloud providers. Regional data transfer costs are charged based on data transfer within a region (intra-region) or data transfer across regions (inter-region). Within each region, charges depend on whether you are communicating within an AZ or across AZs, as shown in Figure 15-9.

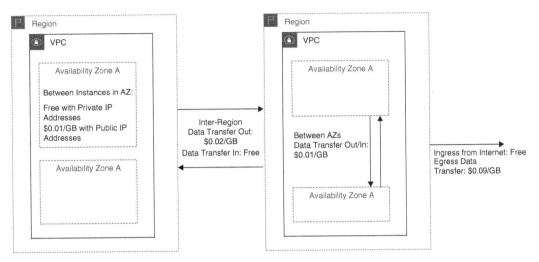

Figure 15-9 AWS Data Transfer Costs Comparison

Accessing AWS Services in the Same Region

Data transfer into any AWS region from the Internet is free of charge. Data transfer out to the Internet from an AWS region is billed at a region-specific tiered data transfer rate. Current EC2 on-demand pricing rates can be found at https://aws. amazon.com/ec2/pricing/on-demand/#Data_Transfer. Data transfer from a source AWS region to another AWS region is charged at a source region–specific data transfer rate. Monthly AWS bills refer to these costs as inter-region inbound and inter-region outbound costs. If the Internet gateway is used to access the public endpoint of the AWS service in this same region, there are no data transfer charges (see Figure 15-10).

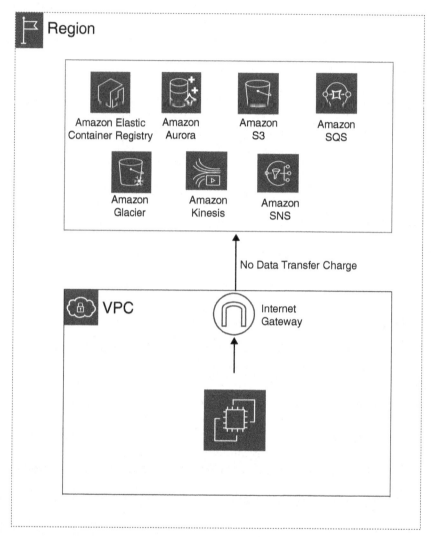

Figure 15-10 Accessing Services Using an Internet Gateway

If a NAT gateway is used to access the same AWS services from a private subnet, there will be a data processing charge per GiB for any data that passes through the NAT gateway (see Figure 15-11).

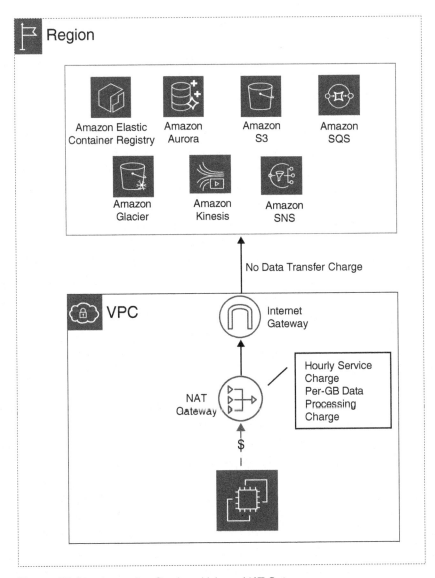

Figure 15-11 Accessing Services Using a NAT Gateway

Workload Components in the Same Region

Data transfer between EC2 instances or containers or with ENIs in the same AZ and VPC using private IPv4 or IPv6 addresses is free. Data transfer between EC2 instances or containers and Amazon S3 storage in the same AZ from the same VPC is also free. For a custom workload design that uses multiple AZs, there will be service-specific pricing for data transfers for cross-AZ communication between the EC2 instances; however, for Amazon RDS designs deployed across multiple AZs and Amazon Aurora, replication of data records across multiple AZs is free. Data transfer charges will be charged for all ingress traffic on both sides of a peering connection that crosses AZs (see Figure 15-12).

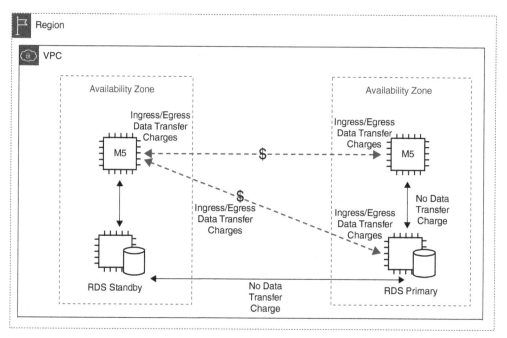

Figure 15-12   Workload Communications Across Availability Zones

A common workload design pattern is to utilize multiple VPCs in the same AWS region. Two methods of VPC-to-VPC communication are VPC peering connections or AWS Transit Gateway. Any data transfer over a VPC peering connection that stays within an AZ is free (see Figure 15-13). An AWS Transit Gateway can interconnect thousands of VPCs together. Transit Gateway costs include an hourly charge for each attached VPC, AWS Direct Connect connection VPN connection, and data processing charges for each GiB of data to the Transit Gateway (see Figure 15-14).

Accessing AWS Services in Different Regions

Workloads that use services in different AWS regions will be charged data transfer fees. Charges will depend on the source and destination regions. For communication across multiple AWS regions using VPC peering connections or Transit Gateway connections, additional data transfer charges will apply. Inter-region data transfer charges will also apply for VPCs peered across regions (see Figure 15-15).

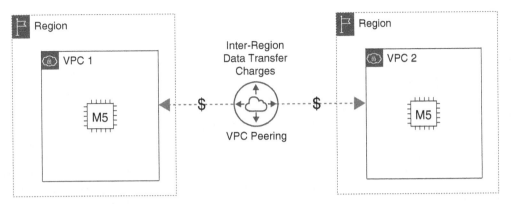

Figure 15-13 VPC Peering Connections and Charges

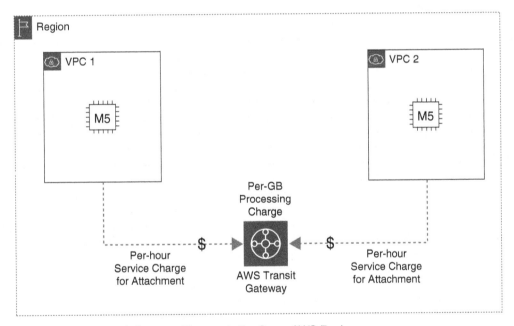

Figure 15-14 Transit Gateway Charges in the Same AWS Region

For Transit Gateway deployments that are peered together (see Figure 15-16), data transfer charges will be charged on one side of the peered connection; for example, data transfer charges do not apply for data sent from the EC2 instance to the Transit Gateway.

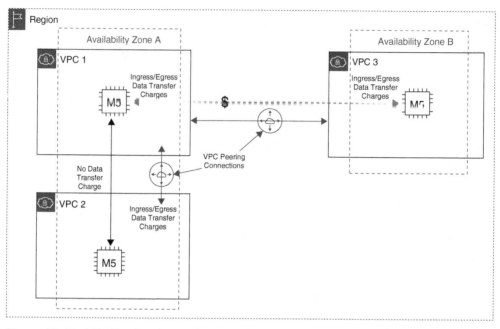

Figure 15-15   VPC Peering Charges Across AWS Regions

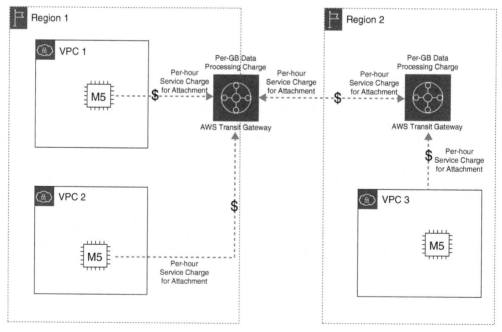

Figure 15-16   Transit Gateway Peering Charges Across AWS Regions

Data Transfer at Edge Locations

Viewer requests into an edge location from the Internet is free of charge. Cached data that is transferred outbound from AWS edge locations to the Internet is billed at region-specific tiered data transfer rates.

There are three services that can be deployed (at additional cost) to improve the speed of data transfer between AWS edge locations and end users:

- **Amazon S3 Transfer Acceleration:** Optimizes transfer of files over long distances between a client location and a single S3 bucket, taking advantage of edge locations; ingress data is routed into an edge location and across Amazon's private network. Upload speeds comparing S3 direct upload speeds to S3 Transfer Acceleration speeds can be found here: http://s3-accelerate-speedtest.s3-accelerate.amazonaws.com/en/accelerate-speed-comparsion.html.

- **AWS Global Accelerator:** Route users' requests across the AWS private network to the AWS application using the closest edge location. AWS Global Accelerator charges a fixed hourly fee and data transfer fees. Additional charges are for each accelerator provisioned and the amount of traffic that flows through the accelerator. There is also an EC2 data transfer out fee charged for application endpoints per hosted region.

- **AWS Site-to-Site VPN:** An AWS Site-to-Site VPN connects to a VPC or AWS Transit Gateway using IPsec tunnels. Charges are for the Site-to-Site VPN connection per hour and data transfer out charges. AWS Global Accelerator can be used with the Accelerated Site-to-site VPN option routing incoming VPN traffic from the on-premises network to the AWS edge location that is closest to your customer gateway.

Consider the following example: There is a Site-to-Site VPN connection to your Amazon VPC in us-east-2 (Ohio) from your on-premises location. The connection is active for 30 days, 24 hours a day. 2,000 GiB is transferred into the VPC; 800 GiB is transferred out through the site-to-site VPN connection.

- **AWS Site-to-Site VPN connection fee:** While connections are active, there is an hourly fee of $0.05 per hour; $36.00 per month in connection fees.

- **Data transfer out fee:** The first 100 GiB transferred out is free; you pay for 700 GiB at $0.09 per GiB, paying $63.00 per month in data transfer out fees.

- **Total charges:** $99.00 per month for the active AWS Site-to-Site VPN connection.

Network Data Transfer

The design of your workload and its use of AWS network services will greatly determine your data transfer costs. Network data transfer costs to understand are as follows:

- AWS services that are hosted in the same region but that are in separate AZs are charged for outgoing data transfer at $0.01 per GiB.

- When data is transferred between AWS services hosted in different AWS regions, the data transfer charge is $0.02 per GiB.

- Data is transferred within the same AWS region and staying within the same AZ is free of charge when using private IP addresses.

- If you are using an AWS-assigned public IP address or an assigned elastic IP public address, there are charges for data transfer out from the EC2 instance. These charges are per GiB transfer, and the minimum charge is $0.01 per GiB.

- Data transfers between EC2 instances, AWS services, or containers using elastic network interfaces in the same availability zone and same VPC using private IPv4 or IPv6 addresses are free of charge. A common example is RDS synchronous database replication from the primary database node to the standby database node. Across AZs, there are data transfer charges for RDS synchronous replication.

NOTE   Always use private IP addresses rather than public IP addresses, sending data with public IP addresses is charged.

- Different AWS regions have different egress data transfer costs. If possible, architect your applications and systems for minimal data transfer across AWS regions or AZs.

NOTE   The AWS pricelist API enables you to query AWS for the current prices of AWS products and services using either JSON or HTML. For example, https://pricing.us-east-1.amazonaws.com/offers/v1.0/aws/AmazonS3/current/us-east-1/index.csv.

Public Versus Private Traffic Charges

Public traffic sent to a public IP address traveling across the Internet will incur a much higher data transfer charge than private IP address traffic. Private traffic traveling within AWS is always cheaper than traffic on a public subnet. Wherever possible, AWS uses the private network for communication.

Private traffic that stays within a single subnet incurs no additional charges, whereas private traffic that travels across multiple private subnets that are hosted by different AZs incurs an egress charge of $0.01 per GiB. One of the tasks to carry out for each hosted application is to create a detailed costing of its design, including charges for the replication of the databases across AZs, the monthly charge, and the traffic flow charges (see Figure 15-17).

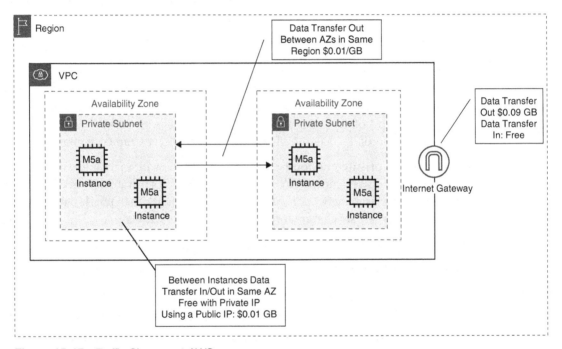

Figure 15-17   Traffic Charges at AWS

Network traffic charges are calculated based on the location of your data records, the location of end users, and the size and volume of all data transfers.

- **Data transfer modeling:** It is important to understand the locations where data transfer occurs during the operation of a workload, as well as the cost of the data transfer. For example, you might have a custom database solution that replicates across multiple AZs within a single region. It would be more cost-effective to deploy a database using Amazon RDS if the database engine you are currently using is supported. One of the advantages of deploying an Amazon RDS database is that there are no additional charges for synchronous replication between the primary and standby database instances. Use AWS Cost Explorer or the AWS Cost and Usage Report to review the details of data transfer costs. (Details on AWS cost and budgeting tools are provided in Chapter 10, "Determining High-Performing Database Solutions.")

- **Use a dedicated network connection:** Perhaps it would be most efficient to establish a dedicated network connection to AWS using an AWS Direct Connect connection. AWS Direct Connect can be ordered in increments from 512 Mbps up to 100 GBps. Advantages include increased security due to the fiber connection being a private connection and faster network performance. Direct Connect involves two charges: port hours used and data transfer. AWS Direct Connect charges are for the bandwidth utilized and the number of connected hours used per month. A 1-GBps connection rate would be $0.30 per hour, whereas a 10-GiBps connection would be slightly over $2.00 per hour. Perhaps the cost of deploying a faster connection is cheaper overall as more data could be processed across a high-speed AWS Direct Connect connection.

- **Changing to private endpoints:** VPC endpoints allow interface and gateway connectivity between most AWS services over Amazon's private network. Data transfer over private network connections is always faster than public data transfer. There are no charges for VPC gateway connections.

 Data Transfer Costs Cheat Sheet

For the AWS Certified Solutions Architect – Associate (SAA-C03) exam, you need to understand the following aspects of improving data transfer costs:

- Operate within the same AWS region. If possible, operate within the AWS region that has the lowest data transfer rates.

- Operate within a single AZ. Operating within the same AZ and the same VPC using private IP addresses incurs no data transfer costs.

- If the users of your application are spread out across a large geographic area and access application data across the Internet, consider using AWS CloudFront. Data transferred out using AWS CloudFront will be less expensive and much faster than public data transfers across the Internet.

- Capture information about IP traffic within a VPC by enabling VPC flow logs.

- Use AWS CloudFront for caching content and reducing the load on the origin servers and data location.

- Avoid using public IPv4 addresses or EIP addresses as costs are higher than private IPv4 addresses.

- RDS Multi-AZ deployments include the data transfer costs for replication between primary and alternate database servers.

- Amazon EFS deployments have both single-AZ or Multi-AZ deployment options. A single-AZ deployment can save up to 40% in storage costs.

- VPC gateway endpoints have no data transfer charges when communicating with Amazon S3 and Amazon DynamoDB within the same region.

- VPC interface endpoints are charged hourly service and data transfer charges.

- Amazon EFS and Amazon RDS deployments have free cross-AZ data transfers.

- Amazon CloudFront has free data transfers for **GET** requests.

- AWS Simple Monthly Calculator allows you to review pricing and data transfer costs for most AWS services.

- AWS Pricing Calculator helps estimate the total price for your workload deployment at AWS.

Exam Preparation Tasks

As mentioned in the section "How to Use This Book" in the Introduction, you have a couple of choices for exam preparation: the exercises here, Chapter 16, "Final Preparation," and the exam simulation questions in the Pearson Test Prep Software Online.

Review All Key Topics

Review the most important topics in the chapter, noted with the Key Topic icon in the margin of the page. Table 15-4 lists these key topics and the page number on which each is found.

Table 15-4   Chapter 15 Key Topics

Key Topic Element	Description	Page Number
Note	An LCU measures the hourly characteristics of network traffic processed by each deployed load balancer.	695
Table 15-2	Cost Comparison for CloudFront Costs	699
Section	CloudFront Pricing Cheat Sheet	699
Figure 15-5	Accessing Elastic Container Registry Using an Interface Endpoint	701
Section	Network Services from On-Premises Locations	703
Section	Accessing AWS Services in the Same Region	707
Section	Accessing AWS Services in Different Regions	710
Section	Data Transfer at Edge Locations	713
Section	Data Transfer Costs Cheat Sheet	716

Define Key Terms

Define the following key terms from this chapter and check your answers in the glossary:

Load Balancer Capacity Unit (LCU), time to live (TTL)

Q&A

The answers to these questions appear in Appendix A. For more practice with exam format questions, use the Pearson Test Prep Software Online.

1. What are the two main components of calculating management service costs at AWS that are applied to every service?

2. What is the key driver behind data transfer costs?

3. What is the term for calculating costs depending on the usage of a service or resource?

4. What are the four dimensions of a Load Balancer Capacity Unit (LCU)?

Final Preparation

Has reading this book made feel prepared and ready to take the AWS Certified Solutions Architect – Associate (SAA-C03) exam? I sure hope so. This chapter gives you specific details on certification prep, including the certification exam itself.

This chapter shares some great ideas on ensuring that you ace your upcoming exam. If you have read this book with the primary goal of mastering the AWS cloud without really considering certification, maybe this chapter will convince you to give the exam a try.

The first 15 chapters of this book covered the technologies, protocols, design concepts, and technical details required to be prepared to pass the AWS Certified Solutions Architect – Associate (SAA-C03) exam. This chapter provides a set of tools and a study plan to help you complete your preparation for the exam to supplement everything you have learned up to this point in the book.

This short chapter has four main sections. The first section provides information on the AWS Certified Solutions Architect – Associate (SAA-C03) exam. The second section shares some important tips to keep in mind to ensure that you are ready for the exam. The third section discusses exam preparation tools that may be useful at this point in the study process. The final section provides a suggested study plan you can implement now that you have completed all the earlier chapters in this book.

Exam Information

Here are details you should be aware of regarding the AWS Certified Solutions Architect – Associate (SAA-C03) exam:

Question types: Multiple-choice and multiple-response

Number of questions: 65

Time limit: 130 minutes

Available languages (at a testing center): English, French, German, Italian, Portuguese, Spanish, Japanese, Simplified Chinese, and Korean

Available languages used by proctors of online exam: English (Pearson VUE/PSI) and Japanese (VUE)

Online exam appointments: 24 hours a day, 7 days a week

Test providers: Pearson VUE or PSI

Exam fee: $150

Exam ID code: SAA-C03

Delivery method: Testing center or online proctored exam from your home or office location

This exam seeks to ensure that a candidate attaining the AWS Certified Solutions Architect – Associate certification has the following required knowledge:

- Knowledge and skills in the following AWS services: compute, networking, storage, and database and deployment and management services

- Knowledge and skills in deploying, managing, and operating AWS workloads and implementing security controls and compliance requirements

- The ability to identify which AWS service meets technical requirements

- The ability to define technical requirements for AWS-based applications

- The ability to identify which AWS services meet a given technical requirement

The exam is broken up into four different domains. Here are those domains and the percentage of the exam for each of the domains:

- **Design Secure Architectures:** 30%

- **Design Resilient Architectures:** 26%

- **Design High-Performing Architectures:** 24%

- **Design Cost-Optimized Architectures:** 20%

Here is the breakdown of the task statements for the domains:

- **Domain 1: Design Secure Architectures**

    - Task Statement 1: Design secure access to AWS resources

    - Task Statement 2: Design secure workloads and applications

    - Task Statement 3: Determine appropriate data security controls

- **Domain 2: Design Resilient Architectures**

  - Task Statement 1: Design scalable and loosely coupled architectures

  - Task Statement 2: Design highly available and/or fault-tolerant architectures

- **Domain 3: Design High-Performing Architectures**

  - Task Statement 1: Design high-performing and/or scalable storage solutions

  - Task Statement 2: Design high-performing and elastic compute solutions

  - Task Statement 3: Determine high-performing database solutions

  - Task Statement 4: Determine high-performing and/or scalable network architectures

  - Task Statement 5: Determine high-performing data ingestion and transformation solutions

- **Domain 4: Design Cost-Optimized Architectures**

  - Task Statement 1: Design cost-optimized storage solutions

  - Task Statement 2: Design cost-optimized compute solutions

  - Task Statement 3: Design cost-optimized database solutions

  - Task Statement 4: Design cost-optimized network solutions

Note the following important information about the AWS Certified Solutions Architect – Associate (SAA-C03) exam:

- You can decide which exam format to take: You can either go to a testing center or take a proctored exam from a personal location like your office or home.

- After you have scheduled your exam, you will receive a confirmation email from the test provider that provides details related to your exam appointment.

- If you are taking the test in person at a testing center, remember to bring two forms of ID on the day of the test. At least one must be a signed ID with a photo, such as a driver's license, passport, or health card. The second ID can be a credit card.

- If you are taking an online proctored exam, make sure to run the system test provided by the selected exam provider to ensure that your computer is acceptable for the exam. Both VUE and PSI have system tests.

- If you are taking an online proctored exam, your exam can be started up to 30 minutes before the scheduled exam time, but if you are more than 15 minutes late for your appointment, you won't be able to start your exam.

- Breaks are allowed when you're taking a test at a testing center, but they are not allowed during an online proctored exam. With an online proctored exam, you are not allowed to move out of the view of your webcam during your appointment.

- Make sure that your exam space at home or at your office remains private. If somebody comes into your office or private space during the exam, you will not be allowed to continue the exam.

Tips for Getting Ready for the Exam

Here are some important tips to keep in mind to ensure that you are ready for the AWS Certified Solutions Architect – Associate exam, some of which apply only to taking the exam at a testing center and others that apply in all cases:

- **Build and use a study tracker:** Consider using the task statements shown in this chapter to build a study tracker for yourself. Such a tracker can help ensure that you have not missed anything and that you are confident for your exam. As a matter of fact, this book offers a sample study planner as a website supplement.

- **Log in to the AWS management portal and write down a quick one-sentence or point-form description of each AWS service:** Writing down this information will put it into long-term memory and will be very helpful when you're trying to decipher test questions.

- **Think about your time budget for questions on the exam:** When you do the math, you will see that, on average, you have 2 minutes per question. Although this does not sound like a lot of time, keep in mind that many of the questions will be very straightforward, and you will take 15 to 30 seconds on those. This leaves you extra time for other questions on the exam.

- **Watch the clock:** Check in on the time remaining periodically as you are taking the exam. You might even find that you can slow down pretty dramatically if you have built up a nice block of extra time.

- **Get some earplugs:** The testing center might provide earplugs, but get some just in case and bring them along. There might be other test takers in the center with you, and you do not want to be distracted by their moans and groans. I personally have no issue blocking out the sounds around me, so I never worry about this, but I know it is an issue for some.

- **Plan your travel time:** Give yourself extra time to find the test center and get checked in. Be sure to arrive early. As you test more frequently at a particular center, you can certainly start cutting it closer time-wise.

- **Get rest:** Most students report that getting plenty of rest the night before the exam boosts their success. All-night cram sessions are not typically successful.

- **Bring in valuables but get ready to lock them up:** The testing center will take your phone, your smartwatch, your wallet, and other such items and will provide a secure place for them.

- **Take notes:** You will be given note-taking implements and should not be afraid to use them. I always jot down any questions I struggle with on the exam. I then memorize them at the end of the test by reading my notes over and over again. I always make sure I have a pen and paper in the car, and I write down the issues in the parking lot just after the exam. When I get home—with a pass or fail—I research those items!

- **Use the FAQs in your study:** The Amazon test authors have told me they love to pull questions from the FAQs they publish at the AWS site. These are a really valuable read anyway, so go through them for the various services that are key for this exam.

- **Brush up with practice exam questions:** This book provides many practice exam questions. Be sure to go through them thoroughly. Don't just blindly memorize answers; use the questions to see where you are weak in your knowledge and then study up on those areas.

Scheduling Your Exam

You can schedule your AWS Certified Solutions Architect – Associate (SAA-C03) exam through the web portal https://www.aws.training/certification; see Figure 16-1. If you haven't yet created an AWS Training and Certification account, you need to create one now, and then you can schedule your exam.

Figure 16-1   Schedule Your AWS Exam

After you've taken your exam, you can return to this portal to download your AWS digital badge, schedule another test, or set up sharing of your transcript to your current or future employer, as shown in Figure 16-2.

Figure 16-2   Viewing Your AWS Training Profile

Tools for Final Preparation

This section provides some information about the available tools and how to access them.

Pearson Test Prep Practice Test Software and Questions on the Website

Register this book to get access to the Pearson Test Prep practice test software, which displays and grades a set of exam-realistic multiple-choice questions. Using Pearson Test Prep practice test software, you can either study by going through the questions in Study mode or take a simulated (timed) AWS Certified Solutions Architect – Associate (SAA-C03) exam.

The Pearson Test Prep practice test software comes with two full practice exams. These practice exams are available to you either online or as an offline Windows application. To access the practice exams that were developed with this book, please see the instructions below.

Accessing the Pearson Test Prep Software Online

The online version of this software can be used on any device with a browser and connectivity to the Internet, including desktop machines, tablets, and smartphones. To start using your practice exams online, simply follow these steps:

Step 1.   Go to www.PearsonTestPrep.com.

Step 2.   Select Pearson IT Certification as your product group.

Step 3.   Enter your email/password for your account. Use the same credentials you used to access this companion website.

Step 4.   In the My Products tab, click the Activate New Product button.

Step 5.   Enter the unique access code found under the product listing in your account page under the Registered Products tab, and click the Activate button to activate your product.

Step 6.   The product will now be listed in your My Products page. Click the Exams button to launch the exam settings screen and start your exam.

Accessing the Pearson Test Prep Software Offline

If you wish to study offline, you can download and install the Windows version of the Pearson Test Prep software. You can find a download link for this software on the book's companion website, or you can just enter this link in your browser for a direct download:

https://www.pearsonitcertification.com/content/downloads/pcpt/engine.zip

To access the book's companion website and the software, simply follow these steps:

Step 1.   Click the Install Windows Version link under the Practice Exams section of the page to download the software.

Step 2.   Once the software finishes downloading, unzip all the files on your computer.

Step 3.   Double click the application file to start the installation, and follow the on-screen instructions to complete the registration.

Step 4.   Once the installation is complete, launch the application and select the Activate Exam button on the My Products tab.

Step 5.   Click the Activate a Product button in the Activate Product Wizard.

Step 6.   Enter the unique access code found under the product listing in your account page under the Registered Products tab, and click the Activate button to activate your product.

Step 7.   Click Next and then the Finish button to download the exam data to your application.

Step 8.   You can now start using the practice exams by selecting the product and clicking the Open Exam button to open the exam settings screen.

The offline and online versions will sync together, so saved exams and grade results recorded in one version will also be available to you on the other.

Customizing Your Exams

When you are in the exam settings screen of Pearson Test Prep, you can choose to take exams in one of three modes:

- Study mode
- Practice Exam mode
- Flash Card mode

Study mode enables you to fully customize an exam and review answers as you are taking the exam. This is typically the mode you use first to assess your knowledge and identify information gaps. Practice Exam mode locks certain customization options in order to present a realistic exam experience. Use this mode when you are preparing to test your exam readiness. Flash Card mode strips out the answers and presents you with only the question stem. This mode is great for late-stage preparation, when you really want to challenge yourself to provide answers without the benefit of seeing multiple-choice options. This mode does not provide the detailed score reports that the other two modes provide, so it is not the best mode for helping you identify knowledge gaps.

In addition to these three modes, you will be able to select the source of your questions. You can choose to take exams that cover all of the chapters, or you can narrow your selection to just a single chapter or the chapters that make up specific parts in the book. All chapters are selected by default. If you want to narrow your focus to individual chapters, simply deselect all the chapters and then select only those on which you wish to focus in the Objectives area.

You can also select the exam banks on which to focus. Each exam bank comes complete with a full exam of questions that cover topics in every chapter. You can have the test engine serve up exams from all four banks or just from one individual bank by selecting the desired banks in the exam bank area.

There are several other customizations you can make to your exam from the exam settings screen, such as the time allowed for taking the exam, the number of questions served up, whether to randomize questions and answers, whether to show the number of correct answers for multiple-answer questions, and whether to serve up only specific types of questions. You can also create custom test banks by selecting only questions that you have marked or questions on which you have added notes.

NOTE The first time you run some test questions, you might find that you do badly. Don't worry about it. Your brain may simply be resisting taking a multiple-choice exam! Run the test engine again, and your brain will eventually give in and start focusing on the questions. Also, remember that as good as Pearson Test Prep and the practice exam questions are, they are not the real exam. That's okay, because what you're actually learning by answering the sample test questions is how to answer multiple-choice questions similar to the questions on the real exam.

Updating Your Exams

If you are using the online version of the Pearson Test Prep software, you should always have access to the latest version of the software as well as the exam data. If you are using the Windows desktop version, every time you launch the software, it will check to see if there are any updates to your exam data and automatically download any changes made since the last time you used the software. This requires that you be connected to the Internet at the time you launch the software.

Sometimes, due to a number of factors, the exam data might not fully download when you activate your exam. If you find that figures or exhibits are missing, you might need to manually update your exams.

To update a particular exam you have already activated and downloaded, simply select the Tools tab and click the Update Products button. Again, this is only an issue with the desktop Windows application.

If you wish to check for updates to the Windows desktop version of the Pearson Test Prep exam engine software, simply select the Tools tab and click the Update Application button. Doing so allows you to ensure that you are running the latest version of the software engine.

Premium Edition

In addition to the free practice exam provided on the website, you can purchase additional exams with expanded functionality directly from Pearson IT Certification. The Premium Edition of this title contains an additional two full practice exams and an eBook (in both PDF and ePub formats). In addition, the Premium Edition includes remediation information for each question and links to the specific part of the eBook that relates to that question.

To view the Premium Edition product page, go to https://www.informit.com/title/9780137941568.

Chapter-Ending Review Tools

Chapters 2 through 15 include several features in the "Exam Preparation Tasks" and "Q&A" sections at the end of the chapter. You might have already worked through these in each chapter. Using these tools again can also be useful as you make your final preparations for the exam.

Suggested Plan for Final Review/Study

This section provides a suggested study plan from the point at which you finish reading through Chapter 15 until you take the AWS Certified Solutions Architect –

– Associate (SAA-C03) exam. You can ignore this plan, use it as is, or take suggestions from it.

The plan involves three steps:

Step 1.   **Review key topics and "Do I Know This Already?" (DIKTA?) questions:** You can use the table that lists the key topics in each chapter or just flip the pages looking for key topics. Also, reviewing the DIKTA? questions from the beginning of the chapter can be helpful for review.

Step 2.   **Review "Q&A" sections:** Go through the Q&A questions at the end of each chapter to identify areas where you need more study.

Step 3.   **Use the Pearson Test Prep to practice:** You can use the Pearson Test Prep practice test engine to study, using a bank of unique exam-realistic questions available only with this book.

Summary

The tools and suggestions provided are meant to help you develop the skills required to pass the AWS Certified Solutions Architect – Associate (SAA-C03) exam. This book has been developed from the beginning to not only tell you the facts but also to help you learn how to apply the facts. No matter what your experience level leading up to taking the exam, I hope that the broad range of preparation tools and the structure of this book help you pass the exam.

Answers to the "Do I Know This Already?" Quizzes and Q&A Sections

Chapter 2

"Do I Know This Already?"

1. b
2. d
3. b
4. a
5. d
6. d

Q&A

1. administrative controls
2. downtime
3. monitoring
4. reliability
5. cost
6. amount, useable
7. horizontally, dynamic
8. template file

Chapter 3

"Do I Know This Already?"

1. b
2. d
3. b

4. b

5. b

6. b

7. b

8. b

9. b

10. b

11. b

12. b

13. c

14. c

Q&A

1. If you're using the root account, you will be able to change your AWS account settings from the management console. You will also be using an email address and password to log into AWS.

2. The best method to provide applications secure access to AWS services is to create an IAM role and assign it to the application by adding the role to the EC2 server where the application is hosted.

3. The advantage of using a resource-based policy is that all of the entities that need access to the resource must be named in the policy. In comparison with an identity-based policy, the IAM user is not named in the policy directly, as the policy is directly attached to the IAM user, thereby allowing a level of access. This could be great; but consider the situation where an IAM policy is mistakenly added to an IAM user and providing access. This situation could not occur with a resource policy, as each entity that requires access must be named within the policy itself.

4. The best method for controlling access to AWS resources is through the use of IAM roles. First, IAM roles provide temporary access to a resource; secondly, the role's access keys are controlled by the secure token service (AWS STS); and finally, using IAM roles means you don't have to create as many IAM users.

5. Although inline policies may serve a need, such as specifying that just a specific IAM user will have access, the issue is documentation; that is, remembering what you may have done. Administrators must carefully document inline policies.

6. The Policy Simulator can be used to check your IAM policies if they are not working properly.

7. AWS Organizations helps you manage multiple AWS accounts in a treelike structure, allowing you to take advantage of consolidated billing, centralized security settings using service control policies, and sharing AWS resources.

8. To run a script at the command-line interface, you must first install the AWS CLI appropriate to your operating system (Linux, Windows, or macOS). Next, you must have the access key and secret access keys of the IAM user that you will be using to execute commands from the command line interface. The final step is that you must execute AWS Configure and enter the AWS region you will be running the script in, and add your access key and secret access key.

Chapter 4

"Do I Know This Already?"

1. c
2. b
3. b
4. c
5. c
6. b
7. a
8. c
9. c
10. a
11. b
12. c

Q&A

1. All networking services provided by AWS are software services. For example, routers and load balancers and all network services are software appliances.

2. A network ACL has the ability to block a specific IP address, whereas a security group does not have that ability.

3. Because CloudTrail provides API authentication and monitoring for all AWS regions where your AWS account is operational, you can track activity in AWS regions in which you do not want to be operating.

4. AWS Secrets Manager allows you to store third-party secrets securely.

5. GuardDuty uses machine learning.

6. A Direct Connect gateway can allow you to connect to multiple VPCs in different AWS regions to provide high-speed connectivity.

7. Network assessment checks do not require the Inspector agent to be installed

8. Purchasing Business support for your AWS account enables all checks for Trusted Advisor.

Chapter 5

"Do I Know This Already?"

1. a
2. b
3. a
4. a
5. c
6. c
7. c
8. c
9. c
10. c

Q&A

1. There is no single-tenant data store service available with AWS. All data stores at AWS are multi-tenant by design. Protection of data records is carried out by enabling encryption.

2. All public access for a newly created S3 bucket is blocked until each organization makes a decision to make the S3 bucket public.

3. SSE-C encryption uses an organization-provided encryption key for both encryption and decryption. The provided key is discarded after use and must be resupplied by the organization each time. Therefore, there is no potential security risk with stored encryption keys at AWS.

4. Envelope encryption involves a hierarchy of security when working with AWS KMS. AWS KMS creates data keys for encryption and decryption that are associated with a specific CMK. The keys cannot work with any other CMK and are controlled by AWS KMS.

5. Amazon S3 Glacier objects are automatically encrypted when stored in vaults.

6. AWS CloudHSM is a hardware storage module that is maintained by AWS. AWS backs up the contents of AWS CloudHSM, but the only person who can access the contents is the assigned organization.

7. AWS KMS does not support the rotation of private keys that were imported.

8. A private CA can be used to create a private CA that can renew and deploy certificates for private-facing resources such as a network load balancer deployed on private subnets.

Chapter 6

"Do I Know This Already?"

1. a

2. b

3. b

4. b

5. b

6. b

7. b

8. c

9. b

10. a

Q&A

1. A sticky session has the advantage of ensuring that the end user who establishes a session with an application server can continue to communicate with that application server for the life of the session. However, the disadvantage is that if the application server fails, the user is sent to another application server, which will know nothing about the previous session. This might not be a huge issue if the user is merely reading reports, as the user could simply start again. However, a user in the midst of purchasing a product would have to start over.

2. One advantage of using a central location to store user state information is that the storage location is redundant, and it operates in memory and therefore is fast. However, the main advantage of using a centralized storage location is that the user state information is stored in an independent location and not at the user location or at the server location, which provides a higher level of redundancy and availability.

3. Because every AWS service allows you to link issues with the associated service directly with SNS, you have the ability to respond to issues at any time, either with manual steps or through automated solution steps.

4. SQS can be a client of SNS notifications. SNS can send messages to specific queues, which have, in turn, application servers as clients. Therefore, an upload of the file to an S3 bucket could prompt a notification, which could be passed on to a queue, which could be processed by the associated application servers automatically.

5. Step Functions allows you to craft workflows using SQS and SNS and a variety of AWS services, through a GUI. Step Functions has a logical component that can interface with the stateless services of a workflow.

6. Utilizing AWS Lambda to respond to notifications enables you to craft automated responses to any notifications that are generated.

7. Using AWS Lambda to create a serverless application allows you to focus on creating functions that map to the tasks in the application. For example, say that you enable an application that has five functions: Login, Search, Save, Download, and Logout. Using Lambda, you could create five separate functions and load those functions into Lambda. Then you could generate an application on your mobile device to call those functions as required. Each function would carry out its specific task when called. You are then charged only when the functions are called.

8. AWS Lambda can be used with API Gateway in this manner: An API call communicates with a custom Lambda function and carries out the tasks, as required, by calling various AWS services.

9. AWS Elastic Beanstalk allows you to deploy the required infrastructure to host an application that you have coded. Both the infrastructure and the hosting of the application can be carried out automatically, including future application and infrastructure updates.

Chapter 7

"Do I Know This Already?"

1. a

2. a

3. b

4. c

5. c

6. c

7. b

8. a

9. b

10. c

11. d

12. c

13. a

14. b

Q&A

1. highly available and reliable

2. localized

3. high availability, fault tolerance, and reliability

4. regions

5. compliance

6. regions

7. traffic flow policies

8. service quota

Chapter 8

"Do I Know This Already?"

1. b

2. b

3. b

4. b

5. b

6. b

7. a

8. b

9. b

10. b

11. b

12. a

13. b

14. a

Q&A

1. EFS storage has no size and sharing constraints. EBS storage can be shared across thousands of EC2 instances across multiple availability zones.

2. Files stored in object storage such as S3 or S3 Glacier are stored and updated as entire files. In contrast, EBS storage can be updated block by block, either as storage changes or by snapshot.

3. EBS io1 and io2 volumes support a feature called multi-attach, which allows you to attach and share the EBS volume to up to 16 instances, as long as all instances are hosted by the Nitro hypervisor.

4. Before a snapshot is deleted, it is analyzed, and only the data that is exclusive to the snapshot copy is retained.

5. The fastest storage that can be ordered at AWS is ephemeral storage, which is temporary storage volumes that are located on the bare-metal server where the instance is hosted. Because the EC2 instance is in exactly the same physical location as the bare-metal server, there is no network to traverse, and therefore the local storage volume is the fastest. However, ephemeral storage is not redundant; when the instance is turned off or fails, the storage is erased.

6. In order to use S3 Lifecycle rules and Same-Region Replication and Cross-Region Replication, you must have versioning enabled.

7. It is possible to share S3 objects with any person who does not have AWS credentials by creating and distributing a pre-signed URL. Temporary access is defined by configuring date and time expiration values.

8. A WORM policy applied to an S3 bucket when operating in Compliance mode can never be removed—not even by Amazon.

Chapter 9

"Do I Know This Already?"

1. c

2. b

3. d

4. b

5. b

6. b

7. c

8. b

9. b

10. b

Q&A

1. template

2. A golden AMI is an image that is as perfect as possible, and no customizations or tweaks need to be made to it. You must have the right processes in place to properly test your images before they go into production. Once your application servers are in production, you do not need to troubleshoot your production servers if your AMIs have been fully tested in preproduction.

3. RAM/CPU, processing time

4. The CloudWatch agent has probably already been deployed. You might want to consider customizing the operation of the CloudWatch agent so that your application logs and system logs are sent to CloudWatch for analysis. CloudWatch can then send notifications when problems arise.

5. Although launch configurations can be used to create EC2 instances that are performed by the Auto Scaling service as required, launch configurations are being deprecated and replaced with launch templates. Launch templates support all features of EC2 instances, whereas launch configurations do not support all current and new EC2 features.

6. The recommended starting point is to deploy a target tracking policy, which allows you to define the level of application performance to be maintained. Auto Scaling adds and removes compute instances to meet this target level.

7. When a workload's compute resources need to be scaled up but not aggressively; for example, an application that requires additional compute resources to be adjusted every 4 hours using a single metric such as CPU utilization. However, after changes have been made, a cooldown period must be observed before any additional changes can be implemented.

8. Step scaling enables you to define the scaling of an application's compute levels based on multiple percentages when scaling both up and down. Therefore, step scaling allows you to carefully tune your scaling requirements.

Chapter 10

"Do I Know This Already?"

1. c
2. d
3. b
4. d
5. b
6. c
7. b
8. c
9. a
10. a
11. d
12. b

Q&A

1. The advantage of using RDS to set up your databases is that after you describe the infrastructure and your needs to AWS, the database infrastructure is automatically set up and maintained for you, and even failover is automatically managed. All you have to do is work with your data records.

2. The disadvantage of using RDS to set up most of your database types is that the standard deployment of RDS is a primary and standby database design. The other disadvantage is that RDS supports a set number of database engines and that's it; there's no flexibility. Of course, nothing stops organizations from building any database infrastructure design that required using custom EC2 instances or using RDS Custom.

3. Read replicas can help improve database performance by taking the load off the primary database instance in regard to queries. The typical RDS deployment has a primary and standby database; however, the standby database is just that—it stands by and waits for disaster and does nothing else but make sure that it's up to date with the primary database instance. That's all well and good, but perhaps your primary database is becoming bogged down by handling all the queries by itself. Adding read replicas in regions where they are needed can increase performance by having the read replicas handle the queries in those specific regions.

4. AWS has two database solutions for multi-region deployments. The first is Amazon DynamoDB, a NoSQL solution that supports global tables that can span multiple AWS regions. The second solution is Amazon Aurora, which can also span multiple AWS regions with a global deployment. The only other option is a database solution that you build yourself using EC2 instances.

5. The difference between eventual consistency and strong consistency in regard to database storage, specifically Dynamo DB, is that you have a choice of living with the reality of replicated data to multiple locations, or you can choose strong consistency, which means that a check will be made to all the storage partitions to see which has the most current copies of data, and those copies will be presented to the application.

6. Amazon Aurora has a huge advantage over a standard MySQL deployment because of the data storage architecture utilizing a virtual SAN composed of SSD drives. The data is also stored in a cluster with multiple writers. As a result, the performance cannot really be compared; Aurora is much faster.

7. Continuous backups for all database solutions at AWS are stored in S3 storage.

8. The advantage of using ElastiCache to store user state information is speed, after all the cache storage is operating in RAM, and reliability. Rather than storing the use state directly on the EC2 instance where the user session is taking place, the user's session information is stored in another location just in case the EC2 instance that the end user is communicating with fails. If there is a failure, and the user begins communicating with another web server, the user's session information can be retrieved from ElastiCache, allowing the continuation of the user's session on the other server.

Chapter 11

"Do I Know This Already?"

1. c

2. c

3. b

4. b

5. a

6. c

7. d

8. b

9. a

10. d

11. d

12. d

13. b

14. b

Q&A

1. CloudFront edge locations are located worldwide, enabling an application hosted in a single AWS region to cache data records to users located anywhere in the world. CloudFront integration with an application allows the caching of requested data records to the edge location closest to the end user.

2. Gateway Load Balancer can be deployed to manage multiple third-party load balancer virtual appliances and manage performance by scaling the virtual appliances up or down, based on demand.

3. The CIDR address range you choose for your VPC should be large enough to host all of the available instances that you will need for your application stack.

4. You should use separate VPCs for development, testing, and production environments.

5. There is no good reason for using public IP addresses for your web servers. Instead, locate your web servers behind load balancers hosted on public subnets. Your web servers should be hosted on private subnets that protect your web servers from direct Internet access.

6. You can move your public IP addresses to AWS by using a bring-your-own IP (BYOIP) address service.

7. All networking services provided by AWS are software services. For example, routers and load balancers and all network services are software appliances.

8. A network ACL has the ability to block a specific IP address, whereas a security group does not.

9. Elastic IP addresses can be used to add static public IP addresses to an EC2 instance or can be assigned to a NAT gateway service.

10. Endpoint interface or gateway connections ensure that traffic to the selected AWS service remains on the AWS private network.

Chapter 12

"Do I Know This Already?"

1. b
2. c
3. b
4. c
5. c
6. c
7. d
8. c
9. d
10. c
11. a
12. d

Q&A

1. The two main components of calculating management service costs at AWS that are applied to every service are the compute and storage used to carry out the management service.

2. Data transfer costs are incurred for the egress traffic from an AWS availability zone or an AWS region to another availability zone or region.

3. Tiered pricing is calculated based on the usage of a service or resource.

4. The two additional components of storage charges, in addition to data transfer charges, are storage and retrieval pricing.

5. After cost allocation tags have been activated, AWS uses the tags to organize and display costs on cost allocation reports, making it easier to track costs.

6. An S3 lifecycle rule defines the management of S3 objects on a defined schedule, such as movement or deletion after a defined timeframe, whereas an AWS Backup lifecycle management policy defines the storage tier location where the backup is stored: either warm storage or cold storage.

7. Backups can be copied to multiple AWS regions on demand or automatically as part of a defined backup plan.

8. An AWS Storage Gateway volume gateway provides block storage to on-premises applications using iSCSI connections that store the volumes in S3. An AWS Storage Gateway file gateway allows storage and retrieval of objects stored in S3 using NFS or SMB protocols.

Chapter 13

"Do I Know This Already?"

1. b
2. b
3. b
4. b
5. d
6. c

Q&A

1. virtual CPU
2. EC2 instance
3. per-VM
4. compute charge
5. pricing discounts
6. capacity reservations
7. regional reservation, anywhere
8. availability zone

Chapter 14

"Do I Know This Already?"

1. b
2. c
3. d
4. b
5. d
6. a

Q&A

1. per request
2. hourly
3. database schema
4. standard SQL queries
5. MongoDB compatibility
6. length of time
7. incremental
8. AWS Backup

Chapter 15

"Do I Know This Already?"

1. a
2. b
3. c
4. a

Q&A

1. The two main components of calculating management service costs at AWS that are applied to every service are the compute and storage used to carry out the management service.

2. The key driver behind data transfer costs is the egress traffic from AWS or from an availability zone or from a region to an external location.

3. With a tiered, or sliding, price point based on usage, costs are calculated depending on the usage of a service or resource.

4. The four dimensions of an LCU are new connections, active connections, processed bytes, and rule evaluations.

AWS Certified Solutions Architect – Associate (SAA-C03) Cert Guide Exam Updates

Over time, reader feedback allows Pearson to gauge which topics give our readers the most problems when taking the exams. To assist readers with those topics, the authors create new materials clarifying and expanding on those troublesome exam topics. As mentioned in the Introduction, the additional content about the exam is contained in a PDF on this book's companion website, at https://www.pearsonITcertification.com/title/9780137941582.

This appendix is intended to provide you with updated information if Amazon makes minor modifications to the exam upon which this book is based. When Amazon releases an entirely new exam, the changes are usually too extensive to provide in a simple update appendix. In those cases, you might need to consult the new edition of the book for the updated content. This appendix attempts to fill the void that occurs with any print book. In particular, this appendix does the following:

- Mentions technical items that might not have been mentioned elsewhere in the book

- Covers new topics if AWS adds new content to the exam over time

- Provides a way to get up-to-the-minute current information about content for the exam

Always Get the Latest at the Book's Product Page

You are reading the version of this appendix that was available when your book was printed. However, given that the main purpose of this appendix is to be a living, changing document, it is important that you look for the latest version online at the book's companion website. To do so, follow these steps:

Step 1.   Browse to https://www.pearsonITcertification.com/title/9780137941582.

Step 2.   Click the Updates tab.

Step 3.   If there is a new Appendix B document on the page, download the latest Appendix B document.

> **NOTE**   The downloaded document has a version number. Comparing the version of the print Appendix B (Version 1.0) with the latest online version of this appendix, you should do the following:
>
> - **Same version:** Ignore the PDF that you downloaded from the companion website.
>
> - **Website has a later version:** Ignore this Appendix B in your book and read only the latest version that you downloaded from the companion website.

Technical Content

The current Version 1.0 of this appendix does not contain additional technical coverage.

Glossary of Key Terms

A

access key   A special set of keys linked to a specific AWS IAM user.

ACID   The storage consistency of a relational database, based on atomicity, consistency, isolation, and durability.

active-active   Multi-region active-active deployment of resources across multiple regions for workloads requiring high availability and failover.

alarm   A warning issued when a single metric crosses a set threshold over a defined number of time periods.

Amazon CloudFront   The AWS content delivery network (CDN) hosted in all edge locations.

Amazon Elastic Block Storage (EBS)   A virtual hard disk block storage device that is attached to Amazon EC2 instances.

Amazon Elastic Compute Cloud (EC2)   A web service that provides secure, resizable compute capacity in the cloud. It enables you to launch and manage virtual servers, called Amazon Elastic Compute Cloud (EC2) instances, in the AWS cloud.

Amazon ElastiCache   A distributed in-memory data store.

Amazon Machine Image (AMI)   A template of an instance's root drive.

application programming interface (API)   A defined set of protocols that enables applications and services to communicate with each other.

archive   An Amazon S3 Glacier grouping of compressed and encrypted files.

asymmetric key   One key of a public/private key pair.

Auto Scaling   An AWS service that adjusts compute capacity to maintain desired performance.

Auto Scaling group   A group of Amazon EC2 instances that is controlled (that is, scaled up, scaled down, or maintained) using the EC2 Auto Scaling service.

availability zone (AZ)   An insulated separate location within a region that contains at least one data center.

AWS Artifact   Allows AWS customers to review the compliance standards supported by AWS.

AWS Direct Connect   A dedicated private fiber connection to AWS VPCs or AWS public services.

AWS EC2access control list (ACL)   A list that enables you to control access to Amazon S3 buckets by granting read/write permissions to other AWS accounts.

AWS Identity and Access Management (IAM)   The hosted security system for the AWS cloud that controls access to AWS resources.

AWS Key Management Service (KMS)   An AWS service that centrally manages AWS customers' cryptographic keys and policies across AWS services that require data encryption.

AWS well-architected framework   A framework for designing, deploying, and operating workloads hosted at AWS.

B

block storage   Data records stored in blocks on a storage area network.

bucket   The storage unit for an Amazon S3 object.

bucket policy   A resource policy that is assigned directly to a storage entity such as an Amazon S3 bucket.

burst capacity   The ability of a storage unit or a compute instance to increase processing power for a short period of time.

burst credits   Performance credits that make it possible to burst above a defined performance baseline.

C

capacity units   A measure of Amazon DynamoDB performance in terms of either reading or writing.

certificate authority (CA)   A company or an entity that validates the identities of websites or domains using cryptographic public/private keys.

CloudWatch log group   A group that logs information in near real time.

codebase   The body of source code for a software program or application.

cold storage   Infrequently accessed storage.

condition   Special rule in a permission policy.

connection draining   The process of deregistering (removing) a registered instance from a load balancer target group.

cooldown period   A defined time period when no changes are allowed.

cost allocation tags   Tags that are used to categorize and track AWS costs displayed with monthly and hourly cost allocation reports.

Cost and Usage Report (CUR)   Tracks your AWS usage and provides estimated charges associated with your account for the current month.

D

data consistency   A definition of how data records are either the same or not the same due to replication.

data transfer   Incoming (ingress) and outgoing (egress) packet flow.

defense in depth (DiD)   Deployment of multiple security controls (physical, administrative, and technical) to protect a hosted workload.

dependencies   Cloud services, applications, servers, and various technology components that depend upon each other when providing a business solution.

Direct Connect   *See* AWS Direct Connect.

distributed session   A user session for which user state information is held in a separate durable storage location.

E

EC2   *See* Amazon Elastic Compute Cloud (EC2).

egress-only Internet gateway (EOIG)   A one-way gateway connection for EC2 instances with IPv6 addresses.

Elastic Block Storage (EBS)   *See* Amazon Elastic Block Storage (EBS).

Elastic IP (EIP) address   A static public IP address that is created and assigned to your AWS account.

ElastiCache   *See* Amazon ElastiCache.

endpoint   A location where communication is made; a private connection from a VPC to AWS services.

ephemeral storage   Temporary local block storage.

event notification   Communications about changes in the application stack.

externally authenticated user   A user that has authenticated outside Amazon before requesting access to AWS resources.

F–H

FedRAMP   Federal Risk and Authorization Management Program, establishes the security requirements for usage of cloud services for federal government agencies.

health check   A status check for availability.

high availability   A group of compute resources that continue functioning even when some of the components fail.

I–K

IAM group   A group of AWS IAM users.

IAM role   A permission policy that provides temporary access to AWS resources.

Identity and Access Management (IAM)   *See* AWS Identity and Access Management (IAM).

immutable   During deployment and updates components are replaced rather than changed.

input/output operations per second (IOPS)   A performance specification that defines the rate of input and output per second when storing and retrieving data.

Internet gateway (IG)   An AWS connection to the Internet for a virtual private cloud (VPC).

Key Management Service (KMS)   *See* AWS Key Management Service (KMS).

key-value   An item of data where the key is the name and the value is the data.

L

Lambda@Edge   A custom-created function to control ingress and egress Amazon CloudFront traffic.

launch template   A set of detailed EC2 instance installation and configuration instructions.

LCU   *See* load balancer capacity unit (LCU).

lifecycle hook   A custom action to be performed before or after an Amazon EC2 instance is added to or removed from an Auto Scaling Group.

lifecycle policy   A set of rules for controlling the movement of Amazon S3 objects between S3 storage classes.

lifecycle rules   Rules that allow customers to transition backups that are stored in warm storage to cheaper cold storage.

listener   A load balancer process that checks for connection requests using the defined protocols and ports.

load balancer capacity unit (LCU)   Defines the maximum resource consumed calculated on new connections, active, connections, bandwidth, and rule evaluations.

Local Zone   A single deployment of compute, storage, and select services close to a large population center.

M

metric   Data collected for an AWS CloudWatch variable.

mount point   A logical connection to a directory in a file system; a method to attach Amazon EFS storage to a Linux workload.

multi-factor authentication (MFA)   Authentication that involves multiple factors, such as something you have and something you know.

multipart upload   An upload in which multiple parts of a file are synchronously uploaded.

N

NAT gateway service   A service that provides indirect Internet access to Amazon EC2 instances that are located on private subnets.

network access control list (NACL)   A stateless subnet firewall that protects both inbound and outbound subnet traffic.

Nitro   The latest AWS hypervisor, which replaces the Xen hypervisor and provides faster networking, compute, encryption, and management services.

NoSQL   A database that does not follow SQL rules and architecture, hence the name "no" SQL.

NVMe   Non-Volatile Memory Express, a standard hardware interface for SSD drives connected using PCI Express bus.

O

object storage   Data storage as a distinct object with associated metadata containing relevant information.

origin access identity (OAI)   A special AWS IAM user account that is provided the permission to access the files in an Amazon S3 bucket.

origin failover   An alternate data source location for Amazon CloudFront distributions.

P

password policy   A policy containing global password settings for AWS account IAM users.

peering connection   A private networking connection between two VPCs or two transit gateways.

Pilot light   An active/passive disaster recovery design that involves maintaining a limited set of compute and data records to be used in case of a disaster to the primary application resources. The compute records are turned off until needed, but the data records are active and are kept up-to-date.

primary database   The primary copy of database records.

Q–R

queue   A redundant storage location for messages and application state data for processing.

read capacity unit   One strongly consistent read per second, or two eventually consistent reads per second, for items up to 4 KB in size.

read replica   A read-only copy of a linked primary database.

recovery point objective (RPO)   A metric that specifies the acceptable amount of data that can be lost within a specified period.

recovery time objective (RTO)   A metric that specifies the maximum length of time that a service can be down after a failure has occurred.

region   A set of AWS cloud resources in a geographic area of the world.

regional edge cache   A large throughput cache found at an edge location that provides extra cache storage.

regional endpoint   A device that provides HTTPS access to AWS services within a defined AWS region.

reliability   The reasonable expectation that an application or service is available and performs as expected.

Reserved instance   An Amazon EC2 instance for which you have prepaid.

RPO   *See* recovery point objective (RPO).

RTO   *See* recovery time objective (RTO).

S

scale out   To increase compute power automatically.

scaling policy   A policy that describes the type of scaling of compute resources to be performed.

security group   A stateful firewall protecting Amazon EC2 instances' network traffic.

Server Message Block (SMB)   A network protocol used by Windows systems on the same network to store files.

serverless   A type of computing in which compute servers and integrated services are fully managed by AWS.

server-side encryption (SSE)   Encryption of data records at rest by an application or a service.

service-level agreement (SLA)   A commitment between a cloud service provider and a customer indicating the minimum level of service to be maintained.

service-level indicator (SLI)   Indicates the quality of service an end user is receiving at a given time. SLIs are measured as a level of performance.

service-level objective (SLO)   An agreement defined as part of each service-level agreement. Objectives could be uptime or response time.

service quota   A defined limit for AWS services created for AWS accounts.

simple scaling   Scaling instances up or down based on a single AWS CloudWatch metric.

SLA   *See* service-level agreement (SLA).

snapshot   A point-in-time incremental backup of an EBS volume.

Snow device   A variety of network-attached storage devices that can be used to transfer and receive data records to and from Amazon S3 storage.

standby database   A synchronized copy of a primary database that is available in the event of a failure.

stateful   Refers to a service that requires knowledge of all internal functions.

stateless   Refers to a self-contained redundant service that has no knowledge of its place in the application stack.

step scaling   Scaling up or down by percentages.

sticky session   A user session for which communication is maintained with the initial application server for the length of the session. It ensures that a client is bound to an individual backend instance.

Structured Query Language (SQL)   The de facto programming language used in relational databases.

subnet   A defined IP address range hosted within a VPC.

symmetric key   A key that can both lock and unlock.

T

T instance   An instance provided with a baseline of compute performance.

table   A virtual structure in which Amazon DynamoDB stores items and attributes.

target group   A group of registered instances that receives specific traffic from a load balancer.

task definition   A blueprint that describes how a Docker container should launch.

Throughput Optimized   An EBS hard disk drive (HDD) volume option that provides sustained throughput of 500 Mb/s.

tiered pricing   The more you use the less you are charged.

time to live (TTL)   A value that determines the storage time of an Amazon CloudFront cache object.

U–V

uptime   the percentage of time that a website is able to function during the course of a calendar year.

user state   Data that identifies an end user and the established session between the end user and a hosted application.

versioning   A process in which multiple copies of Amazon S3 objects, including the original object, are saved.

virtual private cloud (VPC)   A logically isolated virtual network in the AWS cloud.

virtual private gateway (VPG)   The AWS side of a VPN connection to a VPC.

W–Z

warm standby   An active/passive disaster recovery design that maintains a limited set of compute and data records that are both on and functioning. When the primary application resources fail, the warm standby resources are resized to production values.

write capacity unit (WCU)   One write per second for items up to 1 KB in size.

write-once/read-many (WORM)   A security policy that can be deployed on an Amazon S3 bucket or in S3 Glacier storage. The policy indicates that the contents can be read many times but are restricted from any further writes once the policy is enacted.

zonal   Refers to an availability zone location.

Index

E